ARCHAEOLOGY ON THE GREAT PLAINS

ARCHAEOLOGY ON THE GREAT PLAINS

EDITED BY

W. Raymond Wood

Maps by E. Stanley Wood

 University Press of Kansas

To John L. Champe
Pioneer Plains Prehistorian

© 1998 by the University Press of Kansas
All rights reserved
Published by the University Press of Kansas (Lawrence, Kansas 66045),
which was organized by the Kansas Board of Regents and is operated and
funded by Emporia State University, Fort Hays State University, Kansas
State University, Pittsburg State University, the University of Kansas, and
Wichita State University

Library of Congress Cataloging-in-Publication Data

Archaeology on the Great Plains / edited by W. Raymond Wood ; maps by
E. Stanley Wood.
     p.   cm.
   Includes bibliographical references and index.
   ISBN 978-0-7006-0883-6 (cloth : alk. paper)
   ISBN 978-0-7006-1000-6 (pbk. : alk. paper)
     1. Indians of North America—Great Plains—Antiquities.
   2. Excavations (Archaeology)—Great Plains.   3. Great Plains—
Antiquities.   I. Wood, W. Raymond.
   E78.G73A73   1998
   978'.01—DC21   97-52824

British Library Cataloguing in Publication Data is available.

Printed in the United States of America

10 9 8 7 6 5 4 3

CONTENTS

1. Introduction

W. Raymond Wood

Early American settlers and later homesteaders were discouraged, but never wholly beaten, by the heartbreaking problems they faced in settling and wresting a livelihood from the harsh environment of the Great Plains of North America. Life had to have been equally frustrating for their Native American predecessors, who, millennia earlier, also adapted to life there. Droughts and other disasters common to low-moisture regions affected both the Plains environment and the humans dependent on it throughout time, but the evidence suggests that the climate never became severe enough to force its inhabitants to abandon the area. To the contrary, there is a record of continuous human habitation on the Great Plains for the past 11,500 years. This book discusses some of the many Plains cultures that archaeologists have detected in their quest for the past human history of this area.

In late prehistoric times, Native American farmers of the Central and Northern Plains—the northwesternmost horticulturists in Native North America—lived an ample, if not affluent, life, and their distinctive lifeways were among the richest and most colorful of those north of the civilizations of central Mexico. These farmers, their nomadic neighbors, and their predecessors lived in the heart of the North American continent, deep in the great interior grassland that extends from the Gulf of Mexico north to central Canada. This vast area was dominated by perennial grasses and by a multitude of grazing and burrowing animals, of which the most conspicuous was the American bison (*Bison bison*), which ranged over the rolling landscape by the tens of millions. The center of this immense grassland, particularly those areas where rainfall was sparse, has become known as the Plains.

Two contrasting lifeways were followed by the historic Native Americans in this semiarid sea of grass: some were nomadic hunters and gatherers, whereas others were semisedentary village farmers or gardeners, living only in part on products of the hunt. The nomads are well known for their conspicuous role in delaying or aggravating the Euro-American settlement of the West: the Teton Dakota and the "Fighting Cheyenne," for example, are familiar to millions of readers of western history. The village farmers are not as well known. Some of them gained fame or notoriety when, as with the Pawnees, their homelands were crossed by the Oregon Trail or they were mistaken for the descendants of mythical Welsh travelers, as were the Mandans. The villagers nevertheless are as typical of the Plains as their more flamboyant nomadic neighbors, and, although they do not loom as large in popular western history, many of them had been farming on the Plains for hundreds of years before some of the nomadic tribes arrived on the scene in late prehistoric and early historic times.

Several distinctive elements combine to create the image of the historic Plains Indian: the use of the horse, the distinctive skin tipi, the feathered headdress, and bison hunting. This image is so ingrained in western culture that the Plains Indians provide the stereotype for North American Indians (Ewers 1968)—so much so that it is almost axiomatic, for example, that a book on the North American Indian will carry the likeness of a Plains Indian (usually in a feathered headdress) on the cover or dust jacket. Farming does not readily fit the popular view of them, yet farming on at least a limited scale characterized virtually every Indian group in the southeastern half of the North American continent. Plains farmers made a unique adjustment to the land that distinguishes them from the farmers of the eastern forests and prairies, and from the Pueblo and related desert farmers of the Greater Southwest.

The Plains was never an isolated area, centered as it is in North America and lacking any well-defined boundary. The absence of geographic barriers allowed the peoples to be in contact over great distances, principally because of their interest in obtaining nonlocal or otherwise exotic (as well as practical) goods through intertribal trade. Such trade was a major integrative factor in Plains Indian life, abetted by a complicated sign language and by a social network that bound each group to several of its neighbors by intermarriage and adoption ceremonies. This network extended to the continental boundaries (Swagerty 1988). The result was that the Plains Indians were active participants in a pan-continental trade network (Wood 1980), one of the many reasons the area was so dynamic. The Plains can be understood only in relation to the ecological and cultural diversity in which it was embedded and with which it was surrounded. This book provides a descriptive culture history of human groups on the Great Plains, focusing on that environmental and cultural diversity and on the changing archaeological record.

Discussions and "interpretations" of such concepts as ideology provide interesting stories for the general public, but they have little place in a scientific overview, save as speculation, for the data to support them do not exist or, if they do, are subject to many differing and untestable "interpretations." The farther we remove our discussion from the basic data—the artifacts—the less reliable our understanding of them becomes. All too often archaeologists are quick to concoct stories that seemingly accommodate the data at hand when in reality they are way out in front of the data. In fact, many times the data to support (or, just as importantly, to negate) a claim simply do not exist and may never exist. It rarely tells us in a direct way much about anything other than, again, what people made, used, and then threw away, lost, or buried. In our zeal to "reconstruct" the past, we often tend to forget this point. Other aspects of prehistoric life usually must be inferred from the objects recovered and from the contexts that produce the objects—a process that simultaneously opens up an endless number of possibilities and imposes a certain degree of risk on our interpretations. (O'Brien and Wood 1998:2–3) Archaeological reconstruction is much like building a house of cards: no matter how carefully one places the cards, if one of them must be removed, the whole house is liable to collapse. This caveat, however, has not stopped archaeologists from telling stories about the past. The crux of the matter, always, is: Are the propositions that we put forth in our attempts to explain the archaeological record *testable?* If they are *not*, we are doing a disservice both to our profession and to the public, which all too often believes the stories it is told. We have eschewed stories in this volume: as a colleague once said, in a context I have now forgotten, "We must be careful of what we say. Someone is likely to believe us."

Ecology and Great Plains Studies

A century and a half ago, or more, an autumn traveler on the Great Plains would from time to time have seen a procession of Indians, horses, and dogs moving over the landscape in search of bison. Carrying everything they needed on the backs of pack animals or on travois, these groups often were under the leadership of military societies that managed every significant aspect of the hunt. The locale of the hunt would have given our observer some clue to their ethnic identity, and there was tribal variation in some aspects of the hunt, the most conspicuous perhaps being in the organization of the circular encampments of tipis. Nevertheless, an observer too far distant to detect their language or subtleties of tribal style would have been hard-pressed to determine whether these travelers were members of a nomadic group or whether their home base was an earthlodge community along the Missouri River or the Platte River. In either case, the groups were closely attuned to the Great Plains setting—an adaptation of great antiquity.

Ecological studies in anthropology began very early on the Great Plains of North America (Wood 1991). The effects of the dust bowl and the droughts of the 1930s on the Plains were visible to everyone—nationwide—and one regional archaeologist tried to assess the effects of past climate and climate change on its prehistoric inhabitants. An article by Waldo R. Wedel, "Environment and Native Subsistence Economies in the Central Great Plains" (1941), was the first important study to focus specifically on cultural ecology in that area. This paper was followed over the years by many others in a similar vein by a variety of authors, including Symmes C. Oliver's *Ecology and Cultural Continuity as Contributing Factors in the Social Organization of the Plains Indians* (1962). This concern with the interaction between aboriginal Plains Indian culture and environment continues unabated, and *Ecology and Human Organization on the Great Plains* (Bamforth 1988) is one of the latest monographs to use the Great Plains as an ecological laboratory.

Three important aspects of human adaptation to the biophysical environment were established by Paleo-Indian hunters, the first known occupants of the Great Plains: diet, technology, and settlement patterns (Bamforth 1988:1). The way of life led by hunters on the Great Plains is a very ancient one, and it persisted with remarkably little change from Clovis times of 11,500 years ago until the historic arrival of the Old World horse, which diffused north from Spanish sources near Santa Fe.

The early Spanish explorers on the Southern Plains saw pedestrian bison-hunting nomads living on the Plains much as their ancestors had lived for millennia before them. Spanish descriptions of these tipi-dwelling nomads, who followed the "cattle" for their sole livelihood, probably would differ only slightly from accounts of lifeways established 10,000 years earlier—including, in all probability, the use of dogs as pack animals. Dogs are not presently documented for Clovis or Folsom, although they appear in the Plains archaeological record beginning with the Jones–Miller site, a post-Folsom Hell Gap–complex site in Colorado (Stanford 1978). Dog bones occur rarely and irregularly in many later Paleo-Indian sites, but they are common enough to assume that Plains Indians had dogs (and were potentially using them as pack animals) over the past 10,000 years. It probably is only a matter of time before they are documented for Clovis and Folsom as well.

The historic pedestrian Plains lifeway described by the Spanish was to be short-lived, for horses diffused so rapidly beyond the frontiers of the Spanish Southwest that they had become an essential part of Native American culture over most of the Central and Northern Plains well before the appearance there of the first Europeans. Horses so revolutionized Native life that the historical documents on Plains Indians created by the first explorers record an equestrian bison-hunting subsistence that differed conspicuously from the earlier pedestrian period. Horses induced a massive discontinuity in Plains lifeways that is perhaps equivalent in magnitude to the changes brought about by the appearance of European diseases and the subsequent reduction in Native American population and the loss of the knowledge of traditional culture.

The nature of prehorse Plains Indian culture was a controversial topic in early Plains anthropology. The first professional anthropologists beginning work on the Plains had been educated in the East and were impressed with the aridity of the Plains no less than even earlier explorers who had described the region as the "Great American Desert." Because the Plains is a formidable setting for those who do not know it, it was common to believe, as Clark Wissler originally did, that the area was virtually uninhabited before the arrival of horses. This was not an unreasonable assumption at that time, for Wissler (1908)

diet
technology } *hard data*
Settlement patterns

thought that with the exception of the Kiowa, "every tribe" had moved into the Plains from adjacent regions, a belief based on the absence of archaeological knowledge and on the uncritical acceptance of historical accounts and tribal traditions. By 1939, Alfred L. Kroeber had modified this position to accept a prehorse occupation, but he still believed that before the horse "there was no important Plains culture" and that "Plains culture has been one of the well-developed and characterized cultures of North America only since the taking over of the horse from Europeans" (Kroeber 1947:76). The persistence of this mythology is such that one popular book on Plains Indians, written by a scholar with a reputation for sound historical research (Haines 1976:15), alleges that "in AD 1200 there were no Indians anywhere on the Great Plains" and illustrates the point with a map entitled "The Empty Plains, AD 1200"!

This interpretation of an empty or near-empty prehistoric Plains was reinforced by the importance of horses to the historic Plains nomads: the Arapahos, Assiniboins, Blackfeet, Cheyennes, Comanches, Crows, Dakotas, Gros Ventres, Kiowas, Kiowa-Apaches, and other equestrian bison hunters. How, Kroeber asked, "could any good-sized group have lived permanently off the bison on the open plains while they and their dogs were dragging their dwellings, furniture, provisions, and children? How large a tepee could have been continuously moved in this way, how much apparatus could it have contained, how close were its inmates huddled, how large the camp circle? . . . By the standard of the nineteenth century, the sixteenth-century Plains Indian would have been miserably poor and almost chronically hungry" (Kroeber 1947:77). Yet live there they did, and they did so successfully for no less than 11,500 years, although we might note that there is no good archaeological evidence for camp circles anywhere on the Plains: all the data for them are from the historic, posthorse period.

Kroeber and others who tried to interpret the peopling of the Plains imposed their own environmental preconceptions of the area on its occupants, and found it so difficult to believe that the area was habitable before the appearance of horses that they ignored sound archaeological evidence for its long-standing occupation. This is especially curious given the kinds of insights Kroeber accumulated in compiling his monumental *Cultural and Natural Areas of Native North America* (1947), and it tells us much about his biases and how they affected his anthropological interpretation.

The hard data of archaeology, as we have seen, are best suited to studies of diet, technology, and settlement patterns. Under ideal circumstances, sites can provide abundant and unambiguous data for each of these topics. Even more fortunate, they are so intimately interrelated that conclusions based on composite studies permit a level of confidence much higher than individual studies alone could provide. There is remarkable continuity throughout the Paleo-Indian period in precisely these three areas. The major change, in fact, is "a decrease in the diversity of animals hunted after approximately 11,000 years ago

Continuity over 11,500 yrs
↓ in animal diversity is major change

and a series of changes over time in projectile point shape. Neither of these changes seems to indicate any major adaptive shifts," since the change in fauna reflects the loss of extirpated species, "and it is difficult to interpret changes in projectile point style as evidence for substantial changes in other aspects of Paleoindian way of life" (Bamforth 1988:1–2).

It is argued that the adaptive changes that did take place on the Plains involved the human *"organization* within which similar subsistence resources were procured, similar tools were produced and used, and similar locations were selected for occupation" (Bamforth 1988:2, his emphasis). Under most circumstances, human organization is difficult to extract from the archaeological record, especially for hunters and gatherers. Organization is, nonetheless, well illustrated by kill sites. The reason is that many of the most sought-after sites on the High Plains, and those that are often best excavated and reported, are not campsites but bison kill sites. The discovery, driving, entrapment, and killing of large numbers of bison or other ungulates demand a high level of organization, a truism amply documented in the many studies of Plains bison and pronghorn procurement (e.g., Davis and Wilson 1978).

Successful patterns of hunting are likely to persist if conditions for their pursuit do not change. A spectacular example of continuity in hunting patterns appears to be illustrated by the archaeological remains from a 10,000-year-old bison kill site in northeastern Colorado and by accounts of historic bison pounds, or surrounds, on the Northern Plains. A posthole in the center of the bison skeletal remains at the Hell Gap complex, Jones–Miller bison kill site in northeastern Colorado is similar to the solitary "medicine poles" erected in the center of historic pounds. Furthermore, a miniature Hell Gap point (little more than 2 centimeters long) and butchered canid remains were found near the posthole. These offerings may be analogous to the nonfunctional artifacts placed on or near the historic medicine pole by Northern Plains hunters seeking a successful kill. If these analogies are correct, Stanford (1978:95–96) believes that pounding even at that early date was not a fortuitous event, as some students of bison procurement have postulated. Rather, it was a complex, ritualized, and planned event, and here at least we must postulate 10,000 years of some level of socioreligious continuity on the Northern Plains. There were, of course, many different patterns for hunting bison in both time and space, dictated by group differences and by the strikingly different environments in which the beasts were hunted in the varied Plains settings.

It is axiomatic that the historic and late prehistoric Plains are dichotomized between the village-dwelling horticulturists and the nomadic hunting and gathering High Plains groups. Much is made of the differences between them, for the distinction between gardeners and hunters is a basic one in anthropology. The horticultural groups, furthermore, are latecomers to the Plains scene, for villagers were present for only the last millennium of Great Plains history, whereas the nomads represent a way of life that endured for more than ten times that period and persisted on the Western Plains even as the Eastern and Central Plains horticultural tribes developed.

Despite the many contrasts between the two groups, however, the mode of life of the horticulturists was not as profoundly different from that of the nomads as has been claimed. As Wissler (1948:42) pointed out long ago, the villagers characteristically lived in their lodges principally "only while planting, tending, or harvesting the crop. At other times, they took to tipis. Even in midwinter the Omaha and Eastern Dakota lived in tipis." And when villagers were on their annual bison-hunting expeditions away from their lodges, their life scarcely differed from that of their nomadic neighbors. Whether one was a Plains nomad or a villager, the organization of their annual hunts varied only in minor details from tribe to tribe, and in every case was regulated by military societies.

This was true not only of the traditional bison-hunting groups, but of composite groups that developed in the full historic period. Jeffery R. Hanson (personal communication) has pointed out that the hunting technique and organization of two of the Plains bison-hunting groups that developed in post-European times mirrored in many respects those of Plains Indian tribes. The New Mexico villagers known as *ciboleros* (or *comancheros*) and the Northern Plains Métis who went onto the Plains to hunt bison never came into contact with each other, but the parallels in their hunting technique and organization are striking. Both groups went out en masse, during which time they were directed by hunt police, and their hunts shared many other details that were borrowed directly from neighboring Plains Indians. Perhaps the least distinctive visual difference between the traditional Plains Indians and the Métis and *ciboleros* was in transportation. The *ciboleros* used ox-drawn wagons called *carreta*. These wagons were very much like the two-wheeled Red River carts of the Métis, both of which were borrowed from European models. The point here is that if one is to hunt bison on the Plains, and to defend oneself from potential enemies while doing so, the appropriate organization is unlikely to differ significantly from that developed much earlier by Plains Indians, and it is not surprising to find that both the *ciboleros* and the Métis borrowed from a common source.

The contrasts between Plains nomads and villagers, then, have been overdrawn. Towns of the horticultural Plains village tribes differed, for example, very little from the bands that characterized the nomadic groups. Townspeople, of course, lived in substantial earth-covered lodges in semipermanent villages and relied to varying degrees on the produce from their gardens. But, save for the specialized architecture of the earthlodge and the presence of pottery and

farmers more like nomads than not

of gardening tools, the material inventory of any given village was only minutely different from that of an encampment of one of its nomadic neighbors—whether we are speaking of groups on the Northern, Central, or Southern Plains. There is a remarkable monotony of pattern in most aspects of material culture on the Plains, whether of women's products (such as articles of clothing, parfleches, or even tipis [save for a three- or four-pole foundation]) or those presumably made by men (such as arrowpoints and weaponry). Museum curators have found that without specific tribal allocation, it is usually impossible to identify the tribe of origin of a given artifact, for tools and implements used on a daily basis vary only in minor details of style, not of form. Both formal trade and gift giving were important social events on the Plains, and these popular activities led to massive exchanges of every conceivable element of material culture between villagers and nomads (Wood 1980).

Furthermore, each village was politically, socially, and economically autonomous. The political authority of a Mandan chief, for example, was no greater than that of any of the chiefs in the nomadic groups and, like the latter, had no coercive power. Disaffected members of a Mandan town were free to leave one village and join another. Each Mandan community held its own Okipa ceremony (the Mandan equivalent of the Sun Dance), each ran its own annual trade fair, and each conducted its own annual bison hunt in the fall. Plains villages, in short, were markedly similar to the bands that characterized the nomadic groups, save for the presence of stationary architecture, pottery, and a few other artifacts and the dependence on garden produce.

Ethnographic accounts of the Plains horticulturists rarely make explicit the kinds and the extent of social and political relations between individual villages of a tribe. This information is even rarer in historic documents written by travelers, explorers, and missionaries. One reason for this is that intervillage relations were tenuous; another reason is that ethnographers and others tended to examine the kinds of relations between members of a single village, to the detriment of broader connections. To cite one case, the historic Omahas, who for the most part lived in a single town (such as Big Village, in northeastern Nebraska) in the late eighteenth and early nineteenth centuries, have been interpreted as having organized their communal hunts at the "full tribal level" and of having had a central political organization (O'Shea and Ludwickson 1992; Roberts 1964:446, 449–450). Life in one town, of course, makes it difficult to interpret leadership as other than centralized. However, we may be assured that the historic expression of Omaha political organization differed significantly from that in precontact times, when the Omahas lived in an uncertain number of different and probably autonomous villages.

In any event, the traditional dichotomization of the late prehistoric and historic Plains Indians as nomads and as villagers is a legitimate means of describing two differing adaptations to the Plains environment. But it is a deceptive practice that masks many deep-rooted and essential similarities that they shared. In their activities away from their villages, the late Plains horticulturists practiced a lifeway as ancient as that of their nomadic neighbors, and one that drew on many of the same antecedents. There is more unity in the concept of the late Plains Indian than is generally conceded.

The Plains Culture Area and Its Subdivisions

The great interior grassland of the North American continent was designated, very early in the twentieth century, as the Plains. Clark Wissler (1917) was the first to recognize the distinctive nature of the cultures that occupied that vast area, and despite more recent and convincing arguments that culture areas are not "scientific" units, the Plains has continued to be recognized, in one way or another, as a useful (if not valid) cultural entity. We do not defend its use save as a helpful way of organizing data, and here we follow the generally accepted anthropological Plains boundaries and subdivisions (Wedel 1961:Figure 1). The image of the Plains as a "sea of grass" is a visually compelling one, but it must be recognized as a distressingly misleading misnomer; the Plains area is not a "natural monoculture," but a complex mosaic of seasonally and geographically induced patches, varying through time, that were both climatically manipulated by nature and culturally modified by humans (for example, by fire).

As it is traditionally understood, the Plains consists of an arbitrarily circumscribed area that does not correspond, in any one-to-one manner, with physiographic, climatic, or biotic provinces. In physiographic terms, the Plains consists of almost the entirety of the Great Plains province, plus some 200 miles of the western margin of the adjoining Central Lowland (Hunt 1967:Figure 12.1), or, as it is sometimes known, the Prairie Plains. The Plains also closely corresponds to the Northern Interior Grassland (Shelford 1963:328–355), although this unit excludes those parts of this grassland biome within and west of the Rocky Mountains.

The Plains, however defined, is not environmentally homogeneous, and defining the region as it is done here does not reduce its considerable environmental diversity. We may, however, generalize to the extent that (except for such uplifted areas as the Black Hills) the Plains consists of two kinds of grasslands: (1) the short-grass plains that dominate the Great Plains province, and (2) the tall-grass prairies that dominate the western margin of the Central Lowland. A zone of mixed grasses is to be found along the boundary between these two areas (Shelford 1963:Figure 13.1).

The justification for so arbitrarily excising the anthropological Plains from these physiographic and biotic units is that, in cultural terms, it is more productive to think in terms of a Great Plains environment than it is to try to define a Great Plains region. Walter Prescott Webb (1931:1–9) first convincingly espoused this point of view, and it appears to be tacitly accepted by most anthropologists concerned with the Plains. Under this philosophy, we follow Webb in defining the Plains as that part of central North America that is comparatively level and treeless, and has a subhumid or semiarid climate in which the cultivation of domestic crops is precarious, whether practiced by Native American gardeners or by modern farmers. The area that we call the Plains has changed a great deal over the millennia, but there is little doubt that this vast grassland has remained relatively distinctive—at least with respect to the heavily forested areas to the northeast and east—since about 9000 years ago.

flat
treeless
semi-
arid

Life on the Plains would not have been practical, however, without the deciduous forests that lined the major rivers in the grasslands and the lower reaches of most of their tributaries. These gallery forests occupied much of the floodplain of all the major rivers, and it is important to remember that most Plains Indians lived on or near these waterways. The greater percentage of habitation sites are along streams and their associated shelter, fuel, and water.

trees
in
waterways

The Plains has a long culture history. In the Southern Plains, and along its western margin, are sites of the Clovis culture dating to 11,500 years ago. These early hunters, possibly preceded by earlier but as yet undefined peoples, initiated the many thousands of years of subsequent adaptation to the Plains environment. It is unlikely that many successful strategies or technologically sound innovations that they made were lost. We do not subscribe to a catastrophic view of Plains prehistory—that Archaic peoples were "displaced" by Woodland ones, for example. Today we see in the archaeological record a more continuous story than our predecessors did on the basis of their knowledge of far fewer sites: Archaic in most areas is transformed gradually into Woodland, and Woodland, in turn, into the Plains Village traditions. Changes did take place in many spheres of culture, but continuity is often slighted at the expense of discontinuity, primarily because discontinuities often are more "apparent" in the archaeological record precisely because of gaps in that record.

Clovis

Archaic
Woodland
Plains

It is convenient to subdivide the Plains into several cultural subareas. Five major subareas are generally accepted: the Southern Plains, Central Plains, Middle Missouri, Northeastern Plains, and Northwestern Plains (Figure 1.1). These subareas, for the most part, are marked by a particular set of ecological conditions that, in large part, are reflected in the cultural systems of the people who lived within them. That is, each of these geographic subdivisions appears to be an "intelligible unit of study in terms of its culture history" (Lehmer and Caldwell 1966:512), although their histories cannot be divorced from those of their neighbors.

The *Southern Plains* consists of that part of the Plains south of the Arkansas

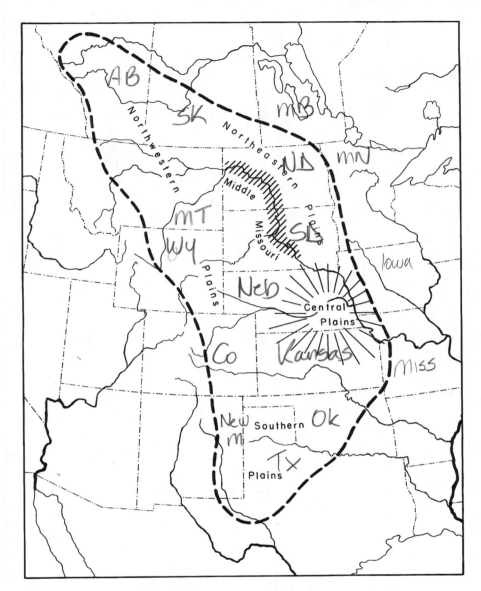

Figure 1.1. Spatial divisions of the Plains area. (After Lehmer 1971:Figure 20)

River, including parts of Kansas, Oklahoma, Texas, and New Mexico. The *Central Plains* includes all of eastern Nebraska and adjoining parts of South Dakota, Iowa, Missouri, and Kansas. The *Middle Missouri* consists of the trench of the Missouri River and the lower reaches of its immediate tributaries, between the mouth of the Yellowstone River, near the Montana–North Dakota boundary, and the mouth of the White River, in south-central South Dakota. The *Northeastern*

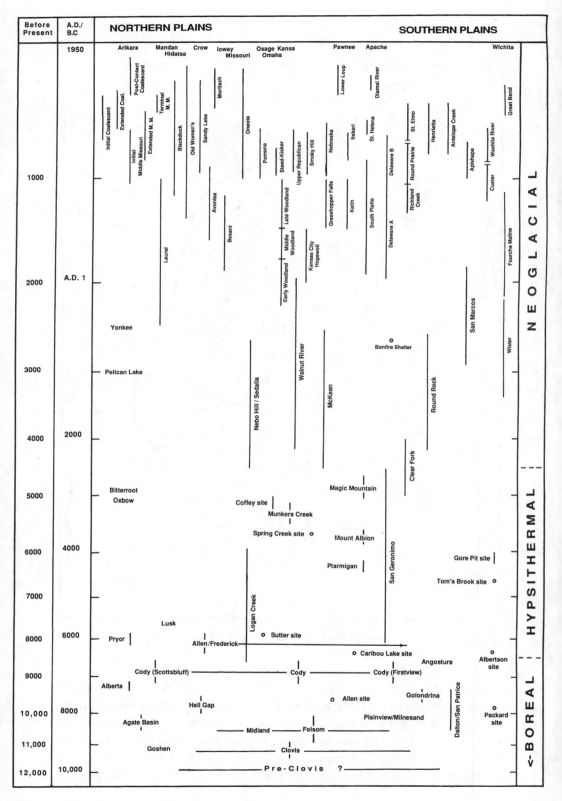

Figure 1.2. The chronology of Plains cultures.

Plains denotes the area northeast of the Middle Missouri subarea and includes the eastern halves of North and South Dakota and adjoining segments of Minnesota, Manitoba, and Saskatchewan. The *Northwestern Plains* comprises the area west of the Missouri River and north of Colorado Springs, Colorado (Wedel 1961:Figure 1).

Because of the nature of the archaeological record, it is inevitable that much of our story consists of inferences from the technological remains of prehistoric peoples, and because these remains are usually embedded in an environmental context, we also necessarily lay heavy stress on the ecological relations of the peoples. Plains cultures, like cultures everywhere, were adaptive systems, enabling human groups to adjust not only to their natural surroundings, but to cultural systems—both their own and those of other peoples. Whereas we normally view cultures as integrated wholes—that is, as systems—this is not to say that cultures are fully internally consistent systems. Like all open systems, cultures are in a constant state of change, so that some parts of the system are always out of phase with the general system. All cultures are constantly in the process of being transformed, so it is necessary for us to slice arbitrary units from the cultural continuum (Figure 1.2).   ρ∩ωρ

Four general culture periods characterize the Plains: Paleo-Indian, Archaic, Woodland, and Plains Village. These four broad periods are based on technology, subsistence, settlement patterns, and, to a lesser degree, social features. Although they are sequential, they have no set temporal or spatial connotations, although such boundaries may be defined for a local sequence. These terms admittedly lack precision, but they are necessary if one is to discuss cultural units beyond the level of component, site, phase, and variant. The term "variant" (Lehmer 1971:32) is used in this book by several authors, as amended by Krause (Chap. 3, this volume), as "a mid-range integrative taxon with less content, greater time span, and greater spatial spread than a phase, but having less time span than a tradition and less spatial spread than a horizon." The concept is used by Johnson and Johnson (Chap. 7, this volume) and Winham and Calabrese (Chap. 9, this volume), but it has wider applicability than it has received to date. Whatever else may be said of the Great Plains, we can be sure that no simple generalization will comprehend both its geographic breadth and the millennia of its cultural record. Today we have a good grasp of the fundamental outlines of its culture history, but every chapter in this book bears witness to the fact that we still have much to learn of this complex area.

The contributors have tried to present a rounded picture of each of the topics covered in each chapter, but the great volume of current literature means that not every culture complex, much less every site, can be mentioned. Efforts, however, have been made to produce a balanced set of references that includes the basic published works. Important manuscripts and archival records are cited, but the intent has been to provide a set of references that can be consulted by the average reader without undue difficulty.

References

Bamforth, D. B.
    1988   *Ecology and Human Organization on the Great Plains.* Plenum, New York.
Davis, L. B., and M. Wilson, eds.
    1978   *Bison Procurement and Utilization: A Symposium.* Plains Anthropologist Memoir
          no. 14.
Ewers, J. C.
    1968   The Emergence of the Plains Indian as the Symbol of the North American In-
          dian. In *Indian Life on the Upper Missouri,* 187–203. University of Oklahoma
          Press, Norman.
Haines, F.
    1976   *The Plains Indians.* Crowell, New York.
Hunt, C. B.
    1967   *Physiography of the United States.* Freeman, San Francisco.
Kroeber, A. L.
    1947   *Cultural and Natural Areas of Native North America.* University of California,
          Publications in American Archaeology and Ethnology, vol. 38. Berkeley.
Lehmer, D. J.
    1971   *Introduction to Middle Missouri Archeology.* National Park Service, Anthropo-
          logical Papers, no. 1. Washington, D.C.
Lehmer, D. J., and W. W. Caldwell
    1966   Horizon and Tradition in the Northern Plains. *American Antiquity* 31:511–516.
O'Brien, M. J., and W. R. Wood
    1998   *The Prehistory of Missouri.* University of Missouri Press, Columbia.
Oliver, S. C.
    1962   *Ecology and Cultural Continuity as Contributing Factors in the Social Organization*
          of the Plains Indians. University of California, Publications in American Ar-
          chaeology and Ethnology, vol. 48, no. 1. Berkeley.
O'Shea, J. M., and J. Ludwickson
    1992   *Archaeology and Ethnohistory of the Omaha Indians: The Big Village Site.* Univer-
          sity of Nebraska Press, Lincoln.
Roberts, J. M.
    1964   The Self-Management of Cultures. In *Explorations in Cultural Anthropology: Es-
          says in Honor of George Peter Murdock,* edited by W. W. Goodenough, 433–454.
          McGraw-Hill, New York.
Shelford, V. E.
    1963   *The Ecology of North America.* University of Illinois Press, Urbana.
Stanford, D. J.
    1978   The Jones–Miller Site: An Example of Hell Gap Bison Procurement Strategy.
          In *Bison Procurement and Utilization: A Symposium,* edited by L. B. Davis and
          M. Wilson, 90–97. Plains Anthropologist Memoir no. 14.
Swagerty, W. R.
    1988   Indian Trade in the Trans-Mississippi West to 1870. In *History of Indian–White
          Relations,* edited by W. E. Washburn, 351–374. Vol. 4 of *Handbook of North*

American Indians, W. C. Sturtevant, general editor. Smithsonian Institution Press, Washington, D.C.

Webb, W. P.
1931   *The Great Plains.* Ginn, Boston.

Wedel, W. R.
1941   Environment and Native Subsistence Economies in the Central Great Plains. *Smithsonian Miscellaneous Collections* 101, no. 3:1–29.

1961   *Prehistoric Man on the Great Plains.* University of Oklahoma Press, Norman.

Wissler, C.
1908   Ethnographic Problems of the Missouri Saskatchewan Area. *American Anthropologist* 10:197–207.

1917   *The American Indian.* McMurtrie, New York.

1948   *North American Indians of the Plains.* American Museum of Natural History, Handbook Series, no. 1. 3rd ed. New York.

Wood, W. R.
1980   Plains Trade in Prehistoric and Protohistoric Tribal Relations. In *Anthropology on the Great Plains,* edited by W. R. Wood and M. Liberty, 98–109. University of Nebraska Press, Lincoln.

1991   Ecology and Great Plains Studies. *Review of Archaeology* 12:30–34.

2. The Great Plains Setting

Marvin Kay

The North American Plains constitutes most of the midcontinental grasslands of Canada and the United States. It is bounded by the Gulf Coastal Plain, the subarctic boreal forests, the Rocky Mountains, and the mixed temperate grasslands and deciduous forests of the Prairie Peninsula (Figure 1.1). The Plains is a vast but far from drab or featureless area. It is a glory of open spaces, clear air, spectacular night skies, and wind that—to be appreciated—must be felt and heard as well as seen. It is varied in landscapes, plants, and animals, but is dominated by grasslands and, until recently, by bison. Its climate is distinctive in that the Plains is more likely to experience drought than adjacent regions. Also, its airstreams, buffeted by strong Pacific westerlies that loose their moisture crossing the Rockies and the winter position of the Arctic Front, largely define the midcontinental grasslands of North America (Borchert 1950; Bryson et al. 1970; see also Shelford 1963:328–372).

Geologically, the Plains is the relatively flat-lying country to the east of the Rockies that formed in Tertiary times as outwash from these eroding mountains; and its surface, where it is not eroded, is still mantled with a veneer of Rocky Mountain gravel. The Plains also includes the glacially modified country to the east and north of these pediment surfaces that today is largely north of the Missouri River. Its eastern border with the Prairie Peninsula marks a more gradual transition from a semiarid to a more humid setting. Denoting this eastern border is as much a philosophical as an analytical issue. Over time, the Plains has been biologically dynamic in response to regional climate. Mammalian species of the modern Plains in whole or in part include the swift fox, the black-footed ferret and its principal prey, the black-tailed prairie dog, plus an infestation of such other rodents as the Plains pocket gopher, the prairie vole, and Franklin's ground squirrel. The heather vole, an ice age denizen, now occurs in the montane and boreal zones to the north and west. To fix the Plains border in prehistoric times (except where it fronts on the Rockies) calls for flexibility and the mapping of past vegetation.

In our usage, the Plains lacks precise margins. Its borders are more to be thought of as where its typical grassland vegetation ends. That sea of grass is laced with bottomland gallery forests along streams both large and small that provide a complex interfingering of prairie–forest ecotones throughout the area (Figure 2.1). For our purposes, we employ three main subdivisions: the Northern, Central, and Southern Plains. The Northern Plains includes the states of

Figure 2.1. Typical Plains view showing the interfingering of stream-bottom vegetation and upland grasslands. In the foreground is the Ray Long site (39FA65), southeast of the South Dakota Black Hills. (Photo by Richard P. Wheeler; National Anthropological Archives)

North and South Dakota along with the prairie parts of Wyoming, Montana, and Minnesota, plus the Canadian provinces of Alberta, Saskatchewan, and Manitoba south of the subarctic boreal forests. We consider the Northern Plains area to the west and northwest of the Missouri River in the Dakotas as the Northwestern Plains; the eastern Dakotas drained by the James River and points farther east, as the Northeastern Plains. The Central Plains is within the states of Kansas and Nebraska, and adjoining parts of Colorado, Iowa, and Missouri; the Southern Plains, the states of Oklahoma, Texas, and parts of New Mexico.

Crosscutting each Plains subdivision is a precipitation-based east-to-west zonal pattern of vegetation and wildlife. Annual moisture and summer temperature control the species of grasses and allow the charting of trends of dominance of six major grass species. These conform to the division between short-grass and tall-grass prairie (Brown and Gersmehl 1985) that centers along the

6 major grass species
short grass + tallgras s

hundredth meridian. The marked east-to-west gradient of decreasing annual precipitation and relative humidity, plus the increasing frequency of prolonged droughts, may largely account for changes in the abundance of birds that winter on the Plains and other wildlife forms.

This chapter extends the reasoning of John R. Borchert and others to an examination of past Plains climates and environments. Its focus is the Plains during and since the last glacial period, the Wisconsin glaciation, which coincides with the initial human migration to and later exploitation of the North American grasslands. Information about these subjects complements other descriptions of Plains environments (Wedel 1961) that convincingly argue that the Plains "culture area" is one of significant diversity and contrast in landforms, vegetation, wildlife, and people. These comments are not a substitute for Waldo Wedel's insights about how late prehistoric, protohistoric, and historic Plains foragers and farmers were affected by often sudden changes in daily temperatures, extended droughts, cyclonic storms, late-winter blizzards, the number of frost-free days, or the topographic and temperature/humidity gradients typical of this area. Rather, the intent is to chart the magnitude and extent of late Quaternary climatic and environmental change—beginning about 14,000 years ago—and their implications for human adaptations to the Plains.

Borchert described four salient features of Plains climate. Each interacts with the others and with the prime "genetic factors" in North American climate: the air-circulation system (Wendland and Bryson 1981), the location of mountain ranges, and the position of the continent in the belt of westerly winds (Borchert 1950:29):

1. Summer rainfall in the Eastern Plains conforms to a decreasing strength of the mean westerly airflow south of the Alberta storm belt.
2. The dry summer continental westerlies in normal years are generally west of the hundredth meridian and maintain the short-grass (steppe) biome.
3. Abnormal low rainfall and high temperature during July lead to subnormal summer rainfall and associated temperature anomalies.
4. During drought years, the prevailing winter westerlies continue unabated *wind* into the summer, producing a "great wedge of spring and summer rainfall deficiency [that extends] from the Great Plains across the mid-West" (Borchert 1950:13).

Borchert's "great wedge" of dry summer air determines the eastern extent of the grasslands, while the late-winter position of the Arctic Front defines their northern extent. This relation between seasonal airstreams (Wendland and Bryson 1981) and vegetation is the "bridge" that links vegetation data to models of past climates (for a detailed exposition, see Bryson et al. 1970). While we cannot directly observe the position of a past airstream, its location may be inferred

Climate doesn't change simultaneously [handwritten]

from the distribution and location of the dominant vegetation on the Plains margins.

Herbert Wright (1983) has noted two basic relationships in past climates. First, late Quaternary climate changes were either sudden or gradual, and of short or long duration. To the extent that climate affects the dynamic balance between people and their environments, its influence on human adaptations to Plains environments should have been dramatic and distinctive at differing times. Second, climate change is time-transgressive (climate does not change simultaneously everywhere) and has effects over much of the northern hemisphere. That is, climate may not have changed at the same time across the Plains and its margins, and its effects on human adaptation would therefore have varied with time. *Adaptations vary based on climate* [handwritten]

We now know the early pronouncements (Kroeber 1939; Wissler 1907) of the Plains as a largely uninhabited, near-desert wasteland in prehistoric times, but one so distinctive in historic times as to be a uniform Native American "culture area," to be doubly wrong. Archaeological investigations convincingly show human habitation of the Plains ever since the lateglacial of no less than 11,200 years ago. The Plains culture area is also one of significant diversity and contrast in landforms, vegetation, wildlife, and people.

One should be reminded also of the eloquent descriptions and insights of Wedel (1961), who was one of Kroeber's students. Wedel had as much to do with changing our perception (if not, ironically, Kroeber's) of the Plains as perhaps any modern scholar. He recognized the intimate tie between Plains weather and the survival of its people. Sudden changes in daily temperatures, extended droughts, cyclonic storms, late-winter blizzards, the number of frost-free days, or the topographic and temperature/humidity gradients typical of this area all affected and, indeed, still affect human existence on the Plains.

As a practical matter, to describe Plains environments is no easy task. Nor can one expect to fully accomplish it in the space allowed here. One must build on the writings of early Euro-American explorers (the most celebrated being those of Lewis and Clark at the beginning of the nineteenth century) and the early-nineteenth-century paintings of George Catlin and Karl Bodmer. One must not overlook also the seminal works of William H. Holmes (1891, 1894, 1919), who recognized the economics of prehistoric stone quarrying in the Plains, or of geographers such as Nevin M. Fenneman (1931, 1938) and John R. Borchert (1950), who wrote of its landscapes and climates. To these, one most certainly would add recent treatments of the Quaternary period and its epochs, the Pleistocene (or glacial) and Holocene (or postglacial). Useful but not exhaustive guides to this literature are Dort and Jones (1970), Graham and Lundelius (1994), Graham and colleagues (1987), Imbrie and Imbrie (1979), Martin and Klein (1984), Morrison (1991), Porter (1983), Ruddiman and Wright (1987), Wright (1983), and less technical summaries (Dawson 1992; Pielou 1991).

Climatic Changes

Our ability to model dynamic atmospheric conditions, or "climate," is far from perfect. It becomes even less so as we go back in time, beyond the record of history, several centuries or thousands of years. Tree rings, pollen, and oxygen isotopes are among the better indirect (or proxy) measures of past temperatures, precipitation, and airstreams. All have been found to faithfully predict known changes in climate, and—in addition to tree rings—occur as annual records in lake varves and, most significantly, in glacial ice. The most elegant oxygen-isotope paleotemperature data are from glacial ice, but even longer records (on the order of hundreds of thousands of years) are from marine sediments. These generally correspond with Milutin Milankovitch's predictions of ice ages from the Earth's orbital cycles. An exception, however, is the Younger Dryas global cooling of 11,500 to 10,750 years ago. The Younger Dryas is only now becoming better understood as the principal climatic oscillation at the end of the ice age. Why renewed glaciation occurred then is ill-defined and hotly debated.

The Plains does not have glacial ice, nor is it well known for pollen or tree rings. But because climatic change can be either sudden *or* gradual and is often global in scope, the Greenland glacial ice cores may actually afford a better knowledge of annually divided Plains climatic history than would ever come from other land or marine sources. Proxy indicators from the Plains and adjacent regions are also instructive. In fact, pollen statistical transfer functions have been used to estimate for the dated period 7200 years ago reduced precipitation at Kirchner Marsh, Minnesota (Webb and Bryson 1972).

Climatic changes during the past millennium in the northern hemisphere with specific reference to the Plains are rather well understood. Two detailed and consistent reconstructions are now available (Porter 1986; Williams and Wigley 1983). Williams and Wigley's record begins about 1300 years ago, during a cold period that continued until the beginning of the twelfth century, the Medieval warm period or optimum (also called the Neo-Atlantic episode), which Porter dates to between 1090 and 1230. The Medieval optimum was followed by the Little Ice Age, which lasted into the mid-nineteenth century. Volcanism was a major climatic forcing mechanism throughout this time (Porter 1986).

The significance of the Medieval optimum to Plains climate and late prehistoric culture change cannot be overestimated. Major changes in regional summer precipitation patterns are likely to have affected different parts of the Plains in a variety of ways (Bryson et al. 1970). Increased summer precipitation in the Texas panhandle and southwestern Oklahoma coincided with the evolution of sedentary farming communities there (Panhandle aspect), whereas much of the Central and Northern Plains experienced drought to one degree or another, leading to other changes in subsistence and settlement. They included an eastward retraction of Upper Republican farmers of the Central Plains, coupled with a change in their settlement from hamlets to homesteads after about A.D. 1250 (Krause 1970). It seems no accident that farming societies in the Plains, the Southwest, and the Southeast changed during or immediately following the Medieval optimum (Euler et al. 1979; Knight 1986).

The following discussion separates the lateglacial Pleistocene epoch from the postglacial Holocene epoch. The transition from one to the other was marked by dramatic climatic and environmental events without parallel in later times. These were forced primarily by the Earth's orbital factors, as first proposed by Milankovitch's astronomical theory of climatic change (Ruddiman 1987). Deglaciation is approximated by changes in vegetation near the present prairie–forest margin as a series of steps at 14,000, 13,500, possibly 12,300, and, most pronounced, 10,000 years ago (Jacobson et al. 1987). The abrupt change from the lateglacial resulted in longer growing seasons, greater or less moisture stress, and increased July mean temperatures. Postglacial changes in climate, vegetation, and landscape were, by comparison, less striking, but they were nonetheless profound for Plains residents who now depended on a new mix and a new distribution of plant and animal resources.

deglaciation → vegetation change

Lateglacial

Lateglacial year-round temperatures were cooler than those of the present, leading to less evaporation of moisture and the stabilization of or increases in pluvial lake levels (Brakenridge 1978). The Laurentide (continental) ice sheet remained in the Northern Plains, but was separated by an arctic tundra from the Cordilleran (mountain) ice sheet of the Rockies in southwestern Alberta. The *Corridor* resulting "ice-free corridor" may have been a significant route of migration into the Plains after 12,000 years ago, coincident with the earliest undisputed evidence of human societies, and had an "open deciduous tree–shrub–herb vegetation . . . dominated by poplar, willow, sage, grass, chenopods, and sedge" (White et al. 1985:184). In contrast to the continental climates of the Holocene, the Pleistocene Plains climate was equable, or one of reduced seasonal temperature extremes (Graham and Mead 1987; Lundelius et al. 1983).

Throughout North America, lateglacial faunas were combinations of arctic and temperate forms that were in ecological balance then, but now are mostly separate. The composition of lateglacial Plains plant and animal communities often lacks a modern analogue. Guthrie's (1982) assessment of the arctic steppe is probably equally appropriate for the lateglacial Plains, since both were patchy, mosaic habitats (in the Plains, a dry, cool wooded parkland) that allowed for a greater concentration and a more diverse composition of herbivores than is true for the Holocene.

About 11,000 years ago, in the eastern part of the Northern Plains, oak, *forest followed ice as it retreated*

aspen, cottonwood, ash, and other hardwoods expanded northward and mixed with spruce. This forest followed the ice retreat northward into southern Manitoba and Saskatchewan. On the western border, between 11,000 and 9000 years ago, the montane conifer forests rapidly expanded their ranges in the Rocky Mountains. These montane forests apparently consisted of small populations of conifers along the lower mountain slopes during glaciation, bounded by tundra or steppe at higher and lower elevations. Pollen data for western Montana, the Powder River basin of Wyoming, and Bear Butte Lake, east of the Black Hills of South Dakota, indicate an unforested Plains lateglacial landscape (Barnowsky et al. 1987).

no forest area

The waning of Pleistocene glacial conditions before 10,000 years ago led, in the Plains, to the disappearance of the lateglacial boreal forest (Wright 1970), of which spruce was characteristic. This forest would have been more a spruce parkland than a closed forest (Ashworth and Cvancara 1983). It was an admixture of ash, oak, and elm, with its open areas dominated by sagebrush. Its migration to the north in the Plains began about 14,000 years ago in western and southwestern Texas, and ended in the prairie provinces of Alberta, Saskatchewan, and Manitoba about 10,000 years ago.

Climate change & megafauna extinction

Lateglacial climatic and vegetational change is tied to the extinction of several Plains megafauna. Included are extinct herbivores (American mastodon, Columbian mammoth, long-nosed peccary, Harlan's ground sloth, horse, camel, and giant bison) and carnivores (dire wolf and saber-toothed tiger), known from the Plains and from middle Mississippi valley Clovis archaeological sites (Graham and Kay 1988; Graham and Mead 1987), as well as a host of other species. On the Plains, Clovis and later Paleo-Indian hunters were clearly responsible for the death of some big-game animals. However, to refer to their hunting as "overkill" (Martin 1984) seems too narrow an explanation for the late Pleistocene extinctions. Reduced habitat diversity coupled with less nutritious foliage increased biological stress and competition among herbivores, especially the many nonruminant ones that died out. The evidence for biological stress is particularly compelling for North American proboscideans (Graham 1986b:168; King and Saunders 1984). It seems likely that the extinct herbivores had too little time to readjust to the abrupt climate-induced changes in plant communities and to the defensive responses of vegetation to grazing and browsing pressures. Herbivores that did survive tended to rapidly increase their population sizes in response to a new mix of habitats and competitive pressures.

More plausible are models that compare the timing and direction of climatic and vegetational changes with responses by individual animal species and competitive plant–animal interactions (Graham 1986a; Graham and Lundelius 1984; Guthrie 1982, 1984; King and Saunders 1984). Extinctions probably first became evident in the south and followed the rapid northward migration of the spruce parkland, in opposition to expectations of the overkill hypothesis. The

bison + C4

patchy southern mosaic of highly nutritious lateglacial vegetation was replaced by habitats with a more restricted suite of less nutritious plants. Differences in plant nutrition generally follow a distinction between two contrastive processes of photosynthesis: C3 and C4. The lateglacial C3 plants were replaced by the less nutritious and often drought-tolerant C4 grasslands (Smith and Epstein 1971).

In the Plains, a chief beneficiary of the new C4-dominated grasslands was bison, which became a Paleo-Indian staple. C4 grasses are better suited to the grazing and nutritional requirements of bison (Peden et al. 1974), so bison, in effect, were "preadapted" to the new grasslands (Graham 1986a:142). As a result of diminished competition with other herbivores and the greater availability of preferred plant foods, bison expanded from small numbers into large herds as grasslands developed. These factors seem to best account for the greater number of bison in postglacial as compared with lateglacial deposits.

Postglacial

Three major North American climatic episodes occurred during the Holocene. Each is time-transgressive and represents a period of climatic similarities that distinguish it from what preceded and followed. The three episodes are the late Pleistocene and early Holocene Early Postglacial, or Boreal; the middle Holocene Altithermal, or Hypsithermal, as redefined by Wright (1976); and the late Holocene Neoglacial, as first described by Deevey and Flint (1957). Profound changes marked the waning of the northern hemisphere ice sheets, for a fundamental reorganization of Plains biota resulted. The patchy mosaic of ice age plants and animals was transformed into a postglacial zonal pattern, what R. Dale Guthrie (1984) has termed a switching from plaids to stripes. A bestiary of large mammals mostly died out, arguably due to climatic change. The few that survived, such as the bison, expanded their numbers and assumed a predominant role in the postglacial world. The postglacial climate also occasioned myriad changes in human adaptation to Plains environments as climate changed in the three major steps from the early Holocene postglacial warming to the late Holocene cooling episode (Figure 2.2).

Warmer + drier conditions

EARLY POSTGLACIAL (CA. 10,000 TO 8500 YEARS AGO)

The retreat of the Laurentide ice sheet marks the Early Postglacial in the Northern Plains, and the general retreat of the Laurentide ice sheet led to the draining of glacial Lake Agassiz. Active stream alluviation between 10,000 and 8000 years ago throughout the tall- and short-grass prairies is attributed to warmer postglacial temperatures and generally drier conditions (Knox 1983).

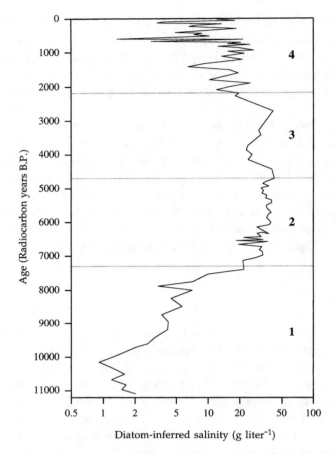

Figure 2.2. Century-scale climatic reconstruction for the past 11,000 years for Moon Lake, a closed-basin lake in the Northern Plains (southeastern North Dakota). Diatom analysis provided an index to lake salinity that suggested four broad climatic zones: (1) an early Holocene period that corresponds with the transition from spruce forest to deciduous parkland to prairie, and suggests a major shift from wet to dry climate; (2) a mid-Holocene period of high salinity, indicating low effective moisture; (3) a period between 4700 and 2200 years ago characterized by poor diatom preservation; and (4) a late Holocene period of variable salinity, indicative of fluctuations in effective moisture (from Laird et al. 1996:Figure 5). It is important to note that no proxy data can provide a Plains-wide record. Conditions would vary in the Southern Plains.

Spruce + pine

About 9600 years ago, spruce colonized the Colorado Front Range at elevations of 11,150 feet, an indication of generally warmer temperatures (Benedict 1985). In the Black Hills, the early Holocene witnessed the immigration of pine and the replacement of the sagebrush-dominated open vegetation by ragweed, goosefoot, and pigweed (Barnowsky et al. 1987). Lateglacial steppe–tundra vegetation apparently did not continue farther south.

The Domebo local fauna of Oklahoma in the Southern Plains (about 11,045 to 10,000 years ago) and the Rex Rodgers local fauna of northwestern Texas were indicative of terminal Pleistocene/early Holocene climates that approached the "modern configuration but with milder winters and cooler summers" (Semken 1983:200). Other faunas from central Texas of probably the same age (Graham 1984; T. Patton 1963; Semken 1983:200–201) and later faunas (9380 to 9000 years ago) from northern Iowa (Hudak 1984) were also typical of more equable climates, a pattern in early Holocene climates that is mirrored in the vegetation history of the southeastern United States (Watts 1980).

About 10,000 years ago, the Llano Estacado probably supported widespread grasslands, and local ponds contained southern bog lemming, whose nearest present habitats are the marshes of either southwestern or northeastern Kansas (Johnson and Holliday 1980). There followed a progressive decrease in effective precipitation, reaching a minimum between 9000 and 8000 years ago (Johnson et al. 1982). Between 8600 and 8300 years ago, some areas on the Llano Estacado were marshlands rimmed by wet meadow that graded into mixed-grass prairie, a change from the earlier rolling prairie (Johnson and Holliday 1981).

Middle Holocene

HYPSITHERMAL (CA. 8500 TO 4000/4500 YEARS AGO) _Atlantic_

Throughout the Plains, the Hypsithermal climatic episode was one of increasing dryness and elevated temperatures, partly brought about by the dominance of an airflow pattern of the Pacific westerlies (Webb and Bryson 1972:108). Another factor was the seasonal peak of solar radiation. The result, depending on latitude, was not one but several seasonally predictable thermal maxima and the dwarfing of critical prey species in the Plains and adjoining Prairie Peninsula (Davis 1984; Purdue 1989). The more drought-tolerant grasslands outcompeted forests on the Plains margins. Grassland-range extensions, lake-level changes, and reduced precipitation document a time-transgressive trend of increasingly warmer and drier, if not full drought, conditions that affected first the Northern Plains and later the Central and Southern Plains. Because of the extension of the prairies beyond their normal range to the north and east, the Hypsithermal is often called the prairie period or prairie maximum.

The Manitoba prairie maximum occurred about 7000 years ago, and did not extend north of latitude 52 degrees north; summer temperatures were as much as 2 degrees Celsius warmer than modern values, and annual precipitation was

drier + warmer

prcipitation below modern levels

about 1 inch less than modern values. At Riding Mountain, Manitoba, in what is now boreal forest, prairie replaced spruce about 10,000 years ago, lasted until about 6130 years ago, and was followed by increasing amounts of oak and hickory until about 3500 years ago, when the modern boreal forest was established (Ritchie 1983:164–165, 1985). At Kirchner Marsh, Minnesota, annual precipitation 7200 years ago was about 2 inches below modern values (Webb and Bryson 1972:107). Summer precipitation values for the Cherokee site in northwestern Iowa between 8460 and 6350 years ago were 1 to 2 inches below modern values (Baerreis 1980:Table 4.2). Prairie replaced forest there after 9000 years ago, followed by its major expansion from 7700 to 3200 years ago. A mid-Holocene drought-ridden landscape is evident at Pickerel Lake in northeastern South Dakota (Watts and Bright 1968; Wright 1970) and in west-central North Dakota (Clayton and Moran 1979; Clayton et al. 1976; Kay et al. 1984:59). Summer precipitation for an eastern prairie outlier at Rodgers Shelter, in southwestern Missouri, is 4 inches below modern values for the period 6700 to 6300 years ago (Baerreis and Theler n.d.). In southwestern Texas, there was a "progressive deterioration of the previous mesic vegetation" between 7000 and 4000 years ago, and probably by 6000 years ago forced human adjustments to "vegetational and climatic conditions that were becoming increasingly" warmer and drier (Bryant and Holloway 1985:56–57). Along the Colorado Front Range, the period from 6700 to 3000 years ago was one of increased summer temperature (Maher 1972:548–550; Peterson and Mehringer 1976:285–286).

The prairie period is illuminated more fully at Elk Lake, Minnesota, than at any other Plains or near-Plains locality. Situated on the boundary between deciduous forest and conifer–hardwood forest just east of the Minnesota prairies, Elk Lake's varved sediments span the past 10,400 years. The prairie period there lasted from 8500 to 3800 years ago, and was a time of the greatest climatic oscillations relative to the rest of the Elk Lake sequence. The prairie period had two dry pulses. It began as a gradual transition to dry conditions and prairie vegetation after 8500 years ago, and ended abruptly 5400 years ago. The time from 5400 to 4800 years ago was relatively wet, and there was a rapid shift to a higher lake level. The second dry pulse was between 4800 and 3800 years ago (Dean et al. 1984:1192).

The wet pulse at Elk Lake from 5400 to 4800 years ago appears to represent a largely unrecognized but significant climatic event, possibly forced, as Benedict (1981) proposed, by an increase in the amount of volcanic aerosols in the global atmosphere 5300 years ago (Bryson and Goodman 1980). The role that volcanism may have played is amplified by Porter's (1986) analysis of Greenland ice-core volcanic acidity compared with the well-dated glacial episodes of the past millennium in the northern hemisphere. Porter notes a lag of 10 to 15 years between increased volcanic acidity in the ice cores and the onset of alpine glaciation such as Benedict (1981) documents for the Colorado Front Range between 5300 and 5150 years ago. Porter believes that volcanic eruptions act as a climatic forcing mechanism on a scale of decades.

Information about the Elk Lake wet episode is more detailed than that for any other middle Holocene climatic event, but there are parallels. LaMarche (1974:Figure 5) has charted the interval from 5150 to 4950 years ago as one of abruptly cooler summers in the White Mountains of southern Nevada and California within a period of relative warmth between 5450 and 3250 years ago. Brakenridge (1980) cites evidence of widespread stream erosion between 5000 and 4900 years ago in the western United States, southwestern Missouri, and central and southwestern Europe. Haynes (1985:11) further evaluates the period from 5400 to 5000 years ago as "a short episode of aggradation" in the Pomme de Terre River drainage of southwestern Missouri. The peak of Denton and Karlen's (1973) first period of northern hemisphere glaciation is 5300 years ago. Correspondence exists as well with the Pre-Piney Creek alluvium of eastern Colorado (Scott 1963) and the alluviation of the Big Blue River in north-central Kansas (Schmits 1978) and the Caney River in northeastern Oklahoma (Artz 1985). Transitions from prairie border to deciduous or coniferous pollen also are described for this interval at Muscotah Marsh in northeastern Kansas (Grüger 1973), Phillips Spring in southwestern Missouri (King 1980), Hackberry Lake in the Nebraska Sand Hills (Sears 1961), and Lake West Okoboji in northwestern Iowa (Van Zant 1979). Wells (1970:200) describes this period in the Nebraska Sand Hills and the Laramie Basin, Wyoming, as one with a "significantly less arid" climate than that of today. In central Texas, "more humid conditions" are posited for 5000 years ago on the basis of otter at the Wunderlich site (Lundelius 1967:312). But on the Llano Estacado of New Mexico and Texas, this period is marked by a return to wind deposition (Holliday 1985) and by falling water tables (Haynes 1975:83; Hester 1972:179) in contrast to mesic conditions to the north and east.

Archaics

NEOGLACIAL (CA. 4000/4500 YEARS AGO TO PRESENT)   moister

The onset of modern or Neoglacial conditions was not uniform, but generally took place earlier in the Northern Plains and in the Rocky Mountains, and parallels the "spread" of the Archaic McKean hunters and gatherers. In the Canadian Rockies of northwestern Alberta, it occurred about 4500 to 4000 years ago (Leonard 1986; Luckman and Kearney 1986). Similarly, the mid-Holocene prairies of northern Alberta and Manitoba were replaced by modern mixed boreal woodlands, oak savanna, or oak savanna followed by boreal forests between 4000 to 3000 years ago, and replacement occurred earliest in the north (Ritchie 1985). At Elk Lake, Minnesota, the prairies were gone by 4500 years ago, but the dry phase continued until about 3800 years ago (Dean et al. 1984). Slightly later, 3700 years ago, an increase in groundwater levels at Swan Lake, in the Nebraska Sand Hills, changed an early to mid-Holocene marshland into a true lake (Wright et al. 1985) and signals the beginning of the Neoglacial in the west-central Plains. In northwestern Iowa, the Lake West Okoboji pollen data define the onset about 3200 years ago (Van Zant 1979). A similar or slightly later time frame is true also for the Pomme de Terre River valley in southwestern Missouri, where Plains vertebrates no longer occur in archaeological sites (McMillan 1976).

The picture in the Southern Plains is not clear. The Neoglacial possibly began in southwestern Texas between 4500 and 3200 years ago, when flooding is noted at Arenosa Shelter (P. Patton 1977). Reduced groundwater levels from 3200 to 2600 years ago at Carnegie Canyon, in southwestern Oklahoma, might also signal the onset of the Neoglacial (Hall and Lintz 1984).

The magnitude of Neoglacial climatic change is less than that of the Hypsithermal, but there were significant changes in climate and environment, especially during the past 1300 years. Three Neoglacial, climate-controlled stream-erosion episodes are identified from widely scattered Plains sites and adjacent areas (Brakenridge 1980). The first of these periods, from 2900 to 2500 years ago, corresponds to the glacial maximum computed by Imbrie and Imbrie (1979:183) of 2800 years ago.

Subsequent Southern Plains climatic trends (Bryant and Holloway 1985; Hall 1982; Hall and Lintz 1984) roughly parallel alpine glaciation in the Colorado Front Range (Benedict 1985; Burke and Birkeland 1983) and at least the second of Brakenridge's (1980) Neoglacial stream-erosion intervals, between 1600 and 1500 years ago. From northeastern Oklahoma to the Texas panhandle, the period from 2000 to 1000 years ago is interpreted as dominated by a moister climate, one that permitted soil formation in Oklahoma and a western range extension of the prairie vole into the Texas panhandle. An open oak woodland with some grassland became established in central Texas about 2400 years ago, a product of more effective moisture that persisted until 1500 years ago, when it was replaced by the drier oak savanna of today (Bryant and Holloway 1985:62–63).

The Plains Setting

This chapter cannot provide a comprehensive and technical review of the Plains setting, but offers a few snapshots—or, perhaps better stated, a postcard—of the Plains, its past and present. However one sees the Plains today, it still manifests a remarkable integrity, a robustness that stands in the face of many alterations. Most recently, these have been occasioned by increasing urbanization and supporting networks of roads, canals and dams, and industrialized agribusiness that has turned many a ranch into a feedlot. One can still find the real Plains—

or, more accurately, the virgin prairies tucked away in shreds and patches, now outlined by irrigated wheat fields. But the search is becoming harder and less rewarding. Even so, the Plains has always undergone change; indeed, change is its one constant. We should lay out a road trip to capture some of what makes the Plains different from other places.

A good place to begin is with the Plains landform. It has truly been a stage of dramatic contrasts in plants, animals, and climate during and since the last glacial ended about 10,000 years ago. In some important ways, the Plains landform has sculpted its vegetation and the animals that feed on it, if not the climate that controls them both. In other ways, the landform has dynamically adjusted to climate and to its life-forms. The Plains landform is the most stable of all, the most tangible and easily grasped. Yet throughout, we must always imagine the Plains landform as quicksilver: solid at one time, liquid the next, and blown to the four cardinal poles. Movements of the continental plates, erosion by the mostly eastward-trending rivers and streams that dissect it, and sculpting by the long-gone glaciers and proglacial lakes that carved its northern frontier and whose wind-blown loess enriched its mantle are the sum total of the Plains landform. But for all of that, the Plains landform is greater still than the sum of its parts (Figure 2.3).

Our postcard must end with no more than a hint of the ways that humans have existed on the Plains. To paraphrase Tip O'Neill, what is true in politics is also true in human ecology: all human adaptation is local. Human adaptation deals with people, places, and the changing circumstances that define daily living and the choices we make. But we tend not to see the relations of local living without a larger view, a view that, if not unique, is ideally suited to our needs. By charting regional and even interregional settlement patterns over time, we can note change in human adaptations. This approach is one used in many Plains studies. I wish to showcase a few of these that highlight late prehistoric and protohistoric agriculture village adaptations in the Central and Northern Plains.

Road Trips

Nothing substitutes for a Plains road trip with a switch or two, as needed, to another conveyance—be it horseback, canoe, train, or airplane. One's trip, ideally, should not go merely from place to place but from season to season. The elemental beauty of the Plains still is seen in spring flowers, the majesty of a summer thunderstorm—nature's prism—filtering a sunset into rainbow hues, the autumn "V" of geese coursing down the Mississippi flyway or cranes along the Platte River and the Sand Hills, or an Alberta clipper as it knifes its way from wintery Calgary to Dallas, scattering blizzards in its wake.

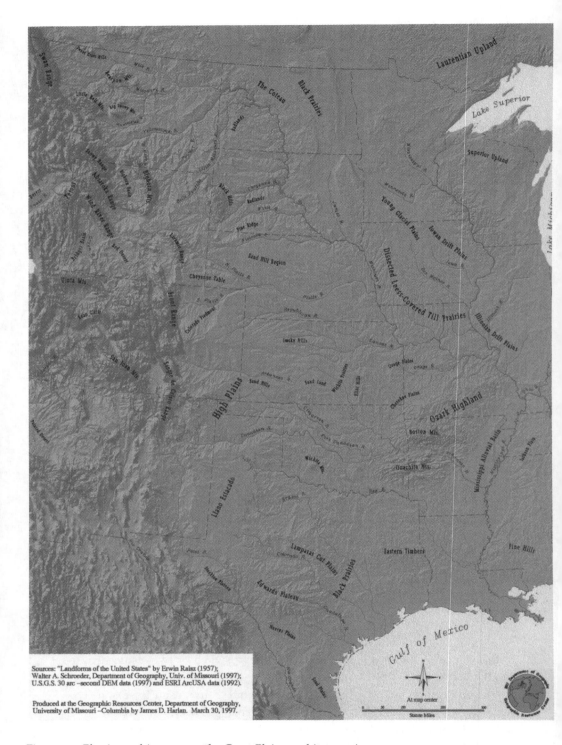

Sources: "Landforms of the United States" by Erwin Raisz (1957);
Walter A. Schroeder, Department of Geography, Univ. of Missouri (1997);
U.S.G.S. 30 arc –second DEM data (1997) and ESRI ArcUSA data (1992).

Produced at the Geographic Resources Center, Department of Geography,
University of Missouri –Columbia by James D. Harlan. March 30, 1997.

Figure 2.3. Physiographic areas on the Great Plains and its margins.

No matter where one goes, the Plains summer can reach near blast-furnace temperatures; its winters, the opposite, offer subzero temperatures and frozen, windswept ground. We often think of the Plains winter as a forbidding time. But even to a Northern Plains forager on foot and with nothing more than a dog travois for transport, the winters may have been better than we would imagine. For one thing, dog-travois travel on snow and ice is more efficient than travel on grassland during summertime, and the cold is less wearing on the dog (Henderson 1994); for another, bison, a prime staple, tended to avoid the forested parkland that borders the Northern Plains because greater snow accumulation made grazing difficult or impossible, and they were more often found on the open prairie (Malainey and Sherriff 1996). Nevertheless, I prefer the spring trip. Life is coming back to the many glacial potholes and sloughs of the Northern Plains, where a host of migratory waterfowl first nest. There are still snowbanks left over from winter, but there is also less chance of being marooned in a late blizzard. Daytime temperatures warm up to shirtsleeve comfort over much of the Central and Southern Plains. The Sand Hills of Nebraska are an emerald-green prairie dotted with lakes that teem with fish and waterfowl. Indian paintbrush and bluebell bud out and burst into flower in the Texas panhandle and western Oklahoma. Depending on the melting snow in spring and rain in early summer, the Northern Plains is an equally colorful carpet of wildflowers that hangs on into August. By August, the prairies in the Northern Plains and High Plains (Fenneman 1938:309–322) parallel to and east of the Rockies from Laramie, Wyoming to Clovis, New Mexico, and points south are a chestnut or rust-brown color and are tinder dry; a lightning bolt or a carelessly thrown, live cigarette butt will set them off in a cycle of fiery renewal. Autumn cools quickly, especially on the High Plains flanked by the Rockies. The autumn chill and even the winter cold can give way to a hot chinook wind that boils down a mountain canyon.

Striking out from St. Joseph, Missouri, we pick up the thread of the Oregon Trail as it heads west across the Central Plains. Other than the Missouri River valley and the Dissected Till Plains of eastern Nebraska and western Iowa, we are mostly in unglaciated country. Eastern Kansas and Nebraska are rolling prairie. They would have been waist deep in tall grasses during the wagon-train days a century or more ago, but today are dotted with farms and small towns, still hanging on but not well. Grand hotels, ballrooms, and banquet halls that once graced even the most modest of these towns are now shuttered. Long ago they gave way to a fast-food burger place, a trailer court, and a dilapidated U-Drop-Inn. The local schools and their football teams are more often than not a thing of memory. The children left for jobs in the cities years ago here and throughout the Plains. In a real sense, the death of their schools spells out a similar fate for these towns. They are hanging on.

Once we leave the Missouri valley, and until we reach the Rockies, the order of the day is truck-stop fast food: instant mashed potatoes and incinerated chicken-fried steak in a library-paste white gravy bordered by thick planks of white-bread Texas toast. An almost singularly Plains place would be the feedlot café buffet. In ways, it is a modern-day version of a bison kill, if only in terms of the quantity of beef served per unit of effort. For some, the new choices might be enough to make one look longingly at the road-killed white-tailed deer, whose expanded range is now throughout the timbered river valleys and into the stubble cornfields, or the ring-necked pheasant, an introduced morsel with a fondness for automobile grillwork. The hardy among us, however, may want to try that modest speed bump, the armadillo, now that it has spread from the Texas Gulf Coastal Plain all the way to southern Nebraska.

The Platte valley in Nebraska, the path of the Oregon and Mormon trails, is more than the main route to the West, because it divides the Central Plains into two major sectors. To its north, the Dissected Till Plains give way gradually to the windblown dunes of the Nebraska Sand Hills, which stretch from just north of Grand Island to the Box Butte tablelands, Pine Ridge, and Pierre Hills near the Wyoming border. Bison no longer exist here, but pronghorn antelope outrace cars and go underneath rather than over a barbed-wire fence. These creatures are distinctive of the short-grass steppe. Their remains tell us that steppe once extended, in the middle Holocene, as far east as northwestern Arkansas and central Missouri. The Sand Hills are drained by branches of the Loup River and, to their north, the Niobrara. Sand Hills archaeology (as is true for much of the Plains overall) has yet to match the physiographic scope and complexity of this area, although recent studies here are adding to our knowledge of different time periods (Koch 1995; Myers 1995). The Nebraska Sand Hills are not, of course, the only Plains dunes, and others are better known for Paleo-Indian campsites and bison kills. But they are the most extensive and, although stabilized by grass, rival in scope the still-active Sand Dunes National Monument near Colorado Springs, Colorado. The permanent Sand Hills lakes are hydrologically controlled; even during drought, some surface water is found here. Beyond the Sand Hills are the badlands along the upper reaches of the White River in the northern panhandle of Nebraska and the ancient and extensive bison-bone bed at the Hudson–Meng site in the Pierre Hills. South of the Platte, a classic braided river, are the mostly unglaciated plains of the meandering Kansas River and its tributaries: the Republican in both Nebraska and Kansas, and in Kansas alone, the Solomon, Saline, and Smoky Hill. These are streams rich in prehistory, and some, notably the Medicine Creek locality of the Republican River in Nebraska and Twelve Mile Creek in the Smoky Hill drainage basin, are conspicuous for both the depth and the age of their buried archaeological sites. The dominant topographic feature south of the Platte is the southward-trending flinthills of southeastern Nebraska and central Kansas that continue into north-central

Southof Platte -
more stone variety

Oklahoma. Naturally enough, the flinthills are source areas for Permian chert, which was regularly used to make chipped-stone tools.

The overall variety and extensiveness of chippable stone from dispersed bedrock sources (Holen 1991) are significantly greater to the south of the Platte than to its north in the Central Plains. This dispersed pattern also is repeated in the Southern Plains, which is dominated by Edwards Chert from central Texas, but also is a source area for Alibates agatized dolomite, Tecovas Jasper, and obsidian (Banks 1990). Northern Plains chippable stone includes an equally diverse suite of obsidian, cherts, silicified mudstones, chalcedonies, quartzites, and orthoquarzites (Ahler 1977; Church 1994, 1996; Francis 1991; Low 1996; Miller 1996) that come mostly from the many mountain basins or from eroded and redeposited sediments. Most famous are the large-scale quarries of the Hartville Uplift (Spanish Diggings) in southeastern Wyoming (Reher 1991) and the Knife River silicified sediment source area in west-central North Dakota (Ahler 1986). Even at a very early date, Knife River Flint was among the most widely exchanged toolstones in North America (Tankersley 1991), but little, if any, is found south of the Platte.

Just beyond the Sand Hills, the vestiges of the High Plains appear in the North and South Platte valleys. The High Plains begins at the foothills of the Rocky Mountains and slopes eastward. Its wide tabular surfaces and mostly calcareous soils are outlined and often deeply incised by river valleys, a pattern seen throughout the High Plains. In western Nebraska, this plain is traversed by the broad, deep North Platte River valley and the smaller valleys of the Niobrara River and Lodgepole Creek, and terminates to the north in the high escarpment of the aptly named Pine Ridge, south of and approximately 1000 feet above the White and Cheyenne river valleys. Surprisingly enough (at least to someone not familiar with the area), pine and juniper forests were relatively common throughout the High Plains, and are now found principally in fire-protected areas. Chimney Rock and the lightly forested Scotts Bluff were among the prominent High Plains remnants first seen by wagon trains heading west on the Oregon Trail. Its wagon ruts still are plainly visible in Mitchell Pass between Scotts Bluff and the adjacent South Bluff. An embayment of Wildcat Ridge, Scotts Bluff is fittingly described as a "great castellated sandstone bluff, dominating the countryside, that has become a shrine of American history . . . its tortuous badlands, sheer walls, frowning battlements and towering crags, looming abruptly eight hundred feet above the river" (Mattes 1945:127). Mattes's words would apply almost equally to many a High Plains remnant. Among those in the Northern Plains are Rainey Buttes and the Killdeer Mountains of North Dakota and Badlands National Monument in South Dakota; in the Southern Plains are outliers of the Caprock Escarpment (of resistant dolomite, gypsum, and calcium carbonate layers above the Permian red beds) in

Texas and Oklahoma. Many of these prominent hills, regardless of their geology, often carry special traditional religious significance to historic Plains Indian cultures.

The Southern High Plains and the rolling prairies of Texas and Oklahoma are underlain by soft bedrock (Permian red beds) interlaced with salt deposits. Throughout the Quaternary and continuing today, the salt often goes into solution, and there are numerous brine springs and salt flats along reaches of the Canadian, Red, and Little Red rivers and other Southern Plains streams. The landscape around Lubbock, Texas, is representative of much of this area, even extending as far north as southwestern Kansas. It is a nearly level plain but with enclosed depressions, the product of a faulted karst landscape created by the subsidence of soluble salt at depth. During the lateglacial and Early Postglacial, this landscape supported pluvial lakes. In western Oklahoma, there is also a cave or two—a notable one is Alibaster Caverns—and entrenched valleys where gypsum has gone into solution. Another point of interest in western Oklahoma is the stratified volcanic ashes that span the Quaternary; the 600,000-year-old ash is found also at Rocky Flats, near Denver, and in eastern Kansas and Nebraska. Southern and Central Plains landscapes postdate these ash falls and are relatively young and highly eroded. The only postglacial volcanic ash of any significance on the Plains is the 6700-year-old Mazama ash. It is restricted mostly to the northwestern plains of Alberta.

South and east of the Permian red beds of the Southern Plains is the extensive limestone country of the Edwards Plateau. The Edwards Plateau is also a karst landscape, but significantly more resistant to erosion than the Permian red beds. Its southern boundary is breached most spectacularly by the entrenched canyons of the Big Bend of the Rio Grand and its tributaries, the Pecos and Devil's Mouth rivers. Its eastern border, the Balcones Escarpment, has numerous karst springs and is dissected by rivers that empty onto the Texas Gulf Coastal Plain.

Northeast of the Edwards Plateau are the Central Lowlands of Texas and Oklahoma, which are drained principally by the Arkansas River. The Central Lowlands and their Osage Plains are dominated by sandstone questas that dip mostly to the southwest and have numerous small caves and rock shelters. Extensive fields of windblown prairie mounds also are characteristic, and many owe their existence to the significantly different climatic conditions of the middle Holocene. The eastern border of the Osage Plains is divided by the Arkansas River, with the Ouachita Mountains to its south and the Ozark Highland to its north. This border area provided a strategic gateway for the movement of material goods and services, if only in late prehistory when Spiro and other Arkansas valley Caddoan chiefdoms prospered.

Until about 14,000 years ago, the combined Cordilleran and Laurentide ice sheets nearly completely covered Canada and Greenland, which, along with Baffin Island, still has remnant ice caps. The Laurentide ice sheet of this time extended south into the Plains states of Montana, North and South Dakota, and northeastern Nebraska. Its Des Moines lobe, which crossed Minnesota and terminated in central Iowa, was a glacial surge of about 14,000 years ago that now marks the eastern border of the Central Plains. By 10,000 years ago, virtually all the Northern Plains was free of Laurentide ice. The ice sheet continued to collapse into the Hudson Bay basin, taking with it successive stages of several 330-foot-deep proglacial lakes in Alberta and Saskatchewan that ultimately drained into Lake Agassiz. Although mostly in Manitoba, Lake Agassiz also extended south into North Dakota and Minnesota, and drained into the Lake Superior basin. A renewed Lake Agassiz covered 124,000 square miles about 9,900 years ago and was the largest Pleistocene lake in North America. Given the volume of glacial meltwater, it is no wonder that the Pleistocene rivers quite literally overran their banks as braided streams or carved cataracts and broad, deep valleys with steep sides. In these respects, they also differ fundamentally from the Holocene rivers, which mostly meander and do not carry the volume of water and sediment of the glacial meltwater streams.

The glaciated Northern Plains landscape varies in age and minimally consists of pre-Wisconsin (mainly Illinoian) and Wisconsin drift. In the Dakotas, the entrenched Missouri River valley cuts through Illinoian drift and is bordered mostly on the east side by Wisconsin till and outwash gravels. Thus it and the valleys of the James and Brown rivers to the east are relatively young, steep sided, and mantled by loess of Wisconsin age and later. They owe their existence to the recession of the Laurentide ice sheet and the draining of Lake Agassiz.

The Missouri and many other Northern Plains waterways are now managed for navigation, flood control, hydroelectric-power generation, and recreation. Earthen dams have impounded them, most spectacularly so in the Dakotas where the Missouri valley is largely inundated. The stretch of the Missouri River at Cross Ranch Wildlife Refuge and Knife River Indian Villages National Historic Site above Bismarck, North Dakota, remains about the only area unimpounded in the Dakotas. Dam construction led to extensive archaeological salvage in the post–World War II years (Lehmer 1971), but the ongoing salvage efforts pale in the face of the wholesale destruction of archaeological sites.

Agricultural Adaptations

Of the 15 cultural traditions that Gordon R. Willey (1966:454–469) identified for North America, the Plains Village tradition is the most closely keyed to a specific landform and is restricted in time to the last millennium. Most North American archaeologists would still agree with Willey's (1966:464) evaluation and description of this agricultural lifeway as being "essentially confined to the suitable river valley locations of the eastern part of the Plains" in the Central and Middle Missouri subareas (principally in the Dakotas), and as a "reintegration and new adaptation of Mississippian traits to a Plains environment."

In essence, the area Willey described is the glaciated part of the Northern or Northeastern plains, together with Central Plains stream valleys in Nebraska, Kansas, and Iowa. This adaptation, which is truly singular in North America, is one that depended on two things. First, lateglacial remodeling of stream valleys provided a suitable environment for villages on the high, flood-free terraces. These villages overlooked floodplain gardens that could be tilled using simple bone hoes, and the river-margin gallery forests that were essential for village life. Second, recent weather patterns allowed for both a sufficient number of frost-free days and the precipitation needed to grow corn, beans, squash, and other staples.

In a review of the Middle Missouri–tradition cultures of Minnesota, Guy Gibbon (Gibbon 1993:183) succinctly frames the puzzle posed by these and other examples of Northern Plains agricultural settlements:

> Although Middle Missouri tradition cultures were present in Minnesota for only a relatively brief period, from about AD 850/900 to 1200/1300, their appearance and disappearance raise intriguing problems of interpretation. Their emergence seems to be a regional expression of a widespread structural transformation that is arguably the most radical culture change in tempo and magnitude to have occurred in the prehistoric upper Midwest; their disappearance seems part of a reorganization of the cultural landscape that was also interregional in scope.

Gibbon calls for a basic evaluation of the context and significance of these changes, but it is beyond the scope of this chapter to address fully his concerns. Yet new data on village population size and movement (Ahler 1993; Roper 1995) may be compared with climate changes for the Central and Northern Plains.

The two studies employ different means to estimate population (Roper: radiocarbon dates organized by century for agricultural villages; Ahler: ceramic production for dated village components) that appear to be appropriately conservative and complementary to each other. They further differ in scale and do not overlap. Roper considers the Central Plains and the Big Bend of the Missouri River near Chamberlain in South Dakota (Figure 2.4); Ahler, the upper Knife–Heart region of the Middle Missouri subarea in North Dakota above Bismarck.

An abstract of Roper's data for the Central Plains shows that the Missouri River area and its tributaries, mainly in western Iowa and Missouri, were among the first areas settled by agricultural villages, and Roper regards them as jumping-off points for further settlement in the Central Plains, beginning in the eleventh century. In Kansas, mainly along the Kansas River and its tributaries (the Republican, Solomon, Saline, and Smoky Hill rivers), agricultural villages reached their peak in the thirteenth century—that is, immediately following the Medieval optimum. The thirteenth century also witnessed the expansion of settlement to the Platte valley and beyond in Nebraska, and along

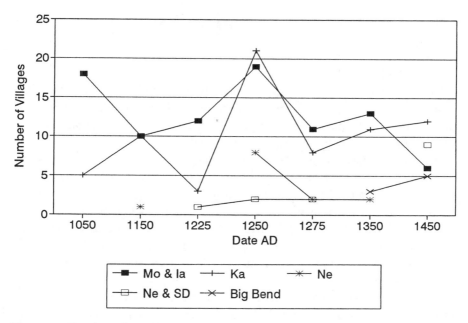

Figure 2.4. Trends in Central Plains agriculture village population (after Roper 1995). Mo & Ia, the Missouri valley and its tributaries in western Missouri and southwest Iowa; Ka, the Kansas River and its tributaries in Kansas and extreme southern Nebraska south of the Platte; Ne, the Platte valley and Loup River in Nebraska; Ne & SD, the Missouri valley in northeastern Nebraska and southeastern South Dakota; Big Bend, the "Grand Detour" of the Missouri River in south-central South Dakota.

1200's major expansion in Central plains
1300-1400's migration to n. Plains

the Missouri River in northeastern Nebraska and southeastern South Dakota. The thirteenth century was, thus, the major time of Central Plains population expansion and the beginning of migration into the Northern Plains of the Middle Missouri subarea. The fourteenth and fifteenth centuries saw an increase of Central Plains village movement that extended into the Big Bend area. The movement into the Big Bend first occurred in the fourteenth century, during a period of climatic amelioration. Toward the end of this period of climatic amelioration, in the early fifteenth century, village population also peaked in the upper Knife–Heart region of North Dakota (Ahler 1993). The dramatic population decline in the late fifteenth century and thereafter in the upper Knife–Heart region coincided with the colder and drier climate of the Little Ice Age.

Conclusion

This outline of the late Quaternary history of the Plains only begins to touch on the literature and conclusions about past climate and environment. Yet understanding the archaeological record depends as much on our success on modeling late Quaternary landscapes and their dynamic biophysical environments as it does on the analysis of artifacts. It is therefore important to remember a number of points.

The lateglacial Plains differed dramatically from the Holocene Plains in climate and environment. The former environment was capable of supporting disharmonious faunas and floras. There was both greater environmental diversity and a more diverse roster of large herbivores.

Abrupt climatic change at the end of the lateglacial signaled the end of many big-game species, several of which were hunted by Clovis and later Paleo-Indian groups. Human predation of big-game animals is not a sufficient explanation for either extinctions or survivals of some herbivores, such as bison, which became a postglacial staple. Models that compare the timing and direction of climatic and vegetative changes with responses by individual animal species and competitive plant–animal interactions provide a more convincing explanation of big-game extinctions.

Gradual and less striking changes in climate, vegetation, and landscape marked the postglacial period. Relative to later events, the Early Postglacial was a more mesic period of continental climate in which more drought-tolerant C4 grasses became established on the Plains. These grasses are better suited to the nutritional needs of bison. The large herds of Holocene bison appear to be a direct consequence of the increased availability of these grasses and the absence of other grazing competitors.

The middle Holocene Hypsithermal period was one of higher temperatures and reduced precipitation that led to a severe, long-term drought over much of the Plains. Relatively deep lakes dried up, accompanied by erosion and alluviation in drainage systems, and the grasslands expanded east and north to their maximum limits. There was a more pronounced west-to-east climatic gradient, which favored a movement to the east of short-grass prairie.

Hypsithermal times included at least one well-defined mesic interval, the Elk Lake, 5400 to 4800 years ago. There may have been other earlier Hypsithermal mesic intervals, but they are not as well established.

The onset of Neoglacial climatic conditions began about 4000 years ago, and were first experienced in the Northern Plains. Neoglacial climatic changes were abrupt and recurring, but were of a lesser magnitude than those of the Hypsithermal.

The well-defined Medieval optimum (or Neo-Atlantic episode) of the twelfth century A.D. was preceded by a period of generally more mesic, if not warmer, conditions. Following the Medieval optimum was the Little Ice Age, which in the Plains reached its peak around the fourteenth and fifteenth centuries.

Dedication and Acknowledgments

This chapter is dedicated to the memory of David A. Baerreis, a pioneer in Plains paleoenvironmental and climatic research. An earlier draft was critically read by Thompson Webb III and two anonymous reviewers. It has also benefited from discussions with, and information provided by, James B. Benedict, G. Robert Brakenridge, Russell W. Graham, Eric C. Grimm, Eileen Johnson, James R. Purdue, and Wayne M. Wendland.

References

Ahler, S. A.
  1977   Lithic Resource Utilization Patterns in the Middle Missouri Subarea. In *Trends in Middle Missouri Prehistory: A Festschrift Honoring the Contributions of Donald J. Lehmer,* edited by W. R. Wood, 132–150. Plains Anthropologist Memoir no. 13.
  1986   *The Knife River Flint Quarries: Excavations at Site 32DU508.* State Historical Society of North Dakota, Bismarck.
  1993   Architecture and Settlement Change in the Upper Knife–Heart Region. In *The Phase I Archeological Research Program for the Knife River Indian Villages National Historic Site.* Part 4, *Interpretation of the Archeological Record,* edited by T. D. Thiessen, 33–55. National Park Service, Midwest Archeological Center, Occasional Studies in Anthropology, no. 27. Lincoln, Nebr.

Artz, J. A.
  1985   A Soil-Geomorphic Approach to Locating Buried Late Archaic Sites in Northeast Oklahoma. *American Archaeology* 5:142–150.

Ashworth, A. C., and A. M. Cvancara
  1983   Paleoecology of the Southern Part of the Lake Agassiz Basin. In *Glacial Lake Agassiz,* edited by J. T. Teller and L. Clayton, 133–156. Geological Association of Canada, Special Paper no. 26. University of Toronto Press, Toronto.

Baerreis, D. A.
  1980   Habitat and Climatic Interpretation Derived from Terrestrial Gastropods at the Cherokee Sewer Site. In *The Cherokee Excavations: Mid-Holocene Paleoecology and Human Adaptation in Northwest Iowa,* edited by D. C. Anderson and H. A. Semken, Jr., 101–122. Academic Press, New York.

Baerreis, D. A., and J. A. Theler
  n.d.   Habitat and Climatic Interpretation from Terrestrial Gastropods at Rodgers Shelter. Manuscript on file, Illinois State Museum, Springfield.

Banks, L. D.
  1990   *From Mountain Peaks to Alligator Stomachs: A Review of Lithic Sources in the Trans-Mississippi South, the Southern Plains, and Adjacent Southwest.* Oklahoma Anthropological Society, Memoir no. 4. Norman.

Barnowsky, C. W., E. C. Grimm, and H. E. Wright, Jr.
  1987   Towards a Postglacial History of the Northern Great Plains: A Review of the Paleoecologic Problems. *Annals of the Carnegie Museum* 56:259–273.

Benedict, J. B.
  1981   Prehistoric Man, Volcanism, and Climatic Change: 7500–5000 C14 Yr. B.P. *Geological Society of America Abstracts with Programs* 13:407.

1985   *Arapaho Pass: Glacial Geology and Archeology at the Crest of the Colorado Front Range.* Center for Mountain Archeology, Research Report no. 3. Ward, Colo.

Borchert, J. R.
1950   The Climate of the Central North American Grassland. *Annals of the Association of American Geographers* 40:1–39.

Brakenridge, G. R.
1978   Evidence for a Cold, Dry Full-Glacial Climate in the American Southwest. *Quaternary Research* 9:22–40.
1980   Widespread Episodes of Stream Erosion During the Holocene and Their Climatic Cause. *Nature* 283:655–656.

Brown, D. A., and P. J. Gersmehl
1985   Migration Models for Grasses in the American Midcontinent. *Annals of the Association of American Geographers* 75:383–394.

Bryant, V. M., Jr., and R. G. Holloway
1985   A Late-Quaternary Paleoenvironmental Record of Texas: An Overview of the Pollen Evidence. In *Pollen Records of North American Sediments*, edited by V. M. Bryant, Jr., and R. G. Holloway, 39–70. American Association of Stratigraphic Palynologists Foundation. Dallas, Tex.

Bryson, R. A., D. A. Baerreis, and W. M. Wendland
1970   The Character of Late-Glacial and Post-Glacial Climatic Changes. In *Pleistocene and Recent Environments of the Central Great Plains*, edited by W. Dort, Jr., and J. K. Jones, Jr., 53–74. University Press of Kansas, Lawrence.

Bryson, R. A., and B. M. Goodman
1980   Volcanic Activity and Climatic Change. *Science* 207:1041–1044.

Burke, R. M., and P. W. Birkeland
1983   Holocene Glaciation in the Mountain Ranges of the Western United States. In *The Holocene*, edited by H. E. Wright, Jr., 3–11. Vol. 2 of *Late Quaternary Environments of the United States.* University of Minnesota Press, Minneapolis.

Church, T.
1994   Ogalalla Orthoquartzite: An Updated Description. *Plains Anthropologist* 39:53–62.
1996   Lithic Resources of the Bearlodge Mountains, Wyoming: Description, Distribution, and Implications. *Plains Anthropologist* 41:135–164.

Clayton, L. S., and S. R. Moran
1979   Oahe Formation. In *Geology and Geohydrology of the Knife River Basin and Adjacent Areas of West-Central North Dakota*, 337–339. North Dakota Geological Survey, Report of Investigation, no. 64. Bismarck.

Clayton, L. S., S. R. Moran, and W. B. Bickley, Jr.
1976   *Stratigraphy, Origin, and Climatic Implications of Late Quaternary Upland Silt in North Dakota.* North Dakota Geological Survey, Miscellaneous Series, no. 54. Bismarck.

Davis, O. K.
1984   Multiple Thermal Maxima During the Holocene. *Science* 225:617–619.

Dawson, A. G.
1992   *Ice Age Earth: Late Quaternary Geology and Climate.* Routledge, London.

Dean, W. E., J. P. Bradbury, R. Y. Anderson, and C. W. Barnowsky
1984   The Variability of Holocene Climate Change: Evidence from Varved Lake Sediments. *Science* 226:1191–1194.

Deevey, E. S., and R. F. Flint
1957   Postglacial Hypsithermal Interval. *Science* 125:182–184.

Denton, G. H., and W. Karlen
  1973   Holocene Climatic Variations—Their Pattern and Possible Cause. *Quaternary Research* 3:155–205.
Dort, W., Jr., and J. K. Jones, Jr., eds.
  1970   *Pleistocene and Recent Environments of the Central Great Plains.* University Press of Kansas, Lawrence.
Euler, R. C., G. J. Gumerman, T. N. V. Karlstrom, J. S. Dean, and R. H. Hevly
  1979   The Colorado Plateaus: Cultural Dynamics and Paleoenvironment. *Science* 205:1089–1101.
Fenneman, N. M.
  1931   *Physiography of Western United States.* McGraw-Hill, New York.
  1938   *Physiography of Eastern United States.* McGraw-Hill, New York.
Francis, J.
  1991   Lithic Resources on the Northwestern High Plains. In *Raw Material Economies Among Prehistoric Hunter-Gatherers*, edited by A. Montet-White and S. Holen, 305–319. University of Kansas, Publications in Anthropology, no. 19. Lawrence.
Gibbon, G.
  1993   The Middle Missouri Tradition in Minnesota: A Review. In *Prehistory and Human Ecology of the Western Prairies and Northern Plains*, edited by J. A. Tiffany, 169–187. Plains Anthropologist Memoir no. 27.
Graham, R. W.
  1984   Environmental Implications of the Quaternary Distribution of the Eastern Chipmunk (*Tamias striatus*) in Central Texas. *Quaternary Research* 21:111–114.
  1986a   Plant–Animal Interactions and Pleistocene Extinctions. In *Dynamics of Extinction*, edited by D. K. Elliott, 131–154. Wiley, New York.
  1986b   Taxonomy of North American Mammoths. In *The Colby Mammoth Site— Taphonomy and Archaeology of a Clovis Kill in Northern Wyoming*, edited by G. C. Frison and L. C. Todd, 165–169. University of New Mexico Press, Albuquerque.
Graham, R. W., and M. Kay
  1988   Taphonomic Comparisons of Cultural and Noncultural Faunal Deposits at the Kimmswick and Barnhart Sites, Jefferson County, Missouri. In *Late Pleistocene and Early Holocene Paleoecology and Archaeology of the Eastern Great Lakes Region*, edited by R. S. Laub, N. G. Miller, and D. W. Steadman, 227–240. Bulletin of the Buffalo Society of Natural Sciences, vol. 33. Buffalo, N.Y.
Graham, R. W., and E. L. Lundelius, Jr.
  1984   Coevolutionary Disequilibrium and Pleistocene Extinctions. In *Quaternary Extinctions: A Prehistoric Revolution*, edited by P. S. Martin and R. G. Klein, 223–249. University of Arizona Press, Tucson.
  1994   *FAUNMAP: A Database Documenting Late Quaternary Distributions of Mammal Species in the United States.* Illinois State Museum, Scientific Papers, vol. 25, nos. 1–2. Springfield.
Graham, R. W., and J. I. Mead
  1987   Environmental Fluctuations and Evolution of Mammalian Faunas During the Last Deglaciation in North America. In *North America and Adjacent Oceans During the Last Deglaciation*, edited by W. R. Ruddiman and H. E. Wright, Jr., 371–402. Vol. K-3 of *The Geology of North America*. Geological Society of America, Boulder, Colo.

Graham, R. W., H. A. Semken, Jr., and M. A. Graham, eds.
  1987   *Late Quaternary Mammalian Biogeography and Environments of the Great Plains and Prairies*. Illinois State Museum, Scientific Papers, vol. 22. Springfield.

Grüger, J.
  1973   Studies on the Late Quaternary Vegetation History of Northeastern Kansas. *Geological Society of America Bulletin* 84:239–250.

Guthrie, D. R.
  1982   Mammals of the Mammoth Steppe as Paleoenvironmental Indicators. In *Paleoecology of Beringia*, edited by D. M. Hopkins, J. V. Matthews, Jr., C. E. Schweger, and S. B. Young, 307–326. Academic Press, New York.

  1984   Mosaics, Allelochemics, and Nutrients: An Ecological Theory of Late Pleistocene Megafaunal Extinctions. In *Quaternary Extinctions: A Prehistoric Revolution*, edited by P. S. Martin and R. G. Klein, 259–298. University of Arizona Press, Tucson.

Hall, S. A.
  1982   Late Holocene Paleoecology of the Southern Plains. *Quaternary Research* 17:391–407.

Hall, S. A., and C. Lintz
  1984   Buried Trees, Water Table Fluctuations, and 3000 Years of Changing Climate in West-Central Oklahoma. *Quaternary Research* 22:129–133.

Haynes, C. V., Jr.
  1975   Pleistocene and Recent Stratigraphy. In *Late Pleistocene Environments of the Southern High Plains*, edited by F. Wendorf and J. J. Hester, 57–96. Fort Burgwin Research Center, Publication no. 9. Ranchos de Taos, N.M.

  1985   *Mastodon-Bearing Springs and Late Quaternary Geochronology of the Lower Pomme de Terre Valley, Missouri*. Geological Society of America, Special Paper no. 204. Boulder, Colo.

Henderson, N.
  1994   Replicating Dog Travois Travel on the Northern Plains. *Plains Anthropologist* 39:145–159.

Hester, J. J.
  1972   *Blackwater Locality No. 1: A Stratified Early Man Site in Eastern New Mexico*. Fort Burgwin Research Center, Publication no. 8. Ranchos de Taos, N.M.

Holen, S. R.
  1991   Bison Hunting Territories and Lithic Acquisition Among the Pawnee: An Ethnohistoric and Archaeological Study. In *Raw Material Economies Among Prehistoric Hunter-Gatherers*, edited by A. Montet-White and S. Holen, 399–411. University of Kansas, Publications in Anthropology, no. 19. Lawrence.

Holliday, V. T.
  1985   New Data on the Stratigraphy and Pedology of the Clovis and Plainview Sites, Southern High Plains. *Quaternary Research* 23:388–402.

Holmes, W. H.
  1891   Aboriginal Novaculite Quarries in Garland Co., Arkansas. *American Anthropologist* 4:313–316.

  1894   *An Ancient Quarry in Indian Territory*. Bureau of American Ethnology Bulletin 21. Washington, D.C.

  1919   *Handbook of Aboriginal American Antiquities*. Part 1, *The Lithic Industries*. Bureau of American Ethnology Bulletin 60. Washington, D.C.

Hudak, C. M.

1984   Paleontology of an Early Holocene Faunal and Floral Assemblage from the Dows Local Biota of North-Central Iowa. *Quaternary Research* 21:351–368.

Imbrie, J., and K. P. Imbrie

1979   *Ice Ages: Solving the Mystery.* Enslow, Hillside, N.J.

Jacobson, G. L., Jr., T. Webb III, and E. C. Grimm

1987   Changing Vegetation Patterns of Eastern North America During the Past 18,000 Years: Inferences from Overlapping Distributions of Selected Pollen Types. In *North America and Adjacent Oceans During the Last Deglaciation,* edited by W. F. Ruddiman and H. E. Wright, Jr., 447–462. Vol. K-3 of *The Geology of North America.* Geological Society of America, Boulder, Colo.

Johnson, E., and V. T. Holliday

1980   A Plainview Kill/Butchering Locale on the Llano Estacado—The Lubbock Lake Site. *Plains Anthropologist* 25:89–111.

1981   Late Paleo-Indian Activity at the Lubbock Lake Site. *Plains Anthropologist* 26:173–193.

Johnson, E., V. T. Holliday, and R. W. Neck

1982   Lake Theo: Late Quaternary Paleoenvironmental Data and a New Plainview (Paleoindian) Date. *North American Archaeologist* 3:113–137.

Kay, M., J. VanNest, S. A. Ahler, C. R. Falk, and C. M. Snyder

1984   Spring Creek Site Descriptions. In *Archaeological Investigations in the Knife River Flint Primary Source Area, Dunn County, North Dakota: 1983–1984 Program,* edited by M. Kay and J. VanNest, 47–161. University of North Dakota, Department of Anthropology and Archaeology, Contribution no. 210. Grand Forks.

King, J. E.

1980   Palynological Investigations at Phillips Spring. In *Holocene Adaptations Within the Lower Pomme de Terre River Valley, Missouri,* edited by M. Kay, 687–699. Report to the United States Army Corps of Engineers, Kansas City District, Kansas City, Mo.

King, J. E., and J. J. Saunders

1984   Environmental Insularity and the Extinction of the American Mastodont. In *Quaternary Extinctions: A Prehistoric Revolution,* edited by P. S. Martin and R. G. Klein, 315–339. University of Arizona Press, Tucson.

Knight, V. J., Jr.

1986   The Institutional Organization of Mississippian Religion. *American Antiquity* 51:675–687.

Knox, J. C.

1983   Responses of River Systems to Holocene Climates. In *The Holocene,* edited by H. E. Wright, Jr., 26–41. Vol. 2 of *Late Quaternary Environments of the United States.* University of Minnesota Press, Minneapolis.

Koch, A.

1995   The McIntosh Fauna: Late Prehistoric Exploitation of Lake and Prairie Habitats in the Nebraska Sand Hills. *Plains Anthropologist* 40:39–60.

Krause, R. A.

1970   Aspects of Adaptation Among Upper Republican Subsistence Cultivators. In *Pleistocene and Recent Environments of the Central Great Plains,* edited by W. Dort, Jr., and J. K. Jones, Jr., 103–115. University Press of Kansas, Lawrence.

Kroeber, A. L.
   1939   *Cultural and Natural Areas of Native North America.* University of California,
            Publications in American Archaeology and Ethnology, vol. 38. Berkeley.
Laird, K. R., S. C. Fritz, E. C. Grimm, and P. G. Mueller
   1996   Century-Scale Paleoclimatic Reconstruction from Moon Lake, a Closed-Basin
            Lake in the Northern Great Plains. *Limnology and Oceanography* 4:890–902.
LaMarche, V. C., Jr.
   1974   Paleoclimatic Inferences from Long Tree-Ring Records. *Science* 183:1043–1048.
Lehmer, D. J.
   1971   *Introduction to Middle Missouri Archeology.* National Park Service, Anthropo-
            logical Papers, no. 1. Washington, D.C.
Leonard, E. M.
   1986   Use of Lacustrine Sedimentary Sequences as Indicators of Holocene Glacial
            History, Banff National Park, Alberta, Canada. *Quaternary Research* 26:218–231.
Low, B.
   1996   Swan River Chert. *Plains Anthropologist* 41:165–174.
Luckman, B. H., and M. S. Kearney
   1986   Reconstruction of Holocene Changes in Alpine Vegetation and Climate in
            the Maligne Range, Jasper National Park, Alberta. *Quaternary Research* 26:244–
            261.
Lundelius, E. L., Jr.
   1967   Late-Pleistocene and Holocene Faunal History of Central Texas. In *Pleistocene
            Extinctions: The Search for a Cause,* edited by P. S. Martin and H. E. Wright, Jr.,
            287–336. Yale University Press, New Haven, Conn.
Lundelius, E. L., Jr., R. W. Graham, E. Anderson, J. Guilday, J. A. Holman, D. W.
Steadman, and S. D. Webb
   1983   Terrestrial Vertebrate Faunas. In *The Late Pleistocene,* edited by S. C. Porter,
            311–353. Vol. 1 of *Late Quaternary Environments of the United States.* University
            of Minnesota Press, Minneapolis.
Maher, L. J., Jr.
   1972   Absolute Pollen Diagram of Redrock Lake, Boulder County, Colorado. *Quater-
            nary Research* 2:531–553.
Malainey, M. E., and B. L. Sherriff
   1996   Adjusting Our Perceptions: Historical and Archaeological Evidence of Winter
            on the Plains of Western Canada. *Plains Anthropologist* 41:333–357.
Martin, P. S.
   1984   Prehistoric Overkill: The Global Model. In *Quaternary Extinctions: A Prehistoric
            Revolution,* edited by P. S. Martin and R. G. Klein, 354–403. University of
            Arizona Press, Tucson.
Martin, P. S., and R. G. Klein, eds.
   1984   *Quaternary Extinctions: A Prehistoric Revolution.* University of Arizona Press,
            Tucson.
Mattes, M. J.
   1945   Hiram Scott, Fur Trader. *Nebraska History* 26:127–162.
McMillan, R. B.
   1976   The Dynamics of Cultural and Environmental Change at Rodgers Shelter,
            Missouri. In *Prehistoric Man and His Environments: A Case Study in the Ozark
            Highland,* edited by W. R. Wood and R. B. McMillan, 211–232. Academic Press,
            New York.

Miller, J. C.

1996 Lithic Sources in the Northwestern Plains. In *Archeological and Bioarcheological Resources of the Northern Plains,* edited by G. C. Frison and R. C. Mainfort, 41–49. Arkansas Archeological Survey, Research Series, no. 47. Fayetteville.

Morrison, R. B.

1991 *Quaternary Nonglacial Geology: Conterminous U.S.* Vol. K-2 of *The Geology of North America.* Geological Society of America, Boulder, Colo.

Myers, T. P.

1995 Paleoindian Occupation of the Eastern Sand Hills. *Plains Anthropologist* 40:61–68.

Patton, P. C.

1977 Geomorphic Criteria for Estimating the Magnitude and Frequency of Flooding in Central Texas. Ph.D. diss., Department of Geology, University of Texas, Austin.

Patton, T. H.

1963 *Fossil Vertebrates from Miller's Cave, Llano County, Texas.* Texas Memorial Museum Bulletin no. 7. Lubbock.

Peden, D. G., G. M. VanDyne, R. W. Rice, and R. M. Hansen

1974 The Trophic Ecology of *Bison bison l.* on Shortgrass Plains. *Journal of Applied Ecology* 11:489–498.

Peterson, K. L., and P. J. Mehringer, Jr.

1976 Postglacial Timberline Fluctuations, La Plata Mountains, Southwestern Colorado. *Arctic and Alpine Research* 8:275–288.

Pielou, E. C.

1991 *After the Ice Age: The Return of Life to Glaciated North America.* University of Chicago Press, Chicago.

Porter, S. C.

1986 Pattern and Forcing of Northern Hemisphere Glacial Variations During the Last Millennium. *Quaternary Research* 26:27–48.

Porter, S. C., ed.

1983 *The Late Pleistocene.* Vol. 1 of *Late Quaternary Environments of the United States.* University of Minnesota Press, Minneapolis.

Purdue, J. R.

1989 Changes During the Holocene in the Size of White-tailed Deer (*Odocoileus virginianus*) from Central Illinois. *Quaternary Research* 32:307–316.

Reher, C. A.

1991 Large Scale Lithic Quarries and Regional Transport Systems on the High Plains of Eastern Wyoming: Spanish Diggings Revisited. In *Raw Material Economies Among Prehistoric Hunter-Gatherers,* edited by A. Montet-White and S. Holen, 251–284. University of Kansas, Publications in Anthropology, no. 19. Lawrence.

Ritchie, J. C.

1983 The Paleoecology of the Central and Northern Parts of the Glacial Lake Agassiz Basin. In *Glacial Lake Agassiz,* edited by J. T. Teller and L. Clayton, 157–170. Geological Association of Canada, Special Paper no. 26. University of Toronto Press, Toronto.

1985 Quaternary Pollen Records from the Western Interior and the Arctic of Canada. In *Pollen Records of Late-Quaternary North American Sediments,* edited by V. M. Bryant, Jr., and R. G. Holloway, 327–352. American Association of Stratigraphic Palynologists Foundation, Dallas, Tex.

Roper, D. C.
   1995   Spatial Dynamics and Historical Process in the Central Plains Tradition. *Plains Anthropologist* 40:203–221.
Ruddiman, W. F.
   1987   Northern Oceans. In *North America and Adjacent Oceans During the Last Deglaciation,* edited by W. F. Ruddiman and H. E. Wright, Jr., 137–154. Vol. K-3 of *The Geology of North America.* Geological Society of America, Boulder, Colo.
Ruddiman, W. F., and H. E. Wright, Jr., eds.
   1987   *North America and Adjacent Oceans During the Last Glaciation.* Vol. K-3 of *The Geology of North America.* Geological Society of America, Boulder, Colo.
Schmits, L. J.
   1978   *The Coffey Site: Environment and Cultural Adaptation at a Prairie-Plains Archaic Site.* Midcontinental Journal of Archaeology, Special Paper no. 1.
Scott, G. R.
   1963   *Quaternary Geology and Geomorphic History of the Kassler Quadrangle, Colorado.* United States Geological Survey, Professional Paper 421-A. Washington, D.C.
Sears, P. B.
   1961   A Pollen Profile from the Grassland Province. *Science* 134:2038–2040.
Semken, H. A., Jr.
   1983   Holocene Mammalian Biogeography and Climatic Change in the Eastern and Central United States. In *The Holocene,* edited by H. E. Wright, Jr., 182–207. Vol. 2 of *Late Quaternary Environments of the United States.* University of Minnesota Press, Minneapolis.
Shelford, V. E.
   1963   *The Ecology of North America.* University of Illinois Press, Urbana.
Smith, B. N., and S. Epstein
   1971   Two Categories of $^{13}C/^{12}$ Ratios for Higher Plants. *Plant Physiology* 47:380–384.
Tankersley, K. B.
   1991   A Geoarchaeological Investigation of Distribution and Exchange in the Raw Material Economies of Clovis Groups in Eastern North America. In *Raw Material Economies Among Prehistoric Hunter-Gatherers,* edited by A. Montet-White and S. Holen, 285–303. University of Kansas, Publications in Anthropology, no. 19. Lawrence.
Van Zant, K.
   1979   Late-Glacial and Postglacial Pollen and Plant Macrofossils from Lake West Okoboji, Northwestern Iowa. *Quaternary Research* 12:358–380.
Watts, W. A.
   1980   Late Quaternary Vegetation History at White Pond on the Inner Coastal Plain of South Carolina. *Quaternary Research* 13:187–199.
Watts, W. A., and R. C. Bright
   1968   Pollen, Seed, and Mollusk Analysis of a Sediment Core from Pickerel Lake, Northeastern South Dakota. *Geological Society of America Bulletin* 79:855–876.
Webb, T., III, and R. A. Bryson
   1972   Late- and Postglacial Climatic Change in the Northern Midwest, U.S.A.: Quantitative Estimates Derived from Fossil Pollen Spectra by Multivariate Statistical Analysis. *Quaternary Research* 2:70–115.
Wedel, W. R.
   1961   *Prehistoric Man on the Plains.* University of Oklahoma Press, Norman.

Wells, P. V.
  1970 Vegetational History of the Great Plains: A Post-Glacial Record of Coniferous Woodland in Southeastern Wyoming. In *Pleistocene and Recent Environments of the Central Great Plains,* edited by W. Dort, Jr., and J. K. Jones, Jr., 185–202. University Press of Kansas, Lawrence.

Wendland, W. M., and R. A. Bryson
  1981 Northern Hemisphere Airstream Regions. *Monthly Weather Review* 109:255–270.

White, J. M., R. W. Mathewes, and W. H. Mathews
  1985 Late Pleistocene Chronology and Environment of the "Ice-Free Corridor" of Northwestern Alberta. *Quaternary Research* 24:173–186.

Willey, G. R.
  1966 *An Introduction to American Archaeology.* Vol. 1, *North and Middle America.* Prentice-Hall, Englewood Cliffs, N.J.

Williams, L. D., and T. M. L. Wigley
  1983 A Comparison of Evidence for Late Holocene Summer Temperature Variations in the Northern Hemisphere. *Quaternary Research* 20:286–307.

Wissler, C.
  1907 Diffusion of Culture in the Plains of North America. *Proceedings, Fifteenth International Congress of Americanists* 2:39–52.

Wright, H. E., Jr.
  1970 Vegetational History of the Great Plains. In *Pleistocene and Recent Environments of the Central Great Plains,* edited by W. Dort, Jr., and J. K. Jones, Jr., 157–172. University Press of Kansas, Lawrence.
  1976 The Dynamic Nature of Holocene Vegetation: A Problem in Paleoclimatology, Biogeography, and Stratigraphic Nomenclature. *Quaternary Research* 6:581–596.

Wright, H. E., Jr., ed.
  1983 *The Holocene.* Vol. 2 of *Late Quaternary Environments of the United States.* University of Minnesota Press, Minneapolis.

Wright, H. E., Jr., J. Almendinger, and J. Grüger
  1985 Pollen Diagram from the Nebraska Sandhills and the Age of the Dunes. *Quaternary Research* 24:115–120.

3. A History of Great Plains Prehistory

Richard A. Krause

This chapter should have been titled "Toward a History of Great Plains Prehistory," for no essay of this length can be comprehensive. Therefore, I cannot detail the events and accomplishments that have made Plains prehistory the
discipline it is today. Instead, I must ignore many of my predecessors' accomplishments and focus on those themes that run through multiple and diverse
past efforts to understand the human occupation of the Great Plains. Thus the
history I shall produce must be understood in a nontraditional sense: as an effort to select those issues in past works that map the areas of analysis and interpretation that still vex us. History in the sense I am contemplating it is an
effort that finds its value in yielding a more precise understanding of the work
yet before us. To accomplish my aim, I must narrow the scope of my vision to a
few tightly focused aspects of past inquiry that I shall identify as themes. There
seem, for instance, to be three of these: the search for an appropriate systematics, the search for a human ecology with explanatory value, and the search for
knowledge of ethnogenesis. Each of these themes, in turn, contains several
trends that add both substance and dynamism to thematic development. Like
the themes they animate, these trends deserve attention and are identified under suitable subheadings. The emergence of both the themes and the trends
were preceded by episodes of inquiry that produced the data necessary for their
very existence. These episodes will be discussed in an introduction to each
theme.

The Search for an Appropriate Systematics

American archaeology traditionally has been a part of anthropology because
Americans bonded elements of a European discipline that was historical to a
form of scholarship that was anthropological. European archaeologists had
a rich body of historical records at their disposal, and many European archaeological finds could be interpreted in the light of documentary accounts. American archaeologists, however, dealt with the remains of preliterate peoples whose
chief testimony lay buried in the earth. Thus the interpretation of American Indian materials in large part depended on recently written ethnographies or the
guiding principles of contemporary ethnological theory.

In the final decades of the nineteenth century, American ethnologists focused on the unilineal succession of social forms and technological events that

presumably marked the course of human history. An emphasis on the making and use of artifacts as "traits" suitable for broad classificatory ends was embedded in this evolutionary perspective. Its most eloquent proponent, Lewis H. Morgan (1977), saw certain social practices, and the artifacts that were a part of them, as markers of progress. The bow and arrow was considered a marker of the stage of Upper Savagery; pottery making, an indicator of Lower Barbarism. Plant or animal domestication, irrigation, and adobe and stone architecture signaled the onset of Middle Barbarism, and iron tools the emergence of Upper Barbarism. Civilization was accompanied by a phonetic alphabet and writing. The inadequacies of this approach have been widely discussed, but Morgan's sequence of stages (with less provocative labels) has been incorporated into North American prehistory, as any introductory text reveals.

While the aims of unilineal evolution provided a stage-organized, time-speculative component to an emergent American archaeology, they did not promote archaeological research in the Plains. Most of the early work in the area was guided by a gentlemanly antiquarianism that occasionally lapsed into vandalism. To be sure, curious homesteaders observed and circulated accounts of burial mounds and earthworks, and we may presume that some residents made desultory inquiries about the "stone age" implements they found (W. Wedel 1981:16–20). But these specimens, at best, were stored, displayed, or described by material of manufacture.

In the last decade of the nineteenth and early years of the twentieth century, the idea of a world-embracing evolutionary order crumbled before an intellectual assault led by Franz Boas (1948:275) This assault stressed field observation as a check on claims to knowledge and turned the attention of American anthropologists to creating a restricted and explicitly historical interpretative format (Harris 1968:250–372). As fieldwork blossomed, ethnographic collections grew, together with an emergent antievolutionism and the idea of geographic categories as museum display units. The first public statement of this trend was Otis T. Mason's (1896) scheme based on similarities among the Native cultures of a region. He regarded the "Plains of the Great West" as such a region, with culture traits that were a response to Great Plains resources. In a later elaboration, McGee and Thomas (1905) argued that the "vast treeless plains" were a convenient dividing line, a no-man's-land, between the Atlantic and the Pacific. Of the two, Mason's view survived and prospered.

While the culture-area idea owed its origin to museum display needs, it was soon used in ethnological theorizing. Mason's culture areas were modified by William H. Holmes (1914) and became central to Clark Wissler's (1917) work in American Indian ethnology. Shortly after, culture areas became "a community product of nearly the whole school of American Anthropologists" (Kroeber 1931:250). The emphasis was still on traits, but they were now arranged in a spatially documented (instead of a temporally) speculative order. Nevertheless, if

Figure 3.1. E. E. Blackman. (Nebraska State Historical
Society)

Culture and Classifications

temporal order was to be inferred, there were both empirical and epistemologi-
cal problems with the culture-area construct (Harris 1968:375–377). Despite
their inadequacies, culture-area formulations directed attention to the ethnological limitations of a trait-list approach and focused interest on human–land
relations. Culture areas therefore were the precursors of attempts to form content-based taxonomies and to subdivide the Plains into meaningful spatial units.

The use of culture areas helped transform traits from time-speculative to
spatially documented units, but this had little immediate effect on the conduct
of Plains archaeology. The concomitant emphasis on systematic fieldwork did,
however, stimulate the first organized archaeological work in the region. During the first decade of the twentieth century, the Nebraska State Historical Society commissioned E. E. Blackman (Figure 3.1) to make a preliminary reconnaissance of the state—a labor he began in 1901 and continued for 30 years

Figure 3.2. Robert F. Gilder. (University of
Nebraska, Lincoln)

Figure 3.3. Frederick H. Sterns. (Reprints in
Anthropology, W. Wedel negative)

Figure 3.4. George F. Will. (Reprints in Anthropology,
W. Wedel negative)

(Blackman 1903, 1907, 1930). In 1903 Robert F. Gilder (Figure 3.2) began a program of reconnaissance and excavation focused on what he called Nebraska
Culture remains near Omaha, Nebraska (Gilder 1907, 1908, 1913, 1926). A little
later, Frederick H. Sterns (Figure 3.3) began a program of reconnaissance and
excavation in southeastern Nebraska, northeastern Kansas, and western Iowa
(Sterns 1914, 1915). Stone-chambered mounds near Kansas City were excavated
in 1907 (Fowke 1910), and a decade later a paper was published on house and
mound sites in southeastern Nebraska (M. Zimmerman 1918).

In the Middle Missouri subarea, Orin G. Libby and A. B. Stout located and
mapped sites along the Missouri River in North Dakota (W. Wedel 1981:23). In
1905 George F. Will (Figure 3.4) and Herbert J. Spinden (1906) tested the Double

Figure 3.5. William H. Holmes. (National Anthropological Archives)

Figure 3.6. Charles R. Keyes. (Reprints in Anthropology, W. Wedel negative)

Ditch Mandan site and later surveyed other sites along the Missouri River (Will 1924). About the same time, Henry Montgomery (1906, 1908) reported the results of his work on earthen mounds on the Northeastern Plains. From 1912 to 1915, William Nickerson also tested mounds in Manitoba (Capes 1963), and elsewhere on the Plains the Bighorn Medicine wheel was examined in northern Wyoming (Simms 1903). To the south, William H. Holmes (Figure 3.5) investigated the Afton Spring in northeastern Oklahoma (Holmes 1903).

The pace of organized fieldwork quickened in the next decade. In 1919 J. Walter Fewkes explored burned rock middens and other sites in central Texas (Pearce 1932:44–54). William E. Myer (1922) dug into mound and village sites near Sioux Falls, South Dakota, and tested Osage sites in western Missouri. In the mid-1920s, Matthew Stirling excavated prehistoric cemetery sites near Mobridge, South Dakota (W. Wedel 1955), Charles R. Keyes (Figure 3.6) organized a productive survey program in Iowa, and Asa T. Hill (Figure 3.7) revitalized the survey work of the Nebraska State Historical Society. Hill also introduced new excavation procedures and, from 1926 to 1929, applied them to Pawnee earthlodges. In 1928 the Smithsonian Institution began a matching-fund program that supported work by the University of Nebraska, whose representatives applied Hill's new techniques to sites along the Missouri, Platte, and Republican rivers. The same Smithsonian program supported the Logan Museum's work on Middle Missouri sites and the Denver Museum–University of Denver's survey of the Colorado High Plains (W. Wedel 1981:25–27). The Nebraska fieldwork resulted in several landmark publications, among them William Duncan Strong's *Introduction to Nebraska Archeology* (1935) and Waldo R. Wedel's "Preliminary Classification for Nebraska and Kansas Cultures" (1934).

From Trait Lists to Taxonomic Hierarchies

Strong (Figure 3.8) completed the manuscript for *An Introduction to Nebraska Archeology* in 1932, before W. C. McKern and his associates introduced the Midwestern Taxonomic System (M.T.S.) to the archaeological community and Wedel (Figure 3.9) introduced it to the Plains. The M.T.S. is a six-unit, content-based hierarchy—a data-arrangement scheme based on strict set inclusion (P. Kay 1971:868)—using as units the component, focus, aspect, phase, pattern, and base (McKern 1939:301–313). In practice, however, only the three lower-level units (component, focus, and aspect) were commonly used. These units were arranged on the basis of shared traits so that one proceeded from units of greatest sharing and least inclusiveness (components) to those of lesser sharing and greater inclusiveness (foci and aspects) (Dunnell 1971:177–183). One important limitation of the M.T.S. was its tendency to mask content variability because its most inclusive units had the least replicated content; its least inclusive units had

like a filing cabinet of labelled drawers

localized detail to large general classes

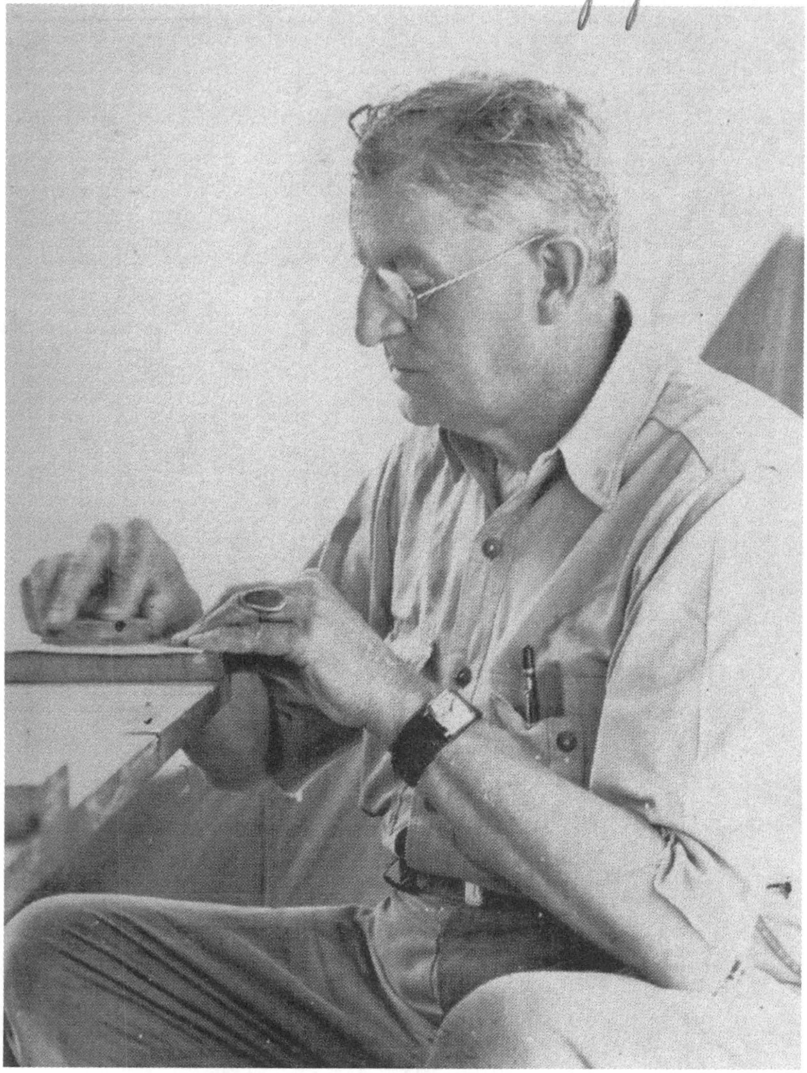

Figure 3.7. Asa T. Hill. (Nebraska State Historical Society)

component is any expression at a site
similar components grouped to foci

the most. Then, too, considerations of time and place were excluded from M.T.S. taxon formation because they could not be handled with the same logic applied to content—a limitation that ultimately led Plains specialists to abandon the system for a more flexible competitor. From the 1930s to the 1950s, however, those limits seemed to be of little consequence.

In his original manuscript, Strong refined Gilder's Nebraska culture, identified an Upper Republican culture, summarized Wedel's work on Pawnee ar-

Figure 3.8. William Duncan Strong. (Reprints in Anthropology, W. Wedel negative)

chaeology, and discussed other regional archaeological cultures. Strong made it clear, as had Gilder before him, that he intended these archaeological cultures to be time- and space-ordered trait clusters. Before publication, however, Strong (1935:1–2) revised and updated his manuscript in the light of Wedel's classification, so in the published version all his original cultures (except Dismal River) were identified not as components or foci but as M.T.S. aspects. Strong's identification of these archaeological cultures as M.T.S. taxa and Wedel's earlier efforts to do the same were admirable first attempts to transform an intuitive systematics into explicitly stated procedures.

As fieldwork continued, taxonomic matters became a greater issue. The year after Strong's monograph appeared, major revisions of his scheme were proposed. G. H. Gilmore (Bell and Gilmore 1936) proposed a Nehawka focus of Strong's Nebraska aspect; John L. Champe (1936) defined a single-component Loup River focus of Strong's Upper Republican aspect; and Paul L. Cooper (1936) removed the St. Helena focus from Strong's Nebraska aspect and placed it in his Upper Republican aspect. Four years later, Wedel (1940) accepted the previous changes, revised Strong's original foci, and grouped the Nebraska and Upper Republican aspects into a Central Plains phase. Wedel's suggestions were adopted by most, but over time, Champe (1961:103) noted "a growing dissatisfaction with the two aspects."

Taxonomic problems and their solutions are, of course, related to the quality and quantity of available data. The data that fueled early taxonomic discussions were collected in the 1920s and 1930s, and during this time the Central Plains became the best known archaeological province in the Great Plains. From the

Figure 3.9. Waldo R. Wedel. (Reprints in Anthropology, W. Wedel negative)

1940s to the 1960s, the construction of dams in the Middle Missouri subarea stimulated a massive archaeological salvage program that diverted time, money, and labor from the Central Plains to the Missouri River valley in the Dakotas. These efforts were organized under the aegis of the Inter-Agency Archeological and Paleontological Salvage Program, which from the late 1940s to the late 1960s coordinated the efforts of an array of federal, state, and local research and educational institutions, chief among them the National Park Service, the Smithsonian Institution's River Basin Surveys, Montana State University, the Nebraska State Historical Society, the Science Museum of St. Paul, the State Historical Society of North Dakota, the University of North Dakota, the University of Idaho, the University of Kansas, the University of Missouri, the University of Nebraska, the University of South Dakota, and the University of Wisconsin (Lehmer 1971:3–7).

Archaeological surveys of the areas to be inundated began in 1947 with the work of Marvin F. Kivett in the Garrison Reservoir and Paul L. Cooper in the Fort Randall Reservoir. A subsequent mixture of survey and limited testing was soon followed by larger-scale research efforts. Between 1950 and 1960, Paul Cooper, William Mulloy, James Howard, Don Hartle, Raymond Wood, Alan Woolworth, Glenn Kleinsasser, G. Hubert Smith, Robert Newman, Gordon Hewes, Wesley Hurt, James Deetz, William Irving, Carlyle Smith, Marvin (Gus) Kivett, Alfred Bowers, David Baerreis, Robert Stephenson, Preston Holder, Warren Caldwell, Waldo Wedel, Franklin Fenenga, Richard Wheeler, Donald Lehmer, and Roscoe Wilmeth contributed their supervisory and analytical talents to the Missouri River basin salvage effort. Then, too, some who participated in this effort as shovel hands—including Robert Hall, Warren Wittry, David Breternitz, William Buckles, George Cowgill, R. E. W. Adams, Karl Heider, Paul Tolstoy, Gary Vescelius, Walter Birkby, Frederick West, Jon Muller, Ward F. Weakly, Tom Witty, Stephen Robinson, Alfred E. Johnson, and Kent Flannery—were later to make more substantial contributions to the discipline.

The large body of data accumulated in the early years of the Inter-Agency Archeological and Paleontological Salvage Program was ordered within the M.T.S.—although with growing difficulty. Some of the emergent classificatory problems were discussed by Gordon Baldwin, J. L. Champe, C. S. Smith, W. R. Hurt, and R. L. Stephenson during a trip to the Fort Randall and Oahe reservoirs in 1953. This discussion led to "a spontaneous, informal gathering upon the party's return to Lincoln."

The deliberations of this informal gathering were circulated as results of the "Accidental (or 10 ½) Plains Conference" later that year. As an aside, it should be noted that this "accidental Plains Conference," as it came to be called, initiated a vigorous summertime series of mid-1950s to early 1960s "Half Plains Conferences," many of them held in Smithsonian Institution quarters at the airport in Pierre, South Dakota (Figure 3.10). The published version of the deliberations of the 10 ½ Plains Conference created 10 foci and six aspects for the Middle Missouri subarea, and eight foci and four new aspects for the Central Plains (Stephenson 1954). The taxa proposed for the Middle Missouri went unchallenged, but a revision of previously defined Central Plains taxa began a controversy that lasted for two decades. At issue was John L. Champe's (Figure 3.11) effort to reduce Strong's Upper Republican and Nebraska aspects to foci of a single new Aksarben aspect.

The battle lines were clearly drawn in 1959 when Wedel reaffirmed his commitment to the earlier two-aspect scheme and added a third, Smoky Hill, aspect to the Central Plains phase. Wedel saw no gain in making Champe's changes; Champe responded by challenging the validity of Strong's original transformations of archaeological "cultures" to M.T.S. aspects. Because Strong had improperly defined foci and aspects, Champe argued, archaeologists should abandon the Omaha and Nehawka foci for a Nebraska focus. This, he claimed, would be an economical solution because "the necessary comparisons of components had

Figure 3.10. Participants in a 1950s "Half Plains Conference" at the airport in Pierre, South Dakota: (*far left*) Wesley R. Hurt, (*third from left*) Harold Huscher, (*background*) Robert L. Stephenson, (*to his right*) Charles R. McNutt and Frank H. H. Roberts, Jr.; the others are unknown. (National Anthropological Archives)

Figure 3.11. John L. Champe. (University of Nebraska, Lincoln)

[handwritten: problem c/MTS was it was based on excavated materials - not allowing for additional newly found materials]

already been made," and "the terms Omaha and Nehawka had little use as focus designations." He suggested a similar new ordering of the Upper Republican materials: abandon the Upper Republican aspect as an M.T.S. category, but identify an Upper Republican focus based on the comparative-trait list used to define the Loup River focus (Champe 1961:103–107).

To summarize: early taxonomic efforts centered on the identification of previously excavated and described materials as M.T.S. aspects and foci, while later arguments focused on the redrawing of taxonomic boundaries to accommodate new materials, some of them considered to be hybrid or transitional. The utility of the M.T.S. was not seriously questioned, nor were there attempts to transcend what Irving Rouse (1960) called the descriptive level of classification. The taxonomic controversies of the 1940s and 1950s did not, however, inhibit the growth of understanding. Before the 1960s those who were dissatisfied with the M.T.S. chose nontaxonomic labels, like "complex" and "culture," to describe the remains at their disposal. Strong's (1935) Dismal River culture and the Holder's Frontier complex are good examples. But it was not long before dissatisfaction with the M.T.S. began to surface. This dissatisfaction was related to the growing body of data pertinent to social development.

[handwritten: Taxonomy · descriptive level of classification]

From a Systemic-Morphological Perspective to a Processual-Interpretive One

Donald J. Lehmer (Figure 3.12) was one of the first to focus his attention on issues of social development. His 1954 synthesis became a prototype for most subsequent studies of the Central and Northern Plains. In this work, he delineated

Figure 3.12. Donald J. Lehmer. (W. R. Wood)

three Willey and Phillips (1958) traditions, or three major lifestyles, that he identified as Central Plains, Middle Missouri, and Coalescent. These traditions, however, did not embody violent contrasts in social, economic, or manufacturing practices. Instead, they reflected subtler distinctions best described as preference clusters or stylistic variations on a set of common themes (Lehmer 1954:140–147). Lehmer's synthesis marked the beginning of a shift from a systematic-morphological to a processual-interpretive perspective.

Lehmer's first attempt to order Middle Missouri archaeological remains was, however, a taxonomic nightmare. It combined the Willey and Phillips (1958) tradition with the M.T.S. focus and the southwestern time–space integrator, the "branch" (Lehmer 1952). This taxonomic arrangement was, at best, inelegant, and Lehmer soon realized that it was simply an ad hoc response to the limits imposed by the M.T.S. Remember, Lehmer saw in his materials several stylistic variations on a set of common themes. To properly express this view, he needed a taxonomic scheme that emphasized content continuities in space and time, an operation the M.T.S. did not facilitate. A similar problem faced Champe (1961) in his struggle to resolve the taxonomic status of "culturally intermediate sites." Champe's solution was to reduce established aspects to foci of a new aspect—that is, to create a unit containing fewer but more inclusive classes. Lehmer (1954:154–159) needed a taxonomic system that would allow him to map content continuities in both time and space: his solution was to substitute the time–space integrator "branch" for the M.T.S. aspect. Champe's proposal retained the logical coherence of the M.T.S. at the expense of empirical utility; Lehmer's retained empirical utility at the expense of logical coherence. Lehmer worried about this state of affairs.

Early in the 1960s, Lehmer collaborated with Warren W. Caldwell to rework and resynthesize Middle Missouri prehistory, an effort that produced the first comprehensive attempt to use Willey and Phillips's (1958) phase-tradition-horizon system in Plains prehistory. The Willey and Phillips formulation is based on taxa created through the interaction of time, space, and content. The basic units are the phase, horizon, and tradition. The phase is a classificatory taxon, and the horizon and tradition are integrative taxa. Phases are basic content units, with space and time given lesser attention. Their relationship to traditions and horizons may be summarized:

1. Phases must always have the greatest content.
2. Traditions must always have the greatest time depth.
3. Horizons must always have the greatest spatial spread.
4. Traditions and horizons may have roughly equal content, but must have less content than any single phase.
5. Phases and traditions may have roughly equal spatial dimensions, but must have less than a horizon.

6. Phases and horizons may have roughly equal time spans, but must be less
   durable than a tradition.   *tradition≠horizon*

   In their pioneering attempt to introduce the Willey and Phillips system,
Lehmer and Caldwell (1966) proposed two major traditions: Middle Missouri
and Coalescent, each of which had Initial, Extended, and Terminal horizons.
Lehmer and Caldwell's use of horizon was, however, a clear violation of principles 3 and 5—violations that vexed Lehmer. While Lehmer pondered the consequences of modifying Willey and Phillips's horizon, Lionel Brown (1966) tried
to reorder Central Plains complexes using Lehmer and Caldwell's scheme. He
integrated three phases: Smoky Hill, Upper Republican, and Nebraska with the
Central Plains tradition, but in doing so he violated principle 2.

   The problems with these early attempts were briefly discussed by Krause
(1969:82–96) as background for revising Central Plains taxonomy. The suggested
revisions can be summarized as follows:

1. Replace the Upper Republican phase with three phases: Solomon River,
   Classic Republican, and Loup River.
2. Replace the Nebraska phase with two phases: Doniphan and Douglas.
3. Retain the designation Central Plains for a subareal tradition and add two
   regional variants: Nebraska and Upper Republican.
4. Recognize a St. Helena phase as a product of fusion between the two regional
   variants.

Krause argued that these changes, based on Lehmer's idea of a variant (devised
in 1968, but not published until 1971) would bring Central Plains classificatory
practices into accord with those used in the Middle Missouri region and with
the provisions of the Willey and Phillips system. Criticism came almost immediately, and centered on how the Nebraska culture materials were to be handled
(Blakeslee and Caldwell 1979).

   In 1971, Lehmer published his *Introduction to Middle Missouri Archeology,*
in which he again turned his attention to taxonomy. He replaced the earlier
Lehmer and Caldwell horizon with the variant, which he described as a unique
and reasonably uniform expression of a cultural tradition that has a greater order of magnitude than a phase and is distinguished from other variants of the
same tradition by its geographic distribution, age, and/or cultural content
(Lehmer 1971:32).

   If Lehmer had characterized the variant as he used it, he would have described it as a mid-range integrative taxon with less content, greater time span,
and greater spatial spread than a phase, but having less time span than a tradition and less spatial spread than a horizon. Thus defined, the variant fits se-
curely within the logic of the Willey and Phillips system. Lehmer used it to provide a lucid and productive comparison of Middle Missouri artifact complexes,

settlement patterns, and village types. With the variant, Lehmer achieved harmony between taxonomy and culture history. Middle Missouri specialists embraced and refined Lehmer's scheme. By separating the Initial variant of the Middle Missouri tradition into eastern and western divisions and by systematically adding phases to most of the variants, they have facilitated a smooth and orderly transition from systematic-morphological to processual-interpretative classifications for the region's post-Woodland remains.

An equivalent shift in taxonomic practices has been uneven in studies of the Central and Southern Plains. Although Kenneth Brown (1984) redefined the Pomona aspect as a variant integrating the Clinton, Wolf Creek, May Brook, and Apple Valley phases, and Mary Adair (1988:33–34) viewed Smoky Hill, Keith, and Kansas City Hopewell as variants, Blakeslee and Caldwell (1979) rejected the use of the taxon in their appraisal of the Nebraska phase. Few Central Plains specialists have used it since. Vis and Henning (1969:253–271) framed cogent arguments for recognizing an early Little Sioux and a later Little Sioux phase for the Mill Creek manifestations. Jack Hofman (1978:6–35) reformulated the Custer and Washita River foci in Oklahoma as phases, and John Ludwickson (1978:94–108) expanded and refined the Loup River phase, ultimately renaming it the Itskari phase. Roger Grange (1979) demonstrated the coherence and interpretative force of a proto-Pawnee Lower Loup phase, and Adair (1988) identified Bemis Creek and Steed–Kisker as phases in her study of the emergence of food production on the Great Plains.

Efforts to form phases from Archaic and Woodland materials have been sporadic. In Nebraska, Wright (1982) identified Kivett's (1962) Logan Creek materials as an Archaic-stage phase. In Kansas, Witty (1982) defined an Archaic Munkers Creek phase; Grosser (1973) introduced a Chelsea phase; Rohn and colleagues (1977), a Colvin phase; and Grosser (1970) and Artz (1981), a Walnut phase. Grosser (1973) defined an El Dorado phase and Schmits (1980) a Black Vermillion phase for Archaic deposits in eastern Kansas; Reid (1983) identified a Nebo Hill phase and M. Kay (1983) a Sedalia phase for similar materials in Missouri. Woodland phases defined for Kansas include Lake City (K. Brown 1981), Trowbridge, Kansas City, Edwardsville (Johnson 1979, 1983), Bowlin (Schmits and Baley 1986), Walnut (Grosser 1977), Hertha (Blakeslee and Rohn 1982), and Butler (Grosser 1973). Reynolds (1977) has also identified a Grasshopper Falls phase; Witty (1982), a Greenwood phase; and Marshall (1972), a Cuesta phase for Kansas Woodland complexes. This listing is but a sampling of recent processual-interpretive classifications. Yet problems remain.

The regional phase structure for the Central and Southern Plains resembles a patchwork quilt and will remain so until attention is focused more firmly on interphase relations. Many Woodland and Archaic manifestations and most Paleo-Indian materials either are unclassified or are classed as M.T.S. aspects or foci (W. Wedel 1961, 1986:49–97), and nontaxonomic labels, some of considerable antiquity, still abound. Then, too, there are still taxonomic difficulties with the proposed Nebraska phase (Blakeslee and Caldwell 1979). The Smoky Hill remains, sometimes classified as a phase, need more attention, as do the Anoka (Witty 1962), Redbird (Wood 1965), Pomona (Witty 1967), and Henrietta foci (Krieger 1947:87–159); the Dismal River (Gunnerson 1960), White Rock (Rusco 1960), Gibson (Bell and Baerreis 1951), Fulton, and Great Bend aspects (W. Wedel 1959:97); and the Bluff Creek and Platte complexes (Witty 1978:63). It is obvious that more must be done vis-à-vis the classification of Great Plains archaeological materials, but for now let us turn to the second of our three themes, the search for a human ecology with explanatory value.

The Search for a Human Ecology with Explanatory Value

The ecological claims made in many early studies were either part of an argument for great antiquity or part of a catastrophist explanatory model. Often, as with Albert Koch's nineteenth-century work in Missouri, the two were combined. Koch's debatable evidence for a human–mastodon association began a mid-nineteenth-century controversy that reached its peak in the 1870s. It did not subside until the early twentieth century and was resolved only by the discovery of a Clovis point directly associated with mastodon remains at Kimmswick, near St. Louis (Graham 1979). Koch's explanation for the association of humans with extinct animals posited an antediluvian paradise that was destroyed by a Noachian catastrophe (McMillan 1976:82–93). Of later date, but no less controversial, were the Nebraska Loess Man (Gilder 1907:35–39), the Pliocene peccary remains identified as the "Western ape" (*Hesperopithecus harold-cooki*), and the 300 "implements" of putative human origin from the same fossil bed in western Nebraska (Osborn 1922, 1927).

The finds excavated in 1926 near Folsom, New Mexico, unequivocally documented human association with an extinct form of bison and renewed interest in the antiquity of humans in the New World (Figgins 1933; Wilmsen and Roberts 1978). The Folsom discoveries were soon followed by others demonstrating an association of humans with mammoths. Two distinct forms of fluted points—Clovis being found primarily with mammoths, and Folsom with extinct bison—and the stratigraphic superposition of the two at the Clovis site (Sellards 1940:29–31) established a sequence of early mammoth and later bison hunters (Figure 3.13).

The food requirements of mammoths presumably exceeded those supplied by the short steppe grasses that now dominate the region; hence, a more luxuriant plant cover was posited and evidence for it was sought. The picture that

Figure 3.13. E. H. Sellards. (*Plains Anthropologist* 6:pt. 1)

emerged was one of a cooler, moister climate that supported a lush prairie grass-land in areas where steppe or desert later prevailed. Many mammoth kills were in or near ancient ponds, streams, or river channels, and many of the beasts slaughtered were female, young, or immature. This evidence led Wedel and others to infer selectivity by the hunters and to posit single mammoth kills at favored hunting stations. With the disappearance of the proboscideans, hunting and harvesting peoples turned to smaller but more abundant grazing animals, chief among them a bison of larger than modern size. Mass kills resembling drives, or pounds, and opportunistic surrounds or ambushes at water holes or in the breaks along watercourses replaced the earlier pattern of repetitious single animal kills (W. Wedel 1961:60–65). This shift may have forced early hunters to adopt principles of personnel management that led to larger and more stable populations. At any rate, a rich diversity of lifestyles emerged from the base they laid.

From Possibilism to Cultural Ecology

For four years in the 1930s, personnel from the United States National Museum conducted surveys and excavations near Kansas City (W. Wedel 1943). This work coincided with a regionwide drought that brought the relations between human cultures and their natural settings into sharp relief. Wedel's "Environment and Native Subsistence Economies in the Central Great Plains" was one consequence of this experience. In this and related papers, he provided classic analyses of environmental and cultural relationships (W. Wedel 1941, 1947, 1963). He had the vision to see that knowledge of environmental variables would be needed for any attempt to understand the patterns of social life on the Plains, but he viewed the natural environment more as a limiting (or leveling) than a creative force—a context within which innovation, diffusion, and migration worked to create divergent or convergent results.

More recent research has centered on the creative force in the interplay among elements of technology, sociology, and environment. Julian Steward (1955), the first to make substantial use of this approach, called it "cultural ecology." Stewart's analysis surpassed traditional approaches by emphasizing functionally interrelated features of environment and culture (Geertz 1963:2). Adaptation became the issue, not trait origin or the mechanisms of trait transmission. It became important to explore those ecological boundaries beyond which a trait or set of traits gained or lost adaptive significance.

In 1967 Steward's perspectives were combined with several newly developed archaeological recovery techniques in a study of two Central Plains–tradition house sites on the Central Plains. In this work, Wood (1969) and his collaborators assumed that population density and distribution, together with domestic group size, composition, and degree of permanency, had adaptive significance. They excavated individual house sites so their data might "be viewed as the product of a meaningful social unit, the household." They took soil samples for pollen, conchological, and other purposes, and used recently popularized flotation techniques on the fill from all features. The two house ruins, one Upper Republican and the other of Nebraska origin, were specifically "chosen to provide maximum geographic and environmental contrasts." From differences in the animal and plant remains, the group argued that Upper Republican peoples were more mobile and more firmly focused on bison hunting than their Nebraska culture compatriots, who were thought to be more firmly committed to growing crops and hunting solitary game animals. Then, too, Wood combined ethnographic and archaeological evidence to suggest that Upper Republican and Nebraska culture peoples shared a cultural heritage of matrilineal, matrilocal communities composed of extended, polygynous families organized into bands led by men holding key kinship positions. While the results of this archaeological experiment were considered controversial by some (W. Wedel 1970), it generated hypotheses about Upper Republican and Nebraska social life that are still being tested.

A year later, Krause (1970:104–115) posited an early Upper Republican occupation of north-central Kansas, typified by hamlet-dwelling groups that built large houses and had difficulty meeting the needs of maize farming and bison hunting under climatically optimal conditions. He introduced the onset of colder and drier weather after A.D. 1250 as an amplifying force that, together with prior ecological stress, worked to produce a stress-relieving pattern of neighborhoods composed of semi-independent, smaller house homesteads or homestead aggregates. Thus, Krause argued, a dispersed pattern of isolated smaller house homesteads or homestead aggregates maximized the efficiency of shifting cultivation in the face of a slowly deteriorating climate.

Lehmer (1970) took a similar approach to the interpretation of events in the Middle Missouri. He considered the rapid expansion of Initial and Extended variant peoples of the Middle Missouri tradition to be a response to favorable Medieval optimum, or Neo-Atlantic episode, climatic conditions. About A.D. 1250, the abundant summer rainfall of Neo-Atlantic times was, however, interrupted by an abrupt change in atmospheric circulation—the introduction of greater amounts of cool dry air, lowered temperatures, and decreased precipitation (Baerreis and Bryson 1965:203–220). Consequently, Lehmer posited a northward withdrawal and concentration of many Middle Missouri populations and a less dense occupation, if not abandonment, of the southern parts of the South Dakota segment of the Missouri valley. He saw an Upper Republican penetration of south-central South Dakota as an additional consequence of this climatic change. Parts of both Lehmer's and Krause's interpretations must, however, be revised in the light of more recent research. An Upper Republican penetration of south-central South Dakota now seems to be earlier than Lehmer posited, and a contrast that Krause drew between an earlier large-house and a later small-house occupation of the Solomon River valley has failed the test of subsequent analysis (Krause 1995:307–352; Lippincott 1978:81–93).

In a yet more recent attempt to explain the relationship between environmental and social variables, Krause argued that all Native American farmers in the Dakota stretch of the Missouri River valley adopted subsistence and settlement strategies that mediated the tension between the centripetal pull of a linear distribution of tillable soils and the centrifugal force of dispersed reserves of foods to hunt and harvest. Yet, he noted, bearers of the Middle Missouri tradition maintained a community design typified by the geographic concentration of households, whereas members of the Coalescent tradition did not. For peoples of the Coalescent tradition, the occasional geographic concentration of households was an ad hoc solution to special problems—a condition to be tolerated only if necessary. Further, when Middle Missouri and Coalescent folk were competing for the same areas and resources, Coalescent peoples spread at the expense of Middle Missouri peoples and did so by spanning their mobility, by the breakup and dispersal of formerly larger and more concentrated populations. Krause attributed the persistence of concentrated Middle Missouri–tradition populations to a willingness to fight both compatriots and outsiders, a commitment to ritual, and managerial or entrepreneurial efforts that promoted conflict (Krause 1994). He attributed Coalescent adaptive success to social practices that promoted the breakup and spread of concentrated popula-

[handwritten] volume resources leads to conflict

tions. He was, however, assuming that fortified Initial Coalescent villages were a response to conflict with Middle Missouri folk. Larry Zimmerman (1985:108–109) has challenged this assumption and backed his claims with evidence from the Crow Creek massacre. The Crow Creek skeletal remains, for instance, showed sufficient nutritional stress for Zimmerman to conclude that Initial Coalescent peoples were competing with one another for limited resources and that such competition caused open and brutal internecine warfare.

There seems, however, to be general agreement that thirteenth- to fifteenth-century environmental conditions on the Southern Plains disadvantaged that region's inhabitants. Dee Ann Story and Sam D. Valestro (1977) argue for drastic dislocations of cultural systems in Texas at this time, although Caddoan groups in the Arkansas River basin may have faced fewer environmental constraints (Brown et al. 1978:176). Yet after assessing the natural and social resources of this area, James Brown and his colleagues conclude that (1) there was a dispersal of households into many small communities as a consequence of attempts to spread the risk of crop failure in a vulnerable growing environment, (2) the location of villages and farmsteads depended on arable soils, (3) there was a tight correlation between settlement size and the amount of arable land, and (4) a growth in system complexity accompanied a favorable climatic cycle, and a collapse in complexity followed climatic reversal.

For some time, cultural ecological research on the Western and Northwestern Plains has focused on the much earlier and more dramatic effects of the Hypsithermal (or Altithermal), a period characterized by generally higher temperatures and lower rainfall than today (Antevs 1955; Deevey and Flint 1957). There are two contrastive views of the Hypsithermal's effects on the human use of the region: most think in terms of abandonment or reduced use, although a few think there was no significant change. Early investigators suggested a cultural hiatus during the period. William Mulloy (Figure 3.14) argued that the region was abandoned and that climatic conditions forced human groups into new settings (Mulloy 1943:433). Human habitation has since been demonstrated (Reeves 1973:123–127), but there seem to be fewer Hypsithermal sites and they tend to cluster in the mountainous parts of the Northwestern Plains or in the Missouri River drainage.

The distribution of Hypsithermal-period sites led Wedel (1961:200) to claim that the carrying capacity of the Central Plains was reduced, thus forcing Archaic-stage Plains dwellers into "oasis" areas or peripheral regions where they developed a diversified hunting and gathering lifestyle. There are, indeed, indications of diminished rainfall. Short-grass communities expanded into areas that now support tall-grass prairies (Reeves 1973:123–127), and parts of the modern short-grass plains in Wyoming had a Great Basin–type ecology (W. Wedel 1978:196). The Simonsen, Lungren, and Logan Creek sites show that

Figure 3.14. William T. Mulloy. (*Plains Anthropologist* 23:pt. 1)

bison were being slaughtered along the Missouri River (Agogino and Frank-forter 1960; W. Wedel 1978:199), although the remains at the Coffey site in north-western Kansas indicate a diversified economy designed to exploit the resources of floodplain settings (Schmits 1978). In the Northwestern Plains, there is evidence for a mountain-oriented hunter-collector economy. Surveys in the Pryor Mountain–Bighorn Canyon region show that Hypsithermal-period peoples occupied higher elevations than their more recent counterparts, a circumstance interpreted as a response to moisture shortages at lower elevations (Loendorf 1971:130). Many bison kill sites in the Bighorn Mountains suggest that this area was an oasis for both bison and bison hunters.

The reduced-carrying-capacity hypothesis has, however, been questioned, and climatological and other data may be cited to the effect that Hypsithermal conditions should not have seriously affected bison populations or altered their potential as a food source. Brian Reeves (1973) has posited a continuation of the Paleo-Indian big-game-hunter pattern and attributed the scarcity and distribution of Hypsithermal sites to sampling bias and poor preservation. In brief, as intriguing as the available evidence might be, the effects of the Hypsithermal have yet to be systematically measured in a full range of Plains contexts, although this work is proceeding at several bison kill and bison hunter campsites in Wyoming (e.g., Benedict and Olson 1978; Frison 1974; Reher 1970).

From Cultural Ecology to Determinism and Interdisciplinary Field Research

In the 1960s and 1970s, a creative role was assigned to the interplay between environment and technology, but it was generally assumed that unless technology and environment alone determined the rest of culture, there was considerable latitude for variation in the social forms associated with a given adaptive pattern. This was considered particularly true for horticultural societies, and one problem confronting the study of such peoples was the selection of those aspects of social life that were functionally related to environmental variables. Another, and perhaps more important, problem lay in determining which of these relations had demonstrable adaptive significance.

Patterned relationships among elements of culture and the ecosystem have always seemed clearest among technologically simple hunting and harvesting societies. This clarity may be more apparent than real; nevertheless, it seems to promote a deterministic view of adaptation in those working with only the remains of hunting and harvesting folk. This tendency is strikingly expressed in the monograph on the Vore bison kill site: "The cumulative effect of adaptive decisions of individual members dictates the ultimate success or failure of a cultural system. Such decisions are primarily based on estimates of energy cost–return ratios along several alternative adaptive strategies. . . . The tendency for these actions to converge toward a productive norm in this sense reflect 'normative' behavior, but adaptive success or failure is more significant than any set of ideological trappings that a people might attach to their behavior" (Reher and Frison 1980:37).

An even more strident view was expressed later: "if the features of a cultural system can be explained by antecedent environmental conditions, this is determinism in a straight forward sense—in spite of any terminological abhorrence" (Reher and Frison 1980:39). The Vore site monograph itself presented an "ecosystemic" interpretation of bison hunting based on variations in (1) effective moisture, (2) short-grass productivity, (3) the population density and distribution of bison, and (4) the density, distribution, and organization of Plains bison hunters.

While the ecologically oriented studies conducted during the 1940s, 1950s, and 1960s used data supplied by experts in various fields, the interdisciplinary part of these ventures was largely confined to the laboratory. In an exemplary use of this approach, Mary Adair argues for two distinct episodes of cultivation in the Central Plains: the first a "domesticatory system" associated with Kansas

City Hopewell, and the second an "agricultural system" initially observed in the Solomon River phase of north-central Kansas, the Bemis Creek phase of south-central Kansas, and the Steed–Kisker phase near Kansas City. She attributes the Steed–Kisker example to migration, but sees the others as indigenously developed. For motivating factors in indigenous development she points to population increases; population packing in valleys; trends to sedentism; complements in the nutritional quality of cultivars and wild foods; compatible scheduling in episodes of crop growing, hunting, and wild-food harvesting; positive genetic transformations in maize; and cognitive awareness of the productive potentials of agriculture (Adair 1988:99–100).

One of the earliest interdisciplinary field efforts reached fruition with the publication of *Prehistoric Man and His Environments* (Wood and McMillan 1976). In this work, the integrated research of specialists in geology, palynology, paleontology, physical anthropology, and archaeology were focused on the lower reaches of the Pomme de Terre River in southwestern Missouri. A fluvial and paleoenvironmental record was developed for the area covering the past 34,000 years, although there was no evidence of human groups until about 10,500 years ago. Archaeological contributors to the volume posited five adaptive patterns for the area's human inhabitants beginning with a Dalton occupation. The investigators found suggestive correlations between changes in Archaic patterns of adaptation and shifts from forest-edge to prairie biotypes, demonstrating the fruitfulness of an integrated in-the-field and interdisciplinary approach to the study of Plains and Plains-margin locales.

While the search for an explanatory human ecology attracted the attention of many Plains archaeologists, it did not distract those who continued the search for a suitable systematics or those who desired a fuller and more systematic understanding of ethnic origins. In many cases, the same Plains scholars worked on all three at the same time. It is to the third of these three themes—the search for knowledge of ethnogenesis—that I now turn.

understanding of tribal origins

The Search for Knowledge of Ethnogenesis

The search for an understanding of tribal origins began, plausibly enough, with attempts to identify historic American Indian village, camp, and burial sites (Dixon 1913:549–577). The work of George F. Will and Herbert J. Spinden (1906), W. E. Myer (1922), Matthew Stirling (W. Wedel 1955), and others was motivated by this aim. In their pioneering study of the Mandans, Will and Spinden used a mixture of oral history, ethnography, history, and archaeology—an approach that later became an integral part of most efforts to summarize Plains archaeology. William Duncan Strong used a similar mix of data in *An Introduction to Nebraska Archaeology* (1935:7–40); Waldo Wedel honed the approach in *An Intro-*

Figure 3.15. Mildred Mott Wedel.
(*Plains Anthropologist* 40)

duction to Pawnee Archeology (1936); and Mildred Mott (Figure 3.15) used it to detail the relations of historic tribes to archaeological manifestations in Iowa (Mott 1938). A little later, Strong (1940) synthesized the ethnographic, historical, and archaeological data for the Arikara, Mandan, and Hidatsa remains in North and South Dakota, and William Mulloy (1942) used a similar integration of sources to suggest a Crow origin for the Hagen site in eastern Montana.

The basic idea in these early works was intellectually demanding and cogent. If historically documented sites could be located and a suitable archaeological sample drawn and analyzed, then (within certain limits) an ethnic identity could be assigned to co-occurring ceramic styles, house types, burial practices, and tool technologies. Once properly attributed to an ethnic group, a recurrent complex of such elements could be used with documentary evidence and migration legends to identify protohistoric villages and camps (M. Wedel 1976). There were expectable problems with sample size, context control, and the choice of analytical ideas and techniques. Then, too, the isomorphism between ethnic groups and their material remains was far from exact. Distinct ethnic groups often shared elements of subsistence technology and lifestyle—a troublesome circumstance at best. In retrospect, many of these similarities can be attributed to residential proximity and borrowing, and others to convergent evolution in a Plains environment (W. Wedel 1977:7–9).

The direct historical approach was and still is a reasonably exact procedure for determining the type of site expected of a given ethnic group (M.

Wedel 1976, 1981). Waldo Wedel (1959) used it to identify the remains expected of Kansa and Wichita Indians (see also Bell and Bastian 1967), and Gunnerson (1960) employed it to claim Plains Apache authorship for the Dismal River aspect. Wood (1971) used the approach to assign, following Strong's (1940) lead, a Cheyenne identity to the Biesterfeldt site and to assess Mulloy's identification of Hagen as a Crow site (Wood and Downer 1977:83–100). By far the most daring use of the direct historical approach, however, came from the Southern Plains, where Jack T. Hughes, in *Prehistory of the Caddoan-Speaking Tribes* (1974), tried to push Caddoan origins back to the Archaic. A major step in his "deep derivation" was the "Woodlandization" of Archaic groups and the continued differentiation of forest from Plains Caddoans.

The nature of archaeological sites in the Western Plains (temporary camps, hunting stations, and kill sites) made a rigorous application of the direct historical approach difficult, if not impossible (Reher and Frison 1980:29–34). But the general idea of working from the historic known to the prehistoric unknown was used to identify loosely defined pottery complexes as Crow (Frison 1976:45–52; Mulloy 1958; W. Wedel 1954:403–409) or Shoshone (A. Kehoe 1959). This loose practice seems to have lapsed into the unfortunate and questionable practice of assigning a linguistic or an ethnic identity to prehistoric projectile-point types (T. Kehoe 1966:827–841).

From the Study of Cultural Dynamics to a Systemic Perspective

If an ethnic identity was to be assigned to pre- and protohistoric archaeological assemblages, the direct historical approach was logically and empirically necessary. When it was combined with the means for ordering the materials identified, Plains prehistorians could offer plausible accounts of Arikara and Mandan cultural dynamics. Wood (1967:165–168), for instance, noted that the major contours of Mandan social life seem to have been shaped by both trade and aggression. As he describes it, military conflict, or the threat of it, amplified perhaps by drought, forced the formerly scattered proto-Mandan populations into large towns. Shortly thereafter, historic Mandan integrative devices—including the multiclan scheduling of ceremonialism, age-graded societies, and the Okipa ceremony—were elaborated in these settlements to meet the need for new forms of social control. Trade with alien village groups and with pedestrian nomads brought wealth to these large towns, providing new models of and for manufacture and conduct—new models that leveled some of the differences between the Mandan and their neighbors. This model was systemic in organization and intent and, in this respect, presaged much of the work to come.

James Deetz brought elements of the "New Archaeology" to the Northern Plains. In his study *The Dynamics of Stylistic Change in Arikara Ceramics* (1965), he argued that Arikara pottery making was a craft transmitted from practitioners to their female offspring, so that if women lived together throughout their careers their products should be quite similar. Thus a tight clustering of ceramic attributes would show a pattern of matrilocal postnuptial residence; a looser clustering would indicate either a neo- or a patrilocal pattern. He therefore interpreted the change from a tight to a looser clustering of attributes in prehistoric Arikara pottery as a consequence of a shift from matri- to patri- or neolocal postnuptial residence. To back this claim, he argued that the dramatic impact of trade, warfare, and disease strengthened the economic position of males and weakened a traditional preference for matrilocality.

Deetz, however, assumed a norm of one practicing potter per household, an undocumented and, at best, questionable assumption. Suppose that most Arikara women knew how to make pottery, but that only a few practiced the craft at a given time and bartered their wares to others in the community. This, too, would produce a tight clustering of ceramic attributes, with variability a consequence of the number of practicing potters per community and the intercommunity diversity of customer preferences. Krause (1967) noted that warfare, disease, and competition for access to new sources of wealth led the Arikara to abandon whole regions and amalgamate formerly separate and independent villages. Hence the trend from a tight to a more diffuse clustering of ceramic attributes may better be interpreted as reflecting an increase in the number of practicing potters and the diversity of customer preference in larger, socially heterogeneous settlements.

Deetz's work came late in the history of the Missouri basin salvage program, and it reflected the confidence that came from the knowledge produced and ideas shared by the community of archaeologists working there. More comprehensive accounts of Arikara ethnogenesis have, however, been proposed. Strong (1940) pioneered this work, and a host of others brought it to maturity. These efforts eventually made possible a systemic model in which each small eighteenth-century Arikara village was viewed as an economically self-sufficient and politically autonomous system maintained by its own inward flow of resources. These resources both supported and were managed by authorities who held their positions by hereditary access to the religious knowledge and power enshrined in a village bundle. The village bundle, with its attendant ritual and high-status representatives, was the focus of annual feasts that integrated the community's various domestic groups into a meaningful social order. Any disruption in the inflow of resources would undermine the religious and economic autonomy of the community and threaten the authority structure that both represented and depended on it. Krause (1972) therefore predicted that threats to the inflow of resources would be met by lifestyle changes intended to secure its maintenance.

In the late eighteenth and early nineteenth centuries, the Arikara faced warfare of a kind and on a scale previously unknown, disease of epidemic proportions, and severe competition for access to sources of natural and human wealth. These forces led them to reshape the design of their villages, abandon whole regions, and combine formerly separate populations. Yet they did not abandon village life, nor were traditional authorities ousted. Further, several groups in the large nineteenth-century historic towns maintained their own identity and authority structure, frequently at the expense of general harmony and efficient collective action. In sum, the rearrangement of personnel and behavior shown by the archaeological and historical records was, indeed, consonant with the predicted pattern of group-specific attempts to maintain an inflow of goods and services (Krause 1972).

Conclusion

If there is a single lesson to be learned from the history of taxonomic efforts in the Plains, it is that taxa are classes and taxonomic orders are logical orders. Taxa are created by definition. They should be justified by the logical fit between the classes formed and the materials for whose study they were created. Achieving an appropriate systematics is not a simple task. It demands that we (1) understand the procedures for class formation, (2) understand the limits and potentials of intertaxa relations, and (3) identify appropriate attributes. We are warranted in assuming that the best target attributes will reflect regularities in past human behavior, but this provides a very rough yardstick for judging the adequacy of taxa and the relationships they imply. Then, too, the taxonomic procedures we adopt and the units we create by adopting them must be consistent with the body of theory we wish them to serve. A taxon that serves one body of theory should not be expected to serve others with equal precision and productivity. The Willey and Phillips tradition, for example, was created to serve the aims of archaeology as culture history. It need not and should not be expected to serve the aims of processual or postprocessual archaeology as well. As Duke and Wilson (1995:11) have observed, "Cultural-historical definitions of tradition are content driven, in that morphological homogeneity defines membership. . . . In contrast, postprocessual traditions are meaning driven, and homogeneity of meaning constitutes membership. Thus, postprocessual traditions can crosscut existing culture-historical traditions. Similarly, culture-historical traditions may encompass several changes in the meaning of the artifact without any corresponding change in artifact morphology."

When I was a graduate student, essays on classification irritated, confused, and bored me. They still irritate, confuse, and bore me. Reading about classification, thinking about classification, and even more so doing something about classification are demanding and, in many respects, thankless tasks. Nevertheless, classification affects what we think and what we believe. If we fail to achieve a workable systematics, if taxonomic issues are ignored, and if the ad hoc labeling practices of our past are continued, both the growth and the precision of our understanding will be inhibited.   *human*

The search for a human ecology with explanatory power has within it two *ecology* clear trajectories: (1) a move toward historical materialist forms of explanation, and (2) a move toward interdisciplinary research. The first trajectory is, in part, a response to empirical and conceptual inadequacies in our view of adaptation and our procedures for measuring its effects. As currently understood, an adaptation is any modification of human action that allows a population to expand at the expense of a competitor or to persist when a competitor fails. Unfortunately, our knowledge of a population's ability to do either is usually the product of prior inquiry rather than the premise of future research. Explanations based on this conception of adaptation seem, therefore, to be ex post facto, and their proponents are perennially on the brink of affirming the consequent. To argue that "the cumulative effect of the adaptive decisions of individual members dictates the ultimate success or failure of a cultural system" (Reher and Frison 1980:37) is no better. Instead, we must be able to specify the prerequisites for making such decisions, foresee the circumstances under which they will occur, and predict their consequences. Further, we must be able to model all of this before beginning the field research that will assess the credibility of our claims. It is in this light that the advent of computer technology and interdisciplinary programs hold exciting prospects. They are needed to both create and evaluate the ecologically oriented models the future will bring. Both the evidentiary and the conceptual shortcomings of our attempts to achieve an understanding of human ecology should preadapt us for this effort. We need no longer worry about the effects of a normative or deterministic view of cultural dynamics. We can instead focus our attention on subtler, yet no less important, issues—among them the identification of critical resources, practices, procedures, and contexts and the role of social persons in creating and exploiting them.   *ethnogenesis*

Perhaps the most cogent lesson to be learned from past attempts to understand ethnogenesis is that the perspective it engendered, the techniques it fostered, and the interest it generated have yet to be fully exploited. The study of ethnogenesis requires an explicitly ethnographic perspective. To be sure, American archaeologists have traditionally depended on ethnographic knowledge: the identification of artifacts, features, and sites frequently proceeds by reference to ethnographic example; archaeological taxa are often correlated with ethnic units; and archaeological syntheses are commonly shaped by ethnographic presuppositions. Many, if not most, of archaeology's theoretical parameters have been set by the potentials and limitations of ethnographically derived measures of significance, and that which is ethnographic has usually been introduced by analogy.

Ethnographic analogy, however, has its drawbacks. If incautiously used, we run the risk of selectively applying historically documented but inappropriate interpretations to the materials of prehistory. To be properly used, ethnographic analogy must be the first step in archaeological inquiry, not the last. Ethnographic data must be used to frame propositions that specify the kinds, quantities, and/or distributions of sites and artifacts to be expected before we conduct the fieldwork that we think will produce them. If we do otherwise—that is, use ethnographic analogy to interpret materials already in hand—we have few, if any, means at our disposal to evaluate the adequacy of our results. In short, we face both evidentiary and conceptual problems in our attempts to understand the human use of the Great Plains. These, however, are not insurmountable. Indeed, future programs of field and laboratory research that are systematically sound, and explicitly designed to refute the test implications of models based on ecological and ethnographic data, may yet bring us the depth and fullness of understanding we all desire.

References

Adair, M.
   1988   *Prehistoric Agriculture in the Central Plains.* University of Kansas, Publications in Anthropology, no. 16. Lawrence.
Agogino, G. A., and W. D. Frankforter
   1960   A Paleo-Indian Bison Kill in Northwestern Iowa. *American Antiquity* 25:414–415.
Antevs, E.
   1955   Geologic-Climatic Dating in the West. *American Antiquity* 20:317–335.
Artz, J.
   1981   Test Excavations at El Dorado Lake, 1978. In *Prehistory and History of the El Dorado Lake Area, Kansas (Phase II),* edited by M. Adair, 54–168. University of Kansas, Museum of Anthropology, Project Report Series, no. 47. Lawrence.
Baerreis, D. A., and R. A. Bryson
   1965   Climatic Episodes and the Dating of the Mississippian Culture. *Wisconsin Archaeologist* 46:203–220.
Bell, E. H., and G. H. Gilmore
   1936   The Nehawka and Table Rock Foci of the Nebraska Aspect. In *Chapters in Nebraska Archaeology,* edited by E. H. Bell, 301–356. University of Nebraska, Lincoln.
Bell, R. E., and D. A. Baerreis
   1951   A Survey of Oklahoma Archaeology. *Bulletin of the Texas Archeological and Paleontological Society* 22:10–14.
Bell, R. E., and T. Bastian
   1967   Survey of Potential Wichita Archaeological Remains in Oklahoma. In *A Pilot Study of Wichita Indian Archeology and Ethnohistory,* compiled by R. E. Bell, E. B. Jelks, and W. W. Newcomb, 119–127. Final report to the National Science Foundation, G.S.-964. University of Oklahoma, Norman.

Benedict, J. B., and B. L. Olson
  1978   *The Mount Albion Complex: A Study of Prehistoric Man and the Altithermal.* Cen-
          ter for Mountain Archeology, Research Report no. 1. Ward, Colo.
Blackman, E. E.
  1903   Report of Department of Archeology. Annual Report, Nebraska State Board
          of Agriculture for 1902, 294–326.
  1907   Prehistoric Man in Nebraska. *Records of the Past* 6:76–79.
  1930   Archaeological Work in 1929. *American Anthropologist* 32:357.
Blakeslee, D. J., and W. W. Caldwell
  1979   *The Nebraska Phase: An Appraisal.* J and L Reprint, Lincoln, Neb.
Blakeslee, D. J., and A. Rohn
  1982   *Man and Environment in Northeastern Kansas: The Hillsdale Lake Project.* Vol. 2.
          Wichita State University, Department of Anthropology. Report to the United
          States Army Corps of Engineers, Kansas City District, Kansas City, Mo.
Boas, F.
  1948   *Race, Language and Culture.* Macmillan, New York.
Brown, K. L.
  1981   Excavations at the Sperry Site, 23JA85. In *Prehistoric Cultural Resources Within
          the Right-of-Way of the Proposed Little Blue River Channel, Jackson County, Mis-
          souri,* compiled by K. L. Brown and R. J. Ziegler, 190–283. United States Army
          Corps of Engineers, Kansas City District, Kansas City, Mo.
  1984   Pomona: A Plains Village Variant in Eastern Kansas and Western Missouri.
          Ph.D. diss., Department of Anthropology, University of Kansas, Lawrence.
Brown, J. A., R. E. Bell, and D. G. Wyckoff
  1978   Caddoan Settlement Patterns in the Arkansas River Drainage. In *Mississippian
          Settlement Patterns,* edited by B. D. Smith, 169–200. Academic Press, New York.
Brown, L. A.
  1966   Temporal and Spatial Order in the Central Plains. *Plains Anthropologist* 11:294–
          301.
Capes, K.
  1963   *The W. B. Nickerson Survey and Excavations, 1912–15, of the Southern Manitoba
          Mounds Region.* National Museum of Canada, Anthropology Paper no. 4.
          Ottawa, Ont.
Champe, J. L.
  1936   The Sweetwater Culture Complex. In *Chapters in Nebraska Archaeology,* edited
          by E. H. Bell, 249–297. University of Nebraska, Lincoln.
  1961   Aksarben. *Plains Anthropologist* 6:103–107.
Cooper, P. L.
  1936   Archaeology of Certain Sites in Cedar County, Nebraska. In *Chapters in Ne-
          braska Archaeology,* edited by E. H. Bell, 11–145. University of Nebraska, Lin-
          coln.
Deetz, J.
  1965   *The Dynamics of Stylistic Change in Arikara Ceramics.* University of Illinois,
          Studies in Anthropology, no. 4. Urbana.
Deevey, E. S., Jr., and R. F. Flint
  1957   Postglacial Hypsithermal Interval. *Science* 125:182–184.
Dixon, R. B.
  1913   Some Aspects of North American Archaeology. *American Anthropologist*
          15:549–577.

Duke, P. and M. C. Wilson
　1995　Processualism and Plains Archaeology. In *Beyond Subsistence: Plains Archaeology and the Postprocessual Critique,* edited by P. Duke and M. C. Wilson, 1–16. University of Alabama Press, Tuscaloosa.
Dunnell, R. C.
　1971　*Systematics in Prehistory.* Free Press, New York.
Figgins, J. D.
　1933　A Further Contribution to the Antiquity of Man in America. *Colorado Museum of Natural History Proceedings* 12, no. 2:4–8.
Fowke, G.
　1910　*Antiquities of Central and Southwestern Missouri.* Bureau of American Ethnology Bulletin 37. Washington, D.C.
Frison, G. C.
　1974　*The Casper Site: A Hell Gap Bison Kill on the High Plains.* Academic Press, New York.
　1976　Crow Pottery in Northern Wyoming. *Plains Anthropologist* 21:29–44.
Geertz, C.
　1963　*Agricultural Involution.* University of California Press, Berkeley.
Gilder, R. F.
　1907　The Nebraska Loess Man. *Records of the Past* 6:35–39.
　1908　Oto Village Site in Nebraska. *American Anthropologist* 10:56–84.
　1913　A Prehistoric "Cannibal" House in Nebraska. *Records of the Past* 12:106–116.
　1926　*The Nebraska Culture Man.* Keiser, Omaha, Neb.
Graham, R. W.
　1979　Paleoclimates and Late Pleistocene Faunal Provinces in North America. In *Pre-Llano Cultures of the Americas: Paradoxes and Possibilities,* edited by R. L. Humphrey and D. J. Stanford, 49–69. Anthropological Society of Washington, Washington, D.C.
Grange, R. T., Jr.
　1979　An Archaeological View of Pawnee Origins. *Nebraska History* 60:134–160.
Grosser, R.
　1970　The Snyder Site: An Archaic-Woodland Occupation in South-Central Kansas. M.A. thesis, Department of Anthropology, University of Kansas, Lawrence.
　1973　A Tentative Cultural Sequence for the Snyder Site, Kansas. *Plains Anthropologist* 18:228–238.
　1977　Late Archaic Subsistence Patterns from the Central Great Plains: A Systemic Model. Ph.D. diss., Department of Anthropology, University of Kansas, Lawrence.
Gunnerson, J. H.
　1960　An Introduction to Plains Apache Archeology: The Dismal River Aspect. *Bureau of American Ethnology Bulletin* 173:131–260.
Harris, M.
　1968　*The Rise of Anthropological Theory.* Crowell, New York.
Hofman, J. L.
　1978　The Development and Northern Relationships of Two Archaeological Phases in the Southern Plains Subarea. In *The Central Plains Tradition: Internal Development and External Relationships,* edited by D. J. Blakeslee, 6–35. University of Iowa, Office of the State Archaeologist, Report no. 11. Iowa City.

Holmes, W. H.
   1903   Flint Implements and Fossil Remains from a Sulphur Spring at Afton,
          Indian Territory. *U.S. National Museum, Report for 1901*, 237–252. Washington,
          D.C.
   1914   Areas of American Cultural Characterization Tentatively Outlined as an Aid
          in the Study of Antiquities. *American Anthropologist* 16:413–416.
Hughes J. T.
   1974   *Prehistory of the Caddoan-Speaking Tribes*. Vol. 13 of *Caddoan Indians*. Edited by
          D. A. Horr. Garland, New York.
Johnson, A. E.
   1979   Kansas City Hopewell: In *Hopewell Archaeology: The Chillicothe Conference*,
          edited by D. Brose and N. Greber, 86–93. Kent State University Press, Kent,
          Ohio.
   1983   Late Woodland in the Kansas City Locality. *Plains Anthropologist* 29:277–288.
Kay, M.
   1983   Archaic Period Research in the Western Ozark Highland, Missouri. In *Archaic
          Hunters and Gatherers in the American Midwest*, edited by J. L. Phillips and J. A.
          Brown, 41–70. Academic Press, New York.
Kay, P.
   1971   Taxonomy and Semantic Contrast. *Language* 47:866–887.
Kehoe, A. B.
   1959   Ceramic Affiliations in the Northwestern Plains. *American Antiquity* 25:237–
          246.
Kehoe, T. F.
   1966   The Small Side-Notched Point System of the Northern Plains. *American Antiq-
          uity* 31:827–841.
Kivett, M. F.
   1962   Logan Creek Complex. Manuscript on file, Nebraska State Historical Society,
          Lincoln.
Krause, R. A.
   1967   Arikara Ceramic Change: A Study of the Factors Affecting Stylistic Change
          in Late 18th and Early 19th Century Arikara Pottery. Ph.D. diss., Department
          of Anthropology, Yale University, New Haven, Conn.
   1969   Correlation of Phases in Central Plains Prehistory. In *Two House Sites in the
          Central Plains: An Experiment in Archaeology*, edited by W. R. Wood, 82–96.
          Plains Anthropologist Memoir no. 6.
   1970   Aspects of Adaptation Among Upper Republican Subsistence Cultivators. In
          Pleistocene and Recent Environments of the Central Plains, edited by W. Dort, Jr.,
          and J. K. Jones, Jr., 103–115. University Press of Kansas, Lawrence.
   1972   *The Leavenworth Site: Archaeology of an Historic Arikara Community*. University
          of Kansas, Publications in Anthropology, no. 3. Lawrence.
   1994   Paper Sacks, Paste-Board Boxes, and Intellectual Bins: The River Basin Sal-
          vage Program and Archaeological Classification. *North Dakota Archaeology*
          5:27–38.
   1995   Attributes, Modes, and Tenth Century Potting in North Central Kansas.
          Plains Anthropologist 40:307–352.
Krieger, A. D.
   1947   The Eastward Extension of Puebloan Datings Toward Cultures of the Missis-
          sippi Valley. *American Antiquity* 12:141–148.

Kroeber, A. L.
    1931   The Culture-Area and Age-Area Concepts of Clark Wissler. In *Methods in So-cial Science,* edited by S. Rice, 248–265. University of Chicago Press, Chicago.
Lehmer, D. J.
    1952   The Fort Pierre Branch, Central South Dakota. *American Antiquity* 17:329–336.
    1954   *Archeological Investigations in the Oahe Dam Area, South Dakota, 1950–51.* Bureau of American Ethnology Bulletin 158. Washington, D.C.
    1970   Climate and Culture in the Middle Missouri Valley. In *Pleistocene and Recent Environments of the Central Plains,* edited by W. Dort, Jr., and J. K. Jones, Jr., 117–129. University Press of Kansas, Lawrence.
    1971   *Introduction to Middle Missouri Archeology.* National Park Service, Anthropo-logical Papers, no. 1. Washington, D.C.
Lehmer, D. J., and W. W. Caldwell
    1966   Horizon and Tradition in the Northern Plains. *American Antiquity* 31:511–516.
Lippincott, K. R.
    1978   Solomon River Upper Republican Settlement Ecology. In *The Central Plains Tra-dition: Internal Development and External Relationships,* edited by D. J. Blakeslee, 81–93. University of Iowa, Office of the State Archaeologist, Report no. 11. Iowa City.
Loendorf, L. L.
    1971   *The Results of the Archaeological Survey in the Pryor Mountain–Bighorn Canyon Recreation Area: 1969 Field Season.* University of Missouri, Department of An-thropology, American Archaeology Division, Columbia.
Ludwickson, J.
    1978   Central Plains Tradition Settlements in the Loup River Basin: The Loup River Phase. In *The Central Plains Tradition: Internal Development and External Relation-ships,* edited by D. J. Blakeslee, 94–108. University of Iowa, Office of the State Archaeologist, Report no. 11. Iowa City.
Marshall, J. O.
    1972   *The Archaeology of the Elk City Reservoir, a Local Archaeological Sequence in South-east Kansas.* Kansas State Historical Society, Anthropological Series, no. 6. Topeka.
Mason, O. T.
    1896   Influence of Environment Upon Human Industries or Arts. *Smithsonian Institu-tion, Annual Report for 1895,* 639–665. Washington, D.C.
McGee, W. J., and C. Thomas
    1905   *Prehistoric North America.* Vol. 19 of *The History of North America,* edited by F. N. Thorpe. Barree, Philadelphia.
McKern, W. C.
    1939   The Midwestern Taxonomic Method as an Aid to Archaeological Study. *Ameri-can Antiquity* 4:301–313.
McMillan, R. B.
    1976   Man and Mastodon: A Review of Koch's 1840 Pomme de Terre Expeditions. In *Prehistoric Man and His Environments: A Case Study in the Ozark Highland,* ed-ited by W. R. Wood and R. B. McMillan, 81–96. Academic Press, New York.
Montgomery, H. W.
    1906   Remains of Prehistoric Man in the Dakotas. *American Anthropologist* 8:640–651.
    1908   Prehistoric Man in Manitoba and Saskatchewan. *American Anthropologist* 10:33–40.

Morgan, L. H.
   1977   *Ancient Society.* World, New York.
Mott, M.
   1938   The Relations of Historic Indian Tribes to Archeological Manifestations in
           Iowa. *Iowa Journal of History and Politics* 36:227–314.
Mulloy, W. T.
   1942   *The Hagen Site: A Prehistoric Village on the Lower Yellowstone.* University of Mon-
           tana, Publications in the Social Sciences, no. 1. Missoula.
   1943   A Prehistoric Campsite Near Red Lodge, Montana. *American Antiquity* 9:170–
           179.
   1958   *A Preliminary Historical Outline for the Northwestern Plains.* University of Wyo-
           ming Publications in Science, vol. 22, no. 1. Laramie.
Myer, W. E.
   1922   Archeological Fieldwork in South Dakota and Missouri. *Smithsonian Miscella-
           neous Collections* 72, no. 15:117–125.
Osborn, H. F.
   1922   Hesperopithecus: The First Anthropoid Primate Found in America. *Museum*
           37:1–5.
   1927   Recent Discoveries Relating to the Origin and Antiquity of Man. *Science*
           65:481–488.
Pearce, J. E.
   1932   The Present Status of Texas Archaeology. *Bulletin of the Texas Archeological and
           Paleontological Society* 4:44–54.
Reeves, B. O. K.
   1973   The Concept of an Altithermal Cultural Hiatus in Northern Plains Prehis-
           tory. *American Anthropologist* 75:1221–1253.
Reher C. A.
   1970   Population Dynamics of the Glenrock *Bison bison* Population. In *The Glenrock
           Buffalo Jump, 48Co304,* edited by G. C. Frison, 51–55. Plains Anthropologist
           Memoir no. 7.
Reher, C. A., and G. C. Frison
   1980   *The Vore Site, 48CK302: A Stratified Buffalo Jump in the Wyoming Black Hills.*
           Plains Anthropologist Memoir no. 16.
Reid, K. C.
   1983   The Nebo Hill Phase: Late Archaic Prehistory in the Lower Missouri Valley.
           In *Archaic Hunters and Gatherers in the American Midwest,* edited by J. A. Brown
           and P. Phillips, 11–39. Academic Press, New York.
Reynolds, J. D.
   1977   Preliminary Report of Archaeological Investigations at Site 14ML307, the
           Range Mound, Glen Elder, Kansas. *Kansas Anthropological Association Newslet-
           ter* 23:1–11.
Rohn, A., C. M. Stein, and G. Glover
   1977   Wolf Creek Archaeology, Coffey County, Kansas. Report on file, Wichita State
           University, Archaeology Laboratory.
Rouse, I.
   1960   The Classification of Artifacts in Archaeology. *American Antiquity* 25:313–323.
Rusco, M. K.
   1960   *The White Rock Aspect.* University of Nebraska, Laboratory of Anthropology,
           Note Book no. 4. Lincoln.

Schmits, L. J.
    1978   The Coffey Site: Environment and Cultural Adaptation at a Plains Archaic
            Site. *Midcontinent Journal of Archaeology* 3:69–185.
    1980   The Williamson Site, 14CF330. In *Salvage Archaeology in the John Redmond Lake,
            Kansas,* edited by T. A. Witty, 13–123. Kansas State Historical Society, Anthro-
            pological Series, no. 8. Topeka.
Schmits, L. J., and B. C. Bailey
    1986   Prehistoric Chronology and Settlement-Subsistence Patterns in the Little
            Blue Valley, Western Missouri. In *Prehistory of the Little Blue River Valley, West-
            ern Missouri: Archaeological Investigations at Blue Springs Lake,* edited by L. J.
            Schmits. 221–251. Report to the United States Army Corps of Engineers,
            Kansas City District, Kansas City, Mo.
Sellards, E. H.
    1940   Early Man in America: Index to Localities and Selected Bibliography. *Geologi-
            cal Society of America Bulletin* 51:373–432.
Simms, S. C.
    1903   A Wheel-Shaped Stone Monument in Wyoming. *American Anthropologist* 5:107–
            110.
Stephenson, R. L.
    1954   Taxonomy and Chronology in the Central Plains–Middle Missouri Area.
            Plains Anthropologist 1:15–21.
Sterns, F. H.
    1914   Ancient Lodge Sites on the Missouri in Nebraska. *American Anthropologist*
            16:135–137.
    1915   A Stratification of Cultures in Eastern Nebraska. *American Anthropologist*
            17:121–127.
Steward, J. H.
    1955   *Theory of Culture Change.* University of Illinois Press, Urbana.
Story, D. A., and S. D. Valestro, Jr.
    1977   Radiocarbon Dating and the George C. Davis Site, Texas. *Journal of Field Ar-
            chaeology* 4:63–89.
Strong, W. D.
    1935   *An Introduction to Nebraska Archeology.* Smithsonian Miscellaneous Collec-
            tions, vol. 93, no. 10. Washington, D.C.
    1940   From History to Prehistory in the Northern Great Plains. *Smithsonian Miscella-
            neous Collections* 100:353–394.
Vis, R. B., and D. R. Henning
    1969   A Local Sequence for Mill Creek Sites in the Little Sioux River Valley. *Plains
            Anthropologist* 14:253–271.
Wedel, M. M.
    1976   Ethnohistory: Its Payoffs and Pitfalls for Iowa Archaeologists. *Journal of the
            Iowa Archaeological Society* 23:1–11.
    1981   *The Deer Creek Site, Oklahoma: A Wichita Village Sometimes Called Ferdinandina:
            An Ethnohistorian's View.* Oklahoma Historical Society, Series in Anthropology,
            no. 5. Oklahoma City.
Wedel, W. R.
    1934   Preliminary Classification for Nebraska and Kansas Cultures. *Nebraska His-
            tory Magazine* 15:251–255.

1936   *An Introduction to Pawnee Archeology.* Bureau of American Ethnology Bulletin 112. Washington, D.C.

1940   Culture Sequences in the Central Great Plains. *Smithsonian Miscellaneous Collections* 100:291–352.

1941   Environment and Native Subsistence Economies in the Central Great Plains. *Smithsonian Miscellaneous Collections* 101, no. 3:1–29.

1943   *Archaeological Investigations in Platte and Clay Counties, Missouri.* Smithsonian Institution, United States National Museum Bulletin no. 183. Washington, D.C.

1947   Prehistory and Environment in the Central Great Plains. *Kansas Academy of Sciences, Transactions* 50:1–18.

1954   Earthenware and Steatite Vessels from Northwestern Wyoming. *American Antiquity* 19:403–409.

1955   Archeological Materials from the Vicinity of Mobridge, South Dakota. *Bureau of American Ethnology Bulletin* 157:69–188.

1959   *An Introduction to Kansas Archeology.* Bureau of American Ethnology, Bulletin 174. Washington, D.C.

1961   *Prehistoric Man on the Great Plains.* University of Oklahoma Press, Norman.

1963   The High Plains and Their Utilization by the Indians. *American Antiquity* 29:1–16.

1970   Some Observations on Two House Sites in the Central Plains: An Experiment in Archaeology. Edited by W. R. Wood. *Nebraska History* 51:225–252.

1977   The Education of a Plains Archeologist. *Plains Anthropologist* 22:1–12.

1978   The Prehistoric Plains. In *Ancient Native Americans,* edited by J. D. Jennings, 183–219. Freeman, San Francisco.

1981   Toward a History of Plains Archeology. *Great Plains Quarterly* 1:16–38.

1986   *Central Plains Prehistory: Holocene Environments and Culture Change in the Republican River Basin.* University of Nebraska Press, Lincoln.

Will, G. F.

1924   Archaeology of the Missouri Valley. *American Museum of Natural History, Anthropological Papers* 22:285–344.

Will, G. F., and H. J. Spinden

1906   *The Mandans.* Harvard University, Peabody Museum of American Archaeology and Ethnology Papers, vol. 3, no. 4. Cambridge, Mass.

Willey, G. R., and P. Phillips

1958   *Method and Theory in American Archaeology.* University of Chicago Press, Chicago.

Wilmsen, E. N., and F. H. H. Roberts, Jr.

1978   *Lindenmeier, 1934–1974: Concluding Report on Investigations.* Smithsonian Contributions to Anthropology, no. 24. Washington, D.C.

Wissler, C.

1917   *The American Indian: An Introduction to the Anthropology of the New World.* McMurtrie, New York.

Witty, T. A.

1962   The Anoka Focus. M.A. thesis, Department of Anthropology, University of Nebraska, Lincoln.

1967   The Pomona Focus. *Kansas Anthropological Association Newsletter* 12:1–5.

1978   Along the Southern Edge: The Central Plains Tradition in Kansas. In *The Central Plains Tradition: Internal Development and External Relationships,* edited by

D. J. Blakeslee, 56–66. University of Iowa, Office of the State Archaeologist, Report no. 11. Iowa City.

1982   *The Slough Creek, Two Dog and William Young Sites, Council Grove Lake, Kansas.* Kansas State Historical Society, Anthropological Series, no. 10. Topeka.

Wood, W. R.

1965   *The Redbird Focus and the Problem of Ponca Prehistory.* Plains Anthropologist Memoir no. 2.

1967   *An Interpretation of Mandan Culture History.* Bureau of American Ethnology Bulletin 198. Washington, D.C.

1971   *Biesterfeldt: A Post-Contact Coalescent Site on the Northeastern Plains.* Smithsonian Contributions to Anthropology, no. 15. Washington, D.C.

Wood, W. R., ed.

1969   *Two House Sites in the Central Plains: An Experiment in Archaeology.* Plains Anthropologist Memoir no. 6.

Wood, W. R., and A. S. Downer

1977   Notes on the Crow–Hidatsa Schism. In *Trends in Middle Missouri Prehistory: A Festschrift Honoring the Contributions of Donald J. Lehmer,* edited by W. R. Wood, 83–100. Plains Anthropologist Memoir no. 13.

Wood, W. R., and R. B. McMillan, eds.

1976   *Prehistoric Man and His Environments: A Case Study in the Ozark Highland.* Academic Press, New York.

Wright, C. M.

1982   An Archaic Site in Osage County, Kansas. *Journal of the Kansas Anthropological Association* 3:7–9.

Zimmerman, L. J.

1985   *Peoples of Prehistoric South Dakota.* University of Nebraska Press, Lincoln.

Zimmerman, M. E.

1918   The Ground-House Indians and Stone-Cist Grave Builders of Kansas and Nebraska. *Kansas State Historical Society, Collections* 14:471–487.

4. The Paleo-Indian Cultures of the Great Plains

Jack L. Hofman and Russell W. Graham

Early Occupations

The origin of Native Americans has been of great interest ever since the time of Columbus, and is still one of the fundamental questions in North American archaeology. However, it was not until 1926 that the great antiquity of Native North American cultures was scientifically demonstrated and accepted at a site on the Plains in eastern New Mexico. Near Folsom, paleontologists from the Denver Museum of Natural History found the bones of fossil bison, believed to have been extinct for thousands of years, in direct association with artifacts later named Folsom points (Cook 1927; Figgins 1927). Suggestions that humans had been associated with extinct Pleistocene fauna had been made much earlier (e.g., Koch 1839, 1857), but scientists at the time recognized the absence of rigor and possible alternative explanations of the evidence offered by Koch (McMillan 1976). Other claims, such as for Lone Wolf Creek in Texas (Cook 1925), were not verified in the field by specialists, although it is now accepted as a genuine site having late-Pleistocene-age fauna and artifacts. In 1895, the Twelve Mile Creek site on the Smoky Hill River in Kansas yielded a fluted point with Pleistocene bison bones (Williston 1902; Rogers and Martin 1984) (Figure 4.1). The point subsequently was lost, and the association was not accepted by archaeologists at the time. Sellards (1952:47), however, recognized Twelve Mile Creek as the first documented direct association between Pleistocene fauna and a human artifact. It was the Folsom site, however, that offered the first incontrovertible and widely accepted proof of geologic association between Pleistocene animal remains and human artifacts. The historical context of this discovery has been detailed by Meltzer (1983, 1994).

Other discoveries of artifacts with extinct mammoths soon followed, in 1932 at Dent, Colorado (Figgins 1933), and at Blackwater Draw near Clovis, New Mexico (Howard 1935). A discussion of the early history of these important discoveries is provided by Wormington (1957). Roberts (1940) coined the term "Paleo-Indian" to differentiate these earliest inhabitants of North America from later archaeologically recognized cultures.

The time that people first occupied the Great Plains is an integral part of the general question of the peopling of the New World. This is a controversial and

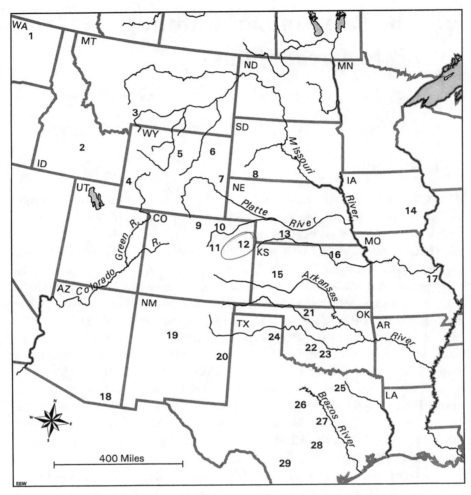

Figure 4.1. Selected pre-11,500 RCYBP sites and Clovis sites on the Great Plains and adjacent areas: *Washington* (1) Ritchie–Roberts; *Idaho* (2) Simon; *Montana* (3) Anzick; *Wyoming* (4) Fenn, (5) Colby, (6) Carter/Kerr–McGee, (7) Sheaman; *South Dakota* (8) Lange–Ferguson; *Colorado* (9) Dent, (10) Drake, (11) Lamb Spring, (12) Selby, Dutton; *Nebraska* (13) La Sena; *Iowa* (14) Rummels–Maske; *Kansas* (15) Twelve Mile Creek, (16) Diskau; *Missouri* (17) Kimmswick; *Arizona* (18) Naco, Lehner, Murray Springs, Escapule, Leikem; *New Mexico* (19) Sandia Cave, (20) Blackwater Draw Locality No. 1; *Oklahoma* (21) Burnham, (22) Cooperton, (23) Domebo; *Texas* (24) Miami, (25) Lewisville, Aubrey, (26) McLean, Yellow Hawk, (27) Gault, (28) Levi Rockshelter, (29) Kincaid Shelter.

debated issue in North American archaeology. Some argue that the Clovis culture, dating after 11,500 years ago, is the earliest good evidence of New World occupation. In the past few decades, there have been numerous discussions of models and important sites throughout North America that pertain to this question (e.g., Bonnichsen and Steele 1994; Bonnichsen and Turnmire 1991; Bryan 1978, 1986; Carlisle 1988; Dincauze 1984; Grayson 1988; MacNeish 1976, 1978; Meltzer 1989; Morlan 1988; Shutler 1983; Stanford 1982; Waters 1985; West 1983). We need not, therefore, give detailed accounts or critiques of all the theories and sites, but it is important to review some of the critical sites on the Plains that have been proposed as evidence for occupation earlier than 11,500 years ago. Meltzer (1989) has suggested that "pre-11,500" be used to characterize sites that generally predate the Clovis cultural complex rather than "pre-Clovis," because not all earlier cultural groups would necessarily be historically connected with the Clovis complex. We prefer to modify this term to "pre-11,500 RCYBP" (radiocarbon years before present) because the date of 11,500 years ago is relative to the radiocarbon time scale, which is not truly absolute.

Like many proposed pre-11,500 RCYBP sites, those on the Plains (Figure 4.1) have been questioned because of uncertainties about dating, stratigraphic context, or identification of artifacts. Stanford (1982, 1983) has reviewed the archaeological records for most of them, and Waters (1985) has reviewed the radiocarbon dates, but several sites deserve special mention. They can provide case examples of the nature of the problems confronting the acceptance of pre-11,500 RCYBP sites in general.

The Selby and Dutton sites, in Yuma County, eastern Colorado, have yielded a record suggestive of human activity before Clovis times (Stanford 1979, 1982, 1983). Both sites contain a similar stratigraphic sequence. Radiocarbon dates on bone collagen from the lowest stratigraphic levels at Selby and Dutton place the age of the upper Peorian Loess between about 17,000 and 13,000 RCYBP. The collagen from mammoth bones at the base of an overlying gleysol at Dutton yielded dates between 11,700 and 7800 RCYBP. Stone tools assigned to the Clovis complex were found associated with remains of extinct fauna in a paleosol overlying the gleysol at Dutton (Stanford 1979:119, Figure 15; Stanford and Graham 1985). The Clovis projectile point from Dutton was removed from its primary context by the mechanical earth moving at the site, but Stanford (1979:116) believes that it was originally in the paleosol that produced other stone artifacts. This would suggest that the 7800 RCYBP date is too young and that the lacustrine deposits, between the Peorian Loess and gleysol, are bracketed between 17,000 and 11,500 RCYBP.

The Peorian Loess levels at both Selby and Dutton yielded the bones of horse (*Equus*), camel (*Camelops*), and bison (*Bison*) that appear to have been butchered (Graham 1981; Stanford 1979; Stanford and Graham 1985). However, none of the bones from the loess appear to have been modified to serve as tools. A large bifacially flaked–stone end scraper was recovered among the disarticulated camel bones from the Peorian Loess at Dutton, but the tool was found at the bottom of a rodent burrow and its association is uncertain (Stanford 1979:111, Figure 5e).

Stanford (1979) initially interpreted the breakage, modification, and spatial patterning of bones in the lacustrine deposits at Selby and Dutton, in part, as the result of human actions. Many fractured bones from these strata at both sites could have been used as expediency tools, made by producing spiral fractures and using the sharp edges for butchering or hide working (Frison 1974; E. Johnson 1977). Seven tiny stone flakes, some of them thermally altered, also were recovered during the screen washing of lacustrine sediments at Dutton. These flakes may have resulted from impact or resharpening of stone tools (Stanford 1979).

Bone specimens similar to those from Selby and Dutton also were found at the Lamb Spring site, near the South Platte River about 10 miles south of Denver, Colorado. Excavations by Wedel in the early 1960s revealed a stratified archaeological sequence spanning from at least Cody times to the historic use of the spring (Rancier et al. 1982). Below the Cody levels were abundant Pleistocene faunal remains and a radiocarbon date of about 13,000 RCYBP on mammoth-bone collagen. In an unpublished report (see Rancier et al. 1982), Wedel suggested that the fragmentation and spatial patterning of the mammoth bones in this level might be the result of human activity.

During new investigations at Lamb Spring in 1979, a 33-pound boulder was found associated with flaked mammoth bone. Other flaked-bone and a few flaked-stone artifacts were recovered from the Pleistocene levels in 1980 and 1981 (Rancier et al. 1982; Stanford 1983; Stanford et al. 1981). However, the excavations in 1981 showed that the upper Cody stratum had cut into the underlying Pleistocene level near where the boulder was found. Therefore, some of the stone artifacts may be fortuitously associated with extinct fauna, and some other stone artifacts may be "geofacts" (Stanford 1983). Finally, a new radiocarbon date of about 11,700 RCYBP on mammoth-bone collagen places the Pleistocene level near the time of the Clovis complex. A summary of modified-bone evidence from Lamb Spring is provided by J. Fisher (1992).

The La Sena site in Frontier County, Nebraska, represents another case of fractured mammoth bones suggestive of human modification (Holen et al. 1990). This bone bed, containing remains of a single mammoth and rodents, is deeply buried in late Wisconsinan loess with radiocarbon dates and stratigraphy indicating an age of about 17,000 RCYBP (May and Holen 1993). No stone tools have been recovered to date, and, while suggestive, the site remains enigmatic. The setting of La Sena is quite different from those of Lamb Spring and Dutton, as it is on a buried surface marked by a weakly developed soil rather than in playa-like deposits. Therefore, it is not in a setting such as a water hole that would have attracted intensive repeated activity of numerous animals, and so trampling may be a less likely candidate for explaining bone modifications.

Most of the evidence for pre-11,500 RCYBP occupations at these sites depends on interpretations of bone breakage and bone-surface modification. Bone specimens nearly the same as those from Selby, Dutton, and Lamb Spring have been produced by butchering, bone-flaking, and utilization experiments on modern elephant bone (Stanford et al. 1981). Gary Haynes (1991), however, has shown that bone modifications similar to those that result from butchering can also be produced by natural processes. For instance, chewing on bones by carnivores can produce spiral fractures, impact notches, scratches and striations, differential polish, and flaking and hinge fractures (G. Haynes 1980, 1983, 1991). Trampling can also be an important contributor to bone breakage and surface modification, especially in the vicinity of water holes or stream crossings where animal activity is focused (Fiorillo 1989). Until the ambiguity about bone modification can be resolved or other types of evidence for human involvement can be demonstrated, these sites do not provide unequivocal evidence for pre-11,500 RCYBP occupation of the Plains (Stanford 1979; Stanford and Graham 1985).

Arguments for a pre-11,500 RCYBP occupation at the Cooperton mammoth site, Kiowa County, Oklahoma (Anderson 1975), are similar to those for Selby, Dutton, and Lamb Spring. Fractured bones of a Columbian mammoth (*Mammuthus columbi*) were found associated with four granitic cobbles, although no flaked-stone artifacts were found. Granite cobbles are abundant in the immediate area of the site, reflecting a colluvial origin of the deposits. Some of the fractured bones were interpreted as probable tools, but more recent taphonomic research and experimental studies have demonstrated that a variety of bone-fracture and -modification types can occur in high-energy depositional settings. Three radiocarbon dates from the site of between 20,400 and 17,500 RCYBP are based on bone apatite (Anderson 1975:156). Radiocarbon dates on the apatite fraction of bone are frequently in error because of isotopic exchange (Hassan et al. 1977; Stafford et al. 1987; Stafford et al. 1991). The age of the Cooperton site is therefore uncertain, and, in fact, it may be older because bone dates commonly give minimum ages.

Although only one of the granitic cobbles shows possible alteration, these cobbles have been interpreted as an anvil and three hammerstones because "their size marks them as foreign to the deposit" (Anderson 1975:147). The lithology of the cobbles is similar to that of the bedrock of the Wichita Mountains, which are about a mile and a half east of the site. Furthermore, Albritton's (1975:133) description of the sediments as "a medium to coarse sand with interbedded granule, pebble, and cobble gravel," and their position at the base of the Wichita Mountains, are more indicative of a colluvial or an alluvial fan than a fine-grained alluvial deposit. Thus the granitic cobbles may be natural constituents of the site. The fractured bones and spatial patterns of the mammoth bones at Cooperton may be the result of natural phenomena. The evidence for human activity, as well as age of the site, is ambiguous.

The Burnham site in northwestern Oklahoma is one of the more recent contenders for pre-11,500 RCYBP human activity on the Plains. Wyckoff and an interdisciplinary team investigated this late Wisconsinan site located on a tributary of the Cimarron River in Woods County (Wyckoff et al. 1990; Wyckoff et al. 1991; Wyckoff and Carter 1994). Fauna includes an extinct species of bison (*Bison chenyi*), with much larger horns than *B. bison antiquus*, as well as a variety of other fauna. The geologic context is complex, with interfingered pond and colluvial deposits that include some coarse sand, gravel, and carbonate lenses in a generally fine matrix. Trampling and differential weathering of the bone is evident. Numerous small chipped-stone pieces are argued to include humanly produced bifacial-reduction flakes, and two possible tools were recovered in screening material near the bison bones. Several radiocarbon dates are not very satisfying and range from 40,000 to 11,500 RCYBP based on snails, sediments, wood, and charcoal. Dates between 28,000 and 24,000 are considered most appropriate for the fauna recovered—a fauna distinctly different from any Clovis fauna from the Southern Plains. Further documentation of the stratigraphic context of artifacts and more precise dating will aid in the evaluation of the Burnham site, which already has proved to be an important site in terms of paleoecological information.

The Levi Rockshelter (Alexander 1963, 1982) in Travis County, Texas, has two presumed pre-11,500 RCYBP levels underlying an occupation identified as Clovis. Utilized flakes were found in these older strata. The complicated nature of the stratigraphy, and the current formation of cave travertine, make straightforward interpretations of occupation levels nearly impossible.

The Clovis-age Lange–Ferguson site in South Dakota is of importance here because of the apparent bone technology represented by a series of bone flakes and worn chopping tools (Hannus 1990a, 1990b). Only a single stone flake was found in the mammoth-bone-bed area at Lange–Ferguson, with diagnostic Clovis points found on the pond margin about 30 feet from the mammoth remains and separated by recent erosion. Had the Clovis points not been recovered, or the site not been well dated to Clovis time, the interpretation of the bone flakes and tools at Lange–Ferguson would have been as problematic as for some samples from pre-11,500 RCYBP sites. In fact, Gary Haynes (1991) questions the Clovis association at Lange–Ferguson. In any case, Lange–Ferguson demonstrates that pre-11,500 RCYBP bone technology may still be a viable concept (Frison 1991a; L. Johnson 1989).

At present, there is simply no unequivocal evidence for pre-11,500 RCYBP human occupation on the Great Plains. It will require more than a long list of suggestive sites to demonstrate human presence in the area before Clovis time. The pre-11,500 RCYBP sites must have (1) good radiometric dating, (2) stratigraphic integrity, (3) indisputable evidence of human involvement, and (4) concordant paleoenvironmental data from a variety of sources (Stanford 1983).

Clovis

The earliest undisputed cultural complex in the Great Plains is Clovis, and the first generally accepted discovery of Clovis points associated with mammoth remains was made near Dent, Colorado, in 1932 (Cassells 1983; Figgins 1933). In the same year, discoveries were made at another important locality, a gravel pit about 14 miles southwest of Clovis, New Mexico (Howard 1935, 1937). Hester (1972) gives a detailed account of the history of discoveries at this site, now known as Blackwater Draw (BWD) Locality No. 1 (see also Sellards 1952). The projectile points first documented in situ with mammoth remains at BWD Locality No. 1 by Cotter (1938), typified by flutes and basal grinding, are now recognized as the type specimens of the Clovis complex (Figure 4.2).

Temporally, the Clovis complex appears to be confined to an interval between 11,300 and 10,900 RCYBP (C. Haynes 1992), but spatially, Clovis artifacts are widespread from northern Mexico, throughout most of the contiguous United States, to southern Canada (West 1983). However, most stratified Clovis sites are restricted to the Plains or southwestern United States (Figure 4.1). The origin of the complex is uncertain (Bonnichsen and Turnmire 1991), but C. Haynes (1970, 1987) believes that Clovis was derived from the technology of adventurous bands of hunters who migrated from Eurasia across the Bering Land Bridge in search of megafauna. This hypothesis would establish Clovis as the first successful human colonization of North America. Haynes (1970) has suggested that the migration may represent multiple groups and many failed attempts, but Meltzer (1989) points out that not all human populations in the New World that date prior to Clovis would necessarily be related genetically or technologically to Clovis.

An alternative explanation for the origins of Clovis is that human populations were already established in North America by 12,000 RCYBP (Bonnichsen and Young 1980; Bryan 1991). Some of these pre-11,500 RCYBP cultures, however, may not have used a recognizable stone technology, but may have relied heavily on bone as a raw material for tools. With the transfer of bone-flaking techniques to stone, the idea of Clovis points was rapidly spread among these preexisting human populations. This does not call for the rapid dispersion of people, but for the dissemination of an idea. The variety of projectile-point forms included in well-dated Clovis samples suggests that there may have been some widespread Clovis progenitors in North America through which the Clovis technological complex, including fluting, diffused rapidly.

Both hypotheses have strengths and weaknesses. The migration model is at-

or followgame?

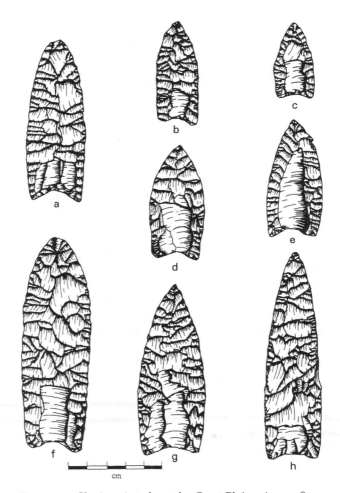

Figure 4.2. Clovis points from the Great Plains: (*a–c, e–f*)
Kansas; (*d*) Boulder County, Colorado; (*g–h*) Dent site,
Colorado.

tractive to those who do not believe that the evidence for pre-11,500 RCYBP culture in North America is well established. Conversely, the lack of clearly defined
antecedent projectile-point forms in the Old World tends to weaken the migration argument. However, C. Haynes (1987) has noted eight shared technological
traits between Clovis and the Upper Paleolithic of eastern Europe and northeastern Asia. Some of these traits include cylindrical bone and ivory shafts that
have been polished, incised, tapered, and beveled at the ends. These artifacts
have been found in sites from Florida to Montana (Stanford 1991) and are interpreted either as foreshafts for stone projectile points or as bone and ivory projectile points (Frison and Craig 1982; Lahren and Bonnichsen 1974). Closely

comparable artifacts have been found in Eurasian Upper Paleolithic sites (C. Haynes 1987; Soffer 1985). A humanly modified end portion of an adult mammoth tusk from Blackwater Draw is also similar to artifacts, known as semifabricates, from Old World Paleolithic sites (Saunders et al. 1990). Semifabricates may have been used in the production of other ivory artifacts like the cylindrical shafts previously mentioned.

A specialized mammoth-bone tool from Murray Springs, a Clovis site in southeastern Arizona, is believed to be a shaft wrench, similar to the *batons de commandement* known from the European Upper Paleolithic (Haynes and Hemmings 1968). It is assumed that these tools were used to straighten the shafts of spears, although some have suggested that they may have been hide or thong stretchers and softeners (Braidwood 1975:76). The bone shaft wrench from Murray Springs is the only New World Paleo-Indian example known. Another distinctive bone artifact of Clovis age is a small bone cylinder from BWD Locality No. 1 that has correlates in Eurasian Upper Paleolithic assemblages (Saunders et al. 1991). *moved south to north*

The rarity of fluted points in the extreme northern latitudes and older radiocarbon dates for southern Clovis sites produce a pattern opposite that to be expected from a southward migration (Clark 1991). This pattern might be more readily explained by an origin of the Clovis culture in the southwestern United States, as suggested by Bonnichsen and Young (1980). This model, however, is criticized for the lack of clearly defined pre-11,500 RCYBP occupations and the apparent absence of pre-11,500 RCYBP technologies, since highly developed stoneworking was an established technology in the Old World well before Clovis times. Sandia Cave site in New Mexico has produced one possible pre-11,500 RCYBP assemblage in the Southwest, with fluted and unfluted bifacial points dating between 14,000 and 11,000 RCYBP (Haynes and Agogino 1986). Alternatively, a southeastern United States origin for fluted points, including Clovis, has been repeatedly suggested (Griffin 1979; Mason 1962; Stanford 1991), based primarily on the high density of fluted-point finds there and the common occurrence of cylindrical bone and ivory foreshafts/points of Clovis form.

There is considerable morphological variation in the shape of Clovis points when those from southeastern Arizona sites are compared with those from Plains sites such as Colby in Wyoming and Domebo in Oklahoma. The significance of this variability for understanding Clovis origins has not been assessed. Miniature points are known from several sites, but the largest and most spectacular Clovis points have been found in caches at such sites as Ritchie–Roberts in Washington, Anzick in Montana, Simon in Idaho, Drake in Colorado, and Fenn near the Wyoming–Idaho border (Frison 1991a; Lahren and Bonnichsen 1974; Mehringer and Foit 1990; Stanford and Jodry 1988; Woods and Titmus 1985). Another important cache or kill site assemblage is the Rummels–Maske collection from Iowa (Anderson and Tiffany 1972). Technological aspects of

Clovis biface production are becoming better understood as a result of studies of Clovis caches and production debris (Bradley 1982). Broad margin-to-margin bifacial flaking is a recurrent characteristic of Clovis technology (e.g., Frison 1991a).

Clovis people, however, were not shadowy figures who simply made stone tools and hunted mammoth. These small bands of hunter-gatherers were resourceful and technologically advanced people with a tremendous aptitude for understanding, observing, and exploiting varied geologic, floral, and faunal resources. The artistic capabilities of Clovis people are certainly reflected in some of their stone and bone technology, and this has been supplemented by recent finds of engraved stones at the Gault site in central Texas (Collins et al. 1991). While these pieces may simply reflect prehistoric doodling, it is possible that record keeping, representational drawings, ritual, or other behaviors are also represented.

Goshen

Throughout most of the Plains, Clovis is followed by Folsom, and the transition between these two complexes is assumed to be a cultural continuum. There is a potential overlap of about 100 years in the radiocarbon dates for Clovis and Folsom, specifically between about 10,900 and 10,800 RCYBP (C. Haynes 1992). In the Northern Plains, this simple transition model is complicated by the Goshen complex, originally named by Irwin (1968), based on an assemblage from the Hell Gap site, Wyoming. Goshen points are unfluted lanceolates having parallel to slightly convex or concave sides and concave bases. They exhibit well-executed parallel horizontal flaking, are basally thinned by the removal of multiple flakes, and are ground along the lower third of their edges (Irwin-Williams et al. 1973:46).

At Hell Gap, Goshen points were stratigraphically below Folsom points, but Clovis materials have not been found in the Hell Gap–site deposits (Irwin-Williams et al. 1973:46). No radiocarbon dates are available for the Goshen complex at Hell Gap. Recent work at the Milliron site in southeastern Montana suggests that Goshen may be relatively widespread. Based on research at Milliron, Frison (1991b, 1996) believes that Goshen is either a Clovis variant or a technological system intermediate between Clovis and Folsom. Technological similarities suggest that Goshen may indeed be the precursor of Folsom on the Northwestern Plains. Radiocarbon dates from the Milliron site do not resolve the problem, because two age groups are represented by dates from both the bison-bone bed and the camp/processing area (Frison 1991b). One set of dates ranges between about 11,500 and 11,200, or essentially Clovis age, whereas the second series of dates is between 10,900 and 10,700, or at the early end of available Folsom radiocarbon ages. The importance of the Goshen complex, in part, is that it suggests (as is the case during the later Paleo-Indian period) the possible coexistence of multiple distinct lithic traditions. We should not assume that Paleo-Indian complexes on the Plains represent a simple unilinear development sequence. There was apparently much experimentation and variability in technological systems, which changed in concert with changing environments and economic orientations. The longevity and success of these techno-complexes was apparently highly variable.

Irwin-Williams and co-workers (1973) also suggested that Goshen was intermediate between Clovis and Folsom, and they proposed that the Goshen projectile point is typologically comparable to the Plainview type, common on the Southern Plains. Chronologically, however, Plainview is usually considered to postdate Folsom on the Southern Plains, but the number of available radiocarbon dates is few and some are of questionable reliability due to the material dated or complex site stratigraphy. It is possible that Plainview overlaps or even partially precedes Folsom in age, as does Goshen (C. Haynes 1991). Judge (1973) has recognized a variety of Folsom points from sites along the central Rio Grande valley in New Mexico that may represent a "transitional variety" between Clovis and Folsom. Clearly, more work with stratified and well-dated sites is necessary before the transition between Clovis and Folsom will be understood.

Goshen an intermediate between Clovis/Folsom or a separate technology

Folsom

The Folsom complex follows Clovis throughout most of the Plains, but, as noted earlier, on the Northwestern Plains the relationships between these two complexes and the Goshen complex remain perplexing. On the Southern Plains, a similar problem exists with Midland, Plainview, and Folsom in that the true chronological, technological, and social relationships among the makers of these different artifact types remains open to debate. Although Folsom sites are widespread on the Plains (Figure 4.3), they are limited in number. Folsom occurs as far south as Bonfire Shelter in Val Verde County, Texas (Dibble and Lorrain 1968), and as far north as the MacHaffie site in west-central Montana (Forbis and Sperry 1952). Surface finds are known from Canada to Mexico (Wormington and Forbis 1965). The Rocky Mountains were primarily the western limit of Folsom, but there are sites in the intermontane basins of the Northwestern Plains and the eastern part of the Great Basin (Davis 1988; Titmus and Woods 1991). The eastern limit of Folsom is not well defined. Folsom points are reported as surface finds in Iowa, Missouri, northern Illinois, and Wisconsin (Alex 1980:113; Chapman 1975; Munson 1990). Stratified radiocarbon-dated sites are limited primarily to the Plains (except for Owl Cave in Idaho [Miller 1982]).

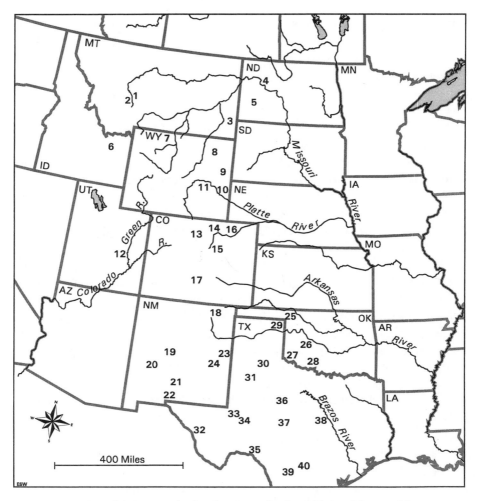

Figure 4.3. Selected Folsom and related sites on the Great Plains: *Montana* (1)
MacHaffie, (2) Indian Creek, (3) Milliron; *North Dakota* (4) Moe, (5) Lake Ilo; *Idaho* (6)
Owl Cave; *Wyoming* (7) Hanson, (8) Carter/Kerr–McGee, (9) Agate Basin/Brewster, (10)
Hell Gap, (11) Rattlesnake Pass; *Utah* (12) Montgomery; *Colorado* (13) Twin Mountain,
(14) Lindenmeier, Johnson, (15) Powars, (16) Fowler–Parrish, (17) Cattle Guard, Linger,
Zapata; *New Mexico* (18) Folsom, (19) Rio Rancho, Correo, Los Lunas, (20) Ake, (21)
Lone Butte, (22) Dona Ana, (23) Blackwater Draw/Mitchell Locality, (24) Elida; *Oklahoma* (25) Waugh, Cooper, (26) Cedar Creek, (27) Winters, (28) Salt Creek; *Texas* (29)
Lipscomb, (30) Lake Theo, (31) Lubbock Lake, (32) Chispa Creek, (33) Shifting Sands,
Winkler No. 1, (34) Scharbauer, (35) Bonfire Shelter, (36) Adair–Steadman, (37)
41RN129, (38) Horn Shelter, (39) Kincaid Shelter, (40) Pavo Real.

About 35 "reliable" Folsom radiocarbon dates indicate that the time frame for this complex is between 10,900 and 10,200 RCYBP (C. Haynes 1992). A number of more recent radiocarbon dates attributed to Folsom are based on sediment or bone and cannot be considered reliable or are from contexts now interpreted as post-Folsom in age (e.g., Holliday and Johnson 1986).

The Folsom type site in New Mexico provided the first definitive evidence for the association between humans and extinct fauna when a Folsom point was found associated with the ribs of an extinct species of bison in 1926 (Wormington 1957). In fact, Clovis points found associated with mammoth and other extinct fauna at Blackwater Draw in 1932 were first called "Folsom-like" because of their stylistic similarity and the uncertainty of their relationships at the time (Cotter 1938:11). Even at this early stage in Paleo-Indian studies, Cotter (1938:13) recognized "classic" Folsom points and other fluted points as "Folsom," and it was not until more than a decade later that the formal distinction was made between Folsom and Clovis (Sellards 1952). The Folsom complex is typified by its diagnostic thin projectile point, usually having pronounced fluting, fine marginal retouch, prominent basal ears, and a deeply concave or recurved base (Figure 4.4*n–p*).

Regional-scale study of Folsom remains—including buried sites, surface collections, and isolated finds—is providing information on land-use patterns that cannot be derived when studies are limited to major sites (Amick 1994; Dawson and Judge 1969; Hofman 1991; Hofman and Ingbar 1988; Judge and Dawson 1972). Also, strict definition of different site types has probably been overly simplistic in some studies, given recent evidence from such sites as Agate Basin, Wyoming, and Cattle Guard, Colorado, which indicate that camps are typically nearby and directly associated with kills (Frison and Stanford 1982; Jodry 1987; Jodry and Stanford 1992). Depending on which areas of sites are sampled through exposure or excavation, particular Folsom assemblages may appear to represent "kill sites" or "campsites" (Hofman et al. 1990). Also, smaller sites and isolated materials can provide important insights into overall land-use patterns (Amick 1991; Hofman and Ingbar 1988; Kornfeld 1988). Studies of lithic raw materials have also added to the understanding of Folsom-period mobility (Hofman 1992; Ingbar 1992; Stanford 1991). Folsom technology was highly curated, with staging in the reduction of cores and preforms, so that much flexibility was retained in the assemblages even after the artifacts had been intensively used and recycled. As with Clovis technology, large bifacial cores of high-quality stone served as sources for a variety of tool forms and provided the flakes and bifaces from which all other tool forms could be derived (Boldurian 1991; Hofman 1992) (Figure 4.4).

The recovery of a T-shaped elk (*Cervus elaphus*) antler tine from the Folsom level at Agate Basin, Wyoming, has led to new thoughts about the methods of fluting Folsom points. Initially, investigators believed that this antler arti-

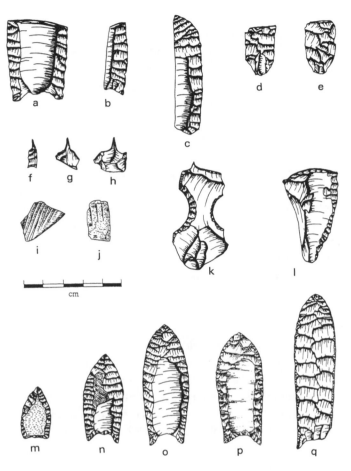

Figure 4.4. Folsom artifacts from the Great Plains: (*a–c*) Folsom preform fragments; (*d–e*) Folsom channel flakes; (*f–h*) Folsom gravers on flakes; (*i–j*) engraved bone pieces; (*k*) spokeshave with graver; (*l*) spurred end scraper; (*m*) pseudo-fluted Folsom point from the Lindenmier site, Colorado; (*n–p*) Folsom points from Colorado, Nebraska, and Texas; (*q*) Midland point from Nebraska.

fact could have been used as a chest punch in a manner originally proposed by Crabtree (1966). Experimentation with an analogue made from a modern elk antler did not replicate "the smooth bulbar surfaces observed on most archaeological Folsom points" (Frison and Bradley 1982:209). Instead, Frison and Bradley found that if the antler tine was used as a punch in a simple lever device, they had greater control of the applied force, and hence they could replicate the morphology of channel flakes on Folsom points (Figure 4.4*d–e*).

As Frison and Bradley (1982:211–212) caution, these experiments are not proof of how fluting was done, but they "provide some means of judging the possibilities and limitations imposed on tool use." Numerous experimenters have replicated Folsom material using a variety of techniques and reduction nuances (Akerman and Fagan 1986; Flenniken 1978; Gryba 1988; Sollberger 1985). These studies also raise interesting questions about the function of fluting. This has been a topic for debate for some time, with suggestions ranging from devising better methods of hafting to enhancing the ability of projectiles to penetrate (Wilmsen and Roberts 1978:176–177). Fluting may also have been an art form, or it may have been done in the realm of ritual (Frison and Bradley 1982). For instance, fluting may have served an important role in the training, teaching, and indoctrination of young hunters. Bamforth (1991) has suggested that fluting was done primarily in the context of multiband aggregations and that fluting specialists were involved. There are counterarguments for all these suggestions, and, in all likelihood, fluting may have served several functions. The notion that the channel flake itself was an important element of Folsom technology (Judge 1973) is supported by the high frequency of utilized channel flakes that occur in some assemblages far removed from good sources of lithic raw material (Hofman et al. 1990).

Pseudo-fluted Folsom points, made as chipped outlines on flakes, are associated with fluted Folsom points at many sites. There is no evidence that their function was different from that of fluted points. At some Folsom sites (for example, Hanson, Cattle Guard, and Lindenmeier), unfluted Folsom points are found associated with fluted ones. One possibility is that the risky fluting process was opted against when there was limited raw material (Hofman 1992). Some unfluted points are virtually indistinguishable from Midland points. Indeed, both classic Folsom and Midland points are found in association at the Midland type site (Wendorf et al. 1955) and at the nearby Shifting Sands site (Hofman et al. 1990). Therefore, the status of the Midland complex, like that of Goshen on the Northern Plains, is uncertain. It is evident that extensive fluting of projectile points was eventually abandoned and that Midland or other unfluted forms (Plainview, Milnesand, and Belen) filled this technological niche.

Midland

The Scharbauer site in Midland County, Texas, at the southern end of the Llano Estacado, is the type site for the Midland complex (Wendorf et al. 1955). The discovery of a partial skull and other human remains in dune deposits in 1953 sparked interest in this site, especially when it became apparent that the bones were "fossilized" and covered with a calcareous accretion. Furthermore, preliminary examination of stratigraphic relations from "four other [adjacent] blowouts showed conclusively that the true Folsom points and other cultural material lie on the contact zone of the Monahan and Judkins sands," and, therefore, any materials from the gray sand that contained the human remains must predate Folsom (Wendorf et al. 1955:4–6). Finally, the recovery of extinct fauna from the gray sand suggested great antiquity for the human remains. Wendorf and his colleagues made every effort to establish the age of the human remains. These included detailed stratigraphic studies, chemical analyses of the human and fossil animal remains, and radiocarbon dating. Even with further investigations (Wendorf and Krieger 1959), it was impossible to determine the age of the human remains. Their age is still uncertain, but it appears from stratigraphic data that they are either Folsom age or older, as originally suggested. For a recent discussion and reevaluation, see Holliday and Meltzer (1996).

The association of the human remains with extinct fauna is somewhat equivocal, however. Wendorf and Krieger (1959:69–70) discuss the possibility of redeposition of fossil vertebrates and conclude that a definitive answer is not possible with the available evidence. They do note that a horse mandible was found in the red sand that overlies the gray sand, and that it would be difficult to explain redeposition of this specimen by wind. Because of the complex geology of the site, it is possible that other natural agents may have caused redeposition, and they cannot be automatically excluded. The question of the association of the human remains with extinct fauna will require further field investigations, and possibly radiocarbon dating with new techniques, before it can be answered with certainty. Also, the remains of extinct fauna that have modifications such as scratches, striations, and polish should be examined in the light of new taphonomic studies before they are accepted as evidence for human activity (Bonnichsen and Sorg 1989).

The Scharbauer site has also stimulated controversy and discussions on point typology. Both classic fluted Folsom points and very thin unfluted points of a general Folsom shape, now called Midland, are found there (Figure 4.4q). All the projectile points originally reported, however, are surface finds, and they were not believed to be contemporaneous with one another or the human remains (Wendorf et al. 1955:65). Later excavations in 1955 by Wendorf and Krieger (1959) documented three artifacts (two scrapers and the basal fragment of an unfluted projectile point) from the gray sand. Other nondiagnostic flint flakes and burned rock also were found in this unit. Other than stratigraphic associations, however, these artifacts cannot be related to the human skeletal remains or the extinct fauna.

It is possible that Midland points are contemporaneous with Folsom and are part of the same complex, as they commonly are found in association. Some may represent reworked Folsom points or channel flakes, while others were made from preforms that were perhaps too thin to flute (Judge 1973; Wendorf et al. 1955:49). Other technological constraints or factors of lithic availability may have influenced decisions about fluting. The close relationship between Folsom and Midland is suggested by the repeated and widespread occurrence of un-fluted points comparable to the Midland type in Folsom contexts, as at the Hell Gap and Hanson sites in Wyoming. The use of the same proportions of distinctive lithic materials in the manufacture of both Folsom and Midland points also lends credence to this proposition (e.g., Brolio 1971; Hofman 1990). Since other tools in the Midland assemblages are also directly comparable to those in Folsom tool kits, it is probable that they represent expressions of a single technological complex with variability resulting from situational, temporal, organizational, and mobility differences within a single tradition.

Midland has, however, been argued to represent a distinct and separate complex (Blaine 1968; Irwin 1971; Irwin-Williams et al. 1973). The presence of sites that produce Midland points to the exclusion of Folsom is one of the primary arguments to support a separate Midland complex (Agogino 1969; Blaine 1968). This is based, however, on the assumption that the full range of point and artifact forms used by a group will be represented at every site they occupy; otherwise, it is possible that the small samples from "pure" Midland sites represent only part of the range of tool forms that might include classic Folsom points (Hofman 1992).

If Midland is a distinct complex, then the sites with classic Folsom and Midland points in association may represent the early stages of the transition from Folsom to Midland. "Pure" Midland sites would then reflect the complete technological evolution of the Midland complex. If this is the case, then "pure" Midland sites should be younger than the sites with both Midland and Folsom points. The possibility of co-traditions also merits further examination. Unfortunately, there are no radiocarbon dates from "pure" Midland sites to determine if they are temporally distinct from Folsom. The Midland-complex problem thus exemplifies recurrent issues in Paleo-Indian studies pertaining to typology, technology, and chronology (Amick 1995).

Plano: Agate Basin, Plainview, Milnesand, and Hell Gap

The Plano complex, originally defined by Jennings (1955), is a general term used to refer to several presumably distinct groups recognized by unfluted, lanceolate projectile points that are known or assumed to date after Clovis and Folsom fluted points. Later, Jennings (1974, 1978) included materials (stemmed and notched projectile points) in Plano that most other researchers would consider as Archaic (Hofman 1989). The unifying theme of the Plano complex, as used here and by most archaeologists, is that it collectively represents late Paleo-Indian (10,200 to 8000 RCYBP) groups that had an economic focus during most of the year on bison hunting (Figure 4.5). As indicated earlier, not all unfluted points are younger than Clovis and Folsom (for example, Goshen), so the

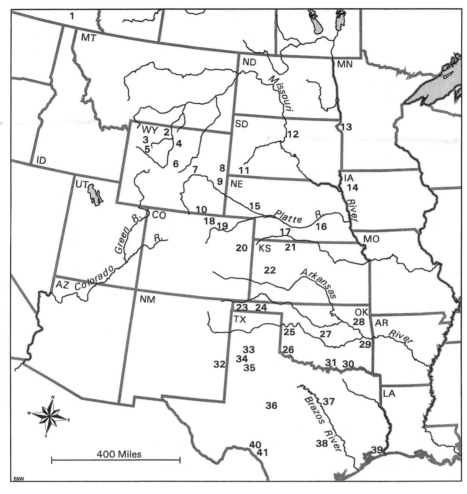

Figure 4.5. Selected late Paleo-Indian sites on the Great Plains: *Alberta* (1) Sibald Creek; *Wyoming* (2) Bottleneck, (3) Mummy Cave, (4) Medicine Lodge Creek, (5) Helen Look-ingbill, (6) Sister's Hill, (7) Casper, (8) Agate Basin, (9) Betty Greene, Hell Gap, (10) James Allen; *South Dakota* (11) Ray Long, (12) Walth Bay, Travis II; *Minnesota* (13) Browns Valley; *Iowa* (14) Cherokee Sewer; *Nebraska* (15) Clary Ranch, (16) Meserve, (17) Lime Creek, Red Smoke; *Colorado* (18) Gordon Creek, (19) Frazier, (20) Jones–Miller; *Kansas* (21) Tim Adrian, (22) Norton; *Oklahoma* (23) Nall, (24) Muncy, (25) Charlie's Terrace, (26) Perry Ranch, (27) Suzanne West, (28) Packard, (29) Billy Ross, (30) Quince, (31) Pumpkin Creek; *New Mexico* (32) Milnesand; *Texas* (33) Lake Theo, Rex Rogers, (34) Plainview, Ryan's, (35) Lubbock Lake, (36) Lone Wolf Creek, (37) Horn Shelter, (38) Wilson–Leonard, (39) McFaddin Beach, (40) Baker Cave, (41) Devil's Mouth.

absence of fluting can no longer be considered an adequate characteristic for inclusion of lanceolate points within Plano. Also, given the absence of fluted-point assemblages in the Old World that might represent Clovis progenitors, New World pre-11,500 RCYBP assemblages very likely included unfluted bifacial points for some unknown period of time (e.g., Dillehay and Collins 1988). Like the older term "Yuma," which was used widely in the 1930s and 1940s for a heterogeneous grouping of unfluted Paleo-Indian points, the term "Plano" may eventually be abandoned, but it remains a useful reference for general consideration of late Plains Paleo-Indian material.

The reinvestigation of Agate Basin, a multicomponent site in Wyoming, has greatly expanded our knowledge of the Agate Basin complex (Frison and Stanford 1982). Wheeler (1954) provided the type description for the Agate Basin projectile point, but like other Paleo-Indian traditions there is a wide range of morphological variation in the projectile points from the Agate Basin level at Agate Basin (Bradley 1982:202–203, Table 3.9). Bradley recognized technological similarities between Agate Basin points (Figure 4.6*f–g*) and the slightly later Hell Gap points, and several points were in fact intermediate between the two.

The Agate Basin complex is well dated to between 10,500 and about 10,000 RCYBP. This age suggests that Agate Basin points may be at least partly contemporaneous with both Folsom and Plainview. Technological similarities between Folsom and Agate Basin have been noted (Frison 1991a; Shelley and Agogino 1983), and it has been suggested that Agate Basin is derived from Folsom. The origins and distribution of the Agate Basin complex are, however, not fully understood. This is partly because projectile points resembling Agate Basin points in form are widely found in the United States and Canada (Chapman 1975; Kunz and Reanier 1996; Wormington and Forbis 1965; Wyckoff 1989), but materials from outside the Plains generally cannot be related technologically with any certainty, or they date to less than 10,000 years (Frison and Stanford 1982).

Krieger (1946) suggested that Plainview projectile points (Figure 4.6*h*), named for the Plainview site in Hale County, Texas, were chronologically and typologically "intermediate" between those of the Folsom and Cody complexes (Figure 4.7). In fact, a comparative analysis of the Plainview-site sample with the Cody collection from the MacHaffie site in Montana shows many similarities between these widely separated assemblages (Knudson 1983). The parallel relationship with Goshen suggested by Irwin-Williams and her colleagues (1973) has already been discussed, and the technological and morphological similarities of some Plainview points with Clovis, Folsom, and Midland points has been noted repeatedly (C. Haynes 1991; Hofman 1989:38). The co-occurrence of Plainview and San Patrice (or Brazos Fish-Tailed) points at the Rex Rodgers site (Willey et al. 1978) in Briscoe County, Texas, also reflects close affiliation between typologically distinctive projectile-point types. The recovery of an Allen

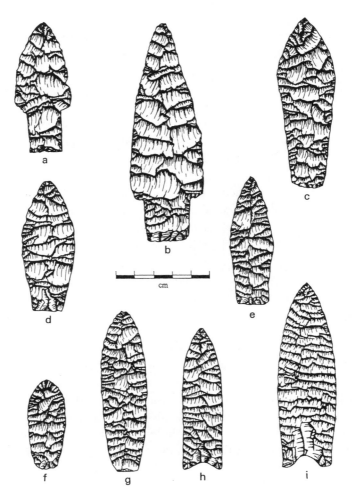

Figure 4.6. Late Paleo-Indian point types from the Great
Plains: (*a–b*) Alberta points from the Hudson–Meng site, Nebraska; (*c–e*) Hell Gap points from the Jones–Miller site, Colorado; (*f–g*) Agate Basin points from the Frazier site, Colorado;
(*h*) Plainview point from Bonner Springs, Kansas; (*i*) Allen
point from the Norton site, Kansas.

point in the bone bed at the Scottsbluff site is intriguing, as are the diverse radiocarbon ages for the Agate Basin– and Cody-complex material (Frison and
Stanford 1982; Frison and Todd 1987). There is repeated evidence for regional
and temporal overlap between a number of late Paleo-Indian projectile-point
types.

Research at Plainview sites in northern Texas—including Plainview (Guffee
1979; Holliday 1986; Speer 1986), Lubbock Lake (E. Johnson 1987), Rex Rodgers

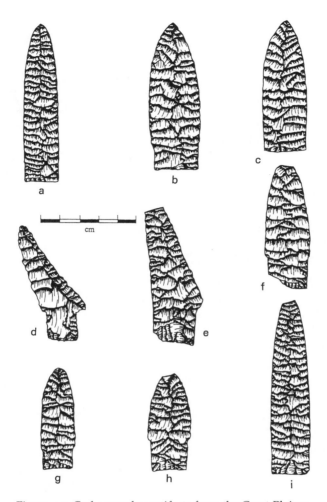

Figure 4.7. Cody-complex artifacts from the Great Plains:
(*a–c*) points from the Olsen–Chubbuck site, Colorado; (*d*)
Cody knife from the Hudson–Meng site, Nebraska; (*e*)
Cody knife from the Claypool site, Colorado; (*f*)
Scottsbluff point from Lime Creek, Nebraska; (*g–i*)
points from the Jurgens site, Colorado.

(Willey et al. 1978), and Lake Theo (Harrison and Killen 1978; Johnson et al.
1982)—have supplied the greatest insights into the age of the Plainview complex
and the lifeways of its people. Radiocarbon dates from these sites cluster around
10,000 years ago, although dates on shell and bone are involved and cannot be
accepted without further supporting evidence. The late date from the Perry
Ranch site in southwestern Oklahoma, for example (Saunders and Penman
1979), was based on bone. A reanalysis of the bone chemistry for this site indi-

cated that almost none of the original bone nitrogen and protein remained and that the date derived had little to do with the age of the bison (Hofman and Todd 1997).

Investigations at the Milnesand site in the 1950s documented an apparent bison kill with projectile points that Sellards (1955) believed to be different from those from Plainview and Scottsbluff. Milnesand points are similar to Plainview points, the primary difference being the basal outline and flaking pattern. Milnesand points usually have straight or squared to slightly convex bases, with many short steep retouch flakes, whereas the base on Plainview points is normally concave and usually has one or several longitudinal thinning flakes (Sellards 1955). Many of the Milnesand-site points have, however, been heavily reworked, which accounts for some of the basal patterns.

The relation of Milnesand to other complexes is unclear, but it may well be a variant of the Plainview or Cody complex. There are no reported radiocarbon dates. Wormington (1957:110–111) reported the co-occurrence of a Milnesand and a Plainview point in a bison-bone bed at the Lone Wolf Creek site in New Mexico. A reexamination of the Plainview point from this site led to the conclusion that "the apparent basal concavity of the incomplete specimen is the result of a single hinge flake having been removed from the base. Otherwise, the broken artifact has the same attributes as the complete Milnesand point" (Johnson and Holliday 1980:103).

Hester (1972:136–137) and others (Agogino et al. 1976:211; Wheat 1972) have reported evidence that Milnesand points occur with and may be closely related to Eden and Scottsbluff (Firstview) points at Blackwater Draw. Hofman (1989:40) suggested that Milnesand may be transitional between Plainview and Firstview, but chronological control is not good for the Milnesand material. Further investigations of artifact variability and occurrences at stratified sites are needed before the relations can be clarified, but again the existence of contemporary distinctive technological and stylistic artifact types must be considered. This has important ramifications for the traditional practice of equating each projectile-point type with a distinct time period or cultural group (e.g., L. Johnson 1989).

Immediately following the Agate Basin complex on the Northern Plains is the Hell Gap complex, which dates between 10,000 and 9500 RCYBP (Frison 1974, 1982a). The type site is Hell Gap in eastern Wyoming (Irwin 1968; Irwin-Williams et al. 1973). Other important localities are bison kill sites such as Casper and Carter/Kerr–McGee (Frison 1974, 1984) in Wyoming, and Jones–Miller (Stanford 1975, 1978) in Colorado. Campsites include Hell Gap and Sister's Hill (Agogino and Galloway 1965) in Wyoming. Hell Gap or closely comparable projectile points are common in the Southern Plains (e.g., Mallouf 1990; Thurmond 1990), but as yet no undisturbed component has been found and studied in the Southern Plains.

Hell Gap points are distinctively shouldered, with a broad tip and a stem that tapers toward the base (Figure 4.6c–e). Flaking patterns often produce a median ridge that results in a lenticular cross section. The base varies from straight to slightly concave, and the stem may be ground for 50 percent of its length (Irwin-Williams et al. 1973:48), especially on specimens with reworked tips. The Hell Gap tool kit is similar to that of late Paleo-Indian assemblages associated with bison hunting. However, Irwin-Williams and co-workers (1973:48, Figure 5) describe and illustrate a "Hell Gap knife" that is known from only the type site. Vaguely similar artifacts were recovered from the Hell Gap component at the Carter/Kerr–McGee site, although these specimens lack the single shoulder of the "Hell Gap knife" (Frison 1984:300).

The Hell Gap complex appears to have been derived directly from Agate Basin (Frison and Stanford 1982:366–367). This contention is supported by the recovery of both Agate Basin and Hell Gap points from the Agate Basin component at the Agate Basin site (Bradley 1982:203). Bradley notes that there are several points of intermediate style in this component.

Cody: Alberta, Scottsbluff, Eden, Firstview, and Kersey

The Cody complex (Figure 4.8), as originally defined by Jepsen (1951), includes a wide range of artifact types, including Cody knives, which have a distinctive stem and transversely retouched blade, and Eden and Scottsbluff points (Figure 4.7d–f). These artifacts were recovered by Jepsen from the Horner site, near Cody, Wyoming. Two areas of this site were excavated at different times by different institutions. In the late 1940s and early 1950s, both Princeton University (Glen Jepsen) and the Smithsonian Institution (Waldo Wedel) carried out excavations in a shallow bison-bone bed now designated as Horner I. In 1977 and 1978, the University of Wyoming investigations revealed another nearby bone bed, Horner II, beneath 6 feet of alluvium that contained an Alberta/Cody component associated with Cody knives (Frison and Todd 1987). Versions of Cody knives on the Southern Plains have been referred to as Red River knives (L. Johnson 1989).

Eden points were named from the Finley site (Howard 1943) near Eden, Wyoming, and Scottsbluff points were named after finds at the Scottsbluff bison kill site in western Nebraska (Schultz 1932). Two variants of Scottsbluff are recognized by Wormington (1957:266–267) and by Satterthwaite (1957:12–17). The co-occurrence of Eden and Scottsbluff points is documented at Horner and at Hell Gap (Frison and Todd 1987; Irwin-Williams et al. 1973). These point types were found with Cody knives at Horner, Hell Gap, Claypool (a campsite in eastern Colorado), Finley, and Medicine Lodge Creek (a campsite in northern Wyoming).

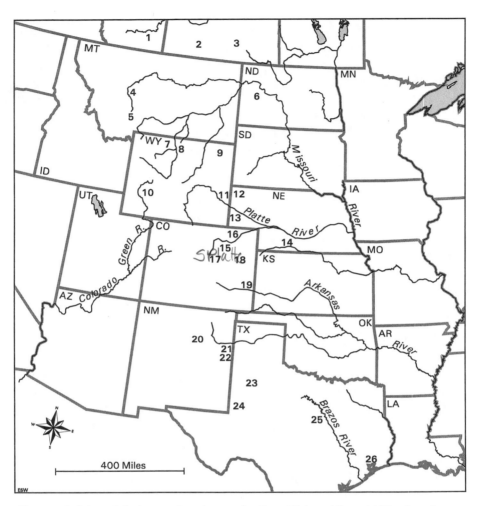

Figure 4.8. Selected Cody-complex sites on the Great Plains: *Alberta* (1) Fletcher; *Saskatchewan* (2) Niska, (3) Dunn; *Montana* (4) MacHaffie, (5) Mammoth Meadow; *North Dakota* (6) Benz; *Wyoming* (7) Horner, (8) Medicine Lodge Creek, (9) Carter/Kerr–McGee, (10) Finley, (11) Hell Gap; *Nebraska* (12) Hudson–Meng, (13) Scottsbluff, (14) Lime Creek; *Colorado* (15) Jurgens, (16) Frasca, (17) Lamb Spring, (18) Claypool, (19) Olsen–Chubbuck; *New Mexico* (20) R-6, (21) San Jon, (22) Blackwater Draw; *Texas* (23) Lubbock Lake, (24) Seminole–Rose, (25) Horn Shelter, (26) McFaddin Beach.

Agenbroad (1978), using finds from the Hudson–Meng site in northwestern Nebraska, was the first to show the association of the Cody knife (Figure 4.7*d–e*) with the Alberta point. He argued that Alberta should be included in the Cody complex as its earliest expression. This idea is supported by recent work at Horner, where the lithic assemblage is considered transitional from Alberta to Cody and is called Alberta/Cody (Bradley and Frison 1987). Alberta points differ from

Hell Gap points because they have abrupt shoulders, with grinding on the parallel-sided or slightly expanding stems (Irwin-Williams et al. 1973:48) (Figure 4.6a–e). The age of the Alberta complex is poorly known because of the dearth of well-dated sites. At Hell Gap, the Alberta material was stratigraphically above the Hell Gap component and below the Cody complex, which was dated about 8850 RCYBP (Irwin-Williams et al. 1973:48). Based on geologic correlations, the Fletcher site, the type site for Alberta, is considered to be 11,000 to 7000 RCYBP (Forbis 1968).

Hudson–Meng is the only site with radiocarbon dates directly associated with a definite Alberta component. Three radiocarbon dates, two on bone and one on charcoal, are reported by Agenbroad (1978:116), who believes that the date of 9820 RCYBP (on charcoal) most accurately reflects the age of the site. Radiocarbon dates for the Alberta/Cody levels at Horner are consistent with a transitional interpretation for this component (Frison and Todd 1987). Alberta thus may be the earliest manifestation of the Cody complex. Recent reinvestigation at the Hudson–Meng site by Todd and Rapson (1991, 1995) has yielded substantive new information and a number of radiocarbon dates averaging about 9700 RCYBP. Todd and Rapson suggest that the large bone bed may represent a natural-death assemblage rather than a kill, and the Alberta artifacts occur above the bone bed.

The Carter/Kerr–McGee site, in Campbell County, Wyoming, contains a badly eroded Cody/Alberta component (Frison 1984). Scottsbluff and Eden points were found in the bison-bone bed, and three Alberta points were at the bottom of the bone bed; no Cody knives were recovered. Two attempts were made to radiocarbon-date the bison bone, but Frison (1984:292) rejects both dates, of about 6950 years ago, as being too young. Frison (1984) believes the site is probably a midwinter meat cache adjoining a kill area that was probably destroyed by erosion.

The Firstview complex was defined on the basis of the Olsen–Chubbuck site, near Firstview, Cheyenne County, Colorado (Wheat 1972). Wheat considers it to be earlier than Cody, and characterized by the Firstview and San Jon points found in the bone bed (Figure 4.7a–c). Firstview points are similar to Scottsbluff points, but lack distinctive shoulders—although grinding on the lower blade edge leaves a subtle change, or "shoulder," in edge outline on some specimens. San Jon points, apparently reworked specimens of the Firstview type, have a more typical Scottsbluff form with a distinct shoulder. San Jon points are named after a specimen from the type site in northeastern New Mexico (Roberts 1942). Reinvestigation of the San Jon site is reported by Hill and others (1995).

One of the more problematic aspects of the Olsen–Chubbuck site is the early radiocarbon date of 10,150 RCYBP (Wheat 1972:156–158). Although this date is not outside the limits for Cody (if Alberta is included), it is not consistent with the dates of about 8600 years ago for stratified Firstview components at Lubbock

Lake (E. Johnson 1987:29). The older Olsen–Chubbuck date may reflect problems with the bison bone that supplied the date (Agogino et al. 1976:221). Dates of 10,060 and 9875 RCYBP from Area II at the Horner site may lend some support to the Olsen–Chubbuck site date and for an early beginning to the Cody complex. The origin, chronological position, and range of the Cody complex remain poorly defined. More recent accelerator mass–spectometric radiocarbon dates on bone from the Olsen–Chubbuck site cluster around 9400 RCYBP (T. W. Stafford, personal communication).

Investigations of several areas at the Jurgens site on the South Platte River in Weld County, northeastern Colorado, revealed camp and butchering areas related to a Cody bison kill (Wheat 1979). Wheat documented much reworking of the points, but considered them to be distinctive from Firstview and named them Kersey points (Figure 4.7g–i). However, Fulgham and Stanford (1982) argue that recognition of a new complex, Kersey, is premature and ascribe the Frasca-site materials, 50 miles northeast of Jurgens, to the Eden and Scottsbluff types within the Cody complex.

The R-6 site, in north-central New Mexico, may represent the southernmost occurrence of Cody knives (Stanford and Patton 1984). The site also yielded projectile points, preforms, scrapers, gravers, hammerstones, and abraders. The manufacture of bifaces for replacing preforms and projectile points was important at this site, but other camp and maintenance activities are also indicated. A semicircular arrangement of large stones associated with artifact and debris concentrations may represent a structure location. Some of the felsite artifacts at Claypool in northeastern Colorado may be derived from the R-6 area (Bradley and Stanford 1987). Farther to the south and east, Cody materials are widely reported from Texas and Oklahoma (L. Johnson 1989; Thurmond 1990; Wyckoff 1992). The best dated stratified site reported from Texas is Lubbock Lake (E. Johnson 1987). Perhaps the most southernmost Cody assemblage is from the Seminole–Rose site in Gaines County, western Texas (Collins et al. 1997). The site was a bison kill and processing location on Seminole Draw.

Component II at the MacHaffie site, near Helena, Montana, is a Cody-complex locality where Scottsbluff points were made. It is important because of the insights it provides into biface-reduction techniques and general campsite activities for the Cody complex (Forbis and Sperry 1952; Knudson 1983). MacHaffie is one of the more northern Cody-complex sites, but important components are also present in the southern Canadian Plains, including Fletcher (Forbis 1968), Dunn (Ebell 1988), and Niska (Meyer 1985).

Sellards (1952:72–74) defined the Portales complex on the basis of 23 points and four scrapers found with bison skeletons at Blackwater Draw. The context in which most of the artifacts were found, and their precise relationships, remain unclear. Hester (1972:137) suggests that the Portales complex as defined by Sellards includes too much time, too much variability in points, and poor context control. As a result, the concept of the Portales complex is of little utility, a conclusion also reached by Johnson and Holliday (1981:188) and Hofman (1989). It is suggested that the Portales complex be abandoned.

There is evidence to support the association among Milnesand, Scottsbluff, and Eden points in the upper bone bed at Station E at Blackwater Draw (Hester 1972). This conclusion is upheld by more recent work at the site (Agogino et al. 1976; Stanford et al. 1986). Wheat (1972:153–154, 1979) includes most of Stratum 5 points from Blackwater Draw in the Firstview complex. There seems little doubt that most of the diagnostic points in Sellards's original definition of the Portales complex primarily represent the Firstview complex.

Bonnichsen and Keyser (1982) have correctly noted that the Cody complex is ambiguously defined and includes an extreme range of morphologically variable hafted bifaces. We believe it may be prudent to recognize a Cody tradition that would include the geographic and temporal variants expressed by these various complexes. Alberta appears to be the earliest expression of this manifestation, and the Alberta/Cody materials at Horner document a transitional stage. The "typical" Cody complex includes Scottsbluff and Eden points, and dates about 9000 RCYBP. Kersey points are recognized as reworked projectiles of the Cody complex. Firstview, including San Jon as reworked specimens and perhaps Milnesand (although its affinities are still unclear), reflect the latest expression of the tradition on the Central and Southern Plains. The Portales complex is dropped because of the heterogeneous nature of the type collection.

Allen/Frederick and Other Terminal Paleo-Indian Complexes

Parallel obliquely flaked lanceolate points, usually with concave bases, appear throughout much of the Plains between 9000 and 8500 RCYBP (Figure 4.5). These artifacts apparently represent the last of the classic Paleo-Indian groups having a highly mobile lifeway and with an economic focus on bison hunting. After 8000 RCYBP, dramatic changes in environment, culture, demography, or a combination of these factors resulted in a widely recognized transition to a more localized foraging way of life, typically called Archaic (Willey and Phillips 1958), Middle Period (Mulloy 1958), or Mesoindian (Forbis 1992; Hofman 1996a). This may be especially evident in Plains-margin groups that occupied the prairie–woodland ecotone (L. Johnson 1989) and those to the west in the Plains–mountain and intermontane region (Frison 1992; Frison and Grey 1980).

Several key sites provide information about this terminal Paleo-Indian period. These include the James (Jimmy) Allen, Mummy Cave, Medicine Lodge Creek, and Hell Gap sites in Wyoming, and the Ray Long site in South Dakota. The James Allen site, near Laramie, supplied the first good documentation of these materials, when lanceolate points with oblique parallel flaking and concave bases were recovered from a bison-bone bed. Allen points (Figure 4.6*i*) are found throughout much of the Great Plains (Hofman 1989:44; Mulloy 1959).

The Frederick complex was defined using materials from the Hell Gap site. Irwin (1968) included the materials from the Allen site in the Frederick complex, and while Irwin-Williams and colleagues (1973:50–51) recognize the similarity of Allen and Frederick points, they note that the two forms are distinct, with more basal concavity on the Allen points. Because of the priority of the Allen studies, and because the Frederick complex is poorly defined, Hofman (1989:44) suggests that the complex be referred to as Allen/Frederick. Evidence from the Hell Gap site suggests that Allen/Frederick people might have used temporary circular dwellings.

The history of the Angostura typology is confusing. Work at the Ray Long site in the Angostura Reservoir, South Dakota, produced an early component with lanceolate points, originally called Long points (Hughes 1949). Wheeler (1954, 1995) carried out further excavations here and restudied the collections, suggesting that the points be renamed Angostura points. Wormington (1957:140) concurred, since "many people have felt that the word 'Long' referred to the length of the points." This action, however, is not consistent with a standard approach to systematic taxonomy. Under such a system, the name of the type materials should not be changed unless it is synonymized with similar materials that were named earlier. This is to prevent capricious changes in name, which generally leads to confusion, as was clearly the case with the Angostura materials. In a formal taxonomic system, the name Angostura would be invalid. To add to this problem, the original type points from the Ray Long site were lost for many years, although casts of some specimens were recently relocated. Furthermore, it was suggested that "points with similar shapes have been found widely distributed from Alaska to Mexico. . . . This term [Angostura] is rapidly, and most unfortunately, replacing Yuma as a name to be applied indiscriminately to all lanceolate points. The writer feels that until more information is available the term should be applied only to points that have the same shape and general thickness and the parallel flaking that typify those from the type station [the Long site]" (Wormington 1957:140). However, Wormington and Forbis (1965:22–23) later concluded that the specimens from the Long site were not typologically like most of the other materials classed as Angostura, but were more like Agate Basin. This constitutes a synonymy of Angostura with Agate Basin, so the names Long and Angostura should be dropped and the materials from the Long site should perhaps be called Agate Basin. Reinvestigation of the Long site by Hannus (1985:96) provided new evidence on the site's deposits and further supported the contention that Angostura as a distinct type was questionable. "Angostura" remains a widely used type in Texas, despite the lack of assemblages from dated contexts or the existence of a clear type assemblage. Recent work at the Richard Beene site in south-central Texas will help clarify the Texas Angostura typology and chronology (Thoms 1993).

The Lusk complex was described by Irwin-Williams and co-workers (1973:51–52) from materials recovered at the Betty Greene site near Lusk, Wyoming. The relations of the Lusk complex are not clear. Irwin-Williams and others (1973) suggest that Lusk is similar to the Allen/Frederick complex and differs from it primarily in the haphazard chipping techniques and the lower width-to-length ratios. They also suggest that the artifacts are similar to materials described as Angostura in the literature. Presently, the position of the Lusk complex in the Paleo-Indian sequence is ambiguous.

Parallel obliquely flaked lanceolate or stemmed points are found at several other Northern Plains sites (Frison 1983, 1992). They include shelter sites along the Bighorn River (Husted 1969) and in the Bighorn Mountains (Frison 1976b, 1992; Frison and Grey 1980), as well as Mummy Cave and Helen Lookingbill in northwestern Wyoming (Larson 1991; McCracken 1979; Wedel et al. 1968). All these sites have stratified deposits, with the terminal Paleo-Indian materials stratigraphically below Archaic forms. The Southern Plains has few well-documented and reported sites of this transitional period (8000 RCYBP). Clearly, this culturally and environmentally dynamic period is of critical importance and deserves a focused research effort. Recent investigations at the Wilson–Leonard site in central Texas will help clarify the complex typological and economic variability in that region between 8000 and 1000 years ago (Collins et al. 1993). It is interesting that the stemmed and notched Wilson points (Early Barbed) appear while lanceolate points are still in use in the area.

Parallel obliquely flaked lanceolate or stemmed points are found at several other Northwestern Plains sites. The Pryor Stemmed complex defined by Frison and Grey (1980) is based on assemblages from foothill and mountain settings (Frison 1992). Sites of the Pryor complex and other terminal Paleo-Indian assemblages are reported from Bighorn River cave sites on the Wyoming–Montana border (Husted 1969), Medicine Lodge Creek and other cave sites in the Bighorn Mountains and foothills (Frison 1976b, 1992; Frison and Grey 1980), Mummy Cave (McCracken 1979; Wedel et al. 1968), and Lookingbill in the Absaroka Mountains (Frison 1983; Larson 1991). These sites include stratified sequences from late Paleo-Indian age through Archaic. The Pryor complex and other foothill–mountain terminal Paleo-Indian assemblages were at least partially contemporary with Plains–intermontane assemblages such as the Cody complex. The potentially distinct settlement and economic patterns and cultural relationships between these early Holocene groups are not well understood.

Similar situations occur along the Southern Plains margin and the eastern prairie–woodland border where the Dalton, San Patrice, and Golondrina cultural complexes are recognized. The Dalton complex is dated between 10,500 and 9400 years ago and occurs at sites well within the Plains region (Goodyear 1982; McMillan and Klippel 1981; Wyckoff 1989) as well as widely distributed along the Southern Plains–woodland border (Chapman 1975; Galm and Hofman 1984; Goodyear 1982; L. Johnson 1989; Morse and Morse 1983; Myers and Lambert 1983; Thurmond 1990; Wetherill 1995). The southern Texas–centered Golondrina complex (L. Johnson 1989; Kelly 1982; Sorrow 1968) has strong similarities with Plainview and Dalton. The San Patrice type (and similar types such as Brazos Fish-Tailed) and related assemblages are common in eastern Texas, but co-occur with Plainview points at the Rex Rodgers bison kill in western Texas, where they are dated to about 9400 years ago (Hester and Newcomb 1990; Willey et al. 1978). The cultural and environmental changes between 10,000 and 8000 years ago made this period a dynamic one. These cultural groups deserve a focused research effort, as they are of critical importance to learning about cultural changes and variability at the transition from Paleo-Indian to Archaic hunter-gatherers.

Paleo-Indian Lifeways

Paleo-Indians lived during a dynamic time of environmental and ecological change that witnessed the extinction of many species and the evolution of various habitats in the region (Graham and Mead 1987; Graham et al. 1987). This dynamic environmental and social context provided for significant changes in human adaptive strategies. Evidence for the lifeways of Paleo-Indians in general, and Clovis in particular, is derived from relatively few artifact forms and a limited number of excavated sites. Information about their social organization and patterns of land use must be derived from analysis of economic resources, patterned use of lithic material, and arrangements, size, and density of material remains at sites and across landscapes. In general, we assume that bands must have come together and interacted at least periodically to exchange information about resources and economic circumstances, to find appropriate mates, and to conduct rites of passage and other ceremonies (Hofman 1994).

The ephemeral nature of the archaeological record for Clovis may reflect, in part, the limited excavations at most sites. Excavations have been more extensive at sites like Murray Springs, Lange–Ferguson, and Aubrey and document the segregation of activities in discrete areas near kill/butchery spots. All site components suggest that the duration of occupations was short or not commonly repeated, perhaps lasting as long as a season when foods were easily available or could be preserved by drying or freezing (Frison 1982b). The probable use by these groups of a broad spectrum of food resources should not distract from the likelihood that they were at least seasonally specialized and focused much of their energy on hunting such first-line, high-return resources as mammoth and bison (Kelly and Todd 1988; West 1983). Their use of a wide variety of lithic sources documents the wide-ranging movements of these early Plains people, but logistical forays and occasional trading probably contributed an unknown dimension to this wide access to lithic material.

Most western Clovis sites that contain faunal remains are associated with mammoths (*Mammuthus* spp.), although bison are associated with Clovis at Aubrey (Ferring 1989), Murray Springs (Hemmings 1970), and BWD Locality No. 1 (Hester 1972). Different hypotheses have been offered for how mammoths were procured. Saunders (1980) suggests that Clovis hunters dispatched entire family groups in a single catastrophic kill event. He believes that the age distributions of mammoth assemblages from some Clovis sites are similar to those of family units of modern African elephants. Frison (1991a), however, suggests that the same data can be interpreted as indicating repetitive kills of individuals at water holes and argues against the feasibility of attacking entire matriarchal groups. Conversely, G. Haynes (1991) believes that Clovis people may not have actively hunted mammoths, but that they merely scavenged animals that were dying as a result of severe environmental changes at the end of the Pleistocene. Distinguishing between killing and scavenging of mammoth in the archaeological record is a long-standing and important problem (Gamble 1986; Mehl 1966).

It might be possible to test these various hypotheses by examining the season of death of individual mammoths as recorded in the incremental growth bands of their tusks (Graham in press). For example, if entire family groups were killed at one time, then the annual increments (e.g., Fisher 1984) of their tusks should record the same year and same season of death. But if Clovis mammoth assemblages reflect attritional accumulations, then the years and seasons of death may vary for individuals. Also, isotopic composition of these growth bands (e.g., Koch et al. 1989) may record various environmental stresses such as starvation (Graham in press).

The utilization of mammoth carcasses offers an interesting glimpse into past lifeways. Based on mammoth-bone piles at Colby, it has been suggested that Clovis people may have cached meat during the fall and winter (Frison 1976a). Similar interpretations have been offered for some Eurasian Upper Paleolithic sites (Shimkin 1978; Soffer 1985). If these bone piles do represent "insurance caches" of meat and marrow, they imply that Clovis people either remained in an area for a time or wanted the security of being able to return to the area if necessary. In either case, such caches would have supplied a resource that would permit the group to stay together for a longer time. G. Haynes (1991) has also observed that the mammoth carcasses at most Clovis sites show little sign of disturbance and processing. He interprets this as a reflection of the abundance of food resources because mammoth carcasses were readily available.

They may also have provided more material than small mobile bands could effectively use.

Clovis subsistence could not have been restricted to mammoths. Bison appear to have been part of the Clovis people's economy at several sites, but little is known about the use of other species. Dermal ossicles of the extinct ground sloth (*Glossotherium harlani*) have been found with Clovis artifacts at the Kimmswick (eastern Missouri) and Aubrey (C. R. Ferring, personal communication) sites. The presence of these ossicles, which are attached to the skin, have been interpreted as possible evidence for the use of skins by Clovis people (Graham and Kay 1988). Clovis people probably used smaller species like snakes, turtles, muskrats, and perhaps even mice, whose remains are frequently recovered from Clovis sites, although demonstrating the use of these species as food may be difficult. Botanical evidence from Clovis sites is even more meager, but plant resources must have been important for food as well as for material to manufacture technological items.

The wide variety of lithic resources found in Clovis tool kits suggests that Clovis people were quite mobile, which would have been advantageous in their exploitation of large game. Lithic resources for Clovis groups, as for most Paleo-Indians on the Plains, were variable but of very high quality. Knife River Flint, Flattop Chalcedony, Alibates Agatized Dolomite, Tecovas Jasper and Quartzite, Dakota Quartzite, and Edwards Chert are typical materials, with specimens made of crystal quartz and obsidian also found. All of the key lithic materials known throughout the Plains region were used by Clovis people.

Clovis artifacts from Anzick include projectile points, especially large flaked bifaces, and beveled ivory foreshafts/points, presumably associated with human remains. Most of the artifacts were coated with ocher, suggesting a ceremonial function. Anzick is interpreted as a Clovis burial site (Lahren and Bonnichsen 1974), and direct dating of bone suggests that at least one of the two human skeletons from this site is of Clovis age (Stafford et al. 1990). Exceptionally large points, bifaces, and other tools have also been found in the Fenn, Ritchie–Roberts, and Simon sites. Again, they are usually associated with red ocher and may well represent ceremonial or burial sites. Red ocher was apparently of considerable significance to Clovis people at key localities, such as the Powars II site in the Heartville Uplift area of eastern Wyoming (Frison 1991b).

Extinct species may be associated with Folsom artifacts at some sites, although Folsom generally postdates the terminal Pleistocene extinctions. For example, the large *Bison bison antiquus* is represented in most Folsom faunas. In their critical review of human utilization of *Camelops*, Haynes and Stanford (1984) conclude that only at Lindenmeier is contemporaneity of *Camelops* and Folsom possible, but the evidence is weak. Wilmsen and Roberts (1978) consider the *Camelops* at Lindenmeier to be intrusive. Haynes and Stanford's critique did not include Agate Basin, which has also yielded remains of *Camelops*. Another extinct species, the flat-headed peccary (*Platygonus compressus*), has been recorded at the Indian Creek and Agate Basin sites (Davis and Greiser 1992; Walker 1982).

At Owl Cave (Wasden site), in Bonneville County, Idaho, Miller (1982) reports three fragmentary fluted points considered to be "typologically Folsom." All three specimens came from the stratum that contains remains of mammoth, camel, and *Bison bison antiquus*. Radiocarbon dates between 12,850 and 10,920 RCYBP on mammoth-bone collagen are reported from this level at Owl Cave. The earlier dates are outside the conventionally accepted age range for Folsom. To at least partly address the question of the contemporaneity of Folsom and extinct species at Owl Cave and other sites, bones of extinct taxa should be radiocarbon-dated directly with new techniques for isolating individual amino acids (Stafford et al. 1987; Stafford et al. 1990; Stafford et al. 1991).

The preservation of bone and antler artifacts at several Folsom sites, especially Agate Basin and Lindenmeier, have added new dimensions to our understanding of Paleo-Indian lifeways (Frison and Stanford 1982; Wilmsen and Roberts 1978). Eyed bone needles were recovered from both sites, as well as from the Hanson site (Frison and Bradley 1980). Bone projectile points are also represented in the Folsom-age bone bed at Agate Basin. Incised bone fragments from all three sites suggest that some Folsom items were made for aesthetic as well as utilitarian purposes. A small bone bead from the Shifting Sands site in western Texas provides a small clue to ornamentation and bone technology in Folsom times (Hofman 1996b). The painted bison skull in the lowest level of the Cooper bison kill in northwestern Oklahoma provides an insight into Folsom hunting ritual (Bement 1997).

Folsom people have been called the "bison hunters of the Plains" because of the frequent association of their artifacts with bison remains. The number of bison at Folsom kill sites ranges from a few isolated individuals, as at Lubbock Lake (Bamforth 1985; E. Johnson 1987), to as many as 55 individuals at the Lipscomb site (Todd et al. 1992). It is not until post-Folsom times that massive kills of hundreds of animals are frequently recorded, which raises interesting paleoecological and cultural questions. The smaller Folsom kills may reflect the lower population levels of bison immediately after the terminal Pleistocene extinction, or, as some suggest, they may indicate the inability of Folsom hunters to manipulate large herds as effectively as later cultures. Both factors may have contributed to site-formation processes. However, it is also quite possible that the lower number of bison at Folsom sites may be due, in part, to other taphonomic factors and incomplete excavations. As larger sites like Lipscomb and Cattle Guard are more fully excavated, it may become apparent that Folsom people did kill and utilize large numbers of bison.

While Folsom people are often considered to have been specialized bison hunters, it is unlikely that any Paleo-Indian culture focused on a single resource to the exclusion of others. As hunters and gatherers, these people had to be opportunistic, but because of preservation and other biases, the archaeological record is skewed toward the preservation of bones from large mammals. Nonbison species in Folsom-age assemblages include antelope, rabbit, and deer. The analysis of blood residue on a series of tools from the Mitchell Locality at Blackwater Draw indicates the use of antelope (Hyland and Anderson 1990). It is nevertheless clear, from Folsom to historic times, that bison played a vital role in shaping the lives and organization of Native Americans on the Plains (e.g., Frison 1991b; Oliver 1962).

Methods of bison procurement were diverse by Hell Gap times. Whether this late diversity is the result of sampling or of development of hunting techniques in response to increasing bison herd size and changing behavior is unknown. An arroyo trap was repeatedly used by Folsom, Agate Basin, and Hell Gap peoples at the Agate Basin site (Frison and Stanford 1982). At the Casper site, Hell Gap people killed bison in a parabolic sand-dune trap (Frison 1974). Landform traps probably did not completely restrain the bison, but merely slowed them enough for hunters to effectively dispatch them (Frison 1982a:266). Bonfire Shelter served as a bison jump from Folsom times until at least the Late Archaic (Dibble and Lorrain 1968). At Jones–Miller, there are no apparent landforms that could be used as a trap (Stanford 1978), and it is suggested that artificial structures such as corrals and diverging fence lines may have been used (Frison 1982a). Extensive bison-bone beds were preserved at all these sites.

Remains of 100 or more individual bison were found in the Agate Basin level at Agate Basin. Analysis of the bison dentition eruption and wear patterns (Frison 1982b) indicates that the animals probably represent more than a single kill. Frison and Stanford (1982) believe that communal efforts were used to trap the bison in an arroyo during the winter, and that the meat was cached on the floodplain. Such winter caching apparently has a long tradition in the Plains, since it may also be known from Clovis sites like Colby (Frison 1976a).

Bison remains are also common at Plainview sites. Johnson and Holliday (1980) believe that the bison remains from the Plainview component at Lubbock Lake reflect processing activities, although evidence of butchering is lacking. A minimum of six bison were identified, and bones of fetal bison suggest that the animals died in the early spring. The number of bison reported at other Plainview sites is greater, but most have not been studied to determine whether they represent single or multiple events.

A diverse faunal assemblage from the Plainview component at Lubbock Lake is indicative of localized pond and stream habitats in a regional savanna environment (E. Johnson 1987:92). The presence of extralimital species like short-tailed shrew (*Blarina*), meadow vole (*Microtus pennsylvanicus*), prairie vole (*Microtus ochrogaster*), and southern bog lemming (*Synaptomys cooperi*) at Lubbock Lake (E. Johnson 1987:91, Table 8.1) and other Plainview sites (Willey et al. 1978) suggests that more moist, and perhaps cooler, environments prevailed on the Southern Plains (Graham 1987). The Firstview component at Lubbock Lake (E. Johnson 1987:91) also produced a wide range of faunal materials that underscore the wide diversity of local fauna.

The large number of bison-bone beds associated with the Cody complex attests to the importance of this species in the Paleo-Indians' economy. Procurement varied, but landform traps were important at some sites. Arroyo traps were especially important, as at Carter/Kerr–McGee. The Finley site, in Sweetwater County, Wyoming, probably was a sand-dune trap like the one at the Hell Gap–age Casper site (Frison 1974:182). Agenbroad (1978:32) believes that at least 474 bison were killed at Hudson–Meng by means of a jump in a V-shaped arroyo trap, but this interpretation is seriously questioned by recent research at the site (Todd and Rapson 1995). Olsen–Chubbuck also involved the use of an arroyo, across which a herd of bison was stampeded, killing at least 190 individuals. Other sites like Horner exhibit no obvious evidence of containment structures or natural features that were used in the kill event (Frison and Todd 1987). Such features may not always be necessary for successful kills, as evidenced at Horner and perhaps Jones–Miller. Brush fences or snowdrifts may have been used, but leave little evidence. The abrupt edge of the dense bone bed at Horner II is suggestive of such features. Most of the sites from which the age structure of the bison populations has been studied indicate winter kills, but an increasing number of kills are being documented that occurred during the spring through the early fall (Todd et al. 1992). The diverse faunal remains from the Firstview component at Lubbock Lake (E. Johnson 1987:91, Table 8.1) illustrate the variety of potential resources available at this time.

For most of the Paleo-Indian cultural complexes on the Plains, we know very little about site structure, dwellings, group organization, intergroup relationships, economic-territory size, alternative or backup subsistence strategies, or mortuary practices. Evidence from Jones–Miller suggests that a ritual may have been associated with bison kills. A diminutive Hell Gap point, a bird-bone whistle or flute, and a butchered dog skeleton (one of the earliest New World records of domestic dog) were found beside a post mold unearthed near the center of the site. These artifacts and associated features are closely comparable to paraphernalia used by shamans of some historic Plains tribes during bison hunts (Stanford 1978). Evidence for ephemeral small, roughly circular dwellings or post patterns with pocked floor areas occur at several sites, including Hell Gap (Irwin 1971), Agate Basin Folsom-level (Frison and Stanford 1982), and Hanson (Frison and Bradley 1980). Red ocher occurs on the floors of some of these small features, and bones are vertically inserted into post molds, apparently to help support the structures.

Another aspect of Paleo-Indian life is represented by the burial of a 25- to 30-year-old female at the Gordon Creek site in north-central Colorado (Breternitz et al. 1971). Several artifacts found with the skeleton are not diagnostic of any specific group, but a date of 9700 RCYBP suggests a Hell Gap affiliation or time frame. The body was placed in a flexed position and covered with red ocher. A fire on or near the body is believed to have been part of the burial ritual. An apparent cremation of Cody age is represented by the Renier site in Wisconsin (Mason and Irwin 1960).

Paleo-Indians lived during a dynamic time of environmental and ecological change that witnessed the extinction of many species and the evolution of various habitats in the region (Graham and Mead 1987; Graham et al. 1987). This dynamic environmental and social context provided for significant changes in human adaptive strategies, some of which were never utilized again on the Plains but helped shape those of later cultural groups.

Future Investigations

From the beginning, Paleo-Indian studies have been interdisciplinary. Because early discoveries involved the association of cultural materials and extinct fauna in stratified deposits, both archaeologists (for example, John Cotter, E. B. Howard, and Frank H. H. Roberts, Jr.) and vertebrate paleontologists (for example, E. H. Barbour, Harold Cook, C. Bertrand Schultz, and Chester Stock) worked with geologists (for example, Ernst Antevs, Kirk Bryan, and Glen Evans). C. V. Haynes (1990) provides an account of these pioneering scholars and their research. It is a foregone conclusion today that Paleo-Indian research demands an interdisciplinary approach with well-defined research questions.

Paleo-Indian research is advancing rapidly with improved interpretive tools derived from studies of animal behavior, taphonomic processes, and geochemistry. The application of radiocarbon dating to archaeology and paleontology in the early 1950s revolutionized Paleo-Indian studies. It not only permitted the establishment of an absolute chronology for human activities, but also allowed the correlation of natural events (paleoclimates, paleoenvironments, and landscape evolution) with these activities. Today, improvements in both technology and methodology of radiocarbon dating allow for more accurate dating of materials like bone, as well as dating much smaller samples. These advances will permit greater refinement in chronologies as well as broaden the radiocarbon database. Other dating techniques (for example, thermoluminescence, electron spin resonance [ESR], and mineral hydration) are generally considered to be more experimental than C-14 dating, but they permit the possibility of dating sites without organic remains.

The study of source areas and the identification of key lithic materials have been improved by geochemical and isotopic analyses of raw materials (e.g., Hoard et al. 1993). These studies will greatly enhance interpretations of group mobility and interaction. Demographic analyses of fossil animal populations will continue to produce new insights into human systems and their interaction with extinct and extant species. In addition, isotopic studies of human and fossil animal bone will open windows into paleodiets and paleoenvironments of these organisms. Studies of blood residue on artifacts and microwear analyses of artifacts promise to reveal a more complete understanding of subsistence strategies.

New approaches to the investigation of the archeological record will yield further knowledge of Paleo-Indian lifeways. To this end, the recognition and documentation of small ephemeral sites and systematic regional-scale study of isolated artifacts as well as larger site studies will be important. The reinvestigation of long-known sites with new methodologies and technologies, including noninvasive remote sensing, is providing critical data. This underscores the importance of preserving and maintaining portions of sites for future investigations. However, extensive horizontal, block excavations are also essential if site use, group organization, and activity patterning are to be documented. This is clearly illustrated by sites like Murray Springs, Agate Basin, and Cattle Guard. This need is further demonstrated by ethnoarchaeological studies of recent hunter-gatherer camp and butchering sites (Fisher and Strickland 1991; O'Connell et al. 1992). Efforts should continue in establishing linkages between excavation and actualistic research.

The Paleo-Indian cultures of the Great Plains extend for some 4000 years, spanning the Pleistocene–Holocene transition. This was a dynamic time of ecological reorganization, with the extinction of numerous terrestrial mammal species, perhaps most notably the proboscideans (mammoth, mastodont, and gomphothere). The speed and pervasiveness of these ecological fluctuations are reflected in rapid and dramatic changes in technology as well as in human subsistence and settlement strategies. Computerized mapping strategies, such as Geographic Information Systems (GIS), offer unique opportunities for integrating complex data sets from a wide variety of disciplines. The Plains is well suited for these types of studies, which not only have the potential to answer long-standing questions, but also can point in new and unanticipated directions for future research. Undoubtedly, within the next few decades our understanding of Paleo-Indian lifeways will increase significantly, but these studies of past systems may also be beneficial in forecasting processes with respect to future environmental changes in our own dynamic world.

Acknowledgments

We wish to thank Malinda Aiello, Carol Archinal, Mary Ann Graham, and Judy Ross for their assistance in preparing the manuscript.

References

Agenbroad, L. D.
  1978   The Hudson–Meng Site: An Alberta Bison Kill in the Nebraska High Plains. *Plains Anthropologist* 23:128–131.
Agogino, G. A.
  1969   The Midland Complex: Is It Valid? *American Anthropologist* 71:1117–1118.
Agogino, G. A., and E. Galloway
  1965   The Sister's Hill Site: A Hell Gap Site in North-Central Wyoming. *Plains Anthropologist* 10:190–195.
Agogino, G. A., D. K. Patterson, and D. E. Patterson
  1976   Blackwater Draw Locality No. 1, South Bank: Report for the Summer of 1974. *Plains Anthropologist* 21:213–223.
Akerman, K., and J. L. Fagan
  1986   Fluting the Lindenmeier Folsom: A Simple and Economical Solution to the Problem, and Its Implications for Other Fluted Point Assemblages. *Lithic Technology* 15:1–6.
Albritton, C. C., Jr.
  1975   Stratigraphy of the Cooperton Site. *Great Plains Journal* 14:133–139.
Alex, L. M.
  1980   *Explaining Iowa's Past: A Guide to Prehistoric Archaeology.* University of Iowa Press, Iowa City.
Alexander, H. L., Jr.
  1963   The Levi Site: A Paleoindian Campsite in Central Texas. *American Antiquity* 28:510–528.
  1982   The Pre-Clovis and Clovis Occupations at the Levi Site. In *Peopling of the New World,* edited by J. E. Ericson, R. E. Taylor, and R. Berger, 133–146. Ballena Press, Los Altos, Calif.
Amick, D. S.
  1991   Folsom Landuse Patterns in the Southern Tularosa Basin. *Current Research in the Pleistocene* 8:3–5.
  1994   Folsom Diet Breadth and Land Use in the American Southwest. Ph.D. diss., Department of Anthropology, University of New Mexico, Albuquerque.
  1995   Patterns of Technological Variation Among Folsom and Midland Projectile Points in the American Southwest. *Plains Anthropologist* 40:23–38.
Anderson, A.D.
  1975   The Cooperton Mammoth: An Early Man Bone Quarry. *Great Plains Journal* 14:130–173.
Anderson, A.D., and J. A. Tiffany
  1972   Rummels–Maske: A Clovis Find Spot in Iowa. *Plains Anthropologist* 18:55–59.
Bamforth, D. B.
  1985   The Technological Organization of Paleo-Indian Small Group Bison Hunting on the Llano Estacado. *Plains Anthropologist* 30:243–258.

1991 Flintknapping Skill, Communal Hunts, and Paleoindian Projectile Point Typology. *Plains Anthropologist* 36:309–322.

Bement, L. C.
1997 The Cooper Site: A Stratified Folsom Bison Kill in Oklahoma. *Plains Anthropologist*, Memoir 29:85–100.

Blaine, J. C.
1968 A Preliminary Report of an Early Man Site in West Texas. In *Transactions of the Third Regional Archaeological Symposium for Southern New Mexico and Western Texas*, 1–11. South Plains Archaeological Society, Lubbock, Tex.

Boldurian, A.
1991 Folsom Mobility and Organization of Lithic Technology: A View from Blackwater Draw, New Mexico. *Plains Anthropologist* 36:281–295.

Bonnichsen, R., and J. Keyser
1982 Three Small Points: A Cody Complex Problem. *Plains Anthropologist* 27:137–144.

Bonnichsen, R., and M. H. Sorg, eds.
1989 *Bone Modification*. University of Maine, Center for the Study of the First Americans, Orono.

Bonnichsen, R., and D. G. Steele, eds.
1994 *Method and Theory for Investigating the Peopling of the Americas*. Oregon State University, Center for the Study of the First Americans, Corvallis.

Bonnichsen, R., and K. L. Turnmire, eds.
1991 *Clovis Origins and Adaptations*. Oregon State University, Center for the Study of the First Americans, Corvallis.

Bonnichsen, R., and D. Young
1980 Early Technological Repertories: Bone to Stone. *Canadian Journal of Anthropology* 1:123–128.

Bradley, B. A.
1982 Flaked Stone Technology and Typology. In *The Agate Basin Site: A Record of the Paleoindian Occupation of the Northwestern High Plains*, edited by G. C. Frison and D. J. Stanford, 181–208. Academic Press, New York.

Bradley, B. A., and G. C. Frison
1987 Projectile Points and Specialized Bifaces from the Horner Site. In *The Horner Site: The Type Site of the Cody Cultural Complex*, edited by G. C. Frison and L. C. Todd, 199–231. Academic Press, Orlando, Fla.

Bradley, B. A., and D. J. Stanford
1987 The Claypool Study. In *The Horner Site: The Type Site of the Cody Cultural Complex*, edited by G. C. Frison and L. C. Todd, 405–434. Academic Press, Orlando, Fla.

Braidwood, R. J.
1975 *Prehistoric Men*. 8th ed. Scott, Foresman, Glenview, Ill.

Breternitz, D. A., A. C. Swedlund, and D. C. Anderson
1971 An Early Burial from Gordon Creek, Colorado. *American Antiquity* 40:86–94.

Brolio, F. J.
1971 An Investigation of Surface Collected Clovis, Folsom, and Midland Projectile Points from Blackwater Draw and Adjacent Localities. M.A. thesis, Department of Anthropology, Eastern New Mexico University, Portales.

Bryan, A. L.
1991 Fluted-Point Tradition in the Americas—One of Several Adaptations to Late

Pleistocene American Environments. In *Clovis Origins and Adaptations*, edited by R. Bonnichsen and K. L. Turnmire, 15–33. Oregon State University, Center for the Study of the First Americans, Corvallis.

Bryan, A. L., ed.
1978   *Early Man in America from a Circum-Pacific Perspective*. University of Alberta, Department of Anthropology, Edmonton.
1986   *New Evidence for the Pleistocene Peopling of the Americas*. University of Maine, Center for the Study of Early Man, Orono.

Carlisle, R. C., ed.
1988   *Americans Before Columbus: Ice Age Origins*. University of Pittsburgh, Department of Anthropology, Ethnology Monographs, no. 12.

Cassells, E. S.
1983   *The Archaeology of Colorado*. Johnson Books, Boulder, Colo.

Chapman, C. H.
1975   *The Archaeology of Missouri*. Vol. 1. University of Missouri Press, Columbia.

Clark, D. W.
1991   The Northern (Alaska–Yukon) Fluted Points. In *Clovis Origins and Adaptations*, edited by R. Bonnichsen and K. L. Turnmire, 35–48. Oregon State University, Center for the Study of the First Americans, Corvallis.

Collins, M. B., C. B. Bousman, P. Goldberg, P. R. Takac, J. C. Guy, J. L. Lanata, T. W. Stafford, and V. T. Holliday
1993   The Paleoindian Sequence at the Wilson–Leonard Site, Texas. *Current Research in the Pleistocene* 10:10–12.

Collins, M. B., T. R. Hester, D. Olstead, and P. J. Headrick
1991   Engraved Cobbles from Early Archeological Contexts in Central Texas. *Current Research in the Pleistocene* 8:13–15.

Collins, M. B., D. J. Stanford, J. L. Hofman, M. A, Jodry, R. O. Rose, L. C. Todd, K. Kibler, and J. M. Blackmar
1997   Cody Down South: The Seminole–Rose Site in West Texas. *Current Research in the Pleistocene* 14:15–17.

Cook, H. J.
1925   Definite Evidence of Human Artifacts in the American Pleistocene. *Science* 62:459–460.
1927   New Geological and Paleontological Evidence Bearing on the Antiquity of Mankind in America. *Natural History* 28:240–247.

Cotter, J. L.
1938   The Occurrence of Flints and Extinct Animals in Pluvial Deposits Near Clovis, New Mexico. Part 4, Report on Excavation at the Gravel Pit, 1936. *Proceedings of the Philadelphia Academy of Natural Sciences* 89:1–16.

Crabtree, D.
1966   A Stoneworker's Approach to Analyzing and Replicating the Lindenmeier Folsom. *Tebiwa* 9:3–39.

Davis, L. B.
1988   Paleoindian Tradition Fluted Points in Montana. *Current Research in the Pleistocene* 5:25–27.

Davis, L. B., and S. T. Greiser
1992   Indian Creek Paleoindians: Early Occupation of the Elkhorn Mountains' Southeast Flank, West-Central Montana. In *Ice Age Hunters of the Rockies*, edited by D. J. Stanford and J. S. Day, 225–283. University Press of Colorado, Boulder.

Dawson, J., and W. J. Judge
  1969   Paleo-Indian Sites and Topography in the Middle Rio Grande Valley of New
          Mexico. *Plains Anthropologist* 14:149–163.
Dibble, D. S., and D. Lorrain
  1968   Bonfire Shelter: A Stratified Bison Kill Site, Val Verde County, Texas. *Texas
          Memorial Museum, Miscellaneous Papers* 1:9–138.
Dillehay, T. D., and M. B. Collins
  1988   Early Cultural Evidence from Monte Verde in Chile. *Nature* 332:150–152.
Dincauze, D.
  1984   An Archaeological Evaluation of the Case for Pre-Clovis Occupations.
          Advances in World Archaeology 3:275–323.
Ebell, S. B.
  1988   The Dunn Site. *Plains Anthropologist* 33:505–530.
Ferring, C. R.
  1989   The Aubrey Clovis Site: A Paleoindian Locality in the Upper Trinity River
          Basin, Texas. *Current Research in the Pleistocene* 6:9–11.
Figgins, J. D.
  1927   The Antiquity of Man in America. *Natural History* 27:229–239.
  1933   *A Further Contribution to the Antiquity of Man in America.* Colorado Museum
          of Natural History Proceedings, no. 12. Denver.
Fiorillo, A. R.
  1989   An Experimental Study of Trampling: Implications for the Fossil Record. In
          Bone Modification, edited by R. Bonnichsen and M. H. Sorg, 61–71. University
          of Maine, Center for the Study of the First Americans, Orono.
Fisher, D. C.
  1984   Taphonomic Analyses of Late Pleistocene Mastodon Occurrences: Evidence
          of Butchery by North American Paleo-Indians. *Paleobiology* 10:338–357.
Fisher, J. W., Jr.
  1992   Observations on the Late Pleistocene Bone Assemblage from the Lamb
          Spring Site, Colorado. In *Ice Age Hunters of the Rockies,* edited by D. J. Stan-
          ford and J. S. Day, 51–80. University Press of Colorado, Boulder.
Fisher, J., and H. Strickland
  1991   Dwellings and Fireplaces: Keys to Efe Pygmy Campsite Structure. In *Ethnoar-
          chaeological Approaches to Mobile Campsites,* edited by C. S. Gamble and W. A.
          Boismier, 215–236. International Monographs in Prehistory, Ethnoarchaeologi-
          cal Series, no. 1. Ann Arbor, Mich.
Flenniken, J. J.
  1978   Reevaluation of the Lindenmeier Folsom: A Replication Experiment in Lithic
          Technology. *American Antiquity* 43:473–480.
Forbis, R. G.
  1968   Fletcher: A Paleo-Indian Site in Alberta. *American Antiquity* 33:1–10.
  1992   The Mesoindian (Archaic) Period in the Northern Plains. *Revista de Ar-
          queología Americana* 5:27–69.
Forbis, R. G., and J. D. Sperry
  1952   An Early Man Site in Montana. *American Antiquity* 18:127–132.
Frison, G. C.
  1974   *The Casper Site: A Hell Gap Bison Kill on the High Plains.* Academic Press, New
          York.
  1976a Cultural Activity Associated with Prehistoric Mammoth Butchering and Pro-
          cessing. *Science* 194:728–730.

1976b   The Chronology of the Paleo-Indian and Altithermal Cultures in the Big Horn Basin, Wyoming. In *Cultural Change and Continuity: Essays in Honor of James Bennet Griffin*, edited by C. E. Cleland, 147–174. Academic Press, New York.

1982a   Radiocarbon Dates. In *The Agate Basin Site: A Record of the Paleoindian Occupation of the Northwestern High Plains*, edited by G. C. Frison and D. J. Stanford, 178–180. Academic Press, New York.

1982b   Paleo-Indian Winter Subsistence Strategies on the High Plains. In *Plains Indian Studies*, edited by D. H. Ubelaker and H. J. Viola, 193–201. Smithsonian Contributions to Anthropology, no. 30. Washington, D.C.

1983   The Lookingbill Site, Wyoming, 48FR308. *Tebiwa* 20:1–16.

1984   The Carter/Kerr–McGee Paleoindian Site: Cultural Resource Management and Archaeological Research. *American Antiquity* 49:288–314.

1991a   *Prehistoric Hunters of the High Plains*. 2nd ed. Academic Press, San Diego, Calif.

1991b   The Goshen Paleoindian Complex: New Data for Paleoindian Research. In *Clovis Origins and Adaptations*, edited by R. Bonnichsen and K. L. Turnmire, 133–151. Oregon State University, Center for the Study of the First Americans, Corvallis.

1992   The Foothills–Mountains and the Open Plains: The Dichotomy in Paleoindian Subsistence Strategies Between Two Ecosystems. In *Ice Age Hunters of the Rockies*, edited by D. J. Stanford and J. S. Day, 323–342. University Press of Colorado, Boulder.

1996   *The Mill Iron Site*. University of New Mexico Press, Albuquerque.

Frison, G. C., and B. A. Bradley
1980   *Folsom Tools and Technology at the Hanson Site, Wyoming*. University of New Mexico Press, Albuquerque.

1982   Fluting of Folsom Projectile Points. In *The Agate Basin Site: A Record of the Paleoindian Occupation of the Northwestern High Plains*, edited by G. C. Frison and D. J. Stanford, 209–212. Academic Press, New York.

Frison, G. C., and C. Craig
1982   Bone, Antler, and Ivory Artifacts and Manufacture Technology. In *The Agate Basin Site: A Record of the Paleoindian Occupation of the Northwestern High Plains*, edited by G. C. Frison and D. J. Stanford, 161–173. Academic Press, New York.

Frison, G. C., and D. C. Grey
1980   Pryor Stemmed, a Specialized Paleo-Indian Ecological Adaptation. *Plains Anthropologist* 25:27–46.

Frison, G. C., and D. J. Stanford
1982   Summary and Conclusions. In *The Agate Basin Site: A Record of the Paleoindian Occupation of the Northwestern High Plains*, edited by G. C. Frison and D. J. Stanford, 361–370. Academic Press, New York.

Frison, G. C., and D. J. Stanford, eds.
1982   *The Agate Basin Site: A Record of the Paleoindian Occupation of the Northwestern High Plains*. Academic Press, New York.

Frison, G. C., and L. C. Todd, eds.
1987   *The Horner Site: The Type Site of the Cody Cultural Complex*. Academic Press, Orlando, Fla.

Fulgham, T., and D. Stanford
1982   The Frasca Site: A Preliminary Report. *Southwestern Lore* 48:1–20.

Galm, J., and J. L. Hofman
   1984   The Billy Ross Site: Analysis of a Dalton Component from the Southern
          Arkansas Basin of Eastern Oklahoma. *Bulletin of the Oklahoma Anthropological
          Society* 33:37–73.
Gamble, C. S.
   1986   *The Paleolithic Settlement of Europe.* Cambridge University Press, Cambridge.
Goodyear, A. C.
   1982   The Chronological Position of the Dalton Horizon in the Southeastern United
          States. *American Antiquity* 47:382–395.
Graham, R. W.
   1981   Preliminary Report on Late Pleistocene Vertebrates from the Selby and
          Dutton Archeological/Paleontological Sites, Yuma County, Colorado.
          University of Wyoming, Contributions to Geology 20:33–56.
   1987   Late Quaternary Mammalian Faunas and Paleoenvironments of the South-
          western Plains of the United States. In *Late Quaternary Mammalian Biogeogra-
          phy and Environments of the Great Plains and Prairies,* edited by R. W. Graham,
          H. A. Semken, Jr., and M. A. Graham, 24–86. Illinois State Museum, Scientific
          Papers, vol. 22. Springfield.
   in press Terminal Pleistocene Environments of the Great Plains. In *Folsom Archaeology,*
          edited by M. A. Jodry and D. J. Stanford. Smithsonian Institution Press,
          Washington, D.C.
Graham, R. W., and M. Kay
   1988   Taphonomic Comparisons of Cultural and Noncultural Faunal Deposits at
          Kimmswick and Barnhart Sites, Jefferson County, Missouri. In *Late Pleistocene
          and Early Holocene Paleoecology and Archeology of the Eastern Great Lakes Region,*
          edited by R. S. Laub, N. G. Miller, and D. W. Steadman, 227–240. Bulletin of
          the Buffalo Society of Natural Sciences, vol. 33. Buffalo, N.Y.
Graham, R. W., and J. I. Mead
   1987   Environmental Fluctuations and Evolution of Mammalian Faunas During the
          Last Deglaciation in North America. In *North America and Adjacent Oceans Dur-
          ing the Last Deglaciation,* edited by W. F. Ruddiman and H. E. Wright, Jr., 371–
          402. University of Minnesota Press, Minneapolis.
Graham, R. W., H. A. Semken, Jr., and M. A. Graham, eds.
   1987   *Late Quaternary Mammalian Biogeography and Environment of the Great Plains and
          Prairies.* Illinois State Museum, Scientific Papers, vol. 22. Springfield.
Grayson, D. K.
   1988   Perspective on the First Americans. In *Americans Before Columbus: Ice Age
          Origins,* edited by R. Carlisle, 107–123. University of Pittsburgh, Department
          of Anthropology, Ethnology Monographs, no. 12.
Griffin, J. B.
   1979   The Origin and Dispersion of American Indians in North America. In *The
          First Americans: Origins, Affinities and Adaptations,* edited by W. Laughlin and
          A. Harper, 43–55. Gustav Fischer, New York.
Gryba, E.
   1988   A Stone Age Pressure Method of Folsom Fluting. *Plains Anthropologist* 33:53–66.
Guffee, E. J.
   1979   *The Plainview Site: Relocation and Archaeological Investigations of a Late
          Paleo-Indian Kill Site in Hale County, Texas.* Llano Estacado Museum,
          Archaeological Research Laboratory, Plainview, Tex.

Hannus, L. A.
   1985   The Lange/Ferguson Site—An Event of Clovis Mammoth Butchery with the
          Associated Bone Tool Technology: The Mammoth and Its Track. Ph.D. diss.,
          Department of Anthropology, University of Utah, Salt Lake City.
   1990a Mammoth Hunting in the New World. In *Hunters of the Recent Past*, edited by
          L. B. Davis and B. O. K. Reeves, 47–67. Unwin Hyman, London.
   1990b The Lange–Ferguson Site: A Case for Mammoth Bone Butchering Tools. In
          Megafauna and Man—Discovery of America's Heartland, edited by L. D. Agen-
          broad, J. I. Mead, and L. W. Nelson, 86–99. Mammoth Site of Hot Springs,
          South Dakota, Scientific Papers, no. 1.
Harrison, B. R., and K. L. Killen
   1978   *Lake Theo: A Stratified Early Man Bison Butchering and Camp Site, Briscoe County,
          Texas.* Panhandle Plains Historical Museum, Special Archaeological Report
          no. 1. Canyon, Tex.
Hassan, A., J. D. Termine, and C. V. Haynes, Jr.
   1977   Mineral Studies on Bone Apatite and Their Implications for Radiocarbon
          Dating. *Radiocarbon* 19:364–374.
Haynes, C. V., Jr.
   1970   Geochronology of Man–Mammoth Sites and Their Bearing on the Origin of
          the Llano Complex. In *Pleistocene and Recent Environments of the Central Great
          Plains,* edited by W. Dort, Jr., and J. K. Jones, Jr., 77–92. University Press of
          Kansas, Lawrence.
   1987   Clovis Origins Update. *Kiva* 52:83–93.
   1990   The Antevs–Bryan Years and the Legacy for Paleoindian Geochronology. In
          Establishment of a Geologic Framework for Paleoanthropology, edited by L. F. Laporte,
          55–68. Geological Society of America, Special Paper no. 242. Boulder, Colo.
   1991   Clovis-Folsom-Midland-Plainview Geochronology, Climatic Change and Ex-
          tinction. Paper presented at the fifty-sixth annual meeting of the Society for
          American Archaeology, New Orleans.
   1992   Contributions of Radiocarbon Dating to the Geochronology of the Peopling
          of the New World. In *Radiocarbon After Four Decades,* edited by R. E. Taylor,
          A. Long, and R. S. Kra, 355–374. Springer-Verlag, New York.
Haynes, C. V., Jr., and G. A. Agogino
   1986   Geochronology of Sandia Cave. *Smithsonian Contributions to Anthropology*
          32:1–32.
Haynes, C. V., Jr., and E. T. Hemmings
   1968   Mammoth-Bone Shaft Wrench from Murray Springs, Arizona. *Science*
          159:186–187.
Haynes, C. V., Jr., and D. Stanford
   1984   On the Possible Utilization of *Camelops* by Early Man in North America.
          Quaternary Research 22:216–230.
Haynes, G.
   1980   Evidence of Carnivore Gnawing of Pleistocene and Recent Mammalian
          Bones. *Paleobiology* 6:341–351.
   1983   Frequencies of Spiral and Green Bone Fractures on Ungulate Limb Bones in
          Modern Surface Assemblages. *American Antiquity* 48:102–114.
   1991   *Mammoths, Mastodonts, and Elephants: Biology, Behavior, and the Fossil Record.*
          Cambridge University Press, Cambridge.

Hemmings, E. T.
1970   Early Man in the San Pedro Valley, Arizona. Ph.D. diss., Department of Anthropology, University of Arizona, Tucson.

Hester, J. J.
1972   *Blackwater Locality No. 1: A Stratified Early Man Site in Eastern New Mexico.* Fort Burgwin Research Center, Publication no. 8. Rancho de Taos, N.M.

Hester, T. R., and S. W. Newcomb
1990   Projectile Points of the San Patrice Horizon on the Southern Plains of Texas. *Current Research in the Pleistocene* 7:17–19.

Hill, M. G., V. T. Holliday, and D. J. Stanford
1995   A Further Evaluation of the San Jon Site, New Mexico. *Plains Anthropologist* 40:369–390.

Hoard, R. J., J. R. Bozell, S. R. Holen, M. D. Glascock, H. Neff, and J. M. Elam
1993   Source Determination of White River Group Silicates from Two Archaeological Sites in the Great Plains. *American Antiquity* 58:698–710.

Hofman, J. L.
1989   Prehistoric Culture History: Hunters and Gatherers in the Southern Great Plains. In *From Clovis to Comanchero: Archeological Overview of the Southern Great Plains,* edited by J. L. Hofman, R. L. Brooks, J. S. Hays, D. W. Owsley, R. L. Jantz, M. K. Marks, and M. H. Manhein, 25–60. Arkansas Archeological Survey, Research Series, no. 35. Fayetteville.

1990   Cedar Creek: A Folsom Locality in Southwestern Oklahoma. *Current Research in the Pleistocene* 7:19–23.

1991   Folsom Land Use: Projectile Point Variability as a Key to Mobility. In *Raw Material Economies Among Prehistoric Hunter-Gatherers,* edited by A. Montet-White and S. Holen, 335–355. University of Kansas, Publications in Anthropology, no. 19. Lawrence.

1992   Recognition and Interpretation of Folsom Technological Variability on the Southern Plains. In *Ice Age Hunters of the Rockies,* edited by D. J. Stanford and J. S. Day, 193–224. University Press of Colorado, Boulder.

1994   Paleoindian Aggregations on the Great Plains. *Journal of Anthropological Archaeology* 13:341–370.

1996a   Early Hunter-Gatherers of the Central Great Plains: Paleoindian and Mesoindian (Archaic) Cultures. In *Archeology and Paleoecology of the Central Great Plains,* edited by J. L. Hofman, 41–100. Arkansas Archeological Survey, Research Series, no. 48. Fayetteville.

1996b   Implications of a Tiny Folsom Bead: Some Big Issues in Paleoindian Research. Paper presented at the sixty-first annual meeting of the Society for American Archaeology, New Orleans.

Hofman, J. L., D. S. Amick, and R. O. Rose
1990   Shifting Sands: A Folsom–Midland Assemblage from a Campsite in Western Texas. *Plains Anthropologist* 35:221–253.

Hofman, J. L., and E. E. Ingbar
1988   A Folsom Hunting Overlook in Eastern Wyoming. *Plains Anthropologist* 33:337–350.

Hofman, J. L., and L. C. Todd
1997   Reinvestigation of the Perry Ranch Plainview Bison Bonebed, Southwestern Oklahoma. In *Southern Plains Bison Procurement and Utilization from Paleoindian*

to Historic, edited by L. C. Bement and K. J. Buehler, 101–117. Plains Anthropologist Memoir no. 29.

Holen, S. R., R. K. Blasing, D. W. May, and C. L. Burres
1990   La Sena Site: A Mammoth Bone Processing Site in Late Wisconsinan Loess. Paper presented at the forty-eighth annual Plains Anthropological Conference, Oklahoma City.

Holliday, V. T., ed.
1986   *Guidebook to the Archaeological Geology of Classic Paleoindian Sites on the Southern High Plains, Texas and New Mexico.* Geological Society of America Guidebook. Texas A&M University, Department of Geography, College Station.

Holliday, V. T., and E. Johnson
1986   Re-evaluation of the First Radiocarbon Age for the Folsom Culture. *American Antiquity* 51:332–338.

Holliday, V. T., and D. J. Meltzer
1996   Geoarchaeology of the Midland (Paleoindian) Site, Texas. *American Antiquity* 61:755–771.

Howard, E. B.
1935   Evidence of Early Man in North America. *Museum Journal* 24:2–3.
1937   The Emergence of the General Folsom Pattern. *25th Anniversary Series, Philadelphia Anthropological Society* 1:111–115.
1943   The Finley Site: Discovery of Yuma Points, in situ, near Eden, Wyoming. *American Antiquity* 7:224–234.

Hughes, J. T.
1949   Investigations in Western South Dakota and Northeastern Wyoming. *American Antiquity* 14:266–277.

Husted, W. M.
1969   *Bighorn Canyon Archeology.* Smithsonian Institution, River Basin Surveys, Publications in Salvage Archeology, no. 12. Lincoln, Neb.

Hyland, D. L., and T. R. Anderson
1990   Blood Residue Analysis of the Lithic Assemblage from the Mitchell Locality, Blackwater Draw, New Mexico. In *Lithic Technology at the Mitchell Locality of Blackwater Draw*, by A. T. Boldurian, 105–110. Plains Anthropologist Memoir no. 24.

Ingbar, E. E.
1992   The Hanson Site and Folsom on the Northwestern Plains. In *Ice Age Hunters of the Rockies*, edited by D. J. Stanford and J. S. Day, 169–192. University Press of Colorado, Boulder.

Irwin, H. T.
1968   The Itama: Early Late Pleistocene Inhabitants of the Plains of the United States and Canada and the American Southwest. Ph.D. diss., Department of Anthropology, Harvard University, Cambridge, Mass.
1971   Developments in Early Man Studies in Western North America, 1960–1970. *Arctic Anthropology* 8:42–67.

Irwin-Williams, C., H. Irwin, G. Agogino, and C. V. Haynes, Jr.
1973   Hell Gap: Paleoindian Occupation on the High Plains. *Plains Anthropologist* 18:40–53.

Jennings, J. D.
1955   *The Archaeology of the Plains: An Assessment (with Special Reference to the Mis-*

souri River Basin). University of Utah, Department of Anthropology, Salt Lake City.

1974   *Prehistory of North America.* 2nd ed. McGraw-Hill, New York.

Jennings, J. D., ed.

1978   *Ancient Native Americans.* Freeman, San Francisco.

Jepsen, G. L.

1951   Ancient Buffalo Hunters in Wyoming. *Archaeological Society of New Jersey News Letter* 24:22–24.

Jodry, M. A.

1987   Stewart's Cattle Guard Site: A Folsom Site in Southern Colorado. M.A. thesis, Department of Anthropology, University of Texas, Austin.

Jodry, M. A., and D. J. Stanford

1992   Stewart's Cattle Guard Site: An Analysis of Bison Remains in a Folsom Kill–Butchery Campsite. In *Ice Age Hunters of the Rockies,* edited by D. J. Stanford and J. S. Day, 101–168. University Press of Colorado, Boulder.

Johnson, E.

1977   Animal Food Resources of Paleoindians. In *Paleoindian Lifeways,* edited by E. Johnson, 65–77. Texas Tech University, Museum Journal. Lubbock.

Johnson, E., ed.

1987   *Lubbock Lake: Late Quaternary Studies on the Southern High Plains.* Texas A&M University Press, College Station.

Johnson, E., and V. T. Holliday

1980   A Plainview Kill/Butchering Locale on the Llano Estacado—The Lubbock Lake Site. *Plains Anthropologist* 25:89–111.

1981   Late Paleo-Indian Activity at the Lubbock Lake Site. *Plains Anthropologist* 26:173–193.

Johnson, E., V. T. Holliday, and R. W. Neck

1982   Lake Theo: Late Quaternary Paleoenvironmental Data and New Plainview (Paleoindian) Date. *North American Archaeologist* 3:113–138.

Johnson, L.

1989   *Great Plains Interlopers in the Eastern Woodlands During Late Paleo-Indian Times.* Texas Historical Commission, Office of the State Archeologist, Report no. 36. Austin.

Judge, W. J.

1973   *The Paleo-Indian Occupation of the Central Rio Grande Valley, New Mexico.* University of New Mexico Press, Albuquerque.

Judge, W. J., and J. Dawson

1972   Paleoindian Settlement Technology in New Mexico. *Science* 176:1210–1216.

Kelly, R. L., and L. C. Todd

1988   Coming into the Country: Early Paleo-Indian Hunting and Mobility. *American Antiquity* 53:231–244.

Kelly, T. C.

1982   Criteria for Classification of Plainview and Golondrina Projectile Point. *La Tierra* 9:2–25.

Knudson, R.

1983   *Organizational Variability in Late Paleo-Indian Assemblages.* Washington State University, Laboratory of Anthropology, Reports of Investigations, no. 60. Pullman.

Koch, A. C.
   1839   Evidences of the Contemporaneous Existence of Man with Mastodon in
          Missouri. *American Journal of Science* 36:198–200.
   1857   Mastodon Remains, in the State of Missouri, Together with Their Evidences
          of the Existence of Man Contemporaneously with the Mastodon. *Transactions
          of the Academy of Science, St. Louis* 1:61–64.
Koch, P. L., D. C. Fisher, and D. Dettman
   1989   Oxygen Isotope Variation in the Tusks of Extinct Proboscideans: A Measure
          of Season of Death and Seasonality. *Geology* 17:515–519.
Kornfeld, M.
   1988   The Rocky Foolsom Site: A Small Folsom Assemblage from the Northwestern
          Plains. *North American Archaeologist* 9:197–222.
Krieger, A.D.
   1946   *Culture Complexes and Chronology in Northern Texas.* University of Texas
          Publication no. 4640. Austin.
Kunz, M. L., and R. E. Reanier
   1996   Paleoindians in Beringia: Evidence from Arctic Alaska. *Science* 263:660–662.
Lahren, L. A., and R. Bonnichsen
   1974   Bone Foreshafts from a Clovis Burial in Southwestern Montana. *Science*
          186:147–150.
Larson, M. L.
   1991   Excavations at 48FR308, the Helen Lookingbill Site: A Preliminary Report.
          Wyoming Archeologist 34:69–82.
MacNeish, R. S.
   1976   Early Man in the New World. *American Scientist* 63:316–327.
   1978   Late Pleistocene Adaptations: A New Look at Early Peopling of the New
          World as of 1976. *Journal of Anthropological Research* 34:475–496.
Mallouf, R. J.
   1990   Hell Gap Points in the Southern Rolling Plains of Texas. *Current Research in
          the Pleistocene* 7:32–35.
Mason, R. J.
   1962   The Paleo-Indian Tradition in Eastern North America. *Current Anthropology*
          3:227–246.
Mason, R. J., and C. Irwin
   1960   An Eden–Scottsbluff Burial in Northeastern Wisconsin. *American Antiquity*
          26:43–57.
May, D. W., and S. R. Holen
   1993   Radiocarbon Ages of Soils and Charcoal in Late Wisconsin Loess,
          South-Central Nebraska. *Quaternary Research* 39:55–58.
McCracken, H., ed.
   1979   *The Mummy Cave Project in Northwestern Wyoming.* Buffalo Bill Historical
          Center, Cody, Wyo.
McMillan, R. B.
   1976   Man and Mastodon: A Review of Koch's 1840 Pomme de Terre Expeditions.
          In *Prehistoric Man and His Environments: A Case Study in the Ozark Highland*,
          edited by W. R. Wood and R. B. McMillan, 81–96. Academic Press, New York.
McMillan, R. B., and W. E. Klippel
   1981   Post-Glacial Environmental Change and Hunting Societies of the Southern
          Prairie Peninsula. *Journal of Archaeological Sciences* 8:215–245.

Mehl, M. G.
  1966 The Domebo Mammoth: Vertebrate Paleomortology. In *Domebo: A Paleo-Indian Mammoth Kill in the Prairie-Plains,* edited by F. C. Leonhardy, 27–30. Museum of the Great Plains Contributions, no. 1. Lawton, Okla.
Mehringer, P. J., Jr., and F. F. Foit, Jr.
  1990 Volcanic Ash Dating of the Clovis Cache at East Wanatchee, Washington. *National Geographic Research* 6:495–503.
Meltzer, D. J.
  1983 The Antiquity of Man and the Development of American Archaeology. In *Advances in Archaeological Method and Theory,* vol. 6, edited by M. B. Schiffer, 1–51. Academic Press, New York.
  1989 Why Don't We Know When the First People Came to North America? *American Antiquity* 54:471–490.
  1994 The Discovery of Deep Time: A History of Views on the Peopling of the Americas. In *Method and Theory for Investigating the Peopling of the Americas,* edited by R. Bonnichsen and D. G. Steele, 7–26, Oregon State University, Center for the Study of the First Americans, Corvallis.
Meyer, D.
  1985 A Component in the Scottsbluff Tradition: Excavations at the Niska Site. *Canadian Journal of Archaeology* 9:1–35.
Miller, S.
  1982 The Archaeology and Geology of an Extinct Megafauna/Fluted-Point Associa- tion at Owl Cave, the Wasden Site, Idaho: A Preliminary Report. In *Peopling of the New World,* edited by J. E. Ericson, R. E. Taylor, and R. Berger, 81–96. Ballena Press, Los Altos, Calif.
Morlan, R.
  1988 Pre-Clovis People? Early Discoveries of America. In *Americans Before Colum- bus: Ice Age Origins,* edited by R. C. Carlisle, 31–43. University of Pittsburgh, Department of Anthropology, Ethnology Monographs, no. 12.
Morse, D. F., and P. A. Morse
  1983 *Archaeology of the Central Mississippi River Valley.* Academic Press, New York.
Mulloy, W. T.
  1958 *A Preliminary Historical Outline for the Northwestern Plains.* University of Wyoming Publications in Science, vol. 22, no. 1. Laramie.
  1959 The James Allen Site, Near Laramie, Wyoming. *American Antiquity* 25:112–116.
Munson, P. J.
  1990 Folsom Fluted Projectile Points East of the Great Plains and Their Bio- geographical Correlates. *North American Archeologist* 11:255–272.
Myers, T. P., and R. Lambert
  1983 Meserve Points: Evidence of a Plainsward Extension of the Dalton Horizon. *Plains Anthropologist* 28:109–114.
O'Connell, J. F., K. Hawks, and N. G. Blurton-Jones
  1992 Patterns in the Distribution, Site-Structure and Assemblage Composition of Hadza Kill-Butchery Sites. *Journal of Archaeological Sciences* 19:319–345.
Oliver, S. C.
  1962 *Ecology and Cultural Continuity as Contributing Factors in the Social Organization of the Plains Indians.* University of California, Publications in American Archaeology and Ethnology, vol. 48. Berkeley.

Rancier, J., G. Haynes, and D. Stanford
  1982   1981 Investigations of Lamb Spring. *Southwestern Lore* 48:1–17.
Roberts, F. H. H., Jr.
  1940   Developments in the Problem of the North American Paleo-Indian. *Smithsonian Miscellaneous Collections* 100:51–116.
  1942   Archeological and Geological Investigations in the San Jon District, Eastern New Mexico. *Smithsonian Miscellaneous Collections* 103, no. 4:1–30.
Rogers, R. A., and L. D. Martin
  1984   The 12 Mile Creek Site: A Reinvestigation. *American Antiquity* 49:757–764.
Satterthwaite, L.
  1957   *Stone Artifacts at and near the Finley Site, Near Eden, Wyoming.* University of Pennsylvania, University Museum, Museum Monographs. Philadelphia.
Saunders, J. J.
  1980   A Model for Man–Mammoth Relationships in Late Pleistocene North America. *Canadian Journal of Anthropology* 1:87–98.
Saunders, J. J., G. A. Agogino, A. T. Boldurian, and C. V. Haynes, Jr.
  1991   A Mammoth-Ivory Burnisher-Billet from the Clovis Level, Blackwater Locality No. 1, New Mexico. *Plains Anthropologist* 36:359–363.
Saunders, J. J., C. V. Haynes, Jr., D. Stanford, and G. A. Agogino
  1990   A Mammoth-Ivory Semifabricate from Blackwater Locality No. 1, New Mexico. *American Antiquity* 55:112–119.
Saunders, R. S., and J. T. Penman
  1979   Perry Ranch: A Plainview Bison Kill on the Southern Plains. *Plains Anthropologist* 24:51–84.
Schultz, C. B.
  1932   Association of Artifacts and Extinct Mammals in Nebraska. *Nebraska Museum Bulletin* 33:171–183.
Sellards, E. H.
  1952   *Early Man in America.* University of Texas Press, Austin.
  1955   Fossil Bison and Associated Artifacts from Milnesand, New Mexico. *American Antiquity* 20:336–344.
Shelley, P., and G. A. Agogino
  1983   Agate Basin Technology: An Insight. *Plains Anthropologist* 28:115–119.
Shimkin, E. M.
  1978   The Upper Paleolithic in North-Central Eurasia: Evidence and Problems. In *Views of the Past: Essays in Old World Prehistory and Paleoanthropology,* edited by L. G. Freeman, 193–315. Mouton, The Hague.
Shutler, R., Jr., ed.
  1983   *Early Man in the New World.* Sage, Beverly Hills, Calif.
Soffer, O.
  1985   *The Upper Paleolithic of the Central Russian Plain.* Academic Press, Orlando, Fla.
Sollberger, J. B.
  1985   A Technique for Folsom Fluting. *Lithic Technology* 14:41–50.
Sorrow, W. M.
  1968   The Devil's Mouth Site: The Third Season—1967. *Papers of the Texas Archeological Salvage Project* 14:1–34.
Speer, R.
  1986   History of the Plainview Site. In *Guidebook to the Archaeological Geology of Clas-*

sic Paleoindian Sites on the Southern High Plains, Texas and New Mexico, edited by V. T. Holliday, 52–59. Geological Society of America Guidebook. Texas A&M University, Department of Geography, College Station.

Stafford, T. W., Jr., P. E. Hare, L. Currie, A. J. T. Jull, and D. J. Donahue

    1990   Accuracy of North American Human Skeletal Ages. *Quaternary Research* 34:111–120.

    1991   Accelerator Radiocarbon Dating at the Molecular Level. *Journal of Archaeological Science* 18:35–72.

Stafford, T. W., Jr., A. J. T. Jull, K. Brendel, R. C. Duhamel, and D. Donahue

    1987   Study of Bone Radiocarbon Dating Accuracy at the University of Arizona NSF Accelerator Facility for Radioisotope Analysis. *Radiocarbon* 29:24–44.

Stanford, D. J.

    1975   The 1975 Excavations at the Jones–Miller Site, Yuma County, Colorado. *Southwestern Lore* 41:34–38.

    1978   The Jones–Miller Site: An Example of Hell Gap Bison Procurement Strategy. In *Bison Procurement and Utilization: A Symposium,* edited by L. B. Davis and M. Wilson, 90–97. Plains Anthropologist Memoir no. 14.

    1979   The Selby and Dutton Sites: Evidence for a Possible Pre-Clovis Occupation on the High Plains. In *Pre-Llano Cultures of the Americas: Paradoxes and Possibilities,* edited by R. L. Humphrey and D. Stanford, 101–123. Washington Anthropological Society, Washington, D.C.

    1982   A Critical Review of Archeological Evidence Relating to the Antiquity of Human Occupation of the New World. In *Plains Indian Studies,* edited by D. H. Ubelaker and H. J. Viola, 202–218. Smithsonian Contributions to Anthropology, no. 30. Washington, D.C.

    1983   Pre-Clovis Occupation South of the Ice Sheets. In *Early Man in the New World,* edited by R. Shutler, Jr., 65–72. Sage, Beverly Hills, Calif.

    1991   Clovis Origins and Adaptations: An Introductory Perspective. In *Clovis Origins and Adaptations,* edited by R. Bonnichsen and K. L. Turnmire, 1–13. Oregon State University, Center for the Study of the First Americans, Corvallis.

Stanford, D. J., R. Bonnichsen, and R. E. Morlan

    1981   The Ginsburg Experiment: Modern and Prehistoric Evidence of a Bone Flaking Technology. *Science* 212:438–440.

Stanford, D. J., and R. W. Graham

    1985   Archeological Investigations of the Selby and Dutton Mammoth Kill Sites, Yuma County, Colorado. *Research Reports* 19:519–541.

Stanford, D. J., C. V. Haynes, Jr., J. J. Saunders, and G. A. Agogino

    1986   Blackwater Draw Locality No. 1: History, Current Research and Interpretations. In *Guidebook to the Archaeological Geology of Classic Paleo-Indian Sites on the Southern High Plains, Texas and New Mexico,* edited by V. T. Holliday, 82–112. Geological Society of America Guidebook. Texas A&M University, Department of Geography, College Station.

Stanford, D. J., and M. A. Jodry

    1988   The Drake Clovis Cache. *Current Research in the Pleistocene* 5:21–22.

Stanford, D. J., and R. Patton

    1984   R-6, a Preliminary Report on a Cody Site in North-Central New Mexico. *New Mexico Archaeological Council Proceedings* 6:189–199.

Thoms, A. V.
    1993   Knocking Sense from Old Rocks: Typologies and the Narrow Perspective of
            the Angostura Point Type. *Lithic Technology* 18:16–27.
Thurmond, J. P.
    1990   *Late Paleoindian Utilization of the Dempsey Divide on the Southern Plains.* Plains
            Anthropologist Memoir no. 25.
Titmus, G. L., and J. C. Woods
    1991   Fluted Points from the Snake River Plain. In *Clovis Origins and Adaptations,*
            edited by R. Bonnichsen and K. L. Turnmire, 119–131. Oregon State Univer-
            sity, Center for the Study of the First Americans, Corvallis.
Todd, L. C., J. L. Hofman, and C. B. Schultz
    1992   Faunal Analysis and Paleoindian Studies: A Reexamination of the Lipscomb
            Bison Bonebed. *Plains Anthropologist* 37:137–165.
Todd, L. C., and D. J. Rapson
    1991   Excavations at the Hudson–Meng Bonebed: Aspects of the Formational His-
            tory. Paper presented at the forty-ninth annual Plains Anthropological Con-
            ference, Lawrence, Kans.
    1995   Formational Analysis of Bison Bonebeds and Interpretation of Paleo-
            indian Subsistence. Paper presented at the symposium "Bison Subsistence
            Through Time: From Middle Paleolithic to Paleoindian Times," Toulouse,
            France.
Walker, D. N.
    1982   Early Holocene Vertebrate Fauna. In *The Agate Basin Site: A Record of Paleo-
            indian Occupation on the Northwestern High Plains,* edited by G. C. Frison and
            D. Stanford, 274–308. Academic Press, New York.
Waters, M. R.
    1985   Early Man in the New World: An Evaluation of the Radiocarbon Dated Pre-
            Clovis Sites in the Americas. In *Environments and Extinctions: Man in Late Gla-
            cial North America,* edited by J. I. Mead and D. J. Meltzer, 125–144. University
            of Maine, Center for the Study of Early Man, Orono.
Wedel, W. R., W. H. Husted, and J. H. Moss
    1968   Mummy Cave: Prehistoric Record from Rocky Mountains of Wyoming. *Sci-
            ence* 160:184–186.
Wendorf, F., and A.D. Krieger
    1959   New Light on the Midland Discovery. *American Antiquity* 25:66–78.
Wendorf, F., A.D. Krieger, C. C. Albritton, and T. D. Stewart
    1955   *The Midland Discovery.* University of Texas Press, Austin.
West, F. H.
    1983   The Antiquity of Man in America. In *The Late Pleistocene,* edited by S. C. Por-
            ter, 364–382. Vol. 1 of *Late Quaternary Environments of the United States.* Univer-
            sity of Minnesota Press, Minneapolis.
Wetherill, R. B.
    1995   A Comparative Study of Paleoindian Evidence at the Bonner Springs Local-
            ity, Lower Kansas River Basin, Kansas. M.A. thesis, Department of Anthropol-
            ogy, University of Kansas, Lawrence.
Wheat, J. B.
    1972   *The Olsen–Chubbuck Site: A Paleoindian Bison Kill.* American Antiquity Memoir
            no. 26.
    1979   *The Jurgens Site.* Plains Anthropologist Memoir no. 15.

Wheeler, R. P.
  1954   Selected Projectile Point Types of the United States II. *Bulletin of the Oklahoma Anthropological Society* 2:1–6.
  1995   *Archeological Investigations in Three Reservoir Areas in South Dakota and Wyoming: Part I, Angostura Reservoir.* J and L Reprint, Lincoln, Neb.
Willey, G. R., and P. Phillips
  1958   *Method and Theory in American Archaeology.* University of Chicago Press, Chicago.
Willey, P. S., B. R. Harrison, and J. T. Hughes
  1978   The Rex Rodgers Site. In *Archaeology of MacKenzie Reservoir,* edited by J. T. Hughes and P. S. Willey, 51–114. Texas Historical Commission, Austin.
Williston, S. W.
  1902   An Arrow-head Found with Bones of *Bison occidentalis* Lucas, in Western Kansas. *American Geologist* 30:313–315.
Wilmsen, E. N., and F. H. H. Roberts, Jr.
  1978   *Lindenmeier, 1934–1974: Concluding Report on Investigations.* Smithsonian Contributions to Anthropology, no. 24. Washington, D.C.
Woods, J. C., and G. L. Titmus
  1985   A Review of the Simon Clovis Collection. *Idaho Archeologist* 8:3–8.
Wormington, H. M.
  1957   *Ancient Man in North America.* Denver Museum of Natural History, Popular Series, no. 4.
Wormington, H. M., and R. G. Forbis
  1965   *An Introduction to the Archaeology of Alberta, Canada.* Denver Museum of Natural History Proceedings, no. 11.
Wyckoff, D. G.
  1989   Accelerator Dates and Chronology at the Packard Site, Oklahoma. *Current Research in the Pleistocene* 6:24–26.
  1992   The Cody Complex in Eastern Oklahoma's Arkansas Basin. *Current Research in the Pleistocene* 9:47–49.
Wyckoff, D. G., G. R. Brakenridge, K. Buehler, B. J. Carter, W. Dort, Jr., L. D. Martin, J. L. Theler, and L. C. Todd
  1991   Interdisciplinary Research at the Burnham Site (34WO73), Woods County, Oklahoma. In *A Prehistory of the Plains Border Region,* edited by B. C. Carter and P. A. Ward, 82–121. Oklahoma State University, Department of Agronomy, Stillwater.
Wyckoff, D. G., and B. J. Carter
  1994   *Geoarchaeology at the Burnham Site: 1992 Investigations at a Pre-Clovis Site.* University of Oklahoma, Oklahoma Archeological Survey, Special Publication. Norman.
Wyckoff, D. G., B. J. Carter, W. Dort, Jr., G. R. Brakenridge, L. D. Martin, J. L. Theler, and L. C. Todd
  1990   Northwestern Oklahoma's Burnham Site: Glimpses Beyond Clovis? *Current Research in the Pleistocene* 7:60–63.

5. The Northwestern and Northern Plains Archaic

George C. Frison

This discussion of Archaic cultural groups encompasses an area that begins in the south at the latitude of the Colorado–Wyoming border and extends to about 52 degrees north latitude in Alberta and Saskatchewan. The eastern boundary extends into western Nebraska, South Dakota, North Dakota, and southwestern Manitoba. The western boundary is more difficult to define. Plains environments extend into areas between mountain ranges, and although these intermontane basins adjoin the Plains they are not true Plains environments. Isolated mountain ranges and uplifted areas are common, and since Archaic groups were not excluded from any of these settings, discussion of the Plains Archaic must include survival practices adapted to several non-Plains environments.

Any close look at the Northwestern and Northern Plains reveals an environment that is not as monotonous as is generally believed. Although dominated by landforms of low relief, there are mountain ranges, lesser uplifts, intermontane basins, erosional remnants, "breaks" formed by major streams and their tributaries, and stream valleys that have much of the basic character of the Plains. In addition, the continental ice sheets that once mantled the land in the north produced other distinctive landforms. These factors created many different environments and allowed for great diversity of plant and animal communities. Precipitation in the area also increases from west to east, resulting in a change from short-grass to tall-grass prairie—an ecotone that shifted from time to time during Archaic times. Plant communities and animal and human carrying capacities also shifted in response to such changes.

The character of the area is influenced by several major river systems, most of which flow generally from west to east. These include the drainages of the Missouri and Platte rivers and, to the north, the basins of the Saskatchewan and Assiniboine rivers. Riparian environments along these streams supplied a wide variety of plant and animal food. The sources of these rivers, and of most of their tributaries, are in the Rocky Mountains, and they influenced the movements of human groups on both a long- and a short-term basis.

Areas that lie in rain shadows of mountain ranges experience low rainfall. Wind patterns are also affected by mountain ranges, influencing, in turn, human occupation at given times of the year. The wind is one's almost constant companion on the open plains. Despite the discomfort it brings, it is an important factor in the winter survival of large ungulates, particularly bison and pronghorn, by clearing areas of snow and exposing grasses for forage. Foothills, breaks, and mountain slopes offer some relief from the incessant winds of the open plains.

Seasonal changes dominate life on the Plains. Animal behavior changes seasonally and had to be understood by Native Americans to ensure success in hunting. Wild plant foods—whether seeds, berries, fruits, leaves, roots, tubers, or blossoms—appear and disappear rapidly, and careful scheduling of group movement in response to their periods of availability was necessary. Late spring through early fall is a time of food abundance, easy travel, and relative comfort. Late fall through early spring is a time of rapid and unpredictable changes in weather and the availability of food. Winter blizzards followed by prolonged periods of subzero weather inhibited normal food procurement, and survival required some food storage. *Winter food storage*

The Northwestern and Northern Plains abut on mountains in distinctive ways. In the Central Plains, the Colorado Front Range rises abruptly, having few outliers to the east. To the north, the terrain is different. High-altitude plains extend between mountain ranges and cross the continental divide for some distance to the south of the Wind River Mountains in Wyoming, so the Wind River and Wyoming basins have a Plains-like environment as far west as the Utah–Idaho border. The Bighorn Basin is an almost isolated enclave of the Plains set between the Bighorn and Absaroka mountains, and it has more of a Great Basin than a Plains environment. Such prominent features as the Black Hills, Little Belt, Big Snowy, Highwood, Bearspaw, Little Rocky Mountains, and Sweetgrass Hills are mountain enclaves completely surrounded by plains. Consequently, the Plains and the mountains cannot be considered separately, since most Archaic groups freely used both settings on a seasonal basis (Figure 5.1).

Historical Perspectives of Plains Archaic Studies

The first evidence of consequence in Plains Archaic studies was from the excavations at Signal Butte in western Nebraska (Strong 1935:224–239). The site, set on top of a prominent butte, was well stratified with diagnostic artifacts and other evidence of human occupation extending back 4500 to 5000 years. A small amount of Archaic material was also recognized at the base of Ash Hollow Cave in western Nebraska in the mid-1940s (Champe 1946).

During the 1940s, excavations also were carried out in a large rock shelter a few miles south of the Yellowstone River near Billings, Montana. The cultural deposits at this shelter, Pictograph Cave, were extensive and well stratified

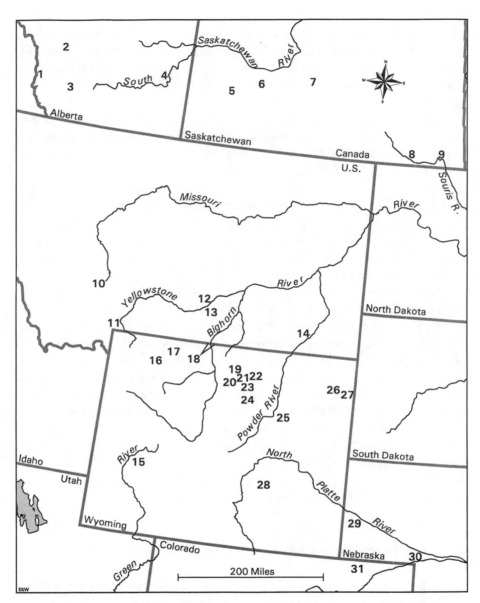

Figure 5.1. Archaic sites on the Northwestern and Northern Plains: *Alberta* (1) Gap, (2) Old Woman's Buffalo Jump, (3) Head-Smashed-In, (4) Cactus Flower; *Saskatchewan* (5) Gull Lake Bison Trap, (6) Gray Burial, (7) Mortlach, (8) Long Creek, (9) Oxbow Dam; *Montana* (10) Schmitt Quarry, (11) Rigler Bluff, (12) Billings Bison Trap, (13) Pictograph Cave, (14) Yonkee Bison Trap; *Wyoming* (15) Wardell Buffalo Trap, (16) Mummy Cave, (17) Dead Indian Creek, (18) Bighorn Canyon caves, (19) Spanish Point Quarry, (20) Medicine Lodge Creek, (21) Beehive, (22) Laddie Creek, (23) Southsider Cave, (24) Spring Creek Cave, (25) Ruby Bison Trap, (26) McKean, (27) Hawken Bison Trap, (28) Muddy Creek Bison Trap; *Nebraska* (29) Signal Butte, (30) Ash Hollow Cave; *Colorado* (31) Dipper Gap.

Figure 5.2. Pictograph Cave, near Billings, Montana, in 1956. (Photo by Paul L. Beaubien, National Park Service)

(Figure 5.2). On the north side of the Yellowstone River, and within the present city limits of Billings, was the stratified Billings Bison Trap. The artifacts from both sites compare quite well typologically, and Mulloy (1958) used both sites (but particularly Pictograph Cave) as a basis for the first serious attempt to establish a historical outline for the Northwestern Plains. This document has been refined as data accumulated, but has withstood the test of time rather well. Mulloy's chronology of Archaic times included a hiatus from about 6000 to about 4500 years ago (Mulloy 1958:220–221), although he recognized that it would probably disappear as more and better data were obtained.

About the same time, Malouf (1958) suggested the term "foragers" to accommodate Archaic groups on the Plains. The term, however, met with resistance and was never accepted, although it seems to be a legitimate and applicable concept. The word was unacceptable largely because at that time it carried a connotation of inferiority on the part of the cultural groups involved.

Several Archaic cultural complexes are recognized by projectile-point types labeled with place names from Saskatchewan. Excavations in a number of

Atlantic Climatic Period

deeply stratified sites in that province took place during the 1950s. The Oxbow complex, recognized at the Oxbow Dam site (Nero and McCorquodale 1958), is dated about 5000 years ago. Pelican Lake and Besant are Late Plains Archaic complexes now recognized by projectile points over the entire Northwestern and Northern Plains, and were named after those from the Mortlach and Long Creek sites (Wettlaufer 1955; Wettlaufer and Mayer-Oakes 1960).

The Smithsonian Institution's Missouri River Basin Surveys initiated federally sponsored archaeological work in 1946 in several western reservoirs, and the results began to add significantly to Archaic studies. The Medicine Creek investigations in south-central Nebraska produced deeply buried materials that appear to be late Paleo-Indian in age but with strong Archaic characteristics. Unfortunately, the materials in the "Frontier complex" assemblage at the Allen site (Holder and Wike 1949) were never completely analyzed or published by its excavators. Bamforth (1991) has been studying the site, and a monograph on the site is nearing completion.

Other Archaic materials appeared in reservoirs farther west, as in the Angostura Reservoir in southwestern South Dakota (J. Hughes 1949). Excavations in the Shoshone Basin of central Wyoming and at the McKean site in northeastern Wyoming (Mulloy 1954a, 1954b) expanded Mulloy's interpretations of the Archaic on the Northwestern Plains. In the 1950s, Wheeler (1957) did extensive work in Angostura and other reservoirs in the Black Hills area of Wyoming and South Dakota, and on the basis of this work he proposed a number of projectile-point types (Wheeler 1954a, 1954b). Mulloy, though, regarded Wheeler's types as being within the range of variation of the McKean lanceolate type instead of as separate types. Each investigator's interpretation can, however, be justified on the basis of the separate bodies of data that each had acquired.

Bison kills compose a large segment of Plains Archaic studies. The Old Woman's Buffalo Jump, a large bison jump with Late Archaic deposits at the bottom and with extensive overlying late prehistoric deposits, was excavated by Forbis (1962) in southern Alberta. Archaic bison jumps and arroyo traps have been major targets of artifact collectors, and few systematic studies have resulted from their activities. Early efforts to excavate such sites recovered a rich body of archaeological and faunal data (Bentzen 1961; Davis and Stallcop 1965) and demonstrated the need for more sophisticated geomorphic studies to interpret the past landforms concerned. About the same time, dry rock shelters in the foothills of the arid western slopes of the Bighorn Mountains began to produce perishable materials that expanded knowledge of the content of Late Archaic cultural assemblages (e.g., Frison 1962, 1965).

The investigation and publication of Plains Archaic data increased significantly after the mid-1960s. After having been largely overlooked for so long, the Northwestern and Northern Plains finally achieved a recognized position in New World archaeology.

Clovis is a culture group

Taxonomy and Climate

Paleolindian a subsistence adaptation

A system of taxonomy is needed to bring order to the otherwise bewildering array of manifestations of human activities. Any classification that aids the investigator may be used, but it is of greater value to devise a system that is mutually understandable and acceptable to all investigators (see Frison 1991:20–24). The term "Archaic" is used here to describe human groups whose subsistence practices are recognizably and quantifiably different from those of other groups as an adaptation, not as a cultural period. When the word is used in this way, the archaeological record should ideally reveal whether a given complex fits into an Archaic category. Since the archaeological record is not always clear, uncertainties creep into the data being analyzed. The archaeological record for the Northwestern and Northern Plains is still incomplete, and a definitive treatment of the Archaic in these areas lies in the future. This discussion of Plains Archaic is therefore a compromise of different concepts and the interpretation of the still inadequate database. It is also biased toward the High Plains, where studies of Archaic groups are less obscured by later and more spectacular horticultural occupations. The bias is reflected also in a greater familiarity of the author with the western part of the area.

Discussion of several issues is necessary. To begin with, and to use Willey and Phillips's (1958:107) concept of the Archaic, there is a convincing body of data to argue for a Plains Archaic between about 41 degrees north latitude (the Colorado–Wyoming boundary) and about 46 degrees north latitude (the North Dakota–South Dakota boundary). The data are progressively less convincing for a Plains Archaic from about 46 degrees north latitude into the Plains of Canada to about 52 degrees north latitude. This problem is addressed by Clark and Wilson (1981:72) in discussing sites in southeastern Montana that, to them, have so far failed to reveal convincing evidence of an Archaic adaptation to diverse foodstuffs. The future may require that the concept of the Archaic not be applied to the Northern Plains or be modified to accommodate Northern Plains conditions.

The concept of a "mountain-adapted culture by at least 6500 B.C., and probably considerably earlier," was proposed by Husted (1969:83), and there is no body of evidence that alters this proposition. Husted's ideas were based on data from Mummy Cave (McCracken 1978; Wedel et al. 1968) and from the Bighorn Canyon caves along the Bighorn River on the Montana–Wyoming border. Data recovered in the 1970s further supports the concept of foothill–mountain groups by at least 8000 years ago and possibly as far back as the Llano complex—groups that appear unquestionably to have been engaged in regularly scheduled hunting and gathering activities in these settings. Also, to date, there is no evidence that these groups were engaged in large-scale animal procurement comparable to the communal bison kills common to the more familiar Paleo-Indian complexes. In fact, present data also show that these foothill–mountain groups did not often frequent the open plains and basins where large-scale hunting was possible. The geographic distribution and age of these groups are postulated on projectile-point typology and radiocarbon dates (Frison 1973a, 1976; Frison and Grey 1980; Husted 1969).

Although the foothill–mountain groups were probably restricted by real or imaginary barriers to certain ecological zones, the same cannot be said for some of the Paleo-Indian groups usually regarded as true Plains hunters—particularly Clovis, Folsom, Alberta, and Cody. Based on the distribution of diagnostic projectile points, these groups were occupying ecological zones from the open plains and intermontane basins to timberline, but whether on regularly scheduled rounds is as yet unclear. It is, however, certain that many late Paleo-Indian groups were living more of an Archaic way of life than was previously thought. Thus it is not possible to determine a realistic beginning for the Plains Archaic based on an analysis of subsistence practices alone. During the time commonly regarded as Paleo-Indian (about 9500 to 8000 years ago), some subsistence practices were of an Archaic nature, while others were not. The "Frontier complex" (Holder and Wike 1949) is of particular significance here, little as we know of it, for its activities were clearly Archaic.

Atlantic The Hypsithermal (or Altithermal, as it is commonly referred to by archaeologists in the western United States) is a concept that has introduced some confusion into Plains archaeology. Antevs (1948, 1955) defined this climatic episode and described its possible effects on the West. However, there is not yet agreement regarding the nature of this episode and its duration, geographic extent, and effects on plants and animals, climate, and landforms (AMQUA 1974), despite its general reputation as a time of higher temperatures and lower precipitation. The Hypsithermal has also been used in a cultural sense because certain diagnostic cultural materials and archaeological sites apparently date to this episode. As a result, the time period "Early Plains Archaic" (Frison 1991:78–88) was proposed to accommodate human occupations on the Northwestern and Northern Plains during the Hypsithermal. The beginning of the Early Plains Archaic appears to coincide not only with the beginning of the Hypsithermal but also with a technological change in projectile-point hafting, as shown by different styles of side notching. The period closes with the end of the Hypsithermal and what appears to be a change to climatic conditions like those of the present.

A noticeable change in projectile-point styles appears at the end of the Early Plains Archaic, about 5000 years ago, in the form of the wide range of variation in the single type found in the McKean complex (Mulloy 1954b) or in the several point types suggested by Wheeler (1954a, 1954b)—whichever view the investigator is inclined to accept. This is the beginning of the Early Middle Prehistoric Period (Mulloy 1958) or Middle Plains Archaic (Frison 1991:88–101), and it lasts until about 3300 years ago, although there are no cultural or climatic changes to establish an abrupt time boundary over the entire area at that time.

The Late Plains Archaic (Frison 1991:101–111) or Late Middle Prehistoric Period was first thought by Mulloy (1958:220) to have begun about A.D. 1. Later, based on better evidence, he revised it to a beginning of about 3300 years ago (Mulloy 1965:25). This period also has no sharply defined end date, but the arrival of the bow and arrow on the Northwestern and Northern Plains provides an appropriate terminus. This event now appears to have begun with some groups as early as shortly after A.D. 1, while other groups were still not using the bow and arrow by A.D. 500. In addition, many groups maintained Archaic subsistence practices until historic times, particularly in the foothill–intermontane basin areas of the Northwestern Plains. But at least one Late Plains Archaic group, Besant, was probably one of the most sophisticated prehistoric bison-hunting groups ever to live on the High Plains (Frison 1971). They were surely also engaged in plant-food gathering during their yearly round, but evidence for this is still lacking.

Archaic Strategies for Survival

The Social Group

There is little, if any, evidence to suggest changes in the complexity of the societal structure of human groups during the 6500 years that Archaic cultures occupied the Northwestern and Northern Plains. The distribution of resources called for continual aggregation and fragmentation of the groups in response to the availability of food, so the band was the highest level of integration reached. There is no evidence to indicate the amalgamation of bands with any temporary authority to organize economic activities or meet the threat of outside aggression, as seen in tribal settings. Even the Late Plains Archaic Besant bison kills that used corrals and religious structures probably did not involve a group of more than about 100 persons for the short time needed for killing and processing the animals. The band apparently fragmented into smaller groups soon afterward.

Different economic activities with varying degrees of predictability from year to year resulted in aggregates of family units. The bison kill required several hunters operating under some form of temporary authority. It was likely also that some plant resources would have allowed the aggregation of families for varying periods of time. Quarrying raw stone for flaking material must have also called for cooperative efforts as well as some means to supply the group during the quarrying period. The uncertainty of results in large-animal procurement required the presence of religious specialists to invoke supernatural help, which was not the case when the results were ensured beforehand—such as harvesting a hillside covered with sego lilies (Aberle 1966).

Subsistence

Subsistence practices are strong determining factors for the economic activities of any cultural group, particularly those at the hunting and gathering level. Archaic groups on the Northern and Northwestern Plains were probably restricted to local territories, and there is little evidence to suggest long-distance movement of such goods as stone-flaking materials, as was the case for certain Paleo-Indian groups (Frison and Stanford 1982). There seems little doubt also that Archaic groups systematically exploited many ecological zones during their yearly round. The productivity and locations of most economic resources were not predictable from year to year, so annual adjustments were necessary.

Scheduling in the sense that Flannery (1968) proposed was necessary, since decisions were required to exploit the economic benefits offered at a given location in any particular season. In addition, two or more resources may have been available at the same time at separate locations, and a decision was needed as to which one to exploit. This probably resulted in long-range scheduling that could be modified by short-term scheduling when the need arose. For example, the grass at one location in early June could indicate the almost certain presence of bison there later, in the early fall. A heavy August hailstorm, however, could affect an area several miles across to such an extent that the bison would shift to another location. The same hailstorm could also strip a promising crop of chokecherries and buffaloberries, or a grasshopper infestation could reduce the forage and cause a similar result—although the insects themselves may have provided a short-term windfall source of food and altered an otherwise carefully scheduled seasonal round.

There is little doubt that Archaic subsistence was dominated by both hunting and gathering. Early Plains Archaic sites strongly suggest that the groups were beginning to exploit plant resources. Manos and metates were present, good evidence for the grinding of plant foods to increase their palatability and food value. In particular, the outer hulls of seeds must be broken so their content can be absorbed by the human digestive system. Grinding implements are present in small numbers in late Paleo-Indian times, but they become more common and attain diagnostic forms during the Early Plains Archaic and proliferate in the Middle and Late Plains Archaic periods.

The relative contributions of plant and animal foods to the diet are not yet decipherable. Percentages undoubtedly shifted from season to season, from year to year, from group to group, from location to location, and from short- to long-term climatic fluctuations. Subsistence changed constantly during the Archaic, but hunting provided the major source of food on the open plains, while gathering may have gained importance in areas where topography and forage were less favorable for large herbivores that favored open grasslands. Fish remains have yet to be found in Archaic sites on the Northwestern or Northern Plains, even though fish were undeniably available. Although this may be a sampling problem because of differential preservation, identifiable fishing gear is lacking. Shellfish were, however, collected along those streams where they could survive, but their contribution to the diet was minimal. Although a clear separation between gathering and hunting may not always be possible, gathering usually consists of those activities associated with plants or with organisms such as shellfish and reptiles that are ineffective in evading humans.

Whether the grinding-tool complex was introduced into the High Plains–foothill–mountain region of the Northwestern Plains or was developed regionally is debatable, but the tools appeared slowly and increased gradually. True manos and metates are present in stratified, dated contexts between 8000 and 7000 years ago. *developed there or migrated?*

Caching of food also seems to have been a common practice in late Paleo-Indian times in the foothill–mountain slope environments, and was carried *caching* through into the Early Plains Archaic. Features dated between 8500 and 8000 years ago at the Medicine Lodge Creek site are located and built in a manner suggesting food-caching areas (Frison 1991:340–343). Similar features appear also in later sites. Caching does not seem to have been undertaken on a scale comparable to the postulated frozen-meat cache of Paleo-Indian hunters (Frison and Stanford 1982). Communal procurement of bison throughout the Archaic, however, strongly suggests the rapid accumulation of meat surpluses that were almost certainly destined to be processed and stored for future use, perhaps during the winter. These sites used natural landforms that needed little or no modification to serve as traps (Bentzen 1961; Frison 1968a; Frison et al. 1976), corrals or pounds (Frison 1971; Lobdell 1974), or bison jumps (Frison 1970; Reeves 1978a, 1983). In addition, bison were regularly taken in smaller numbers, probably for immediate consumption.

Although bison tend to dominate the Archaic faunal assemblage, other species were important, particularly in foothill and mountain-slope environments. Winter deer and mountain sheep were taken with an occasional elk and bison, as at the Middle Plains Archaic Dead Indian Creek site in the Sunlight Basin in northwestern Wyoming (Frison 1991:258–260; Frison and Walker 1984). This is a small, isolated basin within the Absaroka Mountains, and, although hunting methods then are not known, there is assumed to have been day-to-day hunting of animals during the winter. Late Paleo-Indian procurement of mountain sheep is indicated by a juniper-bark cordage net from the Absaroka Mountains that is radiocarbon-dated to about 8800 years ago (Frison, Andrews et al. 1986).

Elk are rare in Archaic sites, and their numbers reach significance only well into the late prehistoric period. But elk antlers were used as quarrying tools in the Early Plains Archaic Spanish Point site (Frison 1991:262), which hints that the lack of elk in sites is due to an inadequate sample and that their real numbers are underrepresented. Small numbers of pronghorn are often found in Archaic faunal assemblages. Smaller animals are also present and, cumulatively, were a significant part of the food supply. Jackrabbits and cottontails are the most common. Rodents—including wood rat, beaver, porcupine, and marmot—are less evident. Occasional carnivores and scavengers include wolf or dog, coyote, fox, bobcat, bear, and badger. The degree to which they represent actual food is questionable.

Plants that may have contributed to the diet are too numerous to consider separately, but included flowers, fruits and berries, seeds, seedpods, leaves, cambium layers, shoots, tubers, and roots. Together, they probably formed an important part of the food supply and one that changed in proportion from area to area and from time to time in response to availability. Some of them were suitable for storage, while others had to be used within a short time.

The element of uncertainty was always present from year to year in the availability and location of plant foods, since temperature is unpredictable. Another factor is elevation. Some plants have a wide tolerance and may be mature at one elevation and still immature at higher elevations, thereby allowing for a long period of exploitation. Other plants are more geographically restricted and may be exploited for only a short time. In general, the use of plants is inferred instead of proved. Rarely, as in dry caves, their use may be demonstrated by the recovery of preserved remains (e.g., Frison and Huseas 1968). The mano and metate are usually considered convincing evidence of plant-food preparation, and small mammals and other items might also have been reduced to a paste using these tools (Mulloy 1954a:59).

TOOLS AND WEAPONS

The tools and weapons used throughout the Archaic for food procurement and preparation were relatively simple and changed little over time. Stone tools were made using raw materials obtained from both local and—such as Knife River Flint—distant sources. The high expenditure of energy needed to remove overburden and to quarry buried deposits reflects a strong desire for high-quality materials. In addition, large amounts of material were available in such settings as river terraces and glacial and lag deposits.

When serious quarrying was started (or became necessary to obtain satisfactory materials) is not known, largely because the study of raw-material sources and procurement is still in its beginning stages. It is known that in Early *quarries*

Plains Archaic times, about 6200 years ago, there were serious efforts at quarrying in the Bighorn Mountains of Wyoming (Frison 1991:291–292). The well-known Spanish Diggings (Holmes 1919) is only a small fraction of the extensive quarrying of quartzite and chert deposits that covered several hundred square miles in southern Wyoming. Much of this quarrying appears to have occurred during later Archaic times, based on the projectile points made of the material. The Schmitt quarry in southwestern Montana reflects intense quarrying activity during the Late Archaic (Ahler 1986; Davis 1982), and the Knife River Flint quarries in western North Dakota were supplying large quantities of raw material in all directions from their source through nearly all prehistoric time (Clayton et al. 1970).

Based on the size of projectile points, the throwing stick and dart was the weapon used during Archaic times. Perishable parts are rare, but were found in Late Archaic contexts in two dry caves (Frison 1965, 1968b). Perishable materials also support the claim that smaller projectile points reflect the use of the bow and arrow (Greer 1978). Sharpened wooden foreshafts are known from another Late Archaic assemblage, and bunt types of wooden foreshafts were found in another (Frison 1962, 1965). Cordage from a Middle Archaic assemblage reveals a wide range of size (Frison and Huseas 1968), and probably reflects the use of nets, snares, and other devices for trapping small animals.

Tool kits are simple and consist of common tool types made of stone, bone, and antler. A diagnostic of the Late Archaic is a biface knife that was systematically resharpened by beveling one edge (Frison 1991:129–132). Other diagnostics are sandstone-slab metates and manos. The rare perishables mentioned earlier provide some insight into the hafting of tools and weapons.

FOOD PROCUREMENT AND PREPARATION

Bison hunting was apparently the single most productive effort during the Archaic, and can be roughly divided into communal operations and single and small-group hunting. Communal kills were accomplished through the planned use of topographic features that were modified if necessary. Arroyo traps, jumps, and pounds are widely scattered over the area (Bentzen 1961; Davis and Stallcop 1965, 1966; Frison 1970, 1971; Frison et al. 1976; Lobdell 1974; Reeves 1978a; Shay 1971). Other methods are known from less visible features (Reeves 1978b) and document single or small groups of hunters who took advantage of the topography and such impermanent features as snowdrifts.

Communal bison hunting indicates the accumulation of surpluses for storage. Seasonality of bison kills is becoming better understood through taphonomic studies, particularly in the larger kills where large-animal population samples are available (Clark and Wilson 1981; Frison 1978; Frison et al.

1976; Reher 1974). Although the relation of communal procurement to other economic activities is still poorly known, communal hunts appear to have been restricted to certain times of the year.

No convincing evidence of large-scale or communal hunting of other large fauna is presently known for the Archaic. A possible exception may be some high-altitude features with lines of large stones that could represent drive lines related to mountain-sheep traps (Frison 1991:248–249). These are older than historic sheep traps in the area, but whether they are Archaic in age has yet to be determined. Special treatments of deer antlers and skulls at the Middle Archaic Dead Indian Creek site (Frison 1991:259–260) strongly suggest an element of ceremonialism that could be related to that in communal hunting, although taphonomy shows that the animals were taken over a long period of time and do not represent a single kill.

Plant-food gathering required only a simple technology. Timing was important; for example, limber-pine seeds may be collected in large numbers with a lodge cover or similar item spread under the tree as the cones are opening, and arrowroot leaves are edible at an early stage of growth. Roots and tubers were available with simple digging tools. A great deal of food can be collected in a short time with a sharpened stick or an elk-antler tine in a field containing sego lilies. The time depth of coiled basketry is unknown, but it has been recovered in both Middle Archaic and Late Archaic sites (Frison, Adovasio et al. 1986; Husted 1978:68, 116) and was probably important in the gathering of plant foods, especially seeds.

Articulated units or complete long bones are rare in Archaic camp- or kill sites, indicating the intense breakdown and use of animal carcasses. Strangely enough, the opening of bison brain cases appears not to have been common until late prehistoric times, and even then may reflect ritualistic instead of economic activity. Fire pits of many shapes and sizes and containing varying amounts of fire-fractured stones are numerous and visible features on the Northwestern Plains, but not as much as on the Northern Plains (Figure 5.3*a*). They usually have been interpreted as ovens or roasting pits (Mulloy 1954a, 1954b), although other possibilities should be considered. If they are food-preparation features, they rarely contain animal bones—although the flesh could have been removed from them before cooking. If they were used to cook plant foods, the kind of plants and the nature of the preparation is not clear. Manos and metates are usually associated with the pits, which could be a strong argument for their use in plant-food preparation. They often occur in groups of two or three, which could reflect separate but related functions. A similar feature containing several bison bones at the late prehistoric Wardell site strongly suggests cooking of bison parts. It was interpreted as a sealed unit that, for some reason, remained unopened (Frison 1991:331–332). It is almost the same as and only slightly younger than many Archaic features.

Figure 5.3. (*a*) Late Archaic slab-lined fire pit (scale = .3048 meter); (*b*) stone circles along the Platte River in southeastern Wyoming (ring diameter, 17 feet) (photo by William Mulloy).

The possibility that these fire pits served several different uses should also be considered. Oxidization rings as much as 5 centimeters thick often are present, suggesting extended periods of burning that may have been undertaken for heating the floor of a small structure. The absence of large, permanent campsites suggests frequent movements of groups, even during the winter. It is difficult to conceive of temporary small structures in winter without some provision to heat them. The heat imparted to a pile of stones and the surrounding earth would have served for both cooking and heating. The decline in frequency of these features to the north of the Wyoming–Montana border may reflect a different winter survival strategy, with increasing reliance on hunting, storing meat, and setting up more permanent winter camps.

SHELTER AND CLOTHING

Caves and rock shelters were used extensively by Archaic groups, although the past desirability of a given shelter is not always clear. Shelters that predictably should have experienced the greatest use were often largely ignored, and seemingly undesirable ones often show the greatest use. Rock shelters are present in only a small part of the Plains area, so other types of shelter were necessary.

A significant discovery in recent years involves Archaic-period pit houses at several locations on the Northwestern Plains and in foothill–mountain areas. With dates as early as 5300 years ago, near the end of the Early Plains Archaic, and extending into the Middle Plains Archaic at about 4400 years ago, these features provide a better model of winter survival (Eakin 1987; Frison 1991:83–85, 100; Harrell and McKern 1986; McGuire et al. 1984).

The most visible archaeological features on the Northwestern and Northern Plains are circular arrangements of stones. Their function has long been a subject of contention (Kehoe 1960; Mulloy 1954a, 1958, 1965), but most are now believed to have been placed to hold down the cover of a conical (or some other type) lodge. The outside diameters of these stone circles vary from about 7 to 36 feet, but most are between 13 and 23 feet. They may consist of single or multiple courses of stones that occur singly or in groups ranging into the hundreds. They may be arranged in lines or clustered together, and may be nearly contiguous or widely spaced. They are found in many topographic settings, but most are common on ridge tops, buttes, and stream terraces, and along mountain flanks (Figure 5.3b).

The number of these circles on the Northwestern and Northern Plains doubtless runs into the hundreds of thousands. Most of them date to the late prehistoric but many are Late Archaic, while a few can be satisfactorily demonstrated as Middle Archaic. They have yet to be firmly established for the Early Archaic.

Stone-filled hearths were alluded to earlier, in the discussion of food preparation, and also as possibly indicating structures. Some hearths are surrounded by stone circles, although most are not. Other hearths have only a few stones—usually to the windward side—which could indicate a less sophisticated structure, such as a windbreak. A major problem in the study of Archaic living shelters is that of seasonality. When the time of year of site occupancy can be determined, better correlations will be possible between various kinds of archaeological features.

Stone circles certainly depended on the availability of stone, for rarely were stones moved more than a short distance. An extensive array of stone circles near the large Muddy Creek Besant bison kill is believed to represent living structures that were occupied during procurement (Reher 1983), while at the Ruby site Besant kill, stone circles are absent (Frison 1971). Stones were readily available at the former site and absent at the latter.

Most stone circles have not been rewarding for study due to the rarity of artifacts in them and the concomitant inability to derive meaningful interpretations. Their study has, however, proliferated in recent years, and many innovative approaches are being tested. The results of a symposium at the thirty-ninth annual Plains Conference provide reason for optimism for future studies (Davis 1983).

Little evidence of clothing is known, but what is available was made from animal hide. Fragments of softened hide sewn with two-strand twisted plant-fiber cordage were recovered from a Middle Archaic component in a dry rock shelter (Frison and Huseas 1968), and a moccasin sewn with twisted sinew was found in a Late Archaic context (Frison 1968b). Footgear of mountain-sheep hide from Mummy Cave dates to the early part of the late prehistoric period (about A.D. 700), and, according to the excavator, it resembles an Eskimo snow boot or mukluk. Items identified as possible grass liners and tailored mountain-sheep-skin clothing were present in the same cultural level (McCracken 1978:13–16). Decorative quillwork was also present by the Late Archaic (Frison 1965:92, 1968b:285). These fragments of clothing are known from only dry rock shelters in a small part of the area. Even so, there is no reason to suspect that anything other than skin clothing was used on the Northwestern and Northern Plains.

Religious Activity *differs from Paleo*

There is little doubt that communal bison procurement resulted in ritual activity. The Ruby site of Besant age in east-central Wyoming is a bison pound with the remains of a large structure beside it; its many features reflect some sort of observance, probably religious. Bison skulls were arranged around one end of the structure, and certain bison bones were given special treatment. There is no evidence that the structure was used for living or any activity associated with the processing of animals killed in the trap (Frison 1970). The arrangement of deer skullcaps and antlers at the Dead Indian Creek site also could reflect ritual behavior (Frison 1991:260).

In other cases, arrangements of stones may have resulted from some form of religious activity. Because of their size or location, some stone circles cannot be interpreted as having been used as lodge-cover weights. Unless datable materials are in good context—which usually is not the case—there is no reliable means of dating these features, but from their context many must date to the Archaic.

Other arrangements of stone besides circles may be related to ritual. Long lines of cairns of various sizes are present in nearly all of Wyoming and at least part of Montana. Although some are known to be of late prehistoric and historic age, others appear to be much older. Some of these cairn lines can be traced for distances up to several miles and have been interpreted as trails (Frison 1981; Loendorf and Brownell 1980), but they are not to be confused with drive-line markers for animal-procurement complexes.

Many locations on the Northwestern and Northern Plains have sandstone and other formations on which are pecked, incised, and painted figures. Dating these manifestations has been a problem, and although there are many studies of rock art, most archaeologists have cautioned against assigning absolute dates. In recent years, however, new rock-art dating methods have been developed and there seems little doubt that some rock art goes back to Late Plains Archaic times and possibly earlier (Francis 1991).

Human Interment

Archaic skeletal material is rare and consists of both primary and secondary interments, usually in shallow pits. One Early Archaic primary, flexed burial from central Wyoming is dated about 5350 to 5250 years ago. This burial was not accompanied by grave offerings, but was associated with a site having at least 60 stone-filled fire pits and an extensive grinding-tool assemblage (Zeimens et al. 1976).

What appears to be an anomaly is the Gray Burial site in southwestern Saskatchewan (Millar et al. 1972). More than 100 individuals were recovered, and it is estimated that an equal number remain interred. Both primary and secondary interments were found in both single and multiple occurrences. Diagnostic materials are of the Oxbow complex, and a radiocarbon date of about 4955 years ago seems to be reliable.

Parts of a human skeleton were placed in shallow pits directly below the cultural levels at both the McKean and the Dead Indian Creek sites (Gill 1984; Mulloy 1954a). They may be bundle burials retrieved from primary interments elsewhere, or they may represent some ritual activity. Both occur in McKean-complex sites.

The Late Archaic is better represented, but the number of inhumations that provide material for meaningful analysis is very low. Remains range from complete skeletons (e.g., Steege 1960) to others—unpublished—that are bundle interments. A Late Archaic cremation, from the grave offerings present, may be of an individual of relatively high status (Frison and Van Norman 1985).

Although the present sample of human skeletal material is limited, there are some indications that morphological characters may be of value in dating (Finnegan 1981; Gill 1991). Better samples and further analyses are needed to refine the methodology.

The Cultural Chronology

Late Paleo-Indian *foothills*

Several radiocarbon dates document the presence of early hunting and gathering groups in foothill areas of mountain ranges in the western part of the Northwestern Plains. The oldest Paleo-Indian date in Mummy Cave is about 9230 years old, and the youngest is 7970 (McCracken 1978). At Medicine Lodge Creek, the dates range from about 9700 to 8050 years ago (Frison 1991:69–70). In the Bighorn Canyon caves, the range is about 8690 to 7560 years ago (Husted 1969) (Figure 5.4).

These stratified rock shelters produce occasional evidence of human habitation in the form of a variety of lanceolate, stemmed, and notched projectile points and of small numbers of tools, some of which are similar to those from classic Paleo-Indian complexes. Most of them have not been given type status, although Husted (1969) suggested "Lovell Constricted" and "Pryor Stemmed" as type names from materials found in Bighorn Canyon caves. Pryor Stemmed has been suggested to represent a cultural complex (Frison and Grey 1980), but Lovell Constricted is not as well known or recognized (Figure 5.5).

Stratigraphic evidence from Mummy Cave, Medicine Lodge Creek (Figure 5.4), and Southsider Cave (Frison 1991:74–76) indicates an unbroken progression from the levels containing late Paleo-Indian projectile points to levels with notched projectile points of the Early Plains Archaic. There is no evidence to suggest sudden changes in lifeways of the groups involved. There is some carryover of the Paleo-Indian tool types that disappear in the Archaic, and grinding tools that begin in late Paleo-Indian times gradually develop in

Figure 5.4. The Medicine Lodge Creek site in north-central Wyoming, which extends about 330 feet along the bluff indicated by the arrow.

Figure 5.5. Stratigraphic order of foothill–mountain Paleo-Indian diagnostics from the Medicine Lodge Creek site. The approximate radiocarbon dates are (*a*) 9700 years ago; (*b*) 9600 years ago; (*e*) 9500 years ago; (*g*) 9350 years ago; (*h*) 8600 years ago; (*l*) Lovell Constricted, 8320 years ago; (*m*) Pryor Stemmed, 8340 years ago; (*o*) 8050 years ago.

Early Plains Archaic. The data suggest continuity between Paleo-Indian and Archaic.

Early Plains Archaic

The Early Plains Archaic and the Hypsithermal climatic episode occupied about the same span of time. Antevs (1948, 1955) pioneered the concept of the Hypsithermal (which he named the Altithermal) and its possible effects on the climate of the West. Since the effects of this warm and dry episode may have severely limited human settlement patterns and subsistence practices, more research is needed to better understand the cultures of the Early Plains Archaic. Many climatic interpretations of the Hypsithermal are based on studies of soil development and alluvial deposits, areas of research in which archaeologists are usually forced to rely on the expertise of specialists in other fields (Haynes 1968; Leopold and Miller 1954).

The effects of a short drought can be demonstrated, and extended periods must have been much worse. A small change in the amount of yearly precipitation brought about disastrous effects for domestic animals and humans on the short-grass prairies during the dust bowl of the 1930s (Weaver 1968). This event lasted for only a few years, and a continuation of such conditions for hundreds or a few thousand years would have had serious effects for people whose choices were limited: they could move to another area or adapt to changing conditions. The latter was possible only if the changed conditions provided a sufficient economic base.

Reeves (1973) has argued that the expanding effects of the Hypsithermal drought created continually changing areas of short-grass plains that would have supplied food for the large herbivores. This might have been true, but it does not provide the answer to the ultimate fate of the human and animal populations living in the original short-grass-prairie areas where, with continually drying conditions, animal carrying capacity would have deteriorated.

Another question not yet satisfactorily answered concerns the kinds of ecological changes that Hypsithermal climates brought to the mountain slopes. If changes resulted in plant communities shifting to higher elevations, human groups should have responded similarly. There is some evidence to support this. Presently, our best evidence for the Early Plains Archaic is found in rock shelters and open sites in the foothill–mountain areas. Conversely, intensive testing of deep, stratified sites in the lower elevations in intermontane basins is beginning to produce evidence of Early Plains Archaic occupations (Armitage et al. 1982). The apparent lack of cultural evidence at lower elevations may be as much a geologic problem as a cultural one. Further resolution of the problem will most likely be realized in continued efforts to explain the geologic processes that resulted from Hypsithermal climatic changes.

Mummy Cave provides the most complete stratified record for the Early Plains Archaic, with radiocarbon dates from about 7630 to 5255 years ago (McCracken 1978). Another rock shelter, Southsider Cave, has almost the same range of dates, 7650 to 5420 years ago (Frison 1991:Table 2.8). Laddie Creek, an open site with stratified Early Archaic levels, has the oldest (dated at about 6830 years ago) and the youngest (at 5700 years ago) (Frison 1991:Table 2.12). These Early Archaic occupations are recognized by distinctive side-notched and occasionally corner-notched and even rarer base-notched projectile points. They are usually called early side-notched, although Husted proposed the type names Pahaska Side-notched and Blackwater Side-notched (Husted and Edgar n.d.). Early side-notched projectile points have also been called Bitterroot Side-notched farther to the west (Swanson et al. 1964).

Farther north in the grasslands and mountains of the Canadian provinces is other evidence of Early Archaic components with diagnostic side-notched projectile points. These include the Stampede, Gap, and Gowen sites (Gryba 1976; Reeves and Dormarr 1972; Walker 1992). Walker (1992) contains a lengthy analysis and discussion of Early Archaic sites and the different early side-notched projectiles.

Two and probably three sites in the Wyoming Black Hills are bison kill sites. One of them, the Hawken site, is a stratified arroyo trap dated to about 6470 to 6270 years ago (Frison et al. 1976). Another arroyo bison kill in the same locality is dated to about 4000 years ago. As a population, the Hawken-site bison were larger than modern bison but significantly smaller than the 10,000-year-old late Pleistocene–early Holocene bison at the Casper site of Hell Gap age (Frison 1974). It is significant that enough bison were present in the Black Hills at this time to allow repeated communal hunting. It is tempting to suggest from this that the Black Hills were something of an oasis for bison during the Hypsithermal, and that large, stable populations could be maintained there. This is not to say that the Black Hills was the only area where bison were able to survive the Hypsithermal in large numbers; areas peripheral to the Northeastern Plains apparently also contained numbers of bison large enough for communal hunting (Anderson and Semken 1980; Shay 1971).

Bison jumping occurred also during the later part of the Hypsithermal. The Head-Smashed-In bison jump in Alberta has radiocarbon dates from about 5600 to 5080 years ago from levels that produced side-notched projectile points that Reeves (1978a) has called the Mummy Cave complex. Oxbow, as described at the type site in Saskatchewan (Nero and McCorquodale 1958), may also be a manifestation of the terminal Early Plains Archaic and the beginning of the Middle Archaic (Figure 5.6).

Figure 5.6. Stratigraphic order of Archaic diagnostics from the Medicine Lodge Creek site. The approximate radiocarbon dates are (a–c) Early Archaic side-notched, no dates recovered; (d–e) Early Archaic corner-notched, no dates recovered; (f–h) McKean, 4000 years ago; (i) 3750 years ago; (k–m) Pelican Lake, 3000 years ago; (n) 1800 years ago; (o) 1360 years ago.

Middle Plains Archaic

[handwritten: archaic is a subsistance adaptation]

The end of the Hypsithermal and the Early Plains Archaic is characterized by a return to climatic conditions similar to those of the present. This is the beginning of the Middle Plains Archaic period, detected by the appearance of new projectile styles and, on the Northwestern Plains, by a marked increase in the tools to prepare plant foods, especially seeds.

The dominant cultural manifestation of the Middle Plains Archaic is the McKean complex, with the type site in southeastern Wyoming (Kornfeld and Todd 1985; Mulloy 1954b). McKean is widely spread over the Northern Plains and into the mountains (Syms 1969). Radiocarbon dates are as early as 4900 years ago from the Rigler Bluffs site in southwestern Montana (Arthur 1966) and as late as 3180 years ago from the Dipper Gap site in northeastern Colorado (Metcalf 1973). Dates from other sites cover this entire range (Frison 1991:Table 2.13).

McKean is definitely a hunting and gathering manifestation and is distinguished by several projectile-point styles, the internal relationships of which are not well understood (Figure 5.6). The Signal Butte site, for example, yielded a projectile point with deep side notches that was given the type name Mallory (Forbis et al. n.d.). These and McKean lanceolates occurred together in a bison pound in central Wyoming (Lobdell 1974). A wide range of projectile-point styles—including lanceolate, stemmed, and side-notched—occurred together at the Dead Indian Creek site in northern Wyoming (Frison and Walker 1984), and the same situation occurred at the McKean site and the Cactus Flower site in southeastern Alberta (Brumley 1975). Wheeler (1954b) felt that his data allowed the designation of several point types, including McKean, Duncan, and Hanna.

[handwritten: complex is au cultural groups Clovis Folsom. Plainview]

Late Plains Archaic

PELICAN LAKE

The relationship between Middle and Late Plains Archaic is conjectural. Pelican Lake is the earliest of the Late Archaic complexes and continued throughout nearly all Late Archaic times (Figure 5.6). Dates on Pelican Lake from the Head-Smashed-In bison jump in Alberta are from 3040 to 1925 years ago (Reeves 1978b:162). Two dates from Medicine Lodge Creek are 3110 and 3020 years ago. Dates between these two extremes are from the Mortlach and Long Creek sites in southern Saskatchewan (Wettlaufer and Meyer-Oakes 1960). Late Plains Archaic materials from Spring Creek Cave in northern Wyoming might also be typologically regarded as Pelican Lake (Frison 1965) and are dated at about 1725 years ago (M-433).

Bison kills in the Powder River basin of Montana and Wyoming designated as Yonkee were first thought to have begun in Middle Plains Archaic times, based on a radiocarbon date of about 4400 years ago at the Yonkee site in southeastern Montana (Bentzen 1961). However, more recent investigations indicate that this date is incorrect, and new dates from the Yonkee site and other related sites indicate that Yonkee should be Late Plains Archaic in age (Bump 1987; Frison 1991:191–194).

The view from the north in Alberta (Reeves 1969:33, 1983) is that Pelican Lake is a phase that is part of a sequence that follows a Hanna phase, which followed a McKean phase. Whatever the facts, Pelican Lake was widespread, covered a long period of time, and its members followed a more Archaic way of life as they progressed southward. There are, also, several Late Plains Archaic sites that produce generally large corner-notched points that may be related to those of Pelican Lake.

BESANT AND AVONLEA

Besant groups made their way well into the central Wyoming area, dating to about 1720±110 years ago at the Muddy Creek site bison pound (Frison 1991:208–211; S. Hughes 1981). The Besant date from Mortlach is about 1570 years ago (Wettlaufer 1955), and Forbis (1962:109) found a Besant level dated at 1650 years ago at the Old Women's Buffalo Jump in Alberta.

Avonlea apparently begins shortly after A.D. 1, judging from a radiocarbon date of 1740 years ago from the Gull Lake site in southwestern Saskatchewan (Kehoe 1973) and from the dates of 1860 and 1840 years ago from the Head-Smashed-In bison jump in Alberta (Reeves 1978a). These dates overlap with Besant.

A regional variant of (or closely related to) Avonlea was present in the Northwestern Plains about A.D. 500, if radiocarbon dates from the bottom level of a bison jump on the Green River in west-central Wyoming are correctly dated at about 1580 years ago (Frison 1973b). A date of 1400 years ago from the Beehive site in north-central Wyoming (Frison 1988:159–162), and another of 1300 years ago from the Irvine site in south-central Wyoming (Duguid 1968), show that terminal Besant and beginning Avonlea may overlap in the south, as they do in the north. Northern Avonlea seems to be less Archaic than its southern counterpart. Although the southern groups were strongly oriented to hunting, typical Archaic grinding tools indicate that a plant-gathering emphasis was important (Davis 1988).

In addition to Avonlea groups, there were large numbers of bow and arrow hunters and gatherers who, based on radiocarbon dates from stone-filled fire pits, persisted until at least A.D. 1000. Better details of their subsistence await further investigation, but present data show no significant change from the earlier groups arbitrarily called Archaic.

Conclusion

The future of archaeological research into the Archaic on the Northwestern and Northern Plains depends largely on the philosophy that is developed in cultural-resource-management programs. All archaeologists must be able to recognize deficiencies that inhibit meaningful programs in research and respond in the best interests of the resource that is threatened.

Several considerations germane to the problem need to be mentioned. The chronology of the Archaic is based largely on radiocarbon dates and on projectile-point typology, and is reasonably well established. The relations between the cultural groups at any given time, however, and from one time period to another are largely hypothetical and are interpreted mainly from similarities in tools, weapons, and economic orientations. In addition, the use of various subsistence models based mainly on ethnographic studies of hunters and gatherers is becoming increasingly popular.

There are nevertheless serious deficiencies, both in the available archaeological data and in the methods used to interpret them. Four areas of research are especially important.

Some progress is being made, especially through taphonomic studies, to determine the seasonality of events. It is necessary to better determine cultural activities on a year-round basis.

Much of the archaeological record on the Plains has been damaged by the geologic effects of the Hypsithermal, which is not yet well understood. This problem cannot be solved by archaeologists alone.

The functions of many of the most visible and numerous archaeological features, such as stone circles and stone-filled fire pits, remain largely unknown. Only recently have the problems of interpreting stone circles been approached with a problem-solving methodology—which is still lacking in the case of the fire pits.

Cultural models as yet fail to allow for some activities that demanded a significant share of the time and energy of Archaic groups. An example is the procurement of stone-flaking materials. Archaic groups expended much time and effort in obtaining such stone, requiring the movement of large numbers of people and provisioning them.

Future research should be directed to the solution of these and related problems, which require continual efforts to improve methodology. Archaeologists must remember that the available information is limited and that gathering

data without reference to specific problems is wasteful of a nonrenewable resource.

References

Aberle, D. F.
    1966   Religico-Magical Phenomena and Power, Prediction, and Control. *Southwest-*
            ern Journal of Anthropology 22:221–229.
Ahler, S. A.
    1986   *The Knife River Flint Quarries: Excavations at Site 32DU508.* State Historical Soci-
            ety of North Dakota, Bismarck.
AMQUA (American Quaternary Association)
    1974   *Abstracts of the Third Biennial Meeting.* University of Wisconsin, Madison.
Anderson, D. C., and H. A. Semken, Jr., eds.
    1980   *The Cherokee Excavations: Holocene Ecology and Human Adaptation in Northwest-*
            ern Iowa. Academic Press, New York.
Antevs, E.
    1948   Climatic Change and Pre-White Man. *Bulletin of the University of Utah* 38:168–
            191.
    1955   Geologic–Climatic Dating in the West. *American Antiquity* 20:317–335.
Armitage, C., S. D. Creasman, and L. C. Mackey
    1982   The Deadman Wash Site: A Multi-Component (Paleo-Indian, Archaic, Late
            Prehistoric) Site in Southwestern Wyoming. *Journal of Intermountain Archaeol-*
            ogy 1:1–11.
Arthur, G. W.
    1966   *An Archeological Survey of the Upper Yellowstone River Drainage, Montana.* Mon-
            tana State University, Economics Research Report no. 26. Bozeman.
Bamforth, D. B.
    1991   Population Dispersion and Paleoindian Technology at the Allen Site. In *Raw*
            Material Economies Among Prehistoric Hunter-Gatherers, edited by A. M. White
            and S. Holen, 357–374. University of Kansas, Publications in Anthropology,
            no. 19. Lawrence.
Bentzen, R. C.
    1961   *The Powers–Yonkee Bison Trap, 24PR5.* Report of the Sheridan Chapter, Wyo-
            ming Archaeological Society.
Brumley, J. H.
    1975   *The Cactus Flower Site in Southeastern Alberta: 1972–1974 Excavations.* National
            Museums of Canada, National Museum of Man, Mercury Series, Archaeologi-
            cal Survey of Canada, Paper no. 46. Ottawa, Ont.
Bump, R. J.
    1987   The Powers–Yonkee Bison Trap: A New Look at an Old (or not so Old) Site.
            Archaeology in Montana 28:27–37.
Champe, J. L.
    1946   *Ash Hollow Cave.* University of Nebraska Studies, n.s., no. 1. Lincoln.
Clark, G. R., and M. Wilson
    1981   The Ayers–Frazier Bison Trap (24PE30): A Late Middle Period Bison Kill on
            the Lower Yellowstone River. *Archaeology in Montana* 22:23–77.

Clayton, L., W. B. Bickley, and W. J. Stone
    1970   Knife River Flint. *Plains Anthropologist* 15:282–290.
Davis, L. B.
    1982   *Archaeology and Geology of the Schmitt Chert Mine, Missouri Headwaters.* Guide-
            book for Field Trip, Thirty-fifth Annual Meeting of the Geological Society of
            America. Montana State University, Bozeman.
Davis, L. B., ed.
    1983   *From Microcosm to Macrocosm: Advances in Tipi Ring Investigations and Interpreta-
            tions.* Plains Anthropologist Memoir no. 19.
    1988   *Avonlea Yesterday and Today: Archaeology and Prehistory.* Brigdens, Regina, Sask.
Davis, L. B., and E. Stallcop
    1965   *The Keaster Site (24PH401): A Stratified Bison Kill Occupation in the Missouri
            Breaks Area of North-Central Montana.* Montana Archaeological Society Memoir
            no. 2. Billings.
    1966   *The Wahkpa Chu'gn Site (24HL101): Late Hunters in the Milk River Valley, Mon-
            tana.* Montana Archaeological Society Memoir no. 3. Billings.
Duguid, J. O.
    1968   The Irvine Site: A Possible Avonlea Site in Eastern Wyoming. *Wyoming Archae-
            ologist* 11:24–34.
Eakin, D. H.
    1987   Final Report of Salvage Investigations at the Split Rock Site (48FR1484). High-
            way Project SCPF-020-2(19), Fremont County, Wyoming, Prepared for the
            Wyoming Highway Department.
Finnegan, M.
    1981   Archaic Skeletal Remains from the Central Plains: Demography and Burial
            Practices. In *Progress in Skeletal Biology of Plains Populations,* edited by R. L.
            Jantz and D. H. Ubelaker, 85–92. Plains Anthropologist Memoir no. 17.
Flannery, K. C.
    1968   Archeological Systems Theory and Early Mesoamerica. In *Anthropological Ar-
            cheology in the Americas,* edited by Betty Meggers, 67–87. Anthropological Soci-
            ety of Washington, Washington, D.C.
Forbis, R. G.
    1962   The Old Women's Buffalo Jump, Alberta. *National Museum of Canada, Contribu-
            tions to Anthropology 1957, Bulletin* 180:119–164.
Forbis, R. G., W. D. Strong, and M. E. Kirkby
    n.d.   Signal Butte and MacHaffie: Two Stratified Sites on the Northern Great
            Plains. Manuscript in possession of the senior author.
Francis, J. E.
    1991   An Overview of Wyoming Rock Art. In *Prehistoric Hunters of the High Plains,*
            edited by G. Frison, 397–430. 2nd ed. Academic Press, San Diego, Calif.
Frison, G. C.
    1962   Wedding of the Waters Cave, 48HO301: A Stratified Site in the Big Horn Basin
            of Northern Wyoming. *Plains Anthropologist* 7:246–265.
    1965   Spring Creek Cave, Wyoming. *American Antiquity* 31:81–94.
    1968a   Site 48SH312: An Early Middle Period Bison Kill in the Powder River Basin of
            Wyoming. *Plains Anthropologist* 13:31–39.
    1968b   Daugherty Cave, Wyoming. *Plains Anthropologist* 13:253–295.
    1970   The Kobold Site, 24BH406: A Post-Altithermal Record of Buffalo Jumping for
            the Northwestern Plains. *Plains Anthropologist* 15:1–35.

1971   The Buffalo Pound in Northwestern Plains Prehistory: Site 48CA302, Wyoming. *American Antiquity* 36:77–91.

1973a   Early Period Marginal Cultural Groups in Northern Wyoming. *Plains Anthropologist* 18:300–312.

1973b   *The Wardell Buffalo Trap, 48SU301: Communal Procurement in the Upper Green River Basin, Wyoming.* University of Michigan, Museum of Anthropology, Anthropological Papers, no. 48. Ann Arbor.

1974   *The Casper Site: A Hell Gap Bison Kill on the High Plains.* Academic Press, New York.

1976   The Chronology of Paleo-Indian and Altithermal Cultures in the Bighorn Basin, Wyoming. In *Cultural Change and Continuity: Essays in Honor of James Bennett Griffin*, edited by C. E. Cleland, 147–173. Academic Press, New York.

1978   Animal Population Studies and Cultural Inference. In *Bison Procurement and Utilization: A Symposium*, edited by L. B. Davis and M. Wilson, 44–52. Plains Anthropologist Memoir no. 14.

1981   Linear Arrangements of Cairns in Wyoming and Montana. In *Megaliths to Medicine Wheels: Boulder Structures in Archaeology*, edited by M. Wilson, K. L. Road, and K. J. Hardy, 133–147. University of Calgary, Department of Archaeology, Proceedings of the eleventh Chacmool Conference.

1988   Avonlea and Contemporaries in Wyoming. In *Avonlea Yesterday and Today: Archaeology and Prehistory*, edited by L. B. Davis, 155–170. Brigdens, Regina, Sask.

1991   *Prehistoric Hunters of the High Plains.* 2nd ed. Academic Press, San Diego, Calif.

Frison, G. C., R. L. Andrews, J, N. Adovasio, R. C. Carlisle, and R. Edgar

1986   A Late Paleoindian Animal Trapping Net from Northern Wyoming. *American Antiquity* 51:352–361.

Frison, G. C., J. M. Adovasio, and R. C. Carlisle

1986   Coiled Basketry from Northern Wyoming. *Plains Anthropologist* 31:163–167.

Frison, G. C., and D. C. Grey

1980   Pryor Stemmed: A Specialized Late Paleo-Indian Ecological Adaptation. *Plains Anthropologist* 25:27–46.

Frison, G. C., and M. Huseas

1968   Leigh Cave, Wyoming: Site 48WA304. *Wyoming Archaeologist* 11:20–33.

Frison, G. C., and D. Stanford, eds.

1982   *The Agate Basin Site: A Record of Paleo-Indian Occupation on the High Plains.* Academic Press, New York.

Frison, G. C., and Z. Van Norman

1985   The Wind River Canyon Burial and Cache. *Archaeology in Montana* 26:43–52.

Frison, G. C., and D. N. Walker, eds.

1984   *The Dead Indian Creek Site: An Archaic Occupation in the Absaroka Mountains of Northwest Wyoming*, Wyoming Archaeologist 27, nos. 1–2.

Frison, G. C., M. Wilson, and D. J. Wilson

1976   Fossil Bison and Artifacts from an Early Altithermal Period Arroyo Trap in Wyoming. *American Antiquity* 41:28–57.

Gill, G. W.

1984   The Partial Skeleton of a Child from Dead Indian Creek. In *The Dead Indian Creek Site: An Archaic Occupation in the Absaroka Mountains of Northwest Wyoming*, edited by G. C. Frison and D. N. Walker, 97. Wyoming Archaeologist 27, nos. 1–2.

1991   Human Skeletal Remains on the Northwestern Plains. In *Prehistoric Hunters of the High Plains,* by G. C. Frison, 431–437. 2nd ed. Academic Press, San Diego, Calif.

Greer, J. W.
  1978   An Avonlea Site in the Bighorn River Canyon, Wyoming. *Archaeology in Montana* 19:1–104.

Gryba, E.
  1976   The Early Side-Notched Component at Site DjOn-26. In *Archaeology in Alberta 1975,* edited by J. M. Quigg and W. J. Byrne, 92–107. Archaeological Survey of Alberta, Occasional Paper no. 1. Edmonton.

Harrell, L. L., and S. T. McKern
  1986   *The Maxon Ranch Site: Archaic and Late Prehistoric Habitation in Southwest Wyoming.* Western Wyoming College, Archaeological Services, Cultural Resource Management Report no. 18. Rock Springs.

Haynes, C. V., Jr.
  1968   Geochronology of Late Quaternary Alluvium. In *Means of Correlation of Quaternary Successions,* edited by R. B. Morrison and H. E. Wright, Jr., 591–631. University of Utah Press, Salt Lake City.

Holder, P., and J. Wike
  1949   The Frontier Complex: A Preliminary Report on a Prehistoric Hunters' Camp in Southwestern Nebraska. *American Antiquity* 14:260–266.

Holmes, W. H.
  1919   *Handbook of Aboriginal American Antiquities.* Bureau of American Ethnology Bulletin 60. Washington, D.C.

Hughes, J. T.
  1949   Investigations in Western South Dakota and Northeastern Wyoming. *American Antiquity* 14:266–277.

Hughes, S. S.
  1981   Projectile Point Variability: A Study of Point Curation at a Besant Kill Site in Southcentral Wyoming. M.A. thesis, Department of Anthropology, University of Wyoming, Laramie.

Husted, W. M.
  1969   *Bighorn Canyon Archeology.* Smithsonian Institution, River Basin Surveys, Publications in Salvage Archeology, no. 12. Lincoln, Neb.
  1978   Excavation Techniques and Culture Layer Analysis. In *The Mummy Cave Project in Northwestern Wyoming,* edited by H. McCracken, 50–132. Buffalo Bill Historical Center, Cody, Wyo.

Husted, W. M., and R. Edgar
  n.d.   The Archeology of Mummy Cave, Wyoming: An Introduction to Shoshonean Prehistory. Manuscript, on file, Buffalo Bill Historical Center, Cody, Wyo.

Kehoe, T. F.
  1960   Stone Tipi Rings in North-Central Montana and the Adjacent Portion of Alberta, Canada: Their Historical, Ethnological, and Archeological Aspects. *Bureau of American Ethnology Bulletin* 173:417–473.
  1973   *The Gull Lake Site: A Prehistoric Bison Drive Site in Southwestern Saskatchewan.* Milwaukee Public Museum, Publications in Anthropology and History, no. 1.

Kornfeld, K., and L. C. Todd, eds.
  1985   *McKean/Middle Plains Archaic: Current Research.* Wyoming Recreational Commission, Occasional Papers on Wyoming Archaeology, no. 4. Cheyenne.

Leopold, L. B., and J. P. Miller
  1954   *A Postglacial Chronology for Some Alluvial Valleys in Wyoming.* United States Geological Survey, Water Supply Paper no. 1261. Washington, D.C.
Lobdell, J. E.
  1974   The Scoggin Site: A Study in McKean Typology. *Plains Anthropologist* 19:123–128.
Loendorf, L. L., and J. L. Brownell
  1980   The Bad Pass Trail. *Archaeology in Montana* 21:11–102.
Malouf, C.
  1958   Outline of Montana Prehistory and History. *Montana Almanac:*106–128.
McCracken, H., ed.
  1978   *The Mummy Cave Project in Northwestern Wyoming.* Buffalo Bill Historical Center, Cody, Wyo.
McGuire, D. A., K. Joyner, R. Kainer, and M. Miller
  1984   Final Report of Archaeological Investigations of the Medicine Bow Mine Archaeological District in the Hanna Basin, Southcentral Wyoming. Mariah Associates, Laramie, Wyo.
Metcalf, M. D.
  1973   Archaeology at Dipper Gap: An Archaic Campsite, Logan County, Colorado. M.A. thesis, Department of Anthropology, Colorado State University, Fort Collins.
Millar, J. F. V., H. Epp, T. W. Foster, and G. Adams
  1972   The Southwestern Saskatchewan Archeological Project. *Napao* 3:14–21.
Mulloy, W. T.
  1954a *Archaeological Investigations in the Shoshone Basin of Wyoming.* University of Wyoming Publications in Science, vol. 18, no. 1. Laramie.
  1954b The McKean Site in Northeastern Wyoming. *Southwestern Journal of Anthropology* 10:432–460.
  1958   *A Preliminary Historical Outline for the Northwestern Plains.* University of Wyoming Publications in Science, vol. 22, no. 1. Laramie.
  1965   *Archaeological Investigations along the North Platte River in Eastern Wyoming.* University of Wyoming Publications in Science, vol. 31, no. 2. Laramie.
Nero, R. W., and B. A. McCorquodale
  1958   Report on an Excavation at the Oxbow Dam Site. *Blue Jay* 16:82–92.
Reeves, B. O. K.
  1969   The Southern Alberta Paleo-Cultural Paleo-Environmental Sequence. In *Post-Pleistocene Man and His Environments on the Northern Plains,* edited by R. G. Forbis, L. B. Davis, O. A. Christensen, and G. Fedirchuk, 6–46. University of Calgary Archaeological Association, Proceedings of the first annual Paleo-Environmental Workshop.
  1973   The Concept of an Altithermal Cultural Hiatus in Northern Plains Prehistory. *American Anthropologist* 75:1121–1153.
  1978a Bison Killing in the Southwestern Alberta Rockies. In *Bison Procurement and Utilization: A Symposium,* edited by L. B. Davis and M. Wilson, 63–78. Plains Anthropologist Memoir no. 14.
  1978b Head-Smashed-In: 5500 Years of Bison Jumping in the Alberta Plains. In *Bison Procurement and Utilization: A Symposium,* edited by L. B. Davis and M. Wilson, 151–174. Plains Anthropologist Memoir no. 14.
  1983   General Remarks on Native Subsistence Adaptations in the Great Plains. In

Man and the Changing Environments in the Great Plains: A Symposium, 115–118. Transactions of the Nebraska Academy of Sciences, vol. 11. Lincoln.

Reeves, B. O. K., and J. F. Dormarr
1972 A Partial Holocene Pedological and Archaeological Record from the Southern Alberta Rocky Mountains. *Arctic and Alpine Research* 4:325–336.

Reher, C. A.
1974 Population Study of the Casper Site Bison. In *The Casper Site: A Hell Gap Bison Kill on the High Plains*, edited by G. C. Frison, 113–124. Academic Press, New York.
1983 Analysis of Spatial Structure in Stone Circle Sites. In *From Microcosm to Macrocosm: Advances in Tipi Ring Investigation and Interpretation*, edited by L. B. Davis, 193–222. Plains Anthropologist Memoir no. 19.

Shay, C. T.
1971 *The Itasca Bison Kill Site: An Ecological Analysis*. Minnesota Historical Society, St. Paul.

Steege, L. C.
1960 Probable Middle Period Burial in Wyoming. *Plains Anthropologist* 5:82–83.

Strong, W. D.
1935 *An Introduction to Nebraska Archeology*. Smithsonian Miscellaneous Collections, vol. 93, no. 10. Washington, D.C.

Swanson, E. H., B. R. Butler, and R. Bonnichsen
1964 *Birch Creek Papers No. 2: Natural and Cultural Stratigraphy in the Birch Creek Valley of Eastern Idaho*. Idaho State University Museum, Occasional Papers, no. 14. Pocatello.

Syms, E. L.
1969 The McKean Complex as a Horizon Marker in Manitoba and on the Northern Great Plains. M.A. thesis, Department of Anthropology, University of Manitoba, Winnipeg.

Walker, E. G.
1992 *The Gowen Site: An Early Archaic Site on the Northern Plains*. National Museums of Canada, National Museum of Man, Mercury Series, Archaeological Survey of Canada, Paper no. 145. Ottawa, Ont.

Weaver, J. E.
1968 *Prairie Plants and Their Environments: A Fifty Year Study in the Midwest*. University of Nebraska Press, Lincoln.

Wedel, W. R., W. M. Husted, and J. Moss
1968 Mummy Cave: Prehistoric Record from the Rocky Mountains of Wyoming. *Science* 160:184–186.

Wettlaufer, B. N.
1955 *The Mortlach Site in the Besant Valley of Central Saskatchewan*. Saskatchewan Museum of Natural History, Anthropological Series, no. 1. Regina.

Wettlaufer, B. N., and W. J. Mayer-Oakes
1960 *The Long Creek Site*. Saskatchewan Museum of Natural History, Anthropological Series, no. 2. Regina.

Wheeler, R. P.
1954a Selected Projectile Point Types of the United States II. *Bulletin of the Oklahoma Anthropological Society* 2:1–6.
1954b Two New Projectile Point Types: Duncan and Hanna Points. *Plains Anthropologist* 1:7–14.

1957   Archeological Remains in Three Reservoir Areas in South Dakota and Wyoming. Manuscript on file, National Park Service, Midwest Archeological Center, Lincoln, Neb.

Willey, G. R., and Philip Phillips
    1958   *Method and Theory in American Archaeology.* University of Chicago Press, Chicago.

Zeimens, G. N., D. N. Walker, T. K. Larson, J. Albanese, and G. W. Gill
    1976   The Dunlap–McMurry Burial, 48NA67, Natrona County, Wyoming. *Wyoming Archaeologist* 22:15–25.

6. The Central and Southern Plains Archaic

Marvin Kay

In the past 30 years, there have been major advances in knowledge about the Archaic period on the Central and Southern Plains. One of the major keys to that advance lies in the recent large-scale excavation programs that are beginning to unlock the secrets of the Archaic hunters and gatherers. The vastly accelerated radiocarbon dating of Archaic sites and sediments of equivalent age is also of paramount importance. It is now possible to recognize some major chronological units and cultural processes that characterized life in the mid-American grasslands during the middle Holocene. Nevertheless, the record is and always will be spotty and very incomplete. The reasons are both poor preservation and inadequate sampling, as Reeves (1973) recognized, along with the likelihood that some Plains areas were actually abandoned during this period.

The Archaic is defined here as lasting from about 8500 to 2500 radiocarbon years before the present. Neither boundary necessarily marks an abrupt change in lifestyle from that which preceded or followed it, although the upper boundary is more defensible on typological grounds as the time when pottery making became widespread on at least the Central Plains. The lower boundary of 8500 years ago is one of convenience, for there are few changes in either artifact style or lifestyle that separate the Archaic from the terminal Paleo-Indian period, although by 8500 years ago there was probably a fully modern Plains fauna. In addition, beginning about 8500 years ago, the Prairie Peninsula started to establish itself on the eastern margin of the Plains (King 1980), and there are the beginnings of complementary cultural developments in both the Plains and the Prairie Peninsula.

The middle Holocene is roughly coeval with the Plains Archaic period, and the Hypsithermal is the major middle Holocene climatic interval—an "episode of warmer and/or drier climate preceding the Neoglaciation [having] continental dimensions but rather indefinite temporal boundaries" (Wright 1976:594). The Hypsithermal is a time-transgressive unit that reached its maximum at varying times and was of unequal duration in different parts of North America.

Evidence of Hypsithermal and early Neoglaciation environment has come from investigations of Plains Archaic sites and from nonarchaeological contexts. These data are important in and of themselves, and they have the additional benefit of defining aspects of the Plains ecosystem that were critical to human survival during the middle Holocene. We also now have a keener appreciation of the dynamic character of Holocene depositional systems that have preserved (as well as destroyed) Archaic sites.

This chapter comments on the Central and Southern Plains Archaic from two perspectives. First, a culture-historical overview of this period is offered for the Central and Southern Plains. In this, the evidence for habitation of the Central Plains heartland during the mid-Holocene drought is heightened by an examination of mainly deeply buried sites from Nebraska to southern Texas and eastern New Mexico. Second, subsistence and settlement data and models are summarized.

Culture History

The Central and Southern Plains are defined as roughly approximating Fenneman's (1931:1–90) Great Plains physiographic province, as well as following conventional archaeological usage. The mountainous and lava-strewn parts of eastern New Mexico and southeastern Colorado with desert shrub vegetation are, however, excluded. But, parts of the western tall-grass prairies of the Central Lowland are added. Our narrative therefore involves five separate sections of the Great Plains that provide a rough framework for our culture history (Figure 6.1).

Central Plains

DISSECTED TILL PLAINS

The Dissected Till Plains includes extreme eastern Nebraska and northeastern Kansas, extending east to near the Mississippi River and south to the Missouri and Kansas rivers in Missouri and Kansas. It is a flat till plain having a relief of 100 to 300 feet or more, mantled by loess, generally a few feet thick, but as much as 90 feet deep near large bordering streams (Fenneman 1938:589). As the distance from the Missouri River increases, the loess mantle gradually thins, but to the east of the river is a belt of loess-modified topography about 40 miles wide. This belt marks the eastern margin of the area we consider here.

The Missouri River valley, its uplands and tributary streams of western Iowa and eastern Nebraska, contain many important Archaic sites. Prominent among them are the multilayered Logan Creek and Cherokee sites, and several related bison kills and human burial sites in Iowa (Anderson et al. 1980). The most extensively analyzed site is Cherokee (Anderson and Semken 1980), but preliminary studies are available for Logan Creek. The most recent discovery extends

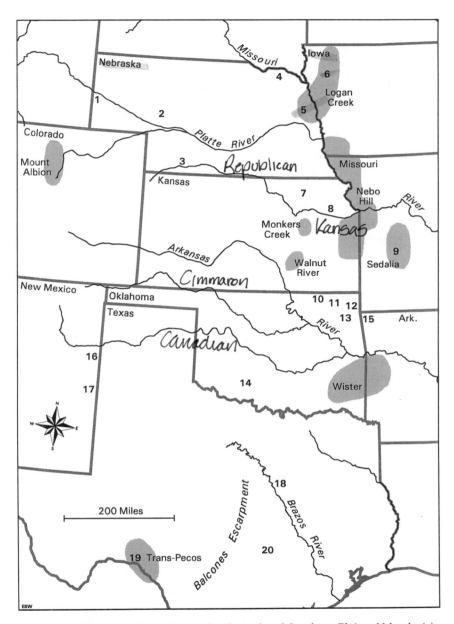

Figure 6.1. Selected Archaic sites on the Central and Southern Plains: *Nebraska* (1) Signal Butte, (2) Dry Lake, (3) Spring Creek, (4) Tramp Deep, (5) Logan Creek; *Iowa* (6) Cherokee; *Kansas* (7) Coffey, (8) Sutter; *Missouri* (9) Rodgers Shelter, Phillips Spring; *Oklahoma* (10) Lizard, (11) Lawrence, (12) Afton, (13) Packard, (14) Gore Pit; *Arkansas* (15) Albertson; *New Mexico* (16) San Jon, (17) Blackwater Draw; *Texas* (18) Bear Creek Shelter, (19) Bonfire Shelter, (20) Wilson–Leonard.

the area of interest farther up the Missouri River to the Rustad Quarry, in south-eastern North Dakota. Logan Creek is nevertheless the most widely known of these sites, and here we refer to these mainly western Iowa and eastern Nebraska sites as the Logan Creek complex because it is the most widely recognized descriptive label.

Radiocarbon dates from Logan Creek, from four other sites in Iowa—Cherokee, Simonsen, Hill, and Lungren—and from Rustad Quarry in North Dakota firmly place the complex between about 8600 and 6000 years ago. Other dates on bone, one as recent as 2815 years ago, are cited for Turin and Lewis Central School, two other Iowa sites that appear to belong to the same complex (Anderson et al. 1980:263). It is unlikely that the Logan Creek complex lasted as long as the latter date suggests, especially in light of the typological evidence for later Archaic materials in eastern Nebraska. For the moment, a terminal date of about 6000 years ago seems the more acceptable alternative.

The Logan Creek complex is described by Anderson and others (1980:261–267), who have defined both its relation to middle Holocene environments and the variability of its artifacts and site usages. Some change in diagnostic artifacts is shown by an early use of lanceolate points, plus the "typical" Logan Creek side-notched point, which is the single element that is consistent over time and space. This point is concave-based, generally with the haft ground on its lateral margins. If the Cherokee site is indicative, the sources of raw materials for chipped-stone tools are in local glacial drift and in a Pennsylvanian chert from southeastern Nebraska and southwestern Iowa. The presence of northern or High Plains raw materials such as Tongue River silicified sediment, Knife River Flint, and Bijou Hills Quartzite does not necessarily imply trade or exchange, as they are found in local glacial deposits. Perhaps the presence of the Pennsylvanian chert denotes a large area of exploitation beyond the area of known sites, but still within the Missouri valley. If so, the area would include the Walker–Gilmore site in Cass County, Nebraska, and might explain the presently enigmatic date of about 6090 years ago on charcoal obtained from a deeply buried hearth there.

Sites of the Logan Creek complex are functionally divided into campsites, bison kills, and human burial sites. The type site plus Cherokee, Hill, Lungren, Rustad Quarry, and Soldow are classed as encampments on the basis of their architecture and technology. Cherokee was repeatedly occupied during the winter months, probably by small multifamily groups dependent primarily on bison, although other species such as deer were also taken. Simonsen Zone 7, dated about 8430 years ago, is interpreted as a bison kill; it yielded a ground-stone ax, anvil stones, knives, and side-notched projectiles. At Pisgah, another bison kill, parts of a single animal were associated with a side-notched point. Turin and Lewis Central School contrast in being human burial sites containing several individuals each. One of the Turin burials, an adolescent, was a primary interment flexed on its right side, sprinkled with red ocher, and having 18 shell beads near its ankles. Lewis Central School is an ossuary of 25 burials with utilitarian grave goods made of locally available resources. A single burial event is inferred of primary and secondary burials, including bundle or broadcast burials (fragmented human bones scattered in an archaeological context as it was being deposited [Wood 1967:112]). The primary burials are flexed on their right sides, as at Turin, but are without ocher.

"Logan Creek" points are often identified in the Plains outside the nuclear area. Indeed, the evidence of medium-size side-notched points supplanting late Paleo-Indian–period lanceolates after 8500 years ago is about the only reason to classify later material assemblages as "Archaic." But until detailed studies are undertaken, it is premature to classify side-notched points from outside the nuclear area as Logan Creek. Anderson and others (1980:261–262) find great variation in these points, both within and between sites. Contrary to other opinions (Benedict 1981; Benedict and Olsen 1978; Grange 1980), there is little reason to accept the premise that most Plains Archaic side-notched points are identifiable as Logan Creek. There is even less justification for accepting arguments for migrations on the Plains during the Hypsithermal if "Logan Creek points" are the primary evidence.

The coherence of Logan Creek as a complex is due to three factors. First is the buried stratigraphic and radiometric contexts of its components for the period about 8600 to 6000 years ago. Second, the technology of its site assemblages implies a common social base, dependent on local resources, with a diagnostic expression chiefly in the Logan Creek point. Third, the diversity of site functions through time and space suggests a successful adaptation to changing Hypsithermal conditions in the eastern prairies.

After Logan Creek, there is a hiatus in the radiocarbon-dated record of Archaic sites in the area, lasting until about 3000 years ago. Investigations in Knox County, Nebraska, of the Tramp Deep and 25KX15 sites produced McKean-like points in preceramic contexts (Howard and Gant 1966). Radiocarbon dates on Tramp Deep charcoal, ranging between about 3000 and 2500 years ago, confirm the probable McKean affiliation and provide a baseline for Central Plains Woodland complexes, since pottery was associated with the most recent date.

A possible age equivalent of the Knox County sites is the Dry Lake Mortuary complex of central and northeastern Nebraska (Carlson and Steinacher 1978:7–8). The type site, Dry Lake, is in the Nebraska Sand Hills; to the south is another site on the Republican River; and two sites are in the Dissected Till Plains to the west of the Missouri valley. None of them is radiocarbon-dated, but all share similarities in grave goods and the use of red ocher. Projectile points are medium in size, with expanding stems; other grave goods include boatstones, marine-shell beads, bone awls, copper staining, and mica. A large sandal-sole gorget of marine shell is regarded as the most diagnostic artifact for dating purposes. Similar artifacts occur in Glacial Kame sites in Canada and the north-eastern United States, believed to predate 3000 years ago. Carlson and Stei-nacher assign a probable age of between 3950 and 2450 years ago for Dry Lake. The complex is among the first in the region to document the interregional exchange of exotic goods.

Farther south in Kansas and Missouri are several radiocarbon-dated Archaic sites or site complexes: sequentially, they are the Sutter and Coffey sites, and the Nebo Hill complex.

Sutter is among the oldest radiocarbon-dated sites in Kansas, with an age of about 7825 years ago. It is on a small tributary of the Kansas River just west of Topeka; occupations associated with bison were at depths of 25 to 30 feet below the surface. Four projectile points are the only diagnostic artifacts and include a lanceolate specimen and three weakly shouldered, straight-stemmed speci-mens (Katz 1971:Figure 12). Katz (1973:168) regards them as similar to points from the late Paleo-Indian Frederick and Cody complexes, although one need not go to the High Plains to find an analogue: all four points resemble speci-mens from sites in the western Missouri Ozarks from the same period.

Deeply buried in alluvium, the multicomponent Coffey site (Schmits 1978) is in the Blue River valley, north of Manhattan, Kansas. The fine-grained stra-tigraphy, the radiocarbon dating of discrete living floors, the good preservation of faunal and floral remains, and the distinctiveness of its artifact assemblages make Coffey an invaluable resource for Plains Archaic studies. The radiocarbon time span for the site is from about 5270 to 5055 years ago.

Coffey's several short-term encampments contain no identified structures, but they may have existed because isolated postholes were defined. Habitation floors typically had multiple hearths. Floral and faunal studies, together with the site's cyclical history of flooding, suggest occupation during drier summer, fall, and winter seasons. The vertebrate fauna is truly impressive. Bison domi-nate the sample, followed in importance by deer, and then by other mammals, although fish and migratory fowl were also exploited. Floral remains are of wild species, including lamb's-quarter, hackberry, bullrushes, grape, knotweed, and Solomon's seal. Subsistence was based on local fauna and flora, placing heavy but not total reliance on bison and seasonal wild seeds, and on migratory wa-terfowl.

Coffey artifacts are paralleled in part by those from Monkers Creek–phase sites to the south, in east-central Kansas (Witty 1982), of which the Coffey-site Horizon II is probably a part. Of the four radiocarbon dates from the type site, William Young, only one date, of about 5400 years ago, is accepted; it corre-sponds in age to the earlier dates from Coffey. Fired mud-dauber nests and a single post mold are evidence of structures at William Young. Witty describes other (undated) sites as representatives of the phase along the eastern margin of, and east of, the Flint Hills, a limestone escarpment that extends from north to south through east-central Kansas and forms the eastern topographic boundary of the High Plains in this region.

Monkers Creek stone tools are made of local materials; cherts from the Flint Hills dominate the chipped stone. Assemblages include a variety of chipped- and ground-stone tools, bone tools, and—significantly—ceramic artifacts. Two fired-clay effigies of human heads were found at William Young. These figurines are at least one millennium older and differ in style from a cache of three ceramic figurines from the Pecos valley in Texas. A tubular bead of fired clay was also recovered from Horizon III-5 at Coffey (Schmits 1978:124). These ceramic items, plus the chipped-stone hoe, gouge, and celt, are suggestive of technological continuity with the later but contrastive Nebo Hill complex, which included the production of fiber-tempered pottery.

To the north and east of the Monkers Creek area is Nebo Hill, a complex whose known sites are principally along the Kansas–Missouri border, with Kansas City near its center. Other sites that have Nebo Hill lanceolates are found to the southeast on the margin of the Dissected Till Plains. Nebo Hill has intrigued Plains archaeologists since its first description (Shippee 1948). The distinctive Nebo Hill lanceolate was at first regarded as a Paleo-Indian form, and later as Early Archaic. Other writers have disagreed about the age of the point. Only recently has radiometric dating assigned Nebo Hill to the period about 4500 to 2600 years ago. Reid (1984) provides the most thorough appraisal of Nebo Hill.

Nebo Hill–phase sites include extensive upland areas bordering the Missouri River valley, smaller lowland encampments on the Missouri's tributaries, and, apparently, isolated upland artifact caches or burial mounds that lack chambers. Reid's (1984) seasonal-use hypothesis, which differentiates between warm-weather social aggregation in the uplands and cold-weather segmentation in the lowlands, is provocative but lacks an empirical foundation other than that accorded by topography. Further confounding the issue is the probability of alluvial encampments being subject to periodic burial by flooding, while upland sites may well have been eroded. Nevertheless, upland encampments are by far the larger, contain greater quantities of material, and are architecturally differentiated from the lowland sites because they lack structures.

Two probable house structures are described for a lowland Nebo Hill site in Kansas. A line of burned clay and probable post molds define the walls of a burned structure. Upland Nebo Hill–site "structures," on the contrary, are inferred from a lack of debris in discrete oval areas between midden and hearth areas. The Kansas houses differ in that each has its own artifact scatter in which there were Nebo Hill points, fiber-tempered pottery, human-effigy fragments of fiber-tempered and untempered pottery, a rolled copper bead, and a lump of galena.

The upland caches and burial mounds near the Iowa–Missouri border include two biface caches and a mortuary site that represent the northernmost extension of probable Nebo Hill sites. An additional biface cache is near the Nebo Hill site. An earthen mound on Wolfden Ridge on the Platte–Clay county line in Kansas City, Missouri, excavated in 1879 by Edward Curtiss of the Peabody Museum, contained burial goods similar to items from the caches, but radiocarbon dating indicates a Middle Woodland age. The mortuary site near the Iowa border contained at least six burials with four fragmentary Etley points. The major items in these cache or mound sites are either large corner-notched Etley points or side-notched Osceola points, most if not all of them of Burlington Chert, which outcrops only in central Missouri; hence in the Kansas City area, it is an exotic raw material. Much of the chipped chert from Nebo Hill habitation sites is from local sources.

Diagnostic Nebo Hill artifacts include manos, three-quarter-grooved axes, bifacial hoes, and lanceolate projectile points. The last are variable in shape, ranging from the "typical" long and narrow lanceolate with a diamond-shape or lenticular cross section to often less distinctive lanceolates that are generally not as long, are broader, and have a biconvex cross section and a concave base. The latter is similar to the Sedalia lanceolate, which is also common on Nebo Hill and other Late Archaic sites.

Fiber-tempered pottery occurs at sites in Missouri, including Nebo Hill itself, and at a site in Kansas. Reid (1984) has described the pottery as having shredded grasses and sedge (but with some grog particles) evenly mixed into the clay as temper. It is undoubtedly of local manufacture and is technologically distinct from contemporary fiber-tempered pottery in the southeastern United States, which often contains a core of plant fibers enveloped by slabs of clay.

Subsistence data for Nebo Hill are limited to the hulls of black walnuts and hickory nuts, the seeds of lamb's-quarter, and a vertebrate fauna minimally of deer, fish, turtle, bird, and squirrel. No tropical cultigens have been recovered, although both cultigens and a fragmentary Nebo Hill lanceolate occur in contemporary contexts in Phillips Spring, a Sedalia-complex site in the western Ozark Highland (Kay 1983). It is therefore best to reserve judgment about specifics of the Nebo Hill hunting and gathering economy.

OSAGE PLAINS

In Kansas, all the other radiocarbon-dated Archaic sites are in the Osage Plains, the southern extension of the Central Lowland Province below the Dissected Till Plains that continues into the Southern Plains of Oklahoma and Texas. The earliest of these is the Stigenwalt site on Big Hill Creek, a tributary of the Verdigris River in Southeastern Kansas. The stream continues into eastern Oklahoma and is noted for other deeply buried Archaic sites. Stigenwalt has large rock-lined hearths and burned-rock scatters buried in alluvium and colluvial fans; an odd assortment of stemmed, basally notched, and one lanceolate projectile point, described (Thies 1990) as the Stigenwalt complex; and an impressive inventory of animal remains that date between 8800 and 7500 years ago. An occasional deer occurs along with the host of small mammals that come from the hearths and are as likely as the deer to be food remains. Equally significant are the Archaic sites along the Walnut River, an affluent of the Arkansas River in Butler County, Kansas. Several stratified sites were found in its alluvium; best known is the Snyder site. The sites postdate Monkers Creek and either predate or are coeval with Nebo Hill. These components are at least superficially similar in artifact types to the Nebo Hill and Sedalia sites, and lanceolates reminiscent of Sedalia are found here and elsewhere in the Osage Plains.

The Walnut River sequence of three preceramic (Chelsea, El Dorado, and Walnut) and one ceramic (Butler) phases near the Iowa–Missouri border was first established at Snyder (Grosser 1977). This sequence has been applied to other Walnut River sites, several of which are now radiocarbon-dated, and to other Osage Plains localities in both the Central and Southern Plains. New stratigraphic and radiocarbon data allow new means to reevaluate this sequence (Leaf 1979:10–11).

The Walnut valley sequence represents a stratified chronicle partly correlated by radiocarbon dating, cross dating of artifact types, and reconstructed subsistence patterns. The sites are primarily habitation sites, but there is reason to suspect that some, especially the Chelsea (4150 to 3980 or 4750 to 3450 years ago) and El Dorado (3980 to 3100 years ago) units at Snyder, might be seasonal base camps with houses and on-site mortuary areas (Grosser 1977:124–129). The mortuary practices of the El Dorado phase and in coeval, eastern Central Plains border sites were primary flexed burials of adult females and adolescents. Unless it is an artifact of site sampling, adult males were perhaps given burial treatment different from that of women and children.

The faunal remains are impressive; they are, indeed, superior to the subsistence records recovered from contemporaneous Nebo Hill sites. A partial list of the animal remains from the Chelsea and El Dorado sites includes bison, deer, antelope, beaver, raccoon and other furbearers, fish, fowl, mussels, and a domestic dog (from a prepared burial). Only deer and bison were recovered from the Walnut phase (3100 to 1970 years ago) sample at Snyder.

No tropical or potential native cultigens are among the plant remains for any of the sites. Wild floral remains from Chelsea and El Dorado contexts include hackberry and two species of goosefoot seeds. Other El Dorado–phase floral remains include pigweed. Both species of goosefoot plus walnut are known from Chelsea-phase contexts. Clearly, for most of the Walnut valley sequence, the broad exploitation of plant and animal species is much like the pattern at Coffey, but without a corresponding emphasis on the seasonal exploitation of waterfowl.

Plains Border

West of the Osage Plains and Dissected Till Plains is the Plains Border, the eastern margin of the High Plains. The region is a wide, irregular zone marked in many places by a scarp, and extends from the Canadian River in Oklahoma to southern Nebraska. The Plains Border is almost terra incognita as far as the Archaic is concerned.

Deeply buried preceramic components are, however, known along tributaries of the Republican River in Frontier County, Nebraska. Several sites on Lime Creek document Paleo-Indian habitations. One of these, Red Smoke, also contained three later occupations that may represent a McKean unit (Davis 1953:383). The Allen site, on Medicine Creek, differs typologically from the Paleo-Indian components at Red Smoke and Lime Creek and has been assigned by Holder and Wike (1949) to the Frontier complex, which may be the earliest Archaic manifestation in western Nebraska. The meaning of the Frontier complex, however, remains in doubt because of a host of typological, stratigraphic, and radiocarbon-dating problems. Recent radiocarbon dating indicates a time frame predating 8500 years ago; subsistence data indicate a "generalized, 'Archaic-like' adaptation" (Bamforth 1991:336).

Farther west is another, and much less ambiguous, terrace site at the confluence of Spring Creek and Red Willow Creek. The Spring Creek site is the best documented and clearly dated Archaic site on the Plains Border. It appears to have been a general-purpose base camp of about 5700 years ago. The settlement contained a series of widely spaced hearths, bone piles, a possible storage pit, and at least one probable post mold (Grange 1980:12–47).

Subsistence remains at Spring Creek are dominated by bison, augmented by deer, antelope, beaver, small mammals, and migratory waterfowl. Bone artifacts include fleshers, socketed digging implements, awls, a shaft wrench, and a bird-bone bead. Ground-stone items consist of a grinding slab and manos that were used, in part, to grind hematite into powder. The major-chipped stone tools are scrapers and points, of which "lanceolate" and side-notched forms are typical. The notched points are similar to those at Logan Creek. Grange (1980:47) regards them as socially linked to but later than Logan Creek points and as the possible product of "a westward movement of hunters and collectors of the Plains Archaic cultural tradition." Site intrusion is not the only—or even the most probable—explanation for similarities in point form, as discussed earlier.

High Plains

The High Plains (including the Osage Plains) extends into the Southern Plains. It is a long narrow region stretching from the boundary of South Dakota almost to the Rio Grande. Its surface in several areas is flat and almost untouched by erosion. There are extensive dune fields, or sand hills, principally in north-central Nebraska, and occasional breaks in the topography such as the Pine Ridge Escarpment in northwestern Nebraska. The Loess Plains to the east and south of the Sand Hills mantle the areas along the generally east-flowing streams. These physiographic divisions have served as useful dividing lines for studies of later cultural periods and probably will also for the Archaic as more work is done.

Recognized Archaic sites are principally of the McKean complex in western Nebraska. Similar and earlier Archaic sites are documented for the Colorado Piedmont and the Colorado Front Range. Sites potentially earlier than McKean are identified at a Kimball County site and at two other sites in Cheyenne County, in western Nebraska, on the basis of "generalized side-notched points that may be related to the Bitterroot and/or Salmon River types" (Carlson and Steinacher 1978:5), which Reeves (1973) estimates to date to about 4950 years ago. Other Logan Creek–like sites are noted to the east in the Sand Hills and Loess Plains (Carlson and Steinacher 1978:Figure 1).

The North Platte River and Lodgepole Creek valleys in western Nebraska compose the main area of High Plains McKean sites (Carlson and Steinacher 1978:Figure 3). McKean sites also extend along the South Platte from just below the Nebraska line to the Denver area, and across the divide into the headwaters of the Arkansas River; others are farther west, in the Colorado Piedmont or at even higher elevations in the Front Range.

McKean components are known at three sites on Lodgepole Creek and at two butte-top camps on the North Platte: Barn Butte and Sheep Mountain. The primary McKean investigations, however, center on two other North Platte sites: Signal Butte (Strong 1935) and Ash Hollow Cave (Champe 1946). Signal Butte's three stratified occupational strata include two preceramic units having diagnostic McKean artifacts and a range of radiocarbon dates from 4550 to 2630 years ago. These dates equate well with other McKean-complex dates from Wyoming, South Dakota, and Colorado, but older dates also occur. The final Signal Butte unit is ceramic. Ash Hollow Cave's preceramic strata are correlated with the second Signal Butte unit (Champe 1946:57), lack radiocarbon dating, and have an identified fauna of antelope, bison, deer, beaver, and jackrabbit. Nearly identical species are recorded at McKean encampments on the Northern Plains (Brumley 1975; Quigg 1986).

Diagnostic McKean artifacts include a variety of projectile points. The dominant forms at Signal Butte are McKean lanceolates. Strong (1935) described stemmed points as varieties of the lanceolate ones, now typed as Duncan and Hanna (Wheeler 1954). Adding to the debate over the validity of these types (Frison 1978:49–50) is Quigg's (1986) report of the southern Saskatchewan Crown site, where McKean and Hanna assemblages are stratigraphically separate.

Another point from the basal unit at Signal Butte is a thin, notched form described as rare, having a broad flange-like butt and a small rounded tip (Strong 1935:233, Plate 25, Figure 1e). This variety also occurs at a central Wyoming bison kill associated with McKean lanceolates, and is described as the Mallory type (Frison 1978:50). It is also found at McKean sites in the Colorado Piedmont (Benedict 1975:6–8, 11).

In sum, the High Plains McKean is a post-Hypsithermal complex occupying both short-grass prairies and mixed prairie–subalpine forests, involving at least seasonal exploitation of high mountain environments. Bison were killed at some sites, especially in Wyoming, but most of the High Plains sites are encampments that were reused periodically. Although data are sketchy, McKean subsistence involved a wide suite of large and small mammals. We have almost no data for plant use. McKean, however, seems to follow the Central Plains Archaic pattern, which capitalized on the local diversity of floral and faunal resources and sought bison wherever and whenever they could be found. The distinctive McKean, Duncan, Hanna, and Mallory points usually occur in the same contexts and may date anywhere from as early as about 4500 to 2500 years ago, and their co-occurence may reflect mixing of deposits—as judged from the Crown site in Saskatchewan (Quigg 1986).

Colorado Piedmont and Front Range

The eroded remnant of the High Plains to the east of the Front Range is the Colorado Piedmont, dissected primarily by the South Platte and Arkansas drainages. This region and the adjacent Front Range have well-defined, although partial, Archaic records that are largely overshadowed by the famous Paleo-Indian discoveries there. The number of preceramic investigations in the Colorado Piedmont is several orders of magnitude greater than for the High Plains.

There is a typological disparity between McKean and Magic Mountain, the unit that immediately precedes McKean in the Colorado Front Range and foothills near Denver (Benedict 1981:114; Irwin-Williams and Irwin 1966). Magic Mountain is dominated by medium-size, convex-based, corner-notched points. Bases are generally ground. Magic Mountain was originally regarded as an eastward extension of the Great Basin Desert culture, but more recent evidence suggests that it is a continuation of Mount Albion, a local complex having corner-notched points similar to those of Magic Mountain (Benedict 1981; Benedict and Olson 1978). Benedict summarizes evidence of a continuation of corner-notched points into the McKean period. Even so, a closer typological analogue for McKean is found in the earlier Oxbow (or Oxbow–McKean) complex of the Northern Plains (Frison 1978:45; Reeves 1973:Figure 6). It is most likely that

McKean ultimately derives from the Northwestern Plains. Whether its southward spread reflects migration or diffusion of a technological complex into existing local Archaic groups is undecided.

Magic Mountain is dated to about 5000 to 4600 years ago, and is potentially even earlier at the type site. Among the better-known components are those in alpine or subalpine settings (Ptarmigan and Coney Lake), including some at lower elevations, such as those along the Dakota Hogback: Magic Mountain, Lo-DaisKa, Willowbrook Shelter, and Van Bibber Creek. The distribution of Magic Mountain components is much the same as that of Mount Albion ones.

Mount Albion has radiocarbon dates from Hungry Whistler and another alpine site, and from two Dakota Hogback sites: Cherry Gulch and Helmer Ranch. These dates are within the interval from 5800 to 5600 years ago. There are no dated Mount Albion units after 5600 years ago, although both LoDaisKa and Magic Mountain are likely candidates. The lower boundary of 5800 years ago appears to be reliable, as a different assemblage of basally ground, concave-based obliquely flaked lanceolates (Frederick or Lusk) is radiocarbon-dated to between 6045 and 5880 years ago at Fourth of July Valley, another alpine site (Benedict 1981:62–92; Benedict and Olson 1973).

Preceding Mount Albion and Fourth of July Valley are even earlier Hypsithermal manifestations from the Colorado Front Range. Ptarmigan has a second component dated at 6450 to 6205 years ago. Possibly associated is a single side-notched point with a lightly ground, slightly convex base (Benedict 1981:103–104, 113). Another site, Caribou Lake, which yielded a large biface and a quartzite point base, is dated to 8460 years ago (Benedict 1974). Benedict describes the point base as probably from a Scottsbluff point.

These early Hypsithermal sites document Archaic high-altitude adaptations on the western Plains Border as well as seemingly abrupt changes in point styles. Best defined is Mount Albion, a Hypsithermal Front Range and Colorado Piedmont adaptation that may serve as a model for the earlier adaptations recorded at Fourth of July Valley, Ptarmigan, and Caribou Lake. In this context, the Mount Albion timberline adaptation may be viewed as distinctive from but related to that of the Colorado Piedmont. Among the more tangible activities is the driving of game at Hungry Whistler, which is complete with drive lines, cairns, and concealment pits (Benedict and Olson 1978). Game drives may have been a major activity, during the summers at least, when their use would not have been hampered by snow pack. Much of the raw material for chipped and ground stone can be traced to either the Dakota Hogback or its vicinity. The general settlement system was one of seasonal transhumance in the eastern parks and foothills of the Front Range. Mount Albion was a successful Hypsithermal adaptation to timberline and lower-elevation habitats. Obviously, neither the Colorado Piedmont nor the Front Range was abandoned because of a possibly adverse climate.

Southern Plains

HIGH PLAINS

The Llano Estacado, or Staked Plains, of Texas and New Mexico comprise an area of about 20,000 square miles, almost untouched by erosion. To the north, the Texas panhandle is entrenched by the Canadian River, and east and south of Amarillo are the headwaters of the Red River. In the central part of the Staked Plains are saucer-like depressions that provide either temporary sources of standing water or more permanent lakes. Dune fields also dot the landscape.

Preceramic sites are found along lake margins and within the dunes, and other sites are present in Yellowhouse and Blackwater draws, the two most famous such localities in the Llano Estacado. As elsewhere on the High Plains, Archaic sites are neither well known nor well documented. Archaic components include at least one bison kill and an encampment, dated to about 5000 years ago (J. Hester 1972:174), at Blackwater Locality No. 1, in New Mexico. An interesting aspect of the Archaic use of Blackwater Draw was the aboriginal hand excavation of about 20 wells, "dug to intersect a fallen water table" (Haynes 1975:83; J. Hester 1972:179). Bison are also noted at San Jon, in eastern New Mexico, in strata that date from about 7500 to 3600 years ago (Hill et al. 1995), but they are lacking at four Texas panhandle sites that postdate 4450 years ago (Dillehay 1974:182–183). Stafford's (1981:561–563) summary evaluates the archaeological potential of the Llano Estacado: The dearth of vertebrate and archaeological remains from between 8000 to 6000 years ago and 2000 to 1000 years ago suggests the reduced use or occupation of the canyons during Archaic and early Ceramic periods. Sedimentology, palynology, and invertebrate paleontology show increasing aridity between about 13,000 and 4900 years ago. How severely this drying cycle affected the environment for humans and animals on the Llano Estacado is unknown. The scarcity of archaeological and paleontological remains between 8000 to 6000 and 2000 years ago implies the decreased use, if not the selective abandonment, of the valleys during that time.

EDWARDS PLATEAU AND CENTRAL TEXAS

The Edwards Plateau lies immediately south of the Llano Estacado. Its level upland varies little from the terrain of the High Plains and is crossed by shallow valleys or draws. Save for where it grades into the Llano Estacado, the plateau's margins are deeply incised outfacing escarpments. The plateau is also entrenched by the 1000-foot-deep canyon of the Pecos River. West of the Pecos, the plateau ends at the Mexican Highland. West of the hundredth meridian, the plateau is a large grass-covered plain resembling the Llano Estacado.

The most famous and best understood Edwards Plateau locality is Trans-Pecos, which has a distinctive rock art, the Pecos River style. Among the most important sites for viewing the overall adaptive pattern, as described by Shafer (1981), are Bonfire Shelter, Hinds Cave, Baker Cave, Devil's Mouth, and Devil's Rockshelter. Although he was speaking of a larger region, Jelks's (1978:71) observation fits the lower Pecos region's nearly continuous Holocene chronicle as "perhaps the most tenaciously conservative prehistoric population in all of North America." This is especially so in terms of human adaptation to middle Holocene climate and environment, but has less validity in reference to diagnostic artifact styles. The most useful artifacts for chronological separation in this locality, and the rest of the Edwards Plateau and central Texas, are chipped-stone points. No uniform agreed-on classification exists for this area.

The Archaic is generally differentiated from Paleo-Indian by the lack of lanceolate forms. But recent excavations of the Wilson–Leonard site near Austin, Texas, document side-notched points greater than 10,000 years in age and replacement by lanceolates until at least 8500 years ago (Figure 6.2b). This site is deeply layered and is now the most meticulously dated of any Southern Plains Paleo-Indian or Archaic site (M. B. Collins, personal communication). Even so, whenever similar Archaic points occur, it is assumed that they are probably coe-

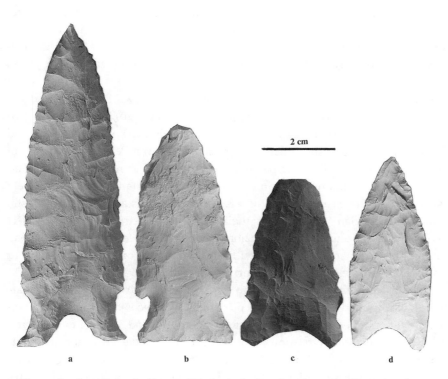

Figure 6.2. Late Paleo-Indian and Early Archaic points from the Central and Southern Plains: (*a*) Dalton; (*b*) Wilson; (*c*) Big Sandy, or Graham Cave Notched; (*d*) Golondrina–Barber.

val, an assumption strengthened by radiocarbon dates. The substance of Trans-Pecos chronology is now available. A complementary but roughly equivalent chronology exists for the eastern Edwards Plateau–central Texas section fronting on the Balcones Escarpment (Weir 1976). For the west Gulf Coastal Plain, Story (1985) uses an Early (7950 to 5450 or 4950 years ago), Middle (5450 or 4950 to 2950 years ago), and Late (2950 to 2150 years ago, extending in some areas to 750 years ago) Archaic format for organizing these data. The chronological units defined by Story and Weir are broad, but have the virtue of being keyed directly to radiocarbon-dated stratigraphy.

Story (1985) defined eight sequential periods for the Trans-Pecos; of these, Periods II through V apply to the Archaic and are roughly correlated with Weir's central Texas Archaic phases. Period II spans the interval from 8950 to 5950 years ago and generally corresponds to the central Texas San Geronimo phase (8000 to 4500 years ago). Stemmed, bifurcated-base forms (Gower and Uvalde) and basally notched points are common to both areas. Period III dates from 5950 to 4450 years ago and overlaps with the Clear Fork phase (5000 to 4000 years ago). For both areas, there is a continuation of stemmed forms (Nolan and Travis) and a lanceolate or weakly shouldered, stemmed variety (Pandale). Contracting-stemmed forms (Langtry, Almagre, and Val Verde) are chiefly found in Period IV (4450 to 2950 years ago) lower Pecos contexts, and an equivalent contracting-stemmed form with a bifurcated base (Pedernales) is the primary marker of the nearly equivalent Round Rock phase (4200 to 2600 years ago).

A seemingly abrupt transition in point styles follows Period IV and the Round Rock phase during Period V (2950 to 2150 years ago), or the San Marcos phase (2800 to 1800 years ago). Basally notched (Shumla) and corner-notched (Marshall and Marcos) specimens are typical in the lower Pecos at this time, but barbed, straight, or expanding-stemmed dart forms (Castroville, Montell, and Lange) are less common here than in central Texas. The latter forms are widely distributed in the eastern Edwards Plateau, central Texas, and Gulf Coastal Plain during the San Marcos phase; their widespread distribution is the subject of considerable speculation about major population movements during the San Marcos phase that may correlate with environmental or climatic change or population increase (Dibble 1975; Story 1985; Weir 1976).

Insights into human adaptation to an increasingly drier Holocene climate are best exemplified by the lower Pecos data. Lower Pecos hunting and gathering adaptation relied heavily on desert succulents as food and as raw materials for textiles and tools. First-line plant resources were plentiful and available throughout the year and included lechuguilla, sotol, and prickly pear leaves. Seasonally available secondary resources included acorns, walnuts, and pecans. As temperatures began to warm in the spring, yucca flowers became available, followed shortly by wild onion, edible forbs, prickly pear fruit, and persimmon.

Except for the Period V bison kill at Bonfire Shelter, "hunting provided a minimal but important amount of the total food intake" (Shafer 1981:136). Small animals were the standard fare and included everything from reptiles and small mammals to aquatic resources. Deer were only rarely taken. The net effect of these endeavors was to allow small human groups to live within the entrenched river systems for millennia in a stable, if not seasonally predictable, way.

The Period V bison kill at Bonfire Shelter has been dated to about 2600 years ago. Some 800 bison were driven off the precipice above the shelter during this time, in one or in several shortly spaced jumps. Because of the sheer number killed and the problems of managing a bison herd, Dibble (1975:109) favors several shortly spaced jumps. The primary weaponry is an assemblage of Montell, Castroville, and Lange dart types. For both the magnitude of the kill and stylistic considerations, Bonfire is an anomaly in the general lower Pecos Archaic adaptation.

Based on stylistic considerations, Dibble (1975:179) regarded the Period V bison hunters to have lived north of the lower Pecos and to have followed the animals south. There may be some basis to Dibble's ideas, since similar point forms co-occur in the Chelsea phase of south-central Kansas (Root 1981) and the coeval Sedalia phase of western Missouri, a millennium or more earlier, and they persist in western Missouri until about 2600 years ago (Kay 1983). Bison hunting is known at least for the Chelsea phase. A complementary argument has been that if a bison-range extension did occur then, it happened during a brief moist period. Story (1985) subscribes to the latter view and uses the mesic-interval idea as a partial explanation for the proliferation of San Marcos–phase sites in the eastern Edwards Plateau and central Texas.

The Edwards Plateau provides other vistas of Archaic culture that overall reflect a riverine-focused adaptation to increased Hypsithermal dryness. Burned rock middens are a common Edwards Plateau site type, although they are by no means restricted to either the Archaic or the region. These are habitation or probable habitation sites with a mounded appearance, apparently resulting from an accretion of living detritus. Other forms include "ring" middens with a depressed center. Most common is the rock-midden mound of variable size and thickness; representative examples are present at least as early as the Clear Fork phase and possibly even in the earlier San Geronimo phase (T. Hester 1971; Wesolowsky et al. 1976). Their presence is not chronologically sensitive, however, as they also occur later in the Archaic and are widely distributed throughout central Texas. Middens of this type are common to the Round Rock phase (Weir 1979).

A second basic midden form is the shell midden. Round Rock– and San Marcos–phase shell accumulations are reported from an unstratified site on a tributary of the Middle Concho River in Tom Green County (Green 1961). Devil's Hollow, on the Colorado River northwest of Austin, is a buried rock and shell ring midden with Bulverde and Bulverde-like points (early Round Rock phase?). Collins (1972:97) suggests a brief period of use for the site, "perhaps during a season of heavy plant-food or river mussel exploitation when deer were killed opportunistically" by a large group that used a communal oven. Despite the possibility of seasonal aggregation, there seems to be a virtue in recognizing the specialized use of the ring or crescent middens as probably communal ovens.

OSAGE PLAINS

South of Kansas, the Osage Plains sweep south and west across central and western Oklahoma and into Texas. Much, but not all, of the Oklahoma Archaic chronicle stems from investigations within this wide belt. Records also exist on its eastern flank in northeastern Oklahoma, northwestern Arkansas, and the Ouachita Mountains. North-central Texas above the Grand Prairie of the Central Texas Section and east of the Llano Estacado completes the picture. The Osage Plains are well watered in both Oklahoma and Texas, and the region is dissected by many small streams, along which most of the Archaic investigations have been made.

The history of Archaic investigations on the Osage Plains of Oklahoma and Texas is a long one, going back at least as far as Holmes's (1903) excavations of the sulfur springs near Afton, in northeastern Oklahoma. A later major phase of work was in the 1930s, with the Depression-era federal programs, especially the Works Project Administration (WPA). Analytical legacies of the WPA efforts are primarily of archival interest (Schambach 1988). These efforts did not strictly follow the Midwestern Taxonomic System, but a fatal objection to them is the haphazard mixing of materials from different time periods. For the Osage Plains Archaic, there continues to be a proliferation of site reports dealing with mixed materials, including an occasional summary that overstates the relevance of a potential Archaic site. Even so, major strides are being made where artifact style, stratigraphy, and radiocarbon dating are all brought to bear.

The oldest radiocarbon-dated Archaic component in the Osage Plains is the Gore Pit site, a buried series of some 30 burned rock middens within the city limits of Lawton, Oklahoma. Two radiocarbon dates are 6145±130 and 6030±300 years ago (Hammatt 1976:267–268).

On the northeastern fringe of the Osage Plains, in Benton County, Arkansas, and Mayes County, Oklahoma, are two other sites with deeply buried late Paleo-Indian/Early Archaic components (Dickson 1991; Wyckoff 1964, 1985, 1989) with radiocarbon dates on charcoal that predate those of Gore Pit. The earlier of the two is from Oklahoma, where Wyckoff has identified the Packard complex of Agate Basin–like lanceolate points and a side-notched dart point in the basal levels of the Packard site. Although originally believed to date to about 9400 years ago, new radiocarbon dating indicates that the Packard complex is from about 9800 years ago. For the most part, the Packard-complex artifacts are stratigraphically below Dalton points (Figure 6.2a) (charcoal from the Dalton zone is now dated to about 9600 years ago), and Wyckoff suggests that they represent an earlier assemblage with analogues to the Agate Basin complex of the Northern Plains. Were it not for differences in lithic materials, the Packard lanceolates would be hard to separate from Agate Basin points. The stratigraphic relations and priority of the Packard-complex artifacts over Dalton, however, are not as clear-cut as Wyckoff would like. One of the Packard lanceolates occurs well within the zone of Dalton materials, and there are substantial vertical differences among refitted specimens from either Packard or Dalton "components" at the site (see Wyckoff 1985).

These facts indicate a strong likelihood of stratigraphic mixing and redeposition of materials of either complex, and neither Dalton nor Packard artifacts should be viewed as being from unambiguous contexts. Thus Packard does not appear to be the kind of site to question the antiquity of the Dalton horizon (Goodyear 1982). Yet it does provide evidence of a seemingly unique early assemblage of Packard lanceolates that strikingly resemble Agate Basin points.

The Albertson site, in Arkansas, has a basal date of 8410±245 years ago from a hearth in deeply stratified alluvium. Associated artifacts include lanceolate points similar to those in Archaic sites of the eastern Plains Border areas.

Later dates for the Archaic of the Osage Plains are available from Texas and Oklahoma sites. A recent date from a Trinity River shell lens associated with a Carrollton point is reported as 3786 years ago (Shaw 1978:232). A slightly older date of 4150 years ago from Bear Creek Shelter, in the central Brazos River area of Hill County, central Texas, potentially may also date Carrollton and Trinity points. In any case, Bear Creek units that are probably coeval with the Round Rock phase lack Pedernales points and have specimens similar to those of Carrollton and Trinity (Lynott 1978:29–32, 84–85). Even discounting the Bear Creek date, the fact that the Trinity River date associated with a Carrollton point is almost two millennia later than the previous estimate (Crook and Harris 1959) is significant, and disagrees with conventional wisdom. If nothing else, this date calls into question the basic point typology for the Trinity River area (McCormick 1976:44, Figure 103), which presupposes that roughly similar forms were present in two sequentially discrete periods, with Carrollton and related forms dropping out by 6000 years ago and Elam and other forms persisting from about 6000 to 4000 years ago.

The Osage Plains of Oklahoma yield few dates that postdate Gore Pit. A date of 2770 years ago came from Area 2 of 34GR12, in Greer County not far from Gore Pit. This site is the basis for the Summers complex (Leonhardy 1966), which remains something of an enigma. A single flexed human burial from Shelby County has an associated date of 3590 years ago (Bell 1968:44, 46). In north-central Oklahoma, a few sites in Nowata and Washington counties are also dated. The Lawrence site in Nowata County has four dates, ranging from 3460 to 2170 years ago. To the west, on a tributary of the Little Caney River in Washington County, the Lizard site has a date of 3810 years ago (Reid and Artz 1984:Table 7.5). The cultural affiliation of these north-central Oklahoma sites is still in doubt, but logically and chronologically equivalent units are found to the northwest in Kansas (Walnut River sites) and to the east or southeast in Arkansas and the Ouachita Mountains of Oklahoma.

A second charcoal date from the Albertson site, in Benton County, Arkansas, is 2850 years ago. This date is on an upper Stratum 4 hearth (Dickson 1991:24). It and the earlier date from Stratum 5 essentially bracket the Archaic sequence at Albertson, which represents a nearly continuous 6000-year chronicle.

The radiocarbon dating of what was first described by Bell (1980; Bell and Baerreis 1951) as Fourche Maline in the Ouachita Mountains has concentrated at five southeastern Oklahoma sites. Galm and Flynn (1978) discuss the radiometric dating of Scott and Wann, two LeFlore County sites. Other data are available for McCutchin–McLaughlin, in Latimer County, and for two sites in Pushmataha County: Bug Hill and 34PU102 (Altschul 1983; Vehik 1982). There are at least 66 radiocarbon dates from these five sites, 29 of which are earlier than 2500 years ago, but only 27 of which are accepted. It is now assumed that Fourche Maline is a ceramic phase or phases that is radiocarbon-dated to between 2150 and 1150 years ago and is preceded by a preceramic phase, the Wister phase, dating to about 3450 to 2150 years ago (Galm and Flynn 1978:155–156; see also Bell 1980; Schambach 1982). On typological and stratigraphic grounds, still earlier Archaic complexes appear to be present in this area (Wyckoff 1970:81–91). Among them is Tom's Brook, which is better defined in Arkansas as a riverine adaptation that dates to about 6600 years ago (Schambach 1988).

Of the Osage Plains Archaic excavations south of Kansas, it is instructive to return to the Gore Pit site. Its analysis and interpretation are representative of the problems and potentials associated with the Archaic. Buried beneath as much as 20 feet of alluvium, Gore Pit has several large circular basins filled with fire-cracked rock, charcoal, mussel shell, and an occasional animal bone. One of these middens, Feature 3, measured 6 by 8 feet and contained two rock and charcoal lenses separated by nearly rock-free sediment. This layering suggests the reuse of a covered earth oven. Shellfish or plant food undoubtedly was baked or steamed in these ovens, after which the blanket of soil and rock that sealed the oven was removed and the food was consumed. Occasionally, the process was repeated in the same oven. A single flexed human burial nearby yielded a bone-apatite date that suggests an Archaic affiliation. No diagnostic artifacts were recovered from the excavated features; the "diagnostic" artifacts were recovered by local collectors from areas around the middens or in zones of displaced hearth-rock refuse. Among the points are Paleo-Indian (Meserve?) to

Late Archaic types (Trinity, Enson, Darl, Ellis, and Gary). Thus the site is stratigraphically, radiometrically, and functionally interpretable, but it is impossible to assign it to a given taxon.

Placing Gore Pit within a regional Archaic taxonomic context, however, is less significant than the facts about the site itself. It is indisputably a Hypsithermal manifestation in the western Osage Plains. In terms of topography and location, it is similar to High Plains sites immediately to the west. Its deeply buried context in stream alluvium is a good example of where sites of similar age are likely to be found in the Southern Plains. Finally, Gore Pit affords valuable insight into local subsistence practices.

Conclusion

For neither the Central nor the Southern Plains is the Archaic a uniform period of cultural development. Rather, it is best conceived as a time of varied responses to a changing Holocene landscape, biota, and climate, on the one hand, and to equally dynamic hunting and gathering systems, on the other. Our understanding of these complex interrelationships is poor at best. Yet it is essential that we continue to examine Archaic lifestyles and development, for it is within this period of about 6000 years that Plains cultures adapted to the postglacial period, responded successfully to Hypsithermal climatic and environmental pressures, established identifiable groups that often conform to regional physiography, first experimented with ceramic technologies and with horticulture, and participated in exchange networks that extended well beyond the Plains.

No comprehensive framework presently exists for Archaic-period culture history. In this chapter, the basic data are presented following the terminology and time markers in general use in specific areas. As a strictly arbitrary division, we employ an Early (8500 or older to 6500 years ago), Middle (6500 to 4500 years ago), and Late (4500 to 2500 years ago) Archaic framework to identify the known complexes, phases, and representative sites in the following discussion of settlement and subsistence models.

Central and Southern Plains Archaic subsistence and settlement information is less than comprehensive, but regional or subregional contrasts are apparent. Site-level subsistence is the clearer of the two, but uncertainty exists in most cases about the seasonal food quest. Moreover, subsistence reconstructions based on single sites or even site complexes exhibit significant biases because of preservation, sampling procedures, and recovery technique so that even our "best" data imperfectly reflect past subsistence. Settlement reconstruction suffers from these and other problems. Chief among them are the inadequacies of intra-and intersite time control; a dearth of primary deposits, architectural features, and typological analysis of artifacts; and a general inability to identify short-lived habitation sites. For these and other reasons, one must approach the subject of Archaic subsistence and settlement with caution.

To the extent that settlement is conditioned by subsistence practices, at least five major settlement strategies are evident: (1) bison hunting that is communal or otherwise undertaken in planned or accidental trap situations; (2) the building and maintenance of hunting facilities that promote better management of large mammals; (3) the use of specialized plant and animal cooking facilities, seemingly during times of peak food abundance; (4) a "mixed" program anchored by food resources of high seasonal or local availability that further capitalizes on annually less predictable resources whose use was restricted to a season or an ecozone; and (5) small-scale horticulture following the introduction of tropical cultigens. It is possible that these five strategies were not mutually exclusive or that four of the five are subsumed by the fourth: the mixed program. For whatever reason, however, the five are usually identified with specific physiographic sections of the Central and Southern Plains or occur principally in one time period.

Sites such as Gore Pit in southwestern Oklahoma and Spring Creek in Nebraska afford a rare glimpse of subsistence and settlement on the Plains during the Hypsithermal. At both sites, subsistence was broadly based and generally conforms to the mixed-program model, although bison were also consumed at Spring Creek. In addition, both sites were deeply buried in alluvium, and their exposure was a direct result of modern construction. Farther to the southwest on the Llano Estacado in eastern New Mexico is the Middle Archaic component at Blackwater Draw, dating to about 5000 years ago. At this time, the draw was in part used as a bison kill, and a seemingly associated encampment significantly relied on hand-dug wells for water during a time of drought. Blackwater Draw is as illuminating an example as we have for the adaptability of Archaic hunters and gatherers to Hypsithermal conditions on the High Plains. These resourceful occupants of the High Plains literally dug in instead of abandoning the area during a time of extreme environmental stress (see also Meltzer 1991). Farther south, on the Edwards Plateau, is the equally irrefutable Hypsithermal chronicle from the lower Pecos. Here again, we see the successful application of the mixed program, in this case with bison absent and deer taken only rarely. The main staple was plant food supplemented by the meat of small animals.

Through the application of a mixed program, Archaic communities could withstand abrupt as well as more gradual environmental changes. Their responses varied according to the adaptational requirements of specific localities on a day-to-day, month-to-month, and year-to-year basis.

Claims for Archaic-period horticulture are justifiably disputed or controversial for the Southern and Central Plains, but there is some evidence of plant husbandry. The least credible are the claims of Archaic corn, or maize, in the Colorado Piedmont. These postulations are associated with several Magic Mountain sites near Denver and, more recently, with a possible Late Archaic burial near Weld, Colorado (Wanner and Brunswig 1992). The problem with the Magic Mountain sites is the high likelihood of stratigraphic mixing; for the Weld burial, the bone-collagen analysis of stable carbon isotopes also does not support maize consumption. It would be essential to use the new advances in radiocarbon dating to decide the issue for individual corn specimens. But none of these sites has unambiguous archaeological contexts that would justify the expense.

On the eastern margin of the Central Plains, the squash and bottle-gourd remains from Phillips Spring have been the subject of several analyses. Among the more recent assessments is Smith's (1992) study of the size and morphology of Phillips Spring squash seed that clearly shows them to be either a wild or a very primitive precursor of modern cultivated varieties. Even so, I regard the Phillips Spring evidence as crucial to the evaluation of Late Archaic horticulture on the eastern margin of the Plains. While there is good reason, as Smith and others have documented, not to accept the squash as a cultigen, the question of horticulture does not rest with the squash, but with its co-occurrence with bottle gourd. Unlike the squash, there is no record of indigenous bottle gourd in the American Midwest. Its presence at Phillips Spring in the same well-defined contexts as squash indicates that both plants were being grown as garden crops.

Acknowledgments

This review was made possible through the efforts of many colleagues who willingly shared information. I am especially indebted to Duane C. Anderson, James B. Benedict, Michael B. Collins, Don Dickson, Roger Grosser, C. Vance Haynes, Marvin F. Kivett, Mark J. Lynott, W. J. Mayer-Oakes, Elizabeth A. Morris, Kenneth C. Reid, Mark J. Root, Harry J. Shafer, Dee Ann Story, Randall M. Thies, Rain Vehik, Thomas A. Witty, and Don G. Wyckoff.

References

Altschul, J. H.
   1983   *Bug Hill: Excavation of a Multicomponent Midden Mound in the Jackfork Valley, Southeast Oklahoma.* New World Research, Report of Investigation, no. 81-1. Pollock, La.
Anderson, D. C., and H. A. Semken, Jr., eds.
   1980   *The Cherokee Investigations.* Academic Press, New York.
Anderson, D. C., R. Shutler, Jr., and W. M. Wendland
   1980   The Cherokee Sewer Site and the Cultures of the Atlantic Climatic Episode. In *The Cherokee Investigations,* edited by by D. C. Anderson and H. A. Semken, Jr., 257–274. Academic Press, New York.
Bamforth, D. B.
   1991   Population Dispersion and Paleoindian Technology at the Allen Site. In *Raw*

Material Economies Among Prehistoric Hunter-Gatherers, edited by by A. Montet-White and S. Holen, 357–374. University of Kansas, Publications in Anthropology, no. 19. Lawrence.

Bell, R. E.
  1968   Dating the Prehistory of Oklahoma. *Great Plains Journal* 7:42–52.
  1980   Fourche Maline: An Archaeological Manifestation in Eastern Oklahoma. In Caddoan and Poverty Point Archaeology: Essays in Honor of C. H. Webb. *Louisiana Archaeology* 6:83–125.

Bell, R. E., and D. A. Baerreis
  1951   A Survey of Oklahoma Archaeology. *Bulletin of the Texas Archeological and Paleontological Society* 22:7–100.

Benedict, J. B.
  1974   Early Occupation of the Caribou Lake Site, Colorado Front Range. *Plains Anthropologist* 19:1–4.
  1975   The Albion Boardinghouse Site: Archaic Occupation of a High Mountain Valley. *Southwestern Lore* 41:1–12.
  1981   *The Fourth of July Valley: Glacial Geology and Archeology of the Timberline Ecotone.* Center for Mountain Archeology, Research Report no. 2. Ward, Colo.

Benedict, J. B., and B. L. Olson
  1973   Origin of the McKean Complex: Evidence from Timberline. *Plains Anthropologist* 18:323–325.
  1978   *The Mount Albion Complex: A Study of Prehistoric Man and the Altithermal.* Center for Mountain Archeology, Research Report no. 1. Ward, Colo.

Brumley, J. H.
  1975   *The Cactus Flower Site in Southeastern Alberta: 1972–1974 Excavations.* National Museums of Canada, National Museum of Man, Mercury Series, Archaeological Survey of Canada, Paper no. 46. Ottawa, Ont.

Carlson, G. F., and T. L. Steinacher
  1978   A Preliminary Culture-Historical Sequence for the Plains Archaic Period in Nebraska. Paper presented at the symposium "Migration and Extinction in the Great Plains," Institute for Tertiary–Quaternary Studies, Lincoln, Neb.

Champe, J. L.
  1946   *Ash Hollow Cave: A Study of Stratigraphic Sequence in the Central Great Plains.* University of Nebraska Studies, n.s., no. 1. Lincoln.

Collins, M. B.
  1972   The Devil's Hollow Site: A Stratified Archaic Campsite in Central Texas. *Bulletin of the Texas Archeological Society* 43:77–100.

Crook, W. W., and R. K. Harris
  1959   C-14 Date for Late Carrollton Focus Archaic Level: 6,000 Years B.P. *Oklahoma Anthropological Society Newsletter* 8, no. 3:1–2.

Davis, E. M.
  1953   Recent Data from Two Paleo-Indian Sites on Medicine Creek, Nebraska. *American Antiquity* 18:380–386.

Dibble, D. S.
  1975   Archeological Investigations at Bonfire Shelter, Texas. Ph.D. diss., Department of Anthropology, Washington State University, Pullman.

Dickson, D. R.
  1991   *The Albertson Site.* Arkansas Archeological Survey Research Series, no. 41. Fayetteville.

Dillehay, T. D.

1974 Late Quaternary Bison Population Changes on the Southern Plains. *Plains Anthropologist* 19:180–196.

Fenneman, N. M.

1931 *Physiography of Western United States.* McGraw-Hill, New York.

1938 *Physiography of Eastern United States.* McGraw-Hill, New York.

Frison, G. C., ed.

1978 *Prehistoric Hunters of the High Plains.* Academic Press, New York.

Galm, J. R., and P. Flynn

1978 *The Cultural Sequence at the Scott (34CF-11) and Mann (34LF-27) Sites and Prehistory of the Wister Valley.* University of Oklahoma, Archaeological Research and Management Center, Research Series, no. 3. Norman.

Goodyear, A. C.

1982 The Chronological Position of the Dalton Horizon in the Southeastern United States. *American Antiquity* 47:382–395.

Grange, R. T., Jr.

1980 *Archeological Investigations in the Red Willow Reservoir.* Nebraska State Historical Society, Publications in Anthropology, no. 9. Lincoln.

Green, F. E.

1961 Archaeological Salvage in the Twin Buttes Reservoir Area, San Angelo, Texas. *Bulletin of the Texas Archeological Society* 30:183–197.

Grosser, R. D.

1977 Late Archaic Subsistence Patterns from the Central Great Plains: A Systemic Model. Ph.D. diss., Department of Anthropology, University of Kansas, Lawrence.

Hammatt, H. H.

1976 The Gore Pit Site: An Archaic Occupation in Southwestern Oklahoma, and a Review of the Archaic Stage in the Southern Plains. *Plains Anthropologist* 21:245–277.

Haynes, C. V.

1975 Pleistocene and Recent Stratigraphy. In *Late Pleistocene Environments of the Southern High Plains,* edited by F. Wendorf and J. J. Hester, 57–96. Fort Burgwin Research Center, Publication no. 9. Ranchos de Taos, N. M.

Hester, J. J.

1972 *Blackwater Locality No. 1: A Stratified Early Man Site in Eastern New Mexico.* Fort Burgwin Research Center, Publication no. 8. Rancho de Taos, N. M.

Hester, T. R.

1971 Archaeological Investigations at the La Jita Site, Uvalde County, Texas. *Bulletin of the Texas Archeological Society* 42:51–148.

Hill, M. G., V. T. Holliday, and D. J. Stanford

1995 A Further Evaluation of the San Jon Site, New Mexico. *Plains Anthropologist* 40:369–390.

Holder, P., and J. Wike

1949 The Frontier Culture Complex: A Preliminary Report on a Prehistoric Hunters' Camp in Southwestern Nebraska. *American Antiquity* 14:260–266.

Holmes, W. H.

1903 Flint Implements and Fossil Remains from a Sulphur Spring at Afton, Indian Territory. *United States National Museum, Report for 1901,* 237–252. Washington, D.C.

Howard, J. H., and R. D. Gant
  1966   *Report of the Archeological Salvage Investigations in the Gavins Point Reservoir Area, Lewis and Clark Lake, Nebraska and South Dakota, 1962 and 1964.* University of South Dakota, South Dakota Museum, Archeological Studies, Circular no. 11. Vermillion.

Irwin-Williams, C. C., and H. J. Irwin
  1966   *Excavations at Magic Mountain.* Denver Museum of Natural History Proceedings, no. 12.

Jelks, E. B.
  1978   Diablo Range. In *Chronologies in New World Archaeology,* edited by by R. E. Taylor and C. W. Meighan, 71–111. Academic Press, New York.

Katz, P. R.
  1971   Archaeology of the Sutter Site in Northwestern Kansas. *Plains Anthropologist* 16:1–19.

  1973   Radiocarbon Dates from the Sutter Site, Northwestern Kansas. *Plains Anthropologist* 18:167–168.

Kay, M.
  1983   Archaic Period Research in the Western Ozark Highland, Missouri. In *Archaic Hunters and Gatherers in the American Midwest,* edited by J. L. Phillips and J. A. Brown, 41–70. Academic Press, New York.

King, J. E.
  1980   Post-Pleistocene Vegetational Changes in the Midwestern United States. In *Prehistory on the Prairie–Plains Border,* edited by A. E. Johnson, 3–11. University of Kansas, Publications in Anthropology, no. 12. Lawrence.

Leaf, G. R.
  1979   A Research Design for Impacted Archeological Sites at El Dorado Lake, Butler County, Kansas. In *Finding, Managing, and Studying Prehistoric Cultural Resources at El Dorado Lake, Kansas (Phase I),* edited by G. R. Leaf, 1–30. University of Kansas, Museum of Anthropology, Research Series, no. 2. Lawrence.

Leonhardy, F. C.
  1966   *Test Excavations in the Magnum Reservoir Area of Southwestern Oklahoma.* Museum of the Great Plains, Contributions, no. 2. Lawton, Okla.

Lynott, M. J.
  1978   *An Archaeological Assessment of the Bear Creek Shelter, Lake Whitney, Texas.* Southern Methodist University, Archaeology Research Program, Research Report, no. 115. Dallas, Tex.

McCormick, O. F.
  1976   The Archaic Period in North Central Texas. In *The Texas Archaic: A Symposium,* edited by by T. R. Hester, 39–45. University of Texas, Center for Archaeological Research, Special Report no. 2. San Antonio.

Meltzer, D. J.
  1991   Altithermal Archaeology and Paleoecology at Mustang Springs, on the Southern High Plains of Texas. *American Antiquity* 56:236–267.

Quigg, J. M.
  1986   *The Crown Site (FhNa-86) Excavation Results.* Saskatchewan Research Council, Nipawan Reservoir Heritage Study, vol. 8. Saskatoon.

Reeves, B. O. K.
  1973   The Concept of an Altithermal Cultural Hiatus in Northern Plains Prehistory. *American Anthropologist* 75:1221–1253.

Reid, K. C.
  1984   *Nebo Hill and Late Archaic Prehistory on the Southern Prairie Peninsula.* University of Kansas, Publications in Anthropology, no. 15. Lawrence.
Reid, K. C., and J. A. Artz
  1984   *Hunters of the Forest Edge: Culture, Time, and Process in the Little Caney Basin.* University of Tulsa, Laboratory of Archaeology, Contributions to Archaeology, no. 14; University of Oklahoma, Oklahoma Archaeological Survey, Studies in Oklahoma's Past, no. 13. Norman.
Root, M. J.
  1981   The Milbourn Site: Late Archaic Settlement in the Southern Flint Hills of Kansas. M. A. thesis, Department of Anthropology, University of Kansas, Lawrence.
Schambach. F. F.
  1982   An Outline of Fourche Maline Culture in Southwest Arkansas. In *Arkansas Archaeology in Review,* edited by N. L. Trubowitz and M. D. Jeter, 132–197. Arkansas Archeological Survey, Research Series, no. 15. Fayetteville.
  1988   The Archaeology of Oklahoma. *Quarterly Review of Archaeology* 9:5–9.
Schmits, L. J.
  1978   *The Coffey Site: Environment and Cultural Adaptation at a Prairie-Plains Archaic Site.* Midcontinental Journal of Archaeology, Special Paper no. 1.
Shafer, H. J.
  1981   The Adaptive Technology of the Prehistoric Inhabitants of Southwest Texas. *Plains Anthropologist* 23:124–138.
Shaw, C.
  1978   Prehistoric Site Testing. In *A Reconnaissance Survey of the Trinity River Basin, 1976–1977,* compiled by J. J. Richner and J. T. Bagot, 218–243. Report to the United States Army Corps of Engineers, Tulsa District, Tulsa, Okla.
Shippee, J. M.
  1948   Nebo Hill, a Lithic Complex in Western Missouri. *American Antiquity* 14:29–32.
Smith, B. D.
  1992   *Rivers of Change.* Smithsonian Institution Press, Washington, D.C.
Stafford, T., Jr.
  1981   Alluvial Geology and Archaeological Potential of the Texas Southern High Plains. *American Antiquity* 46:548–565.
Story, D. A.
  1985   Adaptive Strategies of Archaic Cultures of the West Gulf Coastal Plain. In *Prehistoric Food Production in North America,* edited by R. I. Ford, 19–56. University of Michigan, Museum of Anthropology, Anthropological Papers, no. 75. Ann Arbor.
Strong, W. D.
  1935   *An Introduction to Nebraska Archeology.* Smithsonian Miscellaneous Collections, vol. 93, no. 10. Washington, D.C.
Thies, R. M.
  1990   *The Archeology of the Stigenwalt Site, 14LT351.* Kansas State Historical Society, Contract Archeology Series, Publication no. 7. Topeka.
Vehik, R.
  1982   *The Archaeology of the Bug Hill Site (34PU–116): Pushmataha County, Oklahoma.* University of Oklahoma, Archaeological Research and Management Center, Research Series, no. 7. Norman.

Wanner, J., and R. H. Brunswig, Jr.
  1992   A Late Archaic Skeleton from the Northeastern Colorado High Plains. *Plains Anthropologist* 37:367–383.
Weir, F. A.
  1976   The Central Texas Archaic. Ph.D. diss., Department of Anthropology, Washington State University, Pullman.
  1979   Greenhaw: An Archaic Site in Central Texas. *Bulletin of the Texas Archeological Society* 50:5–67.
Wesolowsky, A. B., T. R. Hester, and D. R. Brown
  1976   Archeological Investigations at the Jetta Court Site (41TX151), Travis County, Texas. *Bulletin of the Texas Archeological Society* 47:25–87.
Wheeler, R. P.
  1954   Two New Projectile Point Types: Duncan and Hanna Points. *Plains Anthropologist* 1:7–14.
Witty, T. A., Jr.
  1982   *The Slough Creek, Two Dog and William Young Sites, Council Grove Lake, Kansas.* Kansas State Historical Society, Anthropological Series, no. 10. Topeka.
Wood, W. R.
  1967   The Fristoe Burial Complex of Southwestern Missouri. *Missouri Archaeologist* 29.
Wright, H. E.
  1976   The Dynamic Nature of Holocene Vegetation: A Problem in Paleoclimatology, Biogeography, and Stratigraphic Nomenclature. *Quaternary Research* 6:581–596.
Wyckoff, D. G.
  1964   *The Cultural Sequence at the Packard Site, Mayes County, Oklahoma.* University of Oklahoma, Oklahoma River Basin Survey Project, Archaeological Site Report no. 2. Norman.
  1970   Archaeological and Historical Assessment of the Red River Basin in Oklahoma. In *Archeological and Historical Resources of the Red River Basin,* edited by by H. A. Davis, 67–134. Arkansas Archeological Survey, Research Series, no. 1. Fayetteville.
  1985   The Packard Complex: Early Archaic, Pre-Dalton Occupations on the Prairie–Woodlands Border. *Southeastern Archaeology* 4:1–26.
  1989   Accelerator Dates and Chronology at the Packard Site, Oklahoma. *Current Research in the Pleistocene* 6:24–26.

7. The Plains Woodland

Ann Mary Johnson and Alfred E. Johnson

Archaeologists working in the Plains have long used the term "Woodland" to refer to prehistoric sites characterized by elongate pottery vessels with conoidal bottoms, corner-notched projectile points, and burial mounds—features recognized as diagnostic of the Woodland archaeological period in the eastern United States. Since its earliest adoption in the area west of the Missouri River, the term "Woodland" has been prefixed by "Plains," in anticipation of the eventual demonstration of unique adaptive responses to the environmental constraints of a grassland–gallery forest setting.

This chapter describes and discusses several of these adaptive responses, although it is possible to choose only a few examples from the many that developed over a millennium of occupation (between about A.D. 1 and 1000) and some 775,000 square miles. We have chosen to present an east-to-west transect of examples from the Central Plains, and overviews of the Northern and Southern Plains (Figure 7.1).

Central Plains: East

The westernmost variant of the Middle Woodland Hopewellian fluorescence of the eastern United States was centered near the junction of the Missouri and Kansas rivers in northwestern Missouri. A recent summary is available (A. E. Johnson 1979), so emphasis is given here to new findings that affect its interpretation. Middle Woodland in the Kansas City area and to the west was long thought to represent a migration up the Missouri River from Hopewellian centers in western Illinois (A. E. Johnson in press). The origins of this variant have recently become somewhat more problematic with the identification of pre–Kansas City Hopewell, Early Woodland sites in the Kansas City locality. The evidence for Early Woodland was detected at four sites along the Little Blue River, a tributary of the Missouri River in Jackson County, Missouri. The best evidence is from the Traff site (Wright 1980), in the form of Black Sand Incised–like pottery (Griffin 1952:98, Plate 28) from a cooking hearth–workshop area with radiocarbon dates of about 500 to 400 B.C. Similar pottery was recovered from the surface of site 23JA36, a site with a radiocarbon date on a buried hearth of about 450 B.C., although no pottery was directly associated with the hearth. The third site, 23JA40, is dated to about 350 B.C.; again, no pottery was associ-

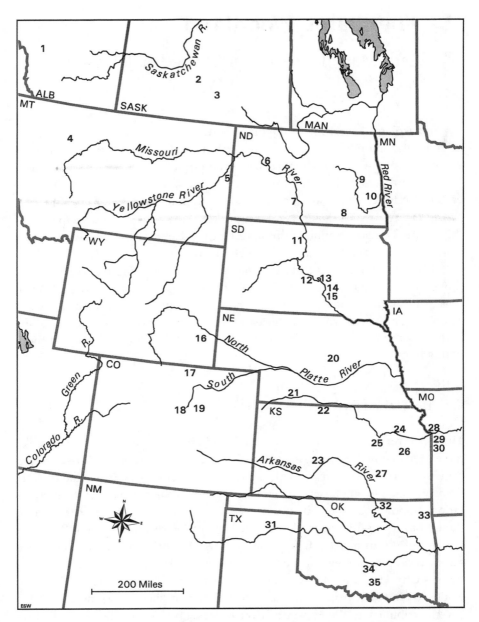

Figure 7.1. Selected Plains Woodland sites: *Alberta* (1) Old Woman's Buffalo Jump; *Saskatchewan* (2) Mortlach, (3) Avonlea; *Montana* (4) Corey Ranch, (5) Goheen; *North Dakota* (6) Nightwalker's Butte, (7) Schmidt Mound, (8) Naze, (9) Baldhill Mounds, (10) Shea; *South Dakota* (11) Arpan Mound, (12) Over's La Roche, (13) Truman Mound, (14) Sitting Crow, (15) Arp; *Wyoming* (16) Greyrocks; *Colorado* (17) Agate Bluff, (18) Bradford House II, Bradford House III, (19) Senac Dam; *Nebraska* (20) Schultz, (21) Doyle; *Kansas* (22) Woodruff Ossuary, (23) 14PA303, (24) Avoca, (25) James Younkin, (26) Wiley, (27) Two Deer; *Missouri* (28) Renner, (29) Sperry, (30) Traff; *Texas* (31) Lake Creek; *Oklahoma* (32) Von Elm, (33) Cooper, (34) Brewer, (35) Pruitt.

ated, although the lithics from the site resemble those from Traff (Ziegler 1981a, 1981b). Finally, a lithic-tool-production area at the Bowlin Bridge site dates to about 500 B.C. (Peterson 1981:389). The relation of these putative Early Woodland occupations to the Late Archaic Nebo Hill phase, with its even earlier fiber-tempered pottery (Reid 1984), has yet to be determined. Radiocarbon dates so far available for Nebo Hill suggest a span from about 2600 to 1000 B.C. (Reeder 1980:63; Schmits et al. 1981:Table 108).

Some 30 radiocarbon dates from Kansas City Hopewell sites (A. E. Johnson 1979:Table 12.1) show that the variant was well established by A.D. 1 and that it lasted as a recognizable entity until A.D. 500. During this time, large (4- to 5-acre) villages were established on streams tributary to the Missouri, as were smaller, probably ancillary hunting and gathering camps. Spacing between clusters of sites suggests hunting and gathering territories. Wild seeds and nuts, fish, deer, raccoon, and turkey were staples, although a wide variety of other wild plants and animals were exploited. Limited evidence for the presence of maize, squash, and marsh elder suggests their addition about A.D. 250 (Adair 1988:Figure 3.9).

Burial features, consisting of central, dry-laid masonry tombs covered with rock and earth mounds, were erected on bluff tops above the villages. Burial goods made from esoteric materials are generally lacking in these mounds, as are artifacts associated with Hopewellian sites to the east (Struever and Houart 1972:47–49), suggesting that Kansas City Hopewell was a marginal participant in the Hopewellian interaction sphere. (The interaction-sphere concept, introduced into the archaeology of the eastern United States by Joseph Caldwell [1964], recognizes intersocietal changes without specifying their exact nature.) The presence of chert from the Boone formation of central Missouri (about 100 miles to the east [Reid 1976]), however, and parallels in both ceramic and projectile-point stylistic change with the Illinois River valley (A. E. Johnson 1979:92) combine to suggest some interaction with peoples to the east.

In a recent overview of the archaeology of Missouri, Kansas City Hopewell was assigned to two phases: Trowbridge and Kansas City (Chapman 1980:29–38). The Trowbridge and Renner sites, type sites for the two phases, were occupied for nearly the entire duration of Kansas City Hopewell (Johnson and Johnson 1975:383–395). The best current criteria for the designation of Kansas City Hopewell phases are ceramic stylistic changes. Recognizing that these changes were gradual and that any divisions will be arbitrary breaks, it would probably be more useful to designate three phases, characterized by the following ceramic elements: pottery rims (1) decorated with cord-wrapped stick impressions, dentate impressions, or plain stick impressions and bosses; (2) decorated with cross-hatching and punctates; and (3) lacking decoration or with crenulations. Rims with the last characteristics indicate that this phase, named Edwardsville, would equate with Early Late Woodland complexes of the eastern

United States dated to A.D. 750 to 1000 (A. E. Johnson 1983:99–108). Stylistic changes in projectile points can probably be correlated with these ceramic variations (Bell 1976:Figure 14; Heffner 1974), thereby adding wider applicability to the taxonomic units.

Detailed evidence has recently begun to accumulate on the occupation of the Kansas City locality following Kansas City Hopewell (A. E. Johnson 1974; Shippee 1967). Identified as Late Woodland, the sites dating to A.D. 750 to 1000 are small hamlets—probably of two or three nuclear-family dwellings—separated by a few hundred yards to perhaps a half-mile. The sites were set along stream margins or on adjoining bluff tops. A similar pattern is described for the Grasshopper Falls phase to the west of Kansas City (Reynolds 1979). Evidence for a greater range of variation for Grasshopper Falls–phase structures is a result of recent excavations at the Avoca site (Baugh 1991:41–47). The Avoca structure has a floor area of about 1431 square feet, and several interior hearths.

Several Late Woodland sites in the Kansas City locality are known. The Sperry site, on the Little Blue River, consisted of a cluster of cooking and storage facilities, associated with cord-roughened pottery and small corner-notched arrowpoints and dates to about A.D. 750 to 800 (Brown 1981; O'Malley 1979). Other dates, clustering between A.D. 700 and 800, are from site 23CL276 at Smithville Lake, north of Kansas City (McHugh 1980:Table 7.5). Although this site also has a later Steed–Kisker phase component, the date cluster is probably associated with thick-walled, grit-tempered, cord-roughened pottery and small corner-notched arrowpoints from an earlier occupation (McHugh 1980:5:1–58; 6:5–12).

Finally, two diagnostic Late Woodland artifact styles (thick-walled, stone-tempered, cord-roughened pottery and small corner-notched projectile points) occasionally occur in late Kansas City Hopewell contexts (A. E. Johnson 1976:15), suggesting continuity and posing an interesting problem in determining the relations between these two manifestations.

Although occasional finds of ceramics in styles similar to those associated with the Early Woodland period of the eastern United States (Griffin 1952) have long been noted from the prairie–Plains border north of Kansas City (Bonney 1970:302–304), recent investigations in Iowa (Benn 1980), Minnesota (Anfinson 1982:73–75), and North Dakota (Gregg 1990:29–44) suggest an importance for this period that was not formerly appreciated. Especially important are the excavations at two stratified sites in northwestern Iowa, Rainbow and MAD (Benn 1980, 1990), on the Floyd and Boyer rivers. These two sites provide the most detailed Woodland sequence available for the Eastern Plains.

The sequence has as its earliest pottery Crawford County ware, dated as early as 395 B.C. at the MAD site. Crawford County Trailed has a cord-roughened surface finish, over which trailed-line decorations were applied. The type is similar to Early Woodland Black Sand Incised pottery from Illinois (Griffin 1952:98, Plate 28). The Middle Woodland period is represented by Valley ware, dated from 50 B.C. to A.D. 350 or 400, and characterized by vertically or obliquely applied cord-roughening on sack-shaped, thick-walled vessels. Decorations, when present, are simple texturing devices applied to the rim. Hopewellian features are lacking in this area during the Middle Woodland period (Benn 1980:3, 23, 33).

Early Late Woodland is characterized by Held ware, dated at the Rainbow site from A.D. 450 to 600 and at MAD to A.D. 500. Held ware is generally similar to Scalp ware, described for the Missouri River valley in South Dakota (Hurt 1952), but vessel walls are thinner, it is made from a finer paste, and the surfaces are smoother—often a result of smoothing over a cord-roughened surface. Vessels also have a somewhat more globular shape, and rims are often outflared. Loseke ware, as defined by Benn, incorporates previously defined types from Nebraska, South Dakota, and western Iowa, including Feye Cord Impressed (Kivett 1952) and Missouri Bluffs Cord Impressed (Keyes 1949). This latest pottery in the sequence is believed to lead directly into the ceramics of Great Oasis and the Plains Village tradition (Benn 1980:7–8, 45).

Soil-geomorphic studies, begun in connection with the excavations at the Rainbow site, have recognized a series of alluvial-fill deposits whose correlations with other sequences indicate nearly synchronous episodes of down-cutting and aggradation throughout the Missouri River basin in Iowa and probably Nebraska as well (Thompson and Bettis 1980:1–60). A tentative sequence spanning the Holocene has now been developed. The implications of this are far-reaching, not only from the standpoint of our increased ability to predict the location of buried prehistoric sites, but for environmental modeling during the Holocene.

Farther to the south, comparable studies are being made in the Arkansas River basin, with equally successful results. At El Dorado Lake in south-central Kansas, for instance, Late Archaic artifacts occur in a buried paleosol that was a slowly aggrading deposit between about 2000 B.C. and A.D. 1, perhaps a function of low-intensity, basinwide floods. From about A.D. 1 to 1000 (the Woodland period in this area), alluvial deposits indicate a period of disequilibrium, probably a result of increased rainfall. By about A.D. 1000, equilibrium had again been achieved, with the establishment of an essentially modern rainfall pattern and stream regimen. Soil, geomorphic, radiocarbon, and archaeological correlations suggest a similar pattern from western Missouri into southwestern Oklahoma (Artz 1980).

Another example of continuity from a local, eastern Central Plains Woodland complex into later developments is becoming apparent in eastern Kansas. Originally named as a focus, the Pomona complex has received enough recent attention to warrant redesignation as a variant (Pankratz 1981:6; Witty 1967). Pomona sites are distributed over eastern Kansas to the Flint Hills, and date from about A.D. 950 to 1350 (Brown 1984:12). Subsistence was based on hunting, gathering, and small-scale horticulture. The bow and arrow was in use, the arrows tipped with small triangular side-notched or unnotched points. Pottery consisted of globular vessels with outflared rims and cord-roughened surfaces. Dwellings are of indefinite form, but most of them were probably oval, with wattle and daub over the wall posts (Bradley 1968:8; Schmits 1980:133–162).

The variant shares many features with the Central Plains tradition (Wedel 1961:92–98), although differences—especially in the absence of the earthlodge—are sufficient to establish a new taxonomic unit. Unity of the Pomona variant over an area as large as eastern Kansas (including some of the prairies of western Missouri) and a time span of 700 years remains to be demonstrated, and some authors have suggested that several phases are represented (Brown 1984; A. E. Johnson 1968).

Many diagnostic features of the Pomona variant are present at 14MM7: wattle-and-daub houses, outside cooking and storage facilities, and triangular side-notched arrowpoints. The site, however, also has features that—on a typological basis—are associated with earlier Woodland complexes (Carrillo 1973). They include small, corner-notched (Scallorn-like) points and pottery vessels with an elongated, sack-like form. An unusual feature of Pomona cord-roughened pottery is the use of a knotted cord.

Material from the Wiley site, in east-central Kansas, suggests the presence of an even earlier complex, related to Woodland—although, unfortunately, it is not dated. Area E of the site is a single-component Woodland occupation. The Woodland pottery from this area is limestone tempered, instead of containing the sand or grog temper common in later pottery, but it bears the distinctive Pomona knotted-cord-roughening (Logan 1980; Witty 1967). The use of some form of calcium carbonate for tempering is a feature of much of the Woodland pottery in the Central Plains (Adair and Brown 1981; Kivett 1953). In summary, recent studies of the archaeology of eastern Kansas suggest a long-standing continuity from a local Plains or Late Woodland complex (as represented at the Wiley site) into the Pomona variant. Site 14MM7 is interpreted as evidence of the transition, as it shares features of both the earlier Woodland and the later Pomona complexes.

Radiocarbon dates for the Grasshopper Falls phase, defined for 124 components along the Delaware River west of Kansas City (Reynolds 1979), range from A.D. 600 to 950, suggesting general contemporaneity with Late Woodland developments in the Kansas City locality. Natural floodplain rises were chosen for sites, with a tendency for sites to be more common along secondary drainages (Reichart 1974:31; Reynolds 1979:73). Excavations at four sites have revealed six structures, marked by oval post-mold patterns enclosing 115 to 448 square feet, probably nuclear-family dwellings. Superstructures were of light poles covered with wattle and daub. Clusters of as many as 12 houses might be present at some sites (Barr 1971; Reichart 1974; Reynolds 1979). Basin-shaped pits, presumably for storage, are both inside and outside the houses, and hearths are outside.

Artifacts, including hunting and butchering tools and grinding stones, suggest that both hunting and gathering were important. Although no horticultural tools have been found, the pattern of dispersed homesteads on or adjoining the best gardening areas may denote some dependence on domesticated plants. Charred maize has been recovered from 14JN349, and maize, domesticated marsh elder, and sunflower seeds from 14JN332 (M. Adair, personal communication). Water flotation at the Bemis Creek–phase, Two Deer site in south-central Kansas produced abundant evidence of maize, gourd, and sunflower—although, again, lacking specialized gardening tools. The Two Deer site dates to A.D. 950 (Adair and Brown 1981).

Grasshopper Falls–phase pottery is in the form of elongate jars with conoidal bases and slightly outflaring rims. Most were tempered with angular rock fragments and cord-roughened on the exterior, although this treatment tends to be smoothed over or obliterated. Decoration is rare, consisting of brushing or simple textured designs (tool impressions and bosses) on the rim. Other tools are large corner-notched or contracting-stemmed projectile points, small corner- or side-notched arrowpoints, drills, chipped-stone celts, gouges, bifacial knives, and scrapers. Ground-stone axes, celts, and grinding stones are also associated (Reynolds 1979:70–73).

Burial mounds are present along the Delaware River, but to date it has not been possible to associate them with the Grasshopper Falls phase (Bass et al. 1967; Reynolds 1979:74).

Recent research has begun to allow us to model Central Plains Woodland subsistence systems. The identification of 44 varieties of animals and 23 kinds of plants, including maize and squash (Adair 1977; E. M. Johnson 1975), is indicative of a broad-spectrum use of local plants and animals by Kansas City Hopewell. The few preserved seeds of tropical cultigens argue against any real importance for horticulture (A. E. Johnson 1976:7–8). Although a variety of microenvironments were exploited to obtain these resources, all are in the immediate vicinity of the Missouri River.

Another data set, reflecting the nature of Plains Woodland faunal exploitation, is available from the Doyle site in southwestern Nebraska (Grange 1980: Table 40). Doyle resembles both the Keith variant and the Massacre Canyon site. Doyle was probably occupied between about 60 B.C. and A.D. 680 (Grange 1980:126–127). Other dates for the Keith variant suggest the date of A.D. 680 as most likely (A. E. Johnson in press). The faunal list from Doyle includes 23 species of large and small mammals, reptiles, waterfowl, and other birds.

Although the contrast in numbers of species utilized in the Kansas City locality (44) and at Doyle (23) is striking, the difference seems attributable mainly to the east-to-west diminution in the quantity and variety of potential natural food resources along the river valleys of the Central Plains. At both sites, the evidence suggests sedentary or semisedentary lifeways, based on the broad-spectrum exploitation of river resources, not a pedestrian nomadic pattern based on bison hunting. One can therefore postulate a reduction in the size of Plains Woodland societies from east to west across the Plains, a function of the diminishing resource base. Data supporting this hypothesis come from studies of the size of villages and burial mounds. Eight Kansas City Hopewell communities range from 9000 to 63,000 square meters (A. E. Johnson 1976:Table 4), while five sites of about the same age in north-central Kansas, 100 miles west of Kansas City, range from 625 to 9000 square meters (A. E. Johnson et al. 1980). This differential is interpreted as an indication of the greater resource potential in the Kansas City area.

Estimates have been calculated of the number of square feet encompassed by nine burial mounds at Kansas City Hopewell sites and by 24 mounds of the Schultz phase (Eyman 1966; Phenice 1969) along the Republican River valley in north-central Kansas. Artifact similarities suggest that these mounds are roughly contemporaneous (O'Brien et al. 1973:54–72). The Kansas City Hopewell mounds range from 254 to 707 square feet (mean = 425), and, with three exceptions, the Schultz mounds range from 28 to 560 square feet (mean = 246). The three exceptions (A. Berry = 1075; Dixon = 1920; and James Younkin = 2636) not only are appreciably larger than the other Schultz mounds, but are significantly larger than the largest Kansas City Hopewell mound (Pearl Mound C = 707 square feet). One explanation for this discrepancy may be that since two of the large Schultz-phase mounds (A. Berry and James Younkin) produced artifacts of two different cultural periods, the original mounds may have been enlarged later. The artifacts from the Dixon mound are attributable to Plains Woodland (Phenice 1969:37). The excavation notes for the Schultz mounds are so poor that mound enlargement over time cannot be disproved. In any event, the cluster of 21 mounds covering between 28 and 560 square feet best represents the Schultz-phase mound size. Larger mounds thus occur to the east.

Burial mounds were the only major sites for disposing of the dead, for excavations in both Kansas City Hopewell and Schultz-phase villages have so far yielded no human burials (A. E. Johnson 1976; Katz 1974; Parks 1978). Inhumations included burial in the flesh, bundle burials, and cremations. The smaller size of the Schultz-phase burial edifices may presumably be attributed to a smaller population size, with population, in turn, governed by the natural-food resources available to Plains Woodland hunters and gatherers in north-central Kansas. It is worth noting that there seems to have been no differential access to mound burial because of age or sex in either complex.

As the result of recent discoveries of sites affiliated with Early Woodland complexes in the Midwest, Woodland expressions in the Central Plains are now known to begin about 500 B.C. These early developments are succeeded about

A.D. 1 by Middle Plains Woodland, best known from studies of Kansas City Hopewell. The Late Plains Woodland development has both early and later phases, with Grasshopper Falls one of the best known of the latter. Late Plains Woodland complexes seem to evolve slowly into Early Plains Village developments, such as the Pomona variant (A.D. 950 to 1350). An adaptive focus on riverine settings seems characteristic of Plains Woodland, with diminution of population sizes from east to west as a function of reduced resource availability.

High Plains

Rather arbitrarily, for the purpose of this chapter, we include within the High Plains those parts of Kansas and Nebraska to the west of the hundredth meridian. This is an area of low relief, with short grasses as the predominant vegetation as a result of the less than 20 inches of precipitation received each year. Throughout much of prehistory, herds of large gregarious animals provided an attraction to human populations.

In keeping with current taxonomic usage for the Plains, the Keith complex (originally defined as a focus of the Orleans aspect, together with the Valley focus [Kivett 1953:135]) is now defined as a variant (A. E. Johnson in press; Lehmer 1971:32). Keith-variant sites extend from the prairie–Plains border on the east into far western Kansas and Nebraska (Bowman 1960; Kivett 1952:24–34; Smith 1949:298–299). The Platte and Arkansas rivers, at the present, seem to be near the northern and southern limits.

Stylistic variability in projectile points and in Harlan Cord Roughened pottery suggest a significant time span for the variant. Projectile points are medium to large corner-notched styles (Wedel 1959:416–422), small and Scallorn-like (Witty 1969:1–2), or a combination of the latter and small, triangular, unnotched arrowpoints (Witty 1966:127–135). Such variability suggests a shift from the use of the atlatl and darts to that of the bow and arrow during Keith-variant times. Ceramic variability also implies change: Harlan Cord Roughened pottery from upper levels of a midden at site 14PA303 near Larned, Kansas, differs in paste and rim form from that in lower levels (E. Monger, personal communication).

Radiocarbon dates for the variant are Woodruff Ossuary, about A.D. 600; 25FT18, A.D. 800; and 25HN12, A.D. 775 (an average of three dates). The Doyle site in southwestern Nebraska, although not assigned to the variant, resembles it in several ways, including sharing Harlan Cord Roughened pottery, and is dated at between 60 B.C. and A.D. 680 (Grange 1980:127).

Keith-variant sites are usually small (less than about an acre), although they sometimes attain some depth. Site 14PA303 near Larned, Kansas, contained a midden that was 1.5 to 3 feet deep, suggesting continued or frequent occupations. Most of the sites, however, are probably short-term camps used for specialized subsistence activities. Occupation sites are on hilltops, buried in river terraces (Bowman 1960; Smith 1949:298–299; Witty 1966:127–135), and in rock shelters (Witty 1962:32–53). Associated features include circular or oval basins with central hearths that are the remains of simple houses (Kivett 1949a:278–284), outside hearths, and storage pits. Specialized burial features include ossuaries (Kivett 1953:103–141) and possibly mounds (Craine 1956:1–4).

Plant remains have yet to be identified at Keith-variant sites, but identified animal bones suggest a broad-spectrum exploitation, including large and small mammals, rodents, birds, and mollusks. Support for this interpretation comes from tools that include hunting, butchering, and grinding implements. Although most artifacts are of local material, shells from the Gulf of Mexico are found at the Pfaff site (a possible burial mound in Ness County) and in the Woodruff Ossuary in Phillips County, Kansas (Craine 1956; Kivett 1953:103–104). Furthermore, a sherd with Hopewellian features from the Pottorff site in Lane County, Kansas (Wedel 1959:381–412), demonstrates that other extra-local contacts were taking place.

Three Plains Woodland pottery types—Ash Hollow Cord Roughened, Valley Cord Roughened, and Harlan Cord Roughened (Champe 1949; Kivett 1949b, 1952:36–37)—are defined for this High Plains area. The presence or numerical superiority of the latter two types are major diagnostics used to identify sites attributable to the Valley variant or the Keith variant.

Sites distributed over very large areas and covering long periods of time are assigned to these variants on the basis of a few pottery features. Yet a reexamination of the pottery from the Schultz site (25VY1) (Hill and Kivett 1940), the type site for the Valley variant, showed more variability than is indicated in the literature (Benn 1980:22). Similarly, two varieties of Harlan Cord Roughened pottery are identified at Doyle, and there are unnamed types at Massacre Canyon (Grange 1980:111, 113–116). The variability of the Woodland pottery at Ash Hollow Cave was pointed out long ago (Champe 1946:112–116).

Assigning sites to spatially and temporally extensive taxonomic units on the basis of only a few ceramic variables is a problem to be dealt with in the future. The reexamination of museum collections will be necessary, as well as excavations to obtain larger samples. As this work progresses, we shall probably see shifts from early elongated vessels with conoidal bottoms, direct rims, overall cordmarking, large amounts of temper, and thick vessel walls, to later vessels with more globular shapes, outflared rims, smoothed-over cord-roughened surfaces, less temper, and thinner vessel walls. Changes of this sort have been noted for northwestern Iowa, southwestern Nebraska, and west-central Kansas (Benn 1980; Grange 1980:116; E. Monger, personal communication).

Although radiocarbon dates from Woodland sites in Colorado are as early as A.D. 100, most of the evidence for Woodland on the High Plains suggests Late

Woodland. The Keith variant, apparently focused on the area between the Platte and Arkansas rivers, is in need of up-to-date studies to assess the range of variation and to add a more substantial and interpretable database.

Central Plains: West

Plains Woodland in the West is a more generalized expression of Woodland than those in neighboring parts of western Nebraska and Kansas. Similarities are in settlement pattern, pottery characteristics such as cord-roughened surface treatment and vessel form, and projectile points. Differences include the absence of specialized pottery characteristics (particularly decoration and temper), the addition of serration to projectile points, subsistence, and sites that indicate shorter occupations. Plains Woodland in the West is equated with Middle Woodland, primarily on the basis of pottery, for no Early or Late Woodland is known.

Geographically, the western Central Plains includes eastern Colorado as far west as the Rocky Mountains' continental divide, and south-central and southeastern Wyoming. Because prehistoric cultural boundaries often fail to coincide with modern political boundaries, the eastern margin particularly is somewhat inexact. Environmentally, the western Central Plains may be divided into three regions: grasslands, foothills (the Front Range), and the montane-alpine. The North Platte, South Platte, and Arkansas rivers and their tributaries create long narrow riverine environments that contrast with the rolling grassy plains through which they flow. The montane-alpine region is mantled primarily in coniferous forest rising to above 7000 feet in elevation. The montane-alpine region receives considerable snow and, during most winters, is assumed to have been inhospitable, with Native Americans moving to lower elevations. The foothills are a mountain–plains ecotone that extends north and south along the mountain front from southern Colorado into central Wyoming.

Our understanding of Plains Woodland throughout this region is uneven. The best known area is in the foothills near Denver and Boulder, while there is almost no modern inventory beyond 25 miles east of the foothills. Dates for Plains Woodland in Colorado range from A.D. 100 to 1050 (Butler 1986).

Sites in northeastern Colorado are assigned to the South Platte phase (Butler 1986, 1988). Settlement includes rock shelters, caves, open sites, and burials.

Pottery is markedly homogeneous and is not divided into types. Cord-roughening on the rim typically has an upper-right to lower-left orientation, but may also be vertical near the rim (Figure 7.2). Temper is usually crushed rock and occasionally sand. Vessels have the classic Middle Woodland form found on the Central Plains. They are rarely decorated; when they are, it consists of simple motifs such as a single row of incising on the lip. Whole or recon-

Figure 7.2. Plains Woodland pottery from Bradford House III (5JF52), Colorado.

structable vessels are rare, but Scott (1963:47–48) reports a vessel almost 2 feet high and 1.5 feet in diameter.

Woodland points are small to medium corner-notched arrowpoints, similar but not identical to the Scallorn type found farther to the east. The blade may be serrated and frequently is asymmetrical. Notches are set at an oblique angle to the blade and, with the long shoulders, have a barbed appearance. Points whose barbs are short appear slightly stemmed (Figure 7.3). These points were also used as hafted knives, and the degree of serration often reflects the amount of wear on the blade.

Thin triangular unnotched bifaces of the general size of the projectile points also are characteristic of Plains Woodland components. Some are preforms. However, in the foothill rock shelters, most thin triangular unnoted bifaces are shorter than the average projectile-point length and probably are knives. Breakage patterns appear to support this function.

Good subsistence data are available only for sites near Denver. In the foot-

Figure 7.3. Plains Woodland corner-notched points from Bradford House III (5JF52), Colorado.

hills, at Bradford House II and III (5JF51 and 5JF52), the faunal assemblage is dominated by deer, with bison, elk, antelope, and mountain sheep. Many smaller species also are present, including canids, rabbit, ground squirrel, gopher, porcupine, beaver, and turkey. Chokecherries and wild plums are present, probably only a few of the many resources gathered. The numerous manos and metates suggest that the use of plants was substantial (O'Neil et al. 1988).

Maize is reported at several sites in the South Platte drainage, and some authors interpret these remains as evidence for experimentation with horticulture (Irwin and Irwin 1957, 1959:132; J. Wood 1967:605). The total of this evidence is a few cobs and a handful of kernels, and it may be significant that cache pits and traditional horticultural tools such as the shoulder-blade hoe are absent. At several sites, the maize cannot be assigned to the Plains Woodland or a later component because the site was dug without making the appropriate provenience records (for example, Lehman Cave on the eastern tip of the Black Forest [Lyons and Johnson 1994]) or rodents may have mixed the deposits. In sum, Plains Woodland subsistence on the western Central Plains appears to be broadly based, but lacking horticulture.

Woodland sites in the grasslands and foothills are near major streams or their tributaries, a pattern like that in Kansas and Nebraska. Montane sites have not been adequately inventoried, but are found in meadows and other forest openings and on major trails through the mountains. Their distribution suggests contacts with the western slope of the Rocky Mountains.

Seasonality data are generally lacking, although the foothills to the west of Denver provide good winter shelter, with the upthrust sandstone hogback buffering the wind and absorbing heat from the sun during the day so that it is several degrees warmer, and more likely to be snow free during the winter, than the surrounding areas. Several sites in the foothills have thick ashy horizons that could be interpreted as winter components.

Primary burials outnumber secondary bundle burials four to one, with all the individuals placed in oval pits. A few, usually nondiagnostic, artifacts may be associated. The shell and bone beads common in Plains Woodland graves to the east are rare and occur in small numbers, if they are present at all (Butler et al. 1986). Burial mounds are absent. The Beacon Hill burial near Pueblo in southeastern Colorado (Black et al. 1991), with its numerous shell disk and *Olivella* beads, is not typical of Colorado Woodland burials and may be affiliated with a Woodland group from Kansas.

Plains Woodland people used houses, although they currently are known from only two sites. At the George W. Lindsay site, local rocks were used to form two rectangular foundations approximately 10 to 12 feet on a side (Nelson 1971). Recent reinvestigations at the Magic Mountain site partially uncovered another Woodland structure (C. Zeir, personal communication), but the kind of superstructure erected on the foundation is unknown.

There may be some westward expansion of Woodland people along the rivers of western Kansas and Nebraska into Colorado and Wyoming (Wedel 1961:284). However, in most of northeastern Colorado, we find no sharp cultural break from the local Late Archaic to Plains Woodland that might denote an influx of new people. Instead, a strong case can be made for a continuum between the Archaic and Woodland populations, with the technological changes accompanying the introduction of the bow and arrow and ceramics. In many foothills rock shelters, multiple Plains Woodland components overlie multiple Archaic components. The contents of these shelters suggest that subsistence, artifact types, and lithic materials vary only slightly between Archaic and Woodland components and that the same lifeway continued essentially unchanged from at least 3500 B.C., if not earlier, to A.D. 1000.

There are differences, of course. One is that Plains Woodland components do not have slab-lined hearths, which typify the Middle Archaic. Late Archaic people also buried their dead in their occupation sites (foothill rock shelters), while Plains Woodland groups did not.

Woodland is not well known in southeastern Colorado. Sites are assigned to the provisional Arkansas phase (Butler 1986), with dry-laid stone houses and possibly horticulture. The post-Woodland Apishapa phase there begins about A.D. 1100, and Apishapa sites may be confused with Woodland, since Apishapa pottery is cord-roughened (but globular in form). Whether the Apishapa phase replaced or absorbed Woodland has not been determined (Butler 1988:462).

Wyoming has minor expressions of Plains Woodland, and sites in its southeastern corner may represent immigration or influences from the Central Plains along tributaries of the North and South Platte rivers (small corner-notched points [Reher 1971]). Other Wyoming sites, such as Grayrocks on the Laramie River (Tibesar 1980), indicate closer relations with Northern Plains Woodland (for example, large side- and corner-notched Besant-like points).

Suggestions about the termination of the local Plains Woodland are unsatisfactory. Sites that were repeatedly occupied by numerous people simply are abandoned without apparent movement to other sites in the general vicinity. The post-Woodland archaeological record in the foothill rock shelters is uniformly thin to absent, suggesting a major shift in population and settlement pattern. There is no clear explanation yet as to why this should have occurred.

Southern Plains

Woodland manifestations in the Southern Plains are not well known, but extend as far south as the Texas panhandle. Woodland components may be difficult to identify, as few sites of this period have been systematically investigated. Furthermore, there is marked diversity between regions, with a general

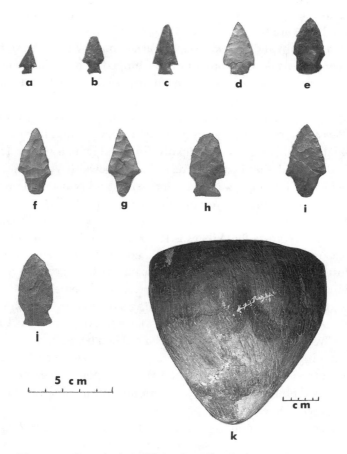

Figure 7.4. Late Archaic/Plains Woodland projectile points and pottery from central Oklahoma: (*a–c*) Scallorn; (*d*) Enser; (*e*) Ellis; (*f–g, i*) Gary; (*h*) Markos; (*j*) Lange; (*k*) Pruitt Cordmarked pottery.

lack of diagnostic artifacts, clear stratigraphy, and radiocarbon dates (Vehik 1984). To complicate identification, pottery may be lacking, projectile points may be carryovers from earlier Archaic times (Gary in the east; Williams/Marcus/Marshall in the west), or some projectiles of probable Woodland age may persist into post-Woodland times (Figure 7.4). The adoption of pottery and arrowpoints by the indigenous groups on the High Plains did not occur simultaneously. Most Oklahoma Woodland falls within a generalized pattern that equates to Middle Woodland elsewhere on the Plains.

In northeastern Oklahoma, Plains Woodland begins about A.D. 1 with the Delaware A focus. Delaware A is characterized by constricting-stemmed points (Gary and Langtry) and Delaware Plain and Delaware Cordmarked pottery.

Vessels are in the form of jars and bowls, tempered with crushed sandstone and/or shell. Delaware B begins about A.D. 900 and ends about A.D. 1300 (Vehik 1984). Delaware Plain and Delaware Cordmarked pottery continue to be made, although there are also several other forms. Chipped stone includes an increasing number of small arrowpoints that are characteristic of the Plains Village tradition.

Overlapping with Delaware A and the later Delaware B is the Cooper phase (Bell and Baerreis 1951); it represents minimal Hopewellian influence in southeastern Oklahoma. Sherds are principally cord-roughened, with a few being smoothed. Decorated sherds closely resemble Hopewellian stamped pottery; techniques include incising, stamping, embossing, and punctation arranged in zones. Cooper points generally resemble the corner-notched Hopewellian Snyders points. Site DL-33 has a radiocarbon date of A.D. 991 (Vehik 1984:181).

The Kaw Reservoir on the Arkansas River has Woodland sites dating from A.D. 100 to 300, characterized by pottery tempered with sand and/or grit, bone, or clay. Most pottery is smoothed, with some sherds being cord-roughened. A few sherds resembling those from the Cooper phase are believed to be trade pieces. The ceramics, storage pits, and grinding stones at the Von Elm site suggest a fairly sedentary lifeway (Hartley 1974), even though no structures have been found. Two structures were identified and dated between A.D. 630 and 990 at the Drumming Sauna site in the nearby Copan Reservoir (Reid and Artz 1984). Dart points include corner-notched Williams points, together with contracting-stemmed points such as Gary. The number of small points such as Scallorn increases with time.

Several burned rock mounds in eastern Oklahoma appear to date to the Woodland period. As few diagnostic artifacts are found in them, identification of cultural affiliation is difficult. Tools associated with plant processing are most consistently present (Vehik and Pailes 1979:207).

In central Oklahoma, the Plains Woodland dates between A.D. 1 and 800, and is characterized by corner-notched arrowpoints, Gary dart points, and grit-tempered, cordmarked pottery (Drass 1988:70). The pottery is coil manufactured with paddle and anvil finishing (Hartley 1974), identified as Pruitt Cordmarked (Drass 1988; Vehik 1984) (Figure 7.4). Tempering material includes, either alone or in combination, sand, limestone, sandstone, or shale. Trade pottery is not present. People emphasized the use of local stone sources (Drass 1988). Large basin-shaped pits are rare in the Woodland period of central Oklahoma, but a partial pit was identified at the Quillan site (Hughes and Briscoe 1987).

About A.D. 800 to 1000, there was a gradual change from Plains Woodland to Plains Village (Central Plains tradition), characterized by unnotched and side-notched arrowpoints, plain pottery (especially shell-tempered plain wares), minor amounts of Caddoan pottery, abraders, bone tools, storage pits, and evidence for increasing dependence on horticulture (maize). Sites bridging the Plains Woodland and Plains Village traditions are classified as Transitional

Plains Village (Drass 1988). The Pruitt and Brewer sites (Barr 1966; Duffield 1953) are now identified as Transitional (Drass 1988).

Plains Woodland in the Texas and Oklahoma panhandles is marked by the addition of arrowpoints and ceramics to the Archaic lifeway, and along the Canadian River there is evidence for the mixing of influences from the Southwest and Plains Woodland in the Lake Creek focus and the Palo Duro complex. Cordmarked pottery occurs with dart points as early as A.D. 250 at the Sanders site in the Palo Duro Reservoir of Texas (Quigg 1997) and at the Medina Rockshelter in southeastern Colorado (Campbell 1969). The Lake Creek focus of the Oklahoma and Texas panhandles dates from about A.D. 500 to 1000 (Hughes 1962). Projectile points are small to medium-size Scallorn and Ellis-like types. Mogollon Jornada Brownware sherds are found at the Lake Creek site (Boyd 1995; Hofman and Brooks 1989).

Transitional Plains Village sites are assigned to the Custer phase in western Oklahoma and the Paoli phase in central Oklahoma. These assemblages show a combination of artifacts that represent a blend of Plains Woodland and Plains Village (Drass 1988).

As is generally true elsewhere on the Plains, Plains Woodland in Oklahoma is marked by the introduction of pottery, and in the eastern and central parts of the state the developments are related to and peripheral to developments in Kansas and Missouri (Hartley 1974:129). There is cultural and biological continuity from the Late Archaic into Plains Woodland, and then into Plains Village. The diversity of material culture through time between regions may be explained as local developments: the stimuli for ceramics and the bow and arrow (Scallorn and other small points) were differentially received and interpreted at different times and places. Although studies emphasize material culture over subsistence data, there seems to be little difference between Archaic and Plains Woodland settlement patterns and subsistence. Bison were present throughout the Texas panhandle during Late Archaic/Woodland time as reflected by a series of bison kills dating between 20 B.C. and A.D. 830 (Lintz et al. 1991; Quigg 1997). Nonetheless, Woodland sites in the Texas–western Oklahoma region are dominated by deer faunal remains. Other foods include turtles and wild plants (Galm 1978).

People were nomadic, returning to campsites possibly on a seasonal basis. Transitional Plains Village sites are apparently more sedentary, with semipermanent four-post houses and greater emphasis on horticulture (Drass 1988).

Northern Plains

The Northern Plains includes the Plains portions of Alberta, Saskatchewan, Manitoba, eastern Montana, North and South Dakota, and eastern Wyoming as far south as the North Platte River.

Early Woodland on the Northern Plains is known from only a few sites and is not well understood. While several Early and Middle Woodland Fox Lake–phase sites are known in eastern South Dakota (Ludwickson et al. 1987), they have yet to be adequately described.

The Naze site, on the James River in eastern North Dakota, contains both Early and Middle Woodland components. The Early Woodland component dates between 550 and 410 B.C. (Gregg 1990:31) and contains Black Sand–like pottery—thick, cord-roughened, and decorated with bosses and trailed lines. Points are of two forms, suggesting a transition from atlatl to bow and arrow: small with diagonal, narrow corner notches (Pelican Lake) and the larger, open-notched Besant-like points. The Naze Early Woodland house has four sets of paired posts as roof supports, but the architecture of the walls or house area could not be determined. The economy of the Early Woodland Naze component is based on species available in or near the adjoining floodplain forest, dominated by bison and elk, and includes the remains of wild grape, chokecherry, chenopodium, and marsh elder.

The Middle Woodland on the Northern Plains begins about A.D. 100 with the addition of ceramics and burial mounds to the Besant phase. Besant belongs to Reeves's (1983) Napikwan cultural tradition, which is found throughout the Northern Plains. The Besant phase and Middle Plains Woodland in the Northern Plains sites often are used interchangeably when sites are burial mounds or contain Woodland pottery (A. E. Johnson in press; Reeves 1983; Wood and Johnson 1973). Middle Plains Woodland burial mounds and pottery do not have the same distribution on the Northern Plains, and they seem to have been transmitted along different routes by different stimuli from the Midwest and Central Plains to local Besant people living in the Dakotas. Burial mounds are rare outside the Dakotas, and while pottery is found throughout the Northern Plains, the frequency of these traits decreases as the distance from the Midwest stimuli increases.

The atlatl-size Besant-type projectile point is broad and corner notched, similar to the generalized Middle Woodland points found throughout the Midwest (Figure 7.5). Knife River Flint is a preferred material for projectile points, even in sites hundreds of miles from the Knife River quarries in west-central North Dakota.

Besant had a bison-hunting economy, using both traps and jumps (Davis and Wilson 1978). Occupation sites show seasonal and probably repeated use, with quantities of bison bones, fire-cracked rock, charcoal, pottery, and lithic debris. North of Nebraska, there is no evidence for horticulture and little for plant utilization. Even grinding stones are rare. Besant people did engage in long-distance trade, obtaining obsidian from Obsidian Cliff (Wyoming) and Bear Gulch (Idaho) and shells from both the Pacific and Gulf coasts.

Northern Plains Middle Woodland pottery is grit tempered and cord-

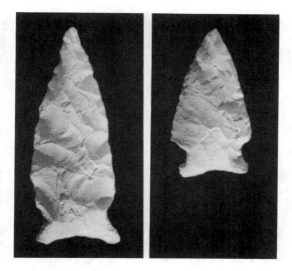

Figure 7.5. Besant points from the Whiskey Hill
site, a single-component Plains Woodland campsite in Montana, with Besant points and Woodland
pottery. (From A. M. Johnson 1977)

roughened, and has a neckless, shoulderless elongated form, like that in contemporary Middle Woodland to the south and east. Vessels are undecorated, or
they may have a single row of interior or exterior bosses encircling the rim below the lip. Due to their general similarity in form, these ceramics are sometimes incorrectly called Valley, although the ceramic decorative diversity and
lifeway of the Central Plains Valley variant are not present on the Northern
Plains (Figure 7.6).

Middle Plains Woodland sites are common on hilltops along the Missouri
River trench (W. Wood 1956; Wood and Johnson 1973). These sites can best be
interpreted as summer camps chosen for the breeze and absence of insects,
as the severity of the winters argues against year-round use of such exposed
camps. Similarly, people would have moved out of winter camps in the river
valleys to avoid spring floods. Other Plains Woodland camps and kill sites are
buried in footslopes and in terraces along the Missouri River (Ahler et al. 1981;
Wheeler and Johnson 1985). Many are stratigraphically below the Middle Missouri–tradition villages (Lehmer et al. 1978). The intaglio turf-cut turtle at the
High Butte site remains a unique site type.

The settlement pattern away from the Missouri River has not been studied,
for most known camps are along the river valleys and their tributaries. There
are extensive tipi-ring sites, showing that Besant groups used the skin tipi for
housing (Davis 1983; Deaver and Deaver 1988). Evidence for more substantial

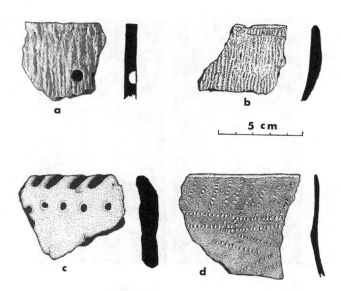

Figure 7.6. Northern Plains Woodland pottery: (*a*) Middle Plains Woodland rim from Whiskey Hill, Montana; (*b, d*) Late Plains Woodland rims from Summit Lake (39GT19) (Lake Benton phase), South Dakota; (*c*) Late Plains Woodland from Hartford Beach (39RO5), South Dakota.

shelter has been found at only the Over's La Roche site in South Dakota (Hoffman 1968). Here, on a Missouri River terrace, an oval dwelling about 23 by 27 feet was outlined by postholes, with a single hearth in the center back of the structure.

There is as yet only one recognized subdivision of the generalized Northern Plains Woodland or Besant phase: the Sonota burial complex. This complex consists of a group of burial mounds and an apparently associated campsite (Stelzer) on the Missouri River in southern North Dakota and northern South Dakota and east to the James River valley (Neuman 1960, 1975) dating from the beginnings of Northern Plains Woodland, from A.D. 100 to 150 until about A.D. 600. As the ceremonial/symbolic artifacts common in the mounds rarely are found in campsites or bison kills, it is not often possible to correlate other sites with mounds. In the absence of demonstrated differences in the basic culture, we support the position (Reeves 1983) that the Besant phase and the Sonota burial complex are the same culture, with the burial mounds representing the burial practices of these people in that part of the Northern Plains. Besant burial practices elsewhere on the Northern Plains are not documented, but do not include mounds.

Sonota mounds contain a rectangular subfloor tomb in which dismembered bodies and secondary burials were placed. Red ocher was liberally placed over the bones. Grave goods include objects that could have been obtained only in trade: obsidian, Gulf coast conch shell, *Olivella, Marginella,* and *Dentalium,* as well as pottery and artifacts with Hopewellian overtones such as carved human palates and worked bear maxillae (Neuman 1975). The pottery has more complex decorations than most Northern Plains Middle Woodland and is reminiscent of some Hopewell ceramics. In sum, the mounds combine Hopewellian construction, burial treatment, and distinctive artifacts with an adaptation of the ceremony to include bison carcasses in the mound fill.

The mounds of the Sonota burial complex obviously reflect an extension of Hopewell influence into the Northern Plains, although they are isolated from other Hopewell centers, the nearest of which are in Iowa. However, this is not viewed as a migration from the Midwest, since only selected parts of the eastern ceremonial constellation are accepted. Other characteristic Hopewellian traits such as rocker-stamped pottery are absent.

Circular mounds, built simply on the ground surface and sometimes in large numbers, are found along major streams in eastern North and South Dakota and southeastern Manitoba. They date from about A.D. 375 to 1100. Most contain secondary burials and sometimes cremations. Grave goods are limited, although artifacts are sometimes found in the mound fill. Bits of copper and cremations suggest contacts with groups to the east. Occasionally, later groups also used these mounds to bury their dead, such as at the Sitting Crow mounds (39BF225) in South Dakota.

There are many other mound sites, particularly in the Dakotas and Manitoba. There have been few modern investigations of these sites, and because many of them lack sufficiently diagnostic artifacts and radiocarbon dates, it usually is not possible to do more than suggest a general relationship to Northern Plains Middle Woodland.

The Avonlea phase is a nomadic bison-oriented Northern Plains culture dating between about A.D. 450 and 1000, assigned to Reeves's Tunaxa tradition. Continuity in lithic preferences and settlement patterns and diminution of the late Pelican Lake point suggest that Avonlea developed out of Pelican Lake (Reeves 1983). Avonlea is easily distinguished by its small, fine, side-notched point (Figure 7.7). There are two distinctive ceramic types (A. M. Johnson 1988),

2 cm

Figure 7.7. Avonlea arrowpoints.

but their disjointed distributions suggest different modes for the transmission of ceramics to Avonlea culture.

Although Avonlea overlaps in time and space with Besant, the nature of their relationship is unknown. Avonlea and Besant are rarely found together in undisturbed components. However, the Truman mound in South Dakota (Neuman 1960) contains parallel-grooved pottery, which suggests contacts between contemporary Plains Woodland and Avonlea peoples.

Fewer than 20 sites have parallel-grooved ceramics. Pottery with this surface treatment is of the Middle Plains Woodland ceramic tradition and rarely is decorated. The parallel-grooved pottery has a south-to-north distribution across the eastern half of Avonlea distribution—the Dakotas, eastern Montana, southern Saskatchewan, and Manitoba—and is so uncommon that it constitutes only an incidental part of the material-culture assemblage. In general, ceramics are very rare and usually absent in Avonlea sites to the south of the international boundary and away from the Missouri River trench.

Avonlea pottery with fabric- or net-impressed surface treatment has a stubby globular form without a distinct neck and with punctate designs on the rim. This form is closer to Late Plains Woodland than Middle Woodland. The dynamics of its addition to Avonlea material culture is unclear, but it has been suggested that pottery is associated with Laurel–Avonlea interactions (Burley et al. 1982:82). Small samples of net-impressed pottery are a common part of assemblages in prairie-province Avonlea camps, but rarely are found south of the international boundary. Smoothed surface treatment may also occur on pottery in Avonlea sites, but is very rare. The Wardell site in Wyoming has such a vessel with smoothed surface treatment and Middle Plains Woodland form (Frison 1973).

From mid-Avonlea times to the historic period, there are local Northern Plains groups that do not share in the Plains Woodland ceramic and cultural traditions. For example, the Saddle Butte phase in northern Montana (Brumley and Rennie 1993) appears in the latter half of the Avonlea period and lasts into the Old Woman's phase.

Late Plains Woodland pottery has a slightly outflaring rim and a more distinct neck and shoulder than that of Middle Plains Woodland. Surface treatment includes smoothing, simple stamping, and cord-roughening. Decorations often consist of multiple rows of cord impressions. In southern South Dakota, several Loseke-variant sites, such as Arp (Gant 1967), contain both generalized Late Plains Woodland and late Late Plains Woodland Great Oasis components.

Middle Plains Woodland in the Dakotas apparently evolved into a currently unnamed Late Woodland culture about which little is known. Culture change may have been stimulated by population pressure from and contact with the Initial Middle Missouri variant. At the Cross Ranch site north of Bismarck, components at two sites with small side-notched projectile points and cord-roughened sherds are interpreted as Late Woodland (Ahler et al. 1981). Other evidence comes from the badlands of western South Dakota, where Late Plains Woodland pottery has a slightly constricted neck and globular vessel form and is associated with side-notched points (A. M. Johnson 1996). That this ceramic tradition and culture is widespread is suggested by a similar but smaller vessel recently found at the Janssen site near Broadus in southern Montana. These Late Plains Woodland vessels are not decorated.

Influences from the northern Midwest (Minnesota and Ontario) are seen (1) in the presence of the Arvilla Burial Mound complex in the Red River valley of North Dakota (E. Johnson 1973); (2) in the intrusion of Middle Woodland Laurel and Late Woodland Blackduck and Sandy Lake peoples into the Northeastern Plains areas of Manitoba, Saskatchewan, and North Dakota; and (3) in the linear mounds along the Missouri River and in eastern North Dakota (Chomko and Wood 1973). Other Woodland movement onto the Plains (Mortlach and Selkirk) are included here, as is the apparently in situ development of the Old Woman's phase.

The Arvilla complex is found from central Minnesota to the Red River of eastern North Dakota and dates from about A.D. 600 to 900. Linear mounds occur as part of the complex and may be related to linear and geometric mounds that are widely distributed over the Northeastern Plains as far as the Missouri River in North Dakota and into Manitoba. Linear mounds may be as much as a quarter of a mile long and 40 feet wide; some of them have tumuli on both ends (Chomko and Wood 1973), and geometric mounds may have radiating spokes (Wheeler n.d.). Linear mounds are inadequately investigated, and more than one culture may be responsible for their construction and use—only one of which may be Late Plains Woodland.

Middle Woodland Laurel begins in Michigan, Minnesota, and Ontario about 400 B.C. and lasts until A.D. 1000. Laurel is found primarily outside the study area in the boreal forests of Saskatchewan and Manitoba (Syms 1977:81). The economy is diversified and includes fishing. Laurel pottery has a smoothed surface treatment with typical Middle Woodland form. Decoration includes dentate stamping, trailing, and bossing. These vessels often break along coil junctions.

The Late Woodland Blackduck follows the Laurel phase from about A.D. 950 and into protohistoric times in Ontario (Syms 1977:101) and on the northeastern edge of the Northern Plains—but not as far as Montana and Saskatchewan. Blackduck has a wild rice–water resources and hunting economic base, with Prairie and Plains Side-notched points (Dyck 1983). Pottery is cord-roughened and globular with shoulders, rounded bases, and thickened lips. Decoration is oriented vertically, obliquely, or horizontally, with cord-wrapped rod impressions, punctations, and lesser amounts of trailing. Different design elements and techniques may be combined on the same vessel.

To the south, following Blackduck, Sandy Lake sites occur in western Minnesota, southern Manitoba, and eastern North Dakota in the prairie–woodland ecotone. Ceramics have smoothed surfaces. Dates range from A.D. 1000 to 1700 (Michlovic 1985). Sandy Lake is believed to be protohistoric Eastern Dakota and/or Assiniboine and may be related to the Siouan occupation of the Northern Plains (Anfinson 1979:176). Most sites contain evidence of hunting and gathering, while the Shea site in eastern North Dakota suggests the presence of horticulture (Michlovic and Schneider 1988).

Following Blackduck is the Pehonan complex in the parklands along the Saskatchewan River. Fur-trade records allow identification of the late prehistoric/historic Pehonan complex as prehistoric and historic Cree (Meyer and McKeand 1994). The projectile points are side notched and triangular unnotched. The ceramics are called Selkirk and are coiled, with indistinct necks and high, vertical rims. Decoration includes punctations and trailing.

The Pehonan people moved from the parklands south to the Plains and north into the boreal forest to exploit a wide range of seasonally available resources and to trade with Mortlach peoples and others.

Most Mortlach sites are south of the Qu'Appelle valley in southern Saskatchewan and west of the Missouri Coteau in northwestern North Dakota and northeastern Montana (Malainey 1991). The Mortlach people successfully hunted bison with small side-notched points. The temporal range of the Mortlach phase is from A.D. 1520 to 1790. Late sites contain small amounts of trade goods. Walde (1994) makes an excellent case for Mortlach being prehistoric and protohistoric Assiniboine.

Mortlach vessels are globular and shouldered, sometimes with a thickened exterior lip and upper rim. Straight rims and vertical profiles of uniform thickness are most common. Occasionally, complex lip forms and S-rims may be present. Shoulders may be decorated. The Mortlach phase is characterized by the great diversity in ceramic attributes and combinations.

In contrast to the Woodland groups that moved out onto the Plains, the Old Woman's phase is a local development. It is found in Montana, Alberta, and Saskatchewan from A.D. 1000 to 1725. The phase is characterized by Saskatchewan Basin–complex pottery (Byrne 1973) and Prairie Side-notched or Plains Side-notched points (Kehoe 1966). Saskatchewan Basin–complex pottery is thick and globular, with deep, smeared cord impressions. The people had a nomadic bison-hunting economy, and Reeves (1983) suggests that the historic Blackfeet are derived from this phase.

Conclusion

Plains Woodland sites in the Northern Plains share characteristics with the Woodland period elsewhere. Early Plains Woodland cultures had a limited presence in southern South Dakota near the Missouri River and the eastern border of the Dakotas, while Middle Woodland culture is widespread. The Middle Plains Woodland tradition in the Missouri River valley and elsewhere is followed by the Late Plains Woodland, which lasts to the protohistoric/historic period, particularly in the eastern prairie provinces and adjoining areas. Early and Middle Plains Woodland economies emphasized bison hunting, and while Late Plains Woodland economies still included bison, a wider range of other resources from fish to beaver played important roles. Early to Late Woodland pottery follows the general decoration and vessel forms so well illustrated in the Central Plains. An indigenous Besant phase accepts Middle Woodland traits of burial mounds and ceramics, while later Plains Woodland is a combination of local groups doing the same, plus movement of people from the northern Midwest out onto the Plains.

There is evidence for interaction between and among these different groups, and it is suggested that the parallel-grooved pottery of Avonlea is derived from or influenced by contact with Central Plains Middle Woodland. Mortlach and Extended Coalescent variant peoples and possibly other Middle Missouri villagers were in contact. Now that a culture history is available, the interactions between groups are beginning to be identified. The complexity of this large area has not been previously appreciated, and the archaeology of the past 2000 years provides a great opportunity for research into cultural dynamics of the Northern Plains.

References

Adair, M. J.
   1977   Subsistence Exploitation at the Young Site. M. A. thesis, Department of Anthropology, University of Kansas, Lawrence.
   1988   *Prehistoric Agriculture in the Central Plains.* University of Kansas, Publications in Anthropology, no. 16. Lawrence.
Adair, M. J., and M. E. Brown
   1981   Late Woodland Occupation at the Two Deer Site (14BU55). In History and Prehistory of the El Dorado Lake Area (Phase II), edited by M. J. Adair. Manuscript on file, University of Kansas, Museum of Anthropology, Lawrence.
Ahler, S. A., C. H. Lee, and C. R. Falk
   1981   *Cross Ranch Archeology: Test Excavations at Eight Sites in the Breaks Zone, 1980–1981 Program.* University of North Dakota, Department of Anthropology and Archaeology, Grand Forks. Report to the National Park Service, Midwest Archeological Center, Lincoln, Neb.
Anfinson, S. F.
   1979   *A Handbook of Minnesota Prehistoric Ceramics.* Minnesota Archaeological Society, Occasional Publications in Minnesota Anthropology, no. 5. Fort Snelling.
   1982   The Prehistoric Archaeology of the Prairie Lake Region. *Journal of the North Dakota Archaeological Association* 1: 65–90.

Artz, J. A.
1980   Soil-Geomorphic Evidence for Environmental Change on the Southeastern Periphery of the Central Plains. Paper presented at the thirty-eighth annual Plains Conference, Iowa City.

Barr, T. P.
1966   *The Pruitt Site: A Late Plains Woodland Manifestation in Murray County, Oklahoma*. University of Oklahoma, Oklahoma River Basin Survey Project, Archaeological Site Report no. 5. Norman.
1971   The Kansas Anthropological Association Fall Dig, 1971. *Kansas Anthropological Association Newsletter* 17, no. 3:1–2.

Bass, W. M., III, D. McWilliams, and B. A. Jones
1967   Archaeological Investigations at Five Sites in Lyon, Jefferson, and Phillips Counties, Kansas. *Transactions of the Kansas Academy of Science* 70:471–489.

Baugh, T. G.
1991   *The Avoca Site (14JN332): Excavation of a Grasshopper Falls Phase Structure, Jackson County, Kansas*. Kansas State Historical Society, Contract Archaeology Series, Publication no. 8. Topeka.

Bell, P.
1976   Spatial and Temporal Variability Within the Trowbridge Site, a Kansas City Hopewell Village. In *Hopewellian Archaeology in the Lower Missouri Valley*, edited by A. E. Johnson, 16–58. University of Kansas, Publications in Anthropology, no. 8. Lawrence.

Bell, R. E., and D. A. Baerreis
1951   A Survey of Oklahoma Archaeology. *Bulletin of the Texas Archeological and Paleontological Society* 22:7–100.

Benn, D. W.
1980   MAD Ceramics. Manuscript on file, Luther College, Archaeological Research Center, Decorah, Iowa.
1990   *Woodland Cultures on the Western Prairies: The Rainbow Site Investigations*. University of Iowa, Office of the State Archaeologist, Report no. 18. Iowa City.

Bonney, R. A.
1970   Early Woodland in Minnesota. *Plains Anthropologist* 15: 302–304.

Bowman, P. W.
1960   *Coal-Oil Canyon, 14LO1*. Kansas Anthropological Association, Bulletin no. 1. Hays.

Boyd, D. K.
1995   The Palo Duro Complex: Redefining the Early Ceramic Period in the Caprock Canyonlands. *Bulletin of the Texas Archeological Society* 66:461–518.

Bradley, L. E.
1968   Archaeological Investigations in the Melvern Reservoir, Osage County, Kansas, 1967. Manuscript on file, University of Kansas, Museum of Anthropology, Lawrence.

Brown, K. L.
1981   Excavations at the Sperry Site, 23JA85. In Prehistoric Cultural Resources Within the Right-of-Way of the Proposed Little Blue River Channel, Jackson County, Missouri, compiled by K. L. Brown and R. J. Ziegler, 190–283. Manuscript on file, University of Kansas, Museum of Anthropology, Lawrence.
1984   Pomona: A Plains Village Variant in Eastern Kansas and Western Missouri. Ph.D. diss., Department of Anthropology, University of Kansas, Lawrence.

Brumley, J. H., and P. Rennie
  1993   Results of Investigations at the King Site Along the East Margins of the Little Rocky Mountains. Consultants report prepared for Fort Belknap College, Fort Belknap, Mont.

Burley, D., J. Prentice, and J. Finnigan
  1982   The Prehistory of the Nipawin Region and Its Relationship to Northern Plains and Boreal Forest Culture History. In *Nipawin Reservoir Heritage Study.* Vol. 3, *Regional Overview and Research Considerations,* edited by D. Burley and D. Meyer, pt. 4, 44–88. Saskatchewan Research Council, Saskatoon.

Butler, W. B.
  1986   Taxonomy in Northeastern Colorado Prehistory. Ph.D. diss., Department of Anthropology, University of Missouri, Columbia.
  1988   The Woodland Period in Northeastern Colorado. *Plains Anthropologist* 33:449–466.

Butler, W. B., S. A. Chomko, and J. M. Hoffman
  1986   The Red Creek Burial, El Paso County, Colorado. *Southwestern Lore* 52:6–27.

Byrne, W.
  1973   *The Archaeology and Prehistory of Southern Alberta as Reflected by Ceramics.* National Museum of Man, Mercury Series, Archaeological Survey of Canada, Paper no. 14. Ottawa, Ont.

Caldwell, J. R.
  1964   Interaction Spheres in Prehistory. In *Hopewellian Studies,* edited by J. R. Caldwell and R. L. Hall, 133–143. Illinois State Museum, Scientific Papers, no. 12. Springfield.

Campbell, R. G.
  1969   Prehistoric Panhandle Culture on the Chaquaqua Plateau, Southeastern Colorado. Ph.D. diss., Department of Anthropology, University of Colorado, Boulder.

Carrillo, R. F.
  1973   14MM7: An Archaeological Site in the Hillsdale Reservoir Area, Eastern Kansas. *Kansas Anthropological Association Newsletter* 19:1–34.

Champe, J. L.
  1946   *Ash Hollow Cave.* University of Nebraska Studies, n.s., no. 1. Lincoln.
  1949   The Sweetwater and Ash Hollow Ceramic Types Re-examined. In *Proceedings of the Fifth Plains Conference for Archeology,* Notebook no. 1:43–44. University of Nebraska, Laboratory of Anthropology, Lincoln.

Chapman, C. H.
  1980   *The Archaeology of Missouri,* Vol. 2. University of Missouri Press, Columbia.

Chomko, S. A., and W. R. Wood
  1973   Linear Mounds in the Northeastern Plains. *Archaeology in Montana* 14:1–19.

Craine, E. R.
  1956   The Pfaff Site: A Preliminary Report. *Kansas Anthropological Association Newsletter* 1:1–4.

Davis, L. B., ed.
  1983   *From Microcosm to Macrocosm: Advances in Tipi Ring Investigation and Interpretation.* Plains Anthropologist Memoir no. 19.

Davis, L. B., and M. Wilson, eds.
  1978   *Bison Procurement and Utilization: A Symposium.* Plains Anthropologist Memoir no. 14.

Deaver, K., and S. Deaver
　1988　Preliminary Report on Pedestrian Sample of the Sprint Line in North Dakota. Ethnoscience, Billings, Mont. Submitted to Dames & Moore, Golden, Colo.

Drass, R. R.
　1988　A Reanalysis of the Brewer Site: An Early Plains Village Settlement in Central Oklahoma. *Bulletin of the Oklahoma Anthropological Society* 37.

Duffield, L. F.
　1953　The Brewer Site: A Preliminary Report. *Bulletin of the Oklahoma Anthropological Society* 1:61–68.

Dyck, I.
　1983　The Prehistory of Southern Saskatchewan. In *Tracking Ancient Hunters: Prehistoric Archaeology in Saskatchewan,* edited by H. T. Epp and I. Dyck, 63–126. Saskatchewan Archaeological Society, Regina.

Eyman, C. E.
　1966　The Schultz Focus: A Plains Middle Woodland Burial Complex in Eastern Kansas. M.A. thesis, Department of Archaeology, University of Calgary.

Frison, G. C.
　1973　*The Wardell Buffalo Trap, 48SU301: Communal Procurement in the Upper Green River Basin, Wyoming.* University of Michigan, Museum of Anthropology, Anthropological Papers, no. 48. Ann Arbor.

Galm, J. R.
　1978　*The Archaeology of the Curtis Lake Site (34LF-5A), LeFlore County, Oklahoma.* University of Oklahoma, Archaeological Research and Management Center, Research Series, no. 2. Norman.

Gant, R.
　1967　*Report of the Archeological Investigations at the Arp Site, 39BR101, Brule County, South Dakota, 1961.* University of South Dakota, South Dakota Museum, Archeological Studies, Circular no. 12. Vermillion.

Grange, R. T., Jr.
　1980　*Salvage Archeology in the Red Willow Reservoir, Nebraska.* Nebraska State Historical Society, Publications in Anthropology, no. 9. Lincoln.

Gregg, M. L.
　1990　An Early Plains Woodland Structure in the Northeastern Plains. *Plains Anthropologist* 35:29–44.

Griffin, J. B.
　1952　Some Early and Middle Woodland Types in Illinois. In *Hopewellian Communities in Illinois,* edited by T. Duel, 95–130. Illinois State Museum, Scientific Papers, no. 5. Springfield.

Hartley, J. D.
　1974　*The Von Elm Site: An Early Plains-Woodland Complex in North-Central Oklahoma.* University of Oklahoma, Oklahoma River Basin Survey Project, Archaeological Site Report no. 28. Norman.

Heffner, M. L.
　1974　Temporal Variability of Some Kansas City Hopewell Projectile Points. Manuscript on file, University of Kansas, Museum of Anthropology, Lawrence.

Hill, A. T., and M. F. Kivett
　1940　Woodland-Like Manifestations in Nebraska. *Nebraska History* 21:146–243.

Hoffman, J. J.
 1968   *The La Roche Sites.* Smithsonian Intsitution, River Basin Surveys, Publications
         in Salvage Archeology, no. 11. Lincoln, Neb.
Hofman, J. L., and R. L. Brooks
 1989   Prehistoric Culture History: Woodland Complexes in the Southern Great
         Plains. In *From Clovis to Comanchero: Archeological Overview of the Southern
         Great Plains,* edited by J. L. Hofman, R. L. Brooks, J. S. Hays, D. W. Owsley,
         R. L. Jantz, M. K. Marks, and M. H. Manhein, 61–70. Arkansas Archeological
         Survey, Research Series, no. 35. Fayetteville.
Hughes, D., and J. M. Briscoe
 1987   Field Investigations of Quillan Site (34 OK-11): Monitoring of Construction,
         1987. Manuscript on file, University of Oklahoma, Oklahoma Archeological
         Survey, Norman.
Hughes, J. T.
 1962   Lake Creek: A Woodland Site in the Texas Panhandle. *Bulletin of the Texas
         Archeological and Paleontological Society* 32:65–84.
Hurt, W. R., Jr.
 1952   *Report of the Investigation of the Scalp Creek Site, 39GR1, and the Ellis Creek Site,
         39GR2, Gregory County, South Dakota.* South Dakota Archaeological Commis-
         sion, Archaeological Studies, Circular no. 4. Vermillion.
Irwin, C., and H. Irwin
 1957   The Archeology of the Agate Bluff Area, Colorado. *Plains Anthropologist*
         8:15–38.
Irwin, H., and C. Irwin
 1959   *Excavations at the LoDaisKa Site in the Denver, Colorado, Area.* Denver Museum
         of Natural History Proceedings, no. 8.
Johnson, A. E.
 1968   *Archaeological Investigations in the Clinton Reservoir Area, Eastern Kansas.* United
         States Department of Commerce, National Bureau of Standards, Institute for
         Applied Technology, Clearinghouse for Federal Scientific and Technical Infor-
         mation, no. 5. Washington, D.C.
 1974   Settlement Pattern Variability in Brush Creek Valley, Platte County, Missouri.
         Plains Anthropologist 19:107–122.
 1976   A Model of the Kansas City Hopewell Subsistence-Settlement System. In
         Hopewellian Archaeology in the Lower Missouri River Valley, edited by A. E.
         Johnson, 7–15. University of Kansas, Publications in Anthropology, no. 8.
         Lawrence.
 1979   Kansas City Hopewell. In *Hopewellian Archaeology: The Chillicothe Conference,*
         edited by D. S. Brose, 86–93. Kent State University Press, Kent, Ohio.
 1983   Late Woodland in the Kansas City Locality. *Plains Anthropologist* 28:99–108.
in press Plains Woodland. In *Plains,* edited by R. J. DeMallie. Vol. 13 of *Handbook of
         North American Indians,* W. C. Sturtevant, general editor. Smithsonian Institu-
         tion Press, Washington, D.C.
Johnson, A. E., and A. S. Johnson
 1975   K-Means and Temporal Variability in Kansas City Hopewell Ceramics. *Ameri-
         can Antiquity* 40:283–295.
Johnson, A. E., C. A. Johnson II, B. Logan, N. O'Malley, and R. J. Ziegler
 1980   Prehistoric Cultural Resources of Tuttle Creek Lake, Kansas. Manuscript on
         file, University of Kansas, Museum of Anthropology, Lawrence.

Johnson, A. M.
　1988　Parallel-Grooved Ceramics: An Additional to Avonlea Material Culture. In *Avonlea Yesterday and Today: Archaeology and Prehistory,* edited by L. B. Davis, 137–144. Brigdens, Regina, Sask.
　1996　The Fog Creek Archeological Sites, Badlands National Park. Report on file, National Park Service, Rocky Mountain Region, Denver.
Johnson, E.
　1973　*The Arvilla Complex.* Minnesota Historical Society, Minnesota Prehistoric Archaeology Series, no. 9. St. Paul.
Johnson, E. M.
　1975　*Faunal and Floral Material from a Kansas City Hopewell Site.* Texas Tech University, Museum, Occasional Papers, no. 36. Lubbock.
Katz, P. R.
　1974　*Kansas City Hopewell Activities at the Diester Site.* University of Kansas, Museum of Anthropology, Research Series, no. 1. Lawrence.
Kehoe, T. F.
　1966　The Small Side-Notched Point System of the Northern Plains. *American Antiquity* 31:827–841.
Keyes, C. R.
　1949　Four Iowa Archaeologies with Plains Affinities. In *Proceedings of the Fifth Plains Conference for Archeology,* Notebook no. 1:96–97. University of Nebraska, Laboratory of Anthropology, Lincoln.
Kivett, M. F.
　1949a　Archaeological Investigations in Medicine Creek Reservoir, Nebraska. *American Antiquity* 14:278–284.
　1949b　A Woodland Pottery Type from Nebraska. In *Proceedings of the Fifth Plains Conference for Archeology,* Notebook no. 1:67–69. University of Nebraska, Laboratory of Anthropology, Lincoln.
　1952　*Woodland Sites in Nebraska.* Nebraska State Historical Society, Publications in Anthropology, no. 1. Lincoln.
　1953　The Woodruff Ossuary, a Prehistoric Burial Site in Phillips County, Kansas. *Bureau of American Ethnology Bulletin* 154:103–141.
Lehmer, D. J.
　1971　*Introduction to Middle Missouri Archeology.* National Park Service, Anthropological Papers, no. 1. Washington, D.C.
Lehmer, D. J., W. R. Wood, and C. L. Dill
　1978　The Knife River Phase. Report to the National Park Service, Interagency Archeological Services, Denver, by Dana College and the University of Missouri, Columbia.
Lintz, C., J. Spath, D. Hughes, and J. Huebner
　1991　Additional Radiocarbon Dates from the Twilla Bison Kill Site. *Bulletin of the Texas Archeological Society* 60:257–266.
Ludwickson, J., D. Blakeslee, and J. O'Shea
　1987　*Missouri River Recreational River: Native American Cultural Resources.* Wichita State University, Publications in Anthropology, no. 3.
Lyons, R. D., and A. M. Johnson
　1994　Lehman Cave. *Southwestern Lore* 60:6–32.
Malainey, M. E.
　1991　Internal and External Relationships of Saskatchewan Plains Pottery Assem-

blages: Circa A.D. 1300 to Contact. M.A. thesis, Department of Anthropology and Archaeology, University of Saskatchewan, Saskatoon.

McHugh, W. P.
1980   Before Smith's Mill: Archaeological and Geological Investigations in the Little Platte River Valley, Western Missouri. GAI Consultants, Monroeville, Pa.

Meyer, D., and P. McKeand
1994   *The Municipal Camp Site (FhNa-113) Excavation Results: Selkirk and Middle Period Components.* Saskatchewan Archaeology 15.

Michlovic, M. G.
1985   The Problem of the Teton Migration. In *Archaeology, Ecology and Ethnohistory of the Prairie–Forest Border Zone of Minnesota and Manitoba,* edited by J. Spector and E. Johnson, 131–145. J and L Reprint, Lincoln, Neb.

Michlovic, M. G., and F. Schneider
1988   The Archaeology of the Shea Site (32CS101). Report submitted to the State Historical Society of North Dakota by Moorhead State University.

Nelson, C. E.
1971   The George W. Lindsay Ranch Site, 5JF11. *Southwestern Lore* 37:1–14.

Neuman, R. W.
1960   The Truman Mound Site, Big Bend Reservoir Area, South Dakota. *American Antiquity* 26:78–92.
1975   *The Sonota Complex and Associated Sites on the Northern Great Plains.* Nebraska State Historical Society, Publications in Anthropology, no. 6. Lincoln.

O'Brien, P. J., C. Larsen, J. O'Grady, B. O'Neill, and A. S. Stirland
1973   The Elliott Site (14GE303): A Preliminary Report. *Plains Anthropologist* 18:54–72.

O'Malley, N.
1979   Subsistence Strategies at the Sperry Site, Jackson County, Missouri. Manuscript on file, University of Kansas, Museum of Anthropology, Lawrence.

O'Neill, B. P., M. J. Tate, P. D. Friedman, and R. J. Mutaw
1988   Data Recovery Program at Site 5AH380 for the City of Aurura Proposed Senac Dam and Reservoir, Arapaho County, Colorado. Powers Elevation Company. Aurora, Colo.

Parks, S. G.
1978   Test Excavations at 14GE41: A Schultz Focus Habitation Site at Milford Lake, Kansas. Manuscript on file, Kansas State University, Department of Sociology, Anthropology, and Social Work, Manhattan.

Peterson, R. R., Jr.
1981   The Bowlin Bridge Site (23JA38). In *Little Blue Prehistory,* edited by L. J. Schmits, 348–392. Manuscript. Soil Systems, Earth Systems Division, Kansas City, Mo.

Phenice, T. W.
1969   *An Analysis of the Human Skeletal Material from Burial Mounds in North-Central Kansas.* University of Kansas, Publications in Anthropology, no. 1. Lawrence.

Quigg, J. M.
1997   The Sanders Site (41HF128): A Single Event Late Archaic Camp/Bison Processing Site in Hansford County, Texas. Technical Report no. 19751. Mariah Associates, Laramie, Wyo.

Reeder, R. L
1980   The Sohn Site: A Lowland Nebo Hill Complex Campsite. In *Prehistory on the*

Prairie–Plains Border, edited by A. E. Johnson, 55–66. University of Kansas, Publications in Anthropology, no. 12. Lawrence.

Reeves, B. O. K.
1983   *Culture Change in the Northern Plains: 1000 B.C.–A.D. 1000.* Archaeological Survey of Alberta, Occasional Paper no. 20. Edmonton.

Reher, C. A.
1971   A Survey of Ceramic Sites in Southeastern Wyoming. M.A. thesis, Department of Anthropology, University of Wyoming, Laramie.

Reichart, M.
1974   The Archeological Resources of Cedar Creek. Manuscript on file, Kansas State Historical Society, Topeka.

Reid, K. C.
1976   Prehistoric Trade in the Lower Missouri River Valley. In *Hopewellian Archaeology in the Lower Missouri Valley,* edited by A. E. Johnson, 63–99. University of Kansas, Publications in Anthropology, no. 8. Lawrence.
1984   *Nebo Hill.* University of Kansas, Publications in Anthropology, no. 15. Lawrence.

Reid, K. C., and J. A. Artz
1984   *Hunters of the Forest Edge: Culture, Time, and Process in the Little Caney Basin.* University of Tulsa, Laboratory of Archeology, Contributions to Archeology, no. 14; University of Oklahoma, Oklahoma Archaeological Survey, Studies in Oklahoma's Past, no. 13. Norman.

Reynolds, J. D.
1979   *The Grasshopper Falls Phase of the Plains Woodland.* Kansas State Historical Society, Anthropological Series, no. 7. Topeka.

Schmits, L. J.
1980   The Dead Hickory Site, 14CF301. In *Salvage Archeology of the John Redmond Lake, Kansas,* edited by T. A. Witty, 133–162. Kansas State Historical Society, Anthropological Series, no. 8. Topeka.

Schmits, L. J., C. A. Wright, and M. J. Adair
1981   Cultural Adaptation in the Little Blue River Valley. In *Little Blue Prehistory,* edited by L. J. Schmits, 589–637. Manuscript. Soil Systems, Earth Systems Division, Kansas City, Mo.

Scott, G. R.
1963   *Quaternary Geology and Geomorphic History of the Kassler Quadrangle, Colorado.* United States Geological Survey, Professional Paper 421-A. Washington, D.C.

Shippee, J. M.
1967   *Archeological Remains in the Area of Kansas City: The Woodland Period, Early, Middle, and Late.* Missouri Archaeological Society, Research Series, no. 5. Columbia.

Smith, C. S.
1949   Archaeological Investigations in Ellsworth and Rice Counties, Kansas. *American Antiquity* 14:257–360.

Struever, S., and G. L. Houart
1972   An Analysis of the Hopewell Interaction Sphere. In *Social Exchange and Interaction,* edited by E. N. Wilmsen, 47–49. University of Michigan, Museum of Anthropology, Anthropological Papers, no. 46. Ann Arbor.

Syms, E. L.
1977   *Cultural Ecology and Ecological Dynamics of the Ceramic Period in Southwestern Manitoba.* Plains Anthropologist Memoir no. 12.

Thompson, D. M., and E. A. Bettis, III
1980   Archeology and Holocene Landscape Evolution in the Missouri Drainage of Iowa. *Journal of the Iowa Archeological Society* 27:1–60.
Tibesar, W. L.
1980   An Intra-Site Discussion of the Grayrocks Archeological Site, 48PL65. M.A. thesis, Department of Anthropology, University of Wyoming, Laramie.
Vehik, S. C.
1984   The Woodland Occupations. In *Prehistory of Oklahoma,* edited by R. E. Bell, 175–197. Academic Press, New York.
Vehik, S. C., and Pailes, R. A.
1979   *Excavations in the Copan Reservoir of Northeastern Oklahoma and Southeastern Kansas (1974).* University of Oklahoma, Oklahoma Archaeological Research and Management Center, Research Series, no. 4. Norman.
Walde, D.
1994   The Mortlach Phase. Ph.D. diss., Department of Archaeology, University of Calgary.
Wedel, W. R.
1959   *An Introduction to Kansas Archeology.* Bureau of American Ethnology Bulletin 174. Washington, D.C.
1961   *Prehistoric Man on the Great Plains.* University of Oklahoma Press, Norman.
Wheeler, R. P.
n.d.   Mounds and Earthworks in the Jamestown Reservoir, North Dakota. Manuscript on file, National Park Service, Midwest Archeological Center, Lincoln, Neb.
Wheeler, R. P., and A. M. Johnson
1985   A Stratified Woodland Site in the Oahe Reservoir Area. South Dakota. *South Dakota Archaeology* 8/9:80–97.
Witty, T. A.
1962   *Archaeological Investigations of the Hell Creek Valley in the Wilson Reservoir, Russell and Lincoln Counties, Kansas.* Kansas State Historical Society, Anthropological Series, no. 1. Topeka.
1966   The West Island Site, 14PH10, a Keith Focus Plains Woodland Site in Kirwin Reservoir, Phillips County, Kansas. *Plains Anthropologist* 11:127–134.
1967   The Pomona Focus. *Kansas Anthropological Association Newsletter* 12:1–5.
1969   The Kansas Anthropological Association Fall Dig, 1969. *Kansas Anthropological Association Newsletter* 16:1–3.
Wood, J. J.
1967   Archaeological Investigations in Northeastern Colorado. Ph.D. diss., Department of Anthropology, University of Colorado, Boulder.
Wood, W. R.
1956   A Woodland Site near Williston, North Dakota. *Plains Anthropologist* 6:21–24.
Wood, W. R., and A. M. Johnson
1973 High Butte, 32ME13: A Missouri Valley Woodland–Besant Site. *Archaeology in Montana* 14:39–83.
Wright, C. A.
1980   Archaeological Investigations in the Proposed Blue Springs Lake Area, Jackson County, Missouri: The Early Woodland Period. Manuscript on file, University of Kansas, Museum of Anthropology, Lawrence.

Ziegler, R. J.
   1981a   Excavations at 23JA40. In Prehistoric Cultural Resources Within the Right-of-
          Way of the Proposed Little Blue River Channel, Jackson County, Missouri,
          compiled by K. L. Brown and R. J. Ziegler, 142–189. Manuscript on file,
          University of Kansas, Museum of Anthropology, Lawrence.
   1981b   Sites Tested. In Prehistoric Cultural Resources Within the Right-of-Way of the
          Proposed Little Blue River Channel, Jackson County, Missouri, compiled by
          K. L. Brown and R. J. Ziegler, 78–141. Manuscript on file, University of Kan-
          sas, Museum of Anthropology, Lawrence.

8. The Central Plains Tradition

Terry L. Steinacher and Gayle F. Carlson

The Central Plains tradition was a lifeway based on the occupation of isolated to small clusters of earthlodges, and whose inhabitants practiced a
diversified subsistence economy. Sites are concentrated in the Central Plains
subarea and span a period from approximately A.D. 900 to about 1450. The beginning of this tradition is marked by the integration of small-scale horticulture
into an older hunting and gathering society. The end of the tradition is marked
by apparent changes in the sociopolitical organization from dispersed settlements to large compact ones. There are numerous syntheses and other statements on the tradition (especially Wedel 1986).

Archaeological research on the Central Plains tradition was severely cur-
tailed after large-scale federal projects ended in the late 1960s. Furthermore,
there have been few major efforts to analyze the large backlog of data collected
by the Works Progress Administration excavations undertaken in the 1930s
and the reservoir salvage efforts conducted in the late 1940s and early 1950s.
Most recent research has been devoted to the long-standing problem of culture-
historical reconstruction, with only minor efforts focused on culture reconstruction and culture process. Furthermore, publication has not kept pace with
research, and much research remains in manuscript form.

There has been considerable debate on the proper application of Willey and
Phillips's (1958) taxonomic scheme for organizing Central Plains–tradition data
(Blakeslee and Caldwell 1979; L. Brown 1966, 1967; Krause 1969, 1982; Lippincott
1976). Thus we make no claim for the primacy of the phase and subphase
classification presented in this chapter, save that it seems to be the most parsimonious means to present the data, and it does not depart radically from existing formulations. And we propose no new taxonomic units, although the definitions of phases used differ in some respects from earlier ones (Figure 8.1).

It is important to note that past and present reconstructions depend heavily
on perceptions of ceramic similarities and differences. Pottery has also been
used in lieu of firm chronological methods for establishing sequences of sites
and deriving relations and trends. Our synthesis follows this approach in that it
is based on a reevaluation of rim form and decoration on pottery from reported
sites having samples of 40 or more rim sherds. It should be kept in mind, however, that if ethnographic analogies (Dunbar 1880; Grinnell 1893) hold true for
the prehistoric period, the current taxonomies are probably based on a female-
dominated craft, so the relations postulated are strongly biased toward a female-

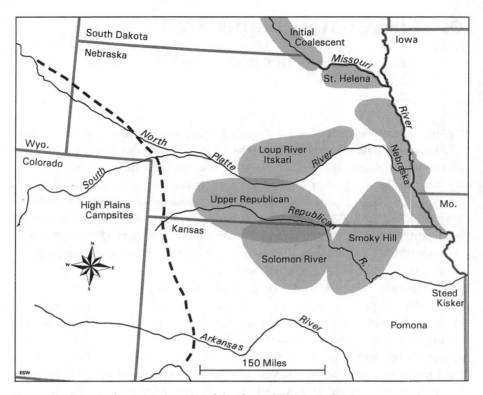

Figure 8.1. Principal taxonomic units of the Central Plains tradition.

interaction system. A more balanced approach is desirable, but too few comparative databases are available for traditionally male-dominated crafts.

Origin and Initial Developments of the Central Plains Tradition

A key element in differentiating the Central Plains tradition from the older
Plains Woodland tradition is the successful adoption of small-scale horticulture,
based primarily on maize. There is some evidence for incipient horticulture in
Plains Woodland, but when it began and how much of an impact it made is still
poorly understood (Adair 1988; Kivett 1952:57–58; Wedel 1943:26). Horticulture
was added to the older pattern of hunting and gathering in the Central Plains
tradition, but at no time does it appear to have supplanted the other two activities. The exact mix of activities at any one time or place has never been specifically demonstrated (Mick 1983), and although various estimates of the importance of maize have been expressed (for example, dominant, about half
gardening and half hunting-gathering), they remain speculative. The adoption

of maize was accompanied by that of other important cultigens: beans, sunflowers, squash, gourds, and tobacco.

The apparent increase in the abundance of sites for this period over earlier times intimates that a population increase accompanied the change in subsistence. This may reflect an increase in the stability of food sources and a dampening of periodic nutritional deficiencies. It may also have had a significant effect on infant and elderly mortality rates by providing additional food. Gardening would also have required at least semipermanent residence, which would have reduced stresses on the newborn and elderly.

Some of the changes in material culture evidenced may have been responses to the adoption of horticulture. The earthlodge may have been a functional response to the more sedentary lifeway and the need for processing, drying, and storage facilities. A number of technological changes in tools would also have resulted in such items as hoes, maize-shelling implements, and milling stones. The appearance of a large number of bell-shaped pits during this period is also believed to be related to the increased need for food storage. Finally, pottery vessels also seem to become more abundant and are increasingly elaborate in form and style, again perhaps reflecting the increased processing and cooking of garden products.

It has been proposed that the earliest maize on the Plains was an eight-rowed variety, originally developed in the southwestern United States, that was particularly adapted to a climate like that of the Central Plains (Cutler and Blake 1973; Galinat and Campbell 1967; Galinat and Gunnerson 1963). That the earliest maize on the Plains ultimately came from a southwestern source is surely correct, but the route it followed and the reasons for its adoption remain to be demonstrated. It appears that the older notion of maize being transmitted to the Plains through a Mississippian movement is incorrect.

Identifying the earliest appearance of Central Plains–tradition sites is still one of the major culture-historical problems faced by archaeology. There are currently two views on where the first sites appear. Most recently, Roper (1995) hypothesized that the Central Plains tradition has its origins along the Missouri River in the vicinity of the Kansas City and Glenwood localities prior to about A.D. 1100 and possibly before A.D. 1000. A second view has suggested that the earliest sites can be found westward, along the Kansas River system in the Smoky Hill and Solomon River phases. This hypothesis has most recently been developed by Krause (1995).

Roper defined two areas with early dates and suggested that the Central Plains tradition expanded from these areas on the Missouri River outward toward the west and north. This hypothesis is based on the reasoning that there are few dates west of the Missouri River for the period before A.D. 1100. One of these areas is centered around the Kansas City locality and includes sites of the Steed–Kisker phase. O'Brien (1993), based on ceramic comparisons with Mississippian sites, places Steed–Kisker at about A.D. 1000 to 1250 and dismisses earlier dating. The second concentration of dates is from the Glenwood locality of the Nebraska phase. Billeck's (1993) analysis of the dating for the Glenwood locality places the earliest occupation by Nebraska-phase peoples there at about A.D. 1150. Whether Roper's analysis of space–time relations accurately reflects the location of the earliest sites seems open to a number of questions. They include the origins of Steed–Kisker and its special relation to the Central Plains tradition. Also, the methodology of Roper's study has been questioned by Ludwickson (1995).

Krause (1995), using a series of dates from sites in north-central Kansas, has arrived at an alternative interpretation. He has proposed a Sumpter subphase of the Solomon River phase dating to about A.D. 850 to 1150. This hypothesis is based on a series of radiocarbon dates that Roper did not include in her analysis. Based on postulated changes in ceramic attributes that he derived experimentally and through observation of ceramic rim construction, Krause has suggested that this early Central Plains–tradition subphase was derived from an earlier indigenous Plains Woodland group, possibly the Keith variant.

If these sites of the Sumpter subphase do represent some of the earliest Central Plains–tradition communities, it appears that maize was transmitted to a basically indigenous population almost certainly derived from a Late Plains Woodland group. Furthermore, the transmittal would seem to have been through an intermediate group, for there is no evidence in any of the Sumpter-subphase sites of southwestern, Caddoan, or Mississippian elements in ceramics or other tool categories.

The namesake of the Sumpter subphase (Sumpter site, 14OB27), of which we have personal knowledge (Carlson 1967), appears to have a bearing on this problem, either as an example of the direct transition from a previous hunting and gathering strategy or as an example of an indigenous Plains Woodland group coming into contact with early Central Plains populations and undergoing change. The site has several small lodges and one large one that may be contemporaneous or may belong to a later component. One area of the site yielded Kansas City Hopewell material that may be contemporaneous with the small lodges or may represent an earlier component. The small lodges yielded generally early radiocarbon dates, and they also contained maize and a ceramic assemblage apparently blending vestiges of Plains Woodland pottery with elements of the early Central Plains tradition.

Solomon River and Upper Republican Phases

The term "Upper Republican" has been given various meanings and taxonomic identities in Central Plains prehistory. In its earlier usage, it included sites primarily in the Republican River drainage of south-central Nebraska. This was later expanded to include sites in central Nebraska that later were placed in the Loup River/Itskari phase (Blakeslee 1988:6; Champe 1936; Strong 1935; Wedel 1935) (Figure 8.2). At one point, Upper Republican was elevated to the level of a "regional variant" that included three sequent phases: Solomon River, Classic Republican, and Loup River (Krause 1969, 1970). However, many researchers prefer to not use the regional variant and keep these as three phases, usually referring to Classic Republican by the earlier appellation Upper Republican. We also prefer this terminology using the Solomon River and Upper Republican phases.

The Solomon River phase has most recently been divided into two sequent subphases (Sumpter and Dubbert) by Krause (1995), with postulated temporal spans of A.D. 1000 ± 150 years and 1200 ± 150 years, respectively. We agree with Krause that the Sumpter site itself is one of the earliest sites in the Solomon River phase, if not the earliest. Whether the site aggregates that Krause proposes

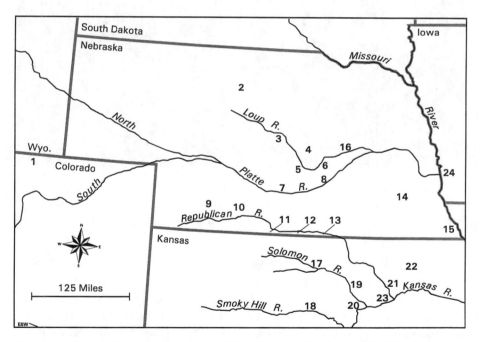

Figure 8.2. Sites of the Central Plains tradition: *Colorado* (1) Agate Bluff; *Nebraska* (2) McIntosh, (3) Sargent, (4) Davis Creek, Sondergaard Ossuary, (5) Sweetwater, (6) Wood River, Schmidt, (7) Flat Rock, (8) Hulme, (9) Red Willow, (10) Medicine Creek, Mowry Bluff, 25FT2, (11) Prairie Dog Creek, Graham Ossuary, Alma Ossuary, (12) Los Creek, (13) Guide Rock, (14) Salt Creek, (15) Nemaha, (16) Burkett; *Kansas* (17) Glen Elder, Sumpter, 14ML11, 14ML15, 14ML16, (18) Root, (19) Minneapolis, (20) Salina Burial Pit, Whiteford, (21) Milford, Miller, Woods, (22) Budenbender, (23) C. C. Witt; *Iowa* (24) Glenwood.

Figure 8.3. Upper Republican–phase House 1 at site 25HN44 being prepared for final photographs. John Champe is on the right; the unfinished Harlan County Reservoir dam is in the far background. (University of Nebraska photograph, 1951)

to include in a Sumpter and a later Dubbert subphase are valid requires further substantiation. In general, sites other than the Sumpter site, in the Glen Elder locality, show broad similarities with Upper Republican sites in Nebraska. However, differences in percentages of ceramic motifs and rim forms, and other minor material-culture variations, appear to warrant a separate Solomon River phase.

The Solomon River phase is located in north-central Kansas along the Solomon and Saline rivers. The Upper Republican phase is located primarily along the central reaches of the Republican River in south-central Nebraska. The material culture of the two phases is very similar, and the geographic position of sites is often more influential than differences in material culture in placing a component in one phase or another. Many of the general characteristics described in this chapter for these two phases are applicable to the other Central

Plains-tradition phases as well, with differences confined primarily to quantity rather than to kind.

Lodges were normally rectangular to subrectangular structures built in shallow pits that may have resulted primarily from the removal of the sod prior to construction. Lodge size ranges from 521.7 to 1206 square feet, with a mean of 868 square feet (based on data in Ludwickson 1980). Entry passages are usually short and are most commonly directed to the east or south. A central fire pit and one or more cache pits are normally associated with the house floors. The subfloor pits usually contain refuse, suggesting that whatever their original function, their final use was as receptacles for household debris (Figure 8.3). Clusters of storage pits occur at some sites outside the lodges, sometimes along terrace edges.

Pottery in earlier sites is usually a sand- and/or grog-tempered, cordmarked ware with a small percentage of the cordmarking being partly to (rarely) heavily smoothed. Vessel form ranges from nearly globular jars to pots with subconoidal bases; shoulders, from those that are angular and well developed to those with gradually rounded forms. Vessel rims either are unthickened or have a thickened bevel or collar. Handles or lugs are rare. Decoration is confined to the outer rim and/or lip, and consists either of incised or excised motifs (usually geometric) or of pinched, applied, or excised nodes (Figures 8.4 and 8.5).

Chipped-stone tools are usually those associated with hunting, processing game, or manufacturing tools. Arrowpoints are small and triangular; they are usually side notched and sometimes base notched as well. Bifacially chipped tools of various forms were used for cutting and chopping. End scrapers,

Figure 8.4. Central Plains–tradition pottery: (*left*) collared vessel; (*right*) unthickened-rim vessel with handles.

Figure 8.5. Central Plains–tradition pottery: (*clockwise*) unthickened-rim vessel with incised shoulder, bowl, miniature vessels.

graver-like tools, drill forms, and retouched and utilized flakes are common. Ground-stone tools include pipes, abraders, hammerstones, spheres, manos, metates/grinding slabs, pitted nutting stones, and disks, as well as processed and raw ocher and hematite (Figure 8.6).

Bone artifacts are dominated by bison-scapula hoes, worked bison-scapula and -ulna tools, awls, shaft wrenches, fishhooks, beads, and tubes. Occasional finds include worked bison toe bones, eagle-bone whistles, and a worked human skull fragment. Antler items are almost equally varied: flakers, awls, handles, drifts, bracelets, shaft wrenches, spatulate objects, and rubbing tools. Shell artifacts consist of spoons, beads, and pendants (Figures 8.7 and 8.8).

In the Glen Elder locality of the Solomon River phase, most of the stone used in making chipped and ground tools comes from local sources (Lippincott 1976:189). Some of the shell artifacts, however, were made from marine shell, denoting at least some extra-local interaction.

Evidence for burial practices in the Solomon River phase comes largely from site 14ML16, a large ossuary pit that contained the remains of about 50 (mostly secondary) human burials. Two clusters of smaller pits were near the ossuary; some of them had served as repositories for individual primary burials that at some point had been transferred to the larger ossuary. Several episodes of burial and reburial are postulated from the jumbled nature of the ossuary materials (Lippincott 1976:181–182). A second and apparently less common pattern of burial was to dispose of the dead in pits within the lodges. A primary child burial and a human skull were recovered at 14ML11 and 14ML15 in the Glen Elder locality under such circumstances.

The settlement pattern for the Solomon River phase has been a focus of much controversy. Krause (1969, 1970) originally postulated three site types for the Glen Elder locality: (1) solitary households, (2) hamlets of two to five lodges, and (3) temporary campsites (that is, sites with no evidence of a permanent dwelling). According to Krause, the small hamlets were generally the earliest sites, and the solitary households and temporary camps came later. The earlier lodges, he said, were generally larger than those at the later sites. Lippincott (1976), though, believed that radiocarbon dates and ceramic seriation show that occupation of the Glen Elder locality can be divided into two periods: one of relatively intense occupation, with all three settlement types represented; and the other of drastically reduced occupation density, consisting of mostly single households and campsites.

Krause's most recent analysis (1995), placing sites in the Sumpter and Dubbert subphases, appears to reflect a realignment of his earlier thinking on settlement. Our review of the data (Carlson 1971; Krause 1969, 1970, 1982, 1995; Lippincott 1976, 1978; Witty 1962), as well as our ceramic analysis and the house-size data collected by Ludwickson (1980), support an early and a late occupation of the Glen Elder locality. However, most of the evidence for an early occupation is based on the Sumpter site. Removal of the Gakushuin dates from the Glen Elder sequence (Blakeslee 1994) will necessitate a reexamination of the dating of the settlement-pattern sequence.

Figure 8.6. Central Plains–tradition worked stone: (*top row*) mano and metate, large biface, elbow pipe; (*middle*) grooved sandstone abrader, polished-stone celt, chipped-stone celt, grooved maul; (*bottom row*) bifacial knives, arrowpoints, drills, scrapers.

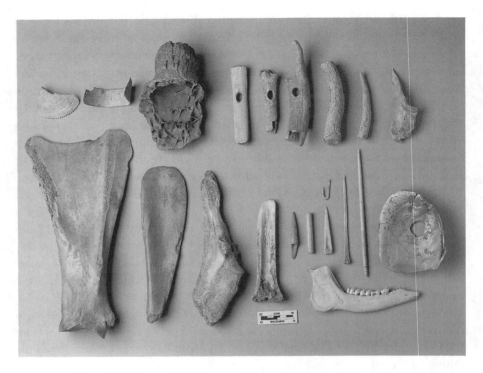

Figure 8.7. Central Plains–tradition bone, antler, and shell work: (*top row*) notched shell, perhaps a scraper; antler bow guard; bison-horn core tool, perhaps a scoop; shaft straighteners; antler tool, perhaps a drift; antler flaking tool; ulna awl; (*bottom row*) bison-scapula hoe; bison-scapula knife; bison-ulna tool; metapodial gouge; antler harpoon head; bone tube; bone fishhook; bone awls; bone matting needle; shell hoe; deer-mandible sickle.

A study of the faunal remains from the Glen Elder locality suggests a difference in the exploitation of game between the hamlets and the isolated homesteads (Sproule 1981). The occupants of the hamlets used a wider range of available resources than those living in homesteads, a difference that Sproule feels supports seasonality of occupation as being the difference between the two settlement types, although she does not discount the possibility that differences may result from time.

The Upper Republican phase (A.D. 1000 to 1350) (Blakeslee 1994) is best represented by numerous sites in south-central Nebraska along the Republican River and its larger tributaries. There are five localities in this area for which information is available: Prairie Dog Creek, Lost Creek, Guide Rock, Medicine Creek, and the Red Willow localities.

Sites of the Upper Republican phase are similar in material-culture content to the later sites of the Solomon River phase. Although Upper Republican sites are abundant throughout the main area of settlement, no systematic surveys have been carried out, so any estimates of the total number of sites or of population density would be speculative. The available evidence suggests that there are hamlets, but the dominant settlement pattern was one of isolated households, although it is sometimes difficult to determine whether some of them may have been loosely grouped into small settlements. Lodge forms have a mean size of 639 square feet.

Ceramics of the Upper Republican phase are also much like those of the Solomon River phase, except there is a stronger tendency for a globular body shape and a higher percentage of collared, decorated rims. Some sites, particularly in the Red Willow locality, that have been called Upper Republican (Grange 1980) have vessels with loop and strap handles and low frequencies of collared rims. These traits suggest closer affinities with the Smoky Hill phase than with

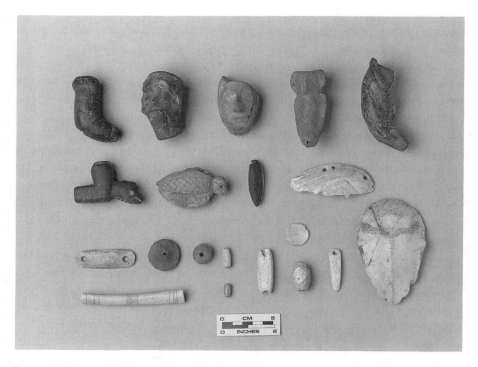

Figure 8.8. Central Plains–tradition decorated objects and items of adornment: (*top row*) fired-clay animal-effigy pipe (stylized reptile or bird–reptile), fired-clay human-effigy pipes, indurated clay human-effigy pipe, fired-clay animal-effigy pipe (with snake around its head); (*middle*) stone animal-effigy pipe with inlaid-shell eyes (stylized reptile or bird–reptile), stone bird-effigy pipe with weeping-eye motif, stone pendant, shell fish-effigy pendant or lure; (*bottom*) bone ornaments, clay beads, bone beads, shell beads, shell disk, shell pendant, deer-cranial-bone pendant (?).

Upper Republican. We do not consider these sites to be a part of the Upper Republican phase. Possible site-unit intrusions such as this may be examples of the weakness of some taxonomic thinking that often relies too heavily on geographic location, potentially masking insights into movement and social interaction.

Nutting stones, common in the Solomon River phase, are rare in the Upper Republican phase, perhaps indicating a difference in local floral resources, in emphasis on their procurement, or in the way they were processed. A second difference is that a few Southeastern Ceremonial–complex motifs and artifacts are associated with sites of the Upper Republican phase (Roll 1968), but not with those of the Solomon River phase. The remainder of the material culture of the Upper Republican phase closely parallels that of the Solomon River phase.

A detailed study of the subsistence activities of an Upper Republican–phase household, based on a well-screened sample, was undertaken at the Mowry Bluff site (Falk 1969). During most of the year, probably fall through spring, a wide range of local species were heavily exploited. At other times, Falk postulated, all or part of the group may have moved onto the adjacent plains to exploit bison and other upland species. This hypothesis is not well supported: no bison kill sites have been reported in the Upper Republican–phase area of concentration, and local hunting camps do not appear to be represented. To date, however, no one has seriously sought potential kill sites and local hunting camps, so it remains a working hypothesis.

Another analysis, at the Hulme site, has a markedly different faunal emphasis. A high proportion of the assemblage consisted of deer and pronghorn, with very few bison remains (Bozell 1991). A more comprehensive study by Bozell (1995), using a broader sample of Central Plains–tradition sites, concludes that the Upper Republican people were locally oriented hunters. A wide variety of game was taken, apparently with an opportunistic hunting strategy. Bison were not specifically targeted except when locally available.

Mortuary patterns for the Upper Republican phase are poorly known, but what evidence exists suggests practices similar to those reported for the Solomon River phase. A large ossuary pit at the Graham site, on Prairie Dog Creek in south-central Nebraska, was badly disturbed by collectors, so no estimate could be made of the number of individuals originally interred in it. There was evidence for primary child burials, but little else could be determined of burial practices. Strong (1935:103–116, 122–123) also reported an apparently similar site, the Alma Ossuary, on the Republican River in south-central Nebraska. He gave no estimate of the number of individuals or the type of interment.

Reconstruction of social organization in this and other phases has been very tentatively addressed. A matrilocal–matrilineal residence and descent pattern has been postulated for the Upper Republican and Nebraska phases (W. Wood 1969). This inference was based on archaeological evidence consisting of ceramic stylistic studies by Deetz (1965) and use of ethnographic analogy. A patrilocal or neolocal pattern has been proposed for a site of the Smoky Hill phase by A. Johnson (1973:293). He based his inference on ceramic patterns showing two distinct wares that he felt represent two female potters at the site.

The termination of the Upper Republican and Solomon River phases may have occurred in a number of ways. The people may have been some of those who took part in the development of the Loup River/Itskari phase, or they may have played a part in the beginning of the St. Helena phase (Cooper 1936:71; Krause 1969:93; Ludwickson 1975, 1978). Alternatively, they may have bypassed the St. Helena–phase area, pushing farther north to settle along the Missouri River as part of the Initial Coalescent tradition, at such sites as Arzberger, South Dakota (Spaulding 1956).

Yet another hypothesis is that they reversed their seemingly steady expansion and traveled southward instead, to participate in the development of cultures in the panhandle of Oklahoma and Texas (Bryson et al. 1970), an explanation that has been questioned by Lintz (1978). Although there is some general relationship between the Central Plains tradition and these Southern Plains groups, it is probably on an early level and has more to do with the origins than the termination of the Central Plains tradition. There may have been some weak ties though time, but the more general trend for the Central Plains tradition was a gradual northerly expansion, not southerly, and any southern ties that once existed would gradually have weakened as time passed. The chronological evidence at hand also favors this possibility (Blakeslee 1994; Eighmy and LaBelle 1996; Kvamme 1982, 1985; Roper 1976, 1985, 1995).

High Plains Campsites

Scattered across the High Plains of western Nebraska and Kansas, eastern Colorado, and southeastern Wyoming are campsites related to the Central Plains tradition. These sites include rock shelters, butte-top camps, and stream-terrace camps (Bell and Cape 1936; Jensen 1973; Reher 1971; Reher et al. 1994; Roper 1990; W. Wood 1971, 1990). Radiocarbon dates suggest an occupation during the period about A.D. 1000 to 1400 (W. Wood 1990). Although comparatively little excavation has been done on these High Plains sites, the material-culture inventory closely parallels that at more easterly earthlodge sites. The more notable differences are the lack of evidence for earthlodges and for horticulture. Gardening implements are completely absent, and only a single maize kernel was found at Agate Bluff (Irwin and Irwin 1957:22); furthermore, no fossil maize pollen was found in the other Upper Republican components investigated in northeastern Colorado (J. Wood 1967).

Rock-shelter sites were usually quite small and probably were occupied intermittently for relatively short periods, possibly serving as base camps from which forays were made for food or raw materials. Butte-top camps probably were occupied partly for the view they afforded of large game in the surrounding area, and possibly for protection from attack by hostile groups. The distance to water would have been a major drawback to such sites, and there would have been little or no protection from the weather unless temporary shelters were built.

Pottery from the High Plains camps appears to be most similar to that of the Upper Republican and Loup River/Itskari phases farther east. The rest of the material culture appears to be substantially the same as that at other Central Plains–tradition sites farther east, except that fewer artifact types are found. The stone tools appear to be made almost entirely from local High Plains sources.

Hypotheses to explain the High Plains sites include:

1. The camps were occupied during periodic or seasonal trips onto the High Plains by earthlodge-dwelling groups from farther east, made to exploit faunal and/or other resources (Eighmy 1994).
2. They were occupied by a previously more easterly group or groups that abandoned their settled way of life and took up residence on the High Plains as hunter-gatherers.
3. They were occupied by indigenous High Plains people who adopted a material culture similar to that farther east as a result of contact.

We reject any idea that the High Plains sites were horticulturally based. An analysis by Roper (1990) based on artifact form and functional classes concludes that the western sites are those of a permanent resident population.

Smoky Hill Phase

Another taxonomic unit closely related to the Upper Republican and Solomon River phases is the Smoky Hill phase. Our definition of the phase encompasses a broader range of sites than do earlier formulations, including many sites that were previously labeled as "hybrid" or affiliated with earlier definitions of the Upper Republican and/or Nebraska phases. Smoky Hill sites are found principally in northeastern Kansas and southeastern Nebraska along the lower reaches of the Smoky Hill, Saline, Solomon, Republican, and Blue river drainages. The chronological span of the phase is based on radiocarbon determinations from Blakeslee (1994) and suggests a date range of about A.D. 1000 to 1350.

The settlement pattern is highly variable. It is characterized by settlement along major and minor streams by small units of one to several lodges. Few of the sites have been extensively investigated to confirm their full contents. Perhaps the most extensive reported work has been at the Miller and Woods sites

(Sperry 1965; Witty 1963). At Woods, two lodges and a shallow midden were excavated; at Miller, one lodge was found, and an area of outside pits with associated post molds was interpreted as a possible second structure destroyed by farming.

Exceptions to the rule of one or a few lodges are the Minneapolis and Whiteford sites, near modern Minneapolis and Salina, Kansas (Wedel 1935, 1959). Minneapolis contained 24 lodges, or mounds indicating the potential presence of houses, and Whiteford had between 12 and 15. Whether all these house features were occupied at the same time, the settlements depart from all other reported sites of the phase in size and composition.

The use of earth- or daub-covered structures is inferred from the architectural evidence. Lodge pattern, as outlined by post molds, varies from circular at Budenbender (A. Johnson 1973) to square or rectangular at most other sites. Most structures were built in a shallow excavation or on the ground surface, with floor areas ranging from 150 to 2710 square feet. They were constructed of closely spaced poles or woven matting, and then covered with mud and grass.

Pottery is more varied than in the Upper Republican phase (Hedden 1994). Vessels include forms similar to those found at Upper Republican sites as well as more globular forms and some with subconical bottoms and high flattened shoulders. Temper is principally grit and/or sand with some grog, shell, or bone and fiber. Rims are straight or flaring or are collared, the former being the more common form. Collared rims are almost always the braced or wedge-shaped variety, with S-rims or channeled rims being rare to absent. Rim embellishment is rare, the few motifs consisting of tool and finger decoration. On simple rims, the decoration is confined to the lip; on collared rims, to the collar edge. Decoration on the upper shoulder, present to some degree at most sites, consists largely of rectilinear opposed-line motifs. Vessel surfaces are cordmarked, but some are partially smoothed. Strap and loop handles, and tabs, occur at most sites.

Based on rim form, surface finish, temper, and shoulder decoration, there seem to be two general wares. One ware, similar to that of the Solomon River and Upper Republican phases, has grit or sand temper, cordmarked surfaces, and simple and collared rims; the other is shell-tempered, with smoothed surfaces and simple undecorated rims, often with shoulder decorations. Both wares appear to be locally made, although the shell-tempered ware shares many attributes with pottery of the Steed–Kisker phase. Motifs on the Smoky Hill forms do appear to differ from those at Steed–Kisker. A ceramic seriation of components in the Milford Reservoir locality, Kansas, indicated that the grit- or sand-tempered and cordmarked forms are earlier than the shell-tempered and smoothed ones (Steinacher 1976a). Two intrusive ceramic items of Caddoan origin have been found—a sherd of the pottery type Crockett Curvilinear Incised, and a human-effigy pipe—both from the Salina Burial pit (Wedel 1959:515–520).

The chipped-stone technology consists largely of forms already described for the Solomon River and Upper Republican phases. The most common forms are triangular, double side-notched and quadruple side-notched arrowpoints, celts, keeled end scrapers, dorsally retouched end scrapers, and flake tools (Steinacher 1975:117–128, 171–177). The most notable difference between the chipped-stone assemblage at the Budenbender site and that at Upper Republican- and Nebraska-phase sites is the greater use of flakes as tools (A. Johnson 1973:295–296). Ground-stone artifacts usually consist of single- or multiple-groove abraders, metates/grinding slabs, celts, and hammerstones.

Bone and antler tools are little represented due to poor preservation. Only one trait is shared by over 50 percent of the sites: splinter awls. Except for bison-bone digging-stick tips found in the Milford Reservoir area and at the Minneapolis site (Sperry 1965:58; Witty 1978:58), the remaining material does not differ from that at other Central Plains–tradition sites. Shell artifacts are restricted to hoes and occasional ornaments. Basketry impressions were found at one site.

Few of the sites have been sampled using microrecovery techniques, so our understanding of the subsistence base is poor. A study by M. Brown (1982), although focusing on butchering patterns, provides some quantifiable information on faunal use. Information from this site indicates that the remains of deer or antelope, bison, and elk dominate, although at least 12 smaller species are present, including fish and mussels. Both maize and beans are reported from Smoky Hill sites.

Individual interments with grave goods are reported from the Salina Burial Pit, a former commercial tourist attraction near the Whiteford site, on a small rise near the Saline River (Wedel 1959). About 140 individuals are represented in this cemetery, accompanied by grave goods. Other individual burials, found in older Plains Woodland mounds in the Milford Reservoir, are also identified as Smoky Hill (Eyman 1966).

O'Brien (1986) and O'Brien and Post (1988) have suggested that the lodge at the C. C. Witt site contained evidence that can be inferred to represent early practices of Pawnee symbolism and cosmological beliefs. This idea has been challenged by Roper (1994).

Smoky Hill–phase sites are geographically located between the Nebraska and Upper Republican phases, and have often been regarded as being intermediate between or "hybrids" of the two phases. This is true to the extent that most traits in one phase can often be duplicated in the other, although this can be said of almost any combination of phases in the Central Plains tradition. Since any phase definition is an artifact of the historical circumstances of where the work was done, distinctions between phases will be muted as intermediate areas are explored. This seems to be particularly true in the case of the Nebraska and Smoky Hill phases, and to a lesser extent between the Solomon River and Smoky Hill phases.

These correspondences can be interpreted in several ways. The origins of Smoky Hill seem tied to the Sumpter subphase of the Solomon River phase, and the end of the phase appears to be related in part to the Nebraska phase. Two possibilities are suggested for the genesis of Smoky Hill. First, it may be a direct outgrowth, through population expansion eastward, of the early subphase of Solomon River. Support for this view may be seen at the Root site (Krause 1995). Both geographically and culturally, it seems to be intermediate between Solomon River and Smoky Hill, although ceramically it is more closely related to the former. The second possibility is that the Smoky Hill phase developed from the same base as Solomon River, but the two groups moved into different areas.

It has been hypothesized that Smoky Hill is ancestral to Upper Republican (Wedel 1959:565). A second idea is that the phase, in part, antedates the Nebraska phase and may be regarded as its principal ancestor (Steinacher 1976a). The process involved seems to have been the spread of population into the Missouri valley from the west, with traits changing through closer interaction with Steed–Kisker and, possibly, with later groups such as Mill Creek and Oneota. Many of the ceramic differences between Smoky Hill and Upper Republican can be regarded as the effects of Smoky Hill contact with Mississippian-related groups (McNerney 1987; Steinacher 1976a). Recent reassessments of the radiocarbon series (Blakeslee 1994; Eighmy and LaBelle 1996) suggest that all three phases developed simultaneously; therefore, ancestral relations are not clear.

Because of the still-poor chronological control of Smoky Hill sites, many of the Smoky Hill people's relations with adjoining groups are based on shared material culture. Smoky Hill appears to have come into contact with the Mississippian-based or -derived Steed–Kisker phase to the east. Contact is reflected in shell-tempered pottery and use of shoulder decoration, although none of the vessel forms or bottles characteristic of the Mississippian occur in Smoky Hill and the designs on the Smoky Hill shell-tempered ware are different from those on Steed–Kisker pottery (Wille 1958). The contact thus appears to have been indirect, although there seems to be an arc some 150 miles wide around Kansas City where Smoky Hill, Nebraska, Pomona, and Steed–Kisker elements occur mixed in sites (Logan and Ritterbush 1994).

A number of sites to the west of the principal concentration of Smoky Hill are ceramically similar, including site 25FT2 in the Medicine Creek locality, sites in the Red Willow Reservoir (Grange 1980; Jelks 1962:71; Steinacher 1976b), and one site in the Glen Elder Reservoir examined by the authors. In addition, the Uncas site, in north-central Oklahoma, shows a striking similarity to the Miller site from the Milford Reservoir area in Kansas (Galm 1979; Sperry 1965; Vehik and Flynn 1982). These long-range similarities suggest either considerable mobility of phase social units or the movement of ceramic elements, perhaps by the movement of women, into areas far removed from the area traditionally defined as Smoky Hill. A number of similarities are also recognized with the Loup River/Itskari phase (Ludwickson 1975; Steinacher and Carlson 1984) and with southerly Pomona-phase sites (K. Brown 1984; Logan and Ritterbush 1994; Steinacher 1976a; Wilmeth 1970; Witty 1978).

What brought about the termination of the phase is not yet clear. It may have developed into or been absorbed by the Nebraska and/or Loup River/Itskari phases. Considering the similarities between Smoky Hill and the Uncas site, it may have been involved in the formation of some southern Caddoan complexes. No subsequent complex appears to have developed in its old locale, and the region seems to have been abandoned by Central Plains–tradition groups by no later than about A.D. 1450.

Nebraska Phase

Sites of the Nebraska phase are found along the Missouri River valley, primarily along its west bank and up tributary streams flowing from the west, from northeastern Nebraska south to northeastern Kansas. A major enclave on the east bank, however, is in the Glenwood locality in southwestern Iowa. Much of the current research for the Central Plains tradition has focused on material from this phase (Anderson and Zimmerman 1976; Anderson and Whitworth 1977; Billeck 1993; Blakeslee 1978, 1989, 1990; Blakeslee and Caldwell 1979; Bozell and Ludwickson 1994; Fulmer 1974; Hotopp 1978a, 1978b; McNerney 1987; Zimmerman 1971, 1977a, 1977b) or with closely related materials (Boylan 1973; GAI Consultants 1980).

Most of the sites we ascribe to the phase are only partly reported, usually in summary statements. Nine localities have been defined by Blakeslee and Caldwell (1979), although the Salt Creek and Nemaha localities include only one site each. We place both these sites in the Smoky Hill phase. The remaining localities parallel the Missouri River, the lower reaches of the Platte River in Nebraska, and Pony and Keg creeks in Iowa. Radiocarbon dates for the phase range from about A.D. 320 to 1760. Using the central grouping of the majority of dates and ignoring extreme dates, following Blakeslee (1994), a range of about A.D. 950 to 1425 is suggested. Radiocarbon determinations from sites in the Glenwood area suggest that this locality was occupied for the 250-year period from about A.D. 1000 to 1250 (Billeck 1993).

The settlement pattern is similar to that of other phases of the tradition: isolated lodges or two or three lodges grouped near one another, with a few aggregates of 20 or more. Whether all lodges in the larger settlements were contemporaneous or all surface indications actually represent lodges is not yet known. Architecture includes rectangular to subrectangular lodge floors ranging from 189 to 2707 square feet, with a mean of 731.7 square feet (Ludwickson 1980) (Figure 8.9). Some circular lodges reported from the Glenwood locality are probably inadequately excavated or interpreted (Hotopp 1978a, 1978b), although a few such lodges are believed to exist on the west bank of the Missouri. A general south-to-north drift of population has been suggested by Blakeslee and Caldwell (1979). The idea of drift has more recently been refined to consider movement as expansion without complete abandonment of former areas (Bozell and Ludwickson 1994; Kvamme 1982, 1985; Roper 1976, 1985, 1995).

Excavations have yet to be undertaken to determine what features may exist between individual lodges. Most lodges were built in excavated pits, in some cases reaching such depths that little of them may have been visible aboveground. Settlement studies have been made on the Glenwood sites (Anderson and Zimmerman 1976; Billeck 1993; Hotopp 1978a, 1978b; Zimmerman 1977b), and larger sites are recognized as part of the overall settlement pattern (Gradwohl 1969).

Analysis of Nebraska-phase subsistence patterns seem to indicate a strategy of exploiting the local area (Bozell 1995; Bozell and Ludwickson 1994; Falk 1969; Green 1990; P. Johnson 1972; Morrow 1995). Large prairie–plains species (bison

Figure 8.9. Nebraska–phase House 4 at site 25CC1, Cass County, Nebraska. (Nebraska State Historical Society photograph, 1937)

and elk) seem to be the primary meat sources, with woodland species secondary. There are scattered reports of cultigens, but little progress has been made in understanding the use of either domestic or wild plant foods. Whether the varieties of maize are similar to those used farther west still awaits investigation. Furthermore, the balance among hunting, gathering, and gardening remains unknown.

The demography of the phase and its burial practices are poorly known. Ossuary burials are present, with some speculations of cannibalism and the scalping of victims. The presence of charnel houses is also suggested (Cook 1977; Gilder 1913, 1926; Hill and Cooper 1938:276–279; Poynter 1915; Strong 1935:173–174).

Nebraska-phase pottery is the most extensively analyzed of that of the Central Plains tradition (Billeck 1993; Bozell and Ludwickson 1994; Gunnerson 1952). However, most of the reports tend to be summary ones, and there are few well-described collections from which one can obtain an appreciation of the range of intrasite variability. Blakeslee and Caldwell's (1979) study is one of the most extensive, yet relies on locality summaries that were used to build an overall chronology. The pottery consists of general wares found in Smoky Hill, but the Nebraska phase differs in having more smoothed vessel surfaces, fewer collared rims, and more decoration on both the rims and the shoulders. Several ceramic seriations suggest that pottery changed over time from a relatively simple assemblage to one of more elaborate form and decoration (Anderson 1961; Blakeslee and Caldwell 1979; Zimmerman 1977a).

There seems little doubt that the shell-tempered ware is an adaptation from the Steed–Kisker complex. Nebraska-phase vessels also seem to be more globular than most of those in Smoky Hill, and appendages are more numerous, including strap and loop handles, lugs, tabs, and effigies. Other ceramic items include pipes, beads, and effigies (Figure 8.6).

Stone and other tool classes follow the general pattern of the other Central Plains phases, and Blakeslee and Caldwell (1979) have shown a general clinal variation in time and space for certain forms.

An early hypothesis was advanced that the Nebraska phase was an outgrowth of the Steed–Kisker phase (Calabrese 1969:219; Krause 1969:84, 91); however, this theory no longer seems tenable (GAI Consultants 1980; O'Brien 1974, 1978a; Steinacher 1976a). A second idea was that the Nebraska phase developed as an eastern movement of the western subsistence adaptation or as a population expanding into new areas, and its differentiation as a cultural unit was due to its relation to the Steed–Kisker phase. The latter phase is still poorly understood, although summaries (O'Brien 1978a, 1978b, 1994; Shippee 1972) and excavation reports (Barnes 1977; Calabrese 1969; GAI Consultants 1980; Wedel 1943) are available. Steed–Kisker is now believed to be derived from and related to a Mississippian complex farther east, possibly Cahokia. In light of reevaluation of dating, an indigenous development out of local Late Plains Woodland groups may be viable for the Nebraska phase.

The termination of the Nebraska phase appears to be, at least in part, related to the St. Helena phase. Blakeslee (1978, 1988) has noted the close similarities between the St. Helena and Nebraska phases, and our ceramic comparisons suggest that St. Helena may be an outgrowth of late elements of the Nebraska phase. The abandonment of southern Nebraska-phase sites may be related to the appearance of such larger groups as Oneota that were competing for the area. The movement of some Nebraska-phase groups into the Loup River and Elkhorn River drainages is also possible, as we discuss later. Suggestions of contacts between Nebraska-phase and Mill Creek– or Initial Middle Missouri–variant components remain to be documented (Blakeslee 1978; Henning 1967).

St. Helena Phase

In spite of its prominence in the literature, there are few reported sites of the St. Helena phase (Blakeslee 1988; Cooper 1936), and only five radiocarbon dates are available. They range from about A.D. 1350 to 1450 (Blakeslee 1994). The settlement pattern differs from that of the adjacent, more southerly Nebraska phase in that at least some of the St. Helena–phase sites are larger. Sites may have from four to 31 lodges or indications of lodges. Whether all of them were occupied at the same time has not been determined. The sites are set on bluffs immediately overlooking the Missouri River valley or on smaller tributary streams nearby. Architecture is similar to that reported for Nebraska-phase sites, and houses were dug 2 to 4 feet into the ground.

Limited faunal information indicates that bison and deer were the two major species hunted (Manz and Blakeslee 1988). Elk and carnivore bones are listed as being raw materials for tools, and fishhooks and objects of freshwater mussel shell reveal that aquatic resources were tapped. Maize kernels were recovered from one site.

Two burial areas are suspected of being associated with the phase. One area contained more than 36 primary semiflexed burials with few associated grave goods. The second area yielded 22 secondary burials mixed in a common ossuary pit, and one primary burial, again with few associated grave goods. Although both areas are called mounds in the original report, neither appears to have had an artificial tumulus erected over the graves. Skeletal analysis suggests close relationships with the Nebraska-phase and Initial Coalescent populations (Jantz 1993; Jantz et al. 1978; Key 1983; McWilliams 1982).

Artifacts from the St. Helena–phase Schulte, Radke, and Wiseman sites in

Cedar County, Nebraska, differ only slightly from those of the Nebraska phase, and some researchers interpret the St. Helena phase as a direct outgrowth of the Nebraska phase. The differences might be explained by contacts with Middle Missouri and Oneota populations (Blakeslee 1978). Oneota sherds found in St. Helena sites provide a link with some of the Nebraska-phase material in the Glenwood locality that also yields occasional Oneota-like ceramics (Anderson 1961; Billeck 1993; Cooper 1936:103; Zimmerman 1977a). In addition, the trend in gross percentage of ceramic decoration and rim form is much the same between St. Helena and the Glenwood locality of the Nebraska phase. St. Helena pottery has a greater number of decorative motifs, many of which are common to sites in the Loup River area.

Blakeslee (1978) has postulated that the St. Helena and Loup River/Itskari phases, and the Middle Missouri and Oneota traditions, participated in a trade network based on food redistribution as a response to localized shortages that may have been instrumental in the development of the Coalescent tradition. A partial test of this hypothesis is based on certain forms of elbow pipes from Nebraska and St. Helena sites believed to reflect the initial development of the Calumet ceremony, which is an integral part of historic accounts of intergroup interactions (Blakeslee 1981).

Loup River/Itskari Phase

The Loup River phase was originally defined by Krause (1969) to encompass the Sweetwater site (Champe 1936), and he regarded Loup River as the latest phase in his Upper Republican regional variant. Subsequent studies have suggested that the phase be expanded to include sites in the Loup River drainage (Ludwickson 1975, 1978). The Loup River phase has also been referred to as the Itskari phase (Blakeslee 1988:6). Although these reinterpretations are stimulating, it must be kept in mind that an empirical base is not yet available in published form: Sweetwater and Flat Rock (Bleed 1974, 1978) are the only well-documented sites. Data on the other putative components come from summary statements. Radiocarbon dates suggest a time span of about A.D. 1100 to 1350 (Blakeslee 1994). No dates are available for the Sweetwater site itself.

The differences believed to separate Loup River/Itskari from other phases include fundamental changes in settlement, subsistence, and artifacts. The sites are larger, having more lodges per site than other phases. Furthermore, the average lodge size has become appreciably smaller: a mean size of 401 square feet is suggested (Ludwickson 1980). There is also a general tendency for some subrectangular lodges. Superposition of successive lodges is found in the Loup River area, one of the few localities where this has been noted in the Central Plains tradition.

On the basis of pottery grave goods, one burial site (Sondergaard Ossuary) in the Loup River valley is believed to relate to the phase (Smith 1946). Thirty-eight graves appear to have been present, containing some 63 burials. The Sargent site, although lacking grave goods, has also been attributed to the phase (O'Shea and Bridges 1989).

A ceramic analysis by the authors using data from sites in the Loup River/Itskari–phase area assessed some of the proposals regarding the enlarged definition of the phase. Sites in the Davis Creek locality provide the bulk of the data, to which we have added data from the Sweetwater, Flat Rock, Schmidt, and Sondergaard Ossuary sites.

Three ceramic groups seem to be present in our sample. These categories were based, where possible, on the contents of individual lodges. Group A sites are primarily in the Davis Creek locality, with one site from the Wood River locality. Its ceramics consist principally of unthickened rims. Group B sites are less numerous and have dominantly collared rims, with more numerous motifs, and decoration is more prevalent. Group C consists of the Sweetwater and Schmidt sites. Although similar in many respects to the second group of sites, it is dominated by cord-impressed decorations. This element is rare to nonexistent at the other sites.

The relation of these three groups to one another is uncertain, in part because the possibility of multicomponent occupations at some of the sites cannot be ruled out. Group B seems to be most closely related to the Upper Republican phase, although the number and complexity of design motifs appear to be greater in the Loup River area. Ceramically, Group A seems to be more similar to the Smoky Hill and Nebraska phases than to Upper Republican. Relations to St. Helena have also been proposed (Ludwickson et al. 1987; Steinacher and Carlson 1984). In this instance, motifs and percentages seem to be closer to those of Group B than to the others. Group C appears to be intermediate between Groups A and B in terms of rim and decoration percentages. It differs in the higher number of motifs present and the use of cord-impressed decoration. Although the origin of the cord-impressed decoration is uncertain, an obvious source is the Middle Missouri tradition. Loup River pottery, however, is well within the manufacturing tradition of the Central Plains tradition.

Subsistence practices for the Loup River/Itskari phase are largely unknown. The McIntosh site, in the Sand Hills of north-central Nebraska, may be related to the Loup River/Itskari phase (Bozell and Ludwickson 1994). The faunal remains from this lakeside site suggests the exploitation of a wide range of species (Koch 1995).

The Loup River phase is the most neglected of the Central Plains-tradition phases and deserves more intensive analysis than it has had to date. Its ceramics and architecture suggest that it has more variability than most of the other phases.

Termination of the Central Plains Tradition

Two hypotheses appear to encompass most of the thinking about the end of the tradition. First, the two latest phases, St. Helena and Loup River/Itskari, terminated when (1) St. Helena peoples moved up the Missouri River to become a part of the Coalescent tradition and to play a role in the development of the historic Arikara, and (2) the Loup River/Itskari phase evolved, in place, into the Lower Loup phase and then into the historic Pawnee. Second, (1) the St. Helena phase followed the preceding scenario, but (2) the Loup River/Itskari–phase people migrated north to the Missouri, to become part of the Coalescent tradition for a time, but returned to central Nebraska as the Lower Loup phase, the ancestor of the historic Pawnee. The reason for the apparent abandonment of the Central Plains has often been attributed to climatic change. Blakeslee (1994) has examined this possibility and also proposed an alternative model based on swidden horticulture.

Much of the speculation concerning the fate of the Central Plains tradition was based on the premise of fusion with the Middle Missouri tradition, resulting in the sequential development into the Coalescent tradition and then into some of the historic tribes such as the Arikara, Pawnee, and Mandan (Lehmer 1971:111; Lehmer and Caldwell 1966:513). The Coalescent concept envisioned a blending of the two traditions to form something new: the Initial Coalescent tradition. However, research today suggests that this scenario is too simplistic. Ceramic studies, radiocarbon dates, and additional descriptive information indicate that coalescence, at least during the "Initial Coalescent," is more apparent than real.

Studies by Steinacher (1983) and Toom (1992) indicate that the Initial Coalescent sites have greater time depth (about A.D. 1250 to 1450) than previously recognized and that the connection with the Central Plains tradition is one of ongoing relations rather than direct developmental replacement. Initial Coalescent sites once regarded as the blending of the two "older" traditions are conceptually better viewed as the equivalent of another Central Plains–tradition phase. Dropping the Initial Coalescent label and returning these sites to one or more of the earlier subtradition names (Anoka focus, Arzberger phase, or Campbell Creek phase) may be a more realistic approach to taxonomy than continuing the misleading idea of "coalescence" (see also Blakeslee and Caldwell 1979:6–7; Steinacher 1983:94–95, 1990:21–23).

The Initial Coalescent tradition or "phase" is similar in its early components to what we term the Loup River/Itskari Group A sites and appears to date to about the same period. Later components appear to be more similar to St. Helena and possibly Loup River/Itskari Group C in motif numbers and types. House forms of the Loup River/Itskari and Initial Coalescent sites also are similar, including the number of houses at sites. That interaction among some of the Loup River/Itskari, St. Helena, and Initial Coalescent sites took place seems likely. However, the form of this interaction is unknown.

That the St. Helena phase did move upriver is supported by present interpretations of the archaeological data. However, the idea that St. Helena people later mixed with groups of the Middle Missouri tradition and became the Initial Coalescent is not tenable. Rather, they appear to have intermingled with closely related groups already established in the Middle Missouri trench.

The hypothesis that Loup River/Itskari remained in place to develop into Lower Loup and then into the historic Pawnee is no longer supportable (Steinacher et al. 1991). There is, in fact, a contrast in material culture and a gap in time between the latest Central Plains–tradition components and the earliest Lower Loup sites. Only one site in Nebraska hints for continuity between these groups: a few rims resembling those of the Central Plains tradition were found at the Lower Loup Burkett site and were thought to be part of the Lower Loup ceramic assemblage (Grange 1968, 1979). This pottery is, however, unlike most known Lower Loup forms, and the possibility that it may be intrusive from an earlier Central Plains–tradition occupation cannot be ruled out.

If the Central Plains tradition evolved into the Pawnee and/or Arikara, the process and the sites that demonstrate it have yet to be identified. Lower Loup does, nonetheless, bear a strong resemblance to Extended Coalescent sites in South Dakota. Many ceramic and other tool forms are widely shared, and intimate contact is implied (Hoffman 1967:63–64; Kivett 1958:134–137). Whether an ultimate development from the South Dakota "Initial Coalescent–Central Plains tradition" through the Extended Coalescent can be shown is still problematic. There continues to be a gap in any developmental sequence from Initial to Extended Coalescent in the Middle Missouri area. How, if at all, the Central Plains and "Initial Coalescent" ultimately gave rise to the "Extended Coalescent" and eventually such historic tribes as the Pawnee and Arikara is still to be resolved. Finally, it cannot be discounted that the Central Plains tradition and Initial Coalescent populations may have been reduced by warfare and other causes to the point of extinction from the archaeological record (Willey 1990; Willey and Emerson 1993; Zimmerman and Bradley 1993). Survivors may have amalgamated with surrounding groups to form the nucleus of some of the later identifiable historic tribes.

The Central Plains tradition occupied the Central Plains for hundreds of years, from possibly as early as about A.D. 900 to 1450. Carriers of this culture appear to have been well adapted to the local environment and were the first groups to significantly use horticulture and to live in permanent settlements there. The bases of stable village life established by the peoples of the Central Plains tradition proved to be a successful pattern of adaptation that continued with minor variations until the late historic period.

References

Adair, M. J.
  1988   *Prehistoric Agriculture in the Central Plains.* University of Kansas, Publications in Anthropology, no. 16. Lawrence.
Anderson, A.D.
  1961   The Glenwood Sequence: A Local Sequence for a Series of Archeological Manifestations in Mills County, Iowa. *Journal of the Iowa Archeological Society* 10:1–101.
Anderson, A.D., and L. J. Zimmerman
  1976   Settlement–Subsistence Variability in the Glenwood Locality, Southwestern Iowa. *Plains Anthropologist* 21:141–154.
Anderson, D. C., and I. Whitworth
  1977   *An Analysis of Ceramics from 13ML155: A Nebraska Phase Earthlodge from Southwestern Iowa.* University of Iowa, Office of the State Archaeologist, Report no. 2. Iowa City.
Barnes, E. J.
  1977   The Calovich Burials (14WY7): The Skeletal Analysis of a Plains Mississippian Population. M.A. thesis, Department of Anthropology, Wichita State University.
Bell, E. H., and R. E. Cape
  1936   The Rock Shelters of Western Nebraska. In *Chapters in Nebraska Archaeology,* edited by E. H. Bell, 357–399. University of Nebraska, Lincoln.
Billeck, W. T.
  1993   Time and Space in the Glenwood Locality: The Nebraska Phase in Western Iowa. Ph.D. diss. Department of Anthropology, University of Missouri, Columbia.
Blakeslee, D. J.
  1978   Assessing the Central Plains Tradition in Eastern Nebraska: Content and Outcome. In *The Central Plains Tradition: Internal Development and External Relationships,* edited by D. J. Blakeslee, 134–143. University of Iowa, Office of the State Archaeologist, Report no. 11. Iowa City.
  1981   The Origin and Spread of the Calumet Ceremony. *American Antiquity* 46:759–768.
  1988   *St. Helena Archaeology: New Data, Fresh Interpretations.* J and L Reprint, Lincoln, Neb.
  1989   On Estimating Household Populations in Archaeological Sites, with an Example from the Nebraska Phase. In *Plains Indian Historical Demography and Health: Perspectives, Interpretations, and Critiques,* edited by G. R. Campbell, 3–16. Plains Anthropologist Memoir no. 23.
  1990   A Model for the Nebraska Phase. *Central Plains Archaeology* 2:29–56.
  1994   Reassessment of Some Radiocarbon Dates from the Central Plains. *Plains Anthropologist* 39:203–210.
Blakeslee, D. J., and W. W. Caldwell
  1979   *The Nebraska Phase: An Appraisal.* J and L Reprint, Lincoln, Neb.
Bleed, P.
  1974   *A Report on 1973 Archeological Investigations in the Wood River Valley, Buffalo County, Nebraska.* Technical Report no. 74-01. University of Nebraska, Department of Anthropology, Division of Archaeological Research, Lincoln.

1978   *Supplemental Data, Subsurface Testing Program, Midstate Irrigation Project.* Techni-
        cal Report no. 78-04. University of Nebraska, Department of Anthropology,
        Division of Archaeological Research, Lincoln.

Boylan, J. R.
1973   A Comparative Analysis of Lithic Industries and Subsistence Patterns in
        Western Iowa from 800 A.D.–1550 A.D. Ph.D. diss., Department of
        Anthropology, Wayne State University, Detroit.

Bozell, J. R.
1991   Fauna from the Hulme Site and Comments on Central Plains Tradition
        Subsistence Variability. *Plains Anthropologist* 36:229–253.
1995   Culture, Environment, and Bison Populations on the Late Prehistoric and
        Early Historic Central Plains. *Plains Anthropologist* 40:145–164.

Bozell, J. R., and J. Ludwickson
1994   *Nebraska Phase Archeology in the South Bend Locality.* Nebraska State Historical
        Society, Lincoln.

Brown, K. L.
1984   Pomona: A Plains Village Variant in Eastern Kansas and Western Missouri.
        Ph.D. diss., Department of Anthropology, University of Kansas, Lawrence.

Brown, L. A.
1966   Temporal and Spatial Order in the Central Plains. *Plains Anthropologist* 11:294–
        301.
1967   *Pony Creek Archeology.* Smithsonian Institution, River Basin Surveys, Publica-
        tions in Salvage Archeology, no. 11. Lincoln, Neb.

Brown, M. E.
1982   Cultural Behavior as Reflected in the Vertebrate Faunal Assemblages of Three
        Smoky Hill Sites. M.A. thesis, Department of Anthropology, University of
        Kansas, Lawrence.

Bryson, R. A., D. A. Baerreis, and W. M. Wendland
1970   The Character of Late-Glacial and Post-Glacial Climatic Changes. In *Pleisto-
        cene and Recent Environments of the Central Great Plains,* edited by W. Dort, Jr.,
        and J. K. Jones, Jr., 53–77. University Press of Kansas, Lawrence.

Calabrese, F. A.
1969   Doniphan Phase Origins. M.A. thesis, Department of Anthropology, Univer-
        sity of Missouri, Columbia.

Carlson, G. F.
1967   Excavations at the Sumter Site (14OB27) in the Glen Elder Reservoir, North
        Central Kansas. *Plains Anthropologist* 12:219–220.
1971   A Local Sequence for Upper Republican Sites in the Glen Elder Reservoir
        Locality, Kansas. M.A. thesis, Department of Anthropology, University of
        Nebraska, Lincoln.

Champe, J. L.
1936   The Sweetwater Culture Complex. In *Chapters in Nebraska Archaeology,* edited
        by E. H. Bell, 249–299. University of Nebraska, Lincoln.

Cook, D. L.
1977   An Inquiry into the Fremont I (25SY1) "Cannibal House." Paper presented at
        the thirty-fifth annual Plains Conference, Lincoln, Neb.

Cooper, P. L.
1936   Archaeology of Certain Sites in Cedar County, Nebraska. In *Chapters in Ne-
        braska Archaeology,* edited by E. H. Bell, 11–145. University of Nebraska, Lincoln.

Cutler, H. C., and L. W. Blake
1973   Plants from Archaeological Sites East of the Rockies. Manuscript on file, Missouri Botanical Garden, St. Louis.

Deetz, J. F.
1965   *The Dynamics of Stylistic Change in Arikara Ceramics.* University of Illinois, Studies in Anthropology, no. 4. Urbana.

Dunbar, J. B.
1880   The Pawnee Indians: Their History and Ethnology. *Magazine of American History* 4:241–281.

Eighmy, J. L.
1994   The Central High Plains: A Cultural Historical Summary. In *Plains Indians, A.D. 500–1500: The Archaeological Past of Historic Groups,* edited by K. H. Schlesier, 224–238. University of Oklahoma Press, Norman.

Eighmy, J. L., and J. M. LaBelle
1996   Radiocarbon Dating of Twenty-Seven Plains Complexes and Phases. *Plains Anthropologist* 41:53–69.

Eyman, C. E.
1966   The Schultz Focus: A Plains Middle Woodland Burial Complex in Eastern Kansas. M.A. thesis, Department of Anthropology, University of Kansas, Lawrence.

Falk, C. R.
1969   Faunal Remains. In *Two House Sites in the Central Plains: An Experiment in Archaeology,* edited by W. R. Wood, 44–51, 80–81, 102. Plains Anthropologist Memoir no. 6.

Fulmer, D. W.
1974   A Central Plains Earthlodge: 13ML124. M.A. thesis, Department of Anthropology, University of Iowa, Iowa City.

GAI Consultants
1980   *Before Smith's Mill: Archaeological and Geological Investigations in the Little Platte River Valley, Western Missouri.* Report to the United States Army Corps of Engineers, Kansas City District, Kansas City, Mo.

Galinat, W. C., and R. G. Campbell
1967   *The Diffusion of Eight-Rowed Maize from the Southwest to the Central Plains.* University of Massachusetts, Agricultural Experiment Station, Monograph Series, no. 1. Amherst.

Galinat, W. C., and J. H. Gunnerson
1963   The Spread of Eight-Rowed Maize from the Prehistoric Southwest. *Harvard University, Botanical Museum Leaflets* 20:117–160.

Galm, J. R.
1979   *The Uncas Site: A Late Prehistoric Manifestation on the Southern Plains.* University of Oklahoma, Archaeological Research and Management Center, Research Series, no. 5. Norman.

Gilder, R. F.
1913   A Prehistoric "Cannibal House" in Nebraska. *Records of the Past* 12:107–166.
1926   *The Nebraska Culture Man.* Kieser, Omaha.

Gradwohl, D. M.
1969   *Prehistoric Villages in Eastern Nebraska.* Nebraska State Historical Society, Publications in Anthropology, no. 4. Lincoln.

Grange, R. T.
   1968   *Pawnee and Lower Loup Pottery.* Nebraska State Historical Society, Publications
          in Anthropology, no. 3. Lincoln.
   1979   An Archeological View of Pawnee Origins. *Nebraska History* 60:134–160.
   1980   *Archeological Investigations in the Red Willow Reservoir.* Nebraska State Histori-
          cal Society, Publications in Anthropology, no. 9. Lincoln.
Green, W., ed.
   1990   *Glenwood Culture Paleoenvironment and Diet: Analysis of Plant and Animal Re-
          mains from the Wall Ridge Earthlodge (13ML176), Mills County, Iowa.* University
          of Iowa, Office of the State Archaeologist, Report no. 15. Iowa City.
Grinnell, G. B.
   1893   *Pawnee Hero Stories and Folk-Tales.* Scribner, New York.
Gunnerson, J. W.
   1952   Some Nebraska Culture Pottery Types. *Plains Archeological Conference News-
          letter* 5:34–44.
Hedden, J. G.
   1994   Riley Cord Roughened Ceramic Variation from Ten Smoky Hill Variant Sites
          in North-Central Kansas. *Central Plains Archaeology* 4:27–42.
Henning, D. R.
   1967   Mississippian Influences on the Eastern Plains Border. *Plains Anthropologist*
          12:184–194.
Hill, A. T., and P. Cooper
   1938   The Archeological Campaign of 1937. *Nebraska History Magazine* 18:237–359.
Hoffman, J. J.
   1967   *Molstad Village.* Smithsonian Institution, River Basin Surveys, Publications in
          Salvage Archeology, no. 4. Lincoln, Neb.
Hotopp, J. A.
   1978a A Reconsideration of Settlement Patterns, Structures, and Temporal Place-
          ment of the Central Plains Tradition in Iowa. Ph.D. diss., Department of An-
          thropology, University of Iowa, Iowa City.
   1978b Glenwood: A Contemporary View. In *The Central Plains Tradition: Internal De-
          velopment and External Relationships,* edited by D. J. Blakeslee, 109–133. Univer-
          sity of Iowa, Office of the State Archaeologist, Report no. 11. Iowa City.
Irwin, C., and H. Irwin
   1957   The Archeology of the Agate Bluff Area, Colorado. *Plains Anthropologist*
          8:15–33.
Jantz, R. L.
   1993   Pawnee–Central Plains Relationships: The Craniometric Evidence. Report to
          the Smithsonian Institution, Repatriation Office, Washington, D.C.
Jantz, R. L., D. W. Owsley, and P. Willey
   1978   Craniometric Relationships of Central Plains Populations. In *The Central
          Plains Tradition: Internal Development and External Relationships,* edited by D. J.
          Blakeslee, 144–156. University of Iowa, Office of the State Archaeologist, Re-
          port No. 11. Iowa City.
Jelks, E. B.
   1962   Notes and News. *Plains Anthropologist* 7:91–98.
Jensen, R. E.
   1973   A Preliminary Report of the Point of Rocks Archeological Survey. In *Archeo-
          logical Salvage and Survey in Nebraska,* by G. F. Carlson and R. E. Jensen, 159–

208. Nebraska State Historical Society, Publications in Anthropology, no. 5. Lincoln.

Johnson, A. E.

1973   Archaeological Investigations at the Budenbender Site, Tuttle Creek Reservoir, North-Central Kansas, 1957. *Plains Anthropologist* 18:271–299.

Johnson, P. C.

1972   Mammalian Remains Associated with Nebraska Phase Earth Lodges in Mills County, Iowa. M.A. thesis, Department of Geology, University of Iowa, Iowa City.

Key, P. J.

1983   *Craniometric Relationships Among Plains Indians: Culture Historical and Evolutionary Implications.* University of Tennessee, Department of Anthropology, Report of Investigations, no. 34. Knoxville.

Kivett, M. F.

1952   *Woodland Sites in Nebraska.* Nebraska State Historical Society, Publications in Anthropology, no. 1. Lincoln.

1958   The Oacoma Site, Lyman County, South Dakota. Manuscript on file, National Park Service, Midwest Archeological Center, Lincoln, Neb.

Koch, A.

1995   The McIntosh Fauna: Late Prehistoric Exploitation of Lake and Prairie Habitats in the Nebraska Sand Hills. *Plains Anthropologist* 40:39–60.

Krause, R. A.

1969   Correlation of Phases in Central Plains Prehistory. In *Two House Sites in the Central Plains: An Experiment in Archaeology*, edited by W. R. Wood, 82–96. Plains Anthropologist Memoir no. 6.

1970   Aspects of Adaptation Among Upper Republican Subsistence Cultivators. In *Pleistocene and Recent Environments of the Central Great Plains*, edited by W. Dort, Jr., and J. K. Jones, Jr., 103–115. University Press of Kansas, Lawrence.

1982   The Central Plains Tradition Revisited: A Critical Review of Recent Interpretations. *Plains Anthropologist* 27:75–82.

1995   Attributes, Modes, and Tenth Century Potting in North Central Kansas. *Plains Anthropologist* 40:307–352.

Kvamme, K. L.

1982   A Reexamination of Roper's Trend-Surface Analysis of Central Plains Radiocarbon Dates. *Plains Anthropologist* 27:305–308.

1985   In Defense of Roper (1976). *Plains Anthropologist* 30:263–264.

Lehmer, D. J.

1971   *Introduction to Middle Missouri Archeology.* National Park Service, Anthropological Papers, no. 1. Washington, D.C.

Lehmer, D. J., and W. W. Caldwell

1966   Horizon and Tradition in the Northern Plains. *American Antiquity* 31:511–516.

Lintz, C.

1978   The Panhandle Aspect and Its Early Relationship with Upper Republican. In *The Central Plains Tradition: Internal Development and External Relationships*, edited by D. J. Blakeslee, 36–55. University of Iowa, Office of the State Archaeologist, Report no. 11. Iowa City.

Lippincott, K. A.

1976   Settlement Ecology of Solomon River Upper Republican Sites in North Central Kansas. Ph.D. diss., Department of Anthropology, University of Missouri, Columbia.

1978 Solomon River Upper Republican Ecology. In *The Central Plains Tradition: Internal Development and External Relationships,* edited by D. J. Blakeslee, 81–93. University of Iowa, Office of the State Archaeologist, Report no. 11. Iowa City.

Logan, B., and L. W. Ritterbush

1994 Late Prehistoric Cultural Dynamics in the Lower Kansas River Basin. *Central Plains Archaeology* 4:1–25.

Ludwickson, J.

1975 The Loup River Phase and the Origins of Pawnee Culture. M.A. thesis, Department of Anthropology, University of Nebraska, Lincoln.

1978 Central Plains Tradition Settlements in the Loup River Basin: The Loup River Phase. In *The Central Plains Tradition: Internal Development and External Relationships,* edited by D. J. Blakeslee, 94–108. University of Iowa, Office of the State Archaeologist, Report no. 11. Iowa City.

1980 Reconsideration of Central Plains Tradition House Floor Areas. Manuscript on file, Nebraska State Historical Society, Lincoln.

1995 The Central Plains Tradition and Radiocarbon Dating. Paper presented at the fifty-third annual Plains Conference, Laramie, Wyo.

Ludwickson, J., D. J. Blakeslee, and J. M. O'Shea

1987 *Missouri National Recreational River: Native American Cultural Resources.* Wichita State University, Publications in Anthropology, no. 3.

Manz, K., and D. J. Blakeslee

1988 The Faunal Remains from Annie's Site and the Limitations of Subsistence Analysis. In *St. Helena Archaeology: New Data, Fresh Interpretations,* edited by D. J. Blakeslee, 157–172. J and L Reprint, Lincoln, Neb.

McNerney, M. J.

1987 The Effigy Complex of the Nebraska Phase and the Problem of Nebraska Phase–Mississippian Relationships. *Journal of the Iowa Archeological Society* 34:23–50.

McWilliams, K. R.

1982 Investigation of the Population of the Arikara. In *Pathways to Plains Prehistory: Anthropological Perspectives of Plains Natives and Their Pasts,* edited by D. G. Wyckoff and J. L. Hofman, 163–172. Oklahoma Anthropological Society, Memoir no. 3. Norman.

Mick, L.

1983 An Ecological Evaluation of Faunal Diversity in the Central Plains Tradition. M.A. thesis, Department of Anthropology, University of Nebraska, Lincoln.

Morrow, T. A.

1995 *Phase III Excavations at 13ML118 and 13ML175, Mills County, Iowa.* University of Iowa, Office of the State Archaeologist, Contract Completion, Report no. 469. Iowa City.

O'Brien, P. J.

1974 A Seriation of Steed–Kisker Ceramics. Paper presented at the thirty-ninth annual meeting of the Society for American Archaeology, Washington, D.C.

1978a Steed–Kisker and Mississippian Influences on the Central Plains. In *The Central Plains Tradition: Internal Development and External Relationships,* edited by D. J. Blakeslee, 67–80. University of Iowa, Office of the State Archaeologist, Report no. 11. Iowa City.

1978b Steed–Kisker: A Western Mississippian Settlement System. In *Mississippian Settlement Patterns*, edited by B. D. Smith, 1–19. Academic Press, New York.

1986 Prehistoric Evidence for Pawnee Cosmology. *American Anthropologist* 88:939–946.

1993 Steed–Kisker: The Western Periphery of the Mississippian Tradition. *Midcontinental Journal of Archaeology* 18:61–96.

O'Brien, P. J., and D. M. Post

1988 Speculations About Bobwhite Quail and Pawnee Religion. *Plains Anthropologist* 33:489–504.

O'Shea, J., and P. S. Bridges

1989 The Sargent Site Ossuary (25CU28), Custer County, Nebraska. *Plains Anthropologist* 34:7–21.

Poynter, S. V.

1915 A Study of Nebraska Crania. *American Anthropologist* 17:509–524.

Reher, C. A.

1971 A Survey of Ceramic Sites in Southeastern Wyoming. *Wyoming Archaeologist* 16, nos. 1–2.

Reher, C. A., L. L. Scheiber, D. J. Wyatt, J. C. Miller, and K. O. Maxfield

1994 The Donovan Site (5LO204): Interim Report on a Stratified Upper Republican Hunting Camp on the Western High Plains. Paper presented at the fifty-second annual Plains Conference, Lubbock, Tex.

Roll, T. E.

1968 Upper Republican Cultural Relationships. M.A. thesis, Department of Anthropology, University of Nebraska, Lincoln.

Roper, D. C.

1976 A Trend-Surface Analysis of Central Plains Radiocarbon Dates. *American Antiquity* 41:181–189.

1985 Some Comments on Kvamme's Reexamination of Roper's Trend-Surface Analysis. *Plains Anthropologist* 30:259–261.

1990 Artifact Assemblage Composition and the Hunting Camp Interpretation of High Plains Upper Republican Sites. *Southwestern Lore* 36:1–19.

1994 A Note on the Quail and the Pawnee. *Plains Anthropologist* 39:73–76.

1995 Spatial Dynamics and Historical Process in the Central Plains Tradition. *Plains Anthropologist* 40:203–221.

Shippee, J. M.

1972 *Archaeological Remains in the Kansas City Area.* Missouri Archaeological Society, Research Series, no. 9. Columbia.

Smith, C. S.

1946 The Sondergaard Burial Site (Hw3). Manuscript on file, Nebraska State Historical Society, Lincoln.

Spaulding, A. C.

1956 *The Arzberger Site, Hughes County, South Dakota.* University of Michigan, Museum of Anthropology, Occasional Contributions, no. 16. Ann Arbor.

Sperry, J. E.

1965 Cultural Relationships of the Miller and Rush Creek Archeological Sites on the Lower Republican River of Kansas. M.A. thesis, Department of Anthropology, University of Nebraska, Lincoln.

Sproule, K.

1981 Fourteen Upper Republican Sites: An Alternate View. In *Breaking from the Tra-*

dition of *Central Plains Archeology: Collected Papers Concerning the Central Plains Tradition*, edited by A. J. Osborn, 1–13. University of Nebraska, Department of Anthropology, Paper no. 5. Lincoln.

Steinacher, T. L.

1975   The Moll Creek Site (14CY102). Manuscript on file, Department of Anthropology, University of Nebraska, Lincoln.

1976a   The Smoky Hill Phase and Its Role in the Central Plains Tradition. M.A. thesis, Department of Anthropology, University of Nebraska, Lincoln.

1976b   Nebraska State Historical Society, Highway Salvage Archaeology Field Report 14. Manuscript on file, Nebraska State Historical Society, Lincoln.

1983   Archeological Investigations at the Whistling Elk Site (39HU242), 1978–1979. In *Archeological Investigations Within Federal Lands Located on the East Bank of the Lake Sharpe Project Area, South Dakota: 1978–1979 Final Report*, edited by C. R. Falk, T. L. Steinacher, and D. L. Toom, vol. 2, sec. A, 1–157. Technical Report no. 83-04. University of Nebraska, Department of Anthropology, Division of Archeological Research, Lincoln. Report to the United States Army Corps of Engineers, Omaha District, Omaha, Neb.

1990   Settlement and Ceramic Variability at the Sommers Site (39ST56), Stanley County, South Dakota. Ph.D. diss., Department of Anthropology, University of Oklahoma, Norman.

Steinacher, T. L., and G. F. Carlson

1984   *Nebraska Highway Archeological and Historical Salvage Investigations 1969–1975*. Nebraska State Historical Society, Publications in Anthropology, no. 10. Lincoln.

Steinacher, T. L., J. Ludwickson, G. F. Carlson, and J. R. Bozell

1991   An Evaluation of Central Plains Tradition–Pawnee Ancestry. Paper presented at the forty-ninth annual Plains Conference. Lawrence, Kans.

Strong, W. D.

1935   *An Introduction to Nebraska Archeology*. Smithsonian Miscellaneous Collections, vol. 93, no. 10. Washington, D.C.

Toom, D. L.

1992   Climate and Sedentism in the Middle Missouri Subarea of the Plains. Ph.D. diss., Department of Anthropology, University of Colorado, Boulder.

Vehik, S. C., and P. Flynn

1982   Archaeological Excavations at the Early Plains Village Uncas Site (34Ka-172). *Bulletin of the Oklahoma Anthropological Society* 31:5–70.

Wedel, W. R.

1935   Contributions to the Archeology of the Upper Republican Valley, Nebraska. *Nebraska History Magazine* 15:132–209.

1943   *Archeological Investigations in Platte and Clay Counties, Missouri*. Smithsonian Institution, United States National Museum Bulletin no. 183. Washington, D.C.

1959   *An Introduction to Kansas Archeology*. Bureau of American Ethnology Bulletin 174. Washington, D.C.

1986   *Central Plains Prehistory: Holocene Environments and Culture Change in the Republican River Basin*. University of Nebraska Press, Lincoln.

Wille, M. E. B.

1958   A Comparative Study of Ceramic Traits Within the Central Plains Phase. M.A. thesis, Department of Anthropology, University of Kansas, Lawrence.

Willey, G. R., and Phillips, P.
　1958　*Method and Theory in American Archaeology.* University of Chicago Press, Chicago.
Willey, P.
　1990　*Prehistoric Warfare on the Great Plains: Skeletal Analysis of the Crow Creek Massacre Victims.* Garland, New York.
Willey, P., and T. E. Emerson
　1993　The Osteology and Archaeology of the Crow Creek Massacre. In *Prehistory and Human Ecology of the Western Prairies and Northern Plains,* edited by J. A. Tiffany, 227–269. Plains Anthropologist Memoir no. 27.
Wilmeth, R.
　1970　*Excavations in the Pomona Reservoir.* Kansas State Historical Society, Anthropological Series, no. 5. Topeka.
Witty, T. A.
　1962　*Archeological Investigations of the Hell Creek Valley in the Wilson Reservoir, Russell and Lincoln Counties, Kansas.* Kansas State Historical Society, Anthropological Series, no. 1. Topeka.
　1963　*The Woods, Avery, and Streeter Archeological Sites, Milford Reservoir, Kansas.* Kansas State Historical Society, Anthropological Series, no. 2. Topeka.
　1978　Along the Southern Edge: The Central Plains Tradition in Kansas. In *The Central Plains Tradition: Internal Development and External Relationships,* edited by D. J. Blakeslee, 56–66. University of Iowa, Office of the State Archaeologist, Report no. 11. Iowa City.
Wood, J. J.
　1967　Archeological Investigations in Northeastern Colorado. Ph.D. diss., Department of Anthropology, University of Colorado, Boulder.
Wood, W. R.
　1969　The Mowry Bluff Site, 25FT35. In *Two House Sites in the Central Plains: An Experiment in Archaeology,* edited by W. R. Wood, 3–11. Plains Anthropologist Memoir no. 6.
　1971　Pottery Sites near Limon, Colorado. *Southwestern Lore* 37:53–85.
　1990　A Query on Upper Republican Archaeology in Colorado. *Southwestern Lore* 56:3–7.
Zimmerman, L. J.
　1971　The Glenwood Taxonomic Problem. M.A. thesis, Department of Anthropology, University of Iowa, Iowa City.
　1977a　The Glenwood Local Sequence: A Reexamination. *Journal of the Iowa Archaeological Society* 24:62–83.
　1977b　*Prehistoric Locational Behavior: A Computer Simulation.* University of Iowa, Office of the State Archaeologist, Report no. 10. Iowa City.
Zimmerman, L. J., and L. E. Bradley
　1993　The Crow Creek Massacre: Initial Coalescent Warfare and Speculations About the Genesis of the Extended Coalescent. In *Prehistory and Human Ecology of the Western Prairies and Northern Plains,* edited by J. A. Tiffany, 215–226. Plains Anthropologist Memoir no. 27.

9. The Middle Missouri Tradition

R. Peter Winham and F. A. Calabrese

Pioneer accounts of Missouri River valley archaeology in modern North and South Dakota date to the late nineteenth and early twentieth centuries, when Theodore H. Lewis mapped a number of village sites and DeLorme W. Robinson mapped the Arzberger site (39HU6) in South Dakota. While most activities at this time can be attributed to antiquarian interest, a notable exception was the excavation in 1905 of a Mandan site (Double Ditch, 32BL8) by George F. Will and Herbert J. Spinden of Harvard University (Will and Spinden 1906).

The term "Middle Missouri" was apparently introduced on a map published by Will and Spinden (1906:Map I) and was subsequently formalized in the archaeological literature by Donald J. Lehmer (1971:26), who defined a Middle Missouri subarea within the Northern Plains that "includes the Missouri Valley from just below the mouth of the White River in South Dakota to just above the mouth of the Yellowstone River in North Dakota."

A series of archaeological surveys and excavations was undertaken intermittently until World War II, and summaries of the archaeology and ethnohistory were formulated. In North Dakota, they were based "on the work of personnel from the State Historical Society . . . the continuing work of the prominent Bismarck businessman, George F. Will; that of Alfred Bowers, for Beloit College; and that of William Duncan Strong, for Columbia University" (Wood 1986:2). In South Dakota, the years 1913 to 1942 have been termed the "W. H. Over period." From 1913 to 1949, Over was curator and director of the University of South Dakota Museum in Vermillion: "His curiosity about the numerous village sites along the Missouri River drew him back to those areas time after time to locate and investigate as many sites as he could" (Helgevold 1981:17).

Near the end of World War II, Congress passed the Flood Control Act of 1944 (U.S. Statutes 1944), and under the Pick–Sloan Plan for the Missouri River basin, major dams were to be built on the Missouri River in both North and South Dakota. Federal and state agencies, as well as national archaeological societies, began planning for the salvage of as many sites as possible. Both the National Park Service and the Smithsonian Institution began devising separate plans until a committee brought the two together, and a "series of cooperative agreements became known as the Inter-Agency Archeological and Paleontological Salvage Program. As a means to carry out its part of this program, the Smithsonian organized a special River Basin Surveys unit under the supervision of the Bureau of American Ethnology" (Helgevold 1981:39–41).

In the 23-year period between 1946 and 1969, intensive archaeological surveys and excavations were undertaken under the auspices of the Inter-Agency Archeological and Paleontological Salvage Program. For those involved in the program, it was an exciting time, with the initiation of a major archaeological project in conjunction with a construction program designed to impound one of the nation's largest rivers. In the process, the destruction of hundreds of major archaeological sites was imminent. The foresight of a few individuals, and their pressure and persistence, led to one of the largest organized archaeological programs since the pre–World War II Civil Works and Works Progress Administration programs. Lehmer's (1971) summary of the history of the salvage program along this part of the Missouri River is an excellent overview of this program and its results, although parts of his synthesis have since been revised. A short history of the work of the Inter-Agency Archeological and Paleontological Salvage Program along the Missouri River is provided by Thiessen (1994).

When the Smithsonian turned the River Basin Surveys unit over to the National Park Service in 1969, the unit was renamed the Midwest Archeological Center. The center continued the salvage mission of the Missouri Basin Project, but not at the pace with which it had been performed in the 1950s and 1960s.

In 1974 Congress authorized the establishment of the Knife River Indian Villages National Historic Site in Mercer County, North Dakota, "to preserve archeological vestiges of the Hidatsa and Mandan Indians and to commemorate the culture history and lifeways of those important native peoples of the Northern Plains" (Thiessen 1993b:v). Since 1976, an extensive program of archaeological and ethnohistorical research has been undertaken at the Knife River Indian Villages National Historic Site (Thiessen 1993a, 1993b, 1993c, 1993d).

The most recent phase of archaeological activity in the Middle Missouri region was initiated when federal preservation legislation mandated that federal land-managing agencies, such as the Army Corps of Engineers, take responsibility for recording and maintaining the cultural resources on lands under their jurisdiction. During the 1970s and 1980s, nearly all federal lands along the Missouri River in North and South Dakota were intensively surveyed. Recently accepted by the National Park Service, a National Historic Landmark Theme Study entitled *Village Sites of the Middle Missouri Subarea A.D. 1000–A.D. 1887* (Winham et al. 1994) provides a synthesis of past work in this region.

Taxonomic Framework

Early attempts to classify Missouri valley village cultures were organized using the Midwestern Taxonomic System (M.T.S.), although in practice only the lower orders of the hierarchy were used: components, foci, and aspects (Krause 1977:6;

Lehmer 1971:25–26; McKern 1939). The M.T.S. does not use temporal and spatial dimensions to define taxonomic units, although researchers inevitably related such units in terms of developmental sequences, often by assigning spatial and temporal limits to them (Stephenson 1954).

The synthesis of Middle Missouri prehistory by Lehmer (1954) introduced new concepts and became a regional standard, lasting until the 1960s. At that time, Lehmer and Caldwell (1966) adapted the Willey and Phillips (1958) taxonomic system to the Missouri River region, using its basic spatial divisions: area, subarea, region, and locality. Lehmer (1971:28) later added the concept of a district. Willey and Phillips's phase, subphase, and component are used in this chapter as originally defined; their integrative units were also adopted, but with a somewhat different interpretation of the tradition and horizon (Krause 1977:8; Lehmer 1971:28). Lehmer and Caldwell's tradition was enlarged, and their horizon was intended to follow that used by Willey and Phillips except that the horizons of some of their traditions had greater time depth than the concept of horizon normally permits. To resolve this problem, Lehmer proposed a taxon he called the variant. A variant, like a phase, is based on time, space, and content—but with greater emphasis on time and space. Conversely, it occupies less time than a tradition, and less space than a horizon (Krause 1977:10). In a more recent consideration of Middle Missouri taxonomy, Tiffany (1983:100) proposed several modifications to the integrative formal and spatial units to accommodate the inclusion of western Iowa sites into the Middle Missouri tradition.

The Lehmer and Caldwell scheme, using a series of subareas instead of regions as first proposed, was later modified by some researchers on the basis of their interests or bias (Krause 1969:84–85), and it was employed by others considering broader, continental interpretations (e.g., Willey 1966:312).

What Lehmer and Caldwell (1966) first defined as "districts" of the Middle Missouri were later redefined and renamed "regions," taking into consideration Krause's (1969) thoughts. Lehmer (1971) defined six major regions in the Middle Missouri subarea: Big Bend, Bad–Cheyenne, Grand–Moreau, Cannonball, Knife–Heart, and Garrison (Figure 9.1). Middle Missouri–tradition remains are found in each of these regions, although its three variants—Initial, Extended, and Terminal—are not equally divided among them.

While the focus of the salvage program and Lehmer's (1971) synthesis was on the broad culture-historical framework, research at the Knife River Indian Villages National Historic Site has shifted attention to the complexities of local regional sequences and, in so doing, focused attention on the need to rethink and redefine much of Lehmer's framework through the development of a well-controlled and well-dated record of material culture at the component and regional level.

A revised, working culture-historic or taxonomic framework for the Plains

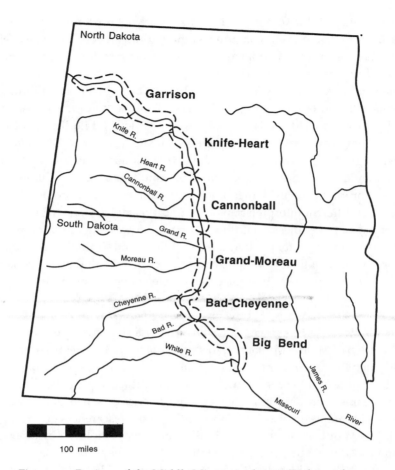

Figure 9.1. Regions of the Middle Missouri subarea. (Redrawn from Lehmer 1971)

Village-tradition archaeological units in the upper Knife–Heart region of the Middle Missouri subarea has been presented by Ahler (1993). Ahler proposes that the Knife–Heart region be redefined as two distinct spatial units, the Knife region and the Heart region, both having equal status as regions. Ahler (1993:58) also defines two new regions, the Lower Yellowstone region and the Little Missouri region, "to further facilitate the discussion of cultural developments in the northern part of the Plains area."

Cultural units in the Knife and Heart regions are defined on the basis of components, phases, and complexes (Ahler 1993:59–62). Lehmer's (1971) use of the term "tradition" has been abandoned in North Dakota for two reasons (Ahler 1993:62–63). First, the word is inappropriate to describe the phenomena under study. Lehmer's Middle Missouri tradition is characterized by, above all else, rectangular house form, and his Coalescent tradition by a nonrectangular or circular house form. However, historically distinct ethnic groups, such as the tribal unit recognized as the Mandans, exhibit a developmental sequence that can be traced through stages that involved the use of both rectangular and circular house forms (Wood 1967:117–144). Thus "we have the curious and confusing instance of historically documented ethnic, social and linguistic traditions which cross-cut Lehmer's archaeological traditions" (Ahler 1993:63). Second, the archaeological record as now known in North Dakota appears quite different from the cultural record in South Dakota:

> In South Dakota the archaeological entities which are assigned to the Middle Missouri and Coalescent traditions are in fact quite contrastive and distinct from each other. . . . Furthermore, the respective oral traditions of the Mandans and Arikaras suggest that the two archeological traditions can in fact be linked convincingly to historical development of the two respective distinct linguistic and ethnic groups. The contrasts between the two traditions, as expressed in South Dakota, are therefore not only supported by archeological data but also by historic and traditional data. In North Dakota this is not so. There is virtually no basis, other than changes in house form, for projecting the existence of the two South Dakota taxonomic units into North Dakota. Oral traditions as well as the archaeological record argue convincingly for unbroken temporal continuity of resident populations throughout the Plains Village period in North Dakota. Positing the existence of temporally sequential distinct "traditions" only tends to obfuscate an already complex record of prehistoric and historic cultural development in North Dakota. (Ahler 1993:63)

A new unit concept introduced in the Knife and Heart regions is that of "Ethnic tradition," which Ahler (1993:63) describes as "the product of synthesis of all available data from oral traditions for resident cultural and ethnic groups with all other available data from the historical and archaeological records."

At the same time that the taxonomic framework has been revised and redefined in the Knife and Heart regions of North Dakota, there have been many attempts to address the origins of the Middle Missouri tradition. One commonly held view is that the Initial variant of the Middle Missouri tradition originated in northwestern Iowa and southwestern Minnesota in the area of the Cambria focus and the Mill Creek culture (Hurt 1951, 1953; Lehmer 1971:97–98; Spaulding 1956:96–99). Tiffany (1983) and others, however, believe that the Mill Creek culture and the Cambria focus are contemporaneous with, and part of, the Initial Middle Missouri variant. D. Henning (1983:4.43–4.66, 1989) identified six phases in the eastern division of the Initial Middle Missouri variant (IMMVe): Great Oasis, Big Sioux Mill Creek, Little Sioux Mill Creek, Brandon Over, James Over, and Cambria (Figure 9.2).

Great Oasis is considered by some to be ancestral to the IMMVe and is viewed as a regional Late Woodland pottery complex. Although it continued un-

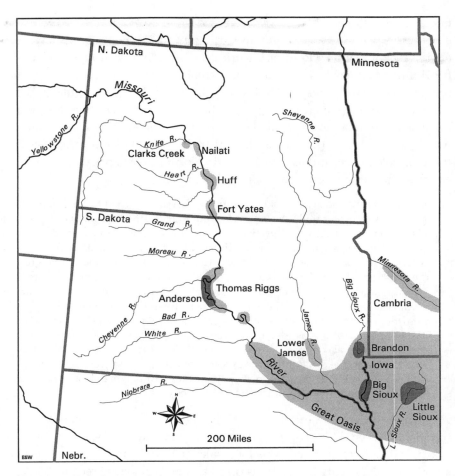

Figure 9.2. Distribution of phases, complexes, and variants. (After Ahler 1993; Johnson 1991; Tiffany 1983, 1991)

til about A.D. 1060, Great Oasis is not now considered by many archaeologists to be part of the IMMVe (Gibbon 1993; Tiffany 1983:97).

Other Woodland groups in the Middle Missouri subarea were also in a position to have played a role in the development or adoption of the Plains Village lifeway. A "Randall phase" recently has been proposed to represent a regional Late Woodland cultural expression in the southern portion of the Northwestern Plains, including the Scalp Creek site (39GR1) and possibly the Arp site on the Missouri River (39BR101) (Haberman 1993:Figure 1).

According to Tiffany (1983:98), "The Initial variant of the Middle Missouri tradition is seen as a simultaneous evolutionary development in the Missouri Trench, eastern South Dakota, northwestern Iowa, and southwestern Minnesota."

Current Research

Research into the Middle Missouri tradition is in a state of flux. Extensive data have been published from the research program at the Knife River Indian Villages National Historic Site (Thiessen 1993a, 1993b, 1993c, 1993d), which includes a revised Plains Village cultural taxonomy for the upper Knife–Heart region (Ahler 1993). In that revision, Ahler (1993:63) states that "there is virtually no basis . . . for projecting the existence of the two South Dakota taxonomic units [Middle Missouri tradition and Coalescent tradition] into North Dakota."

Tiffany (1983) has proposed including the Mill Creek culture and the Cambria focus in Lehmer's (1971) Initial variant, and restated the theory that the Great Oasis aspect may be the ancestor of the Mill Creek culture specifically and of other Initial-variant complexes generally. Tiffany has stressed the role of Mississippian culture in the development of non-Mississippian societies (Tiffany 1991a, 1991b): "As the term Mississippian is used in Iowa and the eastern Plains border, it refers to Middle Mississippian culture as delineated in the Cahokia site sequence. The period of time under consideration is A.D. 900–1200." (Tiffany 1991a:183).

Lehmer's proposed "Modified" Initial variant has not withstood the test of time, but not all the sites originally assigned to the Modified variant have been clearly reassigned, in particular the King site. It has been suggested that this site reflects Central Plains influence on Extended Middle Missouri peoples (Ludwickson n.d.:9).

There recently has been a reevaluation of Plains Village radiocarbon dating in the Middle Missouri subarea (Ahler et al. 1995) and an in-depth study of the village sites along the Missouri River based on geographic position and ceramic seriation—which shortly will be published. That study will undoubtedly require archaeologists working in this region to reevaluate current interpretations.

Toom (1992b:60–161) has addressed the issue of the origins of the Middle Missouri tradition, testing two viewpoints. The first is that the Middle Missouri tradition was a local development among indigenous peoples (R. Alex 1981a, 1981b; Tiffany 1983); the second is that the Middle Missouri tradition in the Middle Missouri subarea proper represents a migration of peoples from the east (e.g., Lehmer 1971; Wood 1967). He examined the development of village life in the Middle Missouri subarea, particularly with regard to the role that the improved climatic conditions of the Medieval optimum, or Neo-Atlantic episode, may have played in this process. Toom (1992b:iii) studied the question of "why was sedentism transferred to and maintained in one of the optimum areas of the world for nomadic hunting and gathering adaptations." His work involved detailed stratigraphic studies of cut-bank exposures at sites along Lake Sharpe, including the following sites assigned to the Middle Missouri tradition: Antelope Dreamer (39LM146), Rousseau (39HU102), Whistling Elk (39HU242), Lost Nation (39LM161), Eagle Feather (39ST228), Stony Point (39ST235), Ghost Lodge (39ST120), and Sitting Buzzard (39ST122) (Figure 9.3). Toom emphasized the role of climatic change in cultural developments at this time, while Tiffany (1991b) has placed greater emphasis on the influence of the Mississippian culture through trade.

A limited program has been initiated by the National Park Service to address sites excavated by the Smithsonian Institution for which no formal site reports have been prepared. Knudson and colleagues (1983) reported on the excavations conducted from 1957 to 1959 at the Anton Rygh site (39CA4), which has an Extended Middle Missouri–variant component. Four Middle Missouri habitation sites that were investigated in the late 1950s were analyzed by Roetzel and Strachan (1986), including the Huston Ranch Village (39HU211), which has an Initial Middle Missouri–variant component.

In 1984 and 1985, the Army Corps of Engineers undertook limited excavations at the Indian Creek site (39ST15) as part of an archaeological program for the public. A report on these excavations, which includes a summary of the Smithsonian Institution's 1952 excavations, has been completed (Winham 1995). This site includes an Extended Middle Missouri–variant component that produced a late date of 450±80 B.P. (I=18,040), which calibrates to A.D. 1444.

One aspect of research in the Missouri River Valley is predictable—that theories and interpretations will change as new research is accomplished. The general overview provided here provides a review of current information that, we hope, will stimulate the reader into pondering the questions still unanswered about the first settled horticulturists of the Middle Missouri subarea.

Revisions in Taxonomy

Village-dwelling horticulturists of the Plains, referred to as the Plains Village tradition, are first recognized in the archaeological record in the Northeastern Plains subarea and adjacent areas of the western Prairie Peninsula of northwestern Iowa, southwestern Minnesota, and southeastern South Dakota. These early village taxa include the Mill Creek culture, the Great Oasis phase (Gibbon 1993) or aspect, the Cambria phase (Gibbon 1993) or focus, and the Over focus, which are estimated to date between A.D. 1000 and 1250 (Lensink 1992, 1993). Collectively, they have been referred to as the eastern division of the Initial Middle Missouri variant (IMMVe).

The western division of the Initial Middle Missouri variant (IMMVw) includes at least one site of the Over focus (Swanson), sites of the Anderson and Grand Detour phases (Wood 1989), and other sites not formally assigned to phases. The IMMVw is dated from about A.D. 1000 to 1300. According to Toom

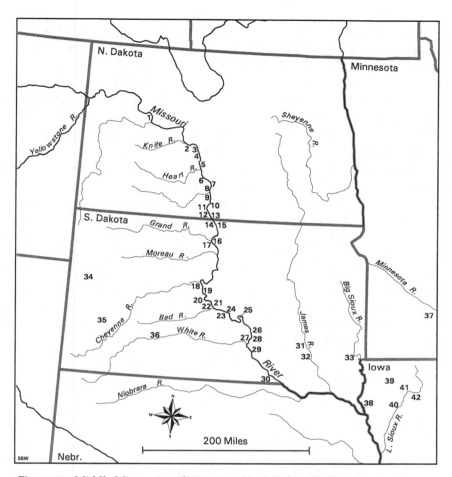

Figure 9.3. Middle Missouri–tradition sites: *North Dakota* (1) Grandmother's
Lodge, (2) Buchfink, White Buffalo Robe, Clark's Creek, (3) Bagnell, Cross Ranch,
(4) PG, (5) Double Ditch, (6) Huff, (7) Shermer, (8) Bendish, (9) South Cannonball,
(10) Tony Glas, (11) Ben Standing Soldier, (12) Paul Brave, Fire Heart Creek, (13)
Havens; *South Dakota* (14) Jake White Bull, (15) Helb, (16) Anton Rygh, (17) Travis
I, Calamity Village, Timber Creek, (18) Cheyenne River Village, Fay Tolton, (19)
Zimmerman, C. B. Smith, (20) H. P. Thomas, Hallam I, Hallam II, (21) Thomas
Riggs, (22) Dodd, Breeden, Indian Creek, (23) Cattle Oiler, Ketchen, Sommers,
Durkin, Eagle Feather, Stony Point, La Roche, Huston Ranch, Sitting Buzzard,
Ghost Lodge, (24) Arzberger, Chapelle Creek, Rousseau, Whistling Elk, (25) Jiggs
Thompson, Langdeau, Hickey Brothers, Antelope Dreamer, Pretty Head, (26)
Crow Creek, (27) King, (28) Swanson, (29) Arp, (30) Scalp Creek, (31) Mitchell,
Goehring, (32) Bloom, Twelve Mile Creek, (33) Brandon, (34) Smiley–Evans, (35)
Phelps, (36) Johnny; *Minnesota* (37) Cambria, Price; *Iowa* (38) Broken Kettle, (39)
Jones, (40) Phipps, Brewster, (41) Wittrock, (42) Chan-Ya-Ta.

(1992b:66), "The Mill Creek culture of northwestern Iowa (e.g., Anderson 1987) and especially the Over focus (Hurt 1951) and Lower James phase (a subunit of the more inclusive Over focus; see Alex 1981b) exhibit the greatest affinity to the IMMVw found in the Middle Missouri subarea proper. Such affinities include similarities in basic technology, subsistence practices, and architectural styles, in addition to clear and unambiguous ceramic-stylistic relationships."

The Extended Middle Missouri variant within the Middle Missouri subarea proper has been described as having northern (EMMVn) and southern (EMMVs) divisions. The EMMVs has considerable spatial and temporal overlap with the IMMVw and includes sites of the Thomas Riggs and other undefined phases. The EMMVn includes sites of the Fort Yates, Clark's Creek, and Nailati phases. Note that Ahler (1993) defines a Middle Missouri complex that includes the Fort Yates and Clark's Creek phases. However, he places the Nailati phase in the Painted Woods complex.

Toom's (1992b:Table 2.2) revised chronology has the Extended Middle Missouri variant dating from A.D. 1100 to 1500, but this may change when the results of recent research are published (Ahler et al. 1995). Revised dating will help address the questions of whether the Initial variant is ancestral to the Extended variant and whether the Terminal variant derives directly from the Extended variant. Toom's revised chronology shows no overlap in time of the Extended and Terminal variants.

Initial Variant

The primary definition of the Middle Missouri tradition is based largely on research in the Missouri River valley, yet the Middle Missouri tradition was not indigenous to the Missouri River valley, but first appeared around A.D. 1000 in the southern part of the Northeastern Plains subarea and adjacent areas of the western Prairie Peninsula. This development is seen as the IMMVe, which rapidly expanded to the northwest along the major stream valleys and into the Big Bend and Bad–Cheyenne regions of the Middle Missouri subarea.

Village sites in this area represent the first major sedentary occupation of the Missouri River. These villages were those of horticultural peoples living in substantial rectangular dwellings. A few sites representing the Initial variant were excavated in the 1940s and 1950s, but most of them were investigated later. The Monroe and Anderson components at the Dodd site (39ST30) are assigned to the Initial variant (Brown 1974; Lehmer 1954). The early component at the nearby Breeden site (39ST16) is roughly contemporaneous with them (Brown 1974). Breeden may in fact represent an occupation intermediate between that of the Monroe and Anderson components at Dodd (Brown 1974:47–50; Caldwell 1966:153). The Fay Tolton site (39ST11) (Wood 1976:42) and the earliest component at the H. P. Thomas site (39ST12) are closely related. These five components presently compose the Anderson phase of the Initial variant.

A second well-defined unit is the Grand Detour phase, represented by several components in the Lower Brule locality of the Big Bend region in central South Dakota. The phase is typified by the Langdeau site (39LM209), component A at Pretty Head (39LM232), and component B at Jiggs Thompson (39LM208) (Caldwell and Jensen 1969).

Ludwickson and his co-workers (1987:143) have discussed the problems of phase-level taxonomy, stating that the "Grand Detour and Anderson phases seem to differ little in terms of any material culture parameter, and the differences perceived between the Missouri Trench sites and the James and Big Sioux sites might change if a single, consistent ceramic typology was applied."

Several Initial variant sites, some of them in the Missouri valley and some of them along the James and Big Sioux rivers in southeastern South Dakota, were termed the Over focus by Hurt (1951:15–16) and the Over phase by Caldwell and Jensen (1969:78, Figure 23). The phase was originally defined using the Brandon (39MH1), Mitchell (39DV2), and Twelve Mile Creek (39HT1) sites (R. Alex 1973; Over 1938; Over and Meleen 1941:41), with the Swanson (39BR16) and Ethan (probably referring to Goehring) sites assigned later (Hurt 1951:13). Component B at Pretty Head may also represent this phase (Caldwell and Jensen 1969:78–79). The Crow Creek component at Crow Creek (39BF11) is closely related to component B at Pretty Head (Kivett and Jensen 1976:67) and the Swanson site. Arp, in the Fort Randall region (Gant 1967), and Twelve Mile Creek, on the James River, are also considered part of the Over phase. Those sites to the west in the Missouri River valley are considered part of the IMMVw. Those along the James and Big Sioux rivers represent the IMMVe.

The Mitchell site has been examined by several investigators (R. Alex 1973, 1981b; Hannus et al. 1987; Over 1938; Winham and Hannus 1988; Winham et al. 1988), but much still remains to be analyzed. Plans to open a research and educational "Archeodome" facility at the site in 1998 mark a step toward the complete analysis of the collections from this national landmark Initial Middle Missouri–variant site. Three sites—Mitchell, Twelve Mile Creek, and Goehring (39HS23, also known as the Sheldonreese site)—and the recently investigated Bloom site (39HS1) (Haug et al. 1994) make up the Lower James phase of the Initial Middle Missouri variant. R. Alex (1981:144) hypothesized that Mitchell, Twelve Mile Creek, and Goehring might represent a single village moving about through time. Recent ceramic seriation data, including the Bloom site, "indicate the possibility that the sites may have been inhabited in a nonsequential geographic pattern" (Haug et al. 1994:69).

Sites of the Over phase are very similar to those assigned to Mill Creek of northwestern Iowa, sufficiently so that it seems logical to assign all the sites to either Over or Mill Creek or refer to them as Mill Creek/Over. Cambria is different from Mill Creek/Over in many respects, particularly in pottery. The Cambria pottery offers several ware groupings (Knudson 1967), none of which is precisely duplicated at Mill Creek/Over sites. However, the stone- and bone-tool assemblages, the density of occupational refuse, and suggested village organization are similar to those of other Initial Middle Missouri–tradition sites.

The data from northwestern Iowa, northeastern Nebraska, southeastern Minnesota, and southeastern South Dakota suggest that Great Oasis is slightly older than other sites assigned to the Initial variant of the Middle Missouri tradition (M. Anderson 1995; D. Henning 1971). Pottery (Henning and Henning 1978) suggests that Great Oasis is clearly ancestral to Mill Creek/Over (E. Henning 1981; Henning and Henning 1982) and Cambria.

Mill Creek/Over sites differ significantly from known Cambria and Great Oasis sites in that many are deeply stratified (up to 12 feet deep) and often are fortified with ditches and stockades. Mill Creek/Over sites are tightly consolidated, often with house floors superimposed on one another, and rarely cover more than a few acres. A number of the sites excavated—Kimball (13PM4) and Broken Kettle (13PM1) on the Big Sioux and Brewster (13CK15), Chan-Ya-Ta (13BV1) (Tiffany 1982), Jones (13CK1), Phipps (13CK21), and Wittrock (13OB4) in the Little Sioux drainage system—are deeply stratified and may offer the full range of dates.

In 1971, Lehmer proposed a "Modified" Initial variant, to which he assigned seven sites in the Big Bend region. But the variant is no longer accepted. Three of the sites—Durkin (39ST238), Hallam I (39ST37), and Ketchen (39ST223)—are now assigned to the Extended variant, although Hallam II (39ST38) is believed to be Initial variant. The assignment of the three other sites—Cattle Oiler (39ST224), King (39LM55), and Sommers (39ST56) (Ehrenhard 1971; Jensen n.d.)—is more difficult (A. Johnson 1979:157–162). The ceramics at Cattle Oiler and King, especially, seem to represent both Initial and Extended varieties, and it is premature to assign them to specific phases, much less to a given variant. The entire concept of the Initial variant must be reassessed when the many excavated but incompletely analyzed Initial-variant sites are reported.

Other sites not assigned to a phase are La Roche, component C (39ST9) (Hoffman 1968), and Chapelle Creek, component C (39HU60).

While the focus of study of the Initial Middle Missouri variant has been on the Missouri River and river valleys to the east, there is a growing body of related material to the west of the Missouri River (A. Johnson 1989, 1993; Sundstrom 1989). The Johnny site (39JK4) is a prehistoric camp in Badlands National Park that has produced Initial Middle Missouri ceramics (Johnson 1989), and a number of other sites with cord-roughened pottery are documented throughout the Badlands. No Initial Middle Missouri sites have been found within the Black Hills interior, but the Phelps site (39CU206) lies along the eastern edge (R. Alex

1981a). The Phelps site produced a large quantity of Initial Middle Missouri pottery as well as *Dentalium* shells and conch columella (A. Johnson 1993:122).

Smiley–Evans (39DU2) is a village on the Belle Fourche River near the Wyoming border. Although this site contained cord-roughened ceramics, middens, a fortification, and possible houses, with a mean age of A.D. 1077, and "the excavators (L. Alex 1979; R. Alex 1981a) were appropriately cautious about assigning this site to the 'classic' Initial Middle Missouri variant . . . [this] author's interpretation of Smiley–Evans is that it most likely represents a nomadic group experimenting with new ideas" (A. Johnson 1993:122–123).

Extended and Terminal Variants

Was the Initial Middle Missouri variant ancestral to the Extended Middle Missouri variant or did the Extended variant of the Middle Missouri tradition develop in situ from a Late Woodland base? The later Extended-variant sites cluster in three groups along the Missouri River. Most of them are in the Bad–Cheyenne region along both banks of the river in central South Dakota. The type site (39HU1) for the Thomas Riggs phase is in this large cluster (Hurt 1953; Johnston 1967; Meleen 1949). Other sites in the region include Zimmerman (39SL41), Cheyenne River (39ST1), C. B. Smith (39SL29), Hallam I (A. Johnson 1979), and the early component at Indian Creek (Lehmer and Jones 1968). Sites in the Grand–Moreau region include Travis I (39CO213), Calamity Village (39DW231), and Timber Creek (39CO201). Most of the data pertaining to the Extended variant in this region are in unpublished or partly completed reports. However, the excavations at Travis I conducted in 1977 and 1978 are published (Haberman 1982). It is mandatory that the Thomas Riggs phase be reassessed when data from these sites become available.

The Hickey Brothers (39LM4) (Caldwell et al. 1964) and King sites were first believed to represent Extended-variant occupation in the Big Bend region (Lehmer 1966:55, 1971:67). Based on recent research, King is more probably an Initial-variant site. King may show Central Plains influence in that "the house excavated was nearly square and possessed an extended entry passage like a Central Plains tradition house, rather than a Middle Missouri tradition interior earthen entry ramp" (Ludwickson n.d.:9). Because of the limited data from Hickey Brothers, its status as Initial or Extended variant is uncertain. The Ketchen, Durkin, and Hallam I sites (all in the Big Bend region), combined with the late component at Cattle Oiler, represent the southernmost Extended-variant occupation on the Missouri River (A. Johnson 1979).

The second cluster of Extended-variant sites consists of five villages on the west bank of the Missouri between the Grand and Moreau rivers south of Mobridge, in north-central South Dakota (Lehmer 1966:55, 1971:67). These include Calamity Village, Travis I (Haberman 1982), and Timber Creek. They are nearly unknown.

The best known and most extensively reported Extended-variant sites are in the Cannonball and the Knife and Heart regions in North Dakota. The Fort Yates phase in the Cannonball region was defined by Lehmer (1966) on the basis of the early component at the Fire Heart Creek site (32SI2), to which he added the Havens (32EM1) and Paul Brave (32SI4) sites (Sperry 1981, 1995; Wood and Woolworth 1964). The Bendish (32MO2) (Thiessen 1975, 1995), Ben Standing Soldier (32SI7), and Tony Glas (32EM3) (Howard 1959) sites also belong to this phase. Other sites—such as South Cannonball (32SI19), Helb (39CA208), and Jake White Bull (39CO6)—await further study (Ahler 1977; Falk and Ahler 1988; Falk and Calabrese 1973). Virtually all the sites assigned to the Fort Yates phase are radiocarbon-dated to between A.D. 1000 and 1300 (Thiessen 1977).

Ahler's (1993:65–67) "Middle Missouri complex" is analogous in material content to Lehmer's (1971) Extended variant of the Middle Missouri tradition. The Middle Missouri complex has a clear expression in both the Stiefel and Clark's Creek components in the Knife region. Two additional components, the PG site (32OL148) and Grandmother's Lodge (32ME59), probably can also be assigned to this complex. All these components have been assigned to the Clark Creek's phase, dated to about A.D. 1200 to 1300 (Ahler 1993:76–77).

Another taxon in the Knife region, the Nailati phase, is based on the Cross Ranch site (32OL14) (Calabrese 1972; Wood 1986). The Nailati phase follows the Clark's Creek phase in the Knife and Garrison regions, dating from about A.D. 1300 to 1400 (Ahler 1993:78). Ahler (1993:67) assigns the Nailati phase to the Painted Woods complex, which is believed to represent an amalgamation of stylistic influences from many far-flung parts of the Northern Plains. Components include Buchfink (32ME9, main component) and White Buffalo Robe (32ME7, early component) (Ahler 1993). The Bagnell site (32OL16), which has an Extended-variant occupation, has not yet been analyzed, but it is roughly contemporaneous with the Cross Ranch site. There is also an Extended-variant component at the White Buffalo Robe site (Lee 1980). Available dates and the artifact assemblage for this component suggest a closer affiliation with the proposed Clark's Creek phase than with the Nailati phase, as proposed by Lee. The most northerly reported Extended-variant site is Grandmother's Lodge, in the lower Garrison region (Woolworth 1956).

The Terminal-variant complexes are the final expression of the Middle Missouri tradition and appear to be contemporaneous with the Coalescent variant. The variant includes several well-known sites, of which Huff (32MO11) (Wood 1967) and Shermer (32EM10) (Sperry 1968) are the best defined. "These components are thought to date in the general period A.D. 1300 to 1500" (Ahler 1993:67). Although Lehmer (1971:121) believed that Jake White Bull and Helb

Figure 9.4. The Helb site, in South Dakota, one of the few fortified Extended Middle Missouri–variant sites. The view is north upstream, along the now-flooded Missouri River. (Photo by Donald J. Lehmer)

(Figure 9.4) were Terminal-variant villages, excavations support an Extended affiliation for both (Ahler 1977; Falk and Calabrese 1973). Ahler (1993:67) comments that "it is presently unclear if components classifiable in Lehmer's Terminal variant of the Middle Missouri tradition should be assigned to this complex [Middle Missouri complex] or to some other complex uniquely expressive of the content of those sites."

Chronology

Most Middle Missouri–tradition sites are best dated by radiocarbon, yet many conflicting dates exist and until recently there was no specific attempt to deal with the situation. Previous syntheses of radiocarbon dates include Lehmer's (1971:20–21) overview of the Smithsonian Institution's Missouri Basin Project chronology program, Thiessen's (1977:59–82) summary of dates for sites in the western division of the Initial Middle Missouri variant, Tiffany's (1981:55–73) compendium for the eastern division, and Toom's (1992a) update for the western division.

Tree-ring dates obtained for the Initial and Extended variants are not considered reliable. Those for the Initial variant range from A.D. 1433 to 1631, and those for the Extended variant, from A.D. 1433 to 1539 (Weakly 1971:42–49). Both sequences are at odds with all chronologies proposed using radiocarbon dates.

A progress statement on the reassessment of the present understanding of radiocarbon-based chronology in the Middle Missouri subarea was presented at the annual meeting of the Society for American Archaeology in 1995:

> A ^{14}C data set has emerged over 15 years that alters our basic understanding of Middle Missouri chronology. Key is (a) 69 dates from the Knife–Heart region produced by the Southern Methodist University laboratory as part of the Knife River Indian Village research program, and (b) 54 dates by the SMU lab and the ETH–Hoenggerberg laboratory produced under the Smithsonian Institution's Repatriation Program. The evaluation of sites lacking primary evidence for long-term occupation allows us to assess reliability and validity for most existing dates. A core set of usable dates emerges, yielding a new chronological framework for village components in the subarea. (Ahler et al. 1995)

The chronology for the Middle Missouri tradition has been considerably revised from that proposed by Lehmer. Comparing Lehmer's (1971:Table 2) chronology with that of Toom (1992b:Table 2.2), it is apparent that the temporal span for the Initial variant has been considerably shortened, from 500 years to 300 years. This involves a later beginning date, about A.D. 1000 rather than A.D. 900. Lehmer's suggested temporal span for the Extended variant of 450 years also has been shortened, and the Terminal variant begins earlier than Lehmer proposed. It is anticipated that the reassessment by Ahler and colleagues (1995) will further alter the chronological framework and hypotheses about culture change and development in the Middle Missouri tradition.

Reassessments of the dating of Great Oasis and the eastern division of the Initial Middle Missouri variant also have been undertaken (M. Anderson 1995; Lensink 1992, 1993). Anderson (1995:43–44) provides a summary:

> Currently published date estimates for the Great Oasis culture establish it as a definable entity no later than A.D. 900, and persisting until almost A.D. 1200 (Anfinson 1987:161; D. Henning 1983:4.49). . . . If this was the case for northwest Iowa, the Great Oasis culture would overlap with nearly the entire radiocarbon range for the Mill Creek phase. . . .
>
> Other researchers suggest a slightly earlier span for the Great Oasis, between A.D. 850–1100 (Tiffany 1983:96), and yet others a slightly shorter span between A.D. 900–1000 (E. Henning 1981:34). Lensink (1992, 1993) has recently reanalyzed the radiocarbon chronology for the Initial Middle Missouri Variant sites, a reanalysis which incorporated the work of Toom (1992a), to suggest that the time interval for the variant should be shortened to span the period from A.D. 1000–1250. . . .
>
> It is . . . proposed that the general time duration and sequence of pottery seriation presented by Peterson (1967) for the Great Oasis culture may be essentially correct. By adding 25–35 years onto the end of the Peterson chronology, a 150–160 year duration for the Great Oasis culture is proposed. This 150–160 years . . . would allow ample time for the development of Great Oasis as a distinct culture from the preced-

ing Late Woodland cultures, the geographically broad distribution of Great Oasis sites throughout the eastern Plains periphery, and the transition into the Initial Middle Missouri Tradition via the Mill Creek and other related cultures. The Great Oasis culture, accepting the weighted average radiocarbon age of A.D. 982 (968 RCYBP) and the median average radiocarbon age of A.D. 995 (955 RCYBP), would effectively span approximately 150–160 years, or between A.D. 900–1060.

Mean radiocarbon dates for the Cambria phase derived from charred wood from the Cambria (21BE2) and Price (21BE36) sites in Minnesota range from A.D. 950 to 1175 (E. Johnson 1991:317).

Dates pertaining to the Extended and Terminal Middle Missouri variants were discussed earlier. Another study based on radiocarbon dates examined the dating of 27 Plains complexes and phases, including the Initial and Extended Middle Missouri variants. The 68 percent confidence interval for the calibrated, pooled, and smoothed probability age range for Initial Middle Missouri was A.D. 969 to 1297 and for Extended Middle Missouri, A.D. 1075 to 1443 (Eighmy and LaBelle 1996:Table 2).

Settlement and Community Patterns

Mill Creek/Over- and Great Oasis–phase houses are generally semi-subterranean, long rectangular structures with two to six central support posts and a central fireplace (Figure 9.5). They often measure up to 20 by 30 feet, have a long entryway, and may contain up to 35 bell-shaped storage pits. Floors are often littered with refuse.

Great Oasis villages are often arranged along a terrace, with no attempt at fortification or purposeful superposition of houses. A Great Oasis village may cover up to 25 acres. There are probably hundreds of Great Oasis villages and burial sites (mounds and ossuaries) in the Des Moines, Skunk, Missouri, and Big Sioux drainage systems and along the prairie lakes of southwestern Minnesota. One important village site is located well outside the documented Great Oasis territory, in Sherman County, Nebraska (Bozell and Rogers 1989).

Although fortifications are not found at Great Oasis sites, Mill Creek/Over sites usually are fortified, with ditches and/or stockades; a few have ramps that allow limited passage to the village within. These small, compact villages are, in a few instances, purposely shaped to form a precise rectangular midden. In contrast to the comparatively numerous Great Oasis sites, there are very few Mill Creek/Over villages; fewer than 50 are recorded. Mill Creek burial probably took place in ossuaries on hilltops above the villages. Burial sites in northwestern Iowa are often confused by a Great Oasis presence.

Some of the known Cambria-phase villages were fortified (E. Johnson 1991), but are not deeply stratified. There are not many Cambria culture sites recorded,

Figure 9.5. A Great Oasis–phase house at the Broken Kettle West site (13PM25), excavated by the University of Nebraska in 1969 under the direction of Dale R. Henning. This semi-subterranean structure had a central fire basin and four heavy interior posts, with a living area measuring 20 by 25 feet. The southeast-facing entrance was partially lost by earlier bulldozing. (Photo courtesy of Dale R. Henning)

and its house type is unknown. Johnson (1991) mentions two large village sites, three smaller adjacent village sites, some prairie-lake and riverine sites (from south-central to southwestern Minnesota) and burial sites, usually in mounds.

Most of the settlements of the western division of the Initial and the Extended variants were built on terrace margins or promontories adjoining and overlooking the Missouri River. Villages were on either bank of the river, although locally one side or the other was preferred. Communities varied in size and plan in both variants, some of them being fortified. The villages in South

Dakota range from 15 to as many as 30 lodges, occupying between 4 and 7 acres. The Sommers site is exceptionally large, having about 90 lodges spread over about 25 acres.

Houses are generally arranged side-by-side in roughly parallel rows. In the larger, usually fortified sites, houses are set close together, whereas in unfortified sites they are more dispersed. House density in the EMMVn sites varies from 2.6 to 5.6 per acre. A central open plaza appears to be present in many villages.

Terminal-variant sites are much larger than those of the Initial and Extended variants. Houses are arranged in irregular rows or lanes, and the village is often laid out with some regularity around a central open plaza. The house density at Huff and Shermer is 8.7 and 11.5 per acre, appreciably greater than in the Extended variant.

One or more margins of fortified villages of the IMMVw and Extended variant often are protected by a steep natural slope of a terrace rim or by a side gully. These boundaries generally were unfortified. Defensive works were produced by digging a ditch around the village area and constructing a vertical post palisade along the inner rim of the ditch. Some ditches around EMMVs villages had bastions at their corners or at 20- to 30-foot intervals along the palisade. The belief that EMMVn villages were not fortified (Lehmer 1971:70) has been dispelled by work at Jake White Bull, Helb, and Tony Glas (Ahler 1977; Falk and Calabrese 1973; Howard 1959).

Elaborate fortifications are the hallmark of the Terminal variant. The Huff site is fortified by a ditch along three sides of the village, with the fourth side facing the steep bank of the Missouri River (Figure 9.6). Here, and at the fortified Shermer site, bastions occur at regular intervals along the ditch.

Examples of fortifications serve to point out some regional defensive patterns. The Initial-variant Jiggs Thompson site is on a terrace spur overlooking the Missouri River floodplain. The western edge of the site is marked on the surface by a ditch that is 35 to 40 feet wide and 1 foot deep, extending, in a U-shape, from the northern to the southern edge of the terrace spur. The Thomas Riggs site has a fortification ditch along the northern, eastern, and southern margins of the village, with a linear line of posts suggesting a palisade along its inner rim (Johnston 1967); Tony Glas also is fortified by a rectangular enclosure. Farther north, Helb was protected on two sides by an irregular line of posts, and immediately below a low earthen embankment were postholes, suggesting the presence of a stockade wall (Falk and Calabrese 1973).

Architectural patterns in all three variants are much the same. Houses are usually semi-subterranean, long rectangular structures with a width about one-third of their length. In the Knife and Heart regions, however, houses often were built on or near the original ground surface (Calabrese 1972; Lehmer et al. 1973). With only rare exceptions, the long axis of the house is oriented so the entry

Figure 9.6. Aerial view of the Huff site, in North Dakota, the best-preserved of the Terminal Middle Missouri–variant sites. The photograph was taken during the excavations in 1960. (From Wood 1967)

passage is directed to the southwest, regardless of the side of the river the site is on; entries as often face away from the river as toward it.

House size varies considerably, and there seems to be a trend for larger dwellings as one moves upriver, for the earlier downriver Initial- and Extended-variant houses are smaller than those in the more northern Extended- and Terminal-variant villages (A. Johnson 1979:137–140). Some smaller structures at Dodd, Swanson, and other southern sites have floor areas of less than 100 square yards. Terminal-variant houses are significantly larger, with those at Huff and Shermer generally having well over 100 square yards of living area.

Most western Middle Missouri–tradition houses were built in pits as much as 3 or 4 feet below the present ground surface, although those at Bagnell were much shallower, and those at Cross Ranch were built on or near the original surface. House floors usually consist simply of tramped earth, although some of them may have been prepared using fire. Raised benches or platforms are sometimes found inside the houses on the front and back floors, and sometimes along the side walls. Wall postholes were on occasion evenly spaced around the perimeter of the house floor (as in the early component at Dodd), but it is more common for them to be set along the side walls. The house ends in these cases appear to have been enclosed by materials that left no visible evidence.

The houses were supported by a central ridgepole. It rested on a king post in the middle rear of the structure, on a center post at the house midline, and on the two large posts that framed the inner end of the entry passage. This passage is flanked by two parallel rows of posts, as much as 15 to 20 feet long, projecting at a right angle from the southwestern end of the house. A step or ramp may extend into the house pit at the inner end of the entry. A screen of posts set in a shallow trench protected the fire in the central hearth from wind blowing through the entrance (Figure 9.7).

Other features on the house floor include a large basin-shaped firepit, one-quarter to one-third of the distance from the entry to the rear wall. Secondary surface or pit hearths are common near the back of the house. Bell-shaped and straight-sided cache pits of varying sizes were dug in the house floor in almost any location.

Whereas most of the houses were supported by a central ridgepole, other

Figure 9.7. Long rectangular House 3 at the Huff site. The view is to the southwest. (From Wood 1967)

houses have auxiliary posts set between the wall lines and the center line, suggesting the presence of an intermediate row of support posts. The exterior form of the house is not yet agreed on, probably because of regional and temporal variation in architecture.

There is always a line of large posts along both of the long walls, either inside or outside the house pit. Suggestions that the posts were bent inward on top to form a quonset-type structure seem precluded by the lack of flexible posts of that size (Wood 1967:104). Vertical side walls, perhaps about 5 feet high, are therefore most probable. Except at Dodd, where the house ends were enclosed, most houses lack large posts at either end. Traces of small timbers indicate that light poles, resting on the ground surface to form end walls, were perhaps covered with light mats or hides instead of the earth that blanketed the roofs of historic earthlodges.

Subsistence

The six centuries of occupation by the peoples of the western Middle Missouri tradition are marked by the relative stability of their subsistence practices (Wood 1974). The changes that took place were principally in the emphases given to different food crops through time. Three basic food sources were exploited to augment their gardens: bison and other game on the High Plains grassland, white-tailed deer and other bottomland species, and migratory game birds. There were, of course, variations in population size and distribution along the Missouri valley during these 600 years. Some models suggest that population shifts were sometimes linked to changes in climatic conditions (Lehmer 1970, 1971:104), as outlined by Bryson and his colleagues (Bryson et al. 1970). Lehmer's model considers the relationship among climatic change, big-game hunting, and the availability of timber.

Griffin (1976:33–45) has argued that even if climatic changes were enough to alter the environment, the Middle Missouri villagers would probably not have been affected to the degree implied by some anthropologists. Floodplain horticulture, he suggests, would be relatively unaffected because available groundwater would not be altered by fluctuating precipitation. Local bison populations, on the contrary, probably fluctuated with the availability of water and pasturage, but there were likely to be large numbers of them. In short, he believes that timber was a more significant resource for maintaining population stability than the availability of food.

The two primary food sources—bison and cultivated plants—combined to provide a generous food supply in a region only marginally suited for horticulture.

The importance of bison cannot be overemphasized. Heavy dependence on this animal is documented for each variant (Calabrese 1972; Chomko 1976; Wood 1967). At many sites, the usable meat represented by bison bone makes up over 90 percent of the total faunal assemblage. The remaining percentage of meat was obtained from a variety of animals: antelope and deer, dog, beaver, porcupine, rabbit, birds, fish, turtle, and freshwater mollusks. Some of them probably simply added variety to the diet. Other animals, such as weasel and fox, supplied pelts or parts for ornamentation. Bison and other large animals also provided clothing (buffalo robes) and raw material for many kinds of tools and weapons.

The domesticated plants found in Middle Missouri–tradition sites include maize, cucurbits, common beans, sunflower, and marsh elder (Benn 1974; Nickel 1974, 1977). In addition, it appears that native weeds and grasses, such as goose-foot, lamb's-quarter, and pigweed, as well as smartweed and dock, were systematically collected or harvested—if not in fact cultivated—especially in the earlier sites.

Supplementing the cultivated crops were many wild species: wild plums and grapes, rose hips, hackberries, chokecherries, and buffaloberries. These and other species helped alleviate the potentially monotonous diet of bison and maize. Other plants contributed raw materials for making dyes, medicines, and other products. In addition, tobacco seeds are reported from the Mitchell site (Benn 1974:58, 66–69), one of the few such finds on the Plains.

There was, to be sure, variation and movement of the Middle Missouri populations—some possibly linked to climatic change, and others to available resources. But abundant multiple resources allowed the tradition to flourish. Although we see variation in the material culture of the successive variants of the tradition, changes were relatively minor, and the story of the Middle Missouri tradition is the history of a population with a stable subsistence.

Material Culture

Pottery

It is not difficult to describe the pottery that is so common in Middle Missouri–tradition sites, but the classifications used for it are rather complicated (Butler and Hoffman 1992). Various approaches have been taken by researchers to the problem of variation in ceramic assemblages (Calabrese 1977). To date, analyses have stressed traditional ceramic typology, although considerable information can be obtained by following other approaches.

Middle Missouri–tradition pottery from all regions is similar in paste. Made from local clays, it is coarse, friable, and porous. It is heavily tempered with grit derived from granite that has been fractured by firing, cooling, and pounding. Vessels were made by lump modeling, using a paddle and an anvil to shape and texture the walls. The outer surfaces generally show impressions resulting from grooved paddles or paddles wrapped with cord, producing vessels with either simple-stamped or cord-roughened surfaces. In the north, check-stamped paddles often were used. These or other surface treatments often are obliterated by smoothing. Large jars are the most common form, with a few bowls and miniature jars. Color ranges widely, with firing clouds present on both the inner and outer surfaces, suggesting variable temperatures and atmospheric conditions during firing. The rims merge into sharp to rounded shoulders, and the bodies into subconical to rounded bottoms.

The greatest variability in pottery is in the form of the rim and the decoration applied to it. Most rims are straight or flared (outcurved and outsloped), with small percentages of S-shaped or recurved forms. The clay is often thickened at the bottom of the upper exterior curve of the S, creating a collar, or "shouldered" appearance. The upper part of the S generally is higher than the lower segment. There is also great variability in the form of the lip. Appendages include triangular to rounded tabs projecting from the lip and, rarely, loop or strap handles attached to the lip and upper shoulder.

Decoration applied to the rim includes trailed lines, single cord impressions, and, less often, cord-wrapped rod or fiber impressions. Clay was also modeled using sharp or pointed tools for incised or punctated designs. The potters used their fingers to pinch and mold the rim, and their fingernails to impress the rim. Motifs produced by these techniques vary considerably. Trailing (lines drawn in soft clay) and single cord impressions were commonly used to create parallel lines on straight rims and on the upper portion of S-rims. The same techniques were used to create triangular or chevron motifs, cross-hatching, and other combinations of lines.

It is more difficult to explain the classificatory schemes used for this pottery. The more common straight and flaring rims are classified into several basic wares, including Chamberlain, Great Oasis High Rim, Anderson, and Riggs. The less popular S-shaped rims are included under three basic wares: Foreman, LeBeau, and Fort Yates (Figure 9.8). These wares vary in popularity by variant and by phase, and are defined according to general vessel form, surface finish, and, above all, basic rim form (Lehmer 1954:41). Types are differentiated on the basis of the technique of decoration (for example, incising and cord impressing) and the pattern they produce (for example, Foreman Cord-impressed Triangle).

Not all researchers have adhered to this terminology. Hurt's (1951) Initial-variant types, for example, were defined with decorative motifs instead of rim form as the ware determinants—the opposite of Lehmer's method. Caldwell and Jensen (1969) also established a new "Grass Rope" ware for variations of one of the Foreman types and "Cable" ware for variations of some Anderson types, a classification followed by Brown (1974).

The pottery of the eastern division of the Initial Middle Missouri tradition

Figure 9.8. Representative pottery vessels from the Extended Middle Missouri–variant Fay Tolton site: (*left*) Anderson Flared Rim ware; (*right*) Foreman S-rim ware. (From Wood 1976)

is fully as complex as that of the western groups. Great Oasis offers two ware groupings, Great Oasis High Rim and Great Oasis Wedge Lip (Henning and Henning 1978); the percentages of each ware grouping appears to vary by region. Some of the ware groupings assigned to Mill Creek/Over appear to have been derived directly from the Great Oasis predecessors (D. Henning 1969; Ives 1962).

Mill Creek/Over Chamberlain ware appears to have its antecedents in Great Oasis High Rim: they share many decorative motifs, the difference being in the precision of application, in which Great Oasis is clearly superior. Sanford ware appears to have evolved out of Great Oasis Wedge Lip. Other Mill Creek/Over ware groupings include the S-rim Foreman ware, Seed Jars, and Mill Creek ware. Seed Jars offer obvious evidence for Cahokia-area Mississippian influence; they are morphologically similar to jars made in the central Mississippi and lower Illinois River valleys, but very few are limestone and shell tempered, as are those made in the central Mississippi valley. Some are painted with red around the lip and upper rim, but most are grit or grit and grog tempered, the local Mill Creek paste. Mill Creek/Over potters were innovative, producing many small vessels, bowls, and even pans and spoons that defy ready classification; they are often grouped under Mill Creek ware.

Pottery from the Cambria site (Knudson 1967) has been divided into types that, because they are based on vessel morphology, would today probably be called ware groupings. Four such groups were defined, some of which suggest some relation to Mill Creek/Over ware groupings. About 14 percent of the Cambria rim sherds are rolled-rim vessels referred to as varieties of Ramey Incised and Powell Plain, two named types in the Cahokia area. Generally, Cambria examples are made of local paste. It is important to note that "Mississippian" pottery has been recovered from only the Cambria site (E. Johnson 1991). The form of these vessels and the lack of other Mississippian-derived elements in the pottery sample, chipped stone, and exotic trade materials (virtually absent) suggest that these forms arrived at the Cambria site via the Red Wing locality, where there is a strong admixture of Oneota and Middle Mississippian traits.

The globular-bodied pottery of the Extended variant differs in some respects from that of the Initial variant. The Foreman S-rims are replaced by Fort Yates S-rims, and Anderson ware is replaced by Riggs ware (for details of the classification of these wares, see Lehmer [1966] and Wood [1967]). Fort Yates ware has a collapsed S-rim, often with a collar on the upper rim, with a deep neck–rim juncture. The height of the convex upper rim is always greater than that of the lower convex part above the neck. The rims of Riggs ware are high, usually with straight to somewhat outcurved cross sections. The dominantly cord-roughened bodies of Initial-variant pottery are replaced on Extended-variant vessels by simple-stamping and smoothing. To the north, in the Knife and Heart regions, Extended-variant surface treatments (simple-stamping and smoothing) are augmented by check-stamping. The key attributes of Ahler's (1993:65) Middle Missouri complex are (1) pottery body sherds in which simple-stamping is the predominant surface treatment and in which less than 5 percent of the body sherds exhibit check-stamped surface treatment; and (2) pottery rim sherds in which combined Fort Yates ware and Riggs ware account for 67 percent or more of the collection.

Terminal-variant ceramics also differ somewhat from Extended-variant pottery, although both Fort Yates and Riggs wares continue to be made. New rim forms, however, appear. The shallow S-rims characteristic of LeBeau ware begin to dominate, and Stanley ware appears (Lehmer 1966:62; Sperry 1968:36–50; Wood 1967:62–75).

Lithics

The general lithic inventory in the Middle Missouri tradition is much the same from beginning to end. Until recently, however, Middle Missouri archaeological studies did not address the potential wealth of information to be obtained from lithic remains. Regional specialists have added significantly to our understanding of both spatial and temporal changes in the lithic technology of different units, as well as the relations between them.

The problem of the utilization patterns of lithic resources on the Missouri River was investigated by Ahler (1977) when he tested Lehmer's (1954:103, 127, 131) assertion that Middle Missouri-tradition populations depended more heavily on Knife River silicified sediment than did the later Coalescent-tradition people. Ahler reviewed 12 lithic types used for chipped-stone tools at two Middle Missouri sites and two Coalescent sites in the Cannonball region. Although his sample was limited, his work supported Lehmer's original hypothesis. The pattern remains to be tested at other sites.

Multivariate statistical techniques were used by Calabrese (1972, 1973) to evaluate the differences in small side-notched projectile points from nine Extended- and Terminal-variant sites. Nailati-phase projectiles differed from those of the Fort Yates phase in both size and shape, while projectiles from the Terminal-variant Huff and Shermer sites have a different haft shape and are smaller than other samples. The differences are believed to reflect variation through time.

Arrowpoints in Middle Missouri–tradition sites either are small bifaces with a triangular outline or are triangular with notches in the lateral edges to form a distinct hafting base. A variety of forms of cutting tools occur. Long narrow bifaces with one convex and one straight edge are believed to have been hafted in slots cut into the edge of bison ribs or vertebrae spines. Some stemmed and side-notched, leaf-shaped, or triangular bifaces were probably also hafted and could have functioned as either knives or spears.

Common Plains snub-nosed end scrapers are a standard part of the inventory of Middle Missouri–tradition sites. These plano-convex flake tools are triangular in outline, with steep pressure flaking on their distal edge opposite the bulb of percussion, and are retouched along most lateral edges. Drills, some of them notched for hafting, have narrow bits and broad bases.

Grooved mauls are also common. They were shaped from granite cobbles by adding a shallow, pecked hafting groove that either encircles the stone or goes around three-quarters of its circumference. Ends were battered from hammering. Pecked- and polished-stone celts of diorite or granite have a wedge-shaped cutting edge and a blunt poll.

Other ground stone includes regularly shaped sandstone shaft smoothers and irregularly shaped smoothing stones of sandstone or clinker. The latter material was taken from the Missouri River, having floated downstream from burned lignite beds on the upper Missouri. Pitted stones, hammerstones, and spherical balls of granite and sandstone are also found, as well as grooved stones, donut-shaped stones, and local fossils.

Bone and Shell

The people of the Middle Missouri tradition depended on bison not only for food, but for raw material for making bone tools. Scapula hoes were fashioned from bison shoulder blades, and occasionally from those of elk. The spine and ridge of the posterior border were removed, and the distal end was sharpened. Some are notched for hafting along the lateral edges near the articular end, and others have holes cut in the center of the blade. Scapulae were also made into knives. Some of them were cut from the center of the shoulder blade to form an L-shaped tool, with the concave margin ground to a sharp cutting edge. Rectangular knives were made with one edge forming the cutting blade, and the opposite edge retaining part of the spine as a grip.

Bone scoops or digging tools were fashioned from bison-horn cores and the adjoining part of the frontal bone. The horn core served as a handle; some of these tools have finger grips cut into the bone. Bone picks, made from bison radii, have distal ends sharpened to a chisel edge. The proximal end of the bone often has a hole excavated through the articular surface to accommodate a handle.

Bison and elk metatarsals were made into fleshers by removing the distal end of the bone and sharpening the shaft to a wedge-shaped bit, which usually was serrated. Ethnographic specimens from the Northern Plains retain the tarsal bones as a handle, although these bones are not always recovered archaeologically, being accidentally separated. L-shaped fleshing adzes were made of elk antler. On ethnographic specimens, metal blades were attached to the short leg of the L; prehistorically, end scrapers were probably used.

Bison ribs were raw materials for many tools. Slotted knife handles were made from segments of large ribs and from vertebrae spines. Crescent-shaped chipped-stone knives were set into the slots along the rib margin. Bison ribs were also split and fashioned into an implement sometimes called a pottery-modeling tool or a quill flattener. Whatever its function, it is common in most sites and must have been used in a variety of tasks. Bison ribs also were made into shaft wrenches. One or more holes were cut in the flat surface of the bone to help hold and straighten shafts, probably of wood.

Most awls were made by splitting deer and antelope metapodials and working one end of the shaft to a sharp point. Fishhooks are common, the upper end grooved to attach the line. Bone beads and tubes were made from bird and mammal long bones, and eagle-wing bones were notched for use as whistles. Bone and antler bracelets and pendants, stone disks, pierced elk canines, and many other elements were used for ornamentation.

There was much trade with external groups. Historically, the Missouri River village Indians acted as intermediaries between the nomadic groups to the east and the west. Much the same pattern must have prevailed prehistorically. Evidence of trade is common at Great Oasis sites, where items of Gulf coast shell and *Anculosa* shell are found in even the earliest components. Mill Creek/Over sites yield shell objects from both the Gulf and the east coast of North America, copper fragments, and even some pottery that is probably derived from Mississippian sites in the central Mississippi valley. The Mill Creek/Over sites yield much more evidence for Mississippian trade and interaction than do Great Oasis sites. In contrast to Great Oasis and Mill Creek/Over, Cambria sites offer little evidence for the receipt of exotic shell, metals, or stone. Many nonlocal goods appear in western Middle Missouri–tradition villages: *Dentalium* shells from the Pacific coast are common, but recent studies in South Dakota have revealed the use of fossil *Dentalium gracile* shells that were available locally (Alex and Martin 1993). Other marine shells, such as *Olivella* from the Pacific coast, and obsidian, probably from the Yellowstone Park area, reflect early trade. There is also evidence of trade to the east and south: native copper, catlinite, and ornaments of *Marginella* and *Anculosa*. Beads and bird silhouettes were cut from Gulf coast conch or whelk shells. Disk and tubular beads were made from either local or imported shell. A study of exotic artifacts from the Cattle Oiler site suggests that "the Initial Middle Missouri was within, but at the edge of, Mississippian trade nets, Extended Middle Missouri was beyond those limits" (Ludwickson et al. 1993:151).

Interpretations: Adaptation, Stability, and Interaction

In this chapter, we have seen a pattern of stable subsistence and of general cultural continuity and equilibrium on the Missouri River from the inception of a village horticultural lifeway to the Terminal variant of the tradition (Calabrese 1972; Wood 1974).

The movements and dynamics of the Middle Missouri populations are not well understood. Both the eastern division and the western division of the Initial variant apparently developed from about A.D. 1000. The eastern division disappeared from the four-state area by about A.D. 1250. Possibly by the late 1100s, the Extended variant was established on the Missouri River, persisting until about 1450. The Extended variant in the Cannonball, Knife, and Heart regions to the north dates from about the twelfth to the fourteenth century, followed in the Cannonball region by the Terminal variant.

There is general agreement that the origins of the Initial variant lie to the east, in northwestern Iowa and southwestern Minnesota. There also is general agreement that the Terminal variant is a direct outgrowth of the Extended variant in the northern part of the Middle Missouri subarea (Lehmer 1971:97,124). The principal disagreement lies in the nature of the relation between the Initial and Extended variants. Both Lehmer (1971:99–103) and Caldwell (1966:154–155) agree that the Initial and Extended variants represent separate populations, if not (as Caldwell notes) a population that overwhelmed or replaced Initial-variant people. Lehmer's argument for two populations seems persuasive, but there are arguments supporting a more parsimonious unilineal development.

Lehmer and others (D. Anderson 1969, 1987; Hurt 1953; Tiffany 1983) suggest that the Initial and Extended variants represent separate migrations out of southwestern Minnesota and northwestern Iowa to the Missouri River in central South Dakota. Lehmer's alternative hypothesis that the Extended variant developed from the Initial is a more plausible view in light of the distribution of sites to the east of the Missouri River.

There is overlap in the radiocarbon dates from Initial and Extended sites. This is, however, not sufficient grounds for refuting the hypothesis of a linear development and/or a split in population on the Missouri River. The distinction between the two variants is based on geographic, temporal, and formal variation—that is, using each of the three formal dimensions of archaeology. The formal differences consist largely of limited variation in architectural details and surface treatment of pottery. These do not appear sufficient to necessitate the introduction of foreign (Caldwell) or alternative (Lehmer) populations to the subarea. These differences could well represent no more than regional variations on a general theme, for the variants obviously are closely related. Furthermore, Initial and Extended sites are not found at the same loci, a circumstance that can be used to argue as strongly for lineal development and/or splitting of groups as it does for two independent populations.

The lack of Extended-variant sites between A.D. 1250 and 1400 in the southern part of the Bad–Cheyenne region was once interpreted as evidence for the abandonment of the area. Several "Modified" Initial–variant sites in this area have recently been reassigned to the Extended variant, so this "abandonment" may be a misinterpretation of the record.

The presence of fortifications at Initial- and Extended-variant sites has suggested to some specialists that there probably was intergroup warfare between different populations. It is now recognized that Coalescent-tradition peoples were on the Missouri River—probably in competition with those of the Middle Missouri tradition—by the beginning of the fourteenth century (Johnson, Chap. 10, this volume). If recent radiocarbon dates for early Coalescent sites are correct, Coalescent populations were on the Missouri River as much as 300 years earlier than previously believed, and could themselves have been the antagonists of the fortified Middle Missouri populations. All of this assumes that village, and not nomadic, peoples inspired the defensive features at the fortified communities.

Many regional specialists (Calabrese 1972; Wood 1974) have argued that the settlement pattern and the subsistence and technological systems of the tradition were in essentially stable equilibrium from the time they first appeared on the Missouri River to the early historic period. Wood has argued that Middle Missouri villages were self-sufficient units with little need for trade in staples among themselves. Most of the artifact inventory is shared by all village peoples, with only minor variation in style and form, from the Initial Middle Missouri variant to the historic period. Villages, whether they are of indigenous settlers or of latecomers to the Missouri (such as the Cheyenne), were built on terrace rims overlooking the Missouri River floodplain, generally in a defensible position. Village placement allowed ready exploitation of the floodplain and river channel, plus the bluffs and uplands away from the river.

The Terminal variant, in any case, was the prehistoric antecedent for the historic Mandan Indians, although the picture appears to be somewhat more complicated with respect to the emerging understanding of Hidatsa prehistory.

References

Ahler, S. A.
   1977   *Archeological Reconnaissance and Test Excavations at the Jake White Bull Site, 39Co6, Oahe Reservoir, South Dakota.* University of North Dakota, Grand Forks. Report to the United States Army Corps of Engineers, Omaha District, Omaha, Neb.
   1993   Plains Village Cultural Taxonomy for the Upper Knife–Heart Region. In *The Phase I Archeological Research Program for the Knife River Indian Villages National Historic Site.* Part 4, *Interpretation of the Archeological Record,* edited by T. D. Thiessen, 57–108. National Park Service, Midwest Archeological Center, Occasional Studies in Anthropology, no. 27. Lincoln, Neb.
Ahler, S. A., C. M. Johnson, H. Haas, and G. Bonani
   1995   Reevaluation of Plains Village Radiocarbon Dating in the Middle Missouri Subarea. Paper presented at the sixtieth annual meeting of the Society for American Archaeology, Minneapolis, Minn.
Alex, L. M.
   1979   39BU2: A Fortified Site in Western South Dakota. *Newsletter of the Archaeological Society of South Dakota* 9:3–7.
Alex, L. M., and J. E. Martin
   1993   The Occurrence of Fossil and Recent *Dentalium* at Four Late Prehistoric Archaeological Sites in the Black Hills Periphery, Western South Dakota. In *Prehistory and Human Ecology of the Western Prairies and Northern Plains,* edited by J. A. Tiffany, 131–143. Plains Anthropologist Memoir no. 27.
Alex, R.
   1973   Architectural Features of Houses at the Mitchell Site (39DV2), Eastern South Dakota. *Plains Anthropologist* 18:149–159.
   1981a   Village Sites off the Missouri River. In *Future of South Dakota's Past,* edited by L. J. Zimmerman and L. C. Stewart, 39–45. South Dakota Archaeological Society, Special Publication no. 2. Vermillion.
   1981b   The Village Cultures of the Lower James Valley, South Dakota. Ph. D. diss., Department of Anthropology, University of Wisconsin, Madison.
Anderson, D. C.
   1969   Mill Creek Culture: A Review. *Plains Anthropologist* 14:137–143.
   1987   Toward a Processual Understanding of the Initial Variant of the Middle Missouri Tradition: The Case of the Mill Creek Culture of Iowa. *American Antiquity* 52:522–537.
Anderson, M.
   1995   *Archaeological Excavations at the Cowan Site: A Phase II Investigation of 13WD88*

Primary Roads Project NHS-75-1(54)—19-97 a.k.a. 91-97060-1, Woodbury County, Iowa. Project Completion Report, vol. 18, no. 10. University of Iowa, Highway Archaeology Program, Iowa City. Report to the Iowa Department of Transportation, Office of Project Planning, Ames.

Anfinson, S. F.
1987   The Prehistory of the Prairie Lakes Region in the Northeastern Plains. Ph.D. diss., Department of Anthropology, University of Minnesota, Minneapolis.

Benn, D. W.
1974   Seed Analysis and Its Implication for an Initial Middle Missouri Site in South Dakota. *Plains Anthropologist* 19:55–72.

Bozell, J. J., and M. K. Rogers
1989   A Great Oasis Fauna from Central Nebraska. *Central Plains Archaeology* 1:3–36.

Brown, L. A.
1974   *The Archeology of the Breeden Site.* Plains Anthropologist Memoir no. 10.

Bryson, R. A., D. A. Baerreis, and W. M. Wendland
1970   The Character of Late-Glacial and Post-Glacial Climatic Changes. In *Pleistocene and Recent Environments on the Central Great Plains,* edited by W. Dort, Jr., and J. K. Jones, Jr., 53–74. University Press of Kansas, Lawrence.

Butler, W. B., and J. J. Hoffman
1992   A Checklist of Plains Ceramic Types and Wares. *South Dakota Archaeology* 16:1–105.

Calabrese, F. A.
1972   Cross Ranch: A Study of Variability in a Stable Cultural Tradition. *Plains Anthropologist* 18:344–349.
1973   Discriminant Analysis of Certain Middle Missouri Tradition Projectiles. *Plains Anthropologist* 18:344–349.
1977   Ceramic Classification in Middle Missouri Prehistory. In *Trends in Middle Missouri Prehistory: A Festschrift Honoring the Contributions of Donald J. Lehmer,* edited by W. R. Wood, 28–37. Plains Anthropologist Memoir no. 13.

Caldwell, W. W.
1966   The Middle Missouri Tradition Reappraised. *Plains Anthropologist* 11:152–157.

Caldwell, W. W., and R. E. Jensen
1969   *The Grand Detour Phase.* Smithsonian Institution, River Basin Surveys, Publications in Salvage Archeology, no. 13. Lincoln, Neb.

Caldwell, W. W., L. G. Madison, and B. Golden
1964   Archeological Investigations at the Hickey Brothers Site (32LM4), Big Bend Reservoir, Lyman County, South Dakota. *Bureau of American Ethnology Bulletin* 189:267–290.

Chomko, S. A.
1976   Faunal Exploitation in the Initial Middle Missouri Variant. In *Fay Tolton and the Middle Missouri Variant,* edited by W. R. Wood, 35–41. Missouri Archaeological Society, Research Series, no. 13. Columbia.

Ehrenhard, J. E.
1971   A Statistical Analysis of Ceramics from Three Sites in South Dakota. M.A. thesis, Department of Anthropology, University of Nebraska, Lincoln.

Eighmy, J. L., and J. M. LaBelle
1996   Radiocarbon Dating of Twenty-Seven Plains Complexes and Phases. *Plains Anthropologist* 41:29–52.

Falk, C. R., and S. A. Ahler
1988   *Archeological Investigations in the Mobridge Area, South Dakota, 1969–1970: Lower Grand (Davis), 39CO14; Walth Bay, 39WW203; and Helb, 39CA208.* University of Missouri, Department of Anthropology, American Archaeology Division, Columbia. Report to the National Park Service, Rocky Mountain Region, Denver.

Falk, C. R., and F. A. Calabrese
1973   Helb: A Preliminary Statement. *Plains Anthropologist* 18:336–343.

Gant, R. D.
1967   *Archeological Investigations at the Arp Site, 39BR101, Brule County, South Dakota.* University of South Dakota, South Dakota Museum, Archaeological Studies, Circular no. 12. Vermillion.

Gibbon, G.
1993   The Middle Missouri Tradition in Minnesota: A Review. In *Prehistory and Human Ecology of the Western Prairies and Northern Plains,* edited by J. A. Tiffany, 169–187. Plains Anthropologist Memoir no. 27.

Griffin, D. E.
1976   A Model of Culture Change for the Middle Missouri Subarea. In *Fay Tolton and the Initial Middle Missouri Variant,* edited by W. R. Wood, 33–35. Missouri Archaeological Society, Research Series, no. 13. Columbia.

Haberman, T. W.
1993   The Randall Phase Component at the Dirt Lodge Village Site, Spink County, South Dakota: Late Woodland/Early Plains Village Transitions on the Northeastern Plains. In *Prehistory and Human Ecology of the Western Prairies and Northern Plains,* edited by J. A. Tiffany, 75–116. Plains Anthropologist Memoir no. 27.

Haberman, T. W., ed.
1982   *Archaeological Excavations at the Travis I Site, 39CO213, Corson County, South Dakota.* South Dakota Archaeological Research Center, Contract Investigations Series, no. 37. Report to the South Dakota Department of Transportation, Federal Highway Administration. Pierre.

Hannus, L. A., E. J. Lueck, and R. P. Winham
1987   *The Mitchell Prehistoric Indian Village, 39DV2: Summary of Studies and Excavations Through 1986.* Augustana College, Archeology Laboratory, Sioux Falls, S.D. Report to the Mitchell Prehistoric Indian Village Preservation Society, Mitchell, S.D.

Haug, J., M. Fosha, J. Abbott, C. Hjort, and R. Mandel
1994   Exploring the Bloom Site, 1993–1994. *South Dakota Archaeology* 18:29–71.

Helgevold, M. K.
1981   *A History of South Dakota Archaeology.* South Dakota Archaeological Society, Special Publication no. 3. Vermillion.

Henning, D. R.
1969   Ceramics from the Mill Creek Sites. *Journal of the Iowa Archeological Society* 16:192–280.
1971   Origins of Mill Creek. *Journal of the Iowa Archeological Society* 18:6–12.
1981   *Excavations in the Proposed Perry Creek Reservoir.* Technical Report no. 81-9. University of Nebraska, Department of Anthropology, Division of Archeological Research, Lincoln.
1983   The Initial Variant of the Middle Missouri Tradition. In *An Archaeological Reconnaissance Survey of the Northern Border Pipeline for the Northern Plains Natural*

Gas Company Minnesota Segment, edited by J. Hudak, D. Henning, E. Henning, C. Hudak, D. Radford, C. Pedersen, and T. Nowak, 4.42–4.65. Archaeological Field Services, Marine on St. Croix, Minn. Report to the Northern Plains Natural Gas Company, Omaha, Neb.

1989   Plains Village Tradition: Eastern Periphery. Manuscript on file, Luther College, Decorah, Iowa.

Henning, D. R., and E. R. Henning

1978   Great Oasis Ceramics. *Occasional Publications in Minnesota Anthropology* 2:2–26.

1982   Mill Creek and Great Oasis Sites. In *Interrelationships of Cultural and Fluvial Deposits in Northwest Iowa,* edited by E. A. Bettis and D. M. Thompson, 15–27. Association of Iowa Archeologists, Iowa City.

Henning, E. R. P.

1981   Great Oasis and the Middle Missouri Tradition. In *The Future of South Dakota's Past,* edited by L. J. Zimmerman and L. Stewart, 33–38. South Dakota Archaeological Society, Special Publication no. 2. Vermillion.

Hoffman, J. J.

1968   *The La Roche Sites.* Smithsonian Institution, River Basin Surveys, Publications in Salvage Archeology, no. 11. Lincoln, Neb.

Howard, J. H.

1959   *Report of the Investigation of the Tony Glas Site, 32EM3. Emmons County, North Dakota.* University of North Dakota, Anthropological Papers, no. 1. Grand Forks.

Hurt, W. R., Jr.

1951   *Report of the Investigation of the Swanson Site, 39BR16, Brule County, South Dakota.* South Dakota Archaeological Commission, Archaeological Studies, Circular no. 3. Pierre.

1953   *Report of the Investigation of the Thomas Riggs Site, 39HU1, Hughes County, South Dakota.* South Dakota Archaeological Commission, Archaeological Studies, Circular no. 5. Pierre.

Ives, J. C.

1962   Mill Creek Pottery. *Journal of the Iowa Archeological Society* 11:3.

Jensen, R. E.

n.d.   Archeology of the Sommers Site (39ST56), Big Bend Reservoir. Manuscript on file, National Park Service, Midwest Archeological Center, Lincoln, Neb.

Johnson, A. M.

1979   *Extended Middle Missouri Components in the Big Bend Region, South Dakota.* South Dakota Archaeological Society, Special Publication no. 1. Vermillion.

1989   An Initial Middle Missouri Campsite in Badlands National Park. *South Dakota Archaeology* 13:1–28.

1993   Initial Middle Missouri in Western South Dakota: A Summary. In *Prehistory and Human Ecology of the Western Prairies and Northern Plains,* edited by J. A. Tiffany, 117–130. Plains Anthropologist Memoir no. 27.

Johnson, E.

1991   Cambria and Cahokia's Northwestern Periphery. In *New Perspectives on Cahokia, Views from the Periphery,* edited by J. B. Stoltman, 307–317. Prehistory Press, Madison, Wis.

Johnston, R. B.

1967   The Thomas Riggs Site (39HU1) Revisited, Hughes County, South Dakota. *American Antiquity* 32:353–395.

Kivett, M. F., and R. E. Jensen

1976   *Archeological Investigations of the Crow Creek Site (39BF11). Fort Randall Reservoir Area, South Dakota.* Nebraska State Historical Society, Publications in Anthropology, no. 7. Lincoln.

Knudson, R. A.

1967   Cambria Village Ceramics. *Plains Anthropologist* 12:247–99.

Knudson, R., J. A. Moe, and A. W. Bowers

1983   *The Anton Rygh Excavations and Assemblage, Campbell County, South Dakota: A Report on Materials Gathered by Alfred W. Bowers in 1957–1959, with Emphasis on the 1958 Collection.* University of Idaho, Laboratory of Anthropology, Anthropological Research Manuscript Series, no. 75. Moscow. Report to the National Park Service.

Krause, R. A.

1969   Correlation of Phases in Central Plains Prehistory. In *Two House Sites in the Central Plains: An Experiment in Archaeology,* edited by W. R. Wood, 82–96. Plains Anthropologist Memoir no. 6.

1977   Taxonomic Practice and Middle Missouri Prehistory: A Perspective on Donald J. Lehmer's Contributions. In *Trends in Middle Missouri Prehistory: A Festschrift Honoring the Contributions of Donald J. Lehmer,* edited by W. R. Wood, 5–13. Plains Anthropologist Memoir no. 13.

Lee, C. H., ed.

1980   *The Archeology of the White Buffalo Robe Site.* 2 vols. Report to Sterns-Roger Engineering Corp., Denver.

Lehmer, D. J.

1954   *Archeological Investigations in the Oahe Area, South Dakota, 1950–51.* Bureau of American Ethnology Bulletin 158. Washington, D.C.

1966   *The Fire Heart Creek Site.* Smithsonian Institution, River Basin Surveys, Publications in Salvage Archeology, no. 1. Lincoln, Neb.

1970   Climate and Culture History in the Middle Missouri Valley. In *Pleistocene and Recent Environments of the Central Great Plains,* edited by W. Dort, Jr., and J. K. Jones, Jr., 117–129. University Press of Kansas, Lawrence.

1971   *Introduction to Middle Missouri Archeology.* National Park Service, Anthropological Papers, no. 1. Washington, D.C.

Lehmer, D. J., and W. W. Caldwell

1966   Horizon and Tradition in the Northern Plains. *American Antiquity* 31:511–516.

Lehmer, D. J., and D. T. Jones

1968   *Arikara Archeology: The Bad River Phase.* Smithsonian Institution, River Basin Surveys, Publications in Salvage Archeology, no. 7. Lincoln, Neb.

Lehmer, D. J., L. K. Meston, and C. L. Dill

1973   Structural Details of a Middle Missouri House. *Plains Anthropologist* 18:160–166.

Lensink, S. C.

1992   Rethinking Mill Creek Radiocarbon Chronology. Paper presented at the fiftieth annual meeting of the Plains Anthropological Conference, Lincoln, Neb. Manuscript on file, University of Iowa, Office of the State Archaeologist, Iowa City.

1993   A Reanalysis of Eastern Initial Middle Missouri Radiocarbon Dates and the Implications for the Timing of Long-Distance Trade with Middle Mississippian Centers. Paper presented at the Midwest Archaeological Conference, Mil-

waukee. Manuscript on file, University of Iowa, Office of the State
Archaeologist, Iowa City.

Ludwickson, J.
n.d.   Origins and Evolution of the Plains Earth Lodge. [Preliminary draft and
notes provided to author, March 1994, for limited citation]

Ludwickson, J., D. J. Blakeslee, and J. M. O'Shea
1987   *Missouri National Recreational River: Native American Cultural Resources.* Wichita
State University, Publications in Anthropology, no. 3.

Ludwickson, J., J. N. Gunderson, and C. Johnson
1993   Select Exotic Artifacts from Cattle Oiler (39ST224): A Middle Missouri Tradition Site in Central South Dakota. In *Prehistory and Human Ecology of the Western Prairies and Northern Plains,* edited by J. A. Tiffany, 151–168. Plains Anthropologist Memoir no. 27.

McKern, W. C.
1939   The Midwestern Taxonomic Method as an Aid to Archaeological Study.
American Antiquity 4:301–313.

Meleen, E. E.
1949   A Preliminary Report on the Thomas Riggs Village Site. *American Antiquity*
14:310–321.

Nickel, R. K.
1974   Plant Resource Utilization at a Late Prehistoric Site in North-Central South
Dakota. M.A. thesis, Department of Anthropology, University of Nebraska,
Lincoln.
1977   The Study of Archeologically Derived Plant Materials from the Middle
Missouri Subarea. In *Trends in Middle Missouri Prehistory: A Festschrift
Honoring the Contributions of Donald J. Lehmer,* edited by W. R. Wood, 53–58.
Plains Anthropologist Memoir no. 13.

Over, W. H.
1938   *A Preliminary Report of the Mitchell Indian Village Site and Burial Mounds.* University of South Dakota, South Dakota Museum, Archaeological Studies, Circu-
lar no. 2. Vermillion.

Over, W. H., and E. E. Meleen
1941   *A Report on the Investigation of the Brandon Village Site and the Split Rock Creek
Mounds.* University of South Dakota, South Dakota Museum, Archaeological
Studies, Circular no. 5. Vermillion.

Peterson, D. A., Jr.
1967   A Ceramic Sequence for Northwest Iowa. B.A. thesis, Harvard College,
Cambridge, Mass. Manuscript on file, University of Iowa, Office of the State
Archaeologist, Iowa City.

Roetzel, K. A., and R. A. Strachan
1986   *Analysis of Collections from the Huston Ranch Site (39HU211), the Amos Shields
Site (39HU220), 39SL22, and 39SL24.* 5 vols. Report to the National Park Service, Rocky Mountain Region, Denver.

Spaulding, A. C.
1956   *The Arzberger Site, Hughes County, South Dakota.* University of Michigan,
Museum of Anthropology, Occasional Contributions, no. 16.
Ann Arbor.

Sperry, J. E.
1968   *The Shermer Site, 32EM10.* Plains Anthropologist Memoir no. 5.

1981   *The Havens Site (32EM1): 1967 and 1968 Excavations.* Report to the National Park Service, Midwest Archeological Center, Lincoln, Neb.

1995   The Havens Site (32EM1): 1967 and 1968 Excavations. In *Two Extended Middle Missouri Village Sites in North Dakota,* edited by F. E. Swensen, 1–94. North Dakota Archaeology 6.

Stephenson, R. L.

1954   Taxonomy and Chronology in the Central Plains–Middle Missouri River Area. *Plains Anthropologist* 1:15–21.

Sundstrom, L.

1989   *Culture History of the Black Hills with Reference to Adjacent Areas of the Northern Great Plains.* J and L Reprint, Lincoln, Neb.

Thiessen, T. D.

1975   The Bendish Site (32Mo2), Morton County, North Dakota. M.A. thesis, Department of Anthropology. University of Nebraska, Lincoln.

1977   A Tentative Radiocarbon Chronology of the Middle Missouri Tradition. In *Trends in Middle Missouri Prehistory: A Festschrift Honoring the Contributions of Donald J. Lehmer,* edited by W. R. Wood, 59–82. Plains Anthropologist Memoir no. 13.

1993a   *The Phase I Archeological Research Program for the Knife River Indian Villages National Historic Site.* Part 1, *Objectives, Methods and Summary of Baseline Studies.* National Park Service, Midwest Archeological Center, Occasional Studies in Anthropology, no. 27. Lincoln, Neb.

1993b   *The Phase I Archeological Research Program for the Knife River Indian Villages National Historic Site.* Part 2, *Ethnohistorical Studies.* National Park Service, Midwest Archeological Center, Occasional Studies in Anthropology, no. 27. Lincoln, Neb.

1993c   *The Phase I Archeological Research Program for the Knife River Indian Villages National Historic Site.* Part 3, *Analysis of the Physical Remains.* National Park Service, Midwest Archeological Center, Occasional Studies in Anthropology, no. 27. Lincoln, Neb.

1993d   *The Phase I Archeological Research Program for the Knife River Indian Villages National Historic Site.* Part 4, *Interpretation of the Archeological Record.* National Park Service, Midwest Archeological Center, Occasional Studies in Anthropology, no. 27. Lincoln, Neb.

1994   A Short History of the Interagency Archeological Salvage Program Work Along the Missouri River. *South Dakota Archaeology* 18:1–5.

1995   The Bendish Site (32Mo2): A Late Prehistoric Village Site in Morton County, North Dakota. In *Two Extended Middle Missouri Village Sites in North Dakota,* edited by F. E. Swensen, 95–294. North Dakota Archaeology 6.

Tiffany, J. A.

1981   A Compendium of Radiocarbon Dates for Iowa Archeological Sites. *Plains Anthropologist* 26:55–73.

1982   *Chan-Ya-Ta, a Mill Creek Village.* University of Iowa, Office of the State Archaeologist, Report no. 15. Iowa City.

1983   An Overview of the Middle Missouri Tradition. In *Prairie Archeology,* edited by G. E. Gibbon, 87–108. University of Minnesota, Publications in Anthropology, no. 3. Minneapolis.

1991a   Models of Mississippian Culture History in the Western Prairie Peninsula: A Perspective from Iowa. In *Cahokia and the Hinterlands, Middle Mississippian Cul-*

tures of the Midwest, edited by T. E. Emerson and R. B. Lewis, 183–192. University of Illinois Press, Chicago.

1991b   Modeling Mill Creek–Mississippian Interaction. In *New Perspectives on Cahokia, Views from the Periphery,* edited by J. B. Stoltman, 319–347. Prehistory Press, Madison, Wis.

Toom, D. L.

1992a   Radiocarbon Dating of the Western Initial Middle Missouri Variant: Some New Dates and a Critical Review of Old Dates. *Plains Anthropologist* 37:115–128.

1992b   Climate and Sedentism in the Middle Missouri Subarea of the Plains. Ph.D. diss., Department of Anthropology, University of Nebraska, Lincoln.

United States Statutes at Large

1944   58 Stat. 534.

Weakly, W. F.

1971   *Tree Ring Dating and Archeology in South Dakota.* Plains Anthropologist Memoir no. 8.

Will, G. F., and H. J. Spinden

1906   *The Mandans: A Study of Their Culture, Archaeology and Language.* Harvard University, Peabody Museum of American Archaeology and Ethnology, Papers, vol. 3, no. 4. Cambridge, Mass.

Willey, G. R.

1966   *An Introduction to American Archaeology.* Vol. 1, *North and Middle America.* Prentice-Hall, Englewood Cliffs, N.J.

Willey, G. R., and P. Phillips

1958   *Method and Theory in American Archaeology.* University of Chicago Press, Chicago.

Winham, R. P., ed.

1995   *Archeological Investigations at the Indian Creek Site (39ST15), Stanley County, South Dakota: A Report on the 1984 and 1985 Excavations.* Augustana College, Archeology Laboratory, Sioux Falls, S.D. Report to the United States Army Corps of Engineers, Omaha District, Omaha, Neb.

Winham, R. P., and L. A. Hannus

1988   *The Mitchell Prehistoric Indian Village, 39DV2: Report of Activities for 1990 and Summary of Field Notes for 1989 and 1990 Excavations at House 7.* Augustana College, Archeology Laboratory, Sioux Falls, S.D. Report to the Mitchell Prehistoric Indian Village Preservation Society, Mitchell, S.D.

Winham, R. P., L. A. Hannus, and K. Watzek

1988   *The Mitchell Prehistoric Indian Village, 39DV2: Summary of Studies and Excavations in 1987.* Augustana College, Archeology Laboratory, Sioux Falls, S.D. Report to the Mitchell Prehistoric Indian Village Preservation Society, Mitchell, S.D.

Winham, R. P., W. R. Wood, and L. A. Hannus

1994   *National Historic Landmark Theme Study. Village Sites of the Middle Missouri Subarea, A.D. 1000–A.D. 1887.* Augustana College, Archeology Laboratory, Sioux Falls, S.D. Report to the State Historical Preservation Center, Vermillion, S.D.

Wood, W. R.

1967   *An Interpretation of Mandan Culture History.* Bureau of American Ethnology Bulletin 198. Washington, D.C.

1974   Northern Plains Village Cultures: Internal Stability and External Relationships. *Journal of Anthropological Research* 30:1–16.

1976   *Fay Tolton and the Initial Middle Missouri Variant.* Missouri Archaeological Society, Research Series, no. 13. Columbia.

1986   Introduction. In *Papers in Northern Plains Prehistory and Ethnohistory, Ice Glider, 32OL110,* edited by W. R. Wood, 1–24. South Dakota Archaeological Society, Special Publication no. 10. Sioux Falls.

1989   Plains Villagers: Middle Missouri Tradition. Manuscript prepared for *Plains,* edited by R. J. DeMallie. Vol. 13 of *Handbook of North American Indians,* W. C. Sturtevant, general editor. Smithsonian Institution Press, Washington, D.C.

Wood, W. R., and A. R. Woolworth

1964   The Paul Brave Site (32SI4), Oahe Reservoir Area, North Dakota. *Bureau of American Ethnology Bulletin* 189:1–66.

Woolworth, A. R.

1956   Archeological Investigations at Site 32ME59 (Grandmother's Lodge). *North Dakota History* 23:78–102.

10. The Coalescent Tradition

Craig M. Johnson

As it was originally envisioned, the Coalescent tradition represented a blending of Central Plains– and Middle Missouri–tradition traits to form a new entity (Lehmer 1954:150–153, 1971:32–33, 115). Four sequential horizons, now called variants, were defined for the Coalescent: Initial (A.D. 1400–1550), Extended (A.D. 1550–1675), Post-Contact (A.D. 1675–1780), and Disorganized (A.D. 1780–1862). Lehmer conceptualized these variants as sequential stages, each developing directly from the previous one.

Recent studies have called into question these basic assumptions of the Coalescent. Research shows that (1) the Initial Coalescent did not develop from a blending of the Central Plains and Middle Missouri traditions, but in its initial form is not distinguishable in most respects from the Central Plains tradition itself; (2) there appears to be a temporal overlap between the Initial and Extended Coalescent variants; and (3) Lehmer's culture-historical model of the Coalescent is not valid along parts of the Missouri River, especially near the Knife River.

The dating of the Initial and Extended variants and the Painted Woods, Heart, and Knife River complexes does not correspond to Lehmer's (1971:33) widely accepted model. Lehmer dated the Initial Coalescent at 1400 to 1550, but more recent research suggests that a range of 1300 to 1600 is perhaps more realistic (Ahler et al. 1994, 1995).

Dates from the Lower Grand, Little Pumpkin, and Demery sites indicate that the Extended variant probably began at least a century earlier than Lehmer believed. The Extended variant can be tentatively dated at 1450/1500 to 1650. These dates overlap those from the Initial Coalescent by 100 years, suggesting that the transition between the two variants, if there was one, may not have been a simple process of replacement, as Lehmer envisioned. Certainly there is discontinuity between Initial-variant ceramic assemblages, with their high number of finger- and tool-impressed lips, and early Extended assemblages, dominated by incised or trailed rims. The origins of the Extended variant from other unidentified sources cannot be ruled out. Key's (1983:90, 94, 100) craniometric study appears to eliminate a Woodland- or Central Plains–tradition origin. Zimmerman and Bradley (1993) support the traditionally accepted replacement model, and Willey (1990:85, 91) is able to establish a biological link between Initial Coalescent and later Arikara populations.

Finally, the chronology for Post-Contact occupations in North Dakota (Lehmer 1971:33, 203–206)—the Heart River phase (1675–1780) followed by the Knife River phase (1780–1845)—is not supported by recent investigations (Ahler

1993a; Ahler et al. 1991). In addition, the commonly accepted date of 1675 (Lehmer 1971:33) for the beginning of the Post-Contact Coalescent is rejected in favor of 1600/1650 (Ahler 1993a:87–89; Ahler and Drybred 1993:290; Ahler and Toom 1995:377; C. Johnson 1994:240–241).

Despite these problems, the concept of the Coalescent as a tradition is retained to maintain continuity with past research and to use as a tool for organizing the late prehistoric and historic sites occupied by the Mandan, Hidatsa, Arikara, and Pawnee. Until viable chronological sequences comparable to the one recently developed for the Knife region become available for other Middle Missouri and Central Plains areas, a basic understanding of the culture history of both subareas will continue to elude us.

Coalescent-tradition sites represent the late prehistoric and historic villages of the Mandan, Hidatsa, Arikara, Pawnee, Cheyenne, and Ponca. Their principal sites are permanent or semipermanent villages of circular earthlodges along the Missouri River in North and South Dakota between the Niobrara and Knife rivers (Figure 10.1). Many sites in this area have been affected by reservoirs (Ebert et al. 1989). A second cluster of sites is along the Platte and Loup rivers in Nebraska. Other Coalescent-related components are along the James and Sheyenne rivers in eastern North Dakota (Wheeler 1963; Wood 1971), on tributaries of the Missouri River in western North and South Dakota and eastern Montana (Cooper 1958; Mulloy 1942), and along the Niobrara, Elkhorn, Big Blue, and Republican rivers in Nebraska and northern Kansas (Wood 1965). With rare exceptions, sites away from core village areas are thought to be either quarries or hunting camps (Ahler 1986; Bozell and Ludwickson 1988; Roper 1989, 1994).

The Mandan, Hidatsa, Arikara, and Pawnee and their proto- and prehistoric ancestors relied on a mixed economy based largely on hunting and gardening. The gathering of wild plants is documented historically and prehistorically. The well-preserved unmodified vertebrate remains found at village sites reveal that bison provided more meat (80 to 95 percent) than any other species. Deer, elk, antelope, canids (dog, wolf, coyote, and fox), birds, and fish have been recovered from many sites (Falk 1977; Snyder 1995). Recent research suggests that bison meat may have overshadowed all other food resources in the diets of at least some of the Coalescent villagers (Tuross and Fogel 1994:285–289).

Early studies of butchering techniques by White (see Falk 1977; Gilbert 1969) indicated a similarity in bison exploitation at Phillips Ranch and Buffalo Pasture, as opposed to Rock Village and the Middle Missouri–tradition occupations at the Dodd site. Wood (1967:183–187) related these differences in butchering techniques to alternative practices among ancestral Mandan, Hidatsa, and Arikara. Although there are differences, there is a general heavy reliance on bison among Coalescent groups, supporting Wood's (1974) general model of Plains Village lifeways (Ahler et al. 1993:270; Bozell 1995:Figure 6; Warren 1986:186). An analysis of microfauna from Plains Village sites, including Coa-

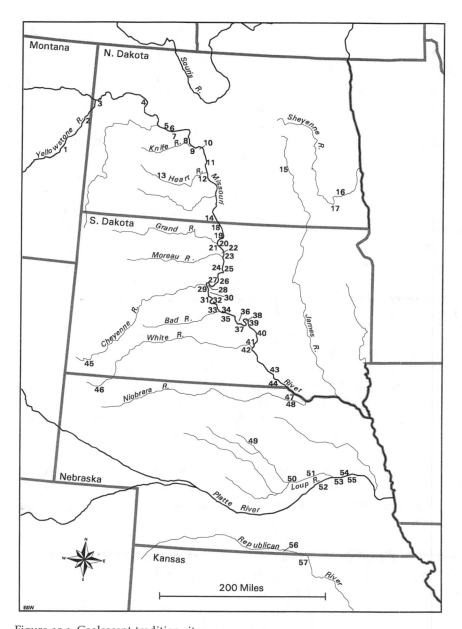

Figure 10.1. Coalescent-tradition sites.
Montana (1) Hagen, (2) Nollmeyer; *North Dakota* (3) Mondrian Tree, (4) Crow Files High, (5) Nightwalker's Butte, (6) Like-a-Fishhook Village, (7) Star Village, Rock Village, (8) Big Hidatsa, Elbee, Sakakawea, Lower Hidatsa, Amahami, (9) White Buffalo Robe, Deapolis, Mahhaha, Fort Clark, (10) Greenshield, (11) Double Ditch, (12) Slant, (13) Koehler, (14) Fire Heart Creek, (15) Hintz, (16) Schultz, (17) Biesterfeldt; *South Dakota* (18) Demery, (19) Nordvold, Leavenworth, (20) Anton Rygh, Bamble, Mobridge, Larson, Spiry, Spiry–Eklo, Blue Blanket Island, (21) Lower Grand, Red Horse Hawk, (22) Potts Village, Fox Island, Molstad, (23) Walth Bay, Payne, Swan Creek, (24) Four Bear, Lahoo-catt, (25) Hosterman, (26) Rosa, (27) No Heart Creek, (28) Coleman, (29) Cheyenne River, 39ST50, 39ST25, Gillette, Black Widow, H. P. Thomas, (30) Sully, (31) Dan Donavan, (32) Oahe Village, Spotted Bear, (33) Buffalo Pasture, Dodd, Phillips Ranch, Indian Creek, Leavitt, (34) Pierre School, Arzberger, McClure, Mush Creek, Whistling Elk, Chapelle Creek, (35) Fort George Village, Bower's/ Over's La Roche, (36) Iron Shooter, Amos Shields, (37) Medicine Creek, Stricker, (38) Black Partizan, Peterson, (39) Cadotte, Medicine Crow, Two Teeth, Farm School, (40) Talking Crow, Crow Creek, (41) Oacoma, (42) Spain, (43) Oldham, Hitchell, (44) Scalp Creek, (45) 39FA45; *Nebraska* (46) Slaughterhouse Creek, (47) Lynch, (48) Redbird II, (49) Goodenow, (50) Palmer, (51) Genoa, Burkett, Wright, Phil Cuba, (52) Clarks, (53) Bellwood, (54) Wolfe, Schuyler (Gray), (55) Linwood, Barcal, (56) Hill; *Kansas* (57) Kansas Monument.

lescent ones, relates changes in these fauna to climatic episodes (Semken and Falk 1987, 1991). It is not clear how these changes in climate affected subsistence activities among the Coalescent peoples.

Plant remains, consisting mostly of cultigens, are reported from most sites. They include maize, beans, squash, sunflower, chokecherry, wild blackberry, cherry, grape, plum, chenopodium, marsh elder, rose, dogwood, buffaloberry, and dock (Nickel 1977). The Northern Flint maize grown prehistorically is similar to varieties grown by historic Plains villagers, and usually had eight or ten rows. Larger row numbers probably represent popcorns, sweetcorns, or Southwestern flints (Cutler 1967; Toom et al. 1995:348–353).

Most Coalescent villages are on upper river terraces, but a few sites are set on floodplains. On rare occasions, villages were built on islands (Stephenson 1969). Many of these lowland sites on the Northern Plains are thought to have been occupied in the winter (Lovick and Ahler 1982:234; Smith and Grange 1958; Stephenson 1969:7). A number of Coalescent villages are found superimposed on earlier Middle Missouri–tradition occupations, such as at the Chapelle Creek, Cheyenne River, Indian Creek, and Cattle Oiler sites. A general overview of Coalescent-tradition material culture can be found in Lehmer (1971) and Wedel (1936). No artifacts have been the subject of more intense study than pottery. Ceramic technology, plus house form, has played a key role in the development of culture-historical models. Pottery vessels are mostly constricted-mouth globular jars, tempered with crushed igneous rock (Figure 10.2). Ceramics are divided into many wares and types to describe the wide range of rim forms and decoration (Butler and Hoffman 1992; Grange 1968; C. Johnson 1980).

Villages contain a wide range of tools made from bone and antler: scapula digging tools, awls, needles, knives, fleshing tools, shaft wrenches, fishhooks, cancellous abrading tools, flaking tools, antler hammers, picks, and bone handles. Nonutilitarian items include bone beads, tubes, whistles, pendants, antler bracelets, ice gliders, and snow snakes. Mussel shell was used primarily for scraping tools or for ornaments such as beads, gorgets, disks, rings, and pendants. *Olivella, Marginella,* and *Dentalium* shells were imported via a trading network from the Pacific, Atlantic, and Gulf coasts for some ornaments (Wood 1980). Chipped-stone tools include small triangular unnotched and side-notched arrowpoints, end scrapers, knives, retouched flakes, cores, drills, gravers, chopping tools, and gunflints. Ground-stone artifacts such as manos, metates, grooved mauls, hammerstones and anvils, abraders, catlinite pipes, and ornaments complete the stone-tool assemblages from Coalescent sites. Euro-American trade goods made from metal and glass are often associated with Post-Contact burials (Orser 1984) and are found in village contexts. Analyses of these items over time and their acceptance by and impact on the Arikara and Hidatsa have been made (Rogers 1990; Toom 1979, 1995:368–371; Weston 1993).

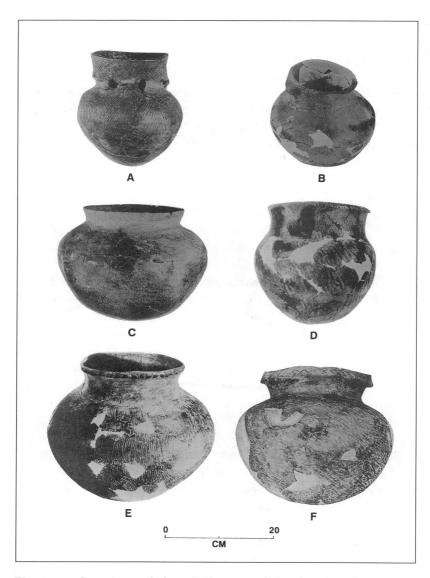

Figure 10.2. Ceramic vessels from Coalescent-tradition sites: (*a, c–d*) Post-Contact Coalescent; (*b*) Extended Coalescent; (*e–f*) Initial Coalescent. (*a, c,* from Grange 1968; *b,* from Hoffman 1967; *d,* from Lehmer 1966; *e,* from Kivett and Jensen 1976; *f,* from Caldwell 1966)

Chronology

Initial Variant

The earliest Coalescent manifestation, the Initial variant (1300–1600), was defined on the basis of five sites in the Big Bend region of central South Dakota—Arzberger, Black Partizan, Crow Creek, Talking Crow, and Farm School—and the Lynch site in northeastern Nebraska. Lehmer (1971:112) includes other Big Bend sites in the variant, and recent work suggests that more villages can be added to the list (Steinacher 1983:48, 64–66). If the radiocarbon dates from the seemingly anomalous Arzberger site are eliminated, the Initial Coalescent would date between 1300 and 1400/1450 (Ahler et al. 1995:27–28). Previous efforts to classify Initial Coalescent components have included the Anoka focus (Witty 1962), Arzberger phase (Caldwell 1966:84–85; Deetz 1965:8, 13–15; Kivett and Jensen 1976:77–78), and Campbell Creek phase (C. Smith 1977:156). Ludwickson and his co-workers (1987:161–168, 218–219) have proposed the "Basal Coalescent" variant, which includes the Loup River/Itskari and St. Helena phases. The Basal variant, which they date at 1250 to 1400, presumably is the progenitor of the Initial variant. Recent research indicates that a viable taxonomic division might be made between early Central Plains–like sites such as Whistling Elk and later Coalescent components like Arzberger (Steinacher 1983).

Perhaps the most distinguishing feature of Initial Coalescent villages is a fortification system composed of a ditch, an interior palisade, and protruding bastions set at 120- to 180-foot intervals (Figure 10.3*a*). All but three of the 10 excavated sites (Farm School, Medicine Creek, and Lynch) are fortified, and only at Talking Crow are there indentations rather than bastions. Many sites were occupied earlier and later by villages of other variants, resulting in mixed assemblages.

Initial Coalescent villages range in size from Black Partizan, with about 10 houses, to Arzberger, with 42 visible houses (Figure 10.3*a*). Village area averages 25.6 acres (excluding Lynch, at 250 to 300 acres) with an average of 1.4 houses per acre, a low density compared with that of other Coalescent variants. Perhaps this low density is because the houses were originally widely scattered, like Central Plains–tradition communities, and later enclosed within fortifications (Lehmer 1971:113). Houses range from typically square structures at Crow Creek (Figure 10.4*b*) and Whistling Elk to more circular ones at Black Partizan and Arzberger (Figure 10.4*a*). Houses are from 16 to 40 feet in diameter, averaging 28.6 feet. House entries generally are parallel to or open in the direction of the Missouri River.

Human burials are occasionally present in Initial Coalescent villages. Black Partizan (Caldwell 1966:15–18), Talking Crow (C. Smith 1977:47–48), and Lynch (Witty 1962:134–136) each yielded a few primary burials. Individuals of both

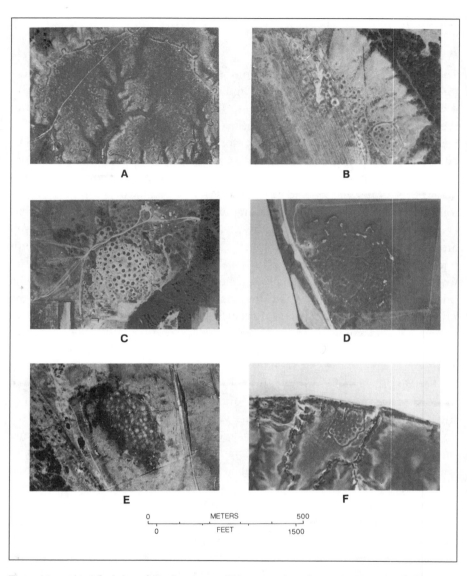

Figure 10.3. Aerial views of Coalescent-tradition sites (north is up): (*a*) Arzberger, an Initial Coalescent village whose fortification system extends between draws on the south side of the site; (*b*) Potts village, an Extended Coalescent, Le Compte–phase village; (*c*) Big Hidatsa, a Knife River–complex, Hidatsa-proper village; (*d*) Double Ditch, a Heart River–complex Mandan village surrounded by the fence of a state park; (*e*) Swan Creek, a Le Beau–phase Arikara village; (*f*) Buffalo Pasture, a Bad River–phase Arikara village. (U.S. Department of Agriculture photographs, 1930s series)

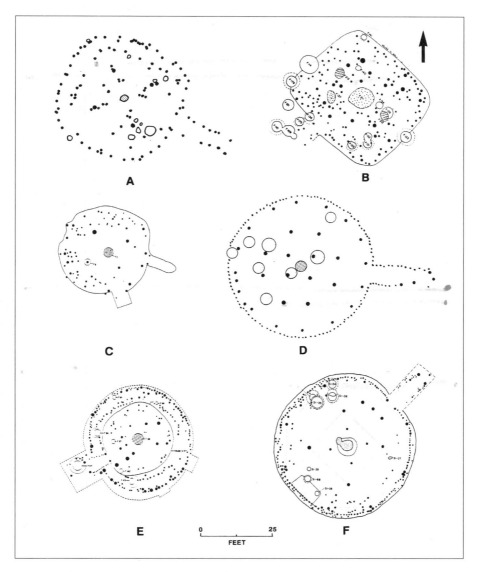

Figure 10.4. Coalescent-tradition house plans (north is up): (*a–b*) Initial houses from Arzberger and Crow Creek; (*c*) Extended house from Over's La Roche; (*d–f*) Post-Contact houses from Gray-Wolfe, Medicine Crow (two houses), and Buffalo Pasture.

315

sexes were found on their sides or backs in flexed or semiflexed positions in ex-
tramural village pits. There were no grave goods. The partially excavated mass
grave from a massacre at Crow Creek, dated at 1297 to 1423 (Ahler et al.
1994:154), yielded at least 486 disarticulated and semiarticulated individuals
who had been dumped in the fortification ditch (Willey and Emerson 1993).
Many of these individuals had been scalped and dismembered (Willey 1990;
Willey and Emerson 1993; Zimmerman and Whitten 1980). It has been suggested that the inhabitants of the village were attacked by other local Initial
Coalescent groups competing for horticultural land (Zimmerman and Bradley
1993). This hypothesis assumes that most of these villages were contemporaneous, which has yet to be demonstrated. Lehmer (1971:125), though, believed that
Initial Coalescent villages were fortified against Extended Middle Missouri
groups, although only a few of the latter sites are in the Big Bend region. A more
viable alternative posits conflicts between Initial Coalescent people and resident
Initial Middle Missouri villagers (C. Johnson 1994:228–229, 317–320).

Initial Coalescent pottery consists of vessels with cord-roughened, simple-
stamped, or smoothed exteriors (Figure 10.2*e–f*) (Steinacher 1983:71–72). Cord-
roughening ranges from 94 percent at Whistling Elk (early) to 12 percent at Arzberger (late). A small amount of check-stamped pottery is present at Arzberger.
Three wares are typically associated with Initial sites: Arzberger, Campbell
Creek, and Hughes (C. Smith 1977:63–67; Spaulding 1956:134–167). Simple or
noncollared rims dominate all Initial Coalescent assemblages, ranging from 73
percent at Arzberger to 99 percent at Black Partizan (Steinacher 1983). Within
this group, most of the pottery is either undecorated or decorated on the lip or
exterior rim by tool or finger impressions (Figure 10.5*b*); horizontal incising or
trailing on the rim exterior ranges from 1 percent to 14 percent. Collared rims
are most common at later sites, and are often trailed with cross-hatched, diagonal, or horizontal lines (Figure 10.5*a*). Overall, the ceramics from early Initial
Coalescent sites such as Whistling Elk resemble Central Plains–tradition assemblages, while the later sites, like Arzberger, have higher percentages of typically
Extended Coalescent pottery.

Initial Coalescent sites contain the usual variety of Plains Village bone and
antler artifacts. Lithic raw materials from Whistling Elk indicate a high reliance
(88 percent) on White River Group silicates (Flattop Chalcedony) from a nonlocal source (Toom 1983), whereas data collected by the writer from the Initial
Coalescent component at Crow Creek (Kivett and Jensen 1976) indicates that the
combined White River Group silicates (Hoard et al. 1993) and plate chalcedony
is well under 25 percent of the assemblage. Locally available materials such as
quartzites, cherts, and chalcedonies were used more extensively. The difference
between these two sites can probably be attributed to varying lengths of occupation.

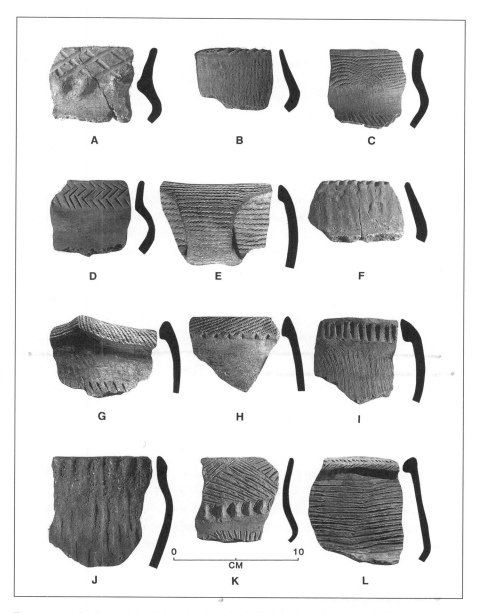

Figure 10.5. Coalescent-tradition rim sherds: (*a–b*) Initial Coalescent; (*d, f, k–l*) Extended Coalescent; (*c, e, g–j*) Post-Contact Coalescent.

Extended Variant

The Extended variant (1400/1450–1650) is represented by more sites than any other Coalescent variant. Lehmer (1971:117) lists 175 components; many others have been discovered in reservoir shoreline surveys. Extended-variant villages are distributed along the Missouri River between the White and Grand rivers, with concentrations at the mouths of the Grand, Moreau, and Cheyenne rivers. One site, Scalp Creek (Hurt 1952), is situated farther south. Related sites, such as those of the Redbird phase (Wood 1965) and campsites such as Slaughterhouse Creek and 39FA45, are along the lower Niobrara, upper White, and Cheyenne rivers (Bozell and Ludwickson 1988). The most recent summary of Extended Coalescent taxonomy proposes four phases: Shannon, Le Compte, La Roche, and Akaska (Lehmer 1971: 120). The Shannon phase includes sites in the Big Bend region, while the Akaska phase encompasses sites in the Grand–Moreau region that show influence from Terminal Middle Missouri and Heart River–complex developments to the north. The Le Compte phase is characterized by villages with houses inside and outside bastioned fortifications, as at the Potts site (Figure 10.3b). Most Extended Coalescent sites, consisting of small unfortified communities with scattered houses, can be assigned to the La Roche phase.

Most Extended Coalescent villages are unfortified communities of loosely arranged houses scattered over large areas. The rare fortified sites are interpreted as refuges for surrounding village groups during times of hostility (Caldwell 1964:3). The median number of houses per village is 15, compared with 31 for the Initial Coalescent. Villages range in size from two houses at Spain to perhaps 200 at the Sully site (about the same number of houses at the latter site were occupied in the Post-Contact period). The average acreage of Extended communities is 14.2, yielding a mean house per acre figure of 4, nearly three times greater than the Initial-variant density of 1.4. Some villages, such as Potts, Molstad, and No Heart Creek, have houses both inside and outside their circular or oval fortifications (Hoffman 1967; Hurt 1970; Stephenson 1971). These villages also have a few irregularly spaced bastions. An exception to the usual curvilinear fortification is the rectangular system at the Lower Grand (Davis) site (Falk and Ahler 1988:18).

Extended Coalescent houses are circular, ranging from 15 to 73 feet in diameter, with a median of 39 feet. There are both large special-purpose "ceremonial" structures and domestic lodges, mean diameters being 55.8 and 31.8 feet (Figure 10.4c). The orientation of house entrances is evenly divided among the east, southeast, and southwest, with almost half facing the Missouri or other rivers. Postholes generally have no recognizable internal pattern, although several villages contain houses with clearly outlined perimeters and four central support posts (Falk and Ahler 1988; Miller 1964:148). There are also cases of superimposed houses showing different rebuilding or occupational episodes.

Burials are represented by only a few examples from Walth Bay, Lower Grand (Falk and Ahler 1988:39, 49), and Molstad (Hoffman 1967:20). The disarticulated and partly articulated remains from the Lower Grand and Molstad sites were in pits both inside and outside houses. One individual from Walth Bay was found partly articulated on a house floor. Grave offerings were found with only the burial at Molstad.

In contrast to Initial Coalescent pottery, Extended Coalescent ceramics are typified by thin-walled vessels with compact, sparsely tempered paste (Figure 10.2b). Simple-stamped or smoothed exterior surfaces predominate (Figure 10.5f). Vertical brushing and incised or trailed decorations on the exterior of the rim are more popular in Extended than in Initial assemblages (Figure 10.5d, i, k–l) (C. Johnson 1980:20–21). The temporal trend is for incised or trailed rim decoration to decline in favor of straight or curved rims with tool-impressed lips. Six major wares, all having duplicate and crosscutting types, are defined for the Extended Coalescent: Talking Crow, Akaska, Iona, La Roche, Le Beau, and Cadotte.

Lithic technology is best understood from Ahler's (1975) work at Walth Bay and Lower Grand, where he demonstrated significant intra- and intersite variation in the function, technology, and style of chipped-stone tools. One of his conclusions stands out in terms of its implication for our methods of developing Plains Village taxonomies. Intersite variation in the style of arrowpoints, tools that denote a male activity, was more significant than that of end scrapers, artifacts that are associated with female-related tasks. These differences raise questions about current culture-historical taxonomies based largely on ceramics, which are associated with women's activities (Ahler 1975:353–361).

Extended Coalescent bone and antler technology is similar to that of the Initial variant, except for the appearance of ice gliders, metatarsal fleshers, and L-shaped antler fleshing adzes. The latter two tools are thought to have been borrowed from Middle Missouri–tradition peoples (Lehmer 1971:119).

Other Late Prehistoric Complexes

Recent work in the Knife and Heart river regions has resulted in the definition of two complexes, Painted Woods and Heart River, dated at 1250 to 1525 and 1450/1500 to 1780, respectively (Ahler 1993a:Figure 25.1). A chronology of the phases assigned to these complexes appears in Ahler and others (1991:27) and Ahler (1993a). The Painted Woods complex is fully prehistoric; Heart River components dating after 1600 are assigned to the Post-Contact period. Although the Painted Woods complex is divided into four phases, only components assigned to the latest two (Scattered Village and Mandan Lake) are traditionally assigned to the Coalescent tradition. Ahler (1993b:33–34) and Lovick and Ahler

(1982:57–65) do not recognize Lehmer's (1971) Coalescent tradition as a valid construct for these regions. They feel that Bowers's (1948, 1950:8–19, 1965:10–25, 476–489) interpretation of Mandan and Hidatsa culture history more fully explains the archaeological remains of these people.

The Painted Woods complex (1250–1525) includes villages within the Knife and Heart river regions and in other locations: the Schultz, Mondrian Tree, Nollmeyer, and Hagen sites. An alternative view of Nollmeyer places it closer to the Extended Coalescent villages of the Le Compte phase (Krause 1996). The complex is defined by the presence of Le Beau ware (Figure 10.5c), and pottery with incised, trailed, or stab-and-drag rim decoration; vessels with flat or T- or L-shaped lips; and/or small quantities of check-stamped pottery (Ahler 1993a:67–68). Some of these traits may have Extended Middle Missouri and Extended Coalescent origins.

Villages assigned to the Scattered Village phase (1400–1450) have pottery with traits resembling those from other Plains areas, perhaps as a result of immigration. Several of these components and those of the later Mandan Lake phase were previously assigned to the Heart River phase (Wood 1986:13–16) and the Scattered Village complex (Ahler and Mehrer 1984).

The Mandan Lake phase (1450–1525) is represented by several large multicomponent earthlodge villages. The transition from rectangular to circular houses may have taken place during this phase (Ahler 1993a:84–85). There is an increase in Le Beau S-rim ware over the Scattered Village phase from 6 to 34 percent, and a decrease in check-stamping from 12 to 6 percent.

Components of the Heart River complex (1450/1500–1780) contain more than half Le Beau S-rim ware, as defined by Wood (1967:67–68). Most of these villages are in the Heart region and represent ancestral Mandan settlements. Sites along the western tributaries of the Missouri River, such as Koehler, are probably Heart River hunting camps (Cooper 1958).

The Hensler phase (1525–1600) includes several villages in the Knife region, some fortified by surrounding ditches (Ahler 1993a:85). Circular house plans are the norm, and Le Beau S-rim ware, most often decorated on the rim with cord impressions, makes up about 80 percent of the pottery.

Post-Contact Variant

The Post-Contact Coalescent is defined by the appearance of Euro-American trade items made of iron, brass, copper, glass, and stone (gunflints). The Post-Contact period has been dated from 1675 to 1862 (Lehmer 1971:3), but recent studies suggest that trade goods first begin to appear in the Middle Missouri and Central Plains subareas as early as 1600 (Ahler 1993a:89; Ahler and Swenson 1985:110; Ahler and Toom 1995:377).

Post-Contact villages tend to be concentrated at the confluences of major rivers and their tributaries. In the Middle Missouri subarea, these include the mouths of the Knife, Heart, Grand, Cheyenne, and Bad rivers. In the Central Plains subarea, sites are along the Platte and Loup rivers. Villages vary greatly in size, ranging from eight houses at Fire Heart Creek to about 163 at Double Ditch (Figure 10.3*d*). Most of the larger villages are assigned to the Heart River complex, occupied between 1450 and 1780 by the Mandan. Median site size is 36 houses, more than double that of Extended Coalescent communities. About one-third of the 98 Post-Contact sites listed in Lehmer (1971:132–135, 173) are fortified by circular or oval ditches without bastions (Will 1924). Several sites are surrounded by multiple ditches, including Swan Creek (Hurt 1957), Larson (39WW2), and Double Ditch (Will and Hecker 1944:82,129). A few sites—such as Leavenworth, H. P. Thomas, and Oacoma—are characterized by two adjacent clusters of houses. There is evidence at some sites of an open "plaza," sometimes next to large "ceremonial" houses. Although it has been suggested that Heart River–complex villages with open central plaza areas were occupied by the Mandan (Lehmer 1971:141, 204), some Hidatsa communities also had plazas (Wood 1986:16). Many Post-Contact villages, particularly those of the Le Beau phase and the Heart River and Knife River complexes, are characterized by thick middens (Lehmer 1971:203–205). These deposits reach depths of 10 feet at Lower Hidatsa, and perhaps more at Double Ditch, suggesting long, intense, and/or continuous occupations (Ahler and Swenson 1985:270; Strong 1940:373; Will and Spinden 1906).

Post-Contact–period houses are 13 to 75 feet in diameter. The median figure of 35 feet is slightly smaller than that of the Extended variant. Post-Contact houses in the Dakotas also can be divided into small and large structures, yielding mean small- and large-structure diameters of 32.8 and 55.7 feet. Many of the larger structures may have served special functions, as shown by their size, central location, or rectangular rear earthen platforms (Figure 10.4*f*). The roofs of these large structures may not have been covered with earth, as were the domestic historic Plains Village houses (Toom and Johnson 1995:217–218). Mean diameters for Lower Loup and Pawnee houses are 38.6 and 41 feet, respectively (Wedel 1979a:91). Bison-skull shrines have also been reported near the rear walls of some domestic houses (Toom and Johnson 1995:Figures 9.4 and 9.7). Like those of earlier periods, Post-Contact house entrances generally face rivers or streams. Post-Contact houses, in contrast to Extended structures, usually have well-defined posthole patterns, with four support posts set in a square around a central hearth. Lower Loup and Pawnee lodges have four, six, eight, or 10 center posts (Figure 10.4*d*). Large "reinforcing" posts often were placed at regular intervals around the wall (Hoffman 1970:8–42). Multiple village occupations or house-rebuilding episodes, indicated by superimposed lodges, are common (Figure 10.4*e*).

There is a substantial literature dealing with Post-Contact Coalescent human remains, much of it involving craniometric analyses to establish relationships within and between large cemetery populations (Bass 1981; Owsley and Jantz 1994). The establishment of cemeteries is thought to have been in response to high mortality rates brought about by the introduction of Euro-American pathogens such as smallpox. Formal reports of burial excavations comparable to village site reports are rare. The Leavenworth cemeteries are the only ones fully reported (Bass et al. 1971), although summary statements and specialized studies are available for other sites (Bass and Rucker 1976; Bass et al. 1971:133–153; Key 1983; O'Shea 1984; Wedel 1955).

Burials at the historic Arikara Leavenworth site provide a baseline for comparisons with earlier Post-Contact cemeteries. Leavenworth was occupied from about 1798 to 1832 (Krause 1972:14–15). Six burial areas were a short distance from the village. The 285 individuals recovered were usually in oval, wood-covered pits. About one-half of the burials were primary, with flexed individuals on their sides or backs; one-third were characterized by scattered or disturbed remains. Infant mortality was high, with one-third of the individuals younger than one year old; three-quarters were dead at 30 years of age. Grave offerings accompanied three-quarters of the burials, with Euro-American trade goods more common than Native artifacts. The Sully cemetery (Bass et al. 1971:133–153) had five separate areas, and yielded 544 individuals in 316 burial pits, usually in flexed positions on their sides or backs. One-third of the pits were covered with wood. Infant mortality and life expectancy were about the same as at Leavenworth.

Excavations at the cemetery associated with the protohistoric Larson site uncovered 267 burial pits and about 611 individuals (Bass and Rucker 1976:36–37). Most were in flexed positions on their backs or sides. Infant mortality was high, with two-fifths of the population dead by one year of age, a figure comparable to those of Leavenworth and Sully. Nearly two-thirds of the population was dead by age 19, and life expectancy at birth was 13.2 years (Owsley and Bass 1979:148–150), high mortality figures compared with those of prehistoric and more recent world populations. Other aspects of the Larson burials include covering the dead with logs or bark and burying utilitarian and imported Native and Euro-American artifacts with many of the dead. Part of the Larson population died a violent death, as indicated by several scalped, mutilated, and dismembered individuals found within the village (Owsley 1994; Owsley et al. 1977).

Compared with those of the earlier Extended period, Post-Contact pottery vessels frequently have thick walls and granular, porous, and liberally tempered paste (Lehmer 1971:143). Surface finish is characterized by simple-stamped or smoothed bodies, and rim exteriors commonly are brushed, simple-stamped, or smoothed (Figure 10.2*a*, *c–d*). Decoration changed with the addition of more cord- and finger-impressed lips or rims, an increase in the number of undecorated vessels, and a dramatic reduction in the percentage of straight or curved rims with horizontal incisions (Figure 10.5*e*, *g–j*).

Much of the work with Post-Contact chipped-stone tools has focused on function, technology, raw material, and context. Artifacts from the Knife River region (Big Hidatsa, Lower Hidatsa, and Sakakawea sites) suggest that the intensity of production and use of chipped-stone tools decreased through time, while ground-stone technology remained stable or increased in intensity (Ahler and Swenson 1985:143–203; Ahler and Toom 1993:255; Ahler and Weston 1981:108–154; Toom 1979). A similar reduction in eighteenth-century Pawnee flintknapping between the Barcal and Linwood sites is documented by Hudson (1993). The reduction in flintknapping at most sites is thought to reflect the introduction of Euro-American metal replacements for Native stone tools.

All Knife River–region chipped-stone assemblages are dominated by Knife River Flint. Sites in South Dakota contain very little of this flint, but substantial quantities of local jaspers/cherts and chalcedonies; nonlocal materials such as Flattop and plate chalcedony are present in smaller amounts (Ahler 1977; C. Johnson 1984). Holen (1991) found that the quantity of materials such as Permian chert and Smoky Hill Silicified Chalk varies greatly in Lower Loup sites (Burkett and Gray), attributable to differing Pawnee-band hunting ranges. Furthermore, there was a shift throughout the eighteenth century in Pawnee lithic-procurement patterns from eastern sources to those farther west (Hudson 1993).

The presence of Euro-American trade items made from metals, glass, clay, and gunflints are Post-Contact horizon or variant markers. The list includes iron, brass, or copper knives and scrapers, projectile points, awls, fleshers, strike-a-lights, axes, hoes, adzes, chisels, mattocks, springs, files, kettle parts, rods, fishhooks, horse bridles, and gun parts. Ornaments include disks, cones, tubes, finger rings, bracelets, and bells. Glass trade beads are found in a wide variety of forms and colors. Earthenware dishes, clay pipes, bottles, buttons, and mirrors are recovered from later sites. Native-made glass pendants and disks, melted and refashioned from glass beads, also are found in late Post-Contact burials (Ubelaker and Bass 1970). Post-Contact villages, especially early ones, usually contain trade materials such as metal sheets and rods made into projectile points, piercing and cutting tools, and various ornaments. Unaltered trade goods are rare. Later sites, particularly cemeteries, contain large quantities and varieties of intact Euro-American artifacts as the result of direct trade. Horses from the southwestern United States are indicated by the presence of horse gear and bones (Lehmer and Jones 1968:98). The "frontiers" of horse and firearm trading reached the Missouri River villages about 1740 (Thiessen 1993:33–34).

The quantity of trade items increased throughout the Post-Contact period.

In the earlier indirect trade period (Ray 1978), villagers received Euro-American goods from other Native groups and passed many of them on to yet others, instead of using and discarding or losing them. During the historic trade period, Native Americans traded directly with Europeans and Americans, accounting for a greater volume and variety of items entering the archaeological record (Lehmer et al. 1978).

The introduction of Euro-American metal tools brought about many changes in Native bone and antler technology. Lehmer (1954:128, 1971:152) attributed the removal of glenoid cavities from bison-scapulae digging tools at the Phillips Ranch site to the use of metal tools. Although metal tools may be lacking at some sites, distinctive cut marks on bone can be viewed as indirect evidence for the increasing presence of Euro-American trade materials through time (Baerreis and Dallman 1961:182–196; Wood 1971:49). Ice gliders and snow snakes began to appear in significant quantities in the Post-Contact period.

There are currently nine phases or complexes recognized for the Post-Contact variant in the Middle Missouri area: Felicia, Talking Crow, Bad River, Le Beau, Knife River, Willows, Minnetaree, Roadmaker, and Four Bears. Four Lower Loup and historic Pawnee-band sequences—Skidi, Grand, Republican, and Tappage—are described for the Central Plains. The Felicia, Talking Crow, Bad River, and Le Beau phases may represent different Arikara-band villages (Parks 1979a:227).

The Felicia phase (Caldwell 1966:80; Smith and Johnson 1968:49) has been dated at 1675 to 1700 (Lehmer 1971:201), and its sites are thought to be the immediate predecessors of the Talking Crow phase, dated at 1700 to 1750 (Lehmer 1971:202). A recent study by C. Johnson (1994:Figures 6.10 and 6.15) suggests that the Felicia and Talking Crow phases probably date somewhat earlier, at 1650 to 1700 and 1675 to 1750, respectively. The approximately 21 known Talking Crow villages are concentrated in the Big Bend region, with several in the Bad–Cheyenne area and below the White River, such as the Hitchell and Oldham sites (Johnston 1967; Lehmer 1971:135, 201–202). They are believed to have been occupied by the protohistoric Arikara, although a small quantity of typical Lower Loup (protohistoric Pawnee) pottery has been recovered from the Oacoma site (Kivett 1958). Talking Crow ware, characterized by straight or curved rims often decorated with only tool impressions on the lip, dominates Talking Crow–phase assemblages.

The Bad River phase consists of about 26 components between the Bad and Cheyenne rivers, with several in the Big Bend region to the south (Figure 10.3*f*). Sites are attributed to the ancestral Arikara (Hoffman and Brown 1967:333–334; Lehmer 1971:135, 202; Lehmer and Jones 1968:82–84). Two subphases are recognized, based on the presence (Bad River 2) or absence (Bad River 1) of fortifications, horse bones, gun parts, large quantities of Euro-American trade items, and Colombe Collared pottery. These subphases are questioned by Hoffman (1970:308–310). Dated at 1675 to 1740 and 1740 to 1795, Bad River 1 and 2 are synonymous with the earlier defined Stanley and Snake Butte foci (Lehmer and Jones 1968:95–100). Evidence for the arrival of Euro-American trade materials in the Middle Missouri subarea beginning around 1650 indicates that a revised span of 1650 to 1800 is perhaps more appropriate for this phase. Ceramic assemblages are characterized by Stanley ware, with straight or curved braced and thickened rims. Undecorated rims or those with tool, finger, or cord impressions on the lips or rim braces occur in equal quantities.

The Le Beau focus was defined using data from the Swan Creek site (Figure 10.3e) (Hurt 1957:27–30). Le Beau–phase sites are concentrated between the Grand and Moreau rivers, particularly at the confluence of the Grand and Missouri; a few major villages are downstream between the Bad and Cheyenne rivers, for a total of about 19 sites (Lehmer 1971:134–135, 202–203). These villages have been dated at 1675 to 1780, but recent dates of 1650 for the appearance of Euro-American items and the thick midden deposits at many of these villages argue for a somewhat longer span of about 1650 to 1785 for the phase. Craniometric analyses suggest that Anton Rygh and other Le Beau–phase components were occupied by the protohistoric Arikara (studies summarized in Bass 1981), although Mandan residence or influence at this and other Le Beau–phase villages cannot be ruled out. Le Beau ware, similar to Stanley ware in rim form and decoration, dominates Le Beau–phase assemblages.

Villages of the Knife River complex (Figure 10.3c), most of them in the Knife River and Garrison regions, are dated at 1600 to 1886. Most were occupied by the Hidatsa, although some of the later villages also included the Mandan and Arikara. They have pottery assemblages dominated by cord-impressed decoration and non-S-rims—for example, Knife River ware, Deapolis Collared, and Transitional ware (Ahler 1993a:69–70). The previously defined Heart River (1450/1675–1780) and Knife River (1780–1845) phases (Lehmer 1971:203–206; Lehmer et al. 1978:422–435; Wood 1986:13–24) are subsumed within the four sequential phases of this complex: Willows, Minnetaree, Roadmaker, and Four Bears.

Villages of the Willows phase (1600–1700) represent various Hidatsa groups that entered the region from sites in eastern Wisconsin and North Dakota such as Hintz (Ahler 1993a:87–89; Ahler et al. 1991). The presence of Euro-American items from indirect trade marks the beginning of this phase, 75 years before the more commonly accepted date for their appearance (Ahler 1993a:87–89; Ahler and Swenson 1985:110). There is also evidence of epidemic diseases at this time (Trimble 1989).

The Minnetaree phase (1700–1785) represents the time when Hidatsa tribal identity was consolidated (Ahler 1993a:89–92). The end date for the phase is after the smallpox epidemic of 1780/1781 that spread throughout the Plains, re-sulting in a dramatic population reduction in Plains Village groups.

Communities of the Roadmaker phase (1785–1830) generally are nucleated and fortified by palisades and an occasional accompanying ditch (Ahler 1993a:92–95). Villages were occupied by the Hidatsa, Mandan, and Arikara, the latter two groups entering the Knife River region from the south to form pro-tective alliances. Several of these and later villages were documented by Lewis and Clark in 1804 to 1806, Catlin in 1832, and Maximilian and Bodmer in 1833 and 1834 (Meyer 1977:36–58). Direct trade with Canadian and St. Louis–based firms began and is reflected in the increase in Euro-American items at the sites (Ahler and Drybred 1993; Thiessen 1993:36–39).

The Four Bears phase (1830–1886) is marked by a further decline in Native population and a consolidation into densely occupied fortified communities (Ahler 1993a:95–97). All Mandan, Hidatsa, and Arikara were living in the Knife River and Garrison regions shortly after 1830. Native pottery and chipped-stone industries decline and disappear during this phase. Sustained direct local trade with American Fur Company and other posts on the upper Missouri marks the beginning of the phase (Thiessen 1993:39–41). The last Native village, Like-a-Fishhook, was abandoned in 1886 (G. Smith 1972:20).

Villages assigned to the Lower Loup phase of eastern Nebraska are concen-trated along the Loup and Platte rivers (Wedel 1938, 1940, 1986). A few, such as Goodenow (Roper 1989), are hunting camps in non-core-village areas. Some of these camps are believed to be Extended Coalescent (J. Ludwickson, personal communication). These protohistoric Pawnee sites date from 1600 to 1750/1775 (O'Shea 1989:93–97). Historic Pawnee villages, dating from 1750/1775 to 1876, are concentrated on the Platte and Loup rivers, with outlying villages on the Big Blue and Republican rivers in southern Nebraska and northeastern Kansas. Only a few reports of excavations of Pawnee and Lower Loup sites exist (Carlson 1973; Dunlevy 1936; Roberts 1975).

O'Shea (1984) examined materials from the Linwood and Clarks sites, two historically documented Pawnee villages dated at 1777 to 1809 and 1820 to 1845. Three rank levels were reflected in the burials from each site: (1) adult males with large quantities of sociotechnic artifacts, (2) adult males, females, and subadults with task-oriented items; and (3) individuals with a few nonornamen-tal artifacts. O'Shea also found evidence for ranking at the Larson site, occupied by the Arikara.

Grange (1968) defined 18 pottery types from Lower Loup and Pawnee sites. Lower Loup assemblages average about 70 percent Nance Flared Rim, a type similar to Talking Crow ware. Minority types include Nance Straight Rim, Wright Collared, Colfax Braced, and Webster Collar Braced, which are similar to Iona Horizontal/Diagonal Incised, Iona S-rim/Caddote Collared, Stanley ware, and Colombe Collared from South Dakota. These and other Lower Loup and Pawnee types also have counterparts in Post-Contact assemblages to the north, particularly those of the Talking Crow phase. Grange (1984) used these types to date Pawnee and Lower Loup sites.

In the prehorse era, 1700 or before on the Central Plains, the protohistoric Pawnee used selective breeding of dogs to serve as beasts of burden and as a supplementary food source (Bozell 1988). After the Pawnee became fully equestrian, domesticated dogs decreased in size and numbers, and became more like the modern dog and coyote, and less similar to the modern wolf. During this period, the dietary consumption of dogs declined in favor of bison, deer, and antelope.

Dating the Lower Loup and Pawnee villages has been a problem. The two radiocarbon dates from Lower Loup sites (Burkett and Wright) fall within the currently accepted periods of occupation. Several Lower Loup sites—including Burkett, Wright, Phil Cuba, Schuyler, and Wolfe—were abandoned about 1750 (O'Shea 1989:93–97), possibly in response to smallpox and measles epidemics in 1734/1735 and 1750 to 1752 (Trimble 1989:50).

Historic Pawnee site locations are summarized by Wedel (1936:9–23, 1979b:278–283) and Grange (1968:118–121). In the last quarter of the eighteenth century, the Pawnee consisted of four bands: the Skidi, Republican, and Grand Pawnee lived at the Palmer, Kansas Monument, and Barcal or Linwood sites, respectively (O'Shea 1989:53–58), while villages occupied by the Tappage band have not been identified, but could lie on the Big Blue River in Gage County, Nebraska. During the smallpox epidemics of 1832 and 1837, the Grand Pawnee were at the Clarks site, with the other three bands occupying villages along the Platte and Loup rivers. By 1859, all four Pawnee bands were living at Genoa Village. It was abandoned in 1876 when the Pawnee left Nebraska for a reservation in Oklahoma.

Origins and Relationships

The following tentative Coalescent-tradition chronology is based, in part, on six regional ceramic seriation of five Initial, 66 Extended, and 75 Post-Contact Coalescent components in South Dakota (C. Johnson 1994). The analyses rely on a detrended correspondence analytic approach based on the frequencies of 13 descriptive rim-sherd types. The remaining regional chronologies are based on the orderings of Lower Loup/Pawnee (O'Shea 1989:93–97).and Knife River–region components (Ahler 1993a). Supplementing these sequences is a large number of radiocarbon dates, a number of which have been run on South Dakota sites.

The earliest Coalescent communities to be established were the Initial-variant

Whistling Elk, Crow Creek, and Talking Crow sites during the fourteenth century. They are covered by a mantle of loess about 2 feet thick, as are many Initial Middle Missouri sites.

Discussions of the origins of the Initial Coalescent began with Strong's (1940:382–383) statement that the Arzberger site represented an Upper Republican-like occupation in the process of changing into a form known from protohistoric Arikara and Pawnee sites. The link between the Initial Coalescent and Central Plains traditions was reinforced by Spaulding (1956:76–79) and others (for a summary of these statements, see Steinacher 1983:51–52, 135–142). This discussion continued to focus on an Upper Republican origin, either by diffusion or by direct migration because of drought (Lehmer 1954:148–150). Some of the latest statements have dropped this link in favor of a generic Central Plains–tradition progenitor (Lehmer 1971:111; Ludwickson 1979:57; C. Smith 1977:152) that exceeded the carrying capacity of the Central Plains (Bozell 1995:159).

These speculations about Initial Coalescent origins are based on impressionistic understandings of the material at hand with little or no presentation of data. Steinacher (1983) and C. Johnson (1994:230–234), however, established through a ceramic seriation a temporal ordering of components beginning with Whistling Elk, continuing through Talking Crow, Black Partizan, and Lynch, and ending with Arzberger. Initial Coalescent components are most similar to Loup River/Itskari-, Smoky Hill-, and Nebraska-phase components of the Central Plains tradition. The old idea of an Upper Republican–Initial Coalescent link, however, is not supported, nor is the view that the Initial variant is a late development occurring after the occupation of the Central Plains by Upper Republican-, Nebraska-, Itskari-, or St. Helena–phase populations. The strength of the ceramic relationships between Central Plains and Initial Coalescent diminished through time. Steinacher (1983:90–95, personal communication) concludes that the Initial variant and the Nebraska, Smoky Hill, and Itskari phases of the Central Plains tradition have a common origin. Whether this involved an incorporation of Central Plains traits by existing groups occupying the Big Bend region or an actual migration of village groups from the Central Plains is not known. A comparison of ceramic and other traits also reveals little evidence for a blending of Central Plains– and Middle Missouri–tradition traits (Steinacher 1983:90–95), commonly accepted as the defining characteristic of the Initial variant (Lehmer 1971:115, 125). Human craniometric studies also suggest some biological affinity between the St. Helena phase and the Initial Coalescent, interpreted to be the result of interaction between these two groups (Key 1983:92). St. Helena and the Initial Coalescent may be related through a common ancestor (Billeck et al. 1995:25). Conversely, St. Helena and sites such as Lynch may represent a reoccupation of northeastern Nebraska by Initial Coalescent villages from South Dakota (Ludwickson et al. 1993:164).

Contemporaneous with the occupations at Black Partizan and Arzberger by late Initial-variant people, a rapid spread of Extended Coalescent groups took place into the Grand–Moreau region to the north during the late fifteenth century. A number of lesser-known Scattered Village–phase (1400–1450) sites in the Knife River region, possibly including the anomalous Elbee site (Ahler 1984), have ceramic similarities with the Extended Coalescent villages. Except for the Le Compte–phase sites of Molstad and Potts, most of these sites were unfortified and lodges were dispersed, suggesting a period of relative calm (Caldwell 1964:3). Because Extended Middle Missouri villages in the area were abandoned by this time, conflict between Coalescent and Middle Missouri groups, which Lehmer (1971:67, 126–127) envisioned, is unlikely. Pottery from these early Extended Coalescent sites is predominantly incised or trailed on S-shaped, curved, or straight rims.

The period from 1500 to 1550 was a time of continued Extended-variant occupations in the Grand–Moreau region and an expansion of villages into the Bad–Cheyenne and Big Bend regions at sites such as Spiry, Black Widow, Leavitt, and Bower's/Over's La Roche. Except for the Payne, Walth Bay, Hosterman, and No Heart Creek sites, these villages were unfortified. The Initial Coalescent site of Arzberger was the last village of this variant to be occupied. From 1550 to 1600, there was a dramatic reduction in the number of sites in the Bad–Cheyenne region, possibly amalgamating at the Sully site, a village of at least 200 lodges. The site, which contains three to four occupational levels, is estimated to span a period of about 125 years (1575–1700). This sequence is supported by the intercemetery chronology (Owsley and Jantz 1978). The reasons for this postulated agglomeration are not clear, although epidemics of infectious diseases, pressure from unidentified nomadic groups, and/or the effects of the Neo-Boreal climatic episode cannot be ruled out (Lehmer 1970:125–128; Trimble 1989:49). Two other major villages that were occupied about as long as Sully, Anton Rygh and Swan Creek, were established at this time. Many of the Extended Coalescent communities in the Big Bend region are late and may represent a movement into the area from the north. Two sites, Scalp Creek in southern South Dakota and Redbird II in northern Nebraska, established about 1550 to 1600, are part of this southern expansion. Coalescent-related Redbird-focus sites have been linked with the historic Ponca (Wood 1965:126–129). Villages of the Mandan Lake and Hensler phases were established in the Knife River region, and many of them show influences from ancestral Mandan Heart River–complex communities that dominated the area from 1525 to 1600 (Ahler 1993a). Heart River influences on the Extended Coalescent peoples in the Grand–Moreau region can be seen in S-shaped rims and cord-impressed pottery. There is evidence to suggest that the Crow and the Hidatsa split began about 1500, the Crow moving westward into Montana to take up a nomadic lifeway (Ahler 1993a:Figure 25.3; Wood and Downer 1977). The Hagen site probably represents one of these Crow villages (Mulloy 1942).

Late Extended-variant villages in South Dakota, dated at 1600 to 1650, continued in areas occupied earlier. Anton Rygh, Swan Creek, and Sully continued their dominance in the Grand–Moreau and Bad–Cheyenne regions. Pierre School and Stricker were also established at this time. There appears to have been an expansion into the lower Big Bend region, at the mouth of the White River, with the establishment of the Spain site. These sites and later Felicia-phase villages (such as Cadotte, Black Partizan, Two Teeth, and McClure) may have contributed populations to Talking Crow and Lower Loup villages. Similar ideas have been proposed by Hoffman (1968:75, 78, 1967:63–643) and Lehmer (1965:107–108, 121). This interpretation rests on ceramic continuities, contemporaneity of late Extended and early Lower Loup communities in about 1650, and the absence of any obvious Lower Loup ancestors in the Central Plains (Grange 1979:134, 157; Lehmer 1954:148; Wedel 1978:160, 1979b:275). This hypothesized downriver movement of village groups from the Bad–Cheyenne and Big Bend regions into Nebraska is supported by Lehmer (1965:107–108), but conflicts with the northward movement of the Arikara proposed by Grange (1981:53).

Extended-variant and Felicia-phase villages in the Big Bend contain pottery with about 20 percent S-shaped or collared rims with incised or trailed opposed-diagonal, diagonal, or herringbone motifs (Figure 10.5d). These motifs are present in small quantities at Lower Loup sites (Wright Collared), but later become the dominant style in historic Pawnee pottery (Webster Collar Braced). The presence of these motifs and significant percentages (70 to 80 percent) of vessels with straight or curved undecorated rims and tool-impressed lips in Extended-variant sites leading up to and contemporaneous with early Lower Loup occupations suggest that at least some of the protohistoric Pawnee may have originated in Coalescent developments in the Middle Missouri subarea. Historic documentation indicates that some Pawnee groups may have been in South Dakota during the protohistoric period (Parks 1979a:228). An alternative hypothesis of mutual contact and influence in this context, however, cannot be excluded (Hurt 1952:34–35).

The search for Lower Loup–phase origins in Nebraska dates back to Strong (1935:277) and his proposed link between Upper Republican and protohistoric Pawnee pottery. The Central Plains–tradition Loup River/Itskari phase (1250–1450) lies between the Upper Republican (1050–1350) and Lower Loup (1600–1750/1775) phases (Ludwickson 1978:102–105, 1979:56, 58). Recent dates put the Itskari phase at 1000 to 1350 (J. Ludwickson, personal communication). Key (1983:927) suggests a possible Itskari Lower Loup–Pawnee sequence on the basis of cranimetric evidence, although a link between Central Plains and Lower Loup/Pawnee has never been demonstrated. Roper (1993:145) also supports a Central Plains–tradition antecedent for the Pawnee, although the mechanisms for this remain unclear.

Oral traditions (summarized in Hughes 1974:43–54) state that the Arikara and Pawnee settled on the Republican River from somewhere to the east, south, or southeast, and then moved to the Platte and Loup rivers. There are no references to a protohistoric Pawnee presence in South Dakota, although oral traditions for this period are very vague, while the historical record is lacking. The Arikara are then said to have split from the Pawnee to move upriver to the Big Bend or Grand River areas. Caddoan language glottochronology suggests a split between the Pawnee and Arikara about 1450 to 1650 (Hughes 1974:84; Parks 1979b:204–208), a period supported by the Extended Coalescent–Lower Loup ceramic evidence.

Major changes took place between 1600 and 1700. Two major Willows-phase villages, Big Hidatsa and Lower Hidatsa—as well as others—were occupied at this time by two Hidatsa bands: the Hidatsa-proper and Awaxawi. Euro-American trade items began to appear around 1600, and there is evidence of epidemic diseases (Ahler 1993a:87–89). Origin traditions have these bands originating in the Devils Lake area, in North Dakota, later settling among the Mandan in the Heart River region, and then moving into villages near the Knife River. The Awatixa Hidatsa claim to have always lived along the Missouri River between the Knife and Heart rivers (Wood 1993). The Mandan, living in Heart River–complex villages at this time, are thought to have their origins in late Extended and Terminal Middle Missouri communities (Wood 1967:116–168). A weaker hypothesis posits an origin for the Awigaxa Mandan and their Heart River–complex descendants in the Le Beau–phase villages (Bowers 1948:97–103, 225–227, 1950:16–17; Strong 1940:380), as reflected in the relatively high number of cord-impressed S-shaped rim sherds from these sites. Craniometric analyses find little evidence for this hypothesis (Lin 1973; Owsley et al. 1981). The Heart River influence in South Dakota also is apparent at earlier Extended Coalescent sites such as Demery (Woolworth and Wood 1964:100–101). It is believed that at the end of this period, the Sully site expanded beyond its carrying capacity, budding off semiautonomous village groups (for example, the Spotted Bear, Coleman, Dodd, Rosa, Oahe Village, and Mush Creek sites) to contribute to the emerging Bad River and Le Beau phases in the Bad–Cheyenne and Grand–Moreau regions. Johnston (1982:47–48) and C. Smith (1977:156) think that the Bad River phase originated in the Felicia or Talking Crow phases, a hypothesis also supported by the available evidence.

The years 1700 to 1785 were a time of continued growth and decline of Plains Village populations (Holder 1970). Post-Contact Coalescent villages increased in number and were distributed over a wide part of the Northern and Central Plains. In the Knife River region, Big Hidatsa, Lower Hidatsa, and Mahhaha continued their long occupational histories, as did the Anton Rygh and Sully sites in the Grand–Moreau and Bad–Cheyenne region. The earliest documented direct European contact with the Northern Plains villagers was between the Mandan and the French explorer La Vérendrye in 1738 (G. Smith

1980). Direct and indirect contacts with the Pawnee also took place during this period (O'Shea 1989:55–56). Nightwalker's Butte, probably representing a Hidatsa splinter group, was occupied at this time, and dissident Hidatsa bands continued to live in their own settlements, such as Crow-Flies-High Village, into the 1870s and 1880s. The Biesterfeldt site, most likely a Cheyenne village, also was occupied at this time (Wood 1971). Several Mandan villages in the Heart River region, including Slant and Double Ditch, were abandoned about 1780 (Chomko 1986:65–69), as was Lower Hidatsa (Ahler and Weston 1981:14). The increase in sites in the Bad–Cheyenne region, some assigned to the Bad River phase (for example, Dodd), may have been partly due to the abandonment of the Sully site late in the previous period. Oahe Village, which may have been inhabited for at least 75 years, may represent another budded group from Sully. Only a few South Dakota villages—such as Bamble, Four Bear, Spiry–Eklo, Red Horse Hawk, Blue Blanket Island, Dan Donavan, and Gillette—remained by 1750. Talking Crow villages south of the Medicine Crow and Peterson sites were abandoned in favor of upriver sites, such as Amos Shields and Iron Shooter, and disappeared before 1750. Fort George Village (Hoffman 1970) and Chapelle Creek (Brown 1967), both outlying communities of the Bad River phase, were occupied during the middle and end of this period, respectively. Lower Loup sites such as Burkett, Wright, Phil Cuba, Schuyler, and Wolfe were abandoned in or before 1750 (O'Shea 1989:93–97). These postulated population reductions and/or movements may have been the result of raids by nomadic groups such as the Dakota, Apache, and Kiowa, and of smallpox and measles epidemics in 1734/1735 and 1750 to 1752 that are documented for other Plains groups (Ramenofsky 1987:134; Trimble 1989:50). These postulated epidemics took place before the major smallpox outbreak of 1780/1781 (previously thought to have been the first one), which commonly is used to mark the end of the Post-Contact variant and the beginning of the Disorganized Coalescent (Lehmer 1971:172–174, 176). The large cemeteries associated with the protohistoric occupation of the Anton Rygh, Larson, Mobridge, and Sully sites are probably a testament to these epidemics and the massive depopulation that ensued.

During the latter part of the eighteenth century, there was a dramatic reduction in the number of protohistoric Arikara communities in South Dakota due to the smallpox epidemic of 1780/1781. Only a few villages remained (Nordvold I, Chapelle Creek, 39ST25, 39ST50), and they were abandoned during an upriver movement to the Greenshield (1795–1798) and Leavenworth (1798–1832) sites. These two Arikara villages were documented during the Lewis and Clark expedition in 1804 (Chomko 1986:70–71, 78–82; Krause 1972:15). Other sites, such as Lahoo-catt and Fire Heart Creek (Chomko 1986:78; Lehmer 1966), also may be attributed to them.

In North Dakota, the Sakakawea (Ahler et al. 1980), Rock Village (Hartle 1960), White Buffalo Robe, and Amahami sites were established by 1785 or shortly after, with a continuing occupation at Big Hidatsa, documented by Lewis and Clark in 1804 and 1805 (Ahler 1993a:92–95). All were occupied by Hidatsa subgroups. The Mandan were living at Fort Clark and Deapolis. Historic Pawnee sites are summarized by Wedel (1936:9–42, 1986:152–185) and Grange (1968:118–121). In the late eighteenth century, four Pawnee bands came to be identified. The Skidi, Republican, and Grand Pawnee lived in a number of villages, including Palmer, Kansas Monument, Bellwood, and the Barcal or Linwood sites; where the Tappage band was living is not known. In 1806, the Republican Pawnee at the Hill site were visited by the Zebulon Pike expedition (O'Shea 1989:53–56).

From 1825/1835 to 1886, only two concentrations of villages remained. The Mandan, Hidatsa, and Arikara were living in the Knife River and Garrison regions, while the Pawnee occupied villages in their traditional homeland along the Platte and Loup rivers. After the Arikara were forced from Leavenworth in 1832, they spent several years with the Pawnee in Nebraska (Wedel 1955:81) before moving in 1838 to Fort Clark, a village that had been abandoned by the Mandan. After the smallpox epidemic of 1837, the Hidatsa established Like-a-Fishhook Village at Fort Berthold in 1845. Some Mandan continued to live at Deapolis, while others moved to be with the Hidatsa at Like-a-Fishhook. By 1862, the rest of the Mandan abandoned Deapolis and the Arikara left Star Village (Metcalf 1963) to join the Hidatsa at Like-a-Fishhook (G. Smith 1972). The three tribes abandoned Like-a-Fishhook—the last such village on the Great Plains—in 1886 when they moved into the nearby Fort Berthold Reservation. During the smallpox epidemics of 1832 and 1837, the Grand Pawnee were at Clarks Village, and the other three bands lived in villages along the Platte and Loup rivers. By 1859, all four Pawnee bands were living at Genoa Village, which was abandoned in 1876 when the Pawnee left Nebraska for a reservation in Oklahoma. Thus ended a 900-year chapter in Plains Village life in the Central and Northern Plains.

Acknowledgments

I thank the following individuals for their comments on several drafts of this chapter: Stanley A. Ahler, Rob Bozell, Carl R. Falk, Roger T. Grange, J. J. Hoffman, John Ludwickson, Carlyle S. Smith, Terry L. Steinacher, Dennis L. Toom, and Larry J. Zimmerman.

References

Ahler, S. A.
  1975   Pattern and Variety in Extended Coalescent Lithic Technology. Ph.D. diss., Department of Anthropology, University of Missouri, Columbia.
  1977   Lithic Resource Utilization Patterns in the Middle Missouri Subarea. In

Trends in Middle Missouri Prehistory: A Festschrift Honoring the Contributions of Donald J. Lehmer, edited by W. R. Wood, 132–150. Plains Anthropologist Memoir no. 13.

1984   Pottery Analysis. In *Archeological Investigations at the Elbee Site, 32ME408, Knife River Indian Villages National Historic Site*, edited by S. A. Ahler, 60–117. University of North Dakota, Department of Anthropology and Archaeology, Contribution no. 209. Grand Forks.

1986   *The Knife River Flint Quarries: Excavations at Site 32DU508.* State Historical Society of North Dakota, Bismarck.

1993a   Plains Village Cultural Taxonomy for the Upper Knife–Heart Region. In *The Phase I Archeological Research Program for the Knife River Indian Villages National Historic Site*. Part 4, *Interpretation of the Archeological Record*, edited by T. D. Thiessen, 57–108. National Park Service, Midwest Archeological Center, Occasional Studies in Anthropology, no. 27. Lincoln, Neb.

1993b   Archeological Study Previous to the KNRI Program. In *The Phase I Archeological Research Program for the Knife River Indian Villages National Historic Site*. Part 1, *Objectives, Methods, and Summaries of Baseline Studies*, edited by T. D. Thiessen, 57–108. National Park Service, Midwest Archeological Center, Occasional Studies in Anthropology, no. 27. Lincoln, Neb.

Ahler, S. A., and A. Drybred
1993   Analysis of Euroamerican Trade Artifacts. In *The Phase I Archeological Research Program for the Knife River Indian Villages National Historic Site*. Part 3, *Analysis of the Physical Remains*, edited by T. D. Thiessen, 289–340. National Park Service, Midwest Archeological Center, Occasional Studies in Anthropology, no. 27. Lincoln, Neb.

Ahler, S. A., C. M. Johnson, H. Haas, and G. Bonani
1994   Radiocarbon Dating Results. In *A Chronology of Middle Missouri Plains Village Sites*, by C. M. Johnson, 97–173. Draft report prepared for the Smithsonian Institution, National Museum of Natural History, Department of Anthropology, Washington, D.C.

Ahler, S. A., and E. L. Mehrer
1984   *The KNRI Small Sites Report: Test Excavations at Eight Plains Village Archeological Sites in the Knife River Indian Villages National Historic Site.* University of North Dakota, Department of Anthropology, Contribution no. 212. Grand Forks.

Ahler, S. A., L. M. Snyder, C. R. Falk, and H. A. Semken, Jr.
1993   KNRI and Upper Knife–Heart Region Unmodified Faunal Remains. In *The Phase I Archeological Research Program for the Knife River Indian Villages National Historic Site*. Part 3, *Analysis of the Physical Remains*, edited by T. D. Thiessen, 263–270. National Park Service, Midwest Archeological Center, Occasional Studies in Anthropology, no. 27. Lincoln, Neb.

Ahler, S. A., and A. A. Swenson
1985   *Test Excavations at Big Hidatsa Village (32ME12), Knife River Indian Villages National Historic Site.* University of North Dakota, Department of Anthropology and Archaeology, Contribution no. 218. Grand Forks.

Ahler, S. A., T. D. Thiessen, and M. K. Trimble
1991   *People of the Willows: The Prehistory and Early History of the Hidatsa Indians.* University of North Dakota Press, Grand Forks.

Ahler, S. A., and D. L. Toom
1993   KNRI and Upper Knife–Heart Region Lithic Artifact Analysis. In *The Phase I*

Archeological Research Program for the Knife River Indian Villages National Historic Site. Part 3, *Analysis of the Physical Remains*, edited by T. D. Thiessen, 173–262. National Park Service, Midwest Archeological Center, Occasional Studies in Anthropology, no. 27. Lincoln, Neb.

1995   Reflections on the Archeology of the Medicine Crow Site Complex. In *Archeology of the Medicine Crow Site Complex (39BF2), Buffalo County, South Dakota*, edited by S. A. Ahler and D. L. Toom, 375–378. Illinois State Museum, Reports of Investigations, no. 52. Springfield.

Ahler, S. A., and T. Weston

1981   *Test Excavations at Lower Hidatsa Village (32ME10), Knife River Indian Villages National Historic Site*. University of North Dakota, Department of Anthropology and Archaeology, Contribution no. 145. Grand Forks.

Ahler, S. A., T. Weston, and K. D. McMiller

1980   *Cutbank Profiling and Test Excavations at Sakakawea Village (32ME11), Knife River Indian Villages National Historic Site*. University of North Dakota, Department of Anthropology and Archaeology, Contribution no. 120. Grand Forks.

Baerreis, D. A., and J. E. Dallman

1961   *Archaeological Investigations near Mobridge, South Dakota*. Society for American Archaeology, Archives of Archaeology, no. 14. Madison, Wis.

Bass, W. M., III

1981   Skeletal Biology on the United States Plains: A History and Personal Narrative. In *Progress in Skeletal Biology of Plains Populations*, edited by R. L. Jantz and D. H. Ubelaker, 3–18. Plains Anthropologist, Memoir no. 17.

Bass, W. M., III, D. R. Evans, and R. L. Jantz

1971   *The Leavenworth Site Cemetery: Archaeology and Physical Anthropology*. University of Kansas, Publications in Anthropology, no. 2. Lawrence.

Bass, W. M., III, and M. D. Rucker

1976   Preliminary Investigation of Artifact Association in an Arikara Cemetery (Larson Site), Walworth County, South Dakota. *National Geographic Society: Research Reports, 1968 Projects:*33–48.

Billeck, W. T., E. B. Jones, S. A. Makseyn-Kelly, and J. W. Verano

1995   Inventory and Assessment of Human Remains and Associated Funerary Objects Potentially Affiliated with the Pawnee in the National Museum of Natural History: Case Report No. 88-007. Smithsonian Institution, National Museum of Natural History, Repatriation Office, Washington, D.C.

Bowers, A. W.

1948   A History of the Mandan and Hidatsa. Ph.D. diss., Department of Anthropology, University of Chicago, Chicago.

1950   *Mandan Social and Ceremonial Organization*. University of Chicago Press, Chicago.

1965   *Hidatsa Social and Ceremonial Organization*. Bureau of American Ethnology Bulletin 194. Washington, D.C.

Bozell, J. R.

1988   Changes in the Role of the Dog in Proto-Historic Pawnee Culture. *Plains Anthropologist* 33:95–111.

1995   Culture, Environment, and Bison Populations on the Late Prehistoric and Early Historic Central Plains. *Plains Anthropologist* 40:145–163.

Bozell, J. R., and J. Ludwickson

1988   Highway Archeological Investigations at the Slaughterhouse Creek Site and

Other Cultural Resources in the Pine Ridge Area. Report prepared by the Nebraska State Historical Society for the Nebraska Department of Roads. Lincoln.

Brown, L.

1967   The Chapelle Creek Site (39HU60), South Dakota. Manuscript on file, National Park Service, Midwest Archeological Center, Lincoln, Neb.

Butler, W. B., and J. J. Hoffman

1992   A Checklist of Plains Ceramic Types and Wares. *South Dakota Archaeology* 16.

Caldwell, W. W.

1964   Fortified Villages in the Northern Plains. *Plains Anthropologist* 9:1–7.

1966   *The Black Partizan Site.* Smithsonian Institution, River Basin Surveys, Publications in Salvage Archeology, no. 2. Lincoln, Neb.

Carlson, G. F.

1973   Excavations at the Linwood Site, 25BU1. In *Archeological Salvage and Survey in Nebraska*, 57–80. Nebraska State Historical Society, Publication in Anthropology, no. 5. Lincoln.

Chomko, S. A.

1986   The Ethnohistorical Setting of the Upper Knife–Heart Region. In *Ice Glider, 32OL110: Papers in Northern Plains Prehistory and Ethnohistory*, edited by W. R. Wood, 59–96. South Dakota Archaeological Society, Special Publication no. 10. Sioux Falls.

Cooper, P. L.

1958   Archeological Investigations in the Heart Butte Reservoir Area, North Dakota. *Bureau of American Ethnology Bulletin* 169:1–40.

Cutler, H. C.

1967   Corn and Squash from Six Sites in North and South Dakota. In *An Interpretation of Mandan Culture History*, by W. R. Wood, 177–182. Bureau of American Ethnology Bulletin 198. Washington, D.C.

Deetz, J.

1965   *The Dynamics of Stylistic Change in Arikara Ceramics.* University of Illinois, Studies in Anthropology, no. 4. Urbana.

Dunlevy, M. L.

1936   A Comparison of the Cultural Manifestations at the Burkett and Gray-Wolfe Sites. In *Chapters in Nebraska Archaeology*, edited by E. H. Bell, 147–247. University of Nebraska, Lincoln.

Ebert, J. I., E. L. Camilli, and L. Wandsnider

1989   Reservoir Bank Erosion and Cultural Resources: Experiments in Mapping and Predicting the Erosion of Archeological Sediments at Reservoirs Along the Middle Missouri River with Sequential Historical Aerial Photographs. Report prepared by Ebert and Associates for the United States Army Corps of Engineers, Washington, D.C.

Falk, C. R.

1977   Analyses of Unmodified Vertebrate Fauna from Sites in the Middle Missouri Subarea: A Review. In *Trends in Middle Missouri Prehistory: A Festschrift Honoring the Contributions of Donald J. Lehmer*, edited by W. R. Wood, 151–161. Plains Anthropologist Memoir no. 13.

Falk, C. R., and S. A. Ahler

1988   *Archeological Investigations in the Mobridge Area, South Dakota, 1969–1970: Lower Grand (Davis), 39CO14; Walth Bay, 39WW203; and Helb, 39CA208.* University of

Missouri, Department of Anthropology, American Archaeology Division, Columbia. Report to the National Park Service, Rocky Mountain Region. Denver.

Gilbert, B. M.

1969   Some Aspects of Diet and Butchering Techniques Among Prehistoric Indians in South Dakota. *Plains Anthropologist* 14:277–294.

Grange, R. T., Jr.

1968   *Pawnee and Lower Loup Pottery.* Nebraska State Historical Society, Publications in Anthropology, no. 3. Lincoln.

1979   An Archeological View of Pawnee Origins. *Nebraska History* 60:134–160.

1981   Ceramic Formula Dating of the Arikara. *South Dakota Archaeological Society, Special Publication,* no. 8:31–55.

1984   Dating Pawnee Sites by the Ceramic Formula Method. *World Archaeology* 15:274–293.

Hartle, D. D.

1960   Rock Village: An Ethnohistorical Approach to Hidatsa Archaeology. Ph.D. diss., Department of Anthropology, Columbia University, New York.

Hoard, R. J., J. R. Bozell, S. R. Holen, M. D. Glascock, H. Neff, and J. M. Elam

1993   Source Determination of White River Group Silicates from Two Archaeological Sites in the Great Plains. *American Antiquity* 58:693–710.

Hoffman, J. J.

1967   *Molstad Village.* Smithsonian Institution, River Basin Surveys, Publications in Salvage Archaeology, no. 4. Lincoln, Neb.

1968   *The La Roche Site.* Smithsonian Institution, River Basin Surveys, Publications in Salvage Archeology, no. 11. Lincoln, Neb.

1970   Two Arikara Villages: A Study in Bad River Phase Material Culture. Manuscript on File, National Park Service, Midwest Archeological Center, Lincoln, Neb.

Hoffman, J. J., and L. A. Brown

1967   The Bad River Phase. *Plains Anthropologist* 12:323–339.

Holder, P.

1970   *The Hoe and the Horse on the Plains.* University of Nebraska Press, Lincoln.

Holen, S. R.

1991   Bison Hunting Techniques and Lithic Acquisition Among the Pawnee: An Ethnohistoric and Archaeological Study. In *Raw Material Economies Among Prehistoric Hunter-Gatherers,* edited by A. Montet-White and S. Holen, 399–411. University of Kansas, Publications In Anthropology, no. 19. Lawrence.

Hudson, L.

1993   Protohistoric Pawnee Lithic Technology. *Plains Anthropologist* 38:265–298.

Hughes, J. T.

1974   *Prehistory of the Caddoan-Speaking Tribes.* Vol. 3 of *Caddoan Indians.* Edited by D. A. Horr. Garland, New York.

Hurt, W. R., Jr.

1952   *Report of the Investigation of the Scalp Creek Site, 39GR1, and the Ellis Creek Site, 39GR2, Gregory County, South Dakota, 1941, 1951.* South Dakota Archaeological Commission, Archaeological Studies, Circular no. 6. Pierre.

1957   *Report of the Investigation of the Swan Creek Site, 39WW7, Walworth County, South Dakota, 1954–1956.* South Dakota Archaeological Commission, Archaeological Studies, Circular no. 7. Pierre.

1970   A Report on the Investigation of the No Heart Creek Site, 39AR2, Dewey County, South Dakota, 1960. *Plains Anthropologist* 15:169–215.

Johnson, C. M.

1980   *Ceramic Classification in the Middle Missouri Subarea of the Plains.* University of Nebraska, Department of Anthropology, Technical Report no. 80-01. Lincoln.

1984   Time, Space and Cultural Tradition as Factors in Lithic Resource Exploitation in the Middle Missouri Subarea. *Plains Anthropologist* 29:289–302.

1994   A Chronology of Middle Missouri Plains Village Sites. Draft report prepared for the Smithsonian Institution, National Museum of Natural History, Department of Anthropology, Washington, D.C.

Johnston, R. B.

1967   *The Hitchell Site.* Smithsonian Institution, River Basin Surveys, Publications in Salvage Archeology, no. 3. Lincoln, Neb.

1982   *Archaeology of the McClure Site (39HU7) and the Protohistoric Period in the Big Bend Region of South Dakota.* Plains Anthropologist Memoir no. 18.

Key, P. J.

1983   *Craniometric Relationships Among Plains Indians: Culture Historical and Evolutionary Implications.* University of Tennessee, Department of Anthropology, Report of Investigations, no. 34. Knoxville.

Kivett, M. F.

1958   The Oacoma Site, Lyman County, South Dakota. Manuscript on file, National Park Service, Midwest Archeological Center, Lincoln, Neb.

Kivett, M. F., and R. E. Jensen

1976   *Archeological Investigations at the Crow Creek Site, Fort Randall Reservoir Area, South Dakota.* Nebraska State Historical Society, Publications in Anthropology, no. 7. Lincoln.

Krause, R. A.

1972   *The Leavenworth Site: Archaeology of an Historic Arikara Community.* University of Kansas, Publications in Anthropology, no. 3. Lawrence.

1996   A Production Stage Grammar of Nollmeyer Potting Practices. *Archaeology in Montana* 36:19–45.

Lehmer, D. J.

1954   *Archeological Investigations in the Oahe Dam Area, South Dakota, 1950–51.* Bureau of American Ethnology Bulletin 158. Washington, D.C.

1965   Salvage Archeology in the Middle Missouri: A Summary and Evaluation. Report on file, National Park Service, Midwest Archeological Center, Lincoln, Neb. ·

1966   *The Fire Heart Creek Site.* Smithsonian Institution, River Basin Surveys, Publications in Salvage Archeology, no. 1. Lincoln, Neb.

1970   Climate and Culture History in the Middle Missouri Valley. In *Pleistocene and Recent Environments in the Central Great Plains,* edited by W. Dort, Jr., and J. K. Jones, Jr., 117–129. University Press of Kansas, Lawrence.

1971   *Introduction to Middle Missouri Archeology.* National Park Service, Anthropological Papers, no. 1. Washington, D.C.

Lehmer, D. J., and D. T. Jones

1968   *Arikara Archeology: The Bad River Phase.* Smithsonian Institution, River Basin Surveys, Publications in Salvage Archeology, no. 7. Lincoln, Neb.

Lehmer, D. J., W. R. Wood, and C. L. Dill

1978   The Knife River Phase. Dana College, Department of Anthropology and Sociology, Blair, Neb.; University of Missouri, Department of Anthropology, American Archaeology Division, Columbia. Report to Interagency Archeological Services, Denver.

Lin, P. M.
 1973   A Study of Arikara Skeletal Populations by Multivariate Analysis: A Problem in Classification. Ph.D. diss., Department of Anthropology, University of Kansas, Lawrence.

Lovick, S. A., and S. A. Ahler
 1982   *Cultural Resource Reconnaissance in the Knife River Indian Villages National Historic Site.* University of North Dakota, Department of Anthropology and Archaeology, Contribution no. 159. Grand Forks.

Ludwickson, J.
 1978   Central Plains Tradition Settlements in the Loup River Basin: The Loup River Phase. In *The Central Plains Tradition: Internal Development and External Relationships,* edited by D. J. Blakeslee, 94–108. University of Iowa, Office of the State Archaeologist, Report no. 11. Iowa City.
 1979   Postulated Late Prehistoric Human Population Movements in the Central Plains: A Critical Review. *Transactions of the Nebraska Academy of Sciences* 7:53–60.

Ludwickson, J., D. J. Blakeslee, and J. O'Shea
 1987   *Missouri National Recreational River: Native American Cultural Resources.* Wichita State University, Publications in Anthropology, no. 3.

Ludwickson, J., J. N. Gunderson, and C. Johnson
 1993   Select Exotic Artifacts from Cattle Oiler (39ST224): A Middle Missouri Tradition Site in Central South Dakota. In *Prehistory and Human Ecology of the Western Prairies and Northern Plains,* edited by J. A. Tiffany, 151–168. Plains Anthropologist Memoir no. 27.

Metcalf, G.
 1963   Star Village: A Fortified Historic Site in Mercer County, North Dakota. *Bureau of American Ethnology Bulletin* 185:57–112.

Meyer, R. W.
 1977   *The Village Indians of the Upper Missouri: The Mandans, Hidatsas and Arikaras.* University of Nebraska Press, Lincoln.

Miller, C. F.
 1964   Archeological Investigations at the Hosterman Site (39PO7), Oahe Reservoir Area, South Dakota, 1956. *Bureau of American Ethnology, Bulletin* 189:139–266.

Mulloy, W.
 1942   *The Hagen Site: A Prehistoric Village on the Lower Yellowstone.* University of Montana, Publications in the Social Sciences, no. 1. Missoula.

Nickel, R. K.
 1977   The Study of Archaeologically Derived Plant Materials from the Middle Missouri Subarea. In *Trends in Middle Missouri Prehistory: A Festschrift Honoring the Contributions of Donald J. Lehmer,* edited by W. R. Wood, 53–58. Plains Anthropologist Memoir no. 13.

Orser, C. E.
 1984   Trade Good Flow in Arikara Villages: Expanding on Ray's "Middleman Hypothesis." *Plains Anthropologist* 29:1–12.

O'Shea, J. M.
 1984   *Mortuary Variability: An Archaeological Investigation.* Academic Press, New York.

1989   Pawnee Archaeology. *Central Plains Archaeology* 1:49–107.

Owsley, D. W.

1994   Warfare in Coalescent Tradition Populations of the Northern Plains. In *Skeletal Biology in the Great Plains: Migration, Warfare, Health, and Subsistence,* edited by D. W. Owsley and R. L. Jantz, 333–343. Smithsonian Institution Press, Washington, D.C.

Owsley, D. W., and W. M. Bass III

1979   A Demographic Analysis of Skeletons from the Larson Site (39WW2) Walworth County, South Dakota: Vital Statistics. *American Journal of Physical Anthropology* 51:145–154.

Owsley, D. W., H. E. Berryman, and W. M. Bass III

1977   Demographic and Osteological Evidence for Warfare at the Larson Site, South Dakota. In *Trends in Middle Missouri Prehistory: A Festschrift Honoring the Contributions of Donald J. Lehmer,* edited by W. R. Wood, 119–131. Plains Anthropologist Memoir no. 13.

Owsley, D. W., and R. L. Jantz

1978   Intracemetery Morphological Variation in Arikara Crania from the Sully Site (39SL4), Sully County, South Dakota. *Plains Anthropologist* 23:139–147.

Owsley, D. W., and R. L. Jantz, eds.

1994   *Skeletal Biology in the Great Plains: Migration, Warfare, Health, and Subsistence,* Smithsonian Institution Press, Washington, D.C.

Owsley, D. W., G. D. Slutzky, M. F. Guagliardo, and L. M. Deitrick

1981   Interpopulation Relationships of Four Post-Contact Coalescent Sites from South Dakota. In *Progress in Skeletal Biology of Plains Populations,* edited by R. L. Jantz and D. H. Ubelaker, 31–42. Plains Anthropologist Memoir no. 17.

Parks, D. R.

1979a   Bands and Villages of the Arikara and Pawnee. *Nebraska History* 60:214–239.

1979b   The Northern Caddoan Languages: Their Subgrouping and Time Depth. *Nebraska History* 60:197–213.

Ramenofsky, A. F.

1987   *Vectors of Death: The Archaeology of European Contact.* University of New Mexico Press, Albuquerque.

Ray, A. J.

1978   History and Archaeology of the Northern Fur Trade. *American Antiquity* 43:26–34.

Roberts, R. L.

1975   The Archaeology of the Kansas Monument Site: A Study in Historic Archaeology on the Great Plains. M.A. thesis, Department of Anthropology, University of Kansas, Lawrence.

Rogers, J. D.

1990   *Objects of Change: The Archaeology and History of Arikara Contact with the Europeans.* Smithsonian Institution Press, Washington, D.C.

Roper, D. C.

1989   Protohistoric Pawnee Hunting in the Nebraska Sand Hills: Archeological Investigations at Two Sites in the Calamus Reservoir. Report to the United States Department of the Interior, Bureau of Reclamation, Billings, Mont.

1993   A Culture-History of the Pawnee. Report to the Smithsonian Institution, Repatriation Office, Washington, D.C.

1994 The Material Culture of 25DS21, a Lower Loup Hunting Camp in the Platte River Valley. *Central Plains Archaeology* 4:55–95.

Semken, H. A., Jr., and C. R. Falk

1987 Late Pleistocene/Holocene Mammalian Faunas and Environmental Changes on the Northern Plains of the United States. In *Quaternary Mammalian Biogeography and Environments of the Great Plains and Prairies,* edited by R. M. Graham, H. A. Semken, Jr., and M. A. Graham, 176–313. Illinois State Museum, Scientific Papers, vol. 22. Springfield.

1991 Micromammal Taphonomy of Three Late Prehistoric Plains Village Tradition Refuse Pits, Walworth County, South Dakota. In *Beamers, Bobwhites, and BluePoints: Tributes to the Career of Paul W. Parmalee,* edited by J. R. Purdue, W. E. Klippel, and B. W. Styles, 111–124. Illinois State Museum, Scientific Papers, vol. 23. Springfield.

Smith, C. S.

1977 *The Talking Crow Site: A Multicomponent Earthlodge Village in the Big Bend Region, South Dakota.* University of Kansas, Publications in Anthropology, no. 9. Lawrence.

Smith, C. S., and R. T. Grange, Jr.

1958 *The Spain Site (39LM301), a Winter Village in Fort Randall Reservoir, South Dakota.* Bureau of American Ethnology, Bulletin no. 169. Washington, D.C.

Smith, C. S., and A. E. Johnson

1968 *The Two Teeth Site.* Smithsonian Institution, River Basin Surveys, Publications in Salvage Archeology, no. 8. Lincoln, Neb.

Smith, G. H.

1972 *Like-a-Fishhook Village and Fort Berthold, Garrison Reservoir, North Dakota.* National Park Service, Anthropological Papers, no. 2. Washington, D.C.

1980 *The Explorations of the La Vérendryes in the Northern Plains, 1738–43.* Edited by W. R. Wood. University of Nebraska Press, Lincoln.

Snyder, L. M.

1995 Assessing the Role of the Domestic Dog as a Native American Food Resource in the Middle Missouri Subarea, A.D. 1000–1840. Ph.D. diss., Department of Anthropology, University of Tennessee, Knoxville.

Spaulding, A. C.

1956 *The Arzberger Site, Hughes County, South Dakota.* University of Michigan, Museum of Anthropology, Occasional Contributions, no. 16. Ann Arbor.

Steinacher, T. L.

1983 Archeological Investigations at the Whistling Elk Site (39HU242), 1978–1979. In *Archeological Investigations Within Federal Lands Located on the East Bank of the Lake Sharpe Project Area, South Dakota: 1978–1979 Final Report,* edited by C. R. Falk, T. L. Steinacher, and D. L. Toom, vol. 2, sec. A, 1–157. Technical Report no. 83-04. University of Nebraska, Department of Anthropology, Division of Archeological Research, Lincoln. Report to the United States Army Corps of Engineers, Omaha District, Omaha, Neb.

Stephenson, R. L.

1969 Blue Blanket Island (39WW9), an Historic Contact Site in the Oahe Reservoir near Mobridge, South Dakota. *Plains Anthropologist* 14:1–31.

1971 The Potts Village Site, Oahe Reservoir, North-Central South Dakota. *Missouri Archaeologist* 33.

Strong, W. D.

1935   *An Introduction to Nebraska Archeology.* Smithsonian Miscellaneous Collec-
        tions, vol. 93, no. 10. Washington, D.C.

1940   From History to Prehistory in the Northern Great Plains. *Smithsonian Miscella-
        neous Collections* 100:353–394.

Thiessen, T. D.

1993   Early Explorations and the Fur Trade at Knife River. In *The Phase I Archeologi-
        cal Research Program for the Knife River Indian Villages National Historic Site.* Part
        2, *Ethnohistorical Studies,* edited by T. D. Thiessen, 29–46. National Park Serv-
        ice, Midwest Archeological Center, Occasional Studies in Anthropology, no.
        27. Lincoln, Neb.

Toom, D. L.

1979   The Middle Missouri Villagers and the Early Fur Trade: Implications for Ar-
        cheological Interpretation. M.A. thesis, Department of Anthropology, Univer-
        sity of Nebraska, Lincoln.

1983   Notes on Prehistoric Lithic Utilization in the Lake Sharpe Area. In *Archeologi-
        cal Investigations Within Federal Lands Located on the East Bank of the Lake Sharpe
        Project Area, South Dakota: 1978–1979 Final Report,* edited by C. R. Falk, T. L.
        Steinacher, and D. L. Toom, vol. 3, sec. I, 1–32. Technical Report no. 83-04.
        University of Nebraska, Department of Anthropology, Division of Archeologi-
        cal Research, Lincoln. Report to the United States Army Corps of Engineers,
        Omaha District, Omaha, Neb.

1995   Summary of Plains Village Archeology. In *Archeology of the Medicine Crow Site
        Complex (39BF2), Buffalo County, South Dakota,* edited by S. A. Ahler and D. L.
        Toom, 361–372. Illinois State Museum, Reports of Investigation, no. 51.
        Springfield.

Toom, D. L., and C. M. Johnson

1995   Plains Village Features and Other Village Excavations. In *Archeology of the
        Medicine Crow Site Complex (39BF2), Buffalo County, South Dakota,* edited by
        S. A. Ahler and D. L. Toom, 191–233. Illinois State Museum, Reports of
        Investigations, no. 51. Springfield.

Toom, D. L., R. K. Nickel, R. E. Warren, and C. R. Falk

1995   Plains Village Subsistence Remains and Miscellaneous Artifacts. In *Archeol-
        ogy of the Medicine Crow Site Complex (39BF2), Buffalo County, South Dakota,*
        edited by S. A. Ahler and D. L. Toom, 343–360. Illinois State Museum,
        Reports of Investigations, no. 51. Springfield.

Trimble, M. K.

1989   Infectious Disease Among the Northern Plains Horticulturists: A Behavioral
        Model. In *Plains Indian Historical Demography and Health: Perspectives, Interpreta-
        tions, and Critiques,* edited by G. R. Campbell, 41–59. Plains Anthropologist
        Memoir no. 23.

Tuross, N., and M. L. Fogel

1994   Stable Isotope Analysis and Subsistence Patterns at the Sully Site. In *Skeletal
        Biology in the Great Plains: Migration, Warfare, Health, and Subsistence,* edited by
        D. W. Owsley and R. L. Jantz, 283–289. Smithsonian Institution Press,
        Washington, D.C.

Ubelaker, D. H., and W. M. Bass III

1970   Arikara Glass Working at the Leavenworth and Sully Sites. *American
        Antiquity* 35:467–475.

Warren, R. E.

1986   Ice Glider Faunal Remains and Yanktonai Ethnohistory. In *Ice Glider: Papers in Northern Plains Prehistory and Ethnohistory,* edited by W. R. Wood, 146–183. South Dakota Archaeological Society, Special Publication, no. 10. Sioux Falls.

Wedel, W. R.

1936   *An Introduction to Pawnee Archeology.* Bureau of American Ethnology Bulletin no. 112. Washington, D.C.

1938   *The Direct-Historical Approach to Pawnee Archeology.* Smithsonian Miscellaneous Collections, vol. 97, no. 7. Washington, D.C.

1940   Culture Sequence in the Central Great Plains. In *Essays in the Historical Anthropology of North America,* 291–352. Smithsonian Miscellaneous Collections, vol. 100. Washington, D.C.

1955   *Archeological Materials from the Vicinity of Mobridge, South Dakota. Bureau of American Ethnology Bulletin* no. 157. Washington, D.C.

1978   Commentary. In *The Central Plains Tradition: Internal Development and External Relationships,* edited by D. J. Blakeslee, 157–162. University of Iowa, Office of the State Archaeologist, Report no. 11. Iowa City.

1979a   House Floors and Native Settlement Populations in the Central Plains. *Plains Anthropologist* 24:85–98.

1979b   Some Reflections on Plains Caddoan Origins. *Nebraska History* 60:272–293.

1986   *Central Plains Prehistory: Holocene Environments and Culture Change in the Republican River Basin.* University of Nebraska Press, Lincoln.

Weston, T.

1993   Acculturation in the Middle Missouri Valley as Reflected in Modified Bone Assemblages. *Plains Anthropologist* 38:79–100.

Wheeler, R. P.

1963   *The Stutsman Focus: An Aboriginal Culture Complex in the Jamestown Reservoir Area, North Dakota.* Bureau of American Ethnology Bulletin no. 185. Washington, D.C.

Will, G. F.

1924   *Archaeology of the Missouri Valley.* American Museum of Natural History, Anthropological Papers, vol. 24, pt. 6. New York.

Will, G. F., and T. C. Hecker

1944   The Upper Missouri River Valley Aboriginal Culture in North Dakota. *North Dakota Historical Quarterly* 11, nos. 1–2.

Will, G. F., and H. J. Spinden

1906   *The Mandans: A Study of Their Culture, Archaeology, and Language.* Harvard University, Peabody Museum of American Archaeology and Ethnology Papers, vol. 3, no. 4. Cambridge, Mass.

Willey, P.

1990   *Prehistoric Warfare on the Great Plains: Skeletal Analysis of the Crow Creek Massacre Victims.* Garland, New York.

Willey, P., and T. E. Emerson

1993   The Osteology and Archaeology of the Crow Creek Massacre. In *Prehistory and Human Ecology of the Western Prairies and Northern Plains,* edited by J. A. Tiffany, 227–269. Plains Anthropologist Memoir no. 27.

Witty, T. A.

1962   The Anoka Focus. M.A. thesis, Department of Anthropology, University of Nebraska, Lincoln.

Wood, W. R.
   1965   *The Redbird Focus and the Problem of Ponca Prehistory.* Plains Anthropologist Memoir no. 2.
   1967   *An Interpretation of Mandan Culture History.* Bureau of American Ethnology Bulletin no. 198. Washington, D.C.
   1971   *Biesterfeldt: A Post-Contact Coalescent Site on the Northeastern Plains.* Smithsonian Contributions to Anthropology, no. 15. Washington, D.C.
   1974   Northern Plains Village Cultures: Internal Stability and External Relationships. *Journal of Anthropological Research* 30:1–16.
   1980   Plains Trade in Prehistoric and Protohistoric Intertribal Relations. In *Anthropology on the Great Plains,* edited by W. R. Wood and M. Liberty, 98–109. University of Nebraska Press, Lincoln.
   1986   Cultural Chronology of the Upper Knife–Heart Region. In *Ice Glider: Papers in Northern Plains Prehistory and Ethnohistory,* edited by W. R. Wood, 7–24. South Dakota Archaeological Society, Special Publication no. 10. Sioux Falls.
   1993   Hidatsa Origins and Relationships. In *The Phase I Archeological Research Program for the Knife River Indian Villages National Historic Site.* Part 2, *Ethnohistorical Studies,* edited by T. D. Thiessen, 11–28. National Park Service, Midwest Archeological Center, Occasional Studies in Anthropology, no. 27. Lincoln, Neb.
Wood, W. R., and A. S. Downer
   1977   Notes on the Crow–Hidatsa Schism. In *Trends in Middle Missouri Prehistory: A Festschrift Honoring the Contributions of Donald J. Lehmer,* edited by W. R. Wood, 83–100. Plains Anthropologist Memoir no. 13.
Woolworth, A. R., and W. R. Wood
   1964   The Demery Site (39CO1), Oahe Reservoir Area, South Dakota. *Bureau of American Ethnology, Bulletin* 189: 67–137.
Zimmerman L. J., and Bradley, L. E.
   1993   The Crow Creek Massacre: Initial Coalescent Warfare and Speculations About the Genesis of Extended Coalescent. In *Prehistory and Human Ecology of the Western Prairies and Northern Plains,* edited by J. A. Tiffany, 215–226. Plains Anthropologist Memoir no. 27.
Zimmerman, L. J., and R. G. Whitten
   1980   Prehistoric Bones Tell a Grim Tale of Indian vs. Indian. *Smithsonian* 11:100–107.

11. The Oneota Tradition

Dale R. Henning

In archaeological research, there is never a "final word." That became blatantly apparent as I read my contribution to this volume, which was put in "final" form several years ago. It was depressingly outdated, partly because of my own recent efforts in Oneota research, but in large measure because of a great and stimulating upsurge of interest in the late prehistoric period by anthropologists and historians of many persuasions. That upsurge was highlighted by the conference "Oneota Archaeology: Past, Present, and Future," held in 1994. Those in attendance included about 150 registrants from both the United States and Canada. They included specialists in anthropology, geography, and history. Papers were presented, and artifacts were spread out on tables, compared, and discussed—all of which amounted to a stimulating learning experience. But to me the highlight of the conference was the general discussion, with input from a host of persons trained in specialized disciplines, all of them focused on the elusive Oneota, who roamed and controlled much of the western Prairie Peninsula for up to seven decades. We all came away from those sessions with renewed focus, enhanced interest, and intent to contribute to the understanding of this dynamic prehistoric period. Needless to say, my dated discussion of the western Oneota written half a decade ago now reflects some of these recent interactions. If interest in Oneota studies persists at the intensity that we find it today, this presentation will be subject to complete revision within another half decade.

Oneota cultural remains are generally defined in terms of a Prairie Peninsula habitat (Borchert 1950; Transeau 1935) and must be viewed, even for this volume with a focus on the Plains, as Peninsula-based (Figure 11.1). Still, when one looks over a collection of characteristic Oneota artifacts from all sites to the west of the Mississippi River and some to the east, the objects themselves suggest many Plains-derived adaptive patterns. Thus we might view Oneota as a "bridging culture" that links the Plains to the eastern Woodlands via the Prairie Peninsula. The concept of Oneota as a culture that links east and west seems especially pertinent when one considers the patterns of climatic change that affected the natural resources on the Plains and Prairie Peninsula in the late Holocene (Baerreis and Bryson 1965; Bryson et al. 1970; Bryson and Wendland 1967). These climatic shifts made parts of the Prairie Peninsula more or less plains-like in available floral and faunal resources through time, with measurable effects on its inhabitants.

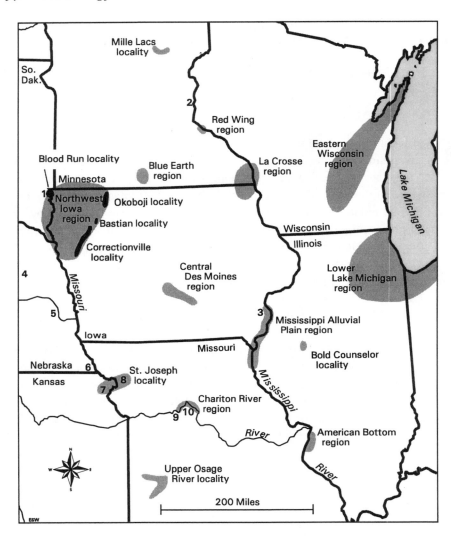

Figure 11.1. Oneota-tradition sites, regions, and localities: *South Dakota* (1) Blood Run; *Minnesota* (2) Sheffield; *Iowa* (3) McKinney; *Nebraska* (4) Stanton, (5) Yutan, (6) Leary; *Kansas* (7) Fanning; *Missouri* (8) King Hill, (9) Gumbo Point, (10) Plattner, (11) Utz.

The Oneota tradition does not lend itself to easy definition, yet it is familiar to most midwestern and Plains archaeologists. The name is derived from an article written by Ellison Orr (1914:231–239) in which he described pottery from northeastern Iowa found along the Oneota River, since named the Upper Iowa River. Charles R. Keyes (1927:214–229) later referred to the pottery and related material as "Oneota." The name has remained in use, but is now applied to a much broader range of materials, both geographically and culturally, than

Keyes and Orr could have dreamed. There is a general similarity in all Oneota remains, but distinctive differences are evident when materials from specific locales are closely compared. Oneota remains do not lend themselves to ease in description, nor do the types developed for them meet with universal approval.

Several sites offer radiocarbon-dated features suggesting Oneota occupancy from A.D. 900. Other sites were occupied into historic times and can be identified with historic tribes. Many Oneota sites probably were occupied intermittently over much of the late prehistoric period, but testable evidence for individual site longevity, coupled with the subtleties of in situ culture change, has not yet been defined for any Oneota site.

Many sites are very large; some show signs of occupation scattered over a hundred acres and more. Very few offer evidence of stockades or fortifications of any kind. Some sites encompass or are located near groups of mounds and earthwork enclosures. Enclosed areas in northeastern Iowa (McKusick 1964; Orr 1963) and in central Missouri (Leaf 1976; Wood 1973) have been tested; some contain good evidence for Oneota construction. Burial mounds were built by Oneota people at the Blood Run site in northwestern Iowa and eastern South Dakota (Harvey 1979); Blood Run also had a 15-acre enclosure. Other mound groups on or near a few other Oneota sites in northwestern Iowa were probably built by Oneota people. Some groups set aside cemetery areas, but burials and fragments of human bone, some cut, split, and burned, may be found at any location on an Oneota site.

On many Oneota sites, the living surface is restricted to the plow zone or extends only a few centimeters below it. The most common features are storage and/or trash pits. Oneota houses are often difficult to locate. Many were destroyed through cultivation; others probably have been missed, even by good archaeologists, because they are difficult to discern and not expected. As more houses are found and described, the better are the possibilities for our seeing evidence for their presence, even if that evidence is just the bottoms of faintly perceived postmolds. Birk and Johnson (1992) describe the differences between summer and winter houses; winter houses found near Mille Lacs were semi-subterranean and are easier to discern, while summer houses were pole structures set into the surface where, in some areas, they could be destroyed by cultivation.

Hollinger (1995) traces the evolution of Oneota houses. The data suggest that during the Emergent and Developmental horizons, habitations were small with simple spatial organization. Houses occupied during the Classic horizon were very large (longhouse styles, some over 100 feet long) and well organized. Hollinger attributes changes in house style to shifts in the preferred postmarital residence pattern. The large longhouse type suggests a matrilineal/matrilocal pattern, and the small square to rectangular types reflect a patrilineal/patrilocal pattern. Shelters recorded for Historic-horizon sites suggest greater variation in form, probably a reflection of the cultural turmoil that characterized the advance of Euro-Americans. Hollinger's model for change through time tests well: Emergent- and Developmental-horizon houses are indeed small, single-family dwellings (Harn 1991; Overstreet 1995:39–42; Santure et al. 1990), and the long, large multifamily Classic-horizon houses (McKusick 1973; O'Gorman 1995) stand to corroborate his thesis. The variability of Historic-horizon houses may be confirmed by examples from Utz (Bray 1991:34–37) that are small, ovoid to rectangular structures that contrast significantly with the long rectangular houses of the Little Osage (Chapman et al. 1985).

Western Oneota sites have not yielded consistent house outlines, aside from the Little Osage long rectangular ones. The post pattern of part of a house that I believe dates to the Developmental horizon (Harvey 1979:63–67, Figure 5:1) suggests a linear structure about 30 feet long and 8 feet wide, constructed of rather heavy posts. The boulder circles and ovoid outlines on the Blood Run site, once estimated (Thomas 1891:38–39) to number in the hundreds (none remain today), probably outlined houses. The Lewis (n.d.) maps suggest circles of 33 to 59 feet in diameter, and one oval outline is over 115 feet long and about 23 feet wide (Henning 1982:30). The single typical Central Plains earthlodge excavated at the Leary site in southeastern Nebraska (Hill and Wedel 1936) is of uncertain authorship, but could be Oneota.

Oneota people were hunters, fishers, and gatherers; the emphasis in resources that they used appears to have been determined by the seasonal availability of resources where they lived. They were consistently maize growers, although beans, squash, sunflower, and indigenous cultivars are recovered from some sites. The quantity of faunal materials on Oneota sites varies with local availability and, of course, with soil and other preservation factors. Bison hunting was very important to most Oneota groups irrespective of their permanent locations. Thus many sites yield large quantities of bison bone, sometimes suggesting articulation when deposited. Judging from ethnographic studies of Plains bison-hunting and butchering practices, the presence of large articulated elements in a village suggests that bison were obtained locally and that parts of the carcass could be carried to the village for processing. Generally, however, bison bone other than elements used for tools is rare in most Oneota components. Blood Run is one of very few Oneota sites that consistently offers evidence for killing bison on or near the village.

Many Oneota components that yield few bison elements other than scapula hoes offer inferred evidence for seasonal bison hunting in the form of end scrapers. I believe that the simple presence of bison scapulae suggests either seasonal expeditions in quest of these large mammals or trade. When both the scapulae and the end scrapers are found in some numbers, the case for bison hunting seems stronger. The small end scrapers were probably hafted in antler or wood handles and used to remove fat and hair from large and heavy hides. The presence of grooved mauls, probably used in processing dried meat, also suggests the importance of bison hunting. They are consistently found in western Oneota components.

Chipped-stone items regularly recovered at Oneota sites include small, simple triangular arrowpoints, end scrapers, side scrapers, bifacial knives, drills, perforators, gravers, occasional "Harahey" knives (western four-edged quadrilateral knives), and a host of flake tools. The quality of the chipped-stone tools at any site is apparently a function of the raw chert available. For instance, chipped-stone tools from sites in central and northwestern Missouri and southeastern Iowa, where fine chert was available, are of exceptional quality and very numerous when compared with those from many other Oneota sites (Figure 11.2).

Ground-stone tools include mortars, manos or handstones, shaft abraders, grooved mauls, celts, and sharpening or abrading stones. Other ground-stone objects include inscribed catlinite plaques (Bray 1963:1–40) and pipes (Hamilton 1967) in a wide range of shapes and sizes. The catlinite plaques are decorated with mythic figures, and a number of elements and striations often are incised over one another. The pipes are often very simple. Some are made of a small block of catlinite, limestone, soapstone, or other soft stone and have two small holes, one for the stem, the other for a bowl. Some are variants of the elbow form, and others are disk-bowl forms. The disk-bowl form is found widely distributed and persists well into the historic period. The Ioway, Osage, and Omaha were curating disk-bowl pipes in "war bundles" well into historic times (Overstreet 1993:169). Omaha and Osage bundle disk-bowl specimens are illustrated by West (1934:760–786).

Bone tools include bison (and sometimes elk) scapula hoes or shovels, punches, awls, eyed needles, scapula knives (also called squash knives), rasps, and shaft wrenches. Ornaments fashioned from bone include bracelets, deer-toe-bone tinklers, tubular beads, and small pendants. Antler was used for digging implements, picks, flaking tools, drifts, and shaft wrenches. Ornaments also were made of cut strips of antler that were bent to form bracelets and complex necklaces of U-shaped strips strung together (Figure 11.3).

Local shell was used for spoons, pendants, and drilled disk beads. Marine-shell ornaments are rare, but include shell mask gorgets (Chapman 1980:Figure 6.9; Overstreet 1993:158–159; W. Wedel 1961:223, Plate 20) and barrel-shaped and large circular disk conch-shell beads, often found in burials. These items seem restricted to the Historic horizon.

Items of European derivation are present at some sites, but generally are rare and suggest restricted trading, both direct and indirect, with whites. Blue and green glass beads, red and white opaque ceramic beads, and copper and brass bracelets, rings, earrings, and pendants occur with small fragments of iron, iron knives, brass and copper kettle fragments, and, at a few sites, seed beads, axes,

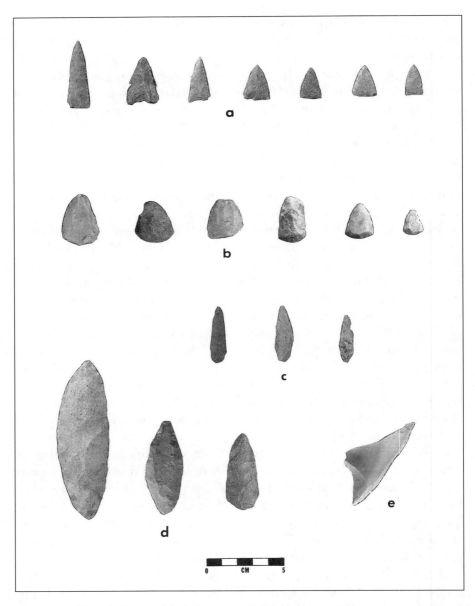

Figure 11.2. Typical Oneota chipped-stone tools (La Crosse–terrace components): (*a*) arrowpoints; (*b*) end scrapers; (*c*) drills or perforators; (*d*) knives; (*e*) flake scraper-graver.

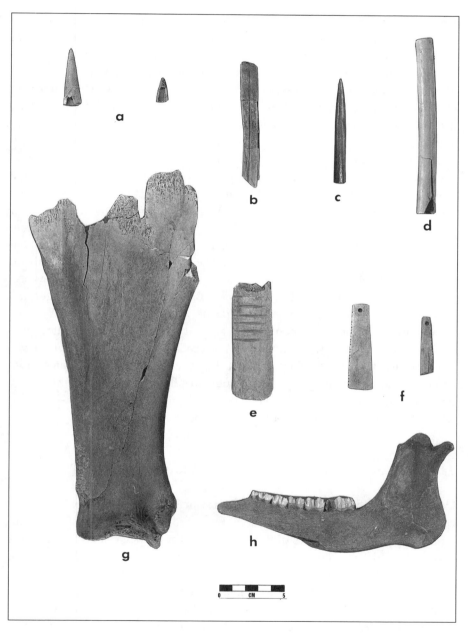

Figure 11.3. Typical Oneota bone and antler tools (La Crosse–terrace components): (*a*) socketed antler-tip projectile points; (*b*) scored antler; (*c*) bone awl; (*d*) bird-bone tube; (*e*) bison-rib rasp; (*f*) notched bone pendants; (*g*) bison-scapula hoe; (*h*) deer-mandible sickle.

hoes, guns, gun parts, and related materials. It should be stressed that none of these items require a Euro-American presence for distribution; Indian exchange systems were fully functional throughout the Oneota tradition, but were especially well developed in the late Classic and early Historic horizons.

Oneota has sometimes been defined as a "pottery culture" (Hall 1962:108; M. Wedel 1959:111), albeit with reluctance by most investigators. Although we decry this dependence on one aspect of material culture, no one has confidently identified an Oneota component without access to a few sherds. Thus we reluctantly rely heavily on ceramics in this chapter. Oneota pottery vessels are generally shell-tempered, globular jars with constricted orifices and rounded bottoms. Plain, broad-mouthed small bowls occur at most sites, but usually are rare. Decoration, if applied to a jar, is confined to the lip or to the inner or outer lip–rim juncture and to the upper body or shoulder. The lip and inner or outer lip–rim juncture may be plain or decorated with punctates, finger and tool impressions, short dashes, or trailed lines. The shoulder area is either plain or decorated with simple line motifs, including vertical lines, triangles, chevrons, and alternating triangles filled with lines (Benn 1989). Punctates, finger and thumb impressions, tool impressions, dashes, concentric circles, and spirals often augment the typical shoulder designs. At one time, Oneota pottery was easy to describe, classify, and interpret. With each new site excavated, however, the complexity increases. Furthermore, the range of radiocarbon dates (from about A.D. 900 to the historic period) from sites that were once believed to be protohistoric or historic has forced severe changes in our past perceptions of what Oneota was all about, if only from the perspective of pottery.

The Oneota Tradition and the Taxa Employed

Oneota is an Upper Mississippian cultural manifestation. The broadly conceived Upper Mississippian tradition (Emerson and Brown 1992:82) encompasses shared characteristics of the Fort Ancient tradition, centered in Indiana and Ohio (Griffin 1943) and the western Oneota tradition, found in parts of Michigan, Indiana, Illinois, Wisconsin, Minnesota, Iowa, South Dakota, Kansas, Nebraska, and Missouri. Both the Oneota and Fort Ancient traditions may span as much as several centuries and offer archaeological evidence of their evolution through time. Sites that are obviously Oneota related also are found in North Dakota, Ontario, and Manitoba.

Numerous early radiocarbon assays combined with the archaeological evidence dictate that Oneota did not evolve directly from a Mississippian ancestor or simply by stimulus from a Mississippian source (Griffin 1943:302, 1946:90, 1960:835; Rodell 1991; Stoltman 1986). Rather, Oneota appears to have evolved as an Emergent Mississippian contemporary, at times contemporaneous with and interacting variously with peoples of the Woodland, Mississippian, Caddoan, Central Plains, Middle Missouri, and Coalescent traditions.

The Oneota tradition may be traced back to A.D. 900 (Boszhardt et al. 1995), culminating 700 years later in the identification of several historic tribes. The tradition probably had its antecedents in regional Woodland groups (Benn 1995), although this has yet to be documented. Some researchers have traced mythological/religious/social traditions that are extant in historic tribes after well over a millennium (Barreca 1992; Salzer 1992, 1993), despite their being masked by significant changes in material culture. The Chiwere-speaking Winnebago, Ioway, Oto, and Missouri have long been identified with the Oneota cultural tradition (Chapman 1980; Griffin 1937; Mott 1938; Overstreet 1995). Some of the Dhegihan speakers—the Osage (Chapman 1959, 1980; Chapman et al. 1985), Kansa (Henning 1970, 1993; W. Wedel 1959:171), and Omaha (Harvey 1979; M. Wedel 1981)—also assumed some trappings of Oneota material culture. The Mdewakonton Dakota (Birk and Johnson 1992:209–211) and, perhaps, the Miami (Herold et al. 1990:99) may also have adapted parts of the Oneota tradition. There is general agreement on some sites assigned to the Ioway and Missouri, but the isolation of specific temporal and cultural traits in those sites is still not universally satisfactory. Other tribal assignments to the Oneota tradition are variously interpreted and are the source of spirited discussion.

The horizon concept (Willey and Phillips 1958) has been applied to the study of the Oneota tradition (Boszhardt 1994; Hall 1962; Overstreet and Richards 1992; M. Wedel 1963). Horizons used are the Emergent (A.D. 900–1000), Developmental (A.D. 1000–1350), Classic (A.D. 1350–1650), and Historic (A.D. 1650–1775); dates vary somewhat by region and researcher. In some regions, there are adequate data to divide some horizons into early, middle, and late subdivisions. Horizon styles mark the advent of each of the named horizons. Horizon styles important to Oneota include such things as the location of decorative elements on pottery, pottery motifs, specific raw materials, pipe styles, tablets, and the presence of historic items. The taxonomic system used here adheres to that of Willey and Phillips (1958).

One integrative unit not employed by Willey and Phillips is specific to Oneota—the group continuity (Hall 1962:94–99). The concept is inclusive, embracing a congeries of traits that are consistent within a locality or region through a period of time. The group continuity satisfies a need in Oneota study for describing grouped traditional elements within defined spatial parameters. It might encompass the traditional activities of a clan, band, or tribe within a locality or a region over a defined period of time.

I also discuss exchange centers. Gibbon (1974:133–137) originally defined "strategic nodal points" that functioned in a variety of ecological niches outside the core zone in the American Bottom as part of the "Ramey symbiotic–extractive exchange system." On a site identified as an exchange center, one cultural manifestation may predominate, but the component should offer evidence of "exchange partners" in the form of traditional materials or a significant percentage of "exotics"—that is, materials or finished artifacts that are not found locally. Oneota exchange centers developed early in the Developmental horizon and persisted into the Historic horizon at a number of locations.

Toward Understanding Oneota

In each regional manifestation, the reader will note the consistency with which researchers suggest that at least one bison hunt was part of the "seasonal round." These seasonal expeditions, most of which probably involved a significant number of people, also required appropriate ceremonies, planning, and preparation of food supplies and equipment. These long and arduous forays, some involving several hundred or more miles on foot and carrying supplies, ended in a successful hunt, processing the spoils of that hunt at the kill site, and carrying them back to the village.

An example of such a hunting expedition is recorded in Bourgmont's journal of an expedition in 1724 to visit the Padoucas in the company of members of the Missouri and Kansa tribes. The group left the Kansa village (Doniphan site, Kansas) on July 24, traveled a league and a half, and then halted. The Kansa chief explained to Bourgmont:

> Do not be surprised that today we are having such a short day of travel. This is our assembly area. We are bringing with us our women and a part of our children, for we have decided among us, with your permission, to take them as far as five or six days' travel from here, where there are plenty of bison. We will kill some, and our women will dry the meat, and then they will return to our village. That will help them to live until our return, and we will continue our journey with you to the Padoucas. (Norall 1988:135)

At least two points important to our understanding of the spread of Oneota culture are made in this account. First, there seems to have been little concern for distance, and, second, working and warfare alliances were possible, even expected, among neighboring tribes, even those that did not speak the same language. Those alliances were notably temporary. It should not be surprising that there is general similarity when the late prehistoric remains across the western Prairie Peninsula are compared. The overview that follows stresses similarities while defining the characteristics that separate the horizons.

Most archaeologists of the Midwest automatically correlate Oneota with shell-tempered pottery, but this cannot be regarded an absolute criterion. Oneota pottery is generally shell tempered, but many classic examples are not. Recent analyses have identified low percentages of grog (sometimes shell-tempered grog) at Mississippi Alluvial Plain sites; grit temper in the Emergent-horizon components of the Door Peninsula; grit temper predominating at the White Rock–phase sites of eastern Kansas and Nebraska; and grit, limestone, grog, and combinations thereof in addition to shell temper (only 21 percent) at the Blood Run site in northwestern Iowa and eastern South Dakota. Oneota pottery from Fort Ridgely, on the Minnesota River, is in all respects comparable to Oneota pottery of the Developmental horizon, but solidly shell-tempered sherds are less than 10 percent of the sample (Anfinson 1987). I am no longer sure that temper is that important to Oneota identification and research, but close analysis coupled with microscopic inspection should continue.

A number of Oneota pottery types have been proposed, only a few of which retain their value to Oneota studies. The literature is filled with discussions of pottery typology (Orton et al. 1993), much of which either is outdated or has little application. I still prefer the ware/type concepts that Donald J. Lehmer developed for the Middle Missouri area. His wares or ware groupings are the most generalized: "wares may be thought of as groups of types which share a majority of basic characteristics including the fabric of the pottery itself, the general vessel form, the surface finish and the basic rim form" (Lehmer 1954:41). Strict adherence to this definition when faced with a tableful of Oneota pottery, however, is virtually impossible. We have to make allowances for variations in the fabric (temper), surface finish (some smooth, some lightly polished, some smoothed-over cordmarked), and rim form (only generalizations of an ideal form are applicable), and find ourselves with two ware groupings—jars and bowls—that are universally applicable to Oneota. As we become more rigorous, subtle differences in jar shape and rim form should allow greater precision in ware definitions, but we are not there yet. The type, again following Lehmer with some modifications, is more applicable to what we need. It is dependent primarily on decorative motifs and the placement of decorative elements on the vessel surface. Motifs and elements should be precisely described, consistently employed, and defined within strict cultural, spatial, and temporal parameters. The type must be distinctive and recognizable wherever found. It should connote relationship to a defined cultural group within a known unit of space and should have been produced within finite temporal limits. Few types are so defined.

Oneota pottery types that conform to these requirements are Carcajou Curvilinear (Hall 1962:60–63), Lake Winnebago Trailed (Hall 1962:171–174; Overstreet 1995:50–52), Grand River Trailed (Hall 1962:65–68; Overstreet 1995:36–37), and the revised definition of Allamakee Trailed (Boszhardt 1994:233–235, Figure 11). A host of other named types are not useful, primarily because they lack spatial and temporal parameters. Unacceptable types include most of the plain types: Grand River Plain, Koshkonong Bold, Perrot Punctate (Hall 1962), Correctionville Trailed (Henning 1961), Blue Earth Trailed (Dobbs 1984; Gibbon 1978), the Van Meter series (Bray 1991; Chapman 1980), and the outdated definitions of Allamakee Trailed (Henning 1961; M. Wedel 1959). Some of these types might be used as indicators of similarity to a norm—Blue Earth Trailed–like, Perrot Punctate–like—but the normative use should be made clear. Some of the notable characteristics of these types, but not the types themselves, can be employed as horizon styles.

A few characteristics on pottery may satisfy our need for definable and understandable Oneota horizon styles. In the Emergent horizon in the Eastern Wisconsin region, jars with notched lips (unless plain) and curvilinear shoulder motifs, especially parallel wavy lines on the upper shoulder, seem to predominate among the rare decorated vessels. A few of these wavy-line motifs are found into the Developmental horizon, but probably are early and rare. In the Developmental horizon wherever it is found, rectilinear motifs (chevrons, grouped oblique parallel lines, vertical and horizontal lines) are often paralleled by tool impressions or punctations, and lip decoration is predominantly tool impressions extending from the lip onto the inner rim. At most Classic-horizon sites, notched lips again predominate, the impressions often made with the fingers or thumb, and there are zones of punctations paralleled by trailed lines, often in conjunction with other motifs, on the jar shoulders (Figures 11.4 and 11.5). Historic-horizon pottery was rapidly replaced by brass, copper, and iron kettles; at the few Historic-horizon sites where pottery is found, it appears to reflect late Classic forms.

There are also a number of nonceramic horizon styles and horizon markers. The Classic horizon is marked by the disk-bowl pipe, which appears in that horizon and survives into the Historic. Data from the La Crosse region suggest that these may be late (Valley View phase) in the Classic horizon (Boszhardt 1994:211). Disk bowls are found in most Classic-horizon components and were shared widely, but not in large numbers, outside the Oneota sphere of influence. For example, large catlinite disk-bowl pipes have been recovered from a prehistoric Cayuga site in New York State, from the Spiro site in northeastern Oklahoma, from the Demery site in north-central South Dakota (Hamilton 1967:24–26), and from the Campbell and McCoy sites in southeastern Missouri (O'Brien 1994).

Incised tablets or plaques may also mark the Classic horizon, with many examples apparently made of catlinite, although other materials, including hematite and limestone, also were used. The tablets are incised with representations of "birdman," anthropomorphic figures, bison, birds, snakes, small animals (often embellished with a weeping eye), lightning, heartlines, and feathers. (Some of these motifs also are found on bone and antler.) One catlinite tablet was collected from the Oto (Howard 1953:133) (Figure 11.6). Boszhardt (1994:191–92) offers evidence for scored deer-rib rasps and copper coils that make their appearance in Oneota contexts late in the Classic horizon, but are also important markers of the Historic horizon. There seems every reason to

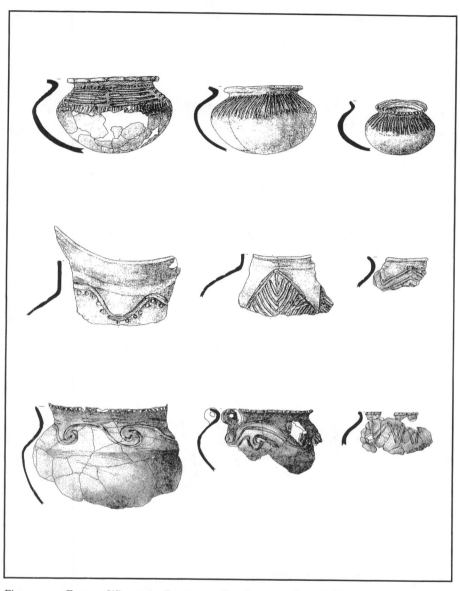

Figure 11.4. Eastern Wisconsin Emergent-, Developmental-, and Classic-horizon pottery (scales vary): *bottom row:* Emergent types, all Carcajou Curvilinear; *middle row:* Developmental types, all Grand River Trailed; *top row:* Classic types, all Lake Winnebago Trailed. Note the prevalence of a notched lip in the Emergent horizon; a plain lip in the Developmental horizon; and a sharply everted rim, notched lip, and bold lines paralleled with tool impressions in the Classic horizon. (After Overstreet 1995)

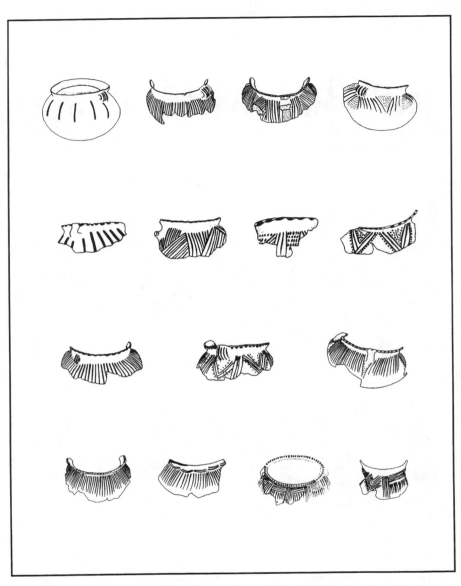

Figure 11.5. La Crosse–terrace Developmental- and Classic-horizon pottery: *fourth row:* late Developmental Brice Prairie phase; *second and third rows:* transitional (early Classic?) Pammel Creek phase; *first row:* late Classic Valley View phase. Note the prevalence of a tool-impressed rim-lip interior and the use of tool impressions parallel to line motifs in the Brice Prairie phase; a notched lip (tool impression on the lip top), the continued use of tool impressions parallel to line motifs, and the beginning use of punctation "zones" in the Pammel Creek phase; and the continued use of a notched lip and punctation zones in the Valley View phase. (After Boszhardt 1994)

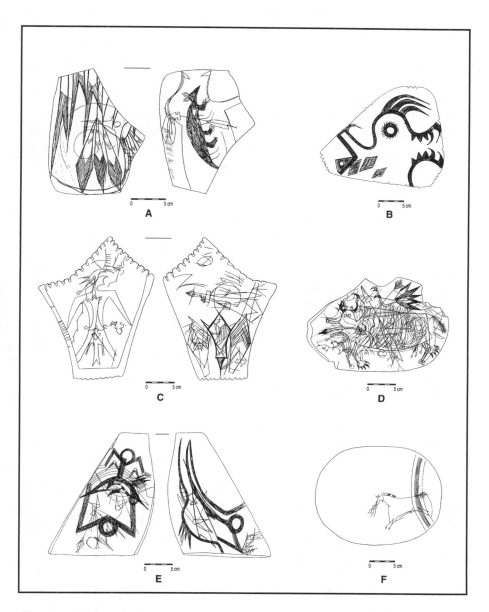

Figure 11.6. Selected plaque motifs: (*a*) tablet no. 5, Bastian site (both sides); (*b*) tablet no. 1, Bastian site (opposed side is smoothed); (*c*) New Albin (Iowa) tablet (both sides); (*d*) tablet no. 2, Bastian site; (*e*) Utz tablet (Missouri) (both sides); (*f*) Oto tablet. (After Bray 1963)

believe that catlinite from quarries in Minnesota was not distributed widely until the Classic horizon and then became very popular. Raw catlinite and finished products appear to have been important into the Historic horizon as well.

Late in the Classic and extending into the Historic horizon, we find Gulf coast conch- or whelk-shell mask gorgets and large circular disks and beads. The presence of these and the incised tablets and disk-bowl pipes suggests the increased importance of interactive ceremonial practices and trade that linked some Historic-horizon Oneota with other groups.

Chiwere and Dhegiha Siouan Archaeology

We revel in our ability to place a tribal name on some Oneota components, allowing us access to a wealth of linguistic and ethnographic data. But the way to truth is fraught with difficulty due to a number of factors, among them disease (Green 1993), pressure from eastern tribes being displaced by Euro-Americans, the rapidity of material-culture change brought about by the introduction of new technology, and traditional patterns of fissioning and shifting alliances that characterize most North American Indian tribes. These factors have wreaked havoc with employing the direct historical approach to confidently relate a prehistoric cultural manifestation to a known historic tribe. R. J. Mason (1976) offers succinct, common-sense procedures for making a genetic connection between a known tribal group and the sites and artifacts of the archaeological record, which he terms "site–unit ethnicity." The requirements he stipulates for this method are paraphrased in the following:

1. There must be a discrete site, or component in a site, associated with iron knives, glass beads, or other evidence of European influence.
2. The component must yield sufficient aboriginal artifacts (pottery, stone and bone tools, and the like) to permit the initiation of an inventory that might be diagnostic of one group rather than many groups of aboriginal peoples.
3. One or more acceptable and appropriate historical documents must provide persuasive, if not wholly unambiguous, dated identification of the locality and its occupants.
4. There must be no serious incompatibility between any two of the foregoing criteria.

Few enough Oneota sites can muster all of the first three criteria, and for none can we claim absolute purity of information. Utz, the historic Missouri village and one of our best examples, offers a mixture of prehistoric and historic components, some of which yield historic trade items; but the prehistoric and historic components remain to be clearly separated and their characteristics defined. The Blood Run site, with good documentation of Omaha presence, may offer some confusing prehistoric components to confuse us and provide additional documentary evidence for more than one tribe (principally Omaha [and Ponca?], but Ioway and, probably, Oto also were there at times). Separating the tribal units archaeologically cannot yet be confidently done, and perhaps never will. The Fanning and King Hill sites (Kansa?) offer European trade items with evidence for short-term, high-intensity occupation by groups well tied to their aboriginal material culture, but have scanty historic documentation. The Astor site in eastern Wisconsin may have a Winnebago connection, but may also have been occupied by the historic Fox or Potawatomi (Overstreet 1995:57). All the historic Osage villages in Missouri are well documented and loaded with European trade items, but yield disappointingly few diagnostics suggestive of their precontact material culture. Gumbo Point, a documented historic Missouri village near Utz, produced only vestiges of the old ways. Even the Upper Iowa River valley, documented home of the Ioways in the late seventeenth century, has too many sites with mixed prehistoric and historic components to be sorted out. Farley village, in the Root River drainage, offers good potential, following the first three requirements, but is not specifically mentioned in an early account. Two Okoboji-phase components, Gillette Grove and Milford, offer data linking the prehistoric material culture and an extensive array of European trade items with fairly good historic documentation of French contact. These are probably Ioway sites occupied shortly after the northeastern Iowa and southeastern Minnesota sites were vacated. The Midewakonton Dakota villages south of Mille Lacs lake (Birk and Johnson 1992) are documented historically, yield historic trade items in quantity, but traditional material-culture remains suggest recent integration of local Sandy Lake with late (probably Ioway-derived) Oneota. This is not a tidy situation, and using Mason's criteria, the Ioway data of the late seventeenth to early eighteenth century are probably the best we have.

The Oneota people were nonetheless related in various ways to some of the tribal entities that emerged in history. Western Europeans once thought that these tribal entities were important and "froze" them in our historic contexts. They were assigned to social units that even in these beginning stages of Oneota research do not allow the flexibility needed to understand or interpret their identification. The Oneota tradition appears to be characterized by shifting ethnic identities in its archaeological record, a phenomenon that persisted into the Historic horizon. Gibbon (1995:180) makes this point clearly: "bounded social units (or tribes) in the early historic period may not be appropriate groupings for studying the social dynamics of the late prehistoric period in many areas." There is every reason to believe that the prehistoric Oneota were extremely fluid in their identity, but the archaeological record does suggest differences in fluidity or willingness to interact. Generally, the Oneota traditionally traveled great distances for taking bison, making war, celebrating social and religions occasions, and trading. They undoubtedly developed networks of interaction and political alliances that shifted through time.

Green (1993) discusses the apparent patterns of precontact depopulation in the upper Midwest, offering several reasons—including climate change, warfare, and disease—for shifting relationships and patterns of interaction. Green points out that from 1300 to 1500 (roughly the Classic horizon), Oneota populations were concentrated in villages around Oshkosh and La Crosse. The record also suggests significant Classic-horizon population concentrations in the lower Blue Earth valley, lower Little Sioux valley, Chariton River region, Mississippi Alluvial Plain, Central Illinois River valley, and Leary site, to name a few. Green offers evidence for population collapse probably attributable to disease, resource depletion, and warfare in the sixteenth and seventeenth centuries, prior to the first face-to-face contacts with whites. Green cites the Winnebago as being particularly hard hit. Seventeenth-century French accounts characterize the Winnebago as a formerly populous and redoubtable nation. The Missouri were also recognized by early explorers as much reduced in numbers. The large, concentrated Classic-horizon villages, the multifamily houses, trade, and other forms of interaction obviously provided the incubators and transmission routes that took their toll. The La Crosse terrace was vacated in the seventeenth century. Most of the Mississippi Alluvial Plain, the central Illinois River valley, the Leary site, and the lower Little Sioux valley were apparently abandoned by this time as well. Warfare was a given in the earliest contacts between Europeans and Indians in the Prairie Peninsula. The indigenous groups, some of which probably were already reduced in numbers and strength by disease, were set upon by well-armed Sauk and Fox, Ojibwa, and Illiniwek. I doubt that the effects of the cool Neo-Boreal (Baerreis and Bryson 1965:217) were nearly as effective as the combined effects of disease and warfare on Oneota populations and interactive patterns.

The Oneota tradition at contact appears to have belonged primarily to Siouan-speaking groups, principally the Chiwere–Winnebago and Dhegiha. Oneota cultural remains have long been identified as "Siouan" (Griffin 1937). Today, some manifestations may be directly tied to the Chiwere speakers, most notably the Ioways and Missouris and, possibly, the Winnebagos, with attenuated ties to the Otos. Furthermore, evidence suggests that the Oneota tradition was assumed by some of the Dhegiha speakers, including the Kansas, Osages, and Omahas. A late Mdewakonton Dakota connection also has been suggested.

Linguistic evidence correlates well with the migration legends of these groups. Springer and Witkowski (1982) offer several insights from historical linguistics that are invaluable to the archaeologist. They suggest three major Siouan subgroups: Eastern, Central, and Western Siouan. All three split from the Proto-Siouans about 500 B.C., the Western Siouans moving in a northwesterly direction, ultimately settling in the Northern Plains (Mandans, Hidatsas, and Crows). The Eastern Siouans broke away about 100 B.C. and moved south (Ofos and Biloxis) and east (Tutelos). The Central Siouan consists of three subgroups—Dakota, Dhegiha, and Chiwere-Winnebago—that began to diverge about A.D. 700 when Proto-Dakota split off. Proto-Dhegiha (Quapaws, Kansas, Osages, and Omahas–Poncas) separated from Proto-Chiwere–Winnebago about A.D. 1000. The Dhegiha languages began to diverge about A.D. 1300 and, about A.D. 1500, Chiwere separated from Winnebago.

Siouan mythology and ethnohistory offer invaluable resources for the Prairie Peninsula archaeologist. A few decades ago, Siouan migration "myths" or legends seemed to have little bearing on how prehistory was being interpreted. With the advent of radiocarbon dating in the 1950s of "late" sites (as all Oneota sites were then regarded), considerable time depth was established for Oneota, making the legends seem more acceptable.

The legends pertinent to the Chiwere-speaking Winnebagos, Ioways, Otos, and Missouris (Dorsey 1886:221–222; McGee 1897:191–196) generally suggest that the Missouris, Ioways, and Otos separated from the Winnebagos near Green Bay, Wisconsin, and proceeded to the Mississippi River. The Ioways stopped at the Iowa River, probably near its confluence with the Mississippi. The Otos and Missouris moved south to the Missouri, establishing themselves near the mouth of the Grand River. Following a quarrel, the latter groups split, the Otos moving up the Missouri River and the Missouris remaining in the lower Missouri River valley.

The Dhegiha speakers—the Osages, Kansas, Omahas, Poncas, and Quapaws—had, according to legend (Dorsey 1886:215), once been a single group, living on or near the Ohio River. They separated, the Quapaws descending the Mississippi and the others proceeding to the mouth of the Missouri, where they lived for a time. Leaving the mouth of the Missouri, they went upstream to the mouth of the Osage River, where the Osages separated. They settled the Osage River headwaters, while the Kansas settled the lower Kansas River. The Omahas and Poncas moved up the Missouri River to what is now northeastern Nebraska. These legends do not lend themselves to close correlation with the archaeological record. However, with the availability of radiocarbon dates that document the antiquity of Oneota remains back to no earlier than A.D. 1000, and the recent work of Hall (1977, 1991) and Salzer (1993) on Siouan mythology, the traditions are more congruent to the archaeological record than they appeared to be in the 1950s.

Henning (1993) once suggested that the Chiwere were the indigenous long-term "core" of the Oneota tradition and that some of the Dhegihan speakers were latecomers who assumed parts of Oneota material culture after their arrival in the western Prairie Peninsula. Modifications are in order. It now seems importune to state that the Oneota tradition is primarily Chiwere-related as we review the length of time over which the tradition evolved, the territorial shifts, and the changing patterns of interrelationships that the prehistoric record affords, and then couple these with the evidence for population decimation by disease and warfare in the precontact period. It is more prudent to suggest that the Chiwere–Winnebago were simply those who emerged as survivors into the contact period, as were the Dhegihan-speaking Osages, Kansas, and Omahas (Omaha–Ponca if these two tribes were still one in 1700).

Still, there are significant differences between the Chiwere–Winnebagos' and the Dhegihan speakers' apparent tenure in the western Prairie Peninsula. The Chiwere appear to have an archaeological link into the prehistoric past, sometimes weak and tenuous. The Dhegiha Osages, Kansas, Omahas, and Poncas as we know them lack any identified late prehistoric antecedents. The sites attributed to them are notable by brevity of occupation; all components appear to have been populated by groups that arrived on site with European trade items. An exception might be Blood Run if the Dhegihan-speaking Omahas are responsible for most of the mounds and features there, but we do not know. Radiocarbon assays suggest that intensive occupation there began as early as A.D. 1500.

So what of the Dhegihan antecedents? Where are they? I have always favored at least a loose adherence to the migration myths that bring the Dheghia speakers out of the Ohio River valley, split off the Quapaws at the Mississippi to settle near the mouth of the Arkansas, and send the others up the Missouri to take up residence approximately where they were met by the first whites. The apparent fact of no identifiable antecedents in the western Prairie Peninsula seems to bolster this concept of a Dhegihan rush to the west, beginning as early as A.D. 1500. Still, there is no antecedent group of components in the Ohio River valley that can be attributed to them. There also is no recognized similarity in the cultural remains from Dhegiha components other than that the Osage sites (Plattner, Hayes, Brown, and Carrington) are comparable, and the two sites tentatively assigned to the early Kansas (King Hill and Fanning) offer similarities.

When we compare the remains from the Osage, Kansa, Omaha, and Ponca sites, though, we find them notably dissimilar. A well-documented Quapaw site has yet to be excavated (Hoffman 1990), but nothing similar to any of the other Dhegihan speakers' components has been found in the documented Quapaw locale of residence. So did the Dhegihan speakers come from the Ohio River valley? I still lean toward placing faith in the migration legends; they have served us well in other instances. But the Dhegiha could have evolved somewhere in the western Prairie Peninsula and, during the period of disruption in the sixteenth and seventeenth centuries, shifted about and altered their archaeologically defined trappings sufficiently to be lost until they appeared, the beneficiaries of European contacts and trade goods, at the sites they occupied historically.

Regional Examination of Oneota

In the following sections, the Oneota tradition will be dealt with by region, outlining defined localities, some sites, the horizons represented, and salient characteristics. Some regions to the east offer little information that pertains directly to the Plains and will be dealt with in summary fashion, although some of the data from eastern contexts are integral to our understanding of Oneota. It should be understood, however, that many Oneota groups, even those located well to the east, probably ventured seasonally toward and onto the Plains in search of bison.

Two regions offer key data to anyone interested in Oneota: the Eastern Wisconsin and La Crosse regions. The Eastern Wisconsin region provides the most detailed information about the Emergent horizon and its relations to a burgeoning Middle Mississippian tradition as well as a well-organized and succinct presentation of the sequence of events there (Overstreet 1995). The La Crosse region has been studied by a number of scholars who provide an organized and testable sequence of events dating from late in the Developmental horizon to the end of the Classic (Boszhardt 1994; Sasso 1993).

Eastern Wisconsin Region

The Eastern Wisconsin region encompasses three localities: Lake Koshkonong, Middle Fox River, and Door Peninsula. Overstreet (1995) defines the sequence of Oneota events in these localities as a group continuity with representative sites from the Emergent, Developmental, Classic, and Historic horizons. At this time, all the best documented and earliest Oneota Emergent-horizon sites are in this region. Still, we see no solid evidence for the generally accepted hypothesis of Oneota development out of Late Woodland (Benn 1995).

In the Lake Koshkonong locality, the Carcajou Point and Crab Apple Point sites; in the Middle Fox River locality, the Old Spring, Alonzo Kellogg, and John Herbst sites; and in the Door Peninsula, the Mero, Porte des Morts, Rock Island, and Little Lake sites are characterized by probable wigwams and small rectangular semi-subterranean houses. Both wall-trench construction and fortification are known at Carcajou Point. Neither mound construction nor mound burial is evident. Burials are in cemeteries and in individual pits at Lake Koshkonong, and below house floors in the Middle Fox River Passageway; no Oneota burials have been found on the Door Peninsula. Pottery generally consists of constricted-orifice jars, variable rim forms with (usually) notched lips, few handles, and a rare decorated upper body (a few curvilinear Ramey-derived motifs occur at Carcajou Point). Pottery is predominantly shell tempered in the Lake Koshkonong and Middle Fox River Passageway localities, and is up to 40 percent grit tempered in the Door Peninsula. Characteristic lithic artifacts include simple triangular arrowpoints, a few end scrapers, and paired sandstone arrowshaft abraders in the Lake Koshkonong and Middle Fox River Passageway localities. Copper awls, copper tubular beads, and pendants are common. Bone awls are common, and shell implements are rare. Maize kernels are found at sites other than in the Door Peninsula. Faunal remains suggest intensive riverine exploitation and the use of upland animals, including deer and elk. There are no data suggesting bison hunting or trade for bison products. Overstreet (1995) states that from A.D. 1050 to 1150, Oneota people left the area, possibly due to a Mississippian presence. The Carcajou Point materials suggest acquaintance with Mississippian pottery decoration, perhaps due to interaction before 1050.

The Developmental horizon is found in the Lake Koshkonong, Middle Fox River Passageway (Grand River phase), and Door Peninsula localities and is characterized by widely scattered settlements. Wigwams were the characteristic house style; the Walker–Hooper site was fortified. The dead were interred in mounds and cemeteries as well as scattered through villages. Pottery consists of jars with constricted orifices and notched lips. Shoulder decoration is rare and consists of meandering trailed lines bordered by punctates. Pinch pots are still fairly common. The artifact inventory is very similar to that of the region's Emergent horizon, with an even higher ratio of arrowpoints to end scrapers. Subsistence patterns remain similar to those of the Emergent horizon, with perhaps even more reliance on shellfish and the addition of beans.

The region's Classic horizon is concentrated solely in the Middle Fox River Passageway locality. Villages are larger and very numerous; possibly, houses were set on low mounds, but house types are unknown. Mortuary practices are unknown. The characteristic pottery is Lake Winnebago Trailed (Hall 1962), with some Koshkonong Bold, rare Perrot Punctate, and decorated pinch pots. Shoulder decoration is found on 90 percent of the vessels, generally composed of vertical and horizontal lines bordered by bold, deep punctations. There are more end scrapers than arrowpoints, and three- or four-sided knives, bifacially chipped–stone disks, shell spoons, shell fish effigies, catlinite disk-bowl pipes, bison-scapula hoes, copper tubular beads, small copper awls, and copper pendants (serpent and talon forms) are common. A few sheet-copper bird effigies are also reported. The presence of the scapulae and the end scrapers suggests that villagers were participating in seasonal bison hunts, returning with only the hard parts desired (for example, scapulae for digging tools), hides, and meat. The presence of a large number of end scrapers suggests that they were processing large hides. With the addition of the hypothetical bison forays, the subsistence pattern closely resembles that of the Developmental horizon. Overstreet (1995) suggests that the population in the Middle Fox River Passageway was large and stable until about A.D. 1600, when it virtually disappears. Pandemic disease (Green 1993), out-migration, and warfare are possible reasons for the decline.

The Historic horizon is "traditionally but not empirically linked to the Winnebago tribe" (Overstreet 1995:56). Many of us have wanted to link the Oneota sequence in the Eastern Wisconsin region to the Winnebagos (Griffin 1960; Lurie 1960; McKern 1945; Overstreet 1993, 1995). C. Mason (1976) and R. Mason (1986, 1993) have urged caution in this assignment, however. There was obviously a distinct disruption in the regional continuity, consistent with early historic accounts of a greatly diminished and weakened Winnebago tribe. Overstreet tentatively proposes a Dandy phase, with four components in the Middle Fox River Passageway and Door Peninsula localities. The component offering the most conclusive data is the Astor site, where pottery similar to Lake Winnebago Trailed was associated with historic items and a single grit-tempered vessel that can be attributed to either Fox or Potawatomi authorship (R. Mason 1986). Overstreet suggests that the site represents a reflection of Winnebago hardship, decline, and ultimate coresidence with some Algonquian group. The components assigned to the Eastern Wisconsin Historic horizon offer material-culture traits that suggest a strong resurgence of old and development of some new trade relationships with both Indians and Europeans. Iron, brass, copper, some silver, gunflints, European clay-pipe fragments, glass beads, and a host of objects made from European trade materials are associated with a few items suggestive of prehistoric everyday material culture. These finds are coupled with Native American trade items, including catlinite beads, at least one catlinite disk-bowl pipe and other worked catlinite, many large conch or whelk beads, a conch-shell mask gorget, and a large number of purple and white shell wampum beads. This resurgence and the introduction of Gulf coast and Eastern Woodlands (wampum) trade items suggest that new trade relations were being developed and is suggestive of the importance of Overstreet's Dandy–phase site occupants (especially the Hanson, Astor, and McCauley components) to both Indian and European trade partners.

It becomes clear as the various Oneota-occupied regions are compared that the Eastern Wisconsin region is distinctive from all others, especially during the Classic horizon. Evidence for communication with the outside world during the Classic, if only as reflected in pottery, is limited. Lake Winnebago Trailed pottery is very distinctive and can be recognized in any Oneota collection, but very few specimens are found outside the core area. Conversely, pottery types characteristic of the Classic horizon elsewhere are rare to absent in components in the Middle Fox River Passageway. This lack of interaction with other Oneota people as well as with contemporaneous Mississippian and Woodland groups throughout the span of this group continuity compares favorably with the recorded traditional and historically recorded attitude of other Indian groups toward the Winnebagos (Hall 1962:161–165). The group continuity in the Eastern Wisconsin region spans seven centuries, making it the longest proposed at this time. It offers the most testable data available about Oneota during the Emergent horizon, making it a vital research area for questions about Oneota origins.

La Crosse Region

A great deal of work has been done in the La Crosse region, on both sides of the Mississippi River, in Iowa, Minnesota, and Wisconsin, offering good site data. Information from the La Crosse terrace has been sufficiently studied that it can stand as comparative data for the Classic horizon. Sasso (1993) suggests that the La Crosse region consists of three localities: the La Crosse terrace and some adjacent portions of western Wisconsin, the lower Root River valley, and the lower Upper Iowa River valley. For the La Crosse–terrace locality, the best known, three sequential phases are proposed: Brice Prairie (late Developmental–early Classic horizon), Pammel Creek (transitional Classic horizon), and Valley View (late Classic) (Boszhardt 1994). The Orr phase is redefined and subsequently identified only in the Root and Upper Iowa river valleys.

A common cultural thread links all the La Crosse–terrace phases with the less well defined occupations in the other localities. Long, ovoid houses are known at the Tremaine site (O'Gorman 1995) on the La Crosse terrace, and at the Grant site (McKusick 1973) in the Upper Iowa River valley. Burial in cemeteries, house floors, and storage or trash pits can be expected. In the Upper Iowa River valley, some burials were defleshed, rearticulated, and buried (Henning and Peterson 1965; Orr 1963). Occasional "trophy" skulls are included with a burial. Grave inclusions are fairly common, and small jars are often included. A broad range of materials is found in Oneota graves (Arzigian et al. 1994; Bray 1961; Collins 1995; M. Wedel 1959), but the later burials, accompanied by historic materials, appear to have the greatest number and range of grave inclusions. A few conical mounds in all localities have burials with Oneota jars, possibly as secondary interments. Human bone is often found on the village surface or in trash pits. All the phases are notable for their dependence on horticulture, principally maize. Riverine resources, deer, elk, smaller mammals, and collected upland resources ensured a solid subsistence. Extensive raised garden beds have been explored on the La Crosse terrace and probably will be found in the Upper Iowa and Root river valleys. We assume that seasonal bison hunts to the west were part of village routine. All these phases and Oneota sites in the other localities yield simple triangular arrowpoints, end scrapers, bifacial knives, flake knives and scrapers, drills, and gravers. The bone tool inventory is, again, very Plains-like, with bison-scapula hoes, bird- and mammal-bone awls and punches, bone tubes, rasps, clamshell spoons, deer-metatarsal socketed projectile points, bone beads, and antler ornaments. Historic materials are not found on the La Crosse terrace, but are found on some components in the Upper Iowa and Root river valleys.

Not all researchers agree that the phases defined for the La Crosse terrace will be found in localities across the Mississippi as further work is conducted, but all agree that the latest Oneota occupations probably are to be found west of the Mississippi and can be identified with the Ioway (Mott 1938).

The Brice Prairie phase dates from A.D. 1300 to 1350 and is assigned to the late Developmental horizon. It is characterized by villages located primarily along terrace edges overlooking the Mississippi River floodplain. No mound construction and no house type has been identified. The characteristic pottery type is Perrot Punctate, which is characterized by tool impressions on the inner lip of the rim, generally exhibits punctate-border elements as embellishments to chevrons and groups of parallel lines, and has paired handles generally set below the lip. The type is often referred to as Blue Earth–like, coupled with the suggestion that its presence indicates its derivation from either the Blue Earth or the Red Wing region, or both. There is obviously a relationship between sites with this pottery style, but I suggest that Perrot Punctate is illustrative of a horizon style rather than a type.

The Classic-horizon Pammel Creek phase dates from A.D. 1350 to 1500. By this time, villages are generally found near the bluffs. There is no evidence for mound construction, and no house type has been identified. Burials are both in cemetery areas and in villages. Associated pottery types are Pammel Creek Trailed and Perrot Punctate.

The late Classic-horizon Valley View phase dates from A.D. 1500 to 1625. Villages are characteristically set back from the terrace edge, assuming more defensible positions. The Valley View site was protected by a palisade. Conical mound construction is established and long, extended-family houses are the norm. Burials in cemeteries, in mounds, in some house floors, and scattered through the village are found. The pottery is "Allamakee Trailed–like": named examples include Allamakee Trailed, Midway Incised, Koshkonong Bold, and Valley View Trailed. Some new artifact types are introduced, including copper coils, mammal-rib rasps, and disk-bowl pipes of catlinite and other materials. The Valley View phase marks the final Oneota occupation of the La Crosse terrace.

The Orr phase was defined long ago (Henning 1961, 1970) following its definition as a focus by M. Wedel (1959). It is in serious need of reanalysis and updating. When Oneota remains from the Upper Iowa River valley were analyzed in the 1950s, they were considered almost contemporaneous with one another and were very late (protohistoric to historic). Thus the collections taken from several components were "lumped" in the definitions, following the meth-

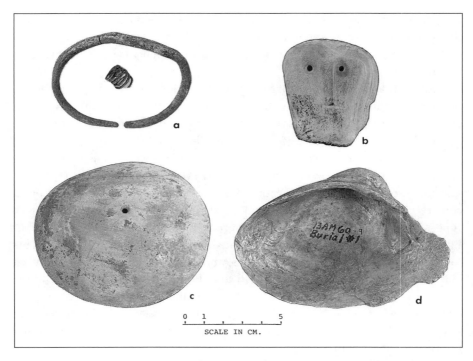

Figure 11.7. Late Classic/early Historic–horizon grave offerings from the Upper Iowa River valley: (*a*) copper or brass bracelet and coil; (*b*) shell mask gorget; (*c*) marine-shell gorget; (*d*) mussel-shell spoon.

odology of the time. This was a serious error, combining materials that possibly span several hundred years. Reanalysis of McKusick's "Grant type" should find that it compares favorably with pottery from the La Crosse–terrace Pammel Creek phase. Pottery from the Lane Enclosure in the Upper Iowa locality (McKusick 1964, 1973:Plates 53 and 54) compares favorably with Allamakee Trailed, as defined by Boszhardt (1994), whose definition I adopt as the new standard. Pottery from Farley village (Gallagher 1990) appears to be Allamakee Trailed. The Farley site may mark the end of Ioway occupations in the La Crosse region. Some components in the Upper Iowa and Root river valleys regularly yield small items suggestive of trade with whites: glass and ceramic beads (never seed beads), brass and copper tubular beads, tinklers, coils, and such small iron items as knives, awls, files, and punches. An occasional iron ax, Jesuit rings, copper or brass bracelets (Figure 11.7), serpents, and large tubes are also found. It is in these late components, especially in burials, that exotic shell items such as barrel-shaped beads, large shell disks, and shell mask gorgets appear, suggesting that these goods were commonly circulated among Oneota groups in the protohistoric period. These items may be accompanied, with increasing frequency, by catlinite objects, including disk-bowl pipes, and tablets with animal and other representations.

Lower Lake Michigan Region

The Lower Lake Michigan region is not as well known as the Eastern Wisconsin region, but is important to the understanding of Oneota and its relation to the Fort Ancient tradition. Emerson and Brown (1992:80–90) suggest that there are two localized traditions (group continuities?) in northern Illinois: Langford and Fisher–Huber. They outline the evolution of these entities and note the late intrusion into the region by an eastern group referred to as Danner.

The Langford tradition probably dates from A.D. 1150 to 1450 (R. Jeske, personal communication). Langford sites are located primarily in the upper Illinois River valley north of Starved Rock and in the Middle Rock River valley between Rockford and Sterling-Rock Falls, as well as along the Fox, Des Plaines, and Du Page rivers (Jeske 1990:224). Langford sites probably represent an upland and small-valley adaptation to northern Illinois (Jeske 1989), often near forest–prairie boundaries. Villages were fairly substantial and composed of rectangular, semi-subterranean structures. Riverine exploitation, hunting of deer, and maize and squash horticulture provided the subsistence base. Jeske (1990) suggests that some bison and elk bone is present in the faunal assemblage. Two types of cemeteries are identified. The first, the accretional mound, is composed of a number of small burial mounds that form a larger mound through accretion. The second type is a flat cemetery that was covered with soil to form a platform for a second cemetery. Each formed a designated mortuary zone; social distinctions based on group affiliation may have been present. Pottery is similar to that of the Grand River phase of eastern Wisconsin, but is always tempered with mafic grit, probably gabbro. The characteristic vessel is a globular jar with an everted, sometimes collared rim. Most rims are undecorated, but some jars have tool impressions on the exterior of the lip. Lobed vessels (Langford Noded) are reported, and lug handles sometimes are present. The vessel surface is either cordmarked or smooth, and is decorated with trailed lines (sometimes bold) and punctates. Chevrons and nested chevrons on the shoulders are common. It is notable that end scrapers are not mentioned, but some bison bone is present. Sherds attributed to Langford-tradition origins have been reported from the Lake Shelbyville Reservoir on the Kaskaskia River, west to the Mississippi, north into southern Wisconsin, and east into northwestern Indiana.

The Fisher "phase" may begin as early as A.D. 1100 and probably did not persist beyond 1350. As it is further studied, the single phase designation will doubtless be refined and others defined. Components are found primarily in northeastern Illinois, with some sites in the lower Rock River to the west and as far east as the St. Joseph River. Late Fisher villages were fairly substantial; the houses may have been semi-subterranean. Both mound and nonmound burials apparently were made. Riverine exploitation, upland hunting, and horticulture were probably supplemented by seasonal bison hunting. Fisher pottery is shell tempered; the globular jars with everted rims are cordmarked and often decorated with punctated lips and curvilinear trailed designs on the shoulder. Typical artifacts include simple triangular arrowpoints, rectangular abraders, and scapula hoes.

The Huber phase probably evolved out of the Fisher, thus reference to Fisher–Huber. The Classic-horizon Huber phase was identifiable from about A.D. 1400 and persisted to no later than 1650 (Emerson and Brown 1992:87). Most Huber sites are on the Sag, Des Plaines, and Little Calumet rivers of northeastern Illinois and northwestern Indiana. Horticulture, broad-based exploitation of regional flora and fauna, combined with probable seasonal bison hunting provided the subsistence base. Huber pottery vessels are smooth-surfaced, shell-tempered globular jars with everted rims. The shoulder motifs of early Huber-phase pottery consist of vertical lines and punctations. Common Huber artifacts include humpbacked knives, triangular arrowpoints, a range of bone tools, bison-scapula hoes, rectangular abraders, catlinite disk-bowl pipes, and copper-wire serpents. Early Huber components offer evidence of strong southern ties in the form of marine shell, Southern Cult objects, and motifs and vessels from the Arkansas area. Some Huber components yield small European-derived items, suggesting at least indirect contact with whites. The Miamis are suggested as Huber-phase authors (Faulkner 1972; Herold et al. 1990), but are rejected by J. Brown (1990:159) and Hall (1995:27) in favor of the Winnebagos.

At this stage in our knowledge, the Langford and Fisher–Huber traditions seem to have enjoyed limited interaction with the rest of the Oneota world until late in Huber times. Although some relations with the Grand River phase of eastern Wisconsin might be drawn through pottery comparisons, the Grand River components are perhaps as much as two centuries earlier. Interactions with Late Mississippian groups to the south and east seem to have been rare. If cultural isolation is truly indicative of Winnebago evolution, these sites are fully as satisfactory in that respect as those in the Eastern Wisconsin region.

The Danner phase is derived from the late prehistoric through historic Fort Ancient complex. The pottery resembles, but is separable from, that of the Fort Ancient Madisonville phase (Griffin 1978). Most sites offer a mixed assemblage, but scapula hoes, end scrapers, and small triangular arrowpoints are always present and associated with a broad range of historic items. Danner subsistence appears to have been dominated by horticulture (maize, beans, even watermelon) and large mammals, including bison. The presence of many elements in addition to scapulae suggest that bison may have been killed and butchered near the Zimmerman site. Usually the only bison bone found on sites east of the

Mississippi are the scapulae used for tools. M. Brown (1975:72) suggests that the Illiniwek groups offer the "strongest possibility" for a tribal connection to the Danner phase in Illinois at this time. This possibility is strengthened by the identification of a Danner-phase Illini village in Clark County, Missouri (Grantham 1993), as the village visited by Marquette and Jolliet in 1673.

Central Des Moines Region

The Central Des Moines region in Iowa is the home of the Moingona phase (Gradwohl 1967). Since Gradwohl's initial report, much work has been done in the Red Rock Reservoir in the central Des Moines River valley, offering many data about this important manifestation (Benn 1989; DeVore 1990; Gradwohl 1974; Moffat et al. 1990; Osborn 1982). A group continuity has not been proposed, and even the definition of probably discontinuous phases is most likely premature in light of the numerous disparate dates (Moffat and Kolderhoff 1990). Thus Moingona remains a "phase" that is much too long. Many radiocarbon assays have been run for sites in the Red Rock Reservoir; they are fraught with problems, with assays that are regarded as far too early and much too late. Corrected dates for most of the dated Oneota sites in the central Des Moines valley tend to group at between A.D. 1175 and 1300. The sites range from small to fairly large. No formal cemeteries were located; two secondary interments in a single pit feature were apparently associated with the remains of a charnel structure (Gradwohl 1974). Human bone fragments are found in the village sites, a characteristic Oneota trait.

Subsistence depended heavily on horticulture: maize, beans, cucurbits, tobacco, little barley, chenopod, sunflower, and marsh elder. Deer remains dominate the faunal assemblage; elk and smaller mammals probably were taken locally; bison likely were hunted on seasonal expeditions to the west. Riverine resources and nuts and seeds were also collected. Pottery is consistently shell tempered; constricted-orifice jars with outflaring rims predominate. Loop and strap handles are common. Depending on the site, varying percentages of the vessels bear smoothed-over cordmarking on the exterior surface. The lips are plain, tool impressed on the lip-rim interior, or (more rarely) notched on the lip. Some have trailed motifs on the inside of the rim. The complex shoulder motifs are often embellished with punctations paralleling the trailed lines. Chevrons and vertical-line and oblique-line combinations predominate. Lithics in the Central Des Moines valley are locally derived, supplemented heavily with Burlington Chert and Warsaw Chert. Arrowpoints, end scrapers, knives, manos, grinding slabs, celts, abraders, and side scrapers are common. A few pendants and pipes have been found. No catlinite is reported. None of the components seems qualified for assignment as an exchange center.

Mississippi Alluvial Plain Region

The Mississippi Alluvial Plain region (Henning 1995) includes "Southeast Iowa" (Tiffany 1979a). The region is redefined to include over 25 Oneota sites on the Iowa side and several on the Illinois side (Conrad and Nolan 1991) of the Mississippi River between Quincy, Illinois, and Muscatine, Iowa. Sites either are on terraces or overlook them from bluff- or hilltops. A loosely defined group continuity is defined on the basis of pottery from five sites (Henning 1995).

Probably due to a combination of sample size and intensive site use over time combined with a century of cultivation, an attempt at site seriation was not entirely satisfactory (Henning 1995). A group continuity is proposed, however, suggesting that the Wever site, late in the Developmental horizon and dated at about A.D. 1300 to 1350, marks the beginning of Oneota occupation in the region, and that the end of those occupations is represented at the McKinney site. My ordering of other sites did not fully agree with the work done by Tiffany (1979a). On the basis of discussions with local collectors (Wapello, Iowa) of items from McKinney, Henning (1961:31) suggested that the site contained a historic component, but neither Tiffany's (1988) excavations nor work in 1995 by a team from the University of Illinois produced any historic material. Even if such artifacts were missed, the termination date for the group continuity is found at McKinney, about A.D. 1450 to 1500 on the basis of radiocarbon assays (Boszhardt et al. 1995).

The Wever terrace, with several village sites, has one separate cemetery area; there are probably others. Some burials found in the Wever village site may be associated with circular structures. Human bone seems indiscriminately scattered throughout the village, usually as fragments, but occasionally as burials or partial burials in trash pits. No burials on the Wever terrace have been formally excavated; thus we know nothing about grave inclusions. No house patterns are known on the alluvial plain; those on the Wever site were destroyed by deep plowing. In a few instances, the orientation of groups of storage pits suggests long ovoid structures. Subsistence patterns indicate strong reliance on riverine resources; hunting of upland animals, including deer and elk; seasonal expeditions for bison; intensive horticulture of maize, beans, squash, and sunflower; and collecting of local plants.

Pottery from Alluvial-Plain Oneota sites is generally shell-tempered jars with constricted orifices and flaring rims. Some large bowls are found as well. Linking between sites can be seen in the pottery; at least a low percentage of the pottery from every site bears evidence of smoothed-over cordmarking on the vessel body, a rare characteristic of pottery from most Oneota sites. Jars from the Wever site are directly comparable to Moingona-phase vessels. Some vessels suggest close relations with Bold Counselor groups to the east; a few Mississippian-derived vessels such as "Crable Plates" and high-necked bottles also occur rarely at Oneota sites in the alluvial plain. End scrapers abound; simple triangular arrowpoints, side scrapers, knives, drills, and gravers are regularly found. Grinding slabs and manos are numerous at some sites, as are sandstone and, occasionally, pumice abrading stones, flintknapping abraders, and paired shaft abraders. Other ground stone includes celts, adze blades, discoidals, paint palettes, and whetstones. Rare small copper objects include rolled tubular beads, Mississippian serpents or feathers, and circlets or "fringe clips."

Similarities between material from the Wever site and that from sites in the central Des Moines River valley suggest a genetic relationship. One working hypothesis is that the Wever terrace was occupied by Oneota groups that came directly from the central Des Moines valley. Radiocarbon assays suggest that this migration occurred about the time that the strength and influence of Mississippian groups centered in the Cahokia area and lower Illinois River valley were declining.

The Wever site is not considered an exchange center. Materials from the Kelley site (Tiffany 1979b) have been summarily analyzed (Henning 1995) and do suggest interaction with people of the Lake Winnebago phase, some Late Mississippian groups, and, perhaps, Bold Counselor–phase people as well. Eric Hollinger (personal communication) suggests exchange-center status for the McKinney site, noting the presence of a Madisonville-phase Fort Ancient rim sherd, a "birdman"-incised tablet, catlinite, Excello Chert (from Missouri), galena (eastern Iowa and Missouri), copper, Hixton silicified sandstone (Wisconsin), and Knife River Flint (North Dakota). The location of the Mississippi Alluvial Plain and the complexity of the remains recovered from other known sites suggest that they also may have functioned as exchange centers.

Bold Counselor Phase

Bold Counselor–phase sites (Santure et al. 1990) are tightly grouped in the central Illinois River valley, about 12 miles north or south of the mouth of the Spoon River. In addition, there is a Bold Counselor–complex component at the Sponemann site in the northern American Bottom (Jackson 1992). Bold Counselor sites may date from A.D. 1275 to 1425, but combine primarily Oneota Developmental horizon with late Middle Mississippian characteristics. The settlement pattern, except for the American Bottom component, is very restricted. Bold Counselor people were obviously contemporaneous and shared space with Crable-phase late Middle Mississippian groups (Conrad 1991:149–154). Judging from cuts and scratches on Bold Counselor skeletal remains, they were summarily dealt with by some of their neighbors. Houses are semi-subterranean and rectangular. Subsistence was strongly dependent on garden products such as maize, beans, squash, chenopodia, knotweed, and little barley, supplemented with local nuts and fruit. Deer, elk, beaver, turkey, aquatic turtles, fish, and waterfowl were also taken.

Tools include arrowpoints, knives, unifacial scrapers, a few end scrapers, drills, Mississippian sword/knives, paired arrowshaft abraders, sandstone abraders, celts, a three-quarter-groove ax, small pipes, a discoidal, polished spheres, plummets, game stones, anvils, and grinding slabs. Shell fish lures, fishhooks, deer-phalanx arrowpoints, bone beads, a hairpin, bird-bone tubes, a sickle, a bone graver, perforators, and possible tattooing needles were also recovered. The inventory is enhanced by the inclusion of grave offerings. Pottery is distinctively Bold Counselor, with jars and bowls found in about equal numbers. Jars are globular with high, angled rims and loop handles. Lip decoration is rare, but the shoulder area is regularly decorated with boldly defined horizontal, angular, or curvilinear elements bordered by rows of punctations. Bowls are large and usually have a notched lip. "Crable Plates" are common, and Mississippian bottles, a beaker, "hybrid" Oneota–Mississippian vessels, and other nonceramic specialized items speak of a close relation between Bold Counselor and Middle Mississippian groups. It is important to note that the distincive Bold Counselor jars and bowls, a few Crable plates, and one red-painted water bottle have been found at the Wever Oneota site in the Mississippi Alluvial Plain. These vessels suggest that Bold Counselor groups were in direct contact with Oneota people in southeast Iowa, thus affording them with Middle Mississippian-derived items or the patterns that were reproduced on their sites.

American Bottom Region

The Oneota tradition was never a significant factor in the American Bottom until after the decline and fall of the Mississippian presence there (Jackson 1992; Milner et al. 1984). Jackson discusses seven sites in the region just above the confluence of the Mississippi, Illinois, and Missouri rivers to a point about 36 miles due southeast, just north of the St. Clair–Monroe county line in western Illinois.

The Groves complex includes Oneota pottery from Cahokia's Powell Tract and Mound 51. The pottery is distinct from materials included in the Vulcan complex. Groves-complex pottery is characterized by shoulder decoration of trailed-line motifs, often the chevron, in conjunction with punctations or tool impressions used as borders.

The Vulcan complex, believed to postdate A.D. 1500, includes components at the Range, Booker T. Washington, and Stolle Quarry sites and is characterized by jars with broad and narrow trailed designs, strap handles, and interior lip-rim finger punctations. The Range site (Milner et al. 1984) is the best known of these sites. The pottery resembles Allamakee Trailed of the Orr phase of the La Crosse region.

For years, the Pere Marquette Lodge site, located just above the confluence of the Illinois and Mississippi rivers, constituted the only Oneota remains so close to Cahokia. Jackson (1992:385) suggests that its pottery is characteristic of the very late Classic horizon. Fragments of catlinite disk-bowl pipes found there serve to corroborate that interpretation.

Oneota occupations in the Cahokia region amounted to little more than sporadic intrusions or "influence" until almost the end of Mississippian domination. The Bold Counselor entradas that took place at that time appear to have been brief. Judging from the artifact descriptions, the Pere Marquette Lodge site was the last Oneota occupation in the American Bottom region.

Red Wing Region

The Red Wing region (Dobbs and Holley 1995; Gibbon 1991; Gibbon and Dobbs 1991; Rodell 1991; Wendt and Dobbs 1989) is located at the confluence of the Cannon, Trimbelle, and Vermillion rivers with the Mississippi River on the Wisconsin–Minnesota border. It is one of the most intriguing and confusing of Oneota or Oneota-related site complexes. Known historically since 1823, the 35-square-mile region was once characterized by over 2000 mounds (Winchell 1911). Some circular, conical, linear, and effigy mounds can probably be attributed to Woodland peoples, but two flat-topped mounds and some of the earthen embankments and/or fortifications are probably the result of Mississippian-inspired and/or Oneota activities. All the conical mounds tested professionally have yielded Oneota and/or Mississippian pottery. Many sites are known: the largest and principal ones are Bartron, Bryan, Silvernale, Energy Park, Adams, and Mero (or Diamond Bluff). They offer evidence for variable relations with Middle Mississippian, Oneota, Cambria, and, perhaps, Woodland groups. Of the village sites, Adams and Bartron are Oneota; the others are either Silvernale phase or dominated by Silvernale components.

The Silvernale phase is characterized by many Mississippian-derived traits, but does not appear to be the result of site–unit intrusions. Gibbon and Dobbs (1991:301) state that major Red Wing settlements may have begun as early as A.D. 1000 when "pure" Oneota occupation began at Bartron and Adams. The Silvernale-phase occupations may be bracketed between A.D. 1100 and 1300, but probably ended earlier. The well-developed Oneota complex is identified as "Blue Earth–like," but does not correlate precisely with sites in the Blue Earth region (Dobbs 1984; Gibbon 1983). The Silvernale phase is thus not derived directly from Blue Earth, nor does it resemble the equally old Emergent or early Developmental horizons defined for the Eastern Wisconsin region.

Red Wing architecture generally is restricted to visible mounds and embankments; at Bryan, a log palisade and semi-subterranean, rectangular house patterns were identified. Subsistence was based on horticulture, including maize, beans, and cucurbits. Riverine collecting and fishing, as well as upland hunting of deer and elk, were also important. Some bison elements indicate seasonal hunting expeditions. Dobbs and Holley's (1995) analysis of "Ramey Incised–like" and "Powell Plain–like" pottery suggests that none of the sherds are directly derived from Middle Mississippian sites, but are the result of imitation and reproduction of a limited range of Mississippian vessels by local potters. A local variety of Blue Earth–like Oneota pottery is found on the Adams and Bartron sites and is mixed with Silvernale-phase ceramics on the others. Cambria pottery is also found in Silvernale contexts. Considering the number of vessel fragments that are obviously Mississippian-inspired, very few other classes of items are probably derived directly from Mississippian sources. Two small "Southern Cult" macelike batons, a silver-colored "pulley" ear spool, a thunderbird shoulder design motif on a high-rim (Oneota?) jar, and the central axis of a shell columella are all privately owned and lack provenience. But some wall-trench structures, a marine-shell Longnosed God mask, and some well-made "copies" of Ramey Incised and Powell Plain jars suggest Mississippian "influence" and trade. Most arrowpoints are simple triangular; some side-notched specimens could be derived from the Plains just as well as from the central Mississippi valley. End scrapers are common; the remaining bone- and stone-tool complex resembles that from Oneota sites to the west rather than Mississippian sites to the south. Silvernale sites probably functioned as parts of "a prairie-oriented northern node in a Mississippian-centered extraction and magico-religious network" (Gibbon and Dobbs 1991:301), linking Initial Middle Missouri–tradition Cambria groups with Oneota and Mississippian. I refer to these "nodes" or "nodal points" as exchange centers.

Blue Earth Region

The Blue Earth region in southern Minnesota (Anfinson 1987; Dobbs 1984; Dobbs and Shane 1982; Gibbon 1983) encompasses the central Blue Earth River valley about 30 miles from its confluence with the Minnesota River. Two geographically separate localities are defined, each about 6 square miles (Dobbs 1984; Dobbs and Shane 1982). Intensive surface survey produced 31 sites in the Willow Creek locality and 33 sites in the Center Creek locality. The Blue Earth complex is casually referred to as a phase, but no definition has been presented. The region seems ripe for definition of a group continuity. Radiocarbon assays from the Vosburg site suggest occupation there from the Emergent into the Historic horizon. Judging from pottery vessel morphology and shoulder decoration, the principal villages, Humphrey and Vosburg, date in the Developmental horizon, about A.D. 1150 to 1350.

It is noteworthy that all sites are to the west of the Blue Earth River, and most larger sites are well away from the valley margin. No house outlines have been defined, nor have cemeteries been professionally excavated. Some burials appear to have been purposefully placed in the Vosburg and Humphrey sites; human bone is often found on the surface of village sites, suggesting either that burials in villages were plowed into or that the villagers followed the common Oneota practice of leaving human bone about in the village. There is no reported evidence for mound burial in the Blue Earth region.

The characteristic pottery is called Blue Earth Trailed and consists primarily of large jars with outflaring rims and a pair of strap or loop handles. Lip-rim decoration includes tool-impressed inner rim lips, some trailed-line motifs on the inner rim, and a few motifs on the outer rim. Shoulders bear rectilinear motifs, including chevrons, vertical lines, and chevrons filled with vertical lines. Curvilinear designs sometimes occur, occasionally as concentric circles below the handles. Tool impressions as embellishments to primary motifs such as the chevrons and grouped parallel lines are characteristic of the Developmental horizon. Celts, sandstone abraders, paint stones, and hammers are found. Arrowpoints and end scrapers are numerous; bifacial knives, side scrapers, and drills are also inventoried. A well-developed bone and antler complex includes scapula hoes, picks, and other implements; antler flakers and picks; bone awls, punches, and tubes; and bone or antler ornaments. Catlinite is rare at the Humphrey and Vosburg sites, but may be more common on other components.

Sheffield Site

The Sheffield site (Gibbon 1973; Henning n.d; Wilford et al. 1969) actually may be several small, closely grouped villages or campsites located on a low terrace adjoining the St. Croix River between Stillwater and Marine on St. Croix, Minnesota. The Sheffield Oneota components are in a very complex area. Some mounds identified as Woodland (Wilford et al. 1969) are closely associated with perhaps 20 small midden mounds, many of which may be Oneota. A single radiocarbon assay from Sheffield suggests a date of about A.D. 1300. One of the Oneota components excavated by Wilford (Gibbon 1973) produced no evidence for a cemetery and no house floors or outlines. The excavated burial mounds on the low terrace yielded no Oneota remains. Only scraps of human bone and a polished, complete male human mandible were recovered in the village excavations. The mandible is polished on the inner surface of the symphyseal area, suggesting that it was a trophy.

Small triangular arrowpoints dominate the chipped-stone-tool inventory, which includes end scrapers, bifacial knives, perforators, lunates, an ax, and a disk. Ground-stone items include a number of sandstone abraders and flaking abraders, hammerstones, a mano, a whetstone, a net sinker, a greenstone bar, sandstone disks, and a small flat sandstone tablet. Bone and antler tools include a bison- or an elk-scapula cleaver, two bison- or elk-scapula knives and a spatula, an elk-metatarsal flesher, a deer-metapodial beamer, fishhooks, awls, needles, shuttles, and bodkins. A copper arrowpoint, a flat "serpent" or "feather" ornament of sheet copper, and a shell disk are also recorded. Pottery was abundant; most was shell-tempered Oneota, but some grit-tempered sherds suggest prior Woodland occupancy. Most of the Oneota vessels are jars with outslanting, fairly high rims and opposing loop and strap handles. Most of the rims are decorated with tool impressions extending from the lip onto the interior of the rim. Vessel shoulders are often decorated with trailed lines; most are rectilinear designs embellished with tool impressions or punctations. A broad range of motifs was employed (Gibbon 1973:45), including chevrons and groups of vertical and oblique lines. Curvilinear motifs are rare, serving principally to embellish the rectilinear elements.

Gibbon (1973) suggests that Sheffield served as a summer base camp for hunting and exploiting the riverine resources. There is little evidence for horticulture. Sheffield-site antecedents and relationships are difficult to determine. Gibbon compares the pottery from the Blue Earth–region Vosburg and Humphrey sites with that from Sheffield, noting that only about 23 percent of the shoulder designs on Sheffield vessels are shared with those from the two Blue Earth sites and suggests that the motifs on Blue Earth vessels are more complex than those on Sheffield pottery. Impressions around the inner lip-rim surface, found on over 90 percent of the Sheffield vessels, occur much less frequently at Humphrey and Vosburg. It is possible that Sheffield ceramics will compare much more positively with pottery from one or more of the many Blue Earth components now identified in that region (Dobbs and Shane 1982), but not written up. Sheffield may fall fairly early in the Developmental horizon. No catlinite is mentioned, no Mississippian traits are recognized, and there is no evidence for exotic materials that would suggest extensive contact with other groups.

Northwest Iowa Region

The Northwest Iowa region (Fishel 1995; Harvey 1979; Henning 1970; Tiffany 1979b) encompasses the Little Sioux River valley, Lake Okoboji, the Big Sioux River valley from Sioux Falls to Sioux City, and the Missouri River valley between its confluence with the Big Sioux and the mouth of the Little Sioux. Oneota components are generally grouped in three undefined localities: along the lower Little Sioux River, around Iowa's "Great Lakes," and on the Big Sioux River east of Sioux Falls. The three localities suggest a definable group continuity in the lower Little Sioux, evidence for early historic components tied principally to the Ioway around the Lakes and the Dhegihan-speaking Omaha and others on the Blood Run site east of Sioux Falls. This line of thinking leaves the Bastian site, just north of Cherokee on the Little Sioux, as a fourth locality. It is physically, temporally, and culturally separate from the others. Oneota occupations in the Northwest Iowa region may have begun as early as A.D. 1250 and ended in the Historic horizon about 1700. I believe that more than one component is found on the earliest (Dixon) site, but most of the calibrated dates from that site suggest an occupation at about A.D. 1300 (Boszhardt et al. 1995). The two Correctionville-site dates (1300–1500) seem very late. The pottery is consistently comparable to that of the Developmental horizon.

The Dixon, Gothier, Anthon, and Correctionville sites in the lower Little Sioux valley are comparable in material culture and are geographically close; they probably comprise a group continuity and are defined as the Correctionville phase. Correctionville-phase villages are on first and second terraces; the Dixon and Correctionville sites are sometimes flooded. At Dixon, one partial house suggests heavy construction and a linear orientation (Harvey 1979). Human bone is found in storage features; one extended burial came from a Correctionville-site village. No cemeteries or mound burials have been found. Some human bone recovered in village sites is cut, scratched, and polished. One large skull fragment from the Dixon site has "birdman" and a four-point star incised on one surface. Artifact and subsistence data from Correctionville and Dixon suggest permanence, perhaps even year-round occupation at Dixon (Fishel 1995:91). Dixon faunal and floral analyses suggest intensive bison hunting away from the village; local deer, elk, and smaller mammals; use of riverine resources, including fish and shellfish; gardening of maize, beans, cucurbits, beans, sunflower, chenopodium, amaranth, and marsh elder; and collecting locally available seeds of little barley, wild rye, barnyard grass, American lotus, burweed, marsh elder, and fruits and nuts such as black nightshade, ground cherry, sumac, rose, blackberry or raspberry, grape, walnut, and hazelnut.

Many grinding slabs, manos, and grooved mauls offer evidence for fairly permanent occupation at Dixon and Correctionville. Hammerstones, discoidals, sandstone shaft abraders, flintknapping abraders, and catlinite (including small pipes and a few tablets) have been recovered. Arrowpoints and many end scrapers characterize the chipped-stone assemblage, but bifacial knives, choppers, drills, gravers, and a host of scrapers are recorded. Chert resource studies (Fishel 1995) suggest that flakable stone at Dixon was derived from local glacial deposits and from sources as far away as the Knife River in North Dakota; parts of South Dakota, Nebraska, and Kansas (Bijou Hills silicified sandstone [Porter 1962] or Ogallala Orthoquartzite [Church 1994]); the Republican River, Nebraska and Kansas (Smoky Hill, Flint Hills Green, and Florence); and Iowa (Pennsylvanian and Burlington cherts), suggesting that the site occupants traveled or traded widely. Fishel (1995) links the acquisition of flakable stone to seasonal hunts away from the village, especially in search of bison to the west. Ogalalla Orthoquartzite—which can be obtained in large working blanks, flakes well, and is a beautiful green (but will not hold a cutting edge)—seems especially popular in western Oneota (as well as in Mill Creek and Great Oasis) sites.

Correctionville-phase pottery is characteristically a jar with a strongly outflaring or outcurving rim. Bowls are often grit tempered and sometimes thickly coated with red ocher. Correctionville-phase jars are sometimes quite large, with low rims, flattened shoulders, and a sharply defined shoulder–lower body juncture. Most jars have two small strap or loop opposed handles. The lip is usually decorated with notches along the top or tool impressed from the lip onto the interior of the rim, occasionally with trailed motifs on the interior and tool impressions on the exterior. The shoulder is generally decorated with trailed lines: opposed diagonals, filled sequential triangles, narrow to very wide finger-trailed vertical lines, and chevrons. The motifs are often embellished with tool impressions and short trailed lines, sometimes by crosses, spirals, and circular depressions. The pottery generally conforms to the decorative modes of the Developmental horizon.

The Bastian locality (Harvey 1979; Henning 1970; Tiffany 1979b) is known from one site, the Bastian site, located just north of Cherokee at the confluence of Mill Creek with the Little Sioux River. On the basis of one radiocarbon assay, the site dates between A.D. 1425 and 1550 (Boszhardt et al. 1995). Although intensively surveyed and tested, the site is poorly known. No associated mounds, cemetery areas, or evidence of house outlines have been found. It is very important because it is geographically separated from the Correctionville locality, the artifacts from it suggest a later time of occupation, and it is the site from which the spectacular Stiles catlinite tablets (Bray 1963) were recovered (Figure 11.6a–b,d).

Bison-scapula hoes, arrowpoints, scrapers, and manos have been recovered. The pottery exhibits fairly high rims and broad strap handles. I once suggested (Henning 1970:153) that it probably evolved out of the Correctionville phase and looked more like Allamakee Trailed, but am less certain today. The 10 Stiles tablets were purchased by Nestor Stiles from a person who said they came from the Bastian site. Since many tablet fragments have since been recovered from the site, the plaques' derivation seems corroborated. The tablets are complete and partial slabs of catlinite ranging in size to 23.5 centimeters long and 19 centimeters wide. Bray (1963:17–32) illustrates the motifs on these plaques, which include "birdman," anthropomorphic figures, serpents, birds, water monsters, bison and other animals, heartlines, weeping eyes, lightning, talleys, feathers, and arrows. Some flat surfaces are devoid of decoration, suggesting that earlier motifs had been "erased" in preparation for others. The tablets' importance to their makers can only be surmised, but the motifs suggest traditional cult-ceremonial activities with roots well in the past that were shared by many North American groups. Bray (1963:Figure 24) illustrates a large catlinite tablet collected from the Oto that has a horse sketched on one side. It is covered with cuts and scratches, suggesting that it once served as a cutting board, perhaps for tobacco. Many of the Stiles tablets and others bear random cuts and scratches on their surfaces.

An Okoboji phase is proposed that includes the Lake Okoboji–Upper Little Sioux locality. All the sites (Harvey 1979; Henning 1970; Tiffany and Anderson 1993) offer material remains that closely resemble those from the late Orr phase in northeastern Iowa, suggesting that they represent movement of the Ioways from the Upper Iowa and Root river valleys to the west (Mott 1938; M. Wedel 1981). The Gillette Grove, Milford, and, possibly, Harriman sites are in the upper Little Sioux River valley. Gillette Grove once boasted 12 low mounds and a circular enclosed area of about 100 yards' diameter, with walls 16 feet wide and 2 feet high. The Harriman site had 12 low mounds, some of them visible in the 1950s. All yield quantities of European trade goods, mostly brass tubular beads, bangles, and tinklers, and glass beads. The Milford site has also yielded copper beads, a discoidal, a buckle, projectile points, a quill flattener, glass beads, silver Jesuit rings, a bead and an Apostle spoon fragment, plus such iron objects as projectile points, fishhooks, trade axes, gun barrels, powder cans, knives, a cross, and gun parts (Anderson 1994). Gunflints, lead shot, and a lead pendant have also been recovered from Milford. Surface collections from Gillette Grove offer materials comparable to those from Milford, along with some turquoise. Gun parts recovered from a field adjacent to the Gillette Grove site suggest a slightly later component.

Blood Run is probably the largest Oneota site on record (Harvey 1979; Henning 1970, 1982, 1993; M. Wedel 1981). Size estimates range from a "core area" of 600 acres to the inclusion of outlying related camp and village sites, amounting to about 1200 acres. Site units are found on both sides of Blood Run Creek and across the Big Sioux River on the South Dakota side, where it is called the Rock Island site. For our purposes, Blood Run will function as an inclusive name. The first written descriptions of the "core area" record 275 large conical mounds, one possible effigy mound, an earthen embankment enclosing about 15 acres, and a large number of circular and ovoid boulder outlines. Thomas (1891:38–39) noted that the boulder outlines outnumbered the mounds by about three to one, suggesting that he saw 150 to 800 outlines, depending upon how much of the site this statement included. Thomas estimated the outlines' diameter at about 30 feet, noting that most had a break perhaps 3 to 4 feet wide, opening toward the southeast, perhaps an entryway. The boulder circles presented an obstacle to cultivation and were removed. The site is notable for the number of pitted boulders found on the surface. One large Sioux Quartzite boulder with several hundred pecked and ground indentations (some still highly polished) is still in place; seven others were removed from the terrace surface and rolled down its sides.

Dating Blood Run is difficult. Radiocarbon assays have been calibrated (Boszhardt et al. 1995), and nine appear to bracket the components between A.D. 1500 and 1700. (I am pushing the calibrated age-range probabilities a bit to accommodate for the known and documented historic occupations.) Blood Run is historically documented (Robinson 1930; M. Wedel 1981) as the principal village of the Omaha tribe from the 1690s until no later than 1714 (O'Shea and Ludwickson 1992:17), when they were living on the Missouri near the mouth of the White River in South Dakota. The Poncas may still have been part of the Omaha tribe during the Blood Run occupation, but functioned separately from shortly after 1700. Historical accounts (Fletcher and La Flesche 1911; M. Wedel 1981) suggest that the Ioways, Otos, Arikaras, and, possibly, Cheyennes were periodic residents or visitors there as well. The archaeology of Blood Run reflects the varied cultural traditions of the occupants. Most of the mounds were built for burial, some with several separate interments, usually extended. All recorded mound contents suggest late interments: glass beads, brass and small iron objects, horse bones, even a dog skeleton wrapped in a hide are recorded (Harvey 1979; Pettigrew n.d.; Starr 1887, 1888). Many of these items probably arrived up to a century before the first French traders arrived at the site. Copper serpents and bracelets, paired sandstone shaft abraders, pottery, arrowpoints, shell beads, *Marginella* beads, conch columella beads, awls, and bone tubes have also been recovered from mounds. Human bone fragments, often bearing cuts and scratches, some articulated elements, and, occasionally, whole skeletons are reported in trash-pit fill. Human bone fragments are common on the surface.

Excavations at the village found mostly storage and trash features—fairly large, often bell-shaped pits, most of which were filled with refuse. Animal bone is common; articulated elements of bison, elk, and many smaller mammals are often present. Dog is common; butchered elements are found in the trash pits. Deer is comparatively rare. The complete skeleton of an adult cow bison was recovered from one storage feature. Even the caudal bones remained, suggesting that it had been killed on-site and stored in the pit without removing the hide. Fish and shellfish were taken from Blood Run Creek and the Big Sioux River. There is consistent evidence for horticulture: maize kernels, beans, and cucurbits are regularly found.

A broad range of stone tools is found at Blood Run, including simple triangular arrowpoints, small end scrapers, bifacial knives, perforators, drills, and bifacial choppers. Ground stone includes a large number of grinding slabs, manos, and grooved mauls, as well as celts, discoidals, sandstone arrowshaft abraders, sandstone and "clinker" abraders, and flat paint palettes. A few full-grooved, long ground-stone axes have been recovered that elsewhere would be relegated to an Archaic context, but are found in sufficient numbers on the surface to suggest Oneota authorship. The many pipes are made of a range of materials, chiefly pipestone and catlinite. Simple elbow, projecting-prow, disk-bowl, and, occasionally, effigy pipes are found. Catlinite is common, usually as small, cut and polished fragments, but occasionally as pipe blanks, preforms, beads, and fragments of tablets. Fragmentary and complete tablets, often made of catlinite, carry a host of motifs, including bison, "birdman," anthropomorphic forms, small animals, serpents, and birds with lightning, forked eyes, feathers, and other embellishments. Catlinite, if properly identified visually (Gundersen 1993), may have come from the quarries near Pipestone, Minnesota, although other nearby sources may have been exploited. Most of the stone used is from glacial outwash, supplemented with quantities of Ogalalla Orthoquartzite (Church 1994), probably from near Chamberlain, South Dakota. This greenish material is commonly shaped into large chopping tools and bifacial knives. A full range of bone and antler tools comparable to Plains Village remains has been recovered from Blood Run. Bison-scapula digging tools abound. Picks, digging tools, "drifts," flaking tools, and ornaments processed from steamed and bent antler are common.

Pottery from Blood Run has been analyzed (Henning 1992), corroborating ethnographic accounts of multiple occupations at the site. Most of the rims suggest small, dark-surfaced Oneota-like jars that are characteristically grit tempered, associated with some shell-tempered Allamakee Trailed–like jars that probably document the Ioway presence on the site. The only restorable vessel is morphologically similar to a generalized Allamakee Trailed jar, with its notched lip and paired handles set below the lip, but is sand and limestone tempered and its exterior body is simple stamped, suggestive of an Arikara presence. This vessel suggests an amalgam of Arikara, Ioway, and, perhaps, Omaha pottery-making traditions and exemplifies the eclectic character of the site.

Blood Run was undoubtedly an exchange center of considerable importance from A.D. 1500 until shortly after 1700. We know from ethnographic accounts (Fletcher and La Flesche 1911) that Dhegihan and Chiwere Siouan–speaking groups met with Caddoan speakers in this location. The site must have been a seasonal rendezvous comparable to those later described for the Cree in the Saskatchewan River valley (Meyer and Thistle 1995). No guns, gun parts, or gunflints are reported, suggesting that occupation ended before guns were regularly distributed locally.

Chariton River Region

The Chariton River region, in Missouri, is the location of the Chariton River group continuity (Henning 1970), which began about A.D. 1350 at the Guthrey Oneota village and ended with the historic Missouri occupations at the Gumbo

Point site, occupied to about 1777. The largest and best known of the eight sites that compose the group continuity is Utz, probably occupied by the Missouris from first contact by Europeans until about 1725. The region is not large; all sites are grouped around the confluences of the Chariton and Grand rivers with the Missouri. The group continuity was defined on the basis of a ceramic continuity based on changes in line width and finishing techniques (wider and well-finished lines, employing smoothing and polishing for the early, to narrow and poorly finished line decorations in the later periods). Most Oneota research in this region has been concentrated on the Utz site (Berry and Chapman 1942; Betancourt 1965; Bray 1963, 1991; Chapman 1946, 1952, 1959, 1980; Chapman et al. 1985; Henning 1970). It is documented as a historic Missouri Indian site and was one of the first sites used to document the relation between some Oneota-culture sites and the Chiwere Siouan speakers (Griffin 1937). The Old Fort, located near Utz, is an earthen enclosure that was probably built by Oneota occupants of that village. Although not defined as part of the regional group continuity, the Little Osage Plattner village site (23SA3) played an important part in regional history.

Oneota occupation in the Chariton River region apparently began at Guthrey in the late Developmental horizon. I am hard-pressed to discern a point of origin for the Guthrey-site materials. The pottery is different from vessels found on any site in the Mississippi Alluvial Plain and from the early forms at Leary, the geographically closest points of derivation. Radiocarbon assays (Boszhardt et al. 1995) suggest occupations around A.D. 1300 (Henning 1970). No mounds or houses are associated with Guthrey, and no burials were found in the excavations. Pottery consists entirely of jars with fairly high outflaring rims, sometimes with a pair of opposed handles attached at or beneath the lip. Most of them have a plain lip; many bear tool impressions on the interior of the rim; some have a notched lip; a few have tool impressions on the exterior of the rim. Shoulders are decorated with parallel-line and chevron combinations, paralleled by punctations and tool impressions. Vessels are well formed and finished, with motifs and embellishments consistent with the Developmental horizon. Chipped-stone tools often employed excellent white chert, possibly from the Crescent Hills quarries along the Mississippi River. Arrowpoints are usually simple triangular, but small-corner notched and side-notched forms were also found. Most chipped-stone tools show exemplary control of flaking techniques, perhaps exhibiting a combination of excellent, probably heat-treated, raw material and considerable expertise. Blade-tool technology was employed in preparing end scrapers, drills, perforators, spokeshaves, gravers, and burins. Manos, a broken celt, a grinding slab, a sandstone mortar fragment, a sandstone shaft abrader, sandstone sharpening and abrading stones, a calcite bead fragment, and some ground hematite pieces were also recovered by excavation at Guthrey. Bone and antler tools include bison-scapula hoes and hoe fragments, deer-mandible sickles, perforated deer phalanges, awls, an antler socketed projectile point, and an antler drift. A cut and polished raccoon mandible, modified dog and human teeth, and shells with notched edges are part of the site inventory. Bison and deer bone predominate; the former includes fragments other than scapulae. Elk, beaver, raccoon, otter, wolf, dog, and muskrat were identified. Fish, turtle, and mollusks suggest intensive use of riverine resources, and charred maize cobs and kernels suggest gardening.

Pottery suggests that the Dowell site (Henning 1970) is later than Guthrey, possibly contemporaneous with components at Utz. Since no historic remains were found, the component is regarded as prehistoric, dating perhaps about A.D. 1450. There was no evidence of house patterns and no human remains. Pottery is less well finished and exhibits narrower lines than that from Guthrey, but decorated shoulder sherds suggest the use of the chevron motif; the parallel lines are bordered with rows of punctations or tool impressions. The site yielded an almost equal number of triangular arrowpoints and end scrapers, found with bifacial knives and gravers. Ground-stone tools include a fragment of a granite grinding slab, sandstone smoothing stones, a sandstone shaft abrader, and ground hematite. A fragment of a bison-scapula hoe and deer-bone fragments were also recovered.

No historic remains have been recovered from the McRoberts site, suggesting that it could be important to our understanding of the Chariton River region group continuity and certainly to ongoing study of the Utz site. There are other Oneota sites in the region for which there are few data.

The Utz site, built on the rolling upland bluffs overlooking the Missouri River valley, has been known for generations (Fowke 1910). Most of the site, which encompasses about 300 acres, has been under cultivation for over a century. It is a well-documented Missouri Indian village and may have been occupied by ancestral Missouri from the time that Oneota people settled in the region. The site is characterized by intensive occupation: storage pits were dug one into another; burials were intruded into by pits; and pits were intruded into by burials and small cemeteries. Utz probably contains much of the entire Oneota sequence in the region to about 1727, but isolating and defining components seems impossible at this time. Utz was obviously an important exchange center through the Classic and into the early Historic horizon, although there is little to no evidence suggesting interaction with the Lake Winnebago, Bold Counselor, Langford, or Fisher phases, all of which were surely contemporaries. The interactions evident at Utz are the shared characteristics of the late Developmental, Classic, and early Historic horizons seen in the Blue Earth, Northwest Iowa, La Crosse, and Mississippi Alluvial Plain regions, and the Leary and Blood Run sites.

Long-term excavation programs carried out at Utz are reported in detail by Bray (1991:34–47). Bray describes floor plans of seven houses; they range from elliptical (up to about 50 feet long and 25 feet wide) to almost square (up to 23 to 26 feet). Two houses date to the Historic horizon, and three are assigned to the Classic horizon (Hollinger 1995); the others could not be assigned. No mounds are known to have been built; small cemeteries and individual (usually extended) burials are found in the village. The Old Fort (Leaf 1976; Wood 1973), a complex earthen enclosure nearby, was probably built by Utz occupants. The Utz and Old Fort sites are adequately discussed (Bray 1991; Wood et al. 1995), making it redundant to offer a list of material-culture characteristics here. Some of the pottery may be distinctive to this region (Yelton 1991), but the subtleties of form have not been well correlated with changes through time. Bray (1991:48–68) lists a series of descriptive types for the site. It is surprising that there is no mention of Ogalalla Orthoquartzite at Utz, especially since it is so common in sites in northwestern Iowa. A full range of cultigens is identified, including watermelon seeds. Watermelon was introduced into Florida as early as 1576 (Bray 1963:129) and may have reached the Prairie Peninsula by the late seventeenth century. It could have come to Utz either through the Mississippi valley or via southwestern origins. It is important to note that the site remains suggest permanence of occupation, probably year-round, and intensive bison hunting.

The Utz site did not function only in Oneota–Oneota interactions; there was contact with other cultural traditions: Caddoan (Spiro phase), Late Mississippian (lower St. Francis River or Memphis area), Puebloan Black on White (Southwest, probably before European contact), and Extended Coalescent (Middle Missouri River) pottery from Utz is documented. Three *Anculosa* beads (probably from the Ohio or Tennessee river valley), a marine whelk labret, and some cowrie, conch, whelk, and marine periwinkle shells from the Gulf coast were recovered. Other items indicative of trade are pieces of catlinite, some with engraved figures sketched on them (Betancourt 1965; Bray 1963), Alibates Agatized Dolomite (from the Canadian River near Amarillo, Texas), two turquoise beads (Southwest), galena (Missouri), Knife River Flint (western North Dakota), copper nuggets (northern Michigan and Wisconsin) and novaculite are noted. Obviously, the breadth of aboriginal trade was established in the early contact period. Late Mississippian sherds suggest that Utz was an intermediate source for the large catlinite disk-bowl pipes recovered from the Late Mississippian Campbell and McCoy villages in southeastern Missouri (O'Brien 1994:Plate 1, 239, 300). Historic items suggest that only very early contacts with Europeans are represented at Utz. Small brass, copper, and iron items; a few bells; and Jesuit rings were recovered. Gun parts are absent. Judging from early historic accounts, the Missouris were already much reduced in number, probably by disease, when first visited by whites, leaving them more vulnerable

to Osage domination than they would have been a century earlier. Further deci-
mated, they left Utz and moved to the Gumbo Point site.

Gumbo Point, a late Missouri Indian village, was probably occupied from
A.D. 1727 to 1789 (Chapman 1959). Two long rectangular structures up to 30 feet
long and 10 feet wide were excavated. Some prehistoric material culture persists
in the form of small shell-tempered jars, chipped triangular arrowpoints, a few
scrapers, a shell spoon, and some bone and antler items. Most artifacts are European trade goods, including glass beads, metal kettle fragments, glass bottles,
iron knives, and gunflints. A cemetery may have been associated with the
Gumbo Point site (O'Brien and Hart 1972). After abandoning Gumbo Point,
some Missouris went to live with the Osages; others joined the Otos on the lower
Platte River (Anonymous 1974:37–38).

The Little Osage village on the Missouri River, the Plattner site, was established about 1727 and abandoned around 1777, principally because of attacks
by the Sauks and Foxes. Plattner may have been associated with earth embankments, pits, and a large mound. Chapman (1959:6–8) offers a number of early
accounts about the site, suggesting that it must have had a number of prominent
surface features and was a notable collecting spot for "relics." Plattner differs
significantly from Gumbo Point in the number of gun parts (hundreds of gun
barrels are reported in early historic accounts), axes, hoes, and iron kettles, associated with bones of buffalo, deer, and turkey (Chapman 1959). Excavations
by a team from the University of Missouri yielded a few items linked to possible
Osage prehistoric material culture, including a few triangular chipped-stone arrowpoints, end scrapers, large ovoid scrapers, bifacial knives, and abrading
stones. A few pieces of pottery, about one-third shell tempered, were found;
some appear to have been impressed with trade cloth. The remainder of the materials are principally derived from trade with whites.

The movement of the Little Osages into Plattner, near the Missouri Indians
at Gumbo Point, was anything but altruistic. The Osages apparently took over
the Missouri-controlled exchange center that had flourished on the lower Missouri River from about A.D. 1300. Their trade with Europeans was obviously
intensive and profitable, if not always legal (Nasatir 1929). The Little Osages
arrived just after Bourgmont departed for France in 1725, armed with guns and
well connected with European traders (Henning 1993). The story of "Ducharme's
invasion" up the Missouri River in the winter of 1772/1773, during Spanish tenure in the area (Nasatir 1929), is an interesting account of trade relations between whites and the Osages and Missouris at this time, in which we are afforded an inventory of the items received by Ducharme over a winter's trade.
Most, by far, were traded to him by the Osages. About 1777, the Little Osages
probably moved to the Hayes, or Coal Pit, site on the Little Osage River, where
they lived near the Big Osages.

Upper Osage River Locality

All Osage sites yield large quantities of trade goods, including guns and gun-related equipment (Chapman 1946, 1952, 1959, 1974). The three major Osage sites in the Upper Osage River locality are Brown, Carrington, and Hayes (or Coal Pit), all in a tightly conscribed locale on the headwaters of the Osage River in Vernon County, Missouri. The Brown and Carrington sites are well-documented Big Osage villages; Hayes is the Little Osage village occupied after that group left the Plattner site on the Missouri River around 1777.

Osage history offers an excellent example of tribal fissioning and restructuring. At the time of first contact by Europeans (DuTisné visited a Big Osage village in Vernon County in 1719), there were two distinct bands: the Big and Little Osages. Just before DuTisné's visit, the Little Osages moved to central Missouri to live near the Missouris at the Plattner site, where they remained until about 1777 (Chapman 1959:6). Then, because of increasing pressure from the Sauks and Foxes and others, they moved to the Hayes site on the Little Osage River. They lived near the Big Osages, but in separate villages. Between 1794 and 1803, the Big Osages were twice subdivided, due in part to internal political problems, and in part to pressures from other Indians. Just before 1808, there was one Big Osage village on the upper Osage and two on the upper Arkansas. Although fissioning was probably accelerated by European pressure, it is the pattern that is important to understanding Oneota site placement and content across the Prairie Peninsula. The potential for splitting, and then subsequent rejoining, was greatest for those who spoke the same or nearly the same dialect, but at times of stress tribal members with different dialects joined, contributing to the archaeological confusion. The Osage data document this pattern very well.

Considering the extent to which Osage sites have been subjected to archaeological investigations, very few burials can be identified as Osage. They may have practiced mound burial (Chapman 1959), for no cemeteries have been located near Osage villages. The Osages built rectangular houses about 15 feet wide and up to 100 feet long, with center poles supporting a ridgepole to which were attached poles extending from the walls; the frame was covered with overlapping rush mats. Doors were in the long walls of the structure, basin-shaped fire pits were along the center line of the house, and cache pits were in other parts of the floor (Chapman and Chapman 1964:99–100; Chapman et al. 1985).

All four Osage sites were extensively tested (Chapman et al. 1985), but only two yielded significant Native pottery and stone tools: Brown and Plattner. The Big Osage Brown site contains shell-tempered pottery that suggests traditional elements, survivals, or direct relations with the Oneota tradition. The incised-line decorations on the pottery were probably applied using iron knives (Henning 1970:34–35). Both Plattner and Brown (Little and Big Osage sites) contain a large number of European trade goods, together with stone and bone tools.

An item characteristic of Osage sites is a mold made of stone, apparently used to cast small objects of silver and pewter.

St. Joseph Locality

A Fanning phase is proposed that would include the King Hill site, on the east side of the Missouri in St. Joseph, Missouri, and the Fanning site, about 3 miles west, across the river in Kansas. Artifacts from these sites are very similar; they are tentatively assigned to the Kansa tribe prior to 1714. The Doniphan site, about 15 miles southwest of King Hill, is probably the Kansa village that Bourgmont visited in 1724. The three sites may constitute a group continuity, based on historic documents and the few Oneota traits that appear to have been retained at Doniphan.

The Fanning site is in northeastern Kansas on a narrow ridge above Wolf Creek. It is tentatively assigned to a Kansa occupation before about A.D. 1700 (W. Wedel 1959:131–171). The site probably covers less than 10 acres. The one dwelling excavated at Fanning is a circular earthlodge. No cemetery was found, no burials were found in the village, and there was no evidence for mounds. The shell-tempered pottery is characteristic of generalized Oneota jar forms. Much of it is hard, well made, and plain, decorated with simple trailed or incised lines and punctates on the lip (Fanning Plain). Fanning Trailed also is decorated on the lip, but has trailed motifs on the shoulder that include chevrons, oblique and vertical groups of parallel lines, and panels filled with punctations. Most jars have two opposed strap or loop handles, often attached below the lip.

A few sherds from Fanning are identified as characteristic of Lower Loup sites in eastern Nebraska. Two shell-tempered rim sherds would be considered Lower Loup except for the uncharacteristic temper. These pieces suggest contact with the Pawnees, a relation borne out by early historic accounts. Furthermore, Grange (1968) records several Oneota sherds from Lower Loup components, including the Barcal, Wright, Burkett, Phil Cuba, Ashland (Occupation C), and Gray sites. None of these sites is historically documented as Pawnee, but the association is clear on the basis of pottery elements, regional association, and application of the direct historical approach. The few shell-tempered rim sherds from Lower Loup sites compare favorably with those from Fanning and King Hill, although they are not out of the range of possibility for derivation from Leary or even some Correctionville-related components.

The artifacts from Fanning compare very closely with those from King Hill. Triangular arrowpoints, many end scrapers, side scrapers, and other chipped-stone tools are generally made of blue-gray, sometimes banded, chert. The ground-stone inventory includes grinding slabs, manos, a celt, fragments of a paired sandstone shaft abrader, sandstone sharpening or flintknapping tools, clinker or pumice abraders, pitted stones, and pounding stones. A few pieces of worked catlinite, including fragments of three pipes and a pipe blank, were also recovered. Bison-scapula hoes and hoe fragments are common. A bison-scapula knife or scraper, shaft straighteners made of bison rib, a slotted knife handle (probably for insertion of a metal blade), needle fragments and awls, bone tubes, socketed deer-antler-tine projectile points, and an antler hammer were also recovered. Historic items included a few iron knife blades and iron fragments; small brass objects, including coils, cones, tubes, and circlets or "fringe clips"; and two blue glass beads.

King Hill is on a hilltop in southern St. Joseph, Missouri, overlooking the Missouri River bottomland to the west. Excavations under the author's direction explored several pits and a deep midden (Raish 1979; Ruppert 1979; Shippee 1967). A size estimate is impossible, but it is doubtful that King Hill was larger than Fanning. A few burials were in the village, but no cemetery has been found. Burial in mounds is not known. On the basis of his faunal study, Ruppert (1979a) suggests that the site was occupied continuously for perhaps less than 25 years. Faunal remains suggest intensive hunting and two annual bison hunts. Bison was the major meat source; deer and dog were also important. Maize is principally Eastern eight-row, with some North American Pop and Mexican Pyramidal Dent or Conical Dent (Blake and Cutler n.d.). Beans, squash, bottle gourd, watermelon seeds, and one peach pit of the type introduced by the Spanish into the Southwest have also been recovered. Blake and Cutler also identified hazelnut, hickory, black walnut, papaw, wild plum, wild grape, blackberry or raspberry, wild sunflower, and acorn.

King Hill pottery (Raish 1979:92) is very similar to that from Fanning, and both samples are distinct from those from other Oneota contexts. A few Lower Loup sherds were present at King Hill. Stone- and bone-tool industries are similar to the list from Fanning and consistent with horticulture and hunting. A few catlinite objects were recovered, and historic trade goods consist of small iron and brass objects comparable to those from Fanning and some glass beads. One Native-made gunflint of local material was recovered from the surface (J. D. Feagins, personal communication), but no gun parts have been found.

King Hill is not a well-documented Kansa site. Bourgmont traveled through the region in 1714 and again in 1724, when he probably visited the Kansa village at Doniphan, but he noted no Kansa villages on the east bank of the Missouri River on either trip. For this reason, one leans toward a pre-1714 date for this putative Kansa site.

Fanning and King Hill are consistently similar and contrast strongly with other nearby Oneota sites (Raish 1979). Judging from correspondence in traditional material culture, similarities in the quality of European trade items found, and the concentrated, rather brief period of time occupied, a Fanning phase including both sites is proposed.

The Doniphan site seems to be a well-documented principal village of the Kansas, probably occupied when they were visited by Bourgmont in 1724 (W. Wedel 1959:100). Stone-covered graves, some of which included European trade goods, were interpreted by Wedel as eighteenth-century Kansas burials. Two houses, identified with the Nebraska phase, probably predate the burials. Fourteen cache or trash pits, most of which yielded some European trade items, did not afford Wedel the desired link between the material culture of the historic Kansas and their protohistoric and prehistoric past. It was a generalized lot, characterized by metal and glass trade items, late-style socketed and grooved club heads, crude shell-tempered pottery, some pieces of protohistoric Lower Loup pottery (probably from eastern Nebraska), and some catlinite. If this material represents the Kansa of about 1724, it suggests the almost total replacement of traditional material culture with Euro-American trade culture and may suggest a significantly smaller population and a less robust culture than is indicated at Fanning and King Hill.

Leary Site

The Leary site, located near the confluence of the Big Nemaha and Missouri rivers in extreme southeastern Nebraska, is in many respects similar to Utz, although it differs in being on low terraces rather than in the uplands. Recent work in southeastern Nebraska has yielded only limited evidence for other Oneota material near Leary (Trisha Nelson, personal communication). Leary covers at least 120 acres. A group of mounds on the summit of a nearby ridge may be associated. A rectangular earthlodge and many cache pits were excavated in the 1930s (Hill and Wedel 1936), yielding a large pottery collection that includes jars that closely resemble two different types: Correctionville Trailed and Allamakee Trailed (Henning 1961). The status of the earthlodge excavated at Leary is equivocal—it may be either Nebraska phase or Oneota. Since the time Leary was excavated, many sites have offered data suggestive of Central Plains–Oneota interaction. In the 1970s, I went through Hill and Wedel's pottery sample from Leary and felt certain I could separate vessels that resembled the two pottery types. Both Mildred and Waldo Wedel kindly suggested that I was mistaken, and perhaps I was, but I still do not think so today. Hill and Wedel illustrate shoulder decorations that are comparable to those of the Classic horizon, but the high percentage of notched lips suggests later placement. Correctionville Trailed–like jar rims were present in a pit excavated later by Shippee (Henning 1970:153), with two radiocarbon dates indicating its age as between A.D. 1200 and 1400 (Boszhardt et al. 1995). These dates suggest that Leary is an early Oneota settlement that may have been occupied for several centuries. The Alla-makee Trailed–like rim sherds suggest that more than one component is present at Leary and that the occupations probably extended into the late Classic hori-zon. The nonpottery-artifact assemblage is comparable to those at other western Oneota sites. There are many grinding slabs and manos, suggesting intensive food processing and fairly permanent residence. Much catlinite, including a tab-let fragment, is reported. The one piece of copper from Leary may be native cop-per, for no other possible Euro-American trade items were found in excavations. A few glass beads have been collected from the surface. Leary appears to date to a time near the end of Gibbon's (1974) period of Mississippianization, about the time the Red Wing exchange center was closing, and at the beginning of the Classic horizon. This probably was the period for development of new large ex-change centers. I believe that Leary and Utz were occupied at about the same time, but that Utz survived into historic times. Leary probably functioned as an exchange center, providing Oneota access to the Central Plains. Leary cannot be assigned to any known historic tribe.

White Rock Phase

Logan (1995) has undertaken an intensive reanalysis of the White Rock–phase material and believes that it represents a late prehistoric migration of Oneota people from the lower Missouri River valley about A.D. 1300 to 1450. White Rock sites are identified in three localities: the Harlan County Lake in south-central Nebraska, and the Waconda and Lovewell reservoirs in north-central Kansas. The complex has always been identified in some way with Oneota remains far-ther to the east, but with qualifications generally involving a low incidence of simple stamping and the almost exclusive use of grit temper in pottery mak-ing. These concerns were expressed long before many collections of Oneota pot-tery were closely examined in search of temper other than shell—which is often there if one looks for it. We now know that significant collections of pottery readily accepted as Oneota have high percentages of grit, limestone, and other temper. For instance, a high percentage of Oneota pottery from the Door Pen-insula and the historic Blood Run site is not shell tempered. It is also notable that recent analyses of White Rock–phase pottery from the White Rock site found that nearly half (42 percent) is exclusively shell tempered. So if the ques-tion of temper and a few simple stamped sherds (also present at Blood Run) are set aside, White Rock settlement and subsistence patterns and the remainder of material culture are very similar to western Oneota assemblages.

The pottery, defined as Walnut Decorated lip (Rusco 1960), consists primar-ily of globular jars with high, slightly flared rims, rounded shoulders, generally smoothed surfaces, a low frequency with simple stamping, and a few with cord-marked surfaces. The shoulder usually is decorated with trailed lines forming oblique sets of parallel lines or chevrons, occasionally accompanied by rows or nests of punctates (Logan 1995). Pottery sample sizes from White Rock sites are small, making generalizations about eastern-derived horizon styles tenuous at best. Bone and stone tools suggest an orientation toward bison hunting and processing with many end scrapers and some grooved mauls. Other faunal remains include deer, canids, rabbits, birds, turtles, and mussels. Gardening is indicated by charred maize and scapula hoes.

Logan (1995) suggests that a group of Oneota-tradition people settled fairly permanently here around A.D. 1300, about the time that Central Plains–tradition groups abandoned the region. Trade and other social contact was carried on with groups of the Northwestern Plains and Plateau regions. Some catlinite suggests contacts with groups to the north and east. According to Logan, 49 percent of the chipped stone recovered in recent excavations by Fishel at the Dixon site may be derived from central Kansas and Nebraska raw materials. Dixon-site occupants were probably contemporaries of the people of the White Rock phase.

Mille Lacs Locality

The Mille Lacs locality in central Minnesota is discussed by Birk and Johnson (1992), who define a Bradbury phase. The Bradbury phase probably evolved from Wilford's (1941:237) Kathio focus, and constitutes the material culture of the well-documented Mdewakanton Dakota (Birk and Johnson 1992:211–219). In the early eighteenth century, this group lived near the outlet of Rum River into Mille Lacs Lake and Lakes Onamia and Ogechie. Possibly as early as 1720, the Mdewakanton left the shores of Mille Lacs for villages in southern Minnesota to avoid direct conflict with the Ojibwa and to establish more continual and favorable trade contacts with Europeans.

The Bradbury phase is of particular interest because it offers solid evidence for French trade, but that trade apparently had little impact on Mdewakanton traditional material culture. Houses were built along the lakeshore. A rectangular summer structure varying from 20 to 40 feet long was built on the shoreline. Winter structures are rectangular and semi-subterranean, with an entry ramp, a central fire pit, and a deep ash pit. The most common features other than the houses and post molds are shallow, circular, basin-shaped pits, most of which are probably wild-rice threshing pits. Large mammals, principally bison, and wild rice supplemented by smaller mammals, turtles, fish, waterfowl, and local plants provided subsistence. Tobacco may have been the only domesticated crop. The Mdewakanton traveled widely in the course of hunting and gathering; seasonal communal hunting parties often left the village for long periods of time.

According to ethnographic accounts, bison were hunted to the south and west of the villages.

The bone- and stone-tool assemblages closely resemble those of the Oneota of northern Iowa. Small triangular arrowpoints, end scrapers, bifacial knives, paired arrowshaft abraders, milling stones, celts, and pipestone elbow pipes are found. The few bone artifacts include deer-ulna awls, bird-bone whistles, barbed points, and awls, but only one bison-scapula hoe. The absence of hoes should not be a surprise if the only cultivated crop was tobacco. Pottery is best described as Oneota-like and is referred to by Ready (1979) as the Ogechie series. Ready suggests that some Ogechie pottery resembles Allamakee Trailed, but some vessels are more crude and not decorated. This pottery has caused some confusion among Minnesota archaeologists (Gibbon 1995:184) and may reflect Oneota influence (from the Ioway?) on the local Sandy Lake ware.

Historical accounts place the Ioway in the southern Minnesota Blue Earth region in the early eighteenth century, when LeSueur encouraged them to settle near his Fort Vert, because the Ioway grew maize, a commodity desired by the French. The Mdewakanton apparently did not grow maize, but were also eager to trade with the French. The Ioway and Mdewakanton probably communicated regularly before LeSueur arrived, but the French presence in Minnesota may have stimulated additional exchanges between those groups and other tribes as well. By 1720, Fort Vert had been abandoned for nearly two decades, but other French traders had established themselves well to the south of the Mille Lacs villages. By this time, the Mdewakanton had surely removed their permanent villages (Birk and Johnson 1992:216–219), and the Ioway had settled in two villages in and near Council Bluffs (M. Wedel 1988).

Northwest Periphery

Gibbon (1995) discusses this intriguing land of marginal Oneota "influence" and summarizes succinctly much of my own reaction to reports and materials from the northwest periphery of the Prairie Peninsula. There is a definitely Oneota "feel" to the adaptive measures at the Shea site (Michlovic and Schneider 1993), for instance, but it is attenuated. This small fortified-village site in southeastern North Dakota, dating to about A.D. 1450, offers evidence for bison hunting, maize remains, a scapula hoe, simple triangular arrowpoints, scrapers, and catlinite pipe fragments. The pottery is a mixed bag, with Sandy Lake and Owego wares dominant and four Oneota-related vessels represented. The Owego ware vessels bear some Oneota-like motifs on the shoulders. Gibbon suggests, citing Flynn (1993), that the Lockport site also has that elusive Oneota "feel." Lockport is on the east bank of the Red River north of Winnipeg, Manitoba, and has yielded maize kernels, scapula hoes, deep storage pits, and evidence for dependence on fish and bison. Occupation by a non-Oneota but Oneota-influenced group that moved into the area and interacted with its local inhabitants is suggested. These villages, others more or less like them, and the fragments of Oneota-like pottery that are found across the Plains periphery can probably be attributed to the movement of people out of Minnesota's Prairie Lake, Central Deciduous Lakes, and Central Coniferous Lakes regions (Anfinson and Wright 1990) and into the Red River valley.

The Oneota "feel" again arises in reviewing the Devils Lake–Sourisford Burial complex (Syms 1979), found in the Northeastern Plains between the Aspen Parkland and the Missouri Coteau around Devils Lake in North Dakota, and extending north into southwestern Manitoba and into south-central and southeastern Saskatchewan. Syms defines the complex, discussing the inclusion of miniature vessels with distinctive decorations (some are illustrated by W. Wedel 1959:Plate 19), some copper items, incised stone tablets, tubular pipes (many of which may be of catlinite), conch-shell mask gorgets, and Gulf coast columella beads. Some of the small pottery jars bear trailed-line motifs on the shoulder reminiscent of Oneota wares, including rectilinear motifs and a thunderbird. Syms suggests that the vessels were personal possessions of persons who had undergone religious experiences rather than strictly made for grave inclusion. He believes that the remains were left by nomadic bison hunters who wintered in the Aspen Parkland and spent the summer on the Plains, even practicing some horticulture. He attributes the remains to Siouan groups that were influenced by Mississippian and Middle Missouri developments from A.D. 900 to 1400, with remnants of the trait complex persisting into the protohistoric and historic periods. I would place much of the complex he defines within a later time bracket, contemporary with the Shea and Lockport sites, on the basis of the presumed catlinite objects and the number of shell mask gorgets recovered from protohistoric to historic contexts (Collins 1995) (Figure 11.7). The Black Partizan–site shell mask gorget is associated with the Arzberger phase of the Initial Coalescent horizon of the Coalescent tradition (Caldwell 1966:85), dating to about A.D. 1400 to 1450. There are a few other shell mask gorgets from South Dakota, as far west as Bear Butte, but most are found in a late prehistoric context (L. Alex and K. Lippincott, personal communications). The gorgets strongly suggest Middle Mississippian influence, even Mississippian contemporaneity. But we find so many of the motifs regularly associated with the Southeastern Ceremonial complex, especially the "weeping" or "forked" eye and various representations of thunderbirds, in protohistoric and historic contexts that we must weigh their ceremonial and status importance to this period as well. Oneota plaques, pipes, and flat pieces of bone and antler embellished with these motifs are found in very late prehistoric and early historic associations, but some of the shell mask gorgets are from undeniable historic contexts (Collins 1995; Howard 1956). The people responsible for the Devils Lake–Sourisford burial complex appear to have been participants in a protohistoric and early historic network that involved personal prestige and status characterized by the distribution of such magicoreligious items as gorgets, tablets, and pipes.

Western Periphery

A number of sites in South Dakota suggest Oneota or Oneota-influenced interactions with local residents. Perhaps the best known example of such contact is found at the Arzberger site (Spaulding 1956), due in great measure to the attention to detail exhibited by Spaulding and his perceptive analyses. Spaulding asserts that their interaction with Oneota groups had an impact on Arzberger residents. The presence of a few shell-tempered body sherds, Oneota-like or -inspired shoulder decorative motifs, a catlinite pipe prow, and a small catlinite tablet are notable in the Arzberger collection. The large pitted stone on the east side of the site is reminiscent of the at least eight such pitted boulders at Blood Run, but few, if any, others are known on the Plains or Prairie Peninsula. Spaulding (1956:Plate 16) illustrates a number of decorated body sherds, most of which carry rectilinear motifs that can be duplicated at Oneota sites in western Iowa, but they constitute a very small part of the sample. Arzberger is a late prehistoric site, assigned to the Initial Coalescent, dating between A.D. 1400 and 1550 (Lehmer 1971:114).

Other South Dakota sites yield small numbers of shell- and grit-tempered rims and body sherds that suggest a relationship with Oneota sites farther east. These sites, two located near Vermillion and 13 on the James River 50 to 80 miles to the northwest, are assigned to the Olivet phase (L. Alex 1994; R. Alex 1981a, 1981b). The sites may be those of hunting parties from the east in search of bison. They were probably in use at the same time as Blood Run, Arzberger, and Black Partizan, and may provide the source for the Oneota-like pottery at Arzberger.

Oneota and the Central Plains Tradition

There is good evidence for Oneota interaction with members of the late Central Plains tradition. The Central Plains tradition may date from A.D. 1050 to 1425. Blakeslee (1978:142) suggests that Oneota- and Middle Missouri–tradition trade items are found in the St. Helena phase (about contemporary with the Kullbom phase, located across the Missouri River) and postulates that there was trade in flakable stone and the exchange of catlinite elbow-shaped pipes with projecting stems from about A.D. 1200. There is Oneota and Oneota-like pottery at the (late) Kullbom site (Billeck 1993) and at other Central Plains–tradition, Nebraska-phase sites south of Council Bluffs. They look Oneota, but I am hard-pressed to identify a source for them.

Conclusion

The Oneota tradition did not evolve on the Plains or develop along the Plains–prairie periphery. The best data suggest that Oneota evolved in eastern Wisconsin, but I still expect to find evidence for simultaneous evolution toward the Oneota tradition elsewhere, including the lower Little Sioux River valley. My expectations are bolstered by the fact that some Plains-like elements are in Oneota inventories even at the late Emergent-horizon sites in eastern Wisconsin. A pattern of prairie–Plains interaction appears to have begun no later than A.D. 1100. Plains material-culture characteristics, notably bison-scapula hoes and end scrapers, are found in most components from that time on. Other artifacts and raw materials from the Eastern Plains appear to have been brought into the central Prairie Peninsula with increasing frequency, especially in the Classic horizon.

Many Oneota sites are inordinately large, and most have no evidence for fortification. The few fortifications that are identified, including some enclosures of heaped-up banks of earth, may be restricted to very late in the Classic and Historic horizons. The size of the sites, seemingly unrestricted by factors other than topography, and the absence of fortifications during the Classic horizon suggest that Oneota people had few concerns for ongoing defensive warfare. The possibility of simultaneous occupation in northwestern Iowa by Oneota- and Initial Middle Missouri–tradition groups seems punctuated by the presence of fortifications on most, if not all, Mill Creek components and the absolute lack of fortifications on the Oneota ones. Was the Oneota presence in northwestern Iowa responsible for the Initial Middle Missouri (Mill Creek/Over) evacuation of the region? None of the sites tested suggests that the groups interacted at all and certainly did not exchange pottery or women who made traditional wares.

Late in Wisconsin's Emergent horizon, there is evidence for some interaction between local Oneota people and Mississippian groups at Carcajou Point (Overstreet 1995:36–44), but this Mississippian influence is not characteristic of the horizon and may date to the early Developmental horizon. Oneota groups appear to have evolved out of, displaced, and replaced regional Woodland groups during this time. There is little evidence for Woodland–Oneota interaction, but Woodland groups were surely an important factor in Oneota daily life and probably lived in nearby villages.

The Middle Mississippian presence in the upper Mississippi River drainage was an important factor in the early Oneota Developmental horizon. Overstreet

(1995) makes a case for the purposeful departure of Oneota people from eastern Wisconsin, followed by their return as Mississippian influence there declined. Mississippian activities in the upper Mississippi valley are well chronicled and date fairly consistently from A.D. 1050 to 1150 or shortly thereafter. Aztalan offers undeniable evidence for close interaction between Middle Mississippian-derived and Woodland groups, who perhaps settled on the Crawfish River to avoid conflict with already established Oneota sites around Lake Koshkonong (Goldstein and Richards 1991). There is no evidence for an Oneota presence there. Aztalan may have persisted until about A.D. 1300 (Baerreis and Bryson 1965).

The Fred Edwards (Finney and Stoltman 1991) site, in southeastern Wisconsin, and the Hartley Fort site, in northeastern Iowa (Tiffany 1982), offer similar evidence for interaction among Mississippian, Woodland, and—at Hartley Fort and other sites in eastern Iowa—Mill Creek Initial Middle Missouri-tradition groups. The Fred Edwards site dates between A.D. 1050 and 1150 (Finney and Stoltman 1991:231). Hartley Fort is dated later, but the assays were done some time ago. The cultural remains are so similar that the two sites must be contemporaneous. Fred Edwards and Hartley Fort are of particular interest because Oneota pottery is not represented, suggesting Oneota exclusion. A similar situation of Woodland–Mississippian (Bennett phase) interaction and amalgamation apparently prevailed along the Apple River in northwestern Illinois from A.D. 1050 to 1200; again, Oneota groups did not participate (Emerson 1991:164–182).

Oneota was definitely part of the Middle Mississippian interaction represented in the Red Wing region in the Silvernale phase, when there is evidence for Oneota–Silvernale–Cambria interaction, ostensibly for trade and magico-religious exchange. Gibbon and Dobbs (1991:301) do not agree on interpretations of the radiocarbon assays; Gibbon suggests a short occupation beginning about A.D. 1100, and Dobbs brackets Silvernale at 1175 to 1300. The information just summarized suggests that the period of intense interactions between Mississippian and other groups in the upper Mississippi valley was brief, probably between A.D. 1050 and 1150. During this time, Oneota–Mississippian interactions were few and were restricted to the Lake Koshkonong locality of southern Wisconsin and the Red Wing region on both sides of the Mississippi.

There was a vital Oneota presence in the central Des Moines River valley (Moingona phase) that is solidly identified and dated to the Developmental horizon. Radiocarbon dates place the Blue Earth–region Vosburg site in the Developmental horizon. The Wever site in the Mississippi Alluvial Plain region dates to late in the Developmental; there are probably several other alluvial-plain components of similar age. Inhabitants of the Wever site apparently interacted sporadically with Bold Counselor and late Mississippian groups in the Central

Illinois River valley. Bold Counselor components near the mouth of the Spoon River date to late in the Developmental horizon and offer evidence for continual interaction with local late Mississippian groups. Neither the Fisher nor the Langford complex of the Lower Lake Michigan region offers evidence for Mississippian interaction and, other than the suggestion of a ceramic relation to the Grand River phase of eastern Wisconsin (Emerson and Brown 1992) for the Langford tradition, provides little evidence for interaction with Oneota groups to the north and west.

Developmental-horizon components are found in the Correctionville locality and at the Leary site. If I am correct in assuming a temporal overlap of Oneota and Mill Creek occupations in northwestern Iowa, Oneota groups in villages less than 50 miles away apparently did not interact with occupants of the nearby Mill Creek villages. Conversely, Mill Creek/Over groups living on their small, fortified middens were in regular contact with Middle Mississippian (Illinois River valley and Cahokia) groups to the southeast and may also have traded and otherwise interacted with Caddoan and Central Plains groups, but those interactions were probably less important. Oneota groups apparently were excluded from the Mill Creek–directed trade relations during the Developmental and early Classic horizons. The Leary site may offer evidence for Oneota–Central Plains interaction during the Oneota Developmental horizon, but temporal data are lacking. The most reliable evidence of Oneota occupations during the Developmental horizon is from eastern Wisconsin, southern Minnesota, and central Iowa, with unproved possibilities in western Iowa and southeastern Nebraska.

The importance of the Middle Mississippian tradition in the central Mississippi valley faded by the beginning of the Oneota Classic horizon, about A.D. 1350. I believe that A.D. 1300 to 1350 marks the initiation of new Oneota settlements—notably in the La Crosse, Mississippi Alluvial Plain, and Chariton River regions—and even allowed some forays into the Cahokia locale. Much of Oneota interaction during the Classic horizon was Oneota–Oneota, apparently with the exclusion of the Lake Winnebago–phase groups centered in eastern Wisconsin and the less well known Langford, then Fisher, and Fisher–Huber groups of northeastern Illinois and northwestern Indiana. The styles of the Classic horizon appear to loosely link the large populations of the La Crosse region, the Mississippi Alluvial Plain region, the Chariton River region, the later Correctionville–phase components of the lower Little Sioux valley, the White Rock phase, and some Leary-site components. Catlinite found on most Classic-horizon components suggests that trade and ceremonial interaction linked these groups.

During the late Classic, Oneota populations decreased sharply and many of the site complexes were vacated, probably due to disease and warfare waged by powerful tribes moving in from the east. Those tribes were apparently well supplied with European trade items, including guns, ammunition, and even horses. These technological advances gave them overwhelming power to dominate the indigenous groups and the trade in furs and meat.

Regions that apparently lost their Oneota populations entirely during the late Classic were the La Crosse, Mississippi Alluvial Plain, and Blue Earth. The Lake Winnebago phase virtually disappeared from northeastern Wisconsin, and the Leary-site occupations apparently ended. Still, out of these changes came a new order, still carrying Oneota hallmarks. Some sites apparently became quite large and important during this period: Blood Run and Utz are among the largest Oneota sites on record and appear to have flourished during this time. As the La Crosse terrace was evacuated, the population moved across the Mississippi to the Upper Iowa and Root river valleys, forming a temporarily powerful entity on the west side of the River. The Huber phase suggests some prosperity in the size of sites and intensity of occupations. Obviously, new trading alliances were developed, along with new locations and shifts in prestige and power. Late in the Classic horizon and extending into the Historic, exchange networks appear to have expanded outside the Prairie Peninsula and the Oneota sphere of influence. This period is marked by the movement of catlinite items (especially pipes and plaques) and Gulf coast shell (large conch-shell beads, shell mask gorgets, and smaller beads) that linked trading partners from the east coast onto the High Plains. These items are often found associated with European trade goods at Blood Run, Utz, and the Upper Iowa and Root river sites. A few conch beads are recovered from Blood Run, but none of the other Dhegihan–related sites yield shell mask gorgets or extensive quantities of large conch beads or Gulf coast items.

For years, the archaeological presence of the Dhegihan Siouan–speaking tribes (Quapaws, Osages, Kansas, Omahas, and Poncas) has been a source of bafflement for archaeologists and ethnohistorians. They seem to have appeared suddenly and without cultural antecedents: the Quapaws near the mouth of the Arkansas River, the Osages in southwestern Missouri, the Kansas in eastern Kansas and western Missouri, the Omahas in northwestern Iowa, and the Poncas in eastern Nebraska. Sites directly attributable to all but the Quapaws have been identified, every one of which offers a significant number of European trade items. Materials from sites tied to any one of these tribes do not compare positively with those from any of the others, suggesting that while these groups shared linguistic, social, and religious elements, time and distance had changed their material-culture inventories. Perhaps they came from the east, arriving at different times; perhaps they evolved somewhere in the Prairie Peninsula and took up residence where they were first found by whites. The relative inventories of European trade items are very different; the elements of traditional culture vary significantly in number, percentage, and quality. Wherever from and under whatever circumstances that brought them to the western Prairie Peninsula, they assumed strong roles. The sudden appearance of Dhegihan speakers in the western Prairie Peninsula gives credence to the suggestion that Oneota may represent several cultures (and at least two linguistic affinities), linked by similar technologies (Tiffany 1991). There seems little doubt, whatever the origin of the Dhegihan speakers, that those tribal entities that emerged in the western Prairie Peninsula were well provided with European trade items. The Osages appear to have been technologically superior to any of their neighbors, with access to guns and ammunition, allowing their preeminence in both environmental exploitation and warfare. My contention is that they arrived in southwestern Missouri well equipped with superior weapons, and with established trade relations that guaranteed them a constant supply.

The Osage villages on the upper Osage River immediately became important exchange centers, and after the arrival of the Little Osages near the Missouris' traditional villages on the Missouri River, all pretense of trade dominance by the Missouris ceased. While not equipped with guns in quantity, the Kansas of the King Hill and Fanning sites were well supplied with small European trade items, some of which probably came from the Southern Plains as well as from the east. To date, the earliest historically documented village occupied by the Omahas is Blood Run. Evidence suggests that Blood Run could have been occupied by ancestral Omahas for up to 200 years before whites found them there, but other Dhegiha sites appear to have been occupied for a much shorter time. Small items indicative of trade with Europeans, but no guns or gun parts, abound at Blood Run. The Poncas may have lived with the Omahas as part of the tribe, but separated from them in the early eighteenth century, ultimately settling in Nebraska near the mouth of the Niobrara River (Wood 1965). Their archaeological remains offer only a few elements of the Oneota tradition.

Years ago, when many of us were young graduate students, we were concerned with what would be left to find, learn, and do in Prairie Peninsula archaeology. Readers of this chapter should have no such questions for their future in Oneota research. Questions about origins, relationships, subsistence, raw materials, social organization, marriage patterns, magicoreligious beliefs, and technologies have, in spite of hundreds of investigations, just been addressed. Should we not turn a spade for a decade, there are collections to reanalyze, hypotheses to develop and test, oral traditions to evaluate, and historic documents to submit to scrutiny—all with value to Oneota studies. Few cultural traditions offer the richness of the ethnohistoric ties combined with the complications wrought by disease, warfare, and the disruption of white entradas.

The Oneota tradition lives on, not simply in an old and lost material culture, but in traditional languages, mythology, and belief systems that have been handed down through the generations. The Oneota tradition as defined by archaeologists was gone and forgotten by its practitioners by 1775, when the last shell-tempered pottery vessel was shaped and fired, the last arrow tipped with a simple triangular point was shot out of a bow, and the last bison hide was scraped with chipped-stone end scrapers. But the traditions endure. The truly important social, linguistic, and religious aspects of the Oneota traditional culture persist today and, we hope, will last forever.

References

Alex, L. M.
　1994　Oneota and the Olivet Phase, South Dakota. *Newsletter of the South Dakota Archaeological Society* 24:1–4.

Alex, R.
　1981a　The Village Cultures of the Lower James River Valley, South Dakota. Ph.D. diss., Department of Anthropology, University of Wisconsin, Madison.
　1981b　Village Sites off the Missouri River. In *The Future of South Dakota's Past*, edited by L. C. Stewart, 39–46. South Dakota Archaeological Society, Special Publication no. 2. Vermillion.

Anderson, D. C.
　1994　*Stone, Glass, and Metal Artifacts from the Milford Site (13KD1): An Early 18th Century Oneota Component in Northwest Iowa.* University of Iowa, Office of the State Archaeologist, Report no. 19. Iowa City.

Anfinson, S. F.
　1987　Investigations at Two Oneota Sites in the Center Creek Locality. *Minnesota Archaeologist* 46:31–45.

Anfinson, S. F., and H. E. Wright
　1990　Climatic Change and Culture in Prehistoric Minnesota. In *The Woodland Tradition in the Western Great Lakes*, edited by G. E. Gibbon, 213–232. University of Minnesota, Publications in Anthropology, no. 4. Minneapolis.

Anonymous
　1974　The Prehistoric and Historic Habitat of the Missouri and Oto Indians. In *Oto and Missouri Indians*, edited by D. A. Horr, 25–76. Garland, New York.

Arzigian, C. M., R. M. Boszhardt, H. P. Halverson, and J. L. Theler
　1994　The Gundersen Site: An Oneota Village and Cemetery in La Crosse, Wisconsin. *Journal of the Iowa Archeological Society* 41:3–75.

Baerreis, D. A., and R. A. Bryson
　1965　Climatic Episodes and the Dating of Mississippian Cultures. *Wisconsin Archeologist* 46:203–220.

Barreca, E.
　1992　The Secret of EB3/47. *Beloit Magazine*, 6–7.

Benn, D. W.
　1989　Hawks, Serpents, and Bird-Men: Emergence of the Oneota Mode of Production. *Plains Anthropologist* 34:233–260.
　1995　Woodland People and the Roots of the Oneota. In *Oneota Archaeology: Past, Present, and Future,* edited by W. Green, 91–140. University of Iowa, Office of the State Archaeologist, Report no. 20. Iowa City.

Berry, B., and C. H. Chapman
　1942　An Oneota Site in Missouri. *American Antiquity* 7:290–305.

Betancourt, P. P.
　1965　A Description of Certain Engraved Artifacts from the Utz Oneota Site. *Plains Anthropologist* 10:256–270.
Billeck, W. T.
　1993　Time and Space in the Glenwood Locality: The Nebraska Phase in Western Iowa. Ph.D. diss., Department of Anthropology, University of Missouri, Columbia.
Birk, D., and E. Johnson
　1992　The Mdewakanton Dakota and Initial French Contact. In *Calumet and Fleur-De-Lys; Archaeology of Indian and French Contact in the Midcontinent,* edited by J. A. Walthall and T. E. Emerson, 203–240. Smithsonian Institution Press, Washington D.C.
Blake, L. W., and H. C. Cutler
　n.d.　Plant Remains from the King Hill Site (23BN1) and Comparison with Those from the Utz Site (23SA2). Manuscript on file, Missouri Botanical Garden, St. Louis.
Blakeslee, D. J.
　1978　Assessing the Central Plains Tradition in Eastern Nebraska: Content and Outcome. In *The Central Plains Tradition: Internal Development and External Relationships.* University of Iowa, Office of the State Archaeologist, Report no. 11. Iowa City.
Borchert, J. R.
　1950　The Climate of the Central North American Grassland. *Annals of the Association of American Geographers* 40:1–39.
Boszhardt, R. F.
　1994　Oneota Group Continuity at La Crosse: The Brice Prairie, Pammel Creek, and Valley View Phases. *Wisconsin Archeologist* 75, nos. 3–4.
Boszhardt, R. F., W. Holtz, and J. Nienow
　1995　A Compilation of Oneota Radiocarbon Dates as of 1995. In *Oneota Archaeology: Past, Present, and Future,* edited by W. Green, 203–217. University of Iowa, Office of the State Archaeologist, Report no. 20. Iowa City.
Bray, R. T.
　1961　The Flynn Cemetery: An Orr Focus Oneota Burial Site in Allamakee County. *Journal of the Iowa Archaeological Society* 4:15–25.
　1963　Southern Cult Motifs from the Utz Site. *Missouri Archaeologist* 25:1–40.
　1991　The Utz Site: An Oneota Village in Central Missouri. *Missouri Archaeologist* 52.
Brown, J. A.
　1990　Ethnohistoric Connections. In *At the Edge of Prehistory: Huber Phase Archaeology in the Chicago Area,* edited by J. A. Brown and P. J. O'Brien, 155–160. Illinois Department of Transportation, Center for American Archeology, Kampsville.
Brown, M. K.
　1975　*The Zimmerman Site: Further Excavations at the Grand Village of the Kaskaskia.* Illinois State Museum, Reports of Investigations, no. 32. Springfield.
Bryson, R. A., D. A. Baerreis, and W. M. Wendland
　1970　The Character of Late-Glacial and Post-Glacial Climatic Changes. In *Pleistocene and Recent Environments of the Central Great Plains,* edited by W. Dort, Jr., and J. K. Jones, Jr., 53–74. University Press of Kansas, Lawrence.

Bryson, R. A., and W. M. Wendland
1967   Tentative Climatic Patterns for Some Late Glacial and Postglacial Episodes in Central North America. In *Life, Land, and Water,* edited by W. J. Mayer-Oakes, 271–298. University of Manitoba Press, Winnipeg.

Caldwell, W. W.
1966   *The Black Partizan Site.* Smithsonian Institution, River Basin Surveys, Publications in Salvage Archeology, no. 2. Lincoln, Neb.

Chapman, C. H.
1946   A Preliminary Survey of Missouri Archaeology. Part 1, Historic Indian Tribes. *Missouri Archaeologist* 10, no. 1.

1952   Culture Sequence in the Lower Missouri Valley. In *Archeology of the Eastern United States,* edited by J. B. Griffin, 139–151. University of Chicago Press, Chicago.

1959   The Little Osage and Missouri Indian Village Sites ca. 1727–77 A.D. *Missouri Archaeologist* 21, no. 1.

1974   Osage Village Locations and Hunting Territories in 1808. In *Osage Indians,* edited by D. A. Horr, 4:173–249. Garland, New York.

1980   *The Archaeology of Missouri.* Vol. 2. University of Missouri Press, Columbia.

Chapman, C. H., L. W. Blake, R. T. Bray, T. M. Hamilton, A. A. Hunter, D. M. Pearsall, J. H. Purdue, E. E. Voigt, R. P. Wiegers, and J. K. Yelton
1985   *Osage and Missouri Indian Life Cultural Change: 1675–1825. Final Performance Report on National Endowment for the Humanities Research Grant RS-20296.* Report on file, University of Missouri, Department of Anthropology, Division of American Archaeology, Columbia.

Chapman, C. H., and E. F. Chapman
1964   *Indians and Archaeology of Missouri.* University of Missouri Press, Columbia.

Church, T.
1994   Ogalalla Orthoquartzite: An Updated Description. *Plains Anthropologist* 39:53–62.

Collins, J. M.
1995   A Shell Mask Gorget from Allamakee County, Iowa. *Plains Anthropologist* 40(153):251–260.

Conrad, L. A.
1991   The Middle Mississippian Cultures of the Central Illinois River Valley. In *Cahokia and the Hinterlands: Middle Mississippian Cultures of the Midwest,* edited by T. E. Emerson and R. B. Lewis, 119–156. University of Illinois Press, Urbana.

Conrad, L. A., and D. J. Nolan
1991   Some Preliminary Observations on the Occurrence of Catlinite in West Central Illinois. Paper presented at the thirty-sixth annual meeting of the Midwest Archaeological Conference, La Crosse, Wis.

Dobbs, C. A.
1984   Oneota Settlement Patterns in the Blue Earth River Valley Minnesota. Ph.D. diss., Department of Anthropology, University of Minnesota, Minneapolis.

Dobbs, C. A., and G. R. Holley
1995   Reclaiming Silvernale: Implications of 12th Century Occupations in the Upper Mississippi. Paper presented at the sixtieth annual meeting of the Society for American Archaeology, Minneapolis.

Dobbs, C. A., and O. C. Shane III
1982   Oneota Settlement Patterns in the Blue Earth River Valley, Minnesota. In

Oneota Studies, edited by G. E. Gibbon, 55–68. University of Minnesota, Publications in Anthropology, no. 1. Minneapolis.

Dorsey, J. O.
1886   Migrations of Siouan Tribes. *American Naturalist* 20:211–222.

Emerson, T. E.
1991   Some Perspectives on Cahokia and the Northern Mississippian Expansion. In *Cahokia and the Hinterlands: Middle Mississippian Cultures of the Midwest,* edited by T. E. Emerson and R. B. Lewis, 221–236. University of Illinois Press, Urbana.

Emerson, T. E., and J. A. Brown
1992   The Late Prehistory and Protohistory of Illinois. In *Calumet and Fleur-de-Lys; Archaeology of Indian and French Contact in the Midcontinent,* edited by J. A. Walthall and T. E. Emerson, 77–128. Smithsonian Institution Press, Washington, D.C.

Faulkner, C. H.
1972   *The Late Prehistoric Occupation of Northwestern Indiana: A Study of the Upper Mississippi Cultures of the Kankakee Valley.* Indiana Historical Society, Prehistoric Research Series, no. 5. Indianapolis.

Finney, F. A., and J. B. Stoltman
1991   The Fred Edwards Site: A Case of Stirling Phase Culture Contact in Southwestern Wisconsin. In *New Perspectives on Cahokia: Views from the Periphery,* edited by J. B. Stoltman, 229–252. Prehistory Press, Madison, Wis.

Fishel, R. L.
1995   *Excavations at the Dixon Site (13WD8): Correctionville Phase Oneota in Northwest Iowa.* University of Iowa, Office of the State Archaeologist, Report no. 442. Iowa City.

Fletcher, A. C., and F. La Flesche
1911   The Omaha Tribe. *Annual Report, Bureau of American Ethnology* 27:17–654.

Fowke, G.
1910   *Antiquities of Central and Southeastern Missouri.* Bureau of American Ethnology Bulletin 37. Washington, D.C.

Gallagher, J. P.
1990   *The Farley Village Site 21Hu2, an Oneota/Ioway Site in Houston County, Minnesota.* University of Wisconsin, Mississippi Valley Archaeology Center, Reports of Investigations, no. 117. La Crosse.

Gibbon, G. E.
1973   *The Sheffield Site: An Oneota Site on the St. Croix River.* Minnesota Historical Society, Minnesota Prehistoric Archaeology Series, no. 10. St. Paul.

1974   A Model of Mississippian Development and Its Implications for the Red Wing Area. In *Aspects of Great Lakes Anthropology,* edited by E. Johnson, 129–137. Minnesota Historical Society, Minnesota Prehistoric Archaeology Series, no. 11. St. Paul.

1978   A Simplified Algorithm Model for the Classification of Silvernale and Blue Earth Phase Ceramics. In *Some Studies of Minnesota Prehistoric Ceramics,* edited by A. R. Woolworth and M. Hall, 3–11. Minnesota Archaeological Society, Occasional Publications in Minnesota Anthropology, no. 2. St. Paul.

1983   The Blue Earth Phase of Southern Minnesota. *Journal of the Iowa Archaeological Society* 30:1–84.

1991   The Middle Mississippian Presence in Minnesota. In *Cahokia and the Hinterlands: Middle Mississippian Cultures of the Midwest,* edited by T. B. Emerson and R. B. Lewis, 206–220. University of Illinois Press, Urbana.

1995   Oneota at the Periphery: Trade, Political Power, and Ethnicity in Northern Minnesota and on the Northeastern Plains in the Late Prehistoric Period. In *Oneota Archaeology: Past, Present, and Future*, edited by W. Green, 175–199. University of Iowa, Office of the State Archaeologist, Report no. 20. Iowa City.

Gibbon, G. E., and C. A. Dobbs

1991   The Mississippian Presence in the Red Wing Area, Minnesota. In *New Perspectives on Cahokia: Views from the Periphery*, edited by J. B. Stoltman, 281–306. Prehistory Press, Madison, Wis.

Goldstein, L. G., and J. D. Richards

1991   Ancient Aztalan: The Cultural and Ecological Context of a Late Prehistoric Site in the Midwest. In *Cahokia and the Hinterlands: Middle Mississippian Cultures of the Midwest*, edited by T. E. Emerson and R. B. Lewis, 193–206. University of Illinois Press, Urbana.

Gradwohl, D. M.

1967   A Preliminary Precis of the Moingona Phase, an Oneota Manifestation in Central Iowa. *Plains Anthropologist* 12:211–212.

1974   Archaeology of the Central Des Moines River Valley: A Preliminary Summary. In *Aspects of Upper Great lakes Anthropology*, edited by E. Johnson, 90–102. Minnesota Historical Society, Minnesota Prehistoric Archaeology Series, no. 11. St. Paul.

Grange, R. T., Jr.

1968   *Pawnee and Lower Loup Pottery*. Nebraska State Historical Society, Publications in Anthropology, no. 3. Lincoln.

Grantham, L.

1993   The Illini Village of the Marquette and Jolliet Voyage of 1773. *Missouri Archaeologist* 54:1–20.

Green, W.

1993   Examining Protohistoric Depopulation in the Upper Midwest. *Wisconsin Archeologist* 73:290–323.

Griffin, J. B.

1937   The Archaeological Remains of the Chiwere Sioux. *American Antiquity* 2:180–181.

1943   *The Fort Ancient Aspect: Its Cultural and Chronological Position in Mississippi Valley Archaeology*. University of Michigan, Museum of Anthropology, Anthropological Papers, no. 28. Ann Arbor.

1946   Cultural Change and Continuity in Eastern United States Archaeology. In *Man in Northeastern North America*, edited by F. Johnson, 27–95. Robert F. Peabody Foundation for Archaeology, Paper no. 3. Phillips Academy, Andover, Mass.

1960   A Hypothesis for the Prehistory of the Winnebago. In *Culture in History: Essays in Honor of Paul Radin*, edited by S. Diamond, 809–868. Columbia University Press, New York.

1978   Late Prehistory of the Ohio Valley. In *Northeast*, edited by B. G. Trigger, 547–559. Vol. 15 of *Handbook of North American Indians*, W. C. Sturtevant, general editor. Smithsonian Institution Press, Washington, D.C.

Gundersen, J. N.

1993   "Catlinite" and the Spread of the Calumet Ceremony. *American Antiquity* 58:560–562.

Hall, R. L.

1962   *The Archeology of Carcajou Point, with an Interpretation of the Development of Oneota Culture in Wisconsin*. 2 vols. University of Wisconsin Press, Madison.

1977   An Anthropocentric Perspective for Eastern United States Prehistory. *American Antiquity* 42:499–518.

1991   Cahokia Identity and Interaction Models of Cahokia Mississippian. In *Cahokia and the Hinterlands: Middle Mississippian Cultures of the Midwest*, edited by T. E. Emerson and R. B. Lewis, 3–34. University of Illinois Press, Urbana.

1995   Relating the Big Fish and the Big Stone: the Archaeological Identity and Habitat of the Winnebago in 1634. In *Oneota Archaeology: Past, Present, and Future*, edited by W. Green, 19–30. University of Iowa, Office of the State Archaeologist, Report no. 20. Iowa City.

Hamilton, H. W.

1967   *Tobacco Pipes of the Missouri Indians.* Missouri Archaeological Society, Memoir no. 5. Columbia.

Harn, A.D.

1991   Comments on Subsistence, Seasonality, and Site Function at Upland Subsidiaries in the Spoon River Area: Mississippianization at Work on the Northern Frontier. In *Cahokia and the Hinterlands: Middle Mississippian Cultures of the Midwest*, edited by T. E. Emerson and R. B. Lewis, 157–163. University of Illinois Press, Urbana.

Harvey, A. E.

1979   *Oneota Culture in Northwestern Iowa.* University of Iowa, Office of the State Archaeologist, Report no. 12. Iowa City.

Henning, D. R.

1961   Oneota Ceramics in Iowa. *Journal of the Iowa Archeological Society* 11, no. 2.

1970   Development and Interrelationships of Oneota Culture in the Lower Missouri River Valley. *Missouri Archaeologist* 32.

1982   *Evaluative Investigations of Three Landmark Sites in Northwest Iowa.* Luther College, Archaeological Research Center, Decorah, Iowa.

1992   A Study of Pottery from the Blood Run Site (13LO2), 1985 Excavations. Manuscript on file, Luther College, Archaeological Research Center, Decorah, Iowa.

1993   The Adaptive Patterning of the Dhegiha Sioux. *Plains Anthropologist* 38:253–264.

1995   Oneota Evolution and Interactions: A Perspective from the Wever Terrace, Southeast Iowa. In *Oneota Archaeology: Past, Present, and Future*, edited by W. Green, 65–88. University of Iowa, Office of the State Archaeologist, Report no. 20. Iowa City.

n.d.   Cemetery Location for Minnesota Indian Affairs Council (Sheffield Mounds, Sheffield Habitation, McKee Mounds). Manuscript on file, Minnesota Indian Affairs Council, St. Paul.

Henning, D. R., and M. Q. Peterson

1965   Re-articulated Burials from the Upper Iowa River Valley. *Journal of the Iowa Archeological Society* 13:1–16.

Herold, E. B., P. J. O'Brien, and D. J. Wenner

1990   Hoxie Farm and Huber: Two Upper Mississippian Archaeological Sites in Cook County, Illinois. In *At the Edge of Prehistory: Huber Phase Archaeology in the Chicago Area*, edited by J. A. Brown and P. J. O'Brien, 3–119. Center for American Archeology Press, Kampsville, Ill.

Hill, A. T., and W. R. Wedel

1936   Excavations at the Leary Indian Village and Burial Site, Richardson County, Nebraska. *Nebraska History Magazine* 17:2–73.

Hoffman, M. P.
  1990   The Terminal Mississippian Period in the Arkansas River Valley and Quapaw
         Ethnogenesis. In *Towns and Temples Along the Mississippi*, edited by D. H. Dye
         and C. A. Cox, 208–226. University of Alabama Press, Tuscaloosa.
Hollinger, R. E.
  1995   Residence Patterns and Oneota Cultural Dynamics. In *Oneota Archaeology:
         Past, Present, and Future*, edited by W. Green, 141–174. University of Iowa,
         Office of the State Archaeologist, Report no. 20. Iowa City.
Howard, J. H.
  1953   The Southern Cult in the Northern Plains. *American Antiquity* 19:130–138.
  1956   The Persistence of Southern Cult Gorgets Among the Historic Kansa. *Ameri-
         can Antiquity* 22:301–303.
Jackson, D.
  1992   Oneota in the American Bottom. In *The Sponemann Site 2: The Mississippian
         and Oneota Occupations (11-Ms-517)*, edited by C. E. Bareis and J. H. Walthall,
         383–392. American Bottom Archaeology, FAI-270 Site Reports, vol. 24. Univer-
         sity of Illinois Press, Urbana.
Jeske, R. J.
  1989   Horticultural Technology and Social Interaction at the Edge of the Prairie
         Peninsula. *Illinois Archaeology* 1:103–120.
  1990   Langford Tradition Subsistence, Settlement, and Technology. *Midcontinent
         Journal of Archaeology* 15:221–249.
Keyes, C. R.
  1927   Prehistoric Man in Iowa. *Palimpsest* 8:215–229.
Leaf, G. R.
  1976   The Function of the Old Fort in Central Missouri Oneota Subsistence and
         Settlement Systems. *Plains Anthropologist* 21:93–110.
Lehmer, D. J.
  1954   *Archeological Investigations in the Oahe Dam Area, South Dakota, 1950–51*. Bureau
         of American Ethnology Bulletin 158. Washington, D.C.
  1971   *Introduction to Middle Missouri Archeology*. National Park Service, Anthropo-
         logical Papers, no. 1. Washington, D.C.
Lewis, T. H.
  n.d.   Field notes. Manuscript on file, Minnesota Historical Society Collections,
         St. Paul.
Logan, B.
  1995   *Phasing White Rock: Archaeological Investigations of the White Rock and Warne
         Sites, Lovewell Reservoir, Jewell County, Kansas, 1994–1995*. University of
         Kansas, Museum of Anthropology, Project Report Series, no. 90. Lawrence.
Lurie, N. O.
  1960   Winnebago Protohistory. In *Culture and History: Essays in Honor of Paul Radin*,
         edited by S. Diamond, 790–808. Columbia University Press, New York.
Mason, C. I.
  1976   Historic Identification and Lake Winnebago Focus Oneota. In *Cultural Change
         and Continuity, Papers in Honor of James B. Griffin*, edited by C. Cleland, 335–
         348. Academic Press, New York.
Mason, R. J.
  1976   Ethnicity and Archaeology in the Upper Great Lakes. In *Cultural Change and
         Continuity: Papers in Honor of James B. Griffin*, edited by C. Cleland, 349–361.
         Academic Press, New York.

1986 Rock Island: Historic Indian Archaeology in the Northern Lake Michigan Basin. Mid-Continent Journal of Anthropology, Special Paper no. 6.

1993 Oneota and Winnebago Ethnogenesis: An Overview. *Wisconsin Archeologist* 74:347–368.

McGee, W. J.

1897 The Siouan Indians: A Preliminary Sketch. *Bureau of American Ethnology, Annual Report* 15:153–204.

McKern, W. C.

1945 Preliminary Report on the Upper Mississippi Phase in Wisconsin. *Milwaukee Public Museum Bulletin* 16:109–285.

McKusick, M.

1964 Prehistoric Man in Northeastern Iowa. *Palimpsest* 45:465–494.

1973 *The Grant Oneota Village.* University of Iowa, Office of the State Archaeologist, Report no. 4. Iowa City.

Meyer, D., and P. C. Thistle

1995 Saskatchewan River Rendezvous Centers and Trading Posts: Continuity in a Cree Social Geography. *Ethnohistory* 42:403–444.

Michlovic, M. G., and F. E. Schneider

1993 The Shea Site: A Prehistoric Fortified Village on the Northeastern Plains. *Plains Anthropologist* 38:117–138.

Milner, G. R., T. E. Emerson, M. W. Mehrer, J. A. Williams, and D. Esarey

1984 Mississippian and Oneota Period. In *American Bottom Archaeology,* edited by C. E. Bareis and J. W. Porter, 158–186. University of Illinois Press, Chicago.

Moffat, C. R., and B. Kolderhoff

1990 Overview of Oneota Studies at Lake Red Rock. In *Archaeological Data Recovery at Five Prehistoric Sites, Lake Red Rock, Marion County, Iowa,* by C. R. Moffat, B. Koldehoff, K. E. Parker, L. S. Kelly, M. R. McCorvie, and J. Craig. 417–465. American Resources Group, Carbondale, Ill.

Moffat, C. R., B. Koldehoff, K. E. Parker, L. S. Kelly, M. R. McCorvie, and J. Craig

1990 *Archaeological Data Recovery at Five Prehistoric Sites, Lake Red Rock, Marion County, Iowa.* American Resources Group, Carbondale, Ill.

Mott, M.

1938 The Relation of Historic Indian Tribes to Archaeological Manifestations in Iowa. *Iowa Journal of History and Politics* 36:227–314.

Nasatir, A. P.

1929 Ducharme's Invasion of Missouri: An Incident in the Anglo-Spanish Rivalry for the Indian Trade of Upper Louisiana. *Missouri Historical Review* 24:3–25.

Norall, F.

1988 *Bourgmont, Explorer of the Missouri, 1698–1725.* University of Nebraska Press, Lincoln.

O'Brien, M. J.

1994 *Cat Monsters and Head Pots: The Archaeology of Missouri's Pemiscot Bayou.* University of Missouri Press, Columbia.

O'Brien, P. J., and K. Hart

1972 The Utlaut Site (23SA162W): An Oneota-Historic Missouri Burial Site. *Missouri Archaeologist* 34:48–66.

O'Gorman, J.

1995 *The Tremaine Site Complex: Oneota Occupation in the La Crosse Locality, Wisconsin.* Vol. 3, *The Tremaine Site (47Lc95).* Archaeological State Historical Society of Wisconsin, Museum Archaeology Program, Madison. Research Series, no. 3.

Orr, E.
 1914 Indian Pottery of the Oneota or Upper Iowa River in Northeastern Iowa. *Iowa Academy of Sciences, Proceedings* 21:231–239.
 1963 *Iowa Archaeological Reports 1934–1939, with an Evaluation and Index by Marshall McKusick.* Society for American Archaeology, Archives of Archaeology, no. 20. University of Wisconsin Press, Madison.

Orton, C., P. Tyers, and A. Vince
 1993 *Pottery in Archaeology.* Cambridge University Press, Cambridge.

Osborn, N. M.
 1982 The Clarkson Site (13WA2), an Oneota Manifestation in the Central Des Moines River Valley. *Journal of the Iowa Archaeological Society* 29:1–108.

O'Shea, J. M., and J. Ludwickson
 1992 *Archaeology and Ethnohistory of the Omaha Indians: The Big Village Site.* University of Nebraska Press, Lincoln.

Overstreet, D. F.
 1993 McCauley, Astor, and Hanson—Candidates for the Provisional Dandy Phase. *Wisconsin Archeologist* 74:120–196.
 1995 The Eastern Wisconsin Oneota Regional Continuity. In *Oneota Archaeology: Past, Present, and Future,* edited by W. Green, 33–64. University of Iowa, Office of the State Archaeologist, Report no. 20. Iowa City.

Overstreet, D. F., and P. B. Richards, eds.
 1992 *Archaeology at Lac Des Puans: The Lake Winnebago Phase, A Classic Horizon Expression of the Oneota Tradition in East-Central Wisconsin.* Great Lakes Archaeological Research Center, Reports of Investigations, no. 280. Great Lakes Archaeological Press, Milwaukee.

Pettigrew, J. W.
 n.d. The Silent City. Manuscript on file, Pettigrew Museum, Sioux Falls, S. D.

Porter, J. W.
 1962 Notes on Four Lithic Types Found in Archaeological Sites near Mobridge, South Dakota. *Plains Anthropologist* 7:267–269.

Raish, C. B.
 1979 *King Hill (23BN1), Fanning (14DP1), and Leary (25RH1): A Study of Oneota Ceramic Variability.* M.A. thesis, Department of Anthropology, University of Nebraska, Lincoln.

Ready, T.
 1979 Ogechie Series. In *A Handbook of Minnesota Prehistoric Ceramics,* edited by S. F. Anfinson, 129–152. Minnesota Archaeological Society, Occasional Publications in Minnesota Anthropology, no. 5. St. Paul.

Robinson, D.
 1930 *History of South Dakota,* Vol. 1. American Historical Society.

Rodell, R. L.
 1991 The Diamond Bluff Site Complex and Cahokia Influence in the Red Wing Locality. In *New Perspectives on Cahokia: Views from the Periphery,* edited by J. B. Stoltman, 253–280. Prehistory Press, Madison, Wis.

Ruppert, M. E.
 1979 Analysis of the Vertebrate Faunal Remains from the King Hill Site, 23BN1. M.A. thesis, Department of Anthropology, University of Nebraska, Lincoln.

Rusco, M. K.
 1960 *The White Rock Aspect.* University of Nebraska, Laboratory of Anthropology, Note Book no. 4. Lincoln.

Salzer, R. J.

1992   Oneota Origins. Paper presented at the thirty-seventh annual Midwest Archaeological Conference, Grand Rapids, Mich.

1993   Oral Literature and Archaeology. *Wisconsin Archeologist* 74:80–119.

Santure, S. K., A. D. Harn, and D. Esarey, eds.

1990   *Archaeological Investigations at the Morton Village and Norris Farms 36 Cemetery.* Illinois State Museum, Reports of Investigations, no. 45. Springfield.

Sasso, R. F.

1993   La Crosse Region Oneota Adaptations: Changing Late Prehistoric Subsistence and Settlement Patterns in the Upper Mississippi Valley. *Wisconsin Archeologist* 74:324–369.

Shippee, J. M.

1967   Belated Archaeological Investigation on King's Hill, St. Joseph, Missouri. *Museum Graphic* 19:5–9.

Spaulding, A. C.

1956   *The Arzberger Site, Hughes County, South Dakota.* University of Michigan, Museum of Anthropology, Occasional Contributions, no. 16. Ann Arbor.

Springer, J. W., and S. R. Witkowski

1982   Siouan Historical Linguistics and Oneota Archaeology. In *Oneota Studies,* edited by G. E. Gibbon, 69–83. University of Minnesota, Publications in Anthropology, no. 1. Minneapolis.

Starr, F.

1887   Mounds and Lodge Circles in Iowa. *American Antiquarian* 9:361–363.

1888   *Mound Explorations in North-western Iowa.* Davenport Academy of Sciences Proceedings, no. 6. Davenport, Iowa.

Stoltman, J. B.

1986   The Appearance of the Mississippian Cultural Tradition in the Upper Mississippi Valley. In *Prehistoric Mound Builders of the Mississippi Valley,* edited by J. B. Stoltman, 26–34. Putnam Museum, Davenport, Iowa.

Syms, E. L.

1979   The Devils Lake–Sourisford Burial Complex on the Northern Plains. *Plains Anthropologist* 24:283–308.

Thomas, C.

1891   Report on the Mounds Explorations of the Bureau of Ethnology. *Bureau of American Ethnology, Annual Report* 12:3–742.

Tiffany, J. A.

1979a   An Overview of Oneota Sites in Southeastern Iowa: A Perspective from the Ceramic Analysis of the Schmeiser Site, 13DM101, Des Moines County, Iowa. *Proceedings of the Iowa Academy of Science* 86:89–101.

1979b   *An Archaeological Survey of the Bastian Oneota Site (13CK28), Cherokee County, Iowa.* University of Iowa, Office of the State Archaeologist, Report no. 1. Iowa City.

1982   Hartley Fort Ceramics. *Proceedings of the Iowa Academy of Science* 89:133–150.

1988   Preliminary Report on Excavations at the McKinney Oneota Village Site (13LA1), Louisa County, Iowa. *Wisconsin Archeologist* 69:228–312.

1991   Models of Mississippian Culture History in the Western Prairie Peninsula: A Perspective from Iowa. In *Cahokia and the Hinterlands: Middle Mississippian Cultures of the Midwest,* edited by T. E. Emerson and R. B. Lewis, 183–192. University of Illinois Press, Urbana.

Tiffany, J. A., and D. Anderson

1993   The Milford Site (13DK1): A Postcontact Village in Northwest Iowa. In *Prehis-*

tory and Human Ecology of the Western Prairies and Northern Plains, edited by
J. A. Tiffany, 283–306. Plains Anthropologist Memoir no. 27.

Transeau, E. N.
1935   The Prairie Peninsula. *Ecology* 16:423–437.

Wedel, M. M.
1959   Oneota Sites on the Upper Iowa River. *Missouri Archaeologist* 21, nos. 2–4.
1963   Note on Oneota Classification. *Wisconsin Archeologist* 44:118–122.
1981   The Ioway, Oto, and Omaha Indians in 1700. *Journal of the Iowa Archeological Society* 28:1–13.
1988   The 1804 "Old Ioway Village" of Lewis and Clark. *Journal of the Iowa Archeological Society* 35:70–71.

Wedel, W. R.
1959   *An Introduction to Kansas Archeology*. Bureau of American Ethnology Bulletin 174. Washington, D.C.
1961   *Prehistoric Man on the Great Plains*. University of Oklahoma Press, Norman.

Wendt, D., and C. A. Dobbs
1989   A Reevaluation of the Mero (Diamond Bluff) Site Complex. *Wisconsin Archeologist* 70:281–308.

West, G. A.
1934   *Tobacco, Pipes and Smoking Customs of the American Indians*. Bulletin of the Public Museum of the City of Milwaukee, vol. 17.

Wilford, L. A.
1941   A Tentative Classification of the Prehistoric Cultures of Minnesota. *American Antiquity* 6:231–249.

Wilford, L. A., E. Johnson, and J. Vicinus
1969   *Burial Mounds of Central Minnesota: Excavation Reports*. Minnesota Historical Society, Minnesota Prehistoric Archaeology Series, no. 1. St. Paul.

Willey, G. R., and P. Phillips
1958   *Method and Theory in American Archaeology*. University of Chicago Press, Chicago.

Winchell, N. H.
1911   *The Aborigines of Minnesota*. Minnesota Historical Society, St. Paul.

Wood, W. R.
1965   *The Redbird Focus and the Problem of Ponca Prehistory*. Plains Anthropologist Memoir no. 2.
1973   Culture Sequence at the Old Fort, Saline County, Missouri. *American Antiquity* 38:101–111.

Wood, W. R., M. J. O'Brien, K. A. Murray, and J. C. Rose
1995   *Holocene Human Adaptations in the Missouri Prairie-Timberlands*. Arkansas Archeological Survey, Research Series, no. 45. Fayetteville.

Yelton, J. K.
1991   Protohistoric Oneota Pottery of the Lower Missouri River Valley: A Functional Perspective. Ph.D. diss., Department of Anthropology, University of Missouri, Columbia.

12. The Southern Plains Villagers

Richard R. Drass

BY A.D. 800 or 900, semisedentary societies appear on the Southern Plains. Sites of this late prehistoric period are part of the Plains Village tradition. This tradition is characterized by permanent houses and small villages occupied for long periods; the development of an economy based on horticulture and hunting, particularly bison hunting; and a diverse artifact assemblage reflecting activities associated with a sedentary lifestyle. Villages are usually near the fertile floodplains of major streams. Some of the villagers are ancestral to the historic Wichita groups documented in the Southern Plains by early Spanish and French explorers. The basic Plains Village economic pattern of growing maize, beans, and squash and hunting bison is evident in the earliest historic accounts of the Wichita groups living in north-central Oklahoma and southern and central Kansas.

There are thousands of villages documented on the Southern Plains, and research on many of these sites began over 60 years ago. The sites exhibit many common characteristics, but a variety of phases and complexes have been identified and studied to varying degrees (Figure 12.1). The best defined units include Antelope Creek, Apishapa, Buried City, and Zimms of the Upper Canark variant in the Texas and Oklahoma panhandles and southeastern Colorado; the Paoli, Washita River, Custer, and Turkey Creek phases of the Redbed Plains variant in central and west-central Oklahoma; the Henrietta complex and Wylie focus in north-central Texas; and the Bluff Creek, Wilmore, and Pratt complexes in southern Kansas. In addition, protohistoric Wichita, the Great Bend aspect, and early historic Wichita villages are identified in Kansas, Oklahoma, and northern Texas. Many other sites have been studied but are not associated with defined complexes (Figure 12.2).

Prehistoric Taxa

Upper Canark Variant

Since the early part of the twentieth century, archaeologists have recognized a distinct cultural pattern at sites along the major drainages in southeastern Colorado, northeastern New Mexico, and the Oklahoma and Texas panhandles. Houses with stone-slab foundations characteristic of this cultural pattern were first described for the Texas panhandle (Eyerly 1907; Moorehead 1921, 1931).

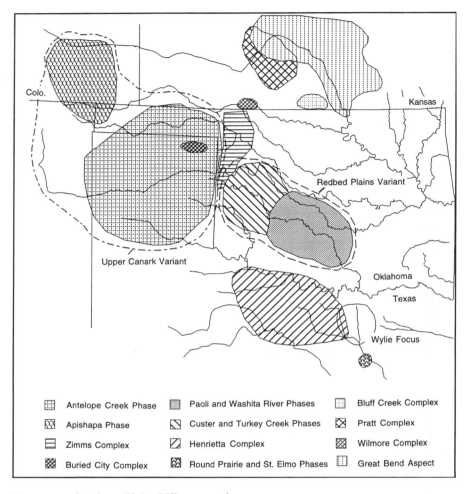

Figure 12.1. Southern Plains Village complexes.

Many survey and excavation expeditions followed, with extensive federally funded (Works Progress Administration and Federal Emergency Relief Administration) excavations in the Texas panhandle during the 1930s (Holden 1929, 1933; Lintz 1986; Studer 1931, 1934, 1955). Krieger (1946) synthesized the data on these sites and proposed the Panhandle aspect for the stone-slab-house sites and Antelope Creek focus for those sites in the Texas panhandle. Watson (1950) subsequently defined the Optima focus in the Oklahoma panhandle as a variant of the Panhandle aspect, and Campbell (1969, 1976) suggested that the Apishapa focus on the Chaquaqua Plateau in southeastern Colorado was part of the Panhandle aspect. Lintz (1986) reviewed the data for the Panhandle

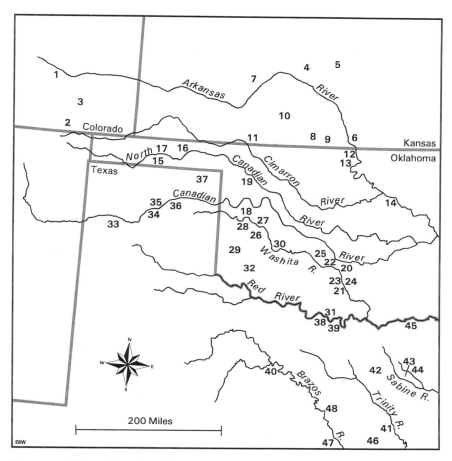

Figure 12.2. Selected Southern Plains Village sites: *Colorado* (1) Cramer, Snake Blakeslee, (2) Trinchera Cave, (3) Medina Rockshelter; *Kansas* (4) Tobias, Thompson, Malone, (5) Marion County sites, (6) Elliot, Arkansas City Country Club, Larcom–Haggard, (7) Larned, Lewis, (8) Armstrong, Hallman, (9) Buresh, Nulik, (10) Pratt, (11) Bell, Booth; *Oklahoma* (12) Deer Creek, Bryson–Paddock, (13) Uncas, (14) Lasley Vore, (15) Stamper, (16) Roy Smith, (17) Two Sisters, (18) Zimms, New Smith, (19) Hedding, (20) Brewer, Patton A, Patton B, Jones, Densmore, Arthur, Carpenter, (21) Currie, (22) Lacy, Lee I, Lee II, (23) Braden, (24) Grant, (25) Brown, (26) Mouse, Shahan, Heerwald, Goodman I, (27) Phillips, (28) Linville II, (29) Edwards II, (30) McLemore, Carl McLemore, (31) Longest, (32) Devil's Canyon; *Texas* (33) Saddleback Mesa, (34) Alibates 28, Coetas Creek Ruin, Antelope Creek Ruin 22, (35) Black Dog Village, Arrowhead Peak, (36) Jack Allen, (37) Buried City, Moorehead, Courson, Kirk Courson, Kit Courson, (38) Coyote, Glass, Spanish Fort, (39) Chicken House, Dillard, (40) Harrell, (41) Bird Point Island, Adams Ranch, (42) Hogge Bridge, Sister Grove, (43) Pearson, (44) Gilbert, (45) Womack, (46) Vinson, (47) Stone, (48) Stansbury.

aspect and revised the classification scheme, defining the Upper Canark variant as consisting of the Antelope Creek phase in the Texas and Oklahoma panhandles and the Apishapa phase in southeastern Colorado and northeastern New Mexico. Later work resulted in the identification of the Buried City complex along Wolf Creek in the Texas panhandle and northwestern Oklahoma (Brooks 1989; Hughes and Hughes-Jones 1987). The Zimms complex in far western Oklahoma (Drass et al. 1987; Flynn 1986) also seems to have many similarities with the Antelope Creek phase, and it may be part of the Upper Canark variant.

The Upper Canark variant extends along the upper reaches of the Canadian River and southern tributaries of the upper Arkansas River in the High Plains of the Texas and Oklahoma panhandles, southeastern Colorado, and northeastern New Mexico (Lintz 1986). Major settlements consist of single and multi-room structures usually constructed with stone-slab foundations. Caves, rock shelters, and small camps are also reported (Campbell 1969; Gunnerson 1987). Artifact assemblages are typical of Southern Plains villagers. Cordmarked globular pots, small triangular side-notched and unnotched points, end and side scrapers, ovate knives, manos and grinding basins, and bison-bone tools are common at these sites. Subsistence is based on hunting and gathering and on horticulture. Bison, antelope, and deer are major game, and there is evidence for cultivation of maize, beans, and squash (Lintz 1984). Dates for the Upper Canark variant range from about A.D. 1100 to 1500 (Lintz 1986).

ANTELOPE CREEK PHASE

Lintz (1986) defined the Antelope Creek phase to include the former Antelope Creek focus and the Optima focus in the Texas and Oklahoma panhandles. Sites concentrate along the Canadian River in the Texas panhandle, but stone-slab houses are found from the Beaver (North Canadian) River in Oklahoma as far south as the Prairie Dog Fork of the Red River. The phase roughly corresponds to the short-grass-prairie setting that extends from about the Texas–Oklahoma border west to at least the edge of the Llano Estacado (Lintz 1986). This phase is one of the best dated complexes on the Southern Plains. Many radiocarbon dates, a few archaeomagnetic determinations, and cross-dated southwestern ceramics indicate occupation between A.D. 1200 and 1500. Hundreds of Antelope Creek–phase sites are recorded, and many have been tested or excavated (J. Hughes 1991). Major components are found at Alibates 28, Antelope Creek 22, Saddleback Mesa, Coetas Creek Ruin 55, Arrowhead Peak, and Black Dog Village in Texas, as well as Stamper, Roy Smith, and Two Sisters in Oklahoma (Lintz 1986).

Research on Antelope Creek has focused on the conspicuous stone-slab-house ruins, but small open camps, rock shelters, and bison kills are reported (J. Hughes 1991). In addition, many of the pits at the Alibates quarries are attributed to the mining of Alibates agatized dolomite by the villagers. Habitation sites include isolated homesteads, small hamlets, and large villages. Large villages may comprise several one-room houses or multiroom structures. House sites occur on terraces, valley walls, or bluffs near major streams; around springs; and, occasionally, on high isolated mesas. Site densities appear highest in the Canadian and North Canadian river valleys. Some of the small sites on low terraces may represent specialized field huts occupied during the summer (Lintz 1984). There may have been a change in settlement pattern through time, with a shift from large contiguous room structures to isolated household units and possibly a move toward more intensive settlement of lateral tributaries near springs and seeps (Lintz 1986:261).

Although the use of stone-slab wall foundations is characteristic of Antelope Creek, there is considerable variability in architecture. In fact, a few houses have no stone construction. Houses may also contain one room or multiple contiguous rooms. The typical Antelope Creek house is a large, rectangular, semi-subterranean structure constructed with single or double rows of vertical rock slabs for the base of the walls. Single-room houses have a central floor channel extending from the east to the west wall, creating wide benches along the north and south walls (Lintz 1984). Entryways extend from the east wall, and a raised platform or altar is found along the west wall. A central hearth and two to four center support posts are associated with the floor channel. Storage pits and walled bins may occur on the benches. Small circular structures with central hearths are also recorded as isolated units or attached to other rooms. Multiple-room structures include houses with one dominant room and small square or circular storage rooms and circular anterooms. Larger buildings may contain over 20 rooms and include semicircular and square storage rooms and stone-lined cists (Lintz 1986). Lintz (1984) suggests that there was little planning involved with the construction of the large buildings. Rooms were simply added when needed, apparently maintaining no specific building configuration (Figure 12.3). The variability in Antelope Creek house forms is related to several factors, including functional differences and engineering limitations, plus shifts through time that reflect cultural adjustments to changing climatic conditions and population pressures (Lintz 1986:255–262).

Cache pits and middens are associated with most house sites. Pits may be basin-shaped or bell-shaped, and some are lined with stone slabs. Burials are found in pits in the village, under or above house floors, and in hilltop cemeteries near villages. Many graves in houses appear to postdate the use of the structures. Most interments are individuals in a flexed or semiflexed position. Graves may be unmarked, covered with rocks, or slab lined (Lintz 1984). Few personal possessions occur with burials, but items of adornment such as beads and pendants and utilitarian items such as points, knives, and pots are reported (Lintz 1986).

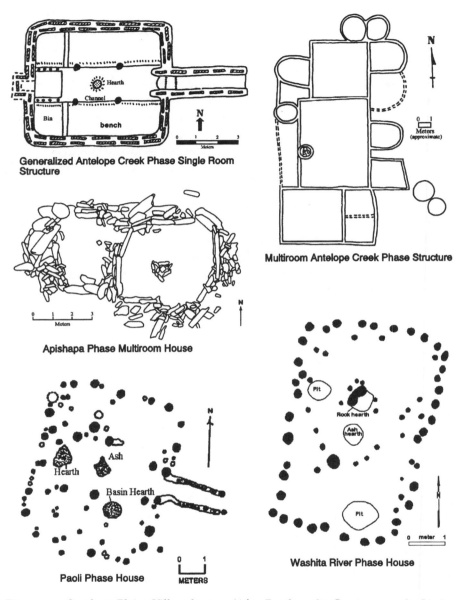

Generalized Antelope Creek Phase Single Room Structure

Multiroom Antelope Creek Phase Structure

Apishapa Phase Multiroom House

Paoli Phase House

Washita River Phase House

Figure 12.3. Southern Plains Village houses. (After Brooks 1987; Gunnerson 1989; Lintz 1986)

Artifacts from Antelope Creek are very similar to those found at Plains Village sites to the east. Projectile points are predominantly small unnotched and side-notched forms (Fresno, Harrell, and Washita). Other chipped stone includes ovate and diamond-beveled knives, expanding-base drills, reamers, and flake cutting and scraping tools. Side and end scrapers are also common, with distinctive "guitar-pick" forms in many assemblages (J. Hughes 1991). The Antelope Creek people probably controlled the Alibates quarries, and most chipped-stone artifacts are made of this local material. Stone elbow pipes, shaft abraders, and a variety of grinding implements are similar to those found at Turkey Creek– and Custer-phase sites to the east. Bison-tibia digging-stick tips, scapula hoes, squash knives, and other bone tools are common. Mussel shell was used for scrapers and spoons.

Pottery from Antelope Creek–phase sites consists primarily of a cord-marked, sand-tempered ware called Borger Cordmarked. Pots are thin, globular, heart-shaped jars with wide mouths and vertical or slightly flaring rims. The cordmarking usually is vertical on the body and rim of the pot. Other decorations are rare, but an incised line or a row of fingernail punctations may encircle the rim–body junction (Suhm and Jelks 1962:15). Perforated sherd disks and clay beads are occasionally found, as well as a few painted pottery sherds originating from pueblos in northern New Mexico (Crabb 1968). Other exotic items—such as obsidian, turquoise, tubular clay pipes, and *Olivella* shell beads—indicate a strong trade network with the Southwest.

Subsistence was based on hunting, gathering, and horticulture. Duffield (1970) has suggested that hunting focused on bison, but antelope and deer were also important. Bison is by far the predominant game animal at the Landergin Mesa site in the western Texas panhandle, and evidence indicates that bison hunting and the processing of grease from bison bone increased through time (Demarcay 1986). A variety of small mammals, waterfowl, fish, and mussels supplemented the diet. Maize, beans, and squash have been recovered from Antelope Creek–phase sites as well as wild plant foods such as plums, persimmons, prickly pear, and various grass seeds (Green 1967:157; J. Keller 1975:22). The presence of maize at most sites and the abundance of bone digging tools indicate that horticultural products were important in the villagers' diet. A study of human bone from Antelope Creek sites shows the C_4 carbon-isotope signatures resulting from a diet rich in maize and bison, although some wild plants such as amaranth, grasses, and cactus are also sources of this carbon isotope (Habicht-Mauche et al. 1994).

There are several models for the origin of the Antelope Creek phase. Initially, researchers suggested that this culture represented a migration of Plains or Southwest groups into the High Plains around A.D. 1200 (Baerreis and Bryson 1965; Bryson et al. 1970; Krieger 1946; Lintz 1976; Watson 1950). In one model (Baerreis and Bryson 1965), increasing precipitation in the southern High Plains coincides with decreasing precipitation in the Central Plains, resulting in a movement of Upper Republican peoples into the western Canadian River valley, where moist conditions were favorable for horticulture. More recent paleoenvironmental studies, however, indicate that the climate in the Southern Plains also was changing toward xeric conditions by the fourteenth century (Lintz 1986). Campbell (1969) suggests that Antelope Creek may be derived from an expansion of the Apishapa phase into the Canadian River valley. Lintz (1986) argues against this proposition, noting that there are considerable cultural differences that cannot be derived from an Apishapa source. It is more likely that Antelope Creek developed from an indigenous Woodland group, probably the Lake Creek complex (J. Hughes 1991). The distinctive architecture represents a borrowing of ideas and construction techniques from Puebloan groups (Lintz 1986).

Population increases in conjunction with drier climatic conditions from A.D. 1300 to 1500 led to changes in adaptation. Antelope Creek people responded to the stresses of population pressure with shifts in settlement patterns, expansion of trade networks, and conflict or warfare to control resources (Lintz 1986). The migration of the Apache into the Southern Plains by A.D. 1500 also may have influenced changes in indigenous groups or resulted in the abandonment of the area by them. By the time of Coronado's expedition, their villages were in ruins and only nomadic groups are recorded in the Texas panhandle. Researchers have been unable to determine if Antelope Creek–phase people remained in the area as nomadic groups or moved elsewhere. Their relation to historic groups requires additional research, but their similarity to other Plains Village people is considered evidence for a Plains Caddoan association (J. Hughes 1991).

APISHAPA PHASE

Stone-slab structures have been documented in southeastern Colorado, and the Apishapa focus was initially defined for late prehistoric sites in this area (Campbell 1976; Withers 1954). Lintz's (1986) reexamination of the Panhandle aspect resulted in the reclassification of this complex as a phase. Its sites are concentrated on mesas and in canyonland settings along the Apishapa and Purgatoire rivers in southeastern Colorado, but the culture extends to the Black Mesa area of the Oklahoma panhandle and possibly to the Cimarron–North Canadian divide in New Mexico (Lintz 1986). Major sites include Snake Blakeslee and Cramer near the Apishapa River (Gunnerson 1989), Avery Ranch near Pueblo, Colorado (Watts 1971), and Trinchera Cave (Wood-Simpson 1976), Medina Rockshelter, and Steamboat Island Fort (Campbell 1976) on tributaries of the Purgatoire River.

Campbell's (1976) survey of the Chaquaqua Plateau recorded stone-foundation structures dated to as early as A.D. 450. He identified Apishapa components as developing from this Woodland culture and dating after about A.D. 1000. After A.D. 1400, there is a decline in Apishapa sites. Lintz's (1989) analysis of 28 radiocarbon dates from sites attributed to the Apishapa phase indicates a temporal span from A.D. 900 to 1390. In contrast, Gunnerson (1989) argues for a "Classic Apishapa," which would date primarily to the thirteenth century. Earlier sites are viewed as ancestral, developing from the Graneros phase, a local Woodland complex. Gunnerson's (1989:53) calibrated radiocarbon dates from two sites, however, range from A.D. 890 to 1410, close to the temporal range suggested by Lintz (1989). The confusion on the time span derives from different definitions of this complex and the lack of radiocarbon dates from many sites. There is general agreement that Apishapa is an indigenous development stemming from a local Woodland culture: the Graneros phase. The long history of stone-slab construction in this area presents problems when attempting to differentiate cultural complexes, but changing tool assemblages, architecture, and subsistence activities indicate the development of a culture that has many similarities to the Antelope Creek phase. Identification of when distinctive changes in cultural patterns occurred in this area and, thus, definition of the time span for the Apishapa phase will require additional research and radiocarbon dates.

Surveys of the Chaquaqua Plateau have noted three kinds of sites: rock shelters and caves, small open encampments, and stone-slab enclosures representing single- and multiple-room structures and barriers or fortifications (Campbell 1976). Petroglyph sites are also known, but none have yet been linked to Apishapa occupations. Many rock shelters have been observed in this area, and testing indicates that they were used as temporary camps. Shelters and caves usually are near springs or water sources and contain hearths and sometimes simple barrier stone walls (Campbell 1976). Open camps tend to be near water and in upper canyons or on mesas (Lintz 1989). These sites have not been excavated, but most are assumed to be temporary camps.

The largest sites are the stone-slab enclosures that usually are found in the upper canyons and on buttes and mesas. Many of these sites are in defendable locations, and stone perimeter walls or fortifications enclose some sites (Campbell 1976). Houses consist primarily of circular single rooms, but paired rooms and buildings containing up to eight contiguous rooms are recorded (Figure 12.3). Rectangular rooms similar to those at Antelope Creek sites are rare, but oval and semicircular floor plans are recorded (Lintz 1986). Rooms vary in size, and some smaller units may have been granaries or storage areas. Construction involved laying wall foundations of horizontal or vertical slabs. Natural rock outcrops and boulders are sometimes incorporated as part of the walls, and floors are the natural ground surface or bedrock. Wooden posts and brush may have served as roofs, and vertical rock slabs are reported as interior roof supports at some sites (Gunnerson 1989). Few structures have identifiable entryways, suggesting access through the roof. Central hearths are recorded in larger rooms, but many units have no interior features. Burials at stone-slab sites and rock shelters consist of flexed individuals interred in pits (Campbell 1976:62). There usually are no grave goods.

Some of the tools typical of Plains Village sites in other areas are rare or absent in Apishapa assemblages. Few diamond-beveled knives, pipes, and bison-bone digging implements (tibia digging-stick tips and scapula hoes) are documented at Apishapa sites. Chipped-stone artifacts are made primarily from quartzites. Alibates represents less than 5 percent of assemblages (Lintz 1989:283). Chipped-stone tools include bifacial knives, snub-nosed end scrapers, side scrapers, expanding-base drills, and modified flakes. Points are predominantly side notched (Washita), with some unnotched arrowpoints. Ground stone is represented by bifacial manos, shallow grinding basins, and abraders. The primary ceramics are globular cordmarked pots, but sherds are not common at many sites. Grit-tempered pots from the Apishapa canyon area appear very similar to Borger Cordmarked, although Gunnerson (1989:71–73) defines them as a new type: Munsell Gray. A few sherds exhibit smoothing of rims, incised lines on rims or lips, or, rarely, appliqué nodes. The most common bone artifacts are awls and tubular beads, but a few bone beamers, digging-stick tips, and shell ornaments are found. Perishable artifacts such as sandals, basketry, mats, bows, cordage, and snares are recovered from rock shelters and caves (Lintz 1989). Trade goods are rare, but assemblages may contain southwestern pottery (corrugated sherds, Taos Plain and Incised, Talpa Black on White, and Rowe Black on White), obsidian, and *Olivella* shell beads (Campbell 1976; Gunnerson 1989).

Apishapa people exploited a variety of settings in hunting small mammals, bison, deer, antelope, and other animals. Bison remains indicate the extensive processing of bone for grease (Hamblin 1989). Wild plants include grasses, sunflower, chokecherry, wild plum, grape, cactus, piñon nuts, pigweed, goosefoot, and purslane (Lintz 1989:283). There is some evidence for the cultivation of plants on the Chaquaqua Plateau. Fragments of maize, beans, and gourds have been recovered, but these plants are found primarily in rock shelters (Campbell 1976). Virtually no maize fragments have been recovered from larger house sites, and there are few bone digging implements. Pollen studies at the Cramer site recovered no maize pollen (Cummings 1989). This evidence suggests that maize and possibly other crops were not grown at or transported to some of the habitation sites. However, most of these sites are near arable land, and many parts of maize plants (including leaves, husks, and shanks [Campbell 1976:37]) have been found in rock shelters, suggesting some local cultivation.

There is general agreement that Apishapa developed locally from the Graneros phase. Woodland sites with small circular houses are present on the Chaquaqua Plateau (Campbell 1976). The Apishapa culture appears to have disappeared from the plateau around A.D. 1400. There is evidence of stone rings, perhaps tipi rings, in the area after this time, but it is not clear if they relate to the previous Apishapa culture.

BURIED CITY COMPLEX

Beginning in 1985, a series of excavations and surveys along Wolf Creek in the Texas panhandle resulted in the identification of the Buried City complex (D. Hughes 1991; Hughes and Hughes-Jones 1987). This complex has stone-foundation houses similar to those at Antelope Creek–phase sites, but there are variations in architecture and artifacts that distinguish the Wolf Creek sites. Major sites include the Buried City or Handley ruins, first defined by Eyerly (1907), and the Moorehead, Courson, Kirk Courson, and Kit Courson ruins. D. Hughes (1991:142) suggests that the main structural sites of the complex occur along a 3-mile reach of Wolf Creek in Ochiltree County. Sites farther east in Ellis County, Oklahoma, also may relate to this complex (Drass and Turner 1989). Dates for the houses indicate occupation between about A.D. 1150 and 1350 (Hughes and Hughes-Jones 1987).

Buried City sites consist primarily of single-room houses built in groups on high terraces, knolls, or bluffs near Wolf Creek. Site densities are high and exceed Antelope Creek–phase densities for the Canadian River basin (D. Hughes 1991). The square houses are basically the same as those described for Antelope Creek sites, but they may be slightly larger, averaging 689 square feet, and the interior wall benches are larger. Wall foundations are constructed of caliche rocks, and some may have been used as footing stones for vertical posts (D. Hughes 1991). Hughes also indicates the presence of circular pit houses that may precede the construction of the square houses. House sites usually contain other features, such as exterior cylindrical storage pits and burials. Burials are semiflexed and often contain beads and tools as grave goods. They typically are covered by rock cairns.

Assemblages are generally similar to Antelope Creek–phase materials. Side-notched projectile points predominate at Buried City sites, but Fresnos and Scallorns are also recorded (D. Hughes 1991). A distinctive characteristic of Buried City assemblages, however, is the pottery. Hughes and Hughes-Jones (1987) describe plain and decorated (Courson Pinched) sherds that usually are not found at Antelope Creek–phase sites. Pottery includes a cordmarked, sand-tempered ware similar to Borger Cordmarked, but smoothed or smoothed-over cordmarked sherds may compose up to half of the assemblage. A similar sand-tempered smoothed pottery in western Oklahoma is defined as Wolf Creek Plain (Drass and Turner 1989:190). A variety of decorations occurs on rims and lips of both the cordmarked and the plain pots. Collared, chevron-incised, crenelated, filleted, pinched, fingernail gouged, and punctated rims are recorded, as are incised or punctated lips (Drass and Turner 1989; Hughes and Hughes-Jones 1987). These decorations resemble those on Geneseo pottery from Great Bend–aspect sites in Kansas (Hughes and Hughes-Jones 1987:78).

Hughes (1991) suggests that the Buried City complex developed locally from Woodland groups in the Wolf Creek valley. The presence of circular pit houses may indicate a gradual development analogous to some of the architectural changes noted for the Apishapa phase. The similarity of Buried City pottery to the Great Bend–aspect wares suggests that these groups may have interacted with people to the east in the Central Plains. Further study of material culture should reveal more information on the relations of the Buried City people to other Plains groups.

ZIMMS COMPLEX

The Zimms complex is defined from a few sites reported in far western Oklahoma (Drass et al. 1987). It is similar to the Antelope Creek phase, and Lintz (1986:29–30) suggests that Zimms sites may be part of that phase. Zimms is distinguished by house patterns similar to those at Antelope Creek–phase sites, but lack stone-slab wall foundations. Assemblages vary slightly from both Antelope Creek and Turkey Creek materials (Drass and Swenson 1986; Moore 1988b). The primary sites for Zimms are Zimms, New Smith, and Lamb–Miller in Roger Mills County, and Hedding in Woodward County, Oklahoma. The extent of the complex awaits further research, but it appears to be confined to the short-grass, rolling plains of western Oklahoma and, possibly, the eastern Texas panhandle. Radiocarbon and archaeomagnetic dates from two sites indicate a range of about A.D. 1250 to 1450 (Brooks et al. 1992:72; Flynn 1984:287), roughly contemporaneous with Antelope Creek and Turkey Creek.

Settlements consist of small hamlets, usually on high terraces or ridges above streams. At least one mortuary site containing burials placed under small arbors is also recorded (Brooks et al. 1992). Houses have been excavated at the Zimms and Hedding sites. Square houses include a recessed central floor trench, benches, and altars typical of Antelope Creek houses, but they are constructed with wall posts and daub instead of stone wall foundations. A similar house is documented at the Jack Allen site in the Texas panhandle. Lintz (1986:92) suggests that Jack Allen is situated in an area where stone was not available. Large caliche rocks also are not found in western Oklahoma near Zimms-complex sites.

The Zimms artifact assemblage differs from that of Antelope Creek in pottery and lithic materials. Zimms ceramic assemblages are dominated by smoothed sherds, as compared with the sand-tempered cordmarked wares that dominate Antelope Creek sites. Similar pottery with fossiliferous shale/shell or limestone temper is found at Turkey Creek sites to the east. However, Turkey

Creek–phase sites have significant amounts of cordmarked sherds, sometimes representing over 28 percent of an assemblage. Lithic assemblages at Zimms sites are marked by significant amounts (about 5 percent) of Florence A Chert from north-central Oklahoma (Drass et al. 1987). Very little Florence A is found at most Turkey Creek and Antelope Creek sites. Alibates is a common lithic material in Zimms assemblages, but most of this stone may have been obtained from local gravels (Flynn 1984:280). Other trade materials are rare, but obsidian, Edwards Chert, Caddoan and Puebloan pottery, and *Olivella* shell beads have been found (Brooks 1989; Brooks et al. 1992).

Redbed Plains Variant

Plains Village sites have been the focus of archaeological investigations in central and western Oklahoma since the WPA work in the late 1930s. Bell and Baerreis (1951) defined the Washita River focus for villages in central Oklahoma and the Custer focus for villages in western Oklahoma. Subsequent research (Brooks 1989; Hofman 1978, 1984a) has redefined these foci into temporally distinct phases: the Washita River and Custer phases. The Custer phase is considered earlier and probably ancestral to the Washita River phase. Further research (Drass and Flynn 1990; Drass and Swenson 1986) has identified additional geographic variations in these late prehistoric complexes. As a result, the Redbed Plains variant has been defined for Plains Village sites in central and west-central Oklahoma (Drass 1995). This variant incorporates four related phases that reflect both temporal distinctions and the eastern and western geographic variations.

The Redbed Plains variant encompasses Plains Village sites along the Washita River and parts of the Canadian River from the Arbuckle Mountains in south-central Oklahoma to the edge of the High Plains in western Oklahoma. Its northern and southern limits are not well defined, but sites in parts of the Red River basin to the south and some in the North Canadian River basin may be included. The core area clearly is the Washita River basin, with villages set on terraces along the river and many of its tributaries. Radiocarbon dates range from A.D. 800 or 900 to 1450. The four divisions of Redbed Plains are the Paoli, Washita River, Custer, and Turkey Creek phases. The Paoli phase is recognized as the early (900–1250) Plains Village society in central Oklahoma, and the Custer phase is restricted to contemporaneous sites in the mixed-grass-prairie settings of western Oklahoma. This geographic division extends through time: the Washita River phase includes the later (1250–1450) villages in central Oklahoma, while Turkey Creek is used for later sites in west-central Oklahoma.

The most extensive research has been conducted on Paoli- and Washita River–phase sites in central Oklahoma. Drass (1995) suggests that the Paoli phase evolved from local Plains Woodland groups and represents the development of sedentary horticulturists in central Oklahoma. Changes in artifact assemblages and settlement and subsistence practices from the Woodland period to the Paoli phase are related to the intensification of plant cultivation and the evolution of technologies, exploitation patterns, and social systems associated with the development of a food-producing society. Many of the changes in tools, subsistence systems, and social organization that mark the growth of the Washita River phase from the Paoli phase are, in turn, a result of the interaction of various environmental factors and technological and social conditions. Changing climatic conditions that affected crops and the availability of bison, in conjunction with increasing human populations concentrating in the Washita River valley, resulted in the specialization of crop production and the intensification of bison hunting over time (Drass 1995). A parallel pattern of development is suggested for the Custer and Turkey Creek phases in western Oklahoma, although less information is available for that area. There is some evidence that Redbed Plains–variant villagers in both central and western Oklahoma continued to occupy the area into the protohistoric period, but more work is needed to identify the changes that took place and the factors influencing these developments.

PAOLI PHASE

The Paoli phase is defined from sites in the Washita and Canadian river basins of central Oklahoma (Drass 1995). All the investigated sites are villages built on terraces or ridges near rivers in the prairie and scrub-oak biotic zones. One site, Brewer, was excavated in the early 1950s, but it was attributed to a Plains Woodland occupation (Duffield 1953). Research in 1986 produced radiocarbon dates that place the site in the early Plains Village period (Drass 1988). Since then, additional sites dating between A.D. 900 and 1250 have been investigated. The major sites are Currie, Lacy, Patton A and B, Jones, and Densmore.

The Paoli phase appears to represent the first sedentary occupation in central Oklahoma. Villages are small, occupying from less than 2.5 acres to up to 10 acres. Villages have not been extensively excavated, but estimates from Patton A indicate a minimum of six houses there. Other sites may contain only two or three structures. Many Paoli-phase villages are buried by recent alluvium, but some terraces in the central Washita River valley have several villages within .3 mile (Drass 1995). Settlements are not documented along tributaries; Paoli groups appear to have concentrated on resources in the larger river floodplains. Lithic workshops and temporary camps are reported from upland areas, but they have not been investigated.

Houses are reported from Patton A, Currie, and Lacy. They are rectangular structures between 20 and 30 feet long and 16 and 26 feet wide. Posts are used for wall construction, and walls and roofs were thatched with grass. Daub is used in some but not all houses. Four center posts and circular or irregular central hearths are characteristic. Structures are aligned roughly north–south, with extended entrys that face east or southeast. Internal posts indicate possible benches and activity areas, but intramural pits are lacking. External features are common, with many pits represented. Pits include cylindrical, bell-shaped, rounded-oval, and shallow basin forms. In addition, there are very large pits, extending over 6 to 10 feet in length (Drass 1995). Pits are typically trash filled, but many were probably used for storage and as roasting pits. Isolated burials have been found at a few Paoli sites. They generally have few grave goods and are scattered in the village area.

Paoli-phase assemblages contain artifacts that appear intermediate in style and technology between earlier Plains Woodland and later Washita River–phase materials. Pottery is divided between plain and cordmarked wares that incorporate a variety of tempers. A stone-or grit-tempered, cordmarked ware (Lindsay Cordmarked) is common at the earliest villages, with smoothed-surface pottery (Lee Plain) increasing through time. The earliest vessels are unshouldered, conical jars that also are found in Woodland sites. Slightly constricted necks, everted rims, and rounded and flat bottoms appear on jars during the Paoli phase. Tempers gradually change, with the inclusion of mixtures of shell and grit. Projectile points include occasional dart points and a variety of arrowpoints. Paoli-phase sites contain mostly corner-notched (Scallorn, Alba, and Bonham) and side-notched (Harrell and Washita) arrowpoints, but later sites also have unnotched (Fresno) points. Other tools include small end scrapers, drills and perforators, manos, grinding basins, U-shaped abraders, and hammerstones. Bone implements consist primarily of ornaments such as bone and shell beads and awls, and shaft wrenches. Stone and clay elbow pipes and pottery disks are also present, but bone digging tools are rare at most Paoli sites.

Although bone digging tools are uncommon, there is direct evidence for the intensive cultivation of maize and other crops (Drass 1993; 1995). Domesticated beans are documented by at least A.D. 1200 (Drass 1993); marsh elder was cultivated, and little barley, maygrass, and knotweed were collected, if not cultivated. A variety of wild plant foods—including goosefoot, dropseed, sunflower, plums, and nuts—also were gathered. Various game animals were hunted, but the emphasis was on resources in river valleys. Few bison are found at Paoli sites, but they are slightly more common at later sites (Drass 1995). Deer, rabbits, and other small game were important, and aquatic resources such as fish and mussels were a significant part of the diet. There is little evidence for trade. Lithic resources are predominantly local cherts and quartzites. Small amounts of Florence A Chert from north-central Oklahoma and Edwards Chert from north-central Texas appear. A few pieces of Caddoan pottery, either imports or local imitations, indicate contact with groups to the east.

The similarity of Paoli-phase material culture to earlier Plains Woodland materials suggests a local origin for this culture. Paoli pottery is closely related to that found in Woodland sites dating from A.D. 1 to 800. Points and other tools also reveal a continuum from Plains Woodland to the Paoli phase. The Pruitt complex was initially defined for Plains Woodland sites in central Oklahoma (Barr 1966), but the major sites for this complex are now attributed to the Plains Village period (Drass 1988). Woodland sites are documented in this area (Hartley and Raymer 1993; Moore 1988a; Vehik 1984), but there is no defined complex. The Paoli phase represents the local development of a sedentary horticultural society from Plains Woodland origins, one that continued to evolve in the Plains Village period, and Paoli is considered ancestral to the Washita River phase, which is so well documented in the same area (Drass 1995).

WASHITA RIVER PHASE

The Washita River focus, as originally defined by Bell and Baerreis (1951), has undergone several revisions, and the Washita River phase is currently defined for sites in the central Washita and in parts of the central Canadian river basins. Many dates are available: occupation occurred between about A.D. 1250 and 1450. This culture is a continuation of the Paoli phase, but is defined by changing adaptations and material assemblages. Villages are found north of the Arbuckle Mountains and as far west as Caddo County. Many Washita River villages are documented, and major excavations have been conducted at the Braden, Grant, Lee I and II, Brown, Arthur, Carpenter, Van Schuyver, and Willingham sites.

Washita River–phase villages are found in the same settings as Paoli villages. The later Washita River sites may be more numerous than Paoli sites and may be larger (Brooks 1989; Hofman 1978). Villages cover up to 15 acres and surveys have indicated that villages are found on average every 1.5 to 2 miles along the Washita River (Brooks 1983). Work at the Arthur site indicates that up to 20 houses may be present, along with sheet middens, pits, hearths, and cemetery areas (Brooks 1987). Villages appear to have been occupied year-round, but special activity sites such as workshops and temporary camps include rock shelters that are also associated with this period. Individual burials are sometimes found in villages, but separate cemeteries are often nearby (Bell 1984a).

There is some variation in the houses excavated at the Braden, Arthur, and Carpenter sites. Six houses at Arthur provide the best information on form. These houses are similar to, but slightly smaller (11 to 15 feet wide and 16 to 21 feet long) than Paoli structures. They are rectangular with two center posts and circular or rectangular, clay-lined central hearths. They lack the extended entryways found in Paoli houses, but they have at least one interior storage pit, usually in the southeast corner (Figure 12.3). In contrast, one house from Carpenter is basically the same as Paoli-phase structures, but it dates to about A.D.

1410. It appears that houses with two center posts, interior pits, and no extended entryway became common during the Washita River phase, but some structures with four center posts continued to be used after A.D. 1250. External pits are abundant and include the same shapes documented for Paoli.

Artifact assemblages are similar to Paoli assemblages, but there is increasing diversity in the Washita River–phase artifacts. Polished celts and diamond-beveled knives are characteristic of Washita River sites, although neither tool is found in large numbers. Unifacial scrapers are abundant, and grooved abraders for smoothing bone tools or sharpening celts are common (Drass 1995). Bone tools include many bison-bone digging implements, such as scapula and horn-core hoes and tibia digging-stick tips. Deer-jaw sickles also appear after about A.D. 1250. Projectile points are predominantly side notched and unnotched. Cordmarked pottery almost disappeared during the Washita River phase, and shell-tempered globular jars (Nocona Plain) became common. They are smoothed but not polished pots with rounded or flat bases and constricted necks. Decorations are infrequent, but Lee and Nocona Plain pots may have lip tabs, handles, appliqué nodes and strips, punctates, or incising. A few Caddoan-type sherds that may be imports or local imitations are found at most Washita River villages.

Contact or trade with surrounding areas is evidenced by the presence of a variety of exotic items. Washita River—phase groups used various materials in making chipped-stone tools, but specific chert resources sometimes were preferred. In the Pauls Valley area, villagers exploited Frisco Chert from a source about 30 miles to the east. Materials were also imported from more distant sources, including Florence A Chert from north-central Oklahoma, Edwards Chert from north-central Texas, and various cherts from eastern Oklahoma (Drass 1995). Although rare, finds of conch-shell ornaments, *Olivella* shell beads, obsidian, exotic pots, and pipestone indicate interaction with groups to the east and west (Bell 1984a). Some exotic pottery and marine shell from burials suggest that there may have been some status differentiation.

Subsistence activities included the typical Plains Village combination of hunting and horticulture. Washita River–phase groups, however, moved toward increasing specialization. High-yield crops such as maize, beans, and probably squash may have increased in importance, while such crops as marsh elder disappeared or became much less significant (Drass 1995). Washita River people also incorporated more bison and possibly less fish in their diet than had Paoli people. Deer and small game remained important sources of protein, and a variety of wild plant foods was collected.

By A.D. 1500, there is a dramatic decrease in the number of villages along the Washita and Canadian rivers in central Oklahoma. Initially, researchers (Bell 1973; Hofman 1978) suggested that Washita River–phase groups abandoned the area and moved north or east to become the modern Wichita. More recent evidence indicates that the area was not completely abandoned and that some Washita River groups may have stayed there. The protohistoric Wheeler phase of central and western Oklahoma is suggested to be Plains Caddoan, and these people may represent descendants of Washita River–phase groups. The presence of Apachean groups in western Oklahoma by A.D. 1500, however, has led to some debate on the ethnic affiliation of some of these sites (Baugh 1986; Hofman 1978, 1984b).

CUSTER AND TURKEY CREEK PHASES

The Custer and Turkey Creek phases are very similar to the Paoli and Washita River phases of central Oklahoma. The Custer focus was initially defined by Bell and Baerreis (1951) for a group of Plains Village sites in Custer County, Oklahoma. Hofman (1978) redefined the focus to a phase and extended its distribution to a larger area of western Oklahoma. The definition of the Paoli phase and geographic variation in artifact assemblages led to the redefinition of the extent of the Custer phase (Drass 1995; Drass and Swenson 1986). Custer sites are found in the mixed-grass prairies of west-central Oklahoma centering along the Washita and Canadian river basins in Custer, Washita, Beckham, and Roger Mills counties (Drass 1995). The Turkey Creek phase is found in the same setting, but radiocarbon dates place Custer from about A.D. 800 to 1250 and the subsequent Turkey Creek from A.D. 1250 to 1450. The primary Custer-phase sites are Mouse, Phillips, Shahan, Hodge, Edwards II, and Linville II. The major Turkey Creek–phase sites are Heerwald, McLemore, Goodman I, Carl McLemore, and Wessner I.

The Custer and Turkey Creek phases are distinguished from the Paoli and Washita River phases by slight variations in artifacts, settlement, and subsistence. Few excavations have been conducted at villages in western Oklahoma, but many villages are recorded. Custer and Turkey Creek villages occur most frequently along tributaries rather than the main rivers, whereas Paoli and Washita River sites in central Oklahoma are almost exclusively in the main river valleys. The western sites appear to be small and may contain from one or two houses up to 10. Only one Custer-phase house has been excavated (at the Mouse site), so there is little information on house patterns. The Mouse-site structure is rectangular, about 15 by 20 feet, but it lacks the four center posts and extended entryway found at Paoli houses. It contains a central rock hearth and possibly an interior storage pit (Buck 1959). Turkey Creek houses have been found at the Heerwald, McLemore, Goodman I, and Goodman II sites (Brighton 1951; Gallaher 1951; Pillaert 1963; Shaeffer 1965). These houses are square to rectangular and are 16 feet wide up to 24 feet long. They include primarily four-center-post structures, but a two-center-post house is reported from the Goodman I site. All houses have central rock or pit hearths. There usually are no interior storage pits, but a variety of external pits are common.

Custer and Turkey Creek assemblages are very similar to those at Paoli and Washita River sites. Ceramic assemblages exhibit some change from cord-marked toward smoothed wares through time in western Oklahoma, but cord-marking continues as a significant part of the later, Turkey Creek–phase pottery assemblages (Drass and Swenson 1986). Turkey Creek sites contain from 12 to 28 percent cordmarked sherds compared with 95 percent smoothed wares at Washita River sites (Drass 1995). Tempers also differ from those used in central Oklahoma. Crushed shales containing fossil shell predominate in the west. Very little pottery contains the crushed mussel-shell temper found in much of the Washita River–phase pottery. Vessel shapes and decorations are similar to those in central Oklahoma assemblages. Corncob-impressed "paint" cups also appear to be slightly more common at western sites.

Lithic tools are basically the same as those found to the east, but with perhaps more diamond-beveled knives in western Oklahoma. Stone elbow pipes may also be more common at Custer and Turkey Creek sites. Lithic material sources consist primarily of local chert and quartzite gravels. Alibates seems to have been a preferred material for making many tools, but this material can be found in gravel deposits along the Canadian River in western Oklahoma (Wyckoff 1993). The Frisco Chert used by many central Oklahoma villagers is not found at most western villages (Drass and Swenson 1986). Bone tools include beads, flakers, awls and pins, and bison-bone hoes and digging-stick tips. Bison-bone digging implements are not common until the Turkey Creek phase (Drass and Moore 1987). Disk beads and inlays made from mussel shell may be characteristic of Custer-phase assemblages.

Subsistence activities for Custer- and Turkey Creek–phase groups included hunting and horticulture, and maize is well documented at some sites (Drass and Flynn 1990). An assortment of wild plants—including sunflower, little barley, and goosefoot—were gathered. Animals hunted included deer, bison, rabbits, birds, and fish. Bison bone appears to be more common at Custer sites compared with similar Paoli sites to the east; bison probably were more abundant in the short- and mixed-grass settings of western Oklahoma. Bison hunting, however, appears to have increased significantly during the Turkey Creek phase, and by A.D. 1400, bison dominate the faunal assemblages (Drass et al. 1987).

The origins of the Custer phase are unclear. It is assumed to derive from local Southern Plains Woodland groups, although few sites of this period are documented in western Oklahoma (Hofman 1978). The Turkey Creek phase derives from the Custer phase, but there is debate on the relationship of later protohistoric sites and Turkey Creek sites. Baugh (1986) suggests that the protohistoric Wheeler-phase sites in western Oklahoma are an indigenous development from local late prehistoric (Turkey Creek phase) groups. These people are viewed as ancestral to the Wichita or one of the tribes that make up the modern Wichita. Other researchers (Gunnerson 1987; Hofman 1978, 1984b) suggest that the Wheeler phase is intrusive, possibly representing the arrival of Apachean groups in the Southern Plains.

Henrietta Complex

The Henrietta focus was initially defined by Krieger (1946) based on the Harrell site and related sites in the upper Red River and Brazos River valleys. Research, however, has been limited at Plains Village sites in northern Texas, and there has been debate on the utility of this focus (Prikryl 1990). There may also be some temporal and regional variation in this manifestation. The Henrietta complex currently is used to identify Plains Village occupations in this area, although there is poorly defined evidence for a sedentary farming and hunting society developing in north-central Texas. Sites attributed to Henrietta are found along the Red River south to the upper Brazos, west to the Wichita and possibly the Peace rivers west of Wichita Falls, and east to the headwater region on the Elm Fork of the Trinity River (Brooks 1989; Krieger 1946). The complex seems to be associated with the prairie and Cross Timbers settings in north-central Texas. Major sites include Harrell, Dillard, Chicken House, Coyote, and Glass.

Dates for Henrietta are not well established. Krieger (1946) suggested a range from A.D. 1450 to 1600 based on Puebloan pottery found at several sites. Lorrain (1967) later argued that the Henrietta focus ended in north-central Texas shortly after A.D. 1400. A few radiocarbon dates are available. Calibrated dates for the Chicken House and Dillard sites on Fish Creek near the Red River range from about A.D. 1100 to 1430 (Martin 1994). A site in Dallas County on the Elm Fork of the Trinity River has yielded a calibrated date of A.D. 1485 (Harris 1959). Prikryl (1990) suggests that late prehistoric sites that would encompass Henrietta date from A.D. 1200 to 1700. The similarity of Henrietta-complex assemblages to Washita River–phase materials may indicate a similar date range, approximately A.D. 1250 to 1450. However, because of the lack of controlled excavations and radiocarbon dates, some Henrietta complex sites may date before A.D. 1200.

Henrietta sites are on terraces and uplands near major streams. Villages may be associated with loose, sandy soils that were easily tilled (Suhm et al. 1954). Small camps and bison kill sites are also associated with Henrietta. Sites vary from less than 2.5 acres up to 30 acres. The larger villages contain houses, hearths, storage pits, and burials. Excavations have not determined village layout, but houses have been exposed at the Glass, Dillard, and Chicken House sites. These houses are oval, 21 to 30 feet long and 16 to 20 feet wide, with wall posts and four major interior support posts (Lorrain 1967, 1969). Rock hearths and cylindrical cache pits are present in most structures (Figure 12.4). Basin hearths, smudge pits, oval and bell-shaped storage pits, and middens are also documented (Lorrain 1969; Martin 1994). Burials are found within villages, possibly in specific areas. They are flexed, semiflexed, or rarely extended (Krieger 1946). They may be individual or group interments. Krieger (1946) reports slab-lined graves from the Harrell site that contained few or no grave goods. Martin (1994), however, reports unlined graves containing many ornamental items such as marine-shell gorgets, *Olivella* shell beads, and tubular bone beads.

The primary characteristic of the Henrietta complex is the shell-tempered plain pottery: Nocona Plain. This pottery is not found at other late prehistoric sites in northern Texas, but similar pottery is found at Washita River–phase sites and at the poorly documented Bryan-focus sites in south-central Oklahoma (Bell and Baerreis 1951:47; Drass and Swenson 1986). Pots are typically rounded or globular jars with rounded or flat bases, constricted necks, and outwardly flaring rims (Lorrain 1969:57). Bowls and untempered, cob-impressed cups or mugs are also found. Decorations on a few pots consist of nodes, finger-nail marks, incised lines, and stamped or punctated impressions, usually on the rims or rim–body junctions. Although shell temper is one of the key characteristics of this period, Prikryl and Perttula (1995:192) note that limestone temper is also common in this pottery.

A few grit- or bone-tempered cordmarked sherds are present in most Henrietta assemblages. Rare examples of southwestern ceramics such as Jornada Mogollon brownwares, Chupadero Black on White, and Rio Grande polychromes and Caddoan pottery are recorded, indicating exchange to the east and west (Krieger 1946; Lorrain 1967; Prikryl and Perttula 1995). Clay figurines, pottery beads and disks, and ceramic pipes are found at many sites. Pipes are long-stemmed and resemble Caddoan pipes, except that they are shell tempered (Lorrain 1969:58–59).

Lithic and bone tools from Henrietta sites are similar to those from other Southern Plains Village complexes, particularly the Washita River phase. Projectile points are predominantly side notched (Washita and Harrell) and unnotched (Fresno) arrowpoints. However, a variety of arrow- and dart-points are found (Martin 1994), possibly indicating some mixing of components at some sites. Other chipped-stone tools include diamond-beveled knives, end and side scrapers, T-shaped or square-based drills, gravers, and spokeshaves. Lithic materials are predominantly local cherts and quartzites, but the presence of some Alibates, Edwards, Reed Springs, novaculite, and obsidian indicates contacts with groups to the west and east. Both trough- and basin-shaped metates are

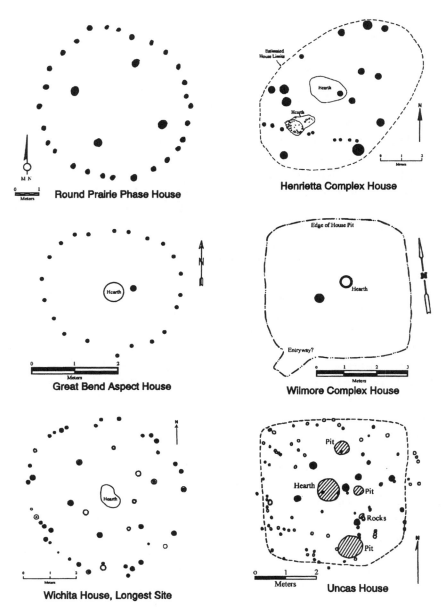

Figure 12.4. Southern Plains village houses, continued. (After Bell and Bastian 1967; Bruseth and Martin 1987a, 1987b; Lorrain 1969; Ranney 1994; Rowlison 1985; Vehik and Flynn 1982)

reported, as are many manos. Celts and elbow pipes are uncommon but appear at several sites. Shaft abraders and sandstone hones are also present. Bone tools are varied and include bison-bone digging implements such as scapula and horn-core hoes and tibia digging-stick tips. Bone awls, rib rasps, ulna flakers, fishhooks, tubular beads, and deer-jaw sickles as well as shell scoops, pendants, beads, and digging tools are found at many sites.

The extent of horticulture among Henrietta-complex groups is difficult to assess. Maize has been recovered from most sites, but there has been no systematic flotation to recover other plant remains. Hoes and digging-stick tips found at most villages are believed to be evidence for the cultivation of crops. Other than nuts, there is no evidence available on the use of wild plants. Hunting appears to have been a major activity, and a variety of animals are represented. Deer and bison are the major game, but there may be some regional variation in the hunting of these animals. Krieger (1946:120) notes the predominance of bison at the Harrell site on the Clear Fork of the Brazos River, but deer bone is four to five times more abundant than bison at the Dillard site on Fish Creek near the Red River (Martin 1994:174). Faunal assemblages at other Fish Creek sites in the Red River basin are also dominated by deer (Lorrain 1969). The different hunting patterns may reflect temporal differences in the presence of bison rather than simply regional variations in bison exploitation. Dillehay (1974) and others (Huebner 1991; Lynott 1979) suggest that the number of bison herds increased on the Southern Plains after about A.D. 1200. More research is needed to determine if subsistence patterns varied based on local environmental settings or if the differences reflect some temporal or cultural variation within Henrietta. Other animals exploited include antelope, rabbits, beaver, turtles, birds, fish, and mussels. Many fish and mussels are present at some sites, and these riverine resources may have been important before bison became abundant.

The limited research on Henrietta-complex sites and the possible regional and temporal variations in assemblages make it difficult to determine the origins of this complex and trace it to historic groups. Martin (1994:190) and Prikryl (1990:83) suggest that late prehistoric sites that encompass Henrietta-complex sites are indigenous, developing from local Late Archaic and subsequent groups that adopted horticulture. The Henrietta complex has been associated with historic Wichita, but the relationship is unclear. The Wichita sites in northern Texas, the Norteño focus, are quite different from Henrietta sites, and they apparently represent the historic movement of Wichita groups from northern and eastern Oklahoma to the Red River area. Lorrain (1967) suggests that Henrietta people were one of the prehistoric Wichita tribes that moved east to the western Caddo area as a result of droughts after A.D. 1400. While this is possible, additional research is needed to determine the relations of Plains Village groups in north-central Texas.

Wylie Focus and the Round Prairie and St. Elmo Phases

The Wylie focus was defined by Stephenson (1952) based on excavations at the Hogge Bridge site and work at other sites along the East Fork of the Trinity River. The original definition of the focus was a late prehistoric horticultural group on the western edge of the Caddo area. Artifact associations are vague, however, and this manifestation is difficult to define. The most distinctive attribute of the focus is the large depressions or pits referred to as "Wylie pits," although these pits are not present at all Wylie-focus sites. The ceramic assemblages contain few of the characteristic Nocona Plain sherds found at Henrietta sites to the west and north, and tool assemblages seem to reflect "a blend of Plains and Caddoan traits" (Suhm et al. 1954:88). Although there are similarities in the artifacts at sites with Wylie pits, there is little contextual evidence for the direct association of these diverse materials, and the artifacts appear to represent a considerable time span (Lynott 1977).

Recent investigations in the Richland Creek area have expanded the known distribution of Wylie pits to the south and resulted in a reexamination of chronologies. It now appears that Wylie sites have a considerable time depth, encompassing Late Archaic and later occupations. The excavations of Wylie pits at the Bird Point Island and Adams Ranch sites indicate that they were roasting pits and cemeteries made by Late Archaic groups (Bruseth and Martin 1987b:284; Prikryl 1993:195). The long time span represented and the problem of the mixing of artifacts limits the usefulness of the Wylie-focus concept, and it has been suggested that it be abandoned (Bruseth and Martin 1987b; Prikryl 1993).

Late prehistoric materials have been found at Wylie sites, and two phases have been defined, Round Prairie and St. Elmo, dating after A.D. 900 in the Richland Creek area. The Round Prairie phase is the earlier, dating from A.D. 900 to 1300, and the St. Elmo phase dates from about A.D. 1300 to 1650. Round Prairie is marked by small hamlets with circular houses from 18 to 23 feet in diameter (Bruseth and Martin 1987a). The houses are constructed of posts with thatch walls and roofs, having four central support posts, central hearths, and, sometimes, storage pits (Figure 12.4). Projectile points are dominated by Alba, Scallorn, and Hayes arrowpoints and Gary dart points. Ceramics include grog- and sand-tempered jars with straight rims and incised and punctated designs resembling Canton Incised pottery found at Caddo sites. Subsistence was based on hunting, primarily deer, and the gathering of nuts and tubers. No maize is recorded at Round Prairie sites. The later St. Elmo–phase components are similar, but represent more seasonal camps at Bird Point Island and Adams Ranch. Maize is found at these later components, but it is considered to have been a supplement to the diet (Bruseth and Martin 1987a:192). Fewer Gary points occur at St. Elmo sites, and contracting-stem Perdiz arrowpoints appear. Pottery is similar to Round Prairie–phase ceramics, but with the addition of carinated bowls, some shell-tempered pots with outflaring rims, and more engraved designs. These phases appear to have developed from local Late Archaic and Woodland complexes, but more work is needed to define their extent and identify relationships with other complexes in north-central and eastern Texas.

Bluff Creek, Pratt, and Wilmore Complexes and the Uncas Site

There are several poorly defined late prehistoric complexes and sites in northern Oklahoma and southern Kansas that represent Plains Village occupation. G. Keller (1961) lumped some of these sites into his Mid-Arkansan complex, but more recent work has identified more variation. This research, however, has not been extensive, and a good definition of complexes and the relationships among these sites awaits further excavation. In addition, the Uncas site and a few sites in the Kaw Lake area of the Arkansas River drainage represent small villages that appear to be distinct from other Southern Plains Village sites (Galm 1979; Vehik and Flynn 1982). In south-central Kansas, the Bluff Creek, Pratt, and Wilmore complexes have been defined on the basis of a few excavated sites and surface collections (Brown and Simmons 1987; Ranney 1994; Rowlison 1985; W. Wedel 1959; Witty 1978). Few radiocarbon dates are available for them, and many of the sites appear to have multiple components (Lees 1991; Monger 1970; Ranney 1994). The Bluff Creek complex is found in the Chikaskia River drainage to the west of the Arkansas River valley, and the Pratt complex occurs to the northwest along the Ninnescah and Pawnee rivers. The Wilmore complex is defined for a few sites along the Cimarron River in southwestern Kansas.

Bluff Creek is considered the earliest of the complexes; it is estimated to date to between A.D. 1000 and 1500 (Thies 1989:175). Three radiocarbon dates for the Buresh and Nulik sites range from A.D. 900 to 1190 (O'Brien 1984:63). However, these dates are from the Gakushuin laboratory, and may be unreliable (Blakeslee 1994). Other major sites include Anderson, Anthony, Hallman, and Armstrong, set on uplands overlooking Bluff Creek, a tributary of the Chikaskia River. The sites are small villages, and a variety of house forms are documented. Oval, square, and rectangular forms were identified at the Buresh site. They appear to have been frame structures plastered with daub (Witty 1978). Hearths are usually absent, but cylindrical storage pits are found inside and outside the houses. Characteristic artifacts include side- and basally notched arrowpoints (Washita, Harrell, and Huffaker) plus a few unnotched points (Fresno). Diamond-beveled knives, end and side scrapers, and shaft abraders are common. Bluff Creek people preferred heat-treated Florence A Chert for making chipped-stone tools (Thies 1989:193). Bone tools are abundant and include bison-bone digging-stick tips, scapula hoes and cleavers, and shaft wrenches. Pottery is plain or cordmarked globular jars with sand or bone temper. Collared rims similar to those on pottery found in Central Plains villages appear on some cord-marked vessels. Decorations are limited to tool-impressed lips (Thies 1989). A few plain vessels with shell temper are found that are very similar to pots from Washita River–phase sites in Oklahoma. These people cultivated maize and probably other crops and hunted, principally bison. Bluff Creek is viewed as having ties with both Central and Southern Plains Village groups (Brown and Simmons 1987; Witty 1978). The origins of the complex may be local Woodland groups, and O'Brien (1984:63) suggests that the complex is similar to the Great Bend aspect and, thus, may be ancestral Wichita.

The Pratt complex may have developed out of Bluff Creek, but there is not enough information to establish this relationship. Southwestern pottery has been used to cross-date Pratt complex sites to A.D. 1400 to 1500 (Brown and Simmons 1987; W. Wedel 1959:510). However, a radiocarbon date from 14PT304 yielded calibrated ages of A.D. 1274 to 1389 and A.D. 1359 to 1392 (Ranney 1994:85). Most researchers suggest that the Pratt complex is ancestral to the Great Bend aspect. Circular to oval grass houses from 10 to more than 16 feet in diameter found at the Lewis and Larned sites are stratigraphically beneath similar Great Bend–aspect houses (Monger 1970; Ranney 1994). The Larned houses have four center posts, a central hearth, and interior storage pits, whereas the Lewis houses have a central hearth but one or no interior posts and no storage pits. This may reflect functional differences in site use (Ranney 1994:87). Artifact assemblages are similar to Bluff Creek materials, but with more trade items. In addition to southwestern pottery, turquoise, obsidian, *Olivella* shell beads, and Gulf marine shell are recovered. Alibates agatized dolomite dominates the Lewis-site lithic collection (Ranney 1994). Ground-stone tools are rare. Cord-marked jars with sand and/or bone tempering, straight to outward-flaring rims, and round or flat bottoms predominate. Subsistence is not well documented, but there is evidence for maize cultivation and bison hunting remained important.

The Wilmore complex is known primarily from two sites: Bell and Booth. This complex may also have its origin in the Bluff Creek complex. It is suggested to date from around A.D. 1370 to 1450, roughly between the dates of the Bluff Creek and Pratt complexes (Brown and Simmons 1987). However, a radiocarbon date from the Bell site yielded an earlier age of A.D. 1170 (Thies 1985), and one from Booth is A.D. 1510 (Lees 1991), indicating a late component at the site. The complex is characterized by pit houses and an assemblage that resembles those from the Pratt and Bluff Creek sites. House are dug about 1 foot below the ground surface. They are approximately 16 feet square with rounded corners and a central hearth. One interior post is near the center of the Bell pit house (Rowlison 1985:123) (Figure 12.4). Artifacts include side-notched arrowpoints and medium-size, corner-notched points similar to Plains Woodland varieties. Wilmore people used diverse lithic materials, including Florence A, Niobrara, and Alibates. Grinding slabs and manos are reported, but there is no evidence of cultivated plants. Pottery is predominantly cordmarked globular jars with sand temper, although some gypsum, bone, and shell tempers are also used. Decorations include pinching in lineal sections, appliqué nodes, incised designs on the neck and shoulder of vessels, scalloped or crenated rims, and stick-impressed lips. Rowlison (1985:125–126) notes some similarity between ceramics of the Wilmore complex and those of the Zimms complex. There are also similarities to materials from Wolf Creek sites in northwestern Oklahoma and Buried City sites in the Texas panhandle.

Uncas is the only major Plains Village site excavated in north-central Oklahoma, and it appears to differ from other manifestations in the region (Galm 1979; Vehik and Flynn 1982). Uncas is situated on a high terrace along the Arkansas River, and similar sites may be present on Beaver Creek, a tributary of the Arkansas. Radiocarbon and archaeomagnetic dates indicate occupation sometime between about A.D. 1100 and 1400, but most likely during the early fourteenth century. Artifacts from Uncas consist of typical Plains Village items, such as side-notched arrowpoints, diamond-beveled knives, and scrapers. Lithics are predominantly Florence A, and contemporary groups in this area may have controlled the Florence A quarries and traded this material to other Plains groups (Vehik 1990). Uncas is distinguished from other manifestations by house form and ceramics. Pottery consists of globular vessels with rounded bases, constricted orifices, and loop handles (Vehik and Flynn 1982). Temper appears to be leached shell, but sand and caliche occur in some pots. Vessels are plain (Uncas Plain) or decorated with parallel incised lines (Coon Creek Incised). Vehik (1994:245) suggests that the ceramics are similar to some types from the Central Plains tradition, specifically the Smoky Hill variant, and the Lower Walnut focus of the Great Bend aspect. Houses, however, differ from others in this area. They are semi-subterranean and square, 13 to 20 feet across, with rounded corners, at least four center posts, and a central basin-shaped hearth (Vehik and Flynn 1982). Bell-shaped storage pits are found in some houses (Figure 12.4). Subsistence is poorly documented. Horticulture is assumed, but no cultivated plants have been recovered. Bone preservation is poor, but bison, deer, and smaller game have been identified.

Protohistoric and Historic Wichita

Many of the late prehistoric manifestations on the Southern Plains are attributed to ancestral Wichita groups, but there is rarely enough evidence to connect prehistoric and historic peoples. There appears to have been a movement or coalescence of people after A.D. 1450, and few early historic accounts are available to help identify groups on the Southern Plains. The earliest records from Spanish and French explorers document people who later are identified as historic

Wichita in north-central Oklahoma and central and south-central Kansas. The record is less clear in other areas, although researchers have suggested that Coronado and Oñate described a Wichita or related Plains Caddoan group in western Oklahoma and the Texas panhandle (Drass and Baugh 1997; Habicht-Mauche 1992; Vehik 1992). The Garza and/or Wheeler phases are argued to be the protohistoric archaeological manifestations of the western Plains Caddoans described by these Spanish explorers. Coronado and Oñate also visited the sedentary villages of Quivira, in central and southern Kansas in the sixteenth and early seventeenth centuries, and subsequent archaeological research has identified protohistoric Wichita sites that are defined as the Great Bend aspect (W. Wedel 1959:571–589). In the early eighteenth century, the French contacted Wichita groups farther south at two sites, Deer Creek and Bryson–Paddock, in north-central Oklahoma (Bell 1984b; M. Wedel 1981). By 1759, under pressure from the Osage and with the promise of more trade with the French in Louisiana, the Wichita groups had moved south to the Red River in south-central Oklahoma and northern Texas. The Norteño focus or phase defined for northern Texas may represent the movement of these groups into the area, or a combination of these people and other Wichita and Caddo groups that occupied the region in the late eighteenth and early nineteenth centuries (Duffield and Jelks 1961; Lorrain 1967; Rohrbaugh 1982).

Great Bend Aspect

W. Wedel (1959) defined two foci, the Little River and Lower Walnut, for the Great Bend aspect. The foci are very similar and are differentiated primarily on location and ceramics. The Little River focus is along the Little Arkansas River and tributaries of the Smoky Hill River in Rice and McPherson counties in central Kansas, and the Lower Walnut focus is on the Lower Walnut River in Cowley County, south-central Kansas. In addition, the Larned site in Pawnee County on the Arkansas River and sites in Marion County on the Cottonwood River are reported as Great Bend (Lees 1988:61; Monger 1970). Some of the most important sites include Malone, Tobias, Thompson, Major, Paint Creek, and Hayes of the Little River focus, and Elliott, Larcom–Haggard, and Arkansas City Country Club of the Lower Walnut focus. The foci are considered contemporaneous, although Wedel (1959:586) suggests that Lower Walnut may have persisted later than Little River. Dates for the Great Bend aspect are based primarily on cross-dated southwestern ceramics and the presence of some historic contact material. Southwestern ceramics indicate occupation between about A.D. 1450 and 1700 (W. Wedel 1959). The presence of chain mail, iron, and copper or brass beads at several Little River sites suggests that they may have been occupied about the time of the Coronado and Oñate expeditions, between A.D. 1541 and

1601. Radiocarbon dates from several Lower Walnut–focus sites range from A.D. 1560 to 1700, supporting the cross-dated ceramics (Hawley 1994:218).

Great Bend–aspect sites are large villages built on terraces or hillsides near streams. Unplowed sites are characterized by large midden or refuse mounds. The Spanish reported that settlements in this area consisted of houses interspersed with gardens and fields of maize. Excavated houses are circular to oval and may be semi-subterranean or surface constructions. They range from less than 10 feet to more than 26 feet in diameter (Lees 1988; Loosle 1991; Monger 1970), and are assumed to be pole and grass-thatch structures similar to those described by Coronado and Oñate. Shallow basin-shaped hearths are present in some houses (Figure 12.4). Pits are abundant and typically are bell shaped. Many are very large, over 6 feet in diameter and up to 10 feet deep (Loosle 1991). Shallow ditches surrounding low mounds, known as council circles, are reported from some Little River sites. The function of these council circles is unclear, but Wedel (1959, 1967) suggests that they may have been ceremonial structures, possibly associated with solstice observations.

Ceramics display the most variation between Little River and Lower Walnut. Wedel (1959:233–245, 359–362) defined Geneseo Plain, Geneseo Simple Stamped, and Geneseo Red Filmed pottery for the Little River focus, and Cowley Plain for the Lower Walnut focus. Geneseo and Cowley pottery generally are similar in vessel form and manufacture. Cowley pottery, however, is tempered predominantly with finely crushed shell, whereas Geneseo wares are tempered predominantly with sand. Pots are jars with vertical or slightly outflaring rims, constricted necks, and round or flat bases. Flat bases may be more common on Cowley Plain than on Geneseo Plain pots. Plain wares predominate for both foci, but Geneseo wares include a few pots with a paddle-stamped design (Geneseo Simple Stamped) or a red slip (Geneseo Red Filmed). Incised lines, fillets, and appliqué nodes are rare. However, incised or punctate designs are common on the lips of both Cowley and Geneseo pots (W. Wedel 1959:575). Loop or strap handles are found on many of the pots. Little River Cord-Roughened pottery also is found at some early Little River sites, and it may be evidence for the local development of Little River from the Pratt-complex or other late prehistoric groups that used cordmarked pottery (Loosle 1991; Ranney 1994).

Most other artifacts from Great Bend–aspect sites are typical of Plains Village assemblages. Unnotched triangular arrowpoints predominate, and ovate and beveled knives, end and side scrapers, and drills are abundant. Grooved mauls, L-shaped stone pipes, and perforated sandstone disks may be characteristic artifacts at Great Bend sites. Bison-scapula hoes are common, as are awls and other bone tools. Little River and Lower Walnut groups, however, may have used different hafting techniques for scapula hoes. Little River groups removed the articular head of the scapula, whereas Lower Walnut people bored sockets or grooved the dorsal surface for hafting (W. Wedel 1959:578). The numerous hoes found at sites are evidence of cultivation, and maize and beans have been recovered. The most important game was bison, but deer, elk, antelope, small mammals, birds, shellfish, and fish were also important.

Many exotic artifacts have been recovered from Great Bend–aspect sites. A variety of southwestern pottery sherds has been recorded at most sites as well as obsidian, turquoise, and *Olivella* shell that may have been traded from the Southwest. Red pipestone pipes indicate contact to the northeast, and Alibates agatized dolomite and Niobrara Jasper are additional evidence of western trade. Great Bend groups also used cherts from the Ozarks to the east. Lower Walnut groups may have controlled the Florence A Chert quarries and traded this material with other groups. In addition to native exotics, European items such as chain mail, an iron ax head, glass beads, and rolled copper beads recovered from Little River sites are attributed to the early Spanish (W. Wedel 1959).

The origins of the Great Bend aspect are unclear. Various researchers have derived this complex from different Southern Plains cultures such as the Custer, Washita River, and Antelope Creek phases (Bell 1973; G. Keller 1961; W. Wedel 1959). Ties with the Neosho focus and the Fort Coffee phase in eastern Oklahoma are also suggested (Bell 1983; Vehik 1976; Wyckoff 1980). Vehik (1976) argues for an indigenous development from the Pratt complex, and more recent work (Hawley 1994; Loosle 1991) suggests that some local development is represented, at least for Lower Walnut. Archaeologists generally accept Great Bend as protohistoric Wichita. Wedel (1959) ties the Little River focus to Coronado's Quivira, and Vehik (1992) suggests that this focus may represent the Tawakoni subdivision of the Wichita. Vehik also connects the Lower Walnut focus to Oñate's Etzanoa and the Wichita subgroup of the Wichita proper. The Taovaya/Tawehash subdivision is associated with the Great Bend–aspect sites in Marion County. The other historic subdivision of the Wichita, Iscani/Waco, is related to the Wheeler and Garza protohistoric complexes in western Oklahoma (Vehik 1992:328). The Kichai, who later joined the Wichita in Texas, are suggested to have originated in eastern Oklahoma and moved southwest into northern Texas as early as the eighteenth century (Rohrbaugh 1982). Some of Norteño-focus sites are probably Kichai. This model of Wichita culture would include many of the late prehistoric and protohistoric complexes known for the Southern Plains, but more research is needed to confirm or refute this view of Wichita culture history.

Historic Wichita

Archaeologists generally believe that the Wichita moved south from Kansas following initial contact with the Spanish. In 1719, French traders visited Wichita groups on the Verdigris River in eastern Kansas and on the Arkansas River near Tulsa, Oklahoma (M. Wedel 1981:26–37, 1982:123–127). The Lasley Vore site south of the Arkansas River may be the Tawakoni village visited by LaHarpe in 1719 (Odell 1990). More extensive European contact was initiated with the Wichita in the mid-eighteenth century when the French established trading posts at two villages in north-central Oklahoma: Deer Creek or Ferdinandina and Bryson–Paddock on the west bank of the Arkansas River are thought to be the two Wichita villages involved (M. Wedel 1981). These groups appear to have been the Taovayas and possibly the Wichita subgroups that had moved south from Kansas (Vehik 1992; M. Wedel 1981:57). However, dates from Bryson–Paddock indicate that it was occupied as early as A.D. 1560 (Bell 1984b). Horses and firearms obtained from Europeans may have increased the importance of bison hunting in the Wichita economy, but the Wichita continued to be sedentary horticulturists who grew maize, beans, and squash and hunted game. The importance of trade increased through time and may have been a major factor in the movement of these groups south to the Red River. The Longest site in Jefferson County, Oklahoma, is one of the major Wichita sites of the mid-eighteenth century, and it may be the Taovaya village attacked by the Spanish in 1759 (Duffield 1965). The Tawakoni may have moved south into Texas after 1719 (M. Wedel 1982:128), and other Wichita groups may have made the move about the same time. Norteño-focus sites in northern Texas—such as Vinson, Stansbury, Stone, Pearson, Spanish Fort, Gilbert, and Womack—represent late-eighteenth- and nineteenth-century Wichita or Kichai villages.

Villages are fairly large at this time and usually are set on high terraces near major streams. Houses excavated at the Bryson–Paddock, Longest (Figure 12.4), Upper Tucker, and Vinson sites (Bell and Bastian 1967; Hartley and Miller 1977; Smith 1993) are circular to oval semi-subterranean structures that resemble those identified at Great Bend–aspect sites. They are assumed to be the beehive-shaped grass houses associated with the Wichita (Bell and Bastian 1967:114). Arbors are probably present at these villages, but none are documented by excavations. Bell-shaped pits found at Great Bend sites also are common at most of the Wichita sites in southern Oklahoma and northern Texas. A distinctive feature at Longest is the earthwork fortification described by the Spanish in 1759 (Duffield 1965). It consists of a circular trench with the dirt piled on the inside to form a parapet, on which logs were placed to form a stockade. No fortifications are found at Great Bend sites, but similar fortifications are noted at earlier Wheeler phase sites in western Oklahoma (Drass and Baugh 1997).

Artifacts associated with the early historic Wichita include many European items, but most of the native tools continued in use into the nineteenth century. Native tool kits for these sites resemble those from other Southern Plains Village complexes, with an abundance of small triangular, unnotched arrowpoints, scrapers, knives, and drills. A distinctive artifact is a very large end and side scraper, usually made from Florence A Chert; it may reflect the emphasis on processing bison meat and hides for trade. Lithic tools represent a diverse assortment of materials, indicating widespread trade. Florence A Chert, Edwards Chert, and Alibates agatized dolomite are documented at the Longest site (Bell and Bastian 1967:115). Pottery includes a shell-tempered plain ware consisting of jars with strap handles, slightly everted rims, and flat bases that resembles Nocona and Cowley Plain pottery. Some sand- and bone-tempered sherds are also present, along with bowls and bottles. In addition, some paddle-marked sherds from the Spanish Fort sites in Texas and Oklahoma resemble pottery from Great Bend–aspect sites in Kansas. Pottery is not common at the northern Texas sites, and aboriginal ceramics probably were being replaced by metal containers at this time (Prikryl and Perttula 1995:194). The Oklahoma and Norteño–focus sites in northern Texas also typically have a decorated pottery (Womack Engraved), plus wares (Emory Punctate and Incised, Nachitoches Engraved, and others) that indicate influence from Caddo groups (Duffield and Jelks 1961; Rohrbaugh 1982). Ceramic elbow pipes with conical bowls, slightly flaring stems, and small spurs at the heel are also characteristic items in Norteño-focus sites (Bastian 1967).

The Wichita continued to live in the vicinity of the Red, Brazos, and Trinity rivers into the nineteenth century. The Leavenworth or Dragoon Expedition in 1834 also identified a Wichita village at Devil's Canyon, in Kiowa County, Oklahoma (Newcomb and Field 1967:292). Epidemics and battles with other Indian groups decreased populations in the early part of the century, and, by 1855, many of the Wichita were established on a reservation along the Brazos River south of Fort Belknap. Conflict with settlers in the 1850s forced the Wichita north into Oklahoma. A Wichita reservation along the Washita River in Caddo County was established in 1859 (Newcomb and Field 1967), and, with the exception of a movement to Kansas during the Civil War, they remain in this area to the present.

Conclusion

By A.D. 900 or 1000, most of the Southern Plains was occupied by sedentary villagers, part of the Plains Village tradition. The Plains Village tradition is marked by the establishment of semipermanent villages and a mixed economy based on horticulture, hunting, and gathering. Although many early studies have attributed these groups to the migration of people from areas outside the Southern Plains, there is growing evidence for the development of early Plains Village people from local Plains Woodland groups. The evolution of various Southern Plains Village societies is similar in many respects. There appears to have been a generally increasing reliance on horticulture and bison hunting through time. However, the diversity of settings and responses to different conditions and resources also resulted in a great deal of variation in adaptations. Antelope Creek–phase people and other societies on the western margins of the prairies were influenced by drier conditions that were less suitable for horticulture but perhaps more favorable for bison herds. These groups also had contact with Puebloan groups to the west, and they incorporated building techniques and probably other aspects of Puebloan culture into a Plains society. In contrast, Washita River–phase and Henrietta-complex people near the eastern edge of the prairies may have had less problems with droughts affecting their crops and more influence from Caddoan groups to the east. Plains Villagers continued to occupy the area into the historic period, when various subgroups of present-day Wichita, along with the Apache in the west, are recorded by early European explorers.

The Wichita people appear to have occupied much of the eastern prairies of the Southern Plains at the time of historic contact, and they were probably present in the west when Coronado traversed the area in 1541. The migration of groups such as the Apache into the Southern Plains—along with droughts, increasing population, and other factors—appears to have resulted in major changes and/or movements of groups around A.D. 1500. Epidemics and movements of people after historic contact resulted in further demographic changes, altering lifestyles and making it difficult for archaeologists and ethnohistorians to associate prehistoric groups with historic tribes. The small amount of archaeological research on early protohistoric sites also has limited our understanding of adaptations and relationships during this volatile period. In addition, there are many areas of the Southern Plains with reported Plains Village sites that have had little or no investigation. Our present database provides interesting clues about the lifestyles of sedentary villagers in the Southern Plains, but many more questions have to be addressed.

References

Baerreis, D. A., and R. A. Bryson
    1965   Historical Climatology of the Southern Plains. *Bulletin of the Oklahoma Anthropological Society* 13:69–75.
Barr, T. P.
    1966   *The Pruitt Site: A Late Plains Woodland Manifestation in Murray County, Oklahoma.* University of Oklahoma, Oklahoma River Basin Survey Project, Archaeological Site Report no. 5. Norman.
Bastian, T.
    1967   Native-Made Artifacts from Historic Sites. In *A Pilot Study of Wichita Indian Archaeology and Ethnohistory,* compiled by R. E. Bell, E. B. Jelks, and W. W. Newcomb, 184–196. University of Oklahoma, Report to the National Science Foundation. Norman.
Baugh, T. G.
    1986   Cultural History and Protohistoric Societies in the Southern Plains. In

Current Trends in Southern Plains Archaeology, edited by T. G. Baugh, 167–187. Plains Anthropologist Memoir no. 21.

Bell, R. E.

1973   The Washita River Focus of the Southern Plains. In *Variation in Anthropology,* edited by D. W. Lathrap and J. Douglas, 171–187. Illinois Archaeological Survey, Urbana.

1983   Reflections on Southern and Central Plains Prehistory. In *Prairie Archaeology: Papers in Honor of David B. Baerreis,* edited by G. E. Gibbon, 1–13. University of Minnesota, Publications in Anthropology, no. 3. Minneapolis.

1984a   The Plains Villagers: The Washita River. In *Prehistory of Oklahoma,* edited by R. E. Bell, 307–324. Academic Press, Orlando, Fla.

1984b   Protohistoric Wichitas. In *Prehistory of Oklahoma,* edited by R. E. Bell, 363–378. Academic Press, Orlando, Fla.

Bell, R. E. and D. A. Baerreis

1951   A Survey of Oklahoma Archaeology. *Bulletin of the Texas Archeological and Paleontological Society* 22:7–100.

Bell, R. E., and T. Bastian

1967   Preliminary Report upon Excavations at the Longest Site, Oklahoma. In *A Pilot Study of Wichita Indian Archaeology and Ethnohistory,* compiled by R. E. Bell, E. B. Jelks, and W. W. Newcomb, 54–118. Report to the National Science Foundation. Norman, Okla.

Blakeslee, D. J.

1994   Reassessment of Some Radiocarbon Dates from the Central Plains. *Plains Anthropologist* 39:203–210.

Brighton, H. D.

1951   Archaeological Sites in Custer County, Oklahoma. *Bulletin of the Texas Archeological and Paleontological Society* 22:164–187.

Brooks, R. L.

1983   Community Structure and Settlement Distributions in the Washita River Phase. Paper presented at the forty-first annual Plains Conference, Rapid City, S.D.

1987   *The Arthur Site: Settlement and Subsistence Structure at a Washita River Phase Village.* University of Oklahoma, Oklahoma Archeological Survey, Studies in Oklahoma's Past, no. 15. Norman.

1989   Village Farming Societies. In *From Clovis to Comanchero: Archeological Overview of the Southern Great Plains,* by J. L. Hofman, R. L. Brooks, J. S. Hays, D. W. Owsley, R. L. Jantz, M. K. Marks, and M. H. Manhein, 71–90. Arkansas Archeological Survey, Research Series, no. 35, Fayetteville.

Brooks, R. L., M. C. Moore, and D. W. Owsley

1992   New Smith, 34RM400: A Plains Village Mortuary Site in Western Oklahoma. *Plains Anthropologist* 37:59–78.

Brown, K. L., and A. H. Simmons, eds.

1987   *Kansas Prehistoric Archaeological Preservation Plan.* University of Kansas, Office of Archaeological Research, Lawrence.

Bruseth, J. E., and W. A. Martin

1987a   Prehistoric Settlements at Bird Point Island. In *The Bird Point Island and Adams Ranch Sites: Methodological and Theoretical Contributions to North Central Texas Archaeology,* edited by J. E. Bruseth and W. A. Martin, 181–198. Southern Methodist University, Institute for the Study of Earth and Man, Archaeology Research Program, Richland Creek Technical Series, vol. 2. Dallas, Tex.

1987b The Wylie Focus: Cultural Reality or Archaeological Myth? In *The Bird Point Island and Adams Ranch Sites: Methodological and Theoretical Contributions to North Central Texas Archaeology,* edited by J. E. Bruseth and W. A. Martin, 267–284. Southern Methodist University, Institute for the Study of Earth and Man, Archaeology Research Program, Richland Creek Technical Series, vol. 2. Dallas, Tex.

Bryson, R. A., D. A. Baerreis, and W. M. Wendland
1970 The Character of Late-Glacial and Post-Glacial Climatic Changes. In *Pleistocene and Recent Environments of the Central Great Plains,* edited by W. Dort, Jr., and J. K. Jones, Jr., 53–77. University Press of Kansas, Lawrence.

Buck, A.D., Jr.
1959 The Custer Focus of the Southern Plains. *Bulletin of the Oklahoma Anthropological Society* 7:1–33.

Campbell, R. G.
1969 Prehistoric Panhandle Culture on the Chaquaqua Plateau, Southeastern Colorado. Ph.D. diss., Department of Anthropology, University of Colorado, Boulder.
1976 *The Panhandle Aspect of the Chaquaqua Plateau.* Texas Tech University, Graduate Studies, no. 11. Lubbock.

Crabb, M.
1968 Some Puebloan Trade Pottery from Panhandle Aspect Sites. *Bulletin of the Texas Archeological Society* 38:83–89.

Cummings, L. S.
1989 Pollen Analysis at the Cramer Site (5PE484). In *Apishapa Canyon Archeology: Excavations at the Cramer, Snake Blakeslee and Nearby Sites,* by J. H. Gunnerson, 259–265. J and L Reprint, Lincoln, Neb.

Demarcay, G. B.
1986 Vertebrate Fauna from Landergin Mesa: An Antelope Creek Period Village Site. M.A. thesis, Department of Anthropology, Texas A&M University, College Station.

Dillehay, T.
1974 Late Quaternary Bison Population Changes on the Southern Plains. *Plains Anthropologist* 19:180–196.

Drass, R. R.
1988 A Reanalysis of the Brewer Site, an Early Plains Village Settlement in Central Oklahoma. *Bulletin of the Oklahoma Anthropological Society* 37:1–110.
1993 Macrobotanical Remains from Two Early Plains Village Sites in Central Oklahoma. *Plains Anthropologist* 38:51–64.
1995 Culture Change on the Eastern Margins of the Southern Plains. Ph.D. diss., Department of Anthropology, University of Oklahoma, Norman.

Drass, R. R., and T. G. Baugh
1997 The Wheeler Phase and Cultural Continuity in the Southern Plains. *Plains Anthropologist* 42:183–204.

Drass, R. R., T. G. Baugh, and P. Flynn
1987 The Heerwald Site and Early Plains Village Adaptations in the Southern Plains. *North American Archaeologist* 8:151–190.

Drass, R. R., and P. Flynn
  1990   Temporal and Geographic Variations in Subsistence Practices for Plains
         Villagers in the Southern Plains. *Plains Anthropologist* 35:175–190.
Drass, R. R., and M. C. Moore
  1987   The Linville II Site (34RM492) and Plains Village Manifestations in the
         Mixed Grass Prairie. *Plains Anthropologist* 32:404–418.
Drass, R. R., and F. E. Swenson
  1986   Variation in the Washita River Phase of Central and Western Oklahoma.
         Plains Anthropologist 31:35–49.
Drass, R. R., and C. L. Turner
  1989   *An Archeological Reconnaissance of the Wolf Creek Drainage Basin, Ellis County,
         Oklahoma.* University of Oklahoma, Oklahoma Archeological Survey,
         Archeological Resource Survey Report no. 35. Norman.
Duffield, L. F.
  1953   The Brewer Site: A Preliminary Report. *Bulletin of the Oklahoma Anthropological
         Society* 1:61–68.
  1965   The Taovayas Village of 1759. *Great Plains Journal* 4:39–48.
  1970   Some Panhandle Aspect Sites in Texas: Their Vertebrates and Paleoecology.
         Ph.D. diss., Department of Anthropology, University of Wisconsin,
         Madison.
Duffield, L. F., and E. B. Jelks
  1961   *The Pearson Site: A Historic Indian Site at Iron Bridge Reservoir, Rains County,
         Texas.* University of Texas, Department of Anthropology, Austin.
Eyerly, T. L.
  1907   Archaeological Work in the Texas Panhandle. *Bulletin of the Canadian Academy
         for 1907.* Canadian, Tex.
Flynn, P.
  1984   Analysis of the 1973 Test Excavations at the Zimms Site (34RM72). In *Archaeol-
         ogy of the Mixed Grass Prairie Phase I: Quartermaster Creek,* edited by T. G.
         Baugh, 215–290. University of Oklahoma, Oklahoma Archeological Survey,
         Archeological Resource Survey Report no. 20. Norman.
  1986   Analysis of Test Excavations at the Zimms Site (34RM72), Western Okla-
         homa. In *Current Trends in Southern Plains Archaeology,* edited by T. G. Baugh,
         129–140. Plains Anthropologist Memoir no. 21.
Gallaher, A.
  1951   The Goodman I Site, Custer County, Oklahoma. *Bulletin of the Oklahoma
         Anthropological Society* 1:188–216.
Galm, J. R.
  1979   *The Uncas Site: A Late Prehistoric Manifestation in the Southern Plains.* University
         of Oklahoma, Archaeological Research and Management Center, Research
         Series, no. 1. Norman.
Green, F. E.
  1967   *Archaeological Salvage in the Sanford Reservoir Area.* National Park Service,
         Report no. 14-10-0333-1126. Washington, D.C.
Gunnerson, J. H.
  1987   *Archaeology of the High Plains.* Bureau of Land Management, Cultural
         Resource Series, no. 19. Denver.
  1989   *Apishapa Canyon Archeology: Excavations at the Cramer, Snake Blakeslee and
         Nearby Sites.* J and L Reprint, Lincoln, Neb.

Habicht-Mauche, J. A.
    1992   Coronado's Querechos and Teyas in the Archaeological Record of the Texas Panhandle. *Plains Anthropologist* 37:247–258.
Habicht-Mauche, J. A., A. A. Levendosky, and M. J. Schoeninger
    1994   Antelope Creek Phase Subsistence: The Bone Chemistry Evidence. In *Skeletal Biology in the Great Plains: Migration, Warfare, Health, and Subsistence,* edited by D. W. Owsley and R. L. Jantz, 291–304. Smithsonian Institution Press, Washington, D.C.
Hamblin, N. L.
    1989   Analysis of the Cramer Site Fauna. In *Apishapa Canyon Archeology: Excavations at the Cramer, Snake Blakeslee and Nearby Sites,* by J. H. Gunnerson, 199–236. J and L Reprint, Lincoln, Neb.
Harris, R. K.
    1959   C-14 Date on Henrietta Focus in Texas. *Oklahoma Anthropological Society Newsletter* 8:2.
Hartley, J. D., and A. F. Miller
    1977   *Archaeological Investigations at the Bryson–Paddock Site: An Early Contact Period Site on the Southern Plains.* University of Oklahoma, Oklahoma River Basin Survey Project, Archaeological Site Report no. 32. Norman.
Hartley, J. D., and L. Raymer
    1993   Test Excavations at the Antioch Bridge Site: A Fluvially Disturbed Woodland Assemblage in Garvin County, Oklahoma. *Bulletin of the Oklahoma Anthropological Society* 41:1–42.
Hawley, M. F.
    1994   *Archeological and Geomorphological Investigations of Sites in the Vicinity of Arkansas City, Cowley County, Kansas.* Kansas State Historical Society, Topeka.
Hofman, J. L.
    1978   The Development and Northern Relationships of Two Archeological Phases in the Southern Plains Subarea. In *The Central Plains Tradition: Internal Development and External Relationships,* edited by D. J. Blakeslee, 6–35. University of Iowa, Office of the State Archaeologist, Report no. 11. Iowa City.
    1984a   The Plains Villagers: The Custer Phase. In *Prehistory of Oklahoma,* edited by R. E. Bell, 287–305. Academic Press, Orlando, Fla.
    1984b   The Western Protohistoric: A Summary of the Edwards and Wheeler Complexes. In *Prehistory of Oklahoma,* edited by R. E. Bell, 347–362. Academic Press, Orlando, Fla.
Holden, W. C.
    1929   Some Explorations and Excavations in Northwest Texas. *Bulletin of the Texas Archeological and Paleontological Society* 1:23–35.
    1933   Excavations at Saddleback Ruin. *Bulletin of the Texas Archeological and Paleontological Society* 5:39–52.
Huebner, J. J.
    1991   Late Prehistoric Bison Populations in Central and Southern Texas. *Plains Anthropologist* 36:343–358.
Hughes, D. T.
    1991   Investigations of the Buried City, Ochiltree County, Texas: With An Emphasis on the Texas Archeological Society Field Schools of 1987 and 1988. *Bulletin of the Texas Archeological Society* 60:107–148.

Hughes, D. T., and A. A. Hughes-Jones
  1987   *The Courson Archeological Projects: Final 1985 and Preliminary 1986.* Innovative
         Publishing, Perryton, Tex.
Hughes, J. T.
  1991   Prehistoric Cultural Developments on the Texas High Plains. *Bulletin of the
         Texas Archeological Society* 60:1–55.
Keller, G. N.
  1961   The Changing Position of the Southern Plains in the Late Prehistory of the
         Great Plains Area. Ph.D. diss., Department of Anthropology, University of
         Chicago.
Keller, J. E.
  1975   *The Black Dog Village Site: A Panhandle Aspect Manifestation in Hutchinson
         County, Texas.* Texas Highway Department, Publications in Archaeology, Re-
         port no. 5. Austin.
Krieger, A.D.
  1946   *Culture Complexes and Chronology in Northern Texas.* University of Texas Publi-
         cation no. 4640. Austin.
Lees, W. B.
  1988   Emergency Salvage Excavations at Site 14MN328, a Great Bend Aspect Site in
         Marion, Kansas. *Kansas Anthropological Association Journal* 9:60–82.
  1991   Chronological Placement of the Booth Site: Implications for the Wilmore
         Complex and Southern Plains Culture History. *Plains Anthropologist* 36:255–
         259.
Lintz, C. R.
  1976   The McGrath Site of the Panhandle Aspect. *Bulletin of the Oklahoma Anthropo-
         logical Society* 25:1–110.
  1984   The Plains Villagers: Antelope Creek. In *Prehistory of Oklahoma*, edited by
         R. E. Bell, 325–346. Academic Press, Orlando, Fla.
  1986   *Architecture and Community Variability Within the Antelope Creek Phase of the
         Texas Panhandle.* University of Oklahoma, Oklahoma Archeological Survey,
         Studies in Oklahoma's Past, no. 14. Norman.
  1989   The Upper Canark Regional Variant: Comparison and Contrast of the Ante-
         lope Creek and Apishapa Phases of the Southwestern Plains. In *In the Light of
         Past Experience: Papers in Honor of Jack T. Hughes,* edited by B. C. Roper, 271–
         294. Panhandle Archeological Society Publication no. 5. Aquamarine
         Publications, Claredon, Tex.
Loosle, B. N.
  1991   Social Interaction Among the Late Plains Village Populations in the Central
         Plains. Ph.D. diss., Department of Anthropology, University of Kansas,
         Lawrence.
Lorrain, D.
  1967   The Glass Site. In *A Pilot Study of Wichita Indian Archaeology and Ethnohistory,*
         compiled by R. E. Bell, E. B. Jelks, and W. W. Newcomb, 24–44. University of
         Oklahoma, Report to the National Science Foundation. Norman.
  1969   *Archaeological Excavations in the Fish Creek Reservoir.* Southern Methodist Uni-
         versity, Contributions in Archaeology, no. 4. Dallas, Tex.
Lynott, M. J.
  1977   Radiocarbon Dating the Wylie Focus North Central Texas. *Plains Anthropolo-
         gist* 22:233–237.

1979   Prehistoric Bison Populations of North Central Texas. *Bulletin of the Texas Archeological Society* 50:89–101.

Martin, E. R.
1994   The Dillard Site, a Late Prehistoric Village on the Red River in Cooke County, Texas. *Bulletin of the Texas Archeological Society* 62:105–200.

Monger, E.
1970   A Preliminary Report of the Larned Site. *Kansas Anthropological Association Newsletter* 15:1–15.

Moore, M. C.
1988a   *Archeological Investigations Within the Central Little River Drainage Basin, Cleveland and Pottawatomie Counties, Oklahoma.* University of Oklahoma, Oklahoma Archeological Survey, Archeological Resource Survey Report no. 31. Norman.
1988b   Additional Evidence for the Zimms Complex? A Reevaluation of the Lamb-Miller Site, 34RM-25, Roger Mills County, Oklahoma. *Bulletin of the Oklahoma Anthropological Society* 37:151–190.

Moorehead, W. K.
1921   Recent Explorations in Northwestern Texas. *American Anthropologist* 23:1–11.
1931   *Archaeology of the Arkansas River Valley.* Yale University Press, New Haven, Conn.

Newcomb, W. W., and W. T. Field
1967   An Ethnographic Investigation of the Wichita Indians in the Southern Plains. In *A Pilot Study of Wichita Indian Archaeology and Ethnohistory*, compiled by R. E. Bell, E. B. Jelks, and W. W. Newcomb, 240–395. University of Oklahoma, Report to the National Science Foundation. Norman.

O'Brien, P. J.
1984   *Archeology in Kansas.* University of Kansas, Museum of Natural History, Public Education Series, no. 9. Lawrence.

Odell, G. H.
1990   *Final Report on Archaeological Excavations Conducted Between May and July, 1988, at the Lasley Vore Site (34TU-65).* Report prepared for Kimberly-Clark Corporation, the Oklahoma State Archeologist, and the Oklahoma State Historical Preservation Office. Tulsa.

Pillaert, E.
1963   The McLemore Site of the Washita River Focus. *Bulletin of the Oklahoma Anthropological Society* 11:1–113.

Prikryl, D. J.
1990   *Lower Elm Fork Prehistory: A Redefinition of Cultural Concepts and Chronologies along the Trinity River, North-Central Texas.* Texas Historical Commission, Office of the State Archeologist, Report no. 37. Austin.
1993   Introduction. In *Archeology in the Eastern Planning Region, Texas: A Planning Document*, edited by N. A. Kenmotsu and T. K. Perttula, 191–204. Texas Historical Commission, Department of Antiquities Protection, Cultural Resource Management Report no. 3. Austin.

Prikryl, D. J., and T. K. Perttula
1995   North Central Texas. In Prehistoric and Historic Aboriginal Ceramics in Texas, edited by T. K. Perttula, M. R. Miller, R. A. Rickles, D. J. Prikryl, and C. Lintz, 189–195. *Bulletin of the Texas Archeological Society* 66.

Ranney, W. H., III
   1994   Redefining the Pratt Complex: Evidence from the Lewis Site. M.A. thesis, De-
           partment of Anthropology, University of Kansas, Lawrence.
Rohrbaugh, C. L.
   1982   An Hypothesis for the Origins of the Kichai. In *Pathways to Plains Prehistory:
           Anthropological Perspectives of Plains Natives and Their Pasts, Papers in Honor of
           Robert E. Bell,* edited by D. G. Wyckoff and J. L. Hofman, 51–61. Oklahoma
           Anthropological Society, Memoir no. 3; Cross Timbers Heritage Association
           Contributions, no. 1. Oklahoma City.
Rowlison, D.
   1985   A Preliminary Report on the Bell Site and the 1984 Kansas Archeology Train-
           ing Program. *Kansas Anthropological Association Journal* 5:117–128.
Shaeffer, J. B.
   1965   Salvage Archaeology in Oklahoma, Volume 1. Papers of the Oklahoma Ar-
           chaeological Salvage Project, Numbers 8–15. *Bulletin of the Oklahoma Anthropo-
           logical Society* 13:77–153.
Smith, J. E., II
   1993   The Vinson Site (41LT1): A Norteño Focus Indian Village in Limestone
           County, Texas. *Bulletin of the Texas Archeological Society* 64:65–162.
Stephenson, R. L.
   1952   The Hogge Bridge Site and the Wylie Focus. *American Antiquity* 17:299–312.
Studer, F. V.
   1931   Archaeological Survey of the North Panhandle of Texas. *Bulletin of the Texas
           Archeological and Paleontological Society* 3:70–75.
   1934   Texas Panhandle Culture Ruin No. 55. *Bulletin of the Texas Archeological and
           Paleontological Society* 6:80–96.
   1955   Archaeology of the Texas Panhandle. *Panhandle-Plains Historical Review*
           28:87–95.
Suhm, D. A., and E. B. Jelks
   1962   *Handbook of Texas Archeology: Type Descriptions.* Texas Archeological Society,
           Special Publication no. 1; Texas Memorial Museum, Bulletin no. 4. Austin.
Suhm, D. A., A.D. Krieger, and E. B. Jelks
   1954   An Introductory Handbook of Texas Archeology. *Bulletin of the Texas Archeo-
           logical Society* 25.
Thies, R. M.
   1985   Radiocarbon Dates from the Bell Site, 14CM407. *Kansas Anthropological
           Association Journal* 6:13–14.
   1989   A Preliminary Report on the Hallman Site and the 1988 Kansas Archeology
           Training Program. *Kansas Anthropological Association Journal* 9(9):174–199.
Vehik, S. C.
   1976   The Great Bend Aspect: A Multivariate Investigation of Its Origins and South-
           ern Plains Relationships. *Plains Anthropologist* 21:199–205.
   1984   The Woodland Occupations. In *Prehistory of Oklahoma,* edited by R. E. Bell,
           175–197. Academic Press, Orlando, Fla.
   1990   Late Prehistoric Plains Trade and Economic Specialization. *Plains Anthropolo-
           gist* 35:125–145.
   1992   Wichita Culture History. *Plains Anthropologist* 37:311–332.
   1994   Cultural Continuity and Discontinuity in the Southern Prairies and Cross
           Timbers. In *Plains Indians, A.D. 500–1500: The Archaeological Past of Historic*

Groups, edited by K. H. Schlesier, 239–263. University of Oklahoma Press, Norman.

Vehik, S. C., and P. Flynn

1982   Archaeological Investigations at the Early Plains Village Uncas Site (34Ka-172). *Bulletin of the Oklahoma Anthropological Society* 31:5–70.

Watson, V.

1950   The Optima Focus of the Panhandle Aspect: Description and Analysis. *Bulletin of the Texas Archeological and Paleontological Society* 21:7–68.

Watts, H. K.

1971   The Archaeology of the Avery Ranch Site on Turkey Creek, Southeastern Colorado. M.A. thesis, Department of Anthropology, University of Denver.

Wedel, M. M.

1981   *The Deer Creek Site, Oklahoma: A Wichita Village Sometimes Called Ferdinandina, An Ethnohistorian's View.* Oklahoma Historical Society, Series in Anthropology, no 5. Oklahoma City.

1982   The Wichita Indians in the Arkansas River Basin. In *Plains Indian Studies: A Collection of Essays in Honor of John C. Ewers and Waldo R. Wedel,* edited by D. H. Ubelaker and H. J. Viola, 118–134. Smithsonian Contributions to Anthropology no. 30. Washington, D.C.

Wedel, W. R.

1959   *An Introduction to Kansas Archeology.* Bureau of American Ethnology Bulletin 174, Washington D.C.

1967   The Council Circles of Central Kansas: Were They Solstice Registers? *American Antiquity* 32:54–63.

Withers, A. M.

1954   University of Denver Archaeological Fieldwork. *Southwestern Lore* 19:1–3.

Witty, T. A.

1978   Along the Southern Edge: The Central Plains Tradition in Kansas. In *The Central Plains Tradition: Internal Development and External Relationships,* edited by D. J. Blakeslee, 56–66. University of Iowa, Office of the State Archaeologist, Report no. 11. Iowa City.

Wood-Simpson, C.

1976   Trinchera Cave; A Rock Shelter in Southeastern Colorado. M.A. thesis, Department of Anthropology, University of Wyoming, Laramie.

Wyckoff, D. G.

1980   Caddoan Adaptive Strategies in the Arkansas Basin, Eastern Oklahoma. Ph.D. diss., Department of Anthropology, Washington State University, Pullman.

1993   Gravel Sources of Knappable Alibates Silicified Dolomite. *Geoarchaeology* 8:35–58.

13. The Late High Plains Hunters

Jeffery R. Hanson

The archaeology of the late prehistoric to historic High Plains nomadic tribes is both a fascinating and a significant field of research in the anthropology of the Great Plains. It is, however, complicated by several factors. First, and perhaps foremost, when it comes to attaching tribal or ethnic identifications to late prehistoric archaeological complexes, one is immediately confronted with the taxonomic inconsistencies encountered in trying to merge archaeology and ethnology. This problem is inevitable, since prehistoric archaeological units (cultures, traditions, phases, and complexes) are built from similarities and differences in artifact attributes, site features, and other physical remains, whereas ethnic or tribal units and subunits are most often delineated by politics, ideology, and symbolism.

The result is that there is rarely a one-to-one correspondence between the archaeological record and ethnic units: tribal identification may not always be archaeologically distinguishable. Second, the "typical" nomadic Plains tribes differed from some of the agricultural village tribes like the Mandans and Pawnees, whose sedentary lifeways resulted in substantial, deeply stratified, and distinctive artifacts and clustering (especially in ceramics and settlement patterns). The late prehistoric and historic High Plains tribes were nomadic hunters and pastoralists whose portable and highly mobile lifestyle rarely left much in the way of accumulated archaeological deposits. Potentially distinctive technologies such as ceramics are rare or absent. Also, in contrast to the relative stability of the horticultural villagers, the historic High Plains tribes are characterized by many migrations and relocations, making them recent occupants in many parts of the Plains. Their mobility makes the conventional practice of associating a historic tribe with the prehistory of a region a dubious one at best. Finally, the historic period on the Great Plains was one of tremendous change for many High Plains tribes. The acquisition of horses and firearms, coupled with the fur trade, devastating epidemic diseases, and American expansion, led to many territorial and ethnic realignments. One cannot therefore uncritically assume that ethnic and tribal units in the historic period were isomorphic with those in late prehistoric times. It is due primarily to these last two factors that the direct historical approach, so successful in extending known historic village tribes into the prehistoric past, is difficult to apply to High Plains tribes. Recent attempts to attribute tribal identity to late High Plains prehistoric complexes attest to the difficulty of merging analytically different units of knowledge: the emics of ethnographic and historical ethnic units, and the etics of archaeological assemblages, taxa, and artifact types (Schlesier 1987, 1994). In short, to be able to match a historical tribal "fingerprint" with a prehistoric component two questions must be answered in the affirmative. First, are the archaeological data in question consistent with the material culture of a historically known tribe? Second, are these data consistent with the tribe to the exclusion of all others? Recent failures in this endeavor stem from the inability to answer the second question. These problems also explain in large part the brevity of this chapter: there is a great deal we simply do not know and, perhaps pessimistically, never will.

What follows is a summary and synthesis of what is known about the archaeology and ethnohistory of Wissler's (1914, 1941) "typical" Plains hunter-gatherers. To this characterization must be added the fact that these tribes were also nomadic pastoralists who used herding to efficiently hunt bison (Oliver 1976). It was pastoralism that gave rise to many of the formal tribal mechanisms shown by most of these tribes, such as chiefs and councils, soldier organizations, and ceremonies like the Sun Dance. While the ethnohistory of these tribes often is rich, the archaeological record is meager and variable at best. Some tribes, for all intents and purposes, are archaeologically invisible, while the evidence for others is tantalizing but equivocal. Sites are rare (Figure 13.1). Because of the difficulty in assigning tribal affiliation to archaeological complexes, and as a matter of convenience, ethnohistoric summaries are used to frame the discussions.

High Plains Groups

The three High Plains groups were historic equestrian bison-hunting nomads, but each is believed to have once been semisedentary horticulturists living in the Northeastern Plains.

Cheyennes

Historic documentation places the Algonquian-speaking Cheyennes in the general area of the Black Hills in the late eighteenth century. In 1795, the fur trader Jean-Baptiste Truteau (1952:301) said that the Cheyennes lived to the west of the Arikara villages along the Cheyenne River in present-day South Dakota. In 1805, Lewis and Clark (1959:6:100) noted that the Cheyennes were a nomadic tribe that lived near the Black Hills. Stephen Long's map of the Plains from his 1823 expedition shows the Cheyennes living in the Black Hills, but it is possible that by this time some Cheyennes were moving south toward the Arkansas River in Colorado (Allen 1987:48, 50). By 1832, the Cheyennes had split into northern and southern divisions, the former ranging the upper Platte River–

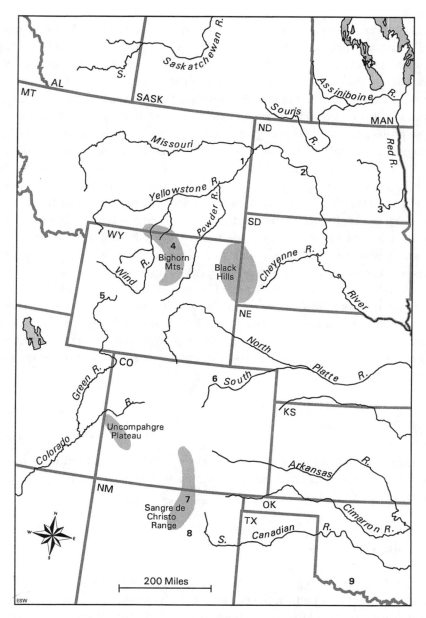

Figure 13.1. Selected sites on the High Plains: *Montana* (1) Hagen; *North Dakota* (2) Ice Glider, (3) Biesterfeldt; *Wyoming* (4) Piney Creek, (5) Eden–Farson; *Colorado* (6) Hatch; *New Mexico* (7) Clinging Cactus, (8) John Alden; *Oklahoma* (9) Cutthroat Gap.

Figure 13.2. Aerial view of the Biesterfeldt site, looking southwest. (From Wood 1971)

Powder River country in Wyoming, while the latter gravitated to Bent's Fort on the Arkansas River (Grinnell 1956:206; Gussow et al. 1974:23).

Cheyenne tradition suggests that before their occupation of the Black Hills as fully adapted equestrian bison hunters, they lived as horticulturists in present-day Minnesota and North Dakota. They began a westward migration in early historic times, establishing several sedentary villages along the Missouri River between the Mandans and the Arikaras before abandoning farming and taking up a nomadic life (Grinnell 1923).

There is some archaeological support for this tradition. While Cheyenne villages along the Missouri River have not been archaeologically verified, there is strong support for a Cheyenne horticultural lifeway in eastern North Dakota. The Biesterfeldt site is a fortified earthlodge village on the bank of the Sheyenne River, a tributary of the Red River in eastern North Dakota (Figure 13.2). In most respects, it resembles Plains Village–tradition sites (especially those of the Arikaras) along the Missouri River and contains historic trade goods. Circumstantial historical evidence suggests that this late-eighteenth-century village was occupied by the Cheyennes. Traditionally, they were driven from the village by the Ojibways, and the archaeological and traditional evidence for its identification appear to be consistent (Wood 1971:55–60). Recent studies have been far more fictional in attributing Cheyenne and Suhtai identity to prehistoric complexes such as Besant, Arvilla, and Blackduck in the Northern Plains (Schlesier 1987, 1994:311). No archaeological manifestation in Minnesota can reliably be attributed to the Cheyenne.

Indeed, if some Cheyennes were still living as earthlodge horticulturists in the late eighteenth century, an interesting problem is raised concerning migration, tribal cohesion, and culture change. By 1794, the Cheyennes were reported living as nomadic hunters far to the west of the Missouri River in the Black Hills. If the Cheyennes migrated en masse, they must have undergone rapid cultural changes within a generation or less, the Plains orientation of village cultures notwithstanding. In 1806, Alexander Henry visited a summer encampment of Cheyennes, complete with camp circle, horses, and Mandan and Hidatsa trading partners (Gough 1988:251–276). A more likely interpretation of their migration is that the Cheyenne village groups, including the cognate Sutais, gradually were pushed out of the Northeastern Plains to the Missouri River and west, where they amalgamated as composite bands with a formal tribal organization of band chiefs and councils.

Arapahos and Gros Ventres

From an ethnographic perspective, the Algonquian-speaking Arapahos and Gros Ventres are very similar in language and culture. They had only dialectal differences in speech, and the Arapahos consider the Gros Ventres to be one of their five aboriginal bands (Kroeber 1902). Some Plains scholars believe that the two groups were a single people who separated in the early historic period. One hypothesis suggests that the Arapahos and Gros Ventres were semisedentary horticulturists living near the Red River before about 1650, and that sometime after this the Gros Ventres migrated to the forks of the Saskatchewan River, while the Arapahos moved to the Missouri River region of Montana (Ewers 1974:53; Trenholm 1970:11).

Although the origins and movements of these two tribes are obscure, by the time they were first observed by Europeans in the eighteenth century they were clearly separated geographically. The Gros Ventres are first mentioned by Anthony Hendry in 1754 as the "Archithinue," living near the Blackfeet at the confluence of the forks of the Saskatchewan River (Ewers 1974:57–58; Trenholm 1970:17). The Gros Ventres, for most of the historic period, ranged north of the Missouri River and south of the North Fork of the Saskatchewan River. The Arapahos are first mentioned by Jean-Baptiste Truteau in 1794. He recorded the "Kananaviche," or Arapahos, living southwest of the Black Hills on the headwaters of the Cheyenne River in present-day southeastern Wyoming (Trenholm 1970:23). While migration histories for these tribes are not available, it is clear that by the late eighteenth century these two tribes, if not culturally distinct, were geographically separated. Later, the Gros Ventres became allied with the Blackfeet in the western Canadian Plains, while the Arapahos drifted south, split into northern and southern groups, and allied themselves with the

Cheyennes in the country between the Arkansas and North Platte rivers. Both groups retained major similarities in language and social organization. For example, each had age-graded military societies, a trait shared with only the Blackfeet, Mandans, and Hidatsas (Hanson 1988).

From an archaeological perspective, the Arapahos and Gros Ventres are invisible: "We know so little about the prehistoric Arapahos that we are unable to point out fundamental differences between their way of life and that of the other Northern Plains Indians" (Trenholm 1970:12–13). This statement echoes one made almost 70 years earlier when Kroeber (1902:4) wrote that "nothing is known of the origin, history, or migrations of the Arapaho." The situation is the same today, since no prehistoric archaeological sites can be assigned to them. Some historical archaeological material from the Denver area may, however, have an Arapaho or a Cheyenne association, since both tribes are known to have camped in the area in about the 1860s (W. B. Butler, personal communication). Circumstantial evidence also suggests that the Hatch site, in northeastern Colorado, which is radiocarbon-dated at 160 years ago, may represent a Cheyenne or an Arapaho habitation (J. Gunnerson 1987:114).

Crows

Historically, the Siouan-speaking Crows had two main subdivisions: the River Crows, who habitually occupied the bison-rich country along the Yellowstone River in present-day Montana; and the Mountain Crows, who preferred the Bighorn Mountains and the valleys of streams that originated there (Lowie 1956).

Both Crow and Hidatsa oral traditions agree that the Crows were once part of the Hidatsas, living and farming in villages along the Missouri River. While the specifics of Crow village life are yet to be worked out, it is generally accepted that the Mountain Crows were part of the Awatixa Hidatsa subgroup, while the River Crows were affiliated with the Hidatsa-proper subgroup (Ahler and Swenson 1985; Bowers 1965; Hanson 1979).

There is a close linguistic connection between the Crows and the Hidatsas; they differ only in dialect. The linguistic affinity argues for a recent separation of the two groups, probably not before 1450 (Wood and Downer 1977). Some time after this, perhaps as recently as the late seventeenth and early eighteenth centuries, the Crows began migrating away from the Missouri River. By 1805, they were living as fully adapted equestrian bison hunters in the general area of the Yellowstone River and the Bighorn Mountains (Hanson 1979; Lewis and Clark 1959:6:103; Medicine Crow 1979; Wood and Thiessen 1985:206–220).

Many archaeological sites in Wyoming and Montana are attributed to the Crows. Some of them, such as the Piney Creek and Big Goose Creek sites in Wyoming, are interpreted as Crow on the basis of pottery (Frison 1976, 1978).

Radiocarbon dates from these sites place occupations in the fourteenth and fifteenth centuries, and are consistent with the proposed linguistic separation of the Crows and Hidatsas. However, the historic Crows did not make pottery, and the ceramics attributed to the Crows may be within the range of Middle Missouri ceramic styles (A. Johnson 1979).

Another site attributed to the Crows is the Hagen site, a prehistoric village on the lower Yellowstone River in eastern Montana. It is identified as Crow for several reasons. First, it is in historic Crow territory. Second, the pottery "falls within the range of variation ascribed to the Mandan and closely related ceramic [that is, Hidatsa Knife River ware] types" (Mulloy 1942:13). Third, the single earthlodge found there conforms to the general architecture of the Plains earthlodge. Fourth, the bone tools (featuring bison-scapula hoes and fishhooks) also are consistent with those from Mandan and Hidatsa sites. But corrected radiocarbon dates for the site appear to place it before the Crows left the Hidatsas (Wood and Downer 1977:87). While circumstantial evidence tends to support the Crow hypothesis, an alternative theory of a seasonal Mandan village also is plausible. If one favors an ethnohistoric view of a recent Crow migration (after 1675), then one might interpret the Hagen site as a Mandan or Hidatsa–Crow village (Figure 13.3).

Northwestern Plains Groups

The Blackfeet are the westernmost of the Algonquian speakers, and the Wind River (or Eastern) Shoshones speak one of the two Uto-Aztecan languages on the Plains (the other being Comanche).

Blackfeet

Historically, the Blackfeet were a loose, informal entity composed of three politically and economically autonomous tribes: the Siksikas or Blackfeet-proper, the Bloods, and the Piegans (Ewers 1974: Kidd 1986). Very little is known of their origins or movements before historic times, although Grinnell states, without citing his authority, that the Blackfeet came from Lesser Slave Lake. They later moved west and south along the Canadian Front Range, where they acquired horses and began to control the region between the Yellowstone River and the North Fork of the Saskatchewan (Grinnell 1962:177–178). Although ethnographic evidence corroborates Grinnell's placement of the Blackfeet between the Yellowstone and Saskatchewan rivers, it was not until about 1832, when the Blackfeet were attracted to Fort Union and the buffalo trade, that they penetrated the Yellowstone country (Ewers 1974:50). Their core territory was between

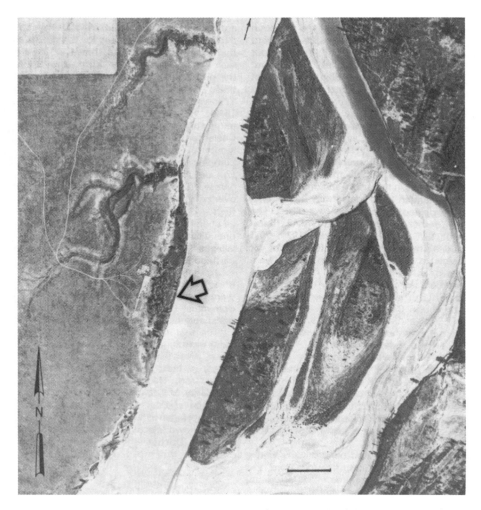

Figure 13.3. U.S. Department of Agriculture aerial photograph of the Hagen site, taken while the 1938 excavations were under way. The bar scale at the lower right is 660 feet long. (From Wood and Downer 1977)

the forks of the Saskatchewan River in Alberta, where they were closely allied with their linguistic relatives, the Algonquian-speaking Gros Ventres to the east and the Athapascan-speaking Sarsis to the north.

If one was to assign late prehistoric or protohistoric archaeological complexes based on known territorial presence of historic groups, one might assign the Old Woman's complex of the prairie regions of Alberta, Saskatchewan, and northern Montana to the Blackfeet (Adams 1978; Reeves 1983). However, this complex could as easily represent the Arapahos or Gros Ventres. Archaeological distinction among these groups is not yet possible. Hannus (1994:197), in

his summary of the prehistory of the Black Hills region (and beyond), empha-
sizes the bittersweet aspect of ethnicity in the archaeological record by quot-
ing Strong: "Once beyond the historic period specific tribal organizations merge
into the complex stream of culture history. The known tribal terminations of
these streams are essential to link history and prehistory. They convert archaeological sequence into historic reality and anchor archaeology to social science.
Yet, from the protohistoric to earlier periods, all tribal and linguistic appella-
tions become increasingly fallacious." This statement can easily apply to the
Blackfeet as well as to the closely related Arapaho and Gros Ventres, who historically ranged within or near the greater Black Hills region. To the northwest
of the Black Hills, where these three tribes interacted historically, some see a
late prehistoric Middle Missouri intrusion (Hidatsa–Crow) in the Mortlach ag-
gregate and the One Gun phase, particularly at Cluny (Vickers 1994:24–26). Another hypothesis, based on ethnographic analogy from the spread of Northern
Plains age-sets, would see Middle Missouri influence coming to the intermediate Arapaho–Gros Ventres and then to the more distant Blackfeet. Thus Mortlach would correspond to the Arapaho–Gros Ventres, while One Gun would
equate with Blackfeet.

Wind River Shoshones

At some point in the late prehistoric or early historic periods, the Eastern
or Prairie Shoshones began to migrate into the Wind River region of present-
day Wyoming. In the process, they adopted a Plains lifestyle to augment their
Great Basin roots. Wright (1978), using ceramic, stratigraphic, and rock-art data,
suggests that Shoshonean populations did not reach southern Wyoming un-
til about the fifteenth century. This is consistent with a recent development of
Plains culture by those Shoshonean bands that became identified as the Wind
River Shoshones. Shimkin (1938:414–415) believes that the historic Wind River
Shoshones consisted of four bands that seasonally fanned out from the Wind
River to the Bighorn Mountains, the Powder River valley, and the Greybull
River. Still, these movements may have been more restrictive than in earlier pe-
riods, when the Shoshones were reported to range as far east as the Black Hills
and as far north as Saskatchewan (Hultkranz 1974:206; Smith 1980:110, 121). The
Wind River Shoshones appear to have been a weakly organized tribe that shared
many typical Plains traits: tribal buffalo hunts in the fall; tribal organization
with a central chief, advisory council, and camp police; and a tribal Sun Dance
(Hultkranz 1974:207).

The Wind River Shoshones are difficult to track archaeologically, for they
are not an aboriginal ethnographic unit; rather, the term refers to the remnant

Prairie Shoshone groups that eventually settled on the Wind River Reservation in the 1870s (Hultkranz 1974:209). A few archaeological sites nevertheless have been interpreted as being Shoshonean or as having a Shoshonean occupation or presence.

Archaeologists in the Northwestern Plains have identified sites as being Shoshonean primarily on the basis of the presence of Intermountain ware pottery. Frison (1971, 1976), for example, infers a Shoshonean occupation at the Eden–Farson site in the Green River basin of southwestern Wyoming, and suggests a possible Shoshonean influence at the Big Goose Creek and Piney Creek sites in northern Wyoming. These occupations are late prehistoric or protohistoric in age (Frison 1971:258; Wright 1978:121). Attributing Intermountain pottery in Wyoming to Shoshoneans is perhaps the most parsimonious inference, but to what branch or band of Shoshones these sites can be attached is not clear. With present evidence, it may not be possible to determine whether these sites, or sites like them, were inhabited by bands of Wind River Shoshones or any other Intermountain ethnic unit. Connections between the historic Shoshones and certain protohistoric rock-art motifs (about 1625 to 1775) in the northwestern Plains—such as the shield-bearing warrior, horse armor, and open-faced horses with upright manes—have been advanced by Keyser (1975, 1987, 1991).

Northeastern Plains Groups

The Lakotas compose the largest of the Dakota, or Sioux, divisions, which were collectively known as the Oceti Xakowin, or Seven Council Fires. The Assiniboins, although derived from the Yanktonais, historically became enemies of their Dakota relations. The Algonquian-speaking Plains Ojibways and Plains Crees once lived in the eastern Woodlands; only historically did they adopt a bison-hunting Plains lifeway.

Lakotas/Dakotas

The Lakotas (also known as the Western or Teton Dakota) were divided into seven large subtribes that, during much of the nineteenth century, ranged from the Missouri River in the east to the Bighorn Mountain–Powder River country in the west, and from the Platte River in the south to the Missouri–Yellowstone region in the north. The seven subtribes were the Oglalas, Brulés (Sicanxu), Sans Arcs (Itaziptce), Hunkpapas, Blackfeet (Sihasapa), Minneconjous, and Two Kettles (Oohenopa). East of the Lakotas, in eastern North and South Dakota, ranged the Yanktonais and Yankton Dakotas, respectively. Ice Glider, a historically documented Yanktonai winter camp dating to 1830 to 1860, is reported from west-central North Dakota (Wood 1986:97–185).

East of the Yanktons, from the prairies of southwestern Minnesota to the Mississippi River, lived the Santee Dakotas, made up of the Sissetons, Wapakutes, Wapatons, and Mdewakantons (Hurt 1974). Unlike the Lakotas, Yanktons, and Yanktonais, who were predominantly nomadic equestrian bison hunters in the historic period, the Santees were semisedentary horticulturists. All the Lakota/Dakota divisions were closely related linguistically and culturally. The traditional viewpoint has been that in terms of culture–area affiliation, the Lakotas were the most Plains-like, while the Santees were the least Plains-like, sharing many Woodland traits with their Chippewa neighbors (Howard 1966). Recent ethnohistorical and archaeological studies have called this interpretation into question, hypothesizing that the Lakota–Santee cultural continuum represents true Plains subsistence and settlement variation (Spector and Johnson 1985).

There are many linguistic and cultural similarities shared by the Lakotas, Yanktonais, Yanktons, and Santees, and many historic records about where these tribes were living in the seventeenth and eighteenth centuries. These parallels have prompted some Plains scholars to postulate an early historic migration of Lakotas from Minnesota to the High Plains west of the Missouri River, centering on the Black Hills. In moving, the Lakotas are thought to have changed their culture from a Plains–Woodland blend like that of the Santees to a typical Plains bison-hunting economy. This argument would imply that the Plains adaptation by the Lakotas was of recent origin, and, by implication, would extend to the Yanktons and Yanktonais (Eggan 1966; Howard 1960; Oliver 1962).

Recent archaeological and ethnohistorical research on the Northeastern Plains and in the prairie–forest border zone of Minnesota suggests that a Plains adaptation by all Lakota/Dakota groups is very old. E. Johnson (1985), for example, has tied Late Woodland Sandy Lake pottery to the historic Santees in Minnesota, and this ceramic style is found westward into the Red and James river valleys in the Dakotas (Wood 1985). Implicit in this association is the hypothesis that prehistoric Dakota groups were already living to the west of the Santees and were adapted to the Plains long before the arrival of Europeans. While it would be difficult to assign specific Lakota/Dakota bands to these archaeological complexes, it is apparent that "the standard view of Dakota migrations onto the Plains does not fit with recently discovered archaeological materials from the Red River area" (Michlovic 1985:136). The Sandy Lake sites on the Northeastern Plains appear to be distinct from other Late Woodland types (suggestive of Algonquian ties) and from Oneota phases such as Orr and Blue Earth (associated with the historic Ioways and Otos). The most parsimonious hypothesis is to regard these sites as ancestral Dakota, giving the Dakotas a presence on the Plains several centuries before European contact. If this is correct, it implies that the cultural changes the Lakotas and Dakotas underwent because of Euro-American factors such as the introduction of horses might not have been as revolutionary as conventional wisdom would lead one to suspect (Michlovic 1985).

Assiniboins

The Assiniboins are believed to have split from their linguistic and cultural cognates, the Yanktonai Dakotas, sometime before 1640 at the headwaters of the Mississippi River (Ewers 1974:77). By this time, they were recognized by the Jesuits as a distinct tribe living near Lake Nipigon in Ontario (Ewers 1974:77; Kennedy 1961:xxv). About this time, the Assiniboins allied themselves with the Crees and the Ojibways, a move that made them inveterate enemies of their Dakota relatives.

With the acquisition of firearms and horses in the mid-eighteenth century, the Assiniboins migrated farther west, where they waged a bitter war with the Blackfeet, Mandans, Hidatsas, and Dakotas for control of the Northern Plains (Kennedy 1961:xxxi). After 1750, the Assiniboins can be regarded as a typical Plains tribe. However, remember that, as once part of the Yanktonai Dakotas, the Assiniboins probably already were well adapted to the Northeastern Plains. Their territory now ranged from eastern Alberta southeast to the confluence of the Assiniboin and Red rivers in southern Manitoba (Ray 1974:22). Their range therefore overlapped that of their Plains Cree and Plains Ojibway allies. By the early nineteenth century, the Assiniboins were pressing the Hidatsas to the south in northern North Dakota, and the Blackfeet to the west along the upper Missouri in Montana (Ray 1974:312).

The Assiniboins did not constitute a "tribe" in an ethnological sense. Like the Plains Crees and Plains Ojibways, the Assiniboins were divided into many economically and politically independent bands, each of which had its own chiefs and soldier societies (Kennedy 1961:15). While the number of Assiniboin bands at any one time is not known, estimates range from a low of five to as high as 33 (Kennedy 1961:190–191; Ray 1974:312).

Archaeologically, almost nothing is known of the Assiniboins. At one time, archaeologists associated the Assiniboins with the Blackduck complex. This connection has been dropped in favor of the western Algonquians (Syms 1985:95). At present, there appear to be no diagnostic criteria to differentiate Assiniboin sites from those of the Crees, Ojibways, Gros Ventres, or Blackfeet, all of whom ranged over the same areas at one time or another. However, Meyer and Hamilton (1994:125–126) have suggested a possible late prehistoric (about 1500) Assiniboin connection with Sandy Lake/Selkirk ceramics in eastern Saskatchewan, where the Assiniboin ranged during the late seventeenth century.

Plains Ojibways and Plains Crees

The Algonquian-speaking Plains Ojibways and Plains Crees are treated together because they represent linguistically and culturally related tribes that
migrated from the Woodland areas of Ontario and Minnesota and adopted a
nomadic bison-hunting lifestyle. These migrations and cultural changes were
of recent origin, probably in the late eighteenth century, and were fueled by the
Canadian fur trade, which provided the Ojibways and Crees with firearms, allowing them to penetrate the Northeastern Plains to trap beaver and hunt bison
for the provisions trade.

The focus of historic Plains Ojibway (or Bungi) territory was the prairie region of eastern Saskatchewan and southern Manitoba (including the southern
reaches of Lake Winnipeg and the Red River) and northeastern North Dakota
(Howard 1977). Ojibway penetration into the Red River region of Manitoba and
North Dakota was well under way by the late eighteenth century. It may have
been earlier if one considers that ancestral Plains Ojibways were responsible for
driving the Cheyennes out of the village known archaeologically as the Biesterfeldt site in eastern North Dakota (Howard 1977; Wood 1971:56).

By the 1830s, the Plains Ojibways were fully adjusted to Plains life and, with
the acquisition of horses, could successfully compete for bison-hunting grounds
in what is now northern North Dakota, northeastern Montana, and their core
range between the Turtle Mountain of North Dakota and the Red River (Howard
1977). The ability of the Plains Ojibways to carve out a niche in the Northern
and Northeastern Plains was also due in part to alliances with the Plains Crees
and Assiniboins, both of whom had large populations and firearms.

The Plains Ojibways were a loose association of autonomous, shifting bands
led by local chiefs. They lacked the formal tribal organization of groups like the
Crows, Arapahos, and Kiowas, but retained the Woodland Ojibway integrative
mechanisms of exogamous patrilineal clans. They added several warrior societies and women's societies to their social structure (Howard 1977:73, 79). Unlike
many other Plains tribes, and no doubt influenced by their Métis neighbors,
the Plains Ojibways made extensive use of Red River carts on their bison hunts.
These carts were commonly placed around the perimeter of camp circles in a defensive posture (Howard 1977:81). Such measures were necessary because, during much of the nineteenth century, the Plains Ojibways were enemies of the
Dakotas, Mandans, Hidatsas, and Blackfeet, on whose traditional bison-hunting
lands they were encroaching.

The Plains Crees, like the Ojibways, were a western Algonquian-speaking
group that expanded out of the Woodland regions of Canada in the historic period. Unlike the Ojibways, who came directly from the east, the Crees in the
mid-eighteenth century were living north of the Canadian Plains in the forest-
lake country of Alberta, Saskatchewan, and Manitoba (Ray 1974:22). The move-

ment of some Crees into the Northern Plains was probably a result of many factors, but two important ones were the depletion of fur-bearers in their forest-lake habitats, and the attraction of the bison trade at posts to the south. By 1800, the Plains Crees had dislodged the Gros Ventres from the forks of the Saskatchewan River and, allied with the Assiniboins, were making inroads into Blackfeet and Hidatsa territory (Ewers 1974:60–70).

The Plains Crees were a loose association of many bands scattered over a large territory. Their social structure was very informal, without centralized tribal leadership or formal status positions. Even their soldier societies lacked the integrative aspects of those of the Plains Ojibways because (unlike the latter) Cree bands tended to have only one soldier society (Mandelbaum 1940:224). The looseness of both Cree and Ojibway social structure was probably due, in part, to their Woodland background as hunter-gatherers whose small populations and nomadic existence fostered flexible kin groups and bands (Oliver 1962).

The assignment of archaeological complexes to the Plains Crees or Plains Ojibways has, for the most part, been unsuccessful. Some investigators have linked the archaeological Blackduck complex with western Algonquian groups, particularly the Ojibways (Syms 1985:95–96). Blackduck sites occur in areas associated with historic Plains Ojibway territory, especially along the lower Red River and near the confluence of the Assiniboin and Souris rivers in southern Manitoba. On geographic and temporal grounds, one might also associate the archaeological Mortlach complex with Plains Ojibways, although, by the same criteria, it could also be tied to the Assiniboins, Arapahos, or Gros Ventres.

Southwestern Plains Groups

The Shoshonean linguistic family encompasses many bands and tribes in the Rocky Mountain region, the Great Basin, and the Southern Plains, including historically known peoples like the Shoshones, Paiutes, Utes, and Comanches. Of immediate relevance are bands of Eastern Shoshones in the Northwestern Plains area of Montana and Wyoming, the Utes of southern Colorado, and the Comanches in the southern Plains of present-day Colorado, New Mexico, Texas, and Oklahoma.

Comanches

The historic Comanches were first recorded in Spanish New Mexico in 1706 when, accompanied by Utes, they appeared in the Santa Fe–Taos region (John 1975:231; Richardson 1933:55). The fact that the Comanches speak a Shoshonean language mutually intelligible with that of the Wind River Shoshones suggests a late prehistoric or protohistoric split with the Wind River bands, perhaps near the headwaters of the North Platte and South Platte rivers in present-day southeastern Wyoming and northeastern Colorado. By the early eighteenth century, Comanche bands were entrenched along the Arkansas River valley in southeastern Colorado and western Kansas and in regions to the south (Richardson 1933). By the mid-eighteenth century, at least five Comanche bands (Yamparikas, Kotsotekas, Nokonis, Quahadis, and Penatekas) ranged over large territories in southeastern Colorado and western Kansas, eastern New Mexico and the Texas panhandle, and south-central Texas (Newcomb 1961; Richardson 1933; Wallace and Hoebel 1952).

Comanche bands were large, economically and politically autonomous units that lacked many of the formal tribal integrative mechanisms of other tribes, such as tribal camp circles, tribal chiefs or councils, or ceremonies like the Sun Dance (Newcomb 1961; Wallace and Hoebel 1952:22–23). Rather, the Comanches were a highly individualistic society whose large bands seldom aggregated (Hanson 1980; Wallace and Hoebel 1953:22).

What little is known archaeologically about the Comanches comes from material culture found in historic-period sites. Most of these sites are burials, and the information from them shows that historic Comanche material culture conformed to a regional Southern Plains style that heavily incorporated Spanish and Mexican trade goods (Hays 1989:257). Most of these trade items came through the Comanchero trade, in which caravans of New Mexican traders established rendezvous camps with Comanches and Kiowas in western Texas in the nineteenth century (Hanson and Hanson 1995; Hays 1989:257; Wallace and Hoebel 1952:267–268). The historic material culture of the Comanches, however, was similar to that of the Kiowas and Kiowa-Apaches (Hays 1989:27). Thus it may be very difficult to differentiate campsites or burials of these tribes without firm historic documentation.

Less is known about earlier periods of Comanche culture history. While protohistoric sites are common in areas that coincide with historic Comanche territory, the Comanches' range also overlapped with that of the Apaches, Kiowas, Cheyennes, and Arapahos. Many of these sites are attributed to the Dismal River culture (putative Plains Apache) (Hofman 1989:91–93). Comanches, Utes, Cheyennes, Arapahos, and Kiowas may be responsible for other sites, such as tipi-ring sites in southeastern Colorado (Hofman 1989:93).

Utes

From their earliest contacts with the Spanish in the late seventeenth century, the Utes are described as essentially a mountain people whose culture expanded dramatically in the direction of the Plains following the introduction of horses

(John 1975). Like the Comanches, the Utes were an informal amalgam of economically and politically independent bands that shared culture, but recognized no centralized overarching tribal authority. Ute bands in closest proximity to Plains culture and influence were the Kapote and Moache, the latter of which was allied with the Comanches from about 1700 to 1735, when a breach between the two tribes turned them into mortal enemies (John 1975:313). After this, Ute core territory remained in the Colorado Rockies and foothills near the headwaters of the Arkansas River (Steward 1974). Archaeologists have had greater success in applying the direct historical approach to Ute prehistoric and historic archaeology than to that of other Plains nomads (Buckles 1971). The Utes were more stable and dominant in their territory in western Colorado than were the other tribes, making them the strongest circumstantial candidates to associate with the late prehistoric and historic complexes. The separation of the Utes from other Numic-speaking groups is difficult to date prior to 1400. After this time, however, several diagnostic artifacts appear to have a Ute association. Most late prehistoric and historic Ute sites occur on the Uncompahgre Plateau and in other parts of western Colorado. Sites dating between 1400 and 1650 have been interpreted as Ute because of the presence of Uncompahgre Brownware pottery, Desert Side-notched points, and Cottonwood Triangular points (Reed 1988:81, 88). Ute associations are based on the presence and distribution of wickiups (a known Ute house type) and the presence of Euro-American artifacts in campsites and burials (Horn 1988; Scott 1988). Rock art in western Colorado also has been attributed to the Utes, particularly that which depicts equestrian scenes, firearms, and Plains stylistic themes (Cole 1988).

Kiowas

The Kiowas have remote linguistic ties to the Tanoan-speaking Pueblo Indians of the Southwest and are the only Plains tribe of this language family. Kiowa legend points to a northern origin, placing them along the Yellowstone River in western Montana in the late seventeenth century. Sometime after, legend holds, the Kiowas migrated south, passing through the Black Hills, later arriving in the Arkansas River valley in present-day eastern Colorado and western Kansas, and eventually moving south of the Arkansas into western Oklahoma and Texas (Harrington 1939; Mayhall 1974; Mooney 1900). It was sometime during this southward migration that the Kiowas were joined by a small band of Plains Apaches who became, in many respects, culturally and politically Kiowas. They are now known as the Kiowa-Apaches.

External sources tend to corroborate parts of the Kiowa migration. They are mentioned (as the Pioya) by the La Vérendrye brothers as one of the Plains tribes living near the Black Hills in 1742 (Smith 1980:106,120). Cheyenne legend also places the Kiowas in the vicinity of the Little Missouri, Powder, and Tongue rivers of Wyoming in the early to mid-eighteenth century (Mayhall 1974:90).

By the late eighteenth century the Kiowas had migrated south to an area between the North Platte and Arkansas rivers, perhaps in responses to Dakota pressure or to gain closer proximity to the source of horses diffusing out to the Spanish Southwest (Mayhall 1974:14–15; Truteau 1952:300–301). By the early 1820s and 1830s, the Kiowas were living along the Arkansas River south to the plains of western Oklahoma and the Staked Plains of Texas and northeastern New Mexico, perhaps to take advantage of the Santa Fe trade. It was here that the Kiowas allied themselves with the Comanches, with whom they shared overlapping territories (Hanson and Chirinos 1989:32).

Historically, the Kiowas were organized into some 10 to 20 bands that gathered into a unified tribe in the summer for the Sun Dance and a communal buffalo hunt. During the Sun Dance, the Keeper of the Taime, or Sun Dance medicine, was formally considered tribal chief. The Kiowas also had several nongraded military societies that functioned as camp police and enforcers of tribal hunt regulations (Mayhall 1974; Oliver 1962) Compared with the Comanches, the Kiowas had a more formally structured society.

Like that of the Comanches, the archaeology of the Kiowas is known almost exclusively through a few historic sites, mostly burials. Even so, it is not clear whether many of the sites are Kiowa, Kiowa-Apache, or Comanche. One site, Cutthroat Gap, is identified as a Kiowa camp (Hays 1989:258). The similarity of Kiowa and Comanche material culture, coupled with their territorial overlap, has probably contributed to the difficulty in isolating diagnostic Kiowa artifacts.

Apacheans

The Kiowa-Apaches, Jicarillas, and Lipans are historic Plains Apache groups that, during the late seventeenth and early eighteenth centuries, were variously described by the Spanish as living in semisedentary villages or rancherias in a vast territory stretching from northeastern New Mexico and the Texas panhandle through southeastern Colorado, western Kansas, and as far north as western Nebraska (J. Gunnerson 1960, 1987; Hanson and Chirinos 1989). Geographically and culturally, the Jicarillas and Lipans had closer ties to each other than to the more remote Kiowa-Apaches.

KIOWA-APACHES

Historically, the Kiowa-Apaches appear never to have had any political connection with either of the other Apache groups discussed here. A linguistic connection to the Jicarillas and Lipans suggests a separation since about 1750. It is speculated that the Kiowa-Apaches were one of several Apache groups living between the forks of the Platte River in the early eighteenth century and were cut off from other Apacheans by the Comanche intrusion into the Southern Plains (Brant 1953:201–202). Their affiliation with the Kiowas may date from this period. Their separation from other Apaches is reflected in their lacking the Pueblo influence characteristic of the Jicarillas. They have been described as a group having an overlay of Plains traits on a southern Athapascan cultural base (Brant 1953; Mooney 1900; Tweedie 1968). If the Kiowa-Apaches are viewed as one of the northernmost groups of Plains Apaches (with groups like the Carlanas, Palomas, and Quartelejos), it is conceivable that they may be the historic representatives of the archaeological culture known as Dismal River in western Nebraska and near the Black Hills (J. Gunnerson 1960, 1987). This bison-hunting and horticultural lifeway, dating from about 1640 to 1725, conforms geographically with the distribution of Plains Apaches described by the Spanish in the early eighteenth century. To date, this association is essentially circumstantial, since by the time the Kiowa-Apaches are known as a historic entity they are full-fledged bison hunters and nomadic pastoralists affiliated with the Kiowas on the Southern Plains.

JICARILLAS

In the ethnographic and historic literature, the Jicarilla Apaches comprise two subdivisions: the Olleros, or Mountain People, and the Llaneros, or Plains People (D. Gunnerson 1974:160–161; Thomas 1974:177; Tiller 1983:441). These subdivisions probably reflect the horticultural and buffalo-hunting polarity of remnant Apache groups of the Central and Southern Plains that, by accretion, became known as Jicarillas. Gunnerson believes that the Olleros probably were the "Jicarilla-proper," who established themselves in the eastern foothills of the Sangre de Cristo Mountains of Colorado, where they lived in flattop adobe houses and irrigated plots of land to grow corn, beans, and squash. The Llaneros probably were remnant Plains Apache groups such as the Carlanas, Palomas, and Quartelejos, who were driven from their semisedentary horticultural and hunting lifestyle in Nebraska and Kansas by the Comanches (D. Gunnerson 1974:164). This amalgamation of Plains Apache with Jicarilla probably took place in the early to mid-eighteenth century, so that about 1750 the Olleros and Llaneros subdivisions lived primarily in the Sangre de Cristo Mountains of southern Colorado, northeastern New Mexico, and southeastern Colorado south of the Arkansas River (Hanson and Chirinos 1989:21).

Archaeologically, J. Gunnerson (1960:105–106) believes that of the various Apache bands, the Palomas represent Dismal River sites in western Nebraska and southwestern South Dakota, while the Carlanas represent Dismal River sites in southeastern Colorado. At this point, the assignment of Dismal River sites to the Llanero subdivision of the Jicarillas is the most parsimonious hypothesis, as it is in agreement chronologically and geographically with Spanish accounts of the distribution of Apaches to the northeast of Santa Fe in the early eighteenth century, as well as with the general description of the semisedentary, rancheria, horticultural and bison-hunting lifestyle of these historic Plains Apache peoples. In addition, pottery from Dismal River sites in northeastern New Mexico, the western Texas panhandle, and southeastern Colorado show similarities with Jicarilla pottery (J. Gunnerson 1987:108, 114). These sites also contain Pueblo pottery, and it is known historically that Jicarillas and Faraons (who were assimilated by the Mescaleros about 1800) often visited and traded at Pecos, Picuris, Nambe, and other pueblos (J. Gunnerson 1987:109, 114). Historic Jicarilla sites, from the early nineteenth century and later, have been identified in the Cimarron region of eastern New Mexico and along the eastern foothills of the Sangre de Cristo Mountains from Raton south to Anton Chico. The Clinging Cactus site, near modern Cimarron, New Mexico, and the John Alden site near Las Vegas are among those attributed to the nineteenth-century Jicarilla Apaches (J. Gunnerson 1987:114).

LIPANS

The Lipan Apaches, according to some investigators, were living in the general area of northeastern New Mexico and the Texas panhandle in the late seventeenth and early eighteenth centuries (Sjoberg 1953; Tweedie 1968). Pressure from the Comanches made the Lipans retreat southward, and by 1732, they were reported in the San Saba region of central Texas (Sjoberg 1953:77). This reconstruction is disputed by Opler (1975:187), who cites evidence to suggest that the Lipans had a much longer tenure in central Texas, where, for example, they are reported as living near and raiding newly founded San Antonio in 1718.

The movements and locations of the Lipans are important in terms of tying them into Dismal River archaeology. Culturally, the Lipans appear to have been dominantly nomadic bison hunters with only a marginal interest in horticulture. They lived almost exclusively in tipis or wikiups. It is primarily on the basis of these features, plus the disdain of Lipans and other Apaches for dog flesh, that Opler (1975) rejected any Lipan association with Dismal River. But the close linguistic connection between the Lipans and the Jicarillas (who have separation dates of between 205 and 227 years)—coupled with similarities in social structure, mythology, and Pueblo connections—suggests a period of living near the Jicarillas in northeastern New Mexico or the Texas panhandle. The changes that the Lipans underwent after moving south to central and southwestern Texas could have resulted in the slow loss of typical Dismal River traits, such as adobe-like structures, pottery, and irrigation horticulture.

Conclusion

This survey of the archaeology of the High Plains nomadic tribes has yielded uneven results. Many of the tribes are either archaeologically invisible or poorly connected to regional complexes. Indeed, these associations become even more tenuous if one adheres strictly to the phase concept as representing distinct sociocultural entities (L. Johnson 1987). For other tribes, however, there exists intriguing circumstantial evidence that has been used to suggest connections between historic tribes and prehistoric complexes. In general, these data seem to hinge on three characteristics. First, connections are more suggestive for tribes that maintained a certain degree of core-territorial stability in the historic period. Such is the case for some Ute bands, Wind River Shoshones, and Blackfeet. Second, the presence of a ceramic tradition increases the chance of bridging the gap between historic and prehistoric. This is certainly true of the Plains Apaches and, to some extent, the Crows, Shoshones, and Utes. Third, historical evidence, if properly used, can yield inferences of tribal affiliation for archaeological assemblages or sites. This applies most strongly to the Cheyennes and Plains Apaches. Whatever chances exist for a particular tribe being recognized in the archaeological record of the High Plains lies in a truly conjunctive application of archaeology, ethnohistory, and ethnography.

References

Adams, G.
    1978   *Tipi Rings in Southern Alberta: The Alkali Creek Sites, Lower Red Deer River.* Archaeological Survey of Alberta, Occasional Paper no. 9. Edmonton.
Ahler, S. A., and A. A. Swenson
    1985   *Test Excavations at Big Hidatsa Village (32ME12), Knife River Indian Villages National Historic Site.* University of North Dakota, Department of Anthropology and Archaeology, Contribution no. 218. Grand Forks.
Allen, J. L.
    1987   Patterns of Promise: Mapping the Plains and Prairies. In *Mapping the North American Plains,* edited by F. C. Luebke, F. W. Kaye, and G. E. Moulton, 41–62. University of Oklahoma Press, Norman.
Bowers, A. W.
    1965   *Hidatsa Social and Ceremonial Organization.* Bureau of American Ethnology Bulletin 194. Washington, D.C.
Brant, C. S.
    1953   Kiowa Apache Culture History: Some Further Observations. *Southwestern Journal of Anthropology* 9:195–202.
Buckles, W. G.
    1971   The Uncompahgre Complex: Historic Ute Archaeology and Prehistoric Archaeology on the Uncompahgre Plateau in West Central Colorado. Ph.D. diss., Department of Anthropology, University of Colorado, Boulder.

Cole, S.
    1988   Ute Rock Art. In *Archaeology of the Eastern Ute: A Symposium,* edited by P. R.
            Nickens, 102–143. Colorado Council of Professional Archaeologists Papers,
            vol. 1. Denver.
Eggan, F.
    1966   *The American Indian.* Aldine, Chicago.
Ewers, J. C.
    1974   *Blackfeet Indians.* Edited by D. A. Horr. Garland, New York.
Frison, G. C.
    1971   Shoshonean Antelope Procurement in the Upper Green River, Wyoming.
            Plains Anthropologist 16:258–284.
    1976   Crow Pottery in Northern Wyoming. *Plains Anthropologist* 21:29–44.
    1978   *Prehistoric Hunters of the High Plains.* Academic Press, New York.
Gough, B. M.
    1988   *The Journal of Alexander Henry the Younger, 1799–1814.* Vol. 1. Chaplain Society,
            Toronto.
Grinnell, G. B.
    1923   *The Cheyenne Indians: Their History and Ways of Life.* 2 vols. Yale University
            Press, New Haven, Conn.
    1956   *The Fighting Cheyennes.* University of Oklahoma Press, Norman.
    1962   *Blackfoot Lodge Tales.* University of Nebraska Press, Lincoln.
Gunnerson, D. A.
    1974   *The Jicarilla Apaches: A Study in Survival.* Northern Illinois University Press,
            De Kalb.
Gunnerson, J. H.
    1960   An Introduction to Plains Apache Archeology: The Dismal River Aspect.
            Bureau of American Ethnology Bulletin 173:131–260.
    1987   *Archeology of the High Plains.* Bureau of Land Management, Cultural Re-
            sources Series, no. 19. Denver.
Gussow, Z., L. R. Hafen, and A. A. Ekirch, Jr.
    1974   *Arapaho-Cheyenne Indians.* Edited by by D. A. Horr. Garland, New York.
Hannus, L. A.
    1994   Cultures of the Heartland: Beyond the Black Hills. In *Plains Indians,* A.D. *500–*
            1500: The Archaeological Past of Historic Groups, edited by K. H. Schlesier, 176–
            198. University of Oklahoma Press, Norman.
Hanson, J. E., and J. R. Hanson
    1995   Ethnogenesis in Colonial Contexts: The Métis of the Red River and the
            Genizaros of New Mexico. Manuscript on file, University of Texas, Depart-
            ment of Sociology and Anthropology, Arlington.
Hanson, J. R.
    1979   Ethnographic Problems in the Crow–Hidatsa Separation. *Archaeology in*
            Montana 20:73–86.
    1980   Structure and Complexity of Medicine Bundle Systems of Selected Plains
            Tribes. *Plains Anthropologist* 25:199–216.
    1988   Age Set Theory and Age Grading Among Historic Plains Indians: A Critical
            Review and Revision. *American Ethnologist* 15:349–364.
Hanson, J. R., and S. Chirinos
    1989   Ethnohistory. In *Nine Rock Art Sites in the Pinyon Canyon Maneuver Site, South-*
            eastern Colorado, edited by L. L. Loendorf, 18–38. University of North Dakota,

Department of Anthropology and Archaeology, Contribution no. 248. Grand Forks.

Harrington, J. P.
   1939   Kiowa Memories of the Northland. In *So Live the Works of Men,* edited by D. D. Brand and F. E. Harvey, 162–176. University of New Mexico Press, Albuquerque.

Hays, J. S.
   1989   Historic Tribal Groups in the Southern Great Plains. In *From Clovis to Comanchero: Archeological Overview of the Southern Great Plains,* edited by J. L. Hofman, R. L. Brooks, J. S. Hays, D. W. Owsley, R. L. Jantz, M. K. Marks, and M. H. Manheim, 247–262. Arkansas Archeological Survey, Research Series, no. 35. Fayetteville.

Hofman, J. L.
   1989   Protohistoric Culture History on the Southern Great Plains. In *From Clovis to Comanchero: Archeological Overview of the Southern Great Plains,* edited by J. L. Hofman, R. L. Brooks, J. S. Hays, D. W. Owsley, R. L. Jantz, M. K. Marks, and M. H. Manheim, 91–100. Arkansas Archeological Survey, Research Series, no. 35. Fayetteville.

Horn, J. C.
   1988   Euroamerican Goods in the Material Culture of the Ute Prior to 1882. In *Archaeology of the Eastern Ute: A Symposium,* edited by P. R. Nickens, 54–63. Colorado Council of Professional Archaeologists Papers, vol. 1. Denver.

Howard, J. H.
   1960   The Cultural Position of the Dakota: A Reassessment. In *Essays in the Science of Culture in Honor of Leslie A. White,* edited by G. E. Dole and R. L. Carneiro, 249–268. Crowell, New York.
   1966   *The Dakota or Sioux Indians.* University of South Dakota, South Dakota Museum, Vermillion.
   1977   *The Plains Ojibwa or Bungi.* J and L Reprint, Lincoln, Neb.

Hultkranz, A.
   1974   The Shoshones in the Rocky Mountain Area. In *Shoshone Indians,* edited by D. A. Horr. Garland, New York.

Hurt, W. R., Jr.
   1974   *Dakota Sioux Indians.* Edited by D. A. Horr. Garland, New York.

John, E.
   1975   *Storms Brewed in Other Mens' Worlds.* University of Nebraska Press, Lincoln.

Johnson, A. M.
   1979   The Problem of Crow Pottery. *Archaeology in Montana* 20:17–29.

Johnson, E.
   1985   The 17th Century Mdewakanton Dakota Subsistence Mode. In *Archaeology, Ecology and Ethnohistory of the Prairie–Forest Border Zone of Minnesota and Manitoba,* edited by J. Spector and E. Johnson, 154–166. J and L Reprint, Lincoln, Neb.

Johnson, L. R., Jr.
   1987   A Plague of Phases. *Bulletin of the Texas Archeological Society* 57:1–26.

Kennedy, M. S., ed.
   1961   *The Assiniboines: From the Accounts of the Old Ones Told to First Boy (James Larpenteur Long).* University of Oklahoma Press, Norman.

Keyser, J. D.
  1975   A Shoshonean Origin for the Plains Shield Bearing Warrior Motif. *Plains
          Anthropologist* 20:207–215.
  1987   A Lexicon for Historic Plains Indian Rock Art: Increasing Interpretive Poten-
          tial. *Plains Anthropologist* 32:43–71.
  1991   A Thing to Tie on the Halter: An Addition to the Plains Rock Art Lexicon.
          Plains Anthropologist 36:261–267.
Kidd, K. E.
  1986   *Blackfoot Ethnography*. Archaeological Survey of Alberta, Manuscript Series,
          no. 8. Edmonton, Alberta.
Kroeber, A. L.
  1902   *The Arapaho*. American Museum of Natural History, Anthropological Papers,
          no. 18. New York.
Lewis, M. and W. Clark
  1959   Ethnology. In *The Original Journals of the Lewis and Clark Expedition*, vol. 6,
          edited by R. G. Thwaites, 80–120. 6. Antiquarian Press, New York.
Lowie, R. H.
  1956   *The Crow Indians*. Holt, Rinehart and Winston, New York.
Mandelbaum, D. G.
  1940   *The Plains Cree*. American Museum of Natural History, Anthropological Pa-
          pers, no. 37. New York.
Mayhall, M. P.
  1974   *The Kiowas*. University of Oklahoma Press, Norman.
Medicine Crow, J.
  1979   The Crow Migration Story. *Archaeology in Montana* 20:63–72.
Meyer, D., and S. Hamilton
  1994   Neighbors to the North: Peoples of the Boreal Forest. In *Plains Indians, A.D.
          500–1500: The Archaeological Past of Historic Groups*, edited by K. L. Schlesier,
          96–127. University of Oklahoma Press, Norman.
Michlovic, M.
  1985   The Problem of Teton Migration. In *Archaeology, Ecology and Ethnohistory of the
          Prairie–Forest Border Zone of Minnesota and Manitoba*, edited by J. Spector and
          E. Johnson, 131–145. J and L Reprint, Lincoln, Neb.
Mooney, J.
  1900   Calendar of the Kiowa Indians. *Smithsonian Annual Report* 17:129–445.
Mulloy, W.
  1942   *The Hagen Site: A Prehistoric Village on the Lower Yellowstone*. University of Mon-
          tana, Publications in the Social Sciences, no. 1. Missoula.
Newcomb, W. W.
  1961   *The Indians of Texas: From Prehistoric to Modern Times*. University of Texas Press,
          Austin.
Oliver, S. C.
  1962   *Ecology and Continuity as Contributing Factors in the Social Organization of the
          Plains Indians*. University of California, Publications in American Archaeol-
          ogy and Ethnology, vol. 48. Berkeley.
  1976   The Plains Indians as Herders. *Anthropology UCLA* 8:35–43.
Opler, M. E.
  1975   Problems in Apachean Culture History with Special Reference to the Lipan.
          Anthropological Quarterly 48:182–192.

Ray, A.
1974 *Indians in the Fur Trade.* University of Toronto Press, Toronto.
Reed, A.D.
1988 Ute Cultural Chronology. In *Archaeology of the Eastern Ute: A Symposium,* edited by P. R. Nickens, 79–101. Colorado Council of Professional Archaeologists Papers, vol. 1. Denver.
Reeves, B. O. K.
1983 *Culture Change in the Northern Plains: 1000 B.C.–A.D. 1000.* Archaeological Survey of Alberta, Occasional Paper no. 20. Edmonton.
Richardson, R. N.
1933 *The Comanche Barrier to South Plains Settlement.* Clark, Glendale, Calif.
Schlesier, K. H.
1987 *Wolves of Heaven; Cheyenne Shamanism, Ceremonies, and Prehistoric Origins.* University of Oklahoma Press, Norman.
1994 Commentary: A History of Ethnic Groups in the Great Plains, A.D. 150–1550. In *Plains Indians, A.D. 500–1500: The Archaeological Past of Historic Groups,* edited by K. L. Schlesier, 308–381. University of Oklahoma Press, Norman.
Scott, D. D.
1988 Conical Timbered Lodges in Colorado, or Wickiups in the Woods. In *Archaeology of the Eastern Ute: A Symposium,* edited by P. R. Nickens, 45–53. Colorado Council of Professional Archaeologists Papers, vol. 1. Denver.
Shimkin, D.
1938 Wind River Shoshone Geography. *American Anthropologist* 40:413–415.
Sjoberg, A. F.
1953 Lipan Apache Culture in Historical Perspective. *Southwest Journal of Anthropology* 9:76–98.
Smith, G. H.
1980 *The Explorations of the La Vérendryes in the Northern Plains, 1738–43.* Edited by W. R. Wood. University of Nebraska Press, Lincoln.
Spector, J., and E. Johnson, eds.
1985 *Archaeology, Ecology and Ethnohistory of the Prairie–Forest Border Zone of Minnesota and Manitoba.* J and L Reprint, Lincoln, Neb.
Steward, J. H.
1974 *Ute Indians.* Vol. 1. Edited by D. A. Horr. Garland, New York.
Syms, E. L.
1985 Fitting People in the Late Prehistory of the Northeastern Plains. In *Archaeology, Ecology and Ethnohistory of the Prairie–Plains Forest Border Zone of Minnesota and Manitoba,* edited by J. Spector and E. Johnson, 73–107. J and L Reprint, Lincoln, Neb.
Thomas, A. B.
1974 The Jicarilla Apache Indians: A History 1598–1888. In *Apache Indians.* Vol. 3. Edited by D. A. Horr. Garland, New York.
Tiller, V. E.
1983 Jicarilla Apache. In *The Southwest,* edited by A. Ortiz, 40–461. Vol. 10 of *Handbook of North American Indians.* W. C. Sturtevant, general editor. Smithsonian Institution Press, Washington, D.C.
Trenholm, V. C.
1970 *The Arapahoes, Our People.* University of Oklahoma Press, Norman.

Truteau, J.-B.
    1952   Journal of Truteau on the Missouri River, 1794–1795. In *Before Lewis and Clark: Documents Illustrating the History of the Missouri, 1785–1804,* edited by A. P. Nasatir, 259–311. 2 vols. St. Louis Historical Documents Foundation, St. Louis, Mo.

Tweedie, M. J.
    1968   Notes on the History and Adaptation of the Apache Tribes. *American Anthropologist* 70:1132–1142.

Vickers, J. R.
    1994   Cultures of the Northwestern Plains: From the Boreal Forest Edge to Milk River. In *Plains Indians, A.D. 500–1500: The Archaeological Past of Historic Groups,* edited by K. K. Schlesier, 3–33. University of Oklahoma Press, Norman.

Wallace, E., and E. A. Hoebel
    1952   *The Comanches, Lords of the South Plains.* University of Oklahoma Press, Norman.

Wissler, C.
    1914   The Influence of the Horse on the Development of Plains Culture. *American Anthropologist* 16:1–25.
    1941   *Indians of the United States.* Doubleday, Doran, New York.

Wood, W. R.
    1971   *Biesterfeldt: A Post-Contact Coalescent Site on the Northeastern Plains.* Smithsonian Contributions to Anthropology, no. 15. Washington, D.C.
    1985   The Plains–Lake Connection: Reflections from a Western Perspective. In *Archaeology, Ecology and Ethnohistory of the Prairie–Forest Border Zone of Minnesota and Manitoba,* edited by J. Spector and E. Johnson, 1–8. J and L Reprint, Lincoln, Neb.

Wood, W. R., ed.
    1986   *Ice Glider, 32OL110: Papers in Northern Plains Prehistory and Ethnohistory.* South Dakota Archaeological Society, Special Publication no. 10. Sioux Falls.

Wood, W. R., and A. S. Downer
    1977   Notes on the Crow–Hidatsa Schism. In *Trends in Middle Missouri Prehistory: A Festschrift Honoring the Contributions of Donald J. Lehmer,* edited by W. R. Wood, 83–100. Plains Anthropologist Memoir no. 13.

Wood, W. R., and T. D. Thiessen
    1985   *Early Fur Trade on the Northern Plains.* University of Oklahoma Press, Norman.

Wright, G. A.
    1978   The Shoshonean Migration Problem. *Plains Anthropologist* 23:113–137.

14. Euro-American Archaeology

Douglas D. Scott

Archaeological research on the Great Plains during the 1940s and 1950s helped spawn the modern subdiscipline of historical archaeology. The Great Plains, so rich in the history of American development—composing as it did a barrier separating Spain from other colonial empires, the "Great American Desert," a crossroad of travel and trade, the breadbasket of America, and the focus of a climatic holocaust, the dust bowl of the 1930s—is nevertheless one of the most poorly studied areas in historical archaeology.

Why has historical archaeology, from a promising beginning, not kept step with advances in the study of prehistory on the Great Plains? Perhaps because the anthropologically trained prehistoric archaeologist sees little value in digging up bits of history that are, by and large, recorded in existing documents. The historian is equally snobbish in dismissing archaeologists as dilettantes concerned with bits of material culture that have no place in a "proper" study of history (Whittenburg 1987). At best, the historical archaeologist is viewed as a handmaiden to history, the one who finds the missing fort, who unearths that fragment of a bowl that provides a tangible link to a renowned personage long dead, or who digs a homestead for which there are no written or oral records. The historical archaeologist has the reputation, somewhat deserved, of "filling in the gaps."

Recently, however, historical archaeology has become a respectable subdiscipline. The inventories called for by environmental- or resource-protection law under the rubrics of "historic preservation" and "cultural-resource management" require that historic sites be given more equal consideration in inventory and mitigation projects.

Historical archaeology is an outgrowth of the two major approaches to the study of the human past. History is, of course, the discipline that uses written and oral records to study the past, whereas archaeology uses a variety of techniques to create culture history and lifeways as a means to understand the dynamics of cultural change. Historical archaeology blends the two disciplines to study the dynamics of culture change in modern society. Culture history is important in that study, but equally important is the attempt to understand the social, cultural, and technological events that led a given people to select and use a particular site, and to trace their success or failure in coping with life there. Both approaches try to construct and understand a given cultural system. Historical archaeologists, of course, have all the tools of the prehistorian at their command plus the use of the historic record.

The Great Plains has always been a frontier—not a frontier in the sense of self-effacing pioneers, but a frontier in the sense of human adaptation to an undeveloped area. Euro-American development of the Great Plains was exploitative and is tied to the theoretical position that frontier growth is economically oriented (McDermott 1967; Steffen 1980). The development of the Great Plains was tied first to the political and economic activities that took place during European expansion in North America, and later to similar American activities. The first European contact with the Great Plains—the contact that begins recorded history—was Coronado's incursion into the area in 1541. Thus the first contact of the Native inhabitants of the Plains with whites was with the Spanish, as both conquerors and traders, although these Europeans left little in the way of artifacts from their brief presence on the Plains.

When the United States purchased Louisiana, a new age of exploration and development began on the Plains. French and Spanish traders had only limited impact on the area, but change now was to come quickly. Next were the explorations of Lewis and Clark, Zebulon Pike, Charles Frémont, and their successors. On the heels of these great discoverers came the fur traders of the upper Missouri and the mountain men of Colorado, Wyoming, and Montana. The decline of the fur trade was followed by the rise of mercantilism and the opening of immigrant trails to the Far West for the seekers of land and gold.

During this era, the Plains was essentially a barrier to be crossed as quickly as possible, for the idea of the "Great American Desert" was still widespread in the East. With the rise of republicanism in the 1850s, the call for free land culminated in the passage of the Homestead Act, and the path was paved for major population expansion onto the Plains. As homesteads were built, there was the simultaneous rise of the livestock rancher dependent on the open range. The stock raiser, and later the farming market, encouraged the railroads to expand their rail coverage. The Timber Culture Act of 1873 and the Stockraising Homestead Entry Act of 1916 further encouraged the reduction of open range and heightened a confrontation between stock raisers and the homesteading farmers. As the range wars died down, the last real threat to Euro-American westward expansion—the Indian—was put on reservations. The Great Plains now entered its final and dominant role, that of the breadbasket of America. This basically rural role continued to the 1960s. Farming, while still a dominant industry, today is experiencing a rapid decline in numbers employed versus production.

There are essentially two schools of historical thought about the Great Plains frontier: one is environmental determinist, and the other is cultural determinist. Frederick Jackson Turner (1893) was the first great advocate of cultural determinism, with his concept of the rugged frontiersman conquering an inhospitable environment. Turner has had many proponents and opponents through the years. His ideas were modified through time, although he has had many supporters of culture as being the dominant force in conquering the Plains (Shannon 1945).

The best known environmental determinist is Walter Prescott Webb (1931), who argued that the Plains environment was the limiting factor to its development. Webb further maintained that people responded to the needs of the Plains with a technology born of the Plains to conquer them. Malin (1947) was a proponent of Webb's, but embellished Webb's ideas and suggested that while Plains development was rooted in the environment, culture was also important. The last major environmental-determinist interpretation for settlement of the Great Plains was made by Kraenzel (1955), who argued that the Plains is an exploited hinterland whose residents display attitudes typical of minority groups. Kraenzel also contended that people must adapt to the Plains or get out. Each of these historical theories is a product of the social thought prevalent at its time. They are today undergoing constant assessment, some parts being discarded and others being revitalized and modernized in a movement identified by some as revisionist history (White 1991).

Three works provide a summary of current historical thought on the growth of the frontier, the result of a reassessment of frontier theory beginning with Pomeroy (1955) and Berkhofer (1964). Each work has a slightly different perspective, but each treats culture and environment as important, if not equal, variables.

McDermott (1967) edited a series of papers on new perspectives on the frontier that took no particular theoretical stance, but provided a forum for discussing and reevaluating frontier theory and development. More recently, Blouet and Luebke (1977) brought together a series of essays on the culture and environment of the Great Plains and the role of each in frontier development. Finally, Steffen (1980) has produced an economic-determinist perspective on frontier development that combines both environment and culture. Steffen establishes a series of subtraditions by which Great Plains development can be studied. His concepts develop the role of the economy in the East as a determining factor in the exploitation of the Plains. These three works provide a modern basis on which to study the Plains as a frontier, for they combine the concepts of culture, environment, and sociological theory. This theoretical orientation sets the stage for the combined historical and anthropological/archaeological study of the western frontier.

The Beginnings of Historical Archaeology on the Great Plains

The archaeology of Euro-American sites on the Great Plains did not begin until the late 1940s and early 1950s, when the Smithsonian Institution's Missouri River Basin Surveys (MRBS) was founded and did its first work on the Plains.

This does not imply that the archaeology of historic sites sprang up overnight, for archaeological work on the Plains had long focused on historic Indian villages in pursuing the direct historical approach—working back in time from the historically known villages to the prehistoric unknown ones (e.g., Wedel 1959). No serious attention, however, was paid to Euro-American sites until the advent of the MRBS.

Great Plains historical archaeology did not develop independently of historical archaeology in other regions or of American archaeology generally. The development of historical archaeology has in fact paralleled that of prehistoric archaeology through the stages defined by Willey and Sabloff (1974), although usually doing so somewhat later. Indeed, it too had birth pangs as it moved into the "new archaeology" (South 1977a).

The principal difference between prehistoric and historical archaeology is not in technique, but in its data. The historical archaeologist in North America retrieves and studies the material remains produced by Euro-Americans or by sites that postdate their arrival. These remains are enhanced by written and oral documentation, so the historical archaeologist often knows who settled or used a site, why they were there, and how long they remained. Given these data, the historical archaeologist should be able to move from the problem of reconstructing culture history to statements on the meaning of cultural patterning in the site.

While historical archaeologists are now examining these and related questions, the beginnings of historical archaeology were not so auspicious. In many ways, the development of historical archaeology on the Great Plains mirrors and parallels its development elsewhere, although the Plains led the way in certain respects. Among the founders of the Society for Historical Archaeology are four pioneers in Plains historical archaeology: Merrill J. Mattes, Carlyle S. Smith, G. Hubert Smith, and Alan R. Woolworth. Historical archaeology on the Plains owes its impetus and continued development in large part to them and their contemporaries.

The focus of the earlier period of historical archaeology on the Plains was on two kinds of sites: fur trade posts and military establishments. Less attention was paid to a third kind of site: the Indian agency. Each of these three historic site types is closely tied to the Plains Indians and their decline as the dominant culture on the Plains, and evoked a romantic image of the trans-Mississippi West—so these sites, like those of the Indian, needed to be saved from construction and flooding by the post–World War II reservoirs. The more common Euro-American sites—homesteads, ranches, small towns, and mines—were too recent or lacked appeal to historians and archaeologists alike. The theoretical orientation necessary to investigate them was lacking, and funds were too sparse to devote them to such "nonessential" goals (Mattes 1960).

Historical archaeology on the Plains, then, began about 1946 with the establishment of the Missouri River Basin Surveys. The orientation of the MRBS was on collecting and classifying data, verifying architectural information, and obtaining objects for study and museum display, especially those objects that shed light on everyday life on the frontier (Mattes 1960:11). During this salvage era, it was important to excavate sites, report the excavations, and describe the artifacts—and wait until later to synthesize the findings. Much of the work focused on fur trade sites on the upper Missouri River, partly because this was the main area of activity of the Missouri River Basin Surveys (Figure 14.1).

Fur Trade Posts

The era of fort archaeology began with the first MRBS excavations in the early 1950s. Both fur trade and military forts were investigated, and, in some ways, this emphasis has continued to the present day. Excavations began in 1951 with the investigation of Fort Lookout II, a "small-time" fur trade post built in 1833 and operated by Joseph La Barge (Mattes 1960:15). Carl F. Miller (1960:50–82) conducted the excavations, which unearthed structural data and recovered a few items of material culture. The information produced by the work is not as important as the fact that this effort launched professional historical archaeology on the Plains.

Fur trade posts continued to be the subject of excavation in 1952, when the MRBS began work at Fort Berthold II. Fort Berthold took several seasons of work because of its multicomponent and bicultural nature. The impetus for excavation slowed in 1953 because of fiscal reductions (Mattes 1960:16), but surged again in 1954 with renewed funding. The MRBS investigated Fort Pierre II and, in later seasons, Fort George, Loisel's Post, and Fort Manuel (G. Smith 1960a, 1968). In 1954 the MRBS and the State Historical Society of North Dakota excavated Fort Berthold I, and the latter institution investigated Kipp's Post during the same season. The two studies reporting this work were contemporary models of a detailed descriptive report (G. Smith 1972; Woolworth and Wood 1960). Attempts were made in both to cross-date and compare structural and artifactual data to develop a basis for dating and subsequent interpretations. The reports produced in the 1960s were essentially descriptive in nature, although comparisons and dating became increasingly more sophisticated. Efforts were also made to standardize publication format.

While the Missouri River basin was the subject of most investigations—because of the availability of salvage funds—other areas of the Plains also witnessed fort archaeology. Probably the best-known fort excavations in this category were those at Bent's Old Fort, on the Arkansas River in southeastern Colorado (Woodward 1956). The work at this famous trading post on the Santa Fe Trail ushered in a new era in Plains historical archaeology—that of restora-

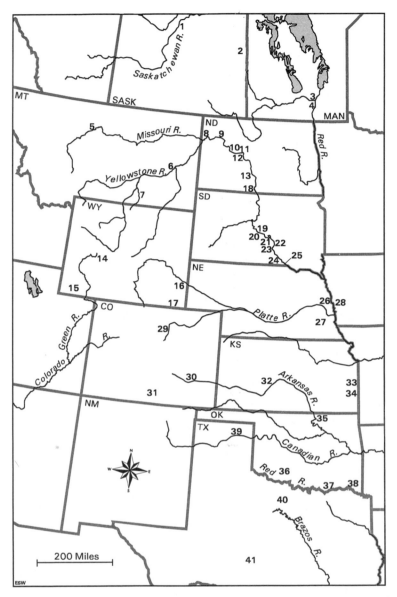

Figure 14.1. Euro-American–period sites on the Plains: *Saskatchewan* (1) Batoche, (2) Fort Pelly; *Manitoba* (3) Upper Fort Garry, Fort Gibraltar, (4) DeLorme House, Garden; *Montana* (5) Fort McKenzie, (6) Powder River Depot, (7) Little Bighorn Battlefield; *North Dakota* (8) Fort Union, Garden Coulee, (9) Kipp's Post, (10) Fort Berthold, Like-a-Fish-hook Village, (11) Fort Stevenson, (12) Ice Glider, (13) Fort Abraham Lincoln; *Wyoming* (14) South Pass, (15) Fort Bridger, (16) Fort Laramie, (17) Fort D. A. Russell; *South Dakota* (18) Fort Manuel, (19) Fort Sully, (20) Fort Pierre, (21) Fort George, (22) Fort Lookout, (23) Red Cloud Agency, (24) Whetstone Agency, (25) Fort Randall; *Nebraska* (26) Fort Atkinson, (27) Lincoln Pottery Works; *Iowa* (28) steamboat *Bertrand*; *Colorado* (29) Fort Vasquez, (30) Bent's Old Fort, (31) Fort Massachusetts; *Kansas* (32) Fort Larned, (33) Mine Creek Battlefield, (34) Fort Scott; *Oklahoma* (35) Deer Creek, Bryson, (36) Kiowa Agency, (37) Fort Washita, (38) Fort Towson; *Texas* (39) Adobe Walls, (40) Fort Richardson, (41) Fort McKavett.

tion archaeology. The first excavations at Bent's Old Fort were undertaken to recover data for the eventual restoration of the post (Dick 1956). The complete excavation by Moore (1973) culminated in the full reconstruction of the fort by the National Park Service and its present status as a national historic site popular with tourists. The intent of restoration archaeology is to recover structural data and material remains in order to enhance documentary data or existing remains, so that a site can be accurately reconstructed or restored and interpreted for the public.

This kind of archaeology continues to be done by many state and federal agencies and is exemplified by efforts at Fort Vasquez in Colorado (G. Baker 1964; Judge 1971). Work at Fort Union Trading Post National Historic Site, on the Montana–North Dakota boundary, was initially undertaken for this purpose (Husted 1971). Extensive mitigation efforts (before fort reconstruction was begun on the original site) were undertaken by the National Park Service from 1986 through 1988 under the direction of William J. Hunt. This effort yielded about 2.5 million artifacts, still being analyzed (Figure 14.2).

Interest in fur trade archaeology has continued, with studies of such sites as Fort McKenzie, Montana, and its trade beads (G. Wood 1977), and the stud-

Figure 14.2. Aerial view to the south of Fort Union Trading Post National Historic Site, showing the walls, bastions, and trade room during excavation. The flagpole and Bourgeois House were reconstructed after earlier investigations by the National Park Service. (Midwest Archeological Center, National Park Service)

ies of Euro-American material culture from underwater contexts (Wheeler et al. 1975) fall into the same category. While the fur trade was studied through such excavations on the Plains, little effort has been made to draw substantive conclusions about the role of these sites in affecting culture change. These interpretations were left, for the most part, to the historian and ethnohistorian. Fur trade archaeology has had further advances in theory based on the work of Toom (1979) and Psyzczyk (1989), who model archaeological and historical data and draw conclusions regarding material-culture use and ethnicity.

Canadian archaeologists are extremely active in the study of their fur trade posts. Trading establishments—including Upper Fort Garry (Priess 1980), Forts Gibraltar I and II (Priess et al. 1986), Fort Pelly I (Klimko 1983), and Rocky Mountain House (Noble 1973)—have been investigated. The most outstanding examples of a synthetic approach are the reports on Kipp's Post (Woolworth and Wood 1960) and Like-a-Fishhook Village (G. Smith 1972) in North Dakota, the Canadian sites of Rocky Mountain House (Noble 1973) and Fort Polly II (Klimko 1983), the effect of trade goods in changing aboriginal lifestyles (Toom 1979), the changes in lifestyles of the Métis as seen in architectural expression (Burley et al. 1988), and the complete excavation and analysis of the late bison-robe trade site of Adobe Walls in Texas (Baker and Harrison 1986).

Military Posts and Sites

The study of military posts has also been a concern of much historical archaeology on the Plains. These sites, like fur trading posts, are self-contained units, easily recognized in the field and of real interest to the historian. Military posts, like fur trade posts, exemplified the western frontier, but are a step nearer to the Euro-American peopling of the Plains. These sites were the most visible manifestation of the role the United States Army played in the West as peacemaker, guardian of the frontier, protector of the trails west, and defender of the immigrant farmer and railroad builder (Utley 1973).

The MRBS also pioneered military fort archaeology on the Plains, beginning with the excavation of Fort Stevenson (occupied from 1867 to 1880) in North Dakota. G. Smith (1960b) describes its excavation and gives a detailed account of the architectural and artifactual remains recovered (Figure 14.3). In his conclusions, he offers a strong argument for continuing investigations at all types of historic sites. Without excavation, much of the detail of history would be lost. He also argues for more excavation to gather comparative data so that broader statements on the meaning of the physical remains can be made.

The MRBS, guided by these statements and by the need to salvage sites before they were flooded, continued to excavate historic military posts. In 1952, Mills (1960) investigated several sites in South Dakota and partly excavated the

Figure 14.3. The exposed foundations and flooring of the commanding officers' quarters at Fort Stevenson, North Dakota, excavated by the Missouri River Basin Project in 1951. (National Anthropological Archives)

site of Fort Randall, first occupied in 1856. He also investigated the military features of the Whetstone Indian Agency and the Lower Brulé Agency, and made an artifact collection at the site of Fort Hale before it was washed away by the Missouri River flood of 1952. G. Smith also explored several other military posts, such as Fort Sully (occupied from 1863 to 1894) in South Dakota, but they have yet to be reported.

Fort archaeology also played a major role in the early work of historical archaeology elsewhere on the Plains. An example is the work by the Nebraska State Historical Society at Fort Atkinson, on the Missouri River near Omaha. The site was first tested in 1956 (Kivett 1959), but was not fully reported until many years later (Carlson 1979). Both works are primarily descriptive, although Carlson's report uses South's (1972) mean ceramic-dating formula to enhance its emphasis on historical reconstruction. More recently, Carlson (1990) reported the excavations and reconstruction of the Fort Atkinson Council House.

Restoration fort archaeology was also carried out in Colorado, Kansas, Oklahoma, and Texas during the same period. The report on Fort Massachusetts

Figure 14.4. The foundations, cellar, and part of the wellhouse tunnel of the block-house at Fort Larned, Kansas, excavated by the National Park Service in 1986. (Midwest Archeological Center, National Park Service)

in Colorado (G. Baker 1968) was entirely descriptive, yielding few interpretive results. Restoration archaeology was the rule rather than the exception in the study of military forts. Most work has been for the purpose of gathering data for reconstruction, restoration, and interpretation by federal, state, or local agencies. Examples of such work are scattered throughout the Plains, and include Fort Larned, Kansas (Scott 1973) (Figure 14.4); Fort Griffin (R. Fox 1975, 1976; Yates 1975), Fort McKavett (Pearson et al. 1975), and Fort Richardson (Lorrain and Giles 1975), Texas; Fort Towson (Lewis 1972; Scott 1975, 1976a, 1976b) and Fort Washita (Lewis 1975), Oklahoma; and Fort Bridger, Wyoming (Meyer 1979).

Among the spinoffs from military fort archaeology is the study of material culture to identify the use of the specimens and to refine the dating of sites by the artifacts they contain. C. Smith's (1954) study of ammunition from Fort Stevenson, North Dakota, is one of the earliest examples of such a study. It was followed by several others, exemplified by Wilson's (1971a, 1981) work with clay pipes and bottles from Fort Laramie, Wyoming; Gettys's (1978) description of a stone pipe from Fort Towson; Gettys and Gettys's (1978) study of lead flint musket-lock patches; and Sudbury's (1978) discussion of tobacco-bag tags.

While the purpose of most restoration fort archaeology was to provide data for the architect and historian, there have been some insightful and innovative anthropologically oriented attempts to study the frontier. Lewis (1972) became the forerunner of the frontier perspective in his early study of Fort Towson, Oklahoma. Recent studies have begun to view the evidence in a more anthropological manner and have used restoration data to build models of frontier adaptation and development.

Most of these efforts have used sources from the East and Far West as models on which to build. Lindsay (1974) used several nineteenth-century military fort–site excavations as a basis for considering the effect of military posts on the development of civilian settlement patterns. Although he used military data, Scott (1977) took a different approach in order to reconstruct, by archaeological means, a nineteenth-century environment and subsistence base. His comparison of the archaeological evidence with a historically derived model resulted in a good correlation of data, but the work stressed the need to view both sets of data as a composite to effectively interpret the sites.

Scott (1978) also proposed a set of hypotheses for the study of frontier military posts using Fort Towson as a model. This work also emphasized the combination of historical and archaeological data to best study frontier adaptations. Additional work based on the excavation of an officer's privy at Fort Larned, Kansas, noted that certain ceramic types—as well as other artifacts commonly found in privies—can provide insight into the perceived and attained status of different groups. Status can be defined using common nineteenth-century artifacts (Scott 1989a). Such studies are by no means alone in using an anthropological approach to these data, as Lees (1988, 1990) has aptly demonstrated.

The 1980s saw a continuing interest in the archaeological study of military sites. The Department of the Air Force contracted for a multiyear study of Fort D. A. Russell/F. E. Warren Air Force Base that resulted in a multivolume report of investigations in 1985. The Corps of Engineers undertook a study of Fort Randall Reservoir in South Dakota, led by Timothy R. Nowak, that very successfully used professional archaeologists and volunteers to excavate several structures (Lees 1991), and Hannus and his colleagues (1986) undertook an innovative study of the Fort Randall cemetery. Gerald Clark of the Bureau of Land Management began a study of the Powder River Depot in Montana, and Richard A. Fox undertook a multiseason excavation project at Fort Abraham Lincoln, North Dakota, in preparation for reconstruction efforts. More recent military sites, such as World War II prisoner-of-war compounds, are now being studied archaeologically (Jepson 1991).

The value of battlefields as archaeological sites containing anthropological data also was recognized in the 1980s. Canadian archaeologists studied parts of the military component of Batoche, a Métis site involved in the Northwest

Rebellion of 1885 (Lee 1983, 1984). The highly publicized study of the Battle of the Little Bighorn was conducted at the same time (Scott et al. 1989). Finally, Lees (1994) used the techniques applied at the Little Bighorn to begin a study of the Civil War battlefield site at Mine Creek, Kansas.

Native American Sites

Indian-related historical archaeology has not fared well on the Plains. Most studies have focused on Euro-American sites, which contributed to the demise of Indian dominance in the area. Where Native historic sites were investigated, the primary purpose was to recover data about the Indian component.

The earliest work in Indian-related historical archaeology was, again, done by the MRBS. Limited excavations were made at the Whetstone Agency and Lower Brulé Agency in South Dakota (Mills 1960). The work recovered only a few artifacts and some data on structures. G. Smith (1968) also carried out excavations in South Dakota to find Red Cloud's Agency, but with little success.

There seems to have been little interest in or opportunity for studying Indian agency remains. The one effort was the investigation of the Kiowa Agency commissaries at Fort Sill, Oklahoma (Crouch 1978). The report summarizes the historical data and archaeological work and, despite limited results from the excavations, tries to integrate the data into a meaningful picture of the site.

The historical archaeology of Native Americans has, with a few exceptions, been applied in two broad areas. One is the study of material culture from Indian-related sites, and the other is the identification and dating of historic Indian burials. In the first area, most of the effort has been on the study of firearms. The primary example of this work is a collection of studies of Indian trade guns dealing with the dating and identification of archaeological examples of guns and firearm components used in the Indian trade (Hamilton 1960). A companion volume expanded the identification criteria for this type of weapon (Hamilton 1968). Hunt (1989) has continued the innovative analysis of firearms in the fur trade. The criminal-investigative technique of firearms identification has recently been applied to archaeological collections with rather spectacular results (Scott 1989b). R. Fox (1993) has recently reassessed the Sioux (Lakota) and Cheyenne accounts of the Battle of the Little Bighorn in light of the archaeological investigations there. His work demonstrates that historians have unfairly and uncritically dismissed Native American accounts of the battle. The work shows the Native American accounts to be much more accurate than previously believed and are well coordinated with the archaeological record.

Huntington's (1967) guide to identifying military equipment also assists in Native American material-culture studies. Similar studies of other subjects appear in archaeological reports (e.g., Jelks 1967; Sudbury 1976) and occasionally as articles on a specific topic. M. Brown's (1971) analysis of an eighteenth-century trade coat is an excellent example of such work.

The studies of historic Indian burials often stress their ethnic identification and provide artifact descriptions used to date the remains (Jackson 1972; Kay 1968; Scott 1976a). Little effort has been made to integrate the data with ethnohistoric or ethnographic accounts of Indian lifeways, to determine the reasons that Euro-American artifacts were used as burial inclusions, or to deal with levels of acculturation.

Some works have, however, tried to assess Euro-American artifacts as indicators of the level of contact, origin of material, and level of acculturation (Rohrbaugh et al. 1971). The work by Toom (1979) tries to determine the effects of Euro-American trade goods on the changing lifeways of early contact village Indians. Earlier works with the same goal have had varying success. For example, Sudbury (1976), using surface collections, identified the Deer Creek and Bryson sites in Oklahoma as early-eighteenth-century contact sites. On the basis of mixed aboriginal and Euro-American artifacts, he speculates on the origin of the trade goods and the identity of the inhabitants. Using historic data and artifact evidence, he builds a model of a protohistoric Wichita occupation of the sites with French contacts, and tries to trace the origin of the inhabitants back in time to a proposed predecessor, the Great Bend aspect. His model is to be tested by excavation.

Current studies of Native American sites have combined traditional archaeological methods with cartographic analyses, documentary research, and ethnohistoric studies that result in model reports. One example of a well-developed and integrated report is the study of the Ice Glider site, a historic Sioux encampment in North Dakota (W. Wood 1986). The spread of smallpox into the Northern Plains was evaluated from an ethnohistorical perspective by Trimble (1986), and G. Fox (1988) built and augmented archaeological data using the tools of the historical archaeologist to evaluate a Hidatsa Indian village, the Garden Coulee site, near Fort Union, North Dakota. Canadian archaeologists have pioneered studies of racially mixed populations, specifically the Métis. They have assessed the effects of acculturation on the Métis at the Delorme House, the Garden site, and several other locations (Brockenshire 1983; Burley et al. 1988; McLeod 1982; McLeod et al. 1983).

Trends in Historical Archaeology

When the MRBS undertook the study and excavation of historic sites on the upper Missouri River, the theoretical orientation was essentially Turner's (1893) view of the frontier. He believed that frontier development had resulted from the rugged individualist carving a niche for himself and his family on the raw frontier. The MRBS historical studies reflect this orientation and were devoted to a study of epic developments on the frontier—the fur trade and the military presence as the dominant factors in the decline of Indian sovereignty on the Plains. The MRBS did not, however, fully ignore the more mundane towns, homes, ranches, and farms. These sites were recorded both on site-data forms and in photographic records (Mattes 1960). With few exceptions, until the advent of cultural-resource management, these sites were almost wholly neglected and were usually written off as inconsequential, not only on the Plains, but in the United States generally.

One of the few to express interest in such nonspectacular sites was Waldo R. Wedel (1963), prompted by his visit to the old mining town of Caribou, Colorado, in the foothills of the Rocky Mountains west of Denver. Although his article was popular in orientation, it sheds light on the potential for historical archaeology of the many modest extant sites. Another archaeologist to pursue such research was Thomas Morley (1960), who used aerial photography to define the remains of the Oregon Trail through Missouri, Nebraska, Kansas, and Wyoming to Fort Laramie.

The idea of the self-reliant individual has also been a subject for archaeological reassessment. J. Brown (1975), discussing the results of an excavation in Kansas, contrasted historic "fact" with archaeological data. Local history told the story of a local judge who was supposed to have lived as the traditional self-reliant rugged individualist. Excavation suggested, instead, that the judge had lived a comfortable life with most of the amenities one would expect in an eastern home. Brown concluded that ruggedness of character might not have carried through in the acquisition of material possessions. This idea was followed by more recent studies of military sites (Scott 1989a), but it has not been widely used in studying the frontier myth.

Cultural-resource-management studies have been the impetus for recording and studying many "common" sites, and they provide a good sample of the current work in historical archaeology. The excavation of the Rustic Hotel at Fort Laramie, Wyoming (Ehrenhard 1973), is an excellent example of a descriptive report that uses an integrated historical and archaeological approach to studying this late-nineteenth-century hotel. The research resulted in the accurate reconstruction of some furnishings and their placement, including data on potables.

Many excavations in historic sites are initiated to enhance the available written records. As is often the case, history may have the "facts," but archaeology finds that local legend has the wrong place or the wrong structure. Cheek's (1976) ethnohistorical and archaeological study of the Honey Springs Battlefield in Oklahoma is a good case in point. The excavation confirmed that a supposed Civil War powder magazine was, in fact, a storehouse built by a local man in 1892. The results were not what the historian expected.

The most ambitious historical archaeological project to date on the Plains was the excavation of the wreck of the steamboat *Bertrand,* which sank in the Missouri River a few miles above Omaha, Nebraska, in 1865. This river packet was loaded with goods meant for the farmers, miners, and merchants in the gold-rush country near Fort Benton, Montana. The river channel having changed since the boat's demise, the remains were found buried in an Iowa bottomland field. Its excavation yielded about 2 million remarkably well preserved artifacts, a time capsule of mid-nineteenth-century frontier mercantile goods. The *Bertrand* is one of the most thoroughly reported historic archaeological sites on the Plains. Petsche (1974) described the history and excavation of the boat, summarized its architecture and cargo, and placed this local story in its broader historical perspective. Some of the cargo was the subject of special studies, including the lead-shot bars, Britannia metal, munitions, butcher knives, Tally Ho buttons, bottles (Switzer 1970, 1971, 1972a, 1972b, 1972c, 1972d, 1974), and passengers' personal possessions (Kjorness 1995). Together, these studies provide significant insight into what was really available to the frontier consumer. The cargo today is on display at the DeSoto Bend National Wildlife Refuge in Iowa.

Until recently, most studies of historic sites were site-specific, but with the arrival of cultural-resource management, inventory has become the more common way to identify historic sites. Very often, the recording of a site is the only study it receives, since many sites are avoided or determined to be trivial by historians; they have forgotten that the commonplace is the rule instead of the exception and that the emphasis on the significant will skew our view of the frontier. Many cultural-resource-management surveys have been able to consider the full range of resources in an area, not only from a historical perspective, but to study changing land-use patterns from prehistory to history (e.g., Ferring 1978).

Many cultural-resource-management studies have also tested a variety of sites to determine their legal significance. This testing has supplied an opportunity to view a variety of historic sites from at least a minimal archaeological perspective. While limited testing has its drawbacks, it also has its advantages: it calls for the archaeologist to make the best possible use of the data, and for economy in both time and money. An excellent example of this is the study of surface-collected artifacts from Separation Station, a railroad site in Wyoming, founded in 1879 and abandoned about 1909. A 3 percent random-sample collection technique and point plot collection of datable artifacts provided data (Fawcett 1979). Since the site is essentially undisturbed, Fawcett could use the data to predict the location of the station house, find a tent city with a possible separate area for Chinese workers, and generate testable questions about socioeconomic patterns. Another Wyoming study has tried an innovative approach to the analysis of the ubiquitous sheep camp, focusing on defining ethnic, seasonal, and temporal variations (Ericson 1979). Kornfeld (1983) has expanded this concept to include the entire stock-raising settlement system. He differentiated between cattle- and sheep-ranching practices and developed an archaeological model for studying their remains. Sites of this type account for over half the archaeological remains recorded in Wyoming cultural-resource-management studies in recent years.

The study of homesteads and urban sites has received little attention for a variety of reasons, funding chief among them. This situation is changing with the inventory and excavation required by cultural-resource management, but all too slowly. Malone (1979) has tested a nineteenth-century pioneer midden, and other homestead-era and farm structures have been investigated. Most recently, Zier (1987) has demonstrated that a site long believed associated with the fur trade is in reality an early Colorado Front Range homestead. Cultural-resource-management activities have also been focused on mining and other industrial sites in Wyoming and other parts of the West. Studies of the human remains of settlers, soldiers, and others are becoming more common as historic sites continue to be investigated. With these studies there is a growing base on pathology, trauma, and diet of the non-Indian residents of the Plains (Gill et al. 1984; Perry 1986).

Urban archaeology on the Plains is in its infancy, although Gillio and Scott (1971) and others have shown through excavations in Denver that there is potential in the anthropological study of late-nineteenth- and early-twentieth-century remains. Studies begun at South Pass City, Wyoming, show the potential for such research (Reiss 1979). The excavation of a major light-industrial site, the Lincoln Pottery Works (Schoen and Bleed 1993), resulted in an interesting study of late-nineteenth- and early-twentieth-century utilitarian pottery technology. They also analyzed the economic implications of the pottery works and its products.

Much remains to be done in Plains historical archaeology, for the area has a wealth of information on frontier development and frontier relations with the more economically developed areas of the country and the world. This can be seen in some recent reports, but more substantive efforts are needed.

The Role of Historical Archaeology

The data derived from historical archaeology have yet to be used effectively by either the historian or the prehistorian. The latter, as a rule, has regarded historical archaeology, at best, as a testing ground for theory or models that can be

applied to prehistory. More often than not, prehistorians have viewed historical archaeology as not having an anthropological orientation. Historians, on the
contrary, have viewed historical archaeology as the handmaiden to history. They
see the value of historical archaeology as filling in the gaps not covered by historical records. To be fair, historical archaeologists often have been devoted to
that goal.

Historical archaeology is a new discipline, having made itself conspicuous
only in the past 25 years. In its earlier stages, it was devoted to the historian's
expectations. In the last few years, however, historical archaeology has taken a
theoretical turn to the quantification of data and the study of that data in an
anthropological perspective (Schuyler 1979; South 1977a, 1977b). The discipline
is undergoing rapid change, with beneficial results. Where frontier history has
evolved from Turner's (1893) concept of the rugged individualist to an economic
view (Steffen 1980), the historical archaeologist has had the opportunity to view
broad patterns of culture continuity and change—patterns that directly affected
modern American social development.

Historical archaeology is concerned with two broad subjects: culture chronology and human behavior. As a new discipline, it considers the dating of a
site or an assemblage of artifacts to be important. Even with the mass of information available in trade catalogs, patent records, and similar sources, the
ages of many once commonplace items are poorly known (Karklins 1981; Pfeiffer 1982). Fragmentary window glass is found in most historic sites, but its value
in dating was recognized only recently. When window glass from sites in the
Northwest was quantified, Roenke (1978) found that there was an increase in
the thickness of single panes through time, a fact of great value when interpreting sites with limited assemblages of datable materials. Schoen (1990) has expanded that work and developed a formula for dating Plains window glass.

Ceramics found at historic sites, and at prehistoric ones, are widely used as
temporal indicators (Gates and Omerod 1982; Gusset 1984; Lofstrom 1976; South
1972). One of the problems in using such ceramics on the Plains is the abundance of whitewares and other nondescript types. An effort was made on the
eastern Plains Border to identify and describe nineteenth-century ceramics in
the eastern Ozarks (Price 1979). In recent years, with the shift of emphasis to
an anthropological view, there has also been a shift in the intent of the study
of material culture and its interpretation. Ceramics continue to be important
in providing insights into how people view themselves. Euro-American culture
is status conscious and has used material objects as easily visible indicators of
one's relative social posture, if not position (Griffiths 1978; Lees et al. 1983;
G. Miller 1980). Innovative studies of mundane blacksmithing slag have revealed the types of metal actually smithed as well as the metalworking techniques used at two sites (Light and Unglik 1987; Gardner et al. 1991).

These efforts are but a beginning for the study of the patterns of recent human behavior and adaptation. Historical archaeology on the Plains is in its infancy, but a promising beginning has been made. It is up to the prehistorian and the historian to treat historical archaeology as an equal in the use of a finite resource base.

The Study of Historical Archaeology on the Plains

The theoretical orientations discussed in this chapter are principally approaches to the study of the region's frontier systems, although there are other approaches to the study of its historical archaeology. One reason for the frontier-system approach is that most Plains historical archaeologists were trained in prehistoric archaeology. Although this training is of great help in their study, archaeologists generally are dismally poor in the use of the necessary historical records (W. Wood 1990).

The intent of historical archaeology is to combine historical documentation with the archaeological record to broaden our picture of the past. Historical archaeologists make use of records and oral-history or archival sources that may provide the data needed, and thus avoid excavation. Digging should be undertaken only when historical data cannot satisfactorily answer questions.

If the view is accepted that Euro-American development on the Plains can be explored as a frontier system, then a definition of "frontier" obviously is in order. Wells (1975) has defined the term as a dynamic social network in which there is continual and structured change over a large geographic area, linking several culturally diversified groups. Wells refines this definition by positing four characteristics that distinguish the system:

1. There is one or more foci of political control and wealth, where the highest status members live in the main communication center. For the Plains, this focus was in the eastern tier of states, where the status, wealth, communication, and political power that controlled or guided much of the development on the Plains was centered.
2. Territorial expansion occurs through systematic migration and resettlement. Such expansion took a variety of forms on the Plains: fur trade posts, military posts, farmsteads, ranching, mining, urban expansion, and wholesale colonial resettlement by large populations.
3. Direct contact and confrontation between Euro-Americans and Plains Indians takes place. The fur trade and military contacts are examples most often cited.
4. A single communication network unifies the frontier. The method of commu-

nication is not as important as the message: on the Plains, economic, political, and, to a lesser degree, religious ideas were important.

There are, of course, subunits or varieties of frontier systems, and the Plains cannot be viewed as having been a single frontier. Rather, its settlement took place by means of a series of waves responding to political and economic stimuli from the east—in essence, the dynamic social network that provided the impetus to westward expansion.

Endless questions can be asked of the archaeological and historical data concerning western frontier expansion. Some archaeologists have begun to study the frontier and develop testable models. Lewis (1977) has suggested a model of colonial frontier history and methods to test it. Although his work was done at eighteenth-century sites in the Carolinas, with appropriate modifications it may be applicable to the Plains. Lewis's study evaluates the Carolina frontier and its agricultural and urban development, including using archaeological data as a means to test cultural generalizations. S. Baker (1978) has proposed a model to study the growth of the Rocky Mountain urban–mining area of Colorado, viewing the development of mining-related subsystems there as part of a broader cultural tradition—the American Victorian frontier. He sees Victorian thought as a product of an urbanizing and industrializing nation and as a major American cultural tradition. Furthermore, this tradition can be seen in the archaeological record in mining localities in the West.

Current theoretical concepts for historical archaeological use have an economic-determinist theoretical base for the development and exploitation of the frontier. They were developed by Steffen (1975, 1980) and have been set in the archaeological realm by Hardesty (1980). Two basic concepts are presented:

1. The driving force behind the development of the trans-Mississippi West was an economically based East striving to expand its wealth and political influence.
2. There is a direct relation between culture change on the frontier and the degree of insulation maintained by a given frontier group. That is, the greater the interaction of the Plains subsystem with the East, the greater the opportunity for change to occur.

The capitalist motivation for peopling the West is also an overriding theme of the New Western historians, or so-called revisionist historians (Limerick 1991; White 1991). They strongly advocate the economic-determinist approach and are particularly forceful in castigating earlier scholars for building on or supporting the Turnerian concept of rugged individuals. They argue that much of the literature on the frontier is perpetuating a myth. This mythological frontier image requires deconstruction and revision from the new point of view. Historical archaeology is in a unique position to use documents and material culture to address many of the theories and tenets of the New Western historians. Historical archaeology has already demonstrated that some western history is based on ill-conceived premises and is in the process of deconstructing frontier myths (R. Fox 1993; Lees 1994). Much more historical archaeological work is needed to fully address the validity of the theoretical stances of either the New Western historians or the old guard.

Steffen (1980) argues that the study of the western frontier cannot be undertaken without a broad perspective on earlier frontier developments in the East and abroad. In addition, the study of change on the western frontier must analyze the interaction of the various links of the system with the parent culture and within the system. He specifically argues for the study of four subsystems on the western frontier: pioneer agriculture, fur trading, ranching, and mining.

The agricultural subsystem, Steffen (1980) maintains, was dependent on technology for its impetus to expand onto the Great Plains, but he also views farmers as essentially a conservative entity in the frontier system. The fur trade is regarded as an economically exploitative subsystem of New World mercantilism, and the ranching subsystem as developing from mercantile capitalism into industrial capitalism, particularly on the Northern Plains. Finally, Steffen sees the mining frontier as a continual process, moving from the early eastern colonial frontier to the western frontier as technology improved and mineral deposits were found.

Other subsystems can be developed, and two are suggested here. The military played a visible role in frontier development and cannot be ignored, for it grew in concert with the rest of the frontier (Tate 1978). The military provides a tightly controlled social substratum of society, and the adaptation of this element of society to the frontier is easily studied by both history and archaeology. Recent studies of the Battle of the Little Bighorn have led to postulating a battlefield archaeology pattern (Fox and Scott 1991; Scott et al. 1989) that allows the identification of individual fighting patterns, unit fighting formations, and opposing combatants (Figure 14.5).

The urban frontier is the other subsystem. A broader study of urban contexts, especially on the frontier (Schuyler 1980), tries to understand the rise of centers of population, economic and political power, and transportation and communication. The concept of urban development is an old one in anthropology and many of the same interests in the rise of urban centers are shared by the prehistorian and the historical archaeologist.

This review of historical archaeology on the Plains makes it apparent that there is a trend for the study of systems. Historians have been developing and reassessing the concept of the frontier for nearly a century. The historical archaeologist has paid heed to historical theory and proposed archaeologically testable

Figure 14.5. Uncovering a soldier's remains at the Little Bighorn Battlefield National Monument. The soldier, whose remains were recovered by the National Park Service in 1984, was one of George Custer's men killed near the Deep Ravine. (Midwest Archeological Center, National Park Service)

models of frontier systems. Lees (1988) has developed and tested models of site-formation processes using Southern Plains and Ozark Highland data. His approach is illustrative of the potential of Plains historical archaeology. The Great Plains provides an ideal area for testing and refining those models, as well as developing new theoretical orientations.

References

Baker, G. R.
    1964   Preliminary Excavation at Fort Vasquez. *Colorado Magazine* 41:58–64.
    1968   Excavating Fort Massachusetts 2. *Colorado Magazine* 45:43–171.
Baker, S. G.
    1978   Historical Archaeology for Colorado and the Victorian Mining Frontier: Review, Discussion, and Suggestions. *Southwestern Lore* 44:11–31.
Baker, T. L., and B. R. Harrison
    1986   *Adobe Walls: The History and Archeology of the 1874 Trading Post.* Texas A&M University Press, College Station.
Berkhofer, R., Jr.
    1964   Space, Time, Culture, and the New Frontier. *Agricultural History* 38:25–37.

Blouet, B. W., and F. Luebke, eds.
    1977   *The Great Plains Environment and Culture.* University of Nebraska Press, Lincoln.
Brown, J.
    1975   Problems with Categories of People: Can Archaeology Help? *Conference on Historic Sites Archaeology Papers 1974* 9:86–95.
Brown, M. K.
    1971   An Eighteenth Century Trade Coat. *Plains Anthropologist* 16:128–133.
Burley, D. V., G. Horsfall, and J. Brandon
    1988   *Stability and Change in Western Canadian Métis Lifeways: An Archaeological and Architectural Study.* Saskatchewan Parks, Recreation, and Culture, Archaeological Resource Management, Heritage Resource Branch, Regina.
Carlson, G. F.
    1979   *Archeological Investigations at Fort Atkinson (25WN9), Washington County, Nebraska, 1956–1971.* Nebraska State Historical Society, Publications in Anthropology, no. 8. Lincoln.
    1990   Archaeology and Reconstruction of the Fort Atkinson Council House. *Central Plains Archaeology* 2:91–131.
Cheek, C. D.
    1976   *Honey Springs, Indian Territory: Search for a Confederate Powder House, An Ethnographic and Archeological Report.* Oklahoma Historical Society, Series in Anthropology, no. 2. Oklahoma City.
Crouch, D. J.
    1978   *Archaeological Investigations of the Kiowa and Commanche Indian Agency Commissaries, 34-CM-232.* Museum of the Great Plains, Contributions, no. 7. Lawton, Okla.
Dick, H. W.
    1956   The Excavations of Bent's Fort, Otero County, Colorado. *Colorado Magazine* 33:181–196.
Ehrenhard, J. E.
    1973   The Rustic Hotel, Fort Laramie National Historic Site, Wyoming. *Historical Archaeology* 7:11–29.
Ericson, K. C.
    1979   Artifact Scatters in South Central Wyoming. Paper presented at the thirty-seventh annual Plains Conference, Kansas City, Mo.
Fawcett, W. B., Jr.
    1979   Separation: Historical Archaeology at a Union Pacific Railroad Station in the Red Desert of Wyoming. Paper presented at the thirty-seventh annual Plains Conference, Kansas City, Mo.
Ferring, C. R., comp.
    1978   *Archaeological Reconnaissance at Fort Sill, Oklahoma.* Museum of the Great Plains, Contributions, no. 6. Lawton, Okla.
Fox, G. L.
    1988   *A Nineteenth Century Village of a Band of Dissident Hidatsa: The Garden Coulee Site (32Wl18).* J and L Reprint, Lincoln, Neb.
Fox, R. A., Jr.
    1975   *Archeological Investigation at Fort Griffin.* Part 2. Archeological Completion Report Series, no. 10. National Park Service, Office of Archeology and Historic Preservation, Washington, D.C.

1976   *Archaeological Investigations at Fort Griffin State Historic Park, Shackelford County, Texas.* University of Texas, Center for Archaeological Research, Archaeological Survey, Report no. 23. San Antonio.

1993   *Archaeology, History, and Custer's Last Battle.* University of Oklahoma Press, Norman.

Fox, R. A., and D. D. Scott

1991   The Post–Civil War Battlefield Pattern: An Example from the Custer Battlefield. *Historical Archaeology* 25:92–103.

Gardner, D. A., D. E. Johnson, and D. Vleck

1991   *Archaeological Investigations at Fort Bonneville.* Western Wyoming College, Archaeological Services, Cultural Resource Management Report, no. 51. Rock Springs.

Gates, W. D., and D. E. Omerod

1982   The East Liverpool Pottery District: Identification of Manufactures and Marks. *Historical Archaeology* 16, nos. 1–2.

Gettys, M.

1978   A Stone Pipe from Fort Towson. *Oklahoma Anthropological Society Newsletter* 26:1–3.

Gettys, M., and A. F. Gettys

1978   Lead Flint Patches from Fort Towson. *Oklahoma Anthropological Society Newsletter* 26:8–12.

Gill, G. W., J. W. Fisher, Jr., and G. M. Zeimens

1984   A Pioneer Burial near the Historic Bordeaux Trading Post. *Plains Anthropologist* 29:229–238.

Gillio, D. A., and D. D. Scott

1971   Archaeological Tests of the Forney Site, Denver, Colorado. *Colorado Anthropologist* 3:24–34.

Griffiths, D. M.

1978   Use-Marks on Historic Ceramics: A Preliminary Study. *Historical Archaeology* 12:78–81.

Gusset, G.

1984   *Stoneware Containers from Some Canadian Prairie Sites.* Parks Canada Research Bulletin, no. 221. Ottawa, Ont.

Hamilton, T. M.

1960   Indian Trade Guns. *Missouri Archaeologist* 22.

1968   *Early Indian Trade Guns: 1625–1775.* Museum of the Great Plains, Contributions, no. 3. Lawton, Okla.

Hannus, L. A., E. J. Lueck, and R. P. Winham

1986   *Cultural Resource Investigation of the Historic Fort Randall Cemetery, Gregory County, South Dakota.* Augustana College, Archeology Laboratory, Archeological Contract Series, no. 20. Sioux Falls, S.D.

Hardesty, D. L.

1980   Historic Sites Archaeology on the Western American Frontier: Theoretical Perspectives and Research Problems. *North American Archaeologist* 2:67–80.

Hunt, W. J.

1989   Firearms and the Upper Missouri Fur Trade Frontier: Weapons and Related Materials from the Fort Union Trading Post National Historic Site (32WI17), North Dakota. Ph.D. diss., Department of American Civilization, University of Pennsylvania, Philadelphia.

Huntington, R. T.
   1967   Dragoon Accouterments and Equipment, 1834–1849: An Identification Guide. *Plains Anthropologist* 12:345–355.
Husted, W. M.
   1971   1970 Excavations at Fort Union Trading Post National Historic Site, North Dakota: A Progress Summary. Manuscript on file, National Park Service, Midwest Archeological Center, Lincoln, Neb.
Jackson, J. B.
   1972   The Jared Site: A Comanche Burial at Fort Sill, Oklahoma. *Plains Anthropologist* 17:316–325.
Jelks, E. B.
   1967   *The Gilbert Site: A Norteño Focus Site in Northwestern Texas.* Texas Archeological Society, Bulletin no. 37. Austin.
Jepson, D. A.
   1991   Camp Carson, Colorado: European Prisoners of War in the American West During World War II. *Midwest Review,* 2nd Ser., 13:32–53.
Judge, W. J.
   1971   The Archaeology of Fort Vasquez. *Colorado Magazine* 48:181–203.
Karklins, K.
   1981   *Glass Trade Beads from a Salvaged Pit in Peter Pond National Historic Site, Saskatchewan.* Parks Canada Research Bulletin, no. 160. Ottawa, Ont.
Kay, M.
   1968   Two Historic Indian Burials from an Open Site, 23AD95, Adair County, Missouri. *Plains Anthropologist* 13:103–114.
Kivett, M. F.
   1959   Excavations at Fort Atkinson, Nebraska: A Preliminary Report. *Nebraska History* 40:39–66.
Kjorness, A. C.
   1995   Material Culture of Nineteenth Century Steamboat Passengers on the *Bertrand* and *Arabia.* M.A. thesis, Department of History, East Carolina University, Greenville, N.C.
Klimko, O.
   1983   *The Archaeology and History of Fort Pelly I, 1824–1856.* Manuscript Series in Archaeology and History, Pastlog no. 5. Regina, Sask.
Kornfeld, M.
   1983   A Model of High Plains and Intermountain Stockraising Settlement Systems. *American Archaeologist* 41:51–62.
Kraenzel, C. F.
   1955   *The Great Plains in Transition.* University of Oklahoma Press, Norman.
Lee, E.
   1983   *Archaeological Investigations at Batoche National Historic Site, 1982.* Parks Canada, Research Bulletin, no. 191. Ottawa, Ont.
   1984   *Archaeological Research at Batoche N.H.S—1983 Field Season.* Parks Canada, Research Bulletin, no. 219. Ottawa, Ont.
Lees, W. B.
   1988   Site Formation Process in Historical Archeology. Ph.D. diss., Department of Anthropology, Michigan State University, Lansing.
   1990   Archeology at Fort Towson. *Chronicles of Oklahoma* 68:54–71.

1991   Archeology of the Subaltern's Quarters, Fort Randall (39GR15), South Dakota. *South Dakota Archaeology* 15:1–72.

1994   When the Shooting Stopped the War Began. In *Look to the Earth: Historical Archaeology and the American Civil War*, edited by C. R. Geier, Jr., and S. E. Winter, 39–59. University of Tennessee Press, Knoxville.

Lees, W. B., K. M. Kimery-Lees, and T. J. Martin

1983   *Fort Towson: The Sutler's Store 1978–1980*. Oklahoma Historical Society Collections, Oklahoma City.

Lewis, K. E.

1972   *Archaeological Investigations at Fort Towson, Choctaw County, Oklahoma*. University of Oklahoma, Oklahoma Archaeological Survey, Studies in Oklahoma's Past, no. 2. Norman.

1975   *Fort Washita from Past to Present: An Archaeological Report*. Oklahoma Historical Society, Series in Anthropology, no. 1. Oklahoma City.

1977   Sampling the Archeological Frontier: Regional Models and Component Analysis. In *Research Strategies in Historical Archeology*, edited by S. South, 151–202. Academic Press, New York.

Light, J. D., and H. Unglik

1987   *A Frontier Fur Trade Blacksmith Shop*. Environment Canada, Canadian Government Publications Center, Hull, Que.

Limerick, P. N.

1991   Making the Most of Words: Verbal Activity and Western America. In *Rethinking America's Western Past*, edited by W. Cronon, G. Mills, and J. Gitling, 72–102. Norton, New York.

Lindsay, R. D.

1974   The Influence of Military Posts upon Historic Settlement Patterns. Paper presented at the seventh annual conference of the Society for Historical Archeology, Orlando, Fla.

Lofstrom, E. U.

1976   An Analysis of Temporal Change in a Nineteenth Century Ceramic Assemblage from Fort Snelling, Minnesota. *Minnesota Archaeologist* 35:16–47.

Lorrain, D., and M. Giles

1975   *Fort Richardson*. National Park Service, Office of Archeology and Historic Preservation, Archeological Completion Report Series, no. 6. Washington, D.C.

McLeod, K. D.

1982   *Archaeological Investigations at the Delorme House (DkLg-18), 1981*. Department of Culture, Heritage, and Citizenship, Historical Resources Branch, Papers in Manitoba Archaeology, Final Report no. 13. Winnipeg.

McLeod, K. D., J. Brockenshire, D. Brown, S. B. Ebell, L. Grant, M. C. Kotecki, P. J. Lambert, and E. Nilson

1983   *The Garden Site, DkLg-16: A Historical and Archaeological Study of a Nineteenth Century Métis Farmstead*. Department of Culture, Heritage, and Citizenship, Historical Resources Branch, Papers in Manitoba Archaeology, Final Report no. 16. Winnipeg.

Malin, J. C.

1947   *The Grassland of North America: Prolegomena to its History*. Privately published by the author, Lawrence, Kans.

Malone, J. A.

1979   Investigations of a Nineteenth Century Pioneer Midden, Marion County, Kansas: A Study in Historic Archaeology. M.A. thesis, Department of Anthropology, Wichita State University.

Mattes, M. J.
  1960 Historical Sites Archeology on the Upper Missouri. *Bureau of American Ethnology Bulletin* 176:5–24.

McDermott, J. F., ed.
  1967 *The Frontier Re-examined.* University of Illinois Press, Urbana.

Meyer, M.
  1979 Flagpole Excavation at Fort Bridger, 48UT29, Wyoming. Paper presented at the thirty-seventh annual Plains Conference, Kansas City, Mo.

Miller, C. F.
  1960 The Excavation and Investigation of Fort Lookout Trading Post II (39LM57) in the Fort Randall Reservoir, South Dakota. *Bureau of American Ethnology Bulletin* 176:49–82.

Miller, G. L.
  1980 Classification and Economic Scaling of 19th Century Ceramics. *Historical Archaeology* 14:1–41.

Mills, J. E.
  1960 Historic Sites Archeology in the Fort Randall Reservoir, South Dakota. *Bureau of American Ethnology Bulletin* 176:25–48.

Moore, J. W., Jr.
  1973 *Bent's Old Fort: An Archeological Study.* Pruett, Boulder, Colo.

Morley, T.
  1960 The Independence Road to Fort Laramie by Aerial Photographs. *Plains Anthropologist* 6:242–251.

Noble, W. C.
  1973 The Excavation and Historical Identification of Rocky Mountain House. *Canadian Historic Sites Occasional Papers in Archaeology and History,* no. 6:55–164.

Pearson, E. L., S. A. Carter, M. R. Eiserer, W. G. Payne, and R. L. Stribe
  1975 Archeological Investigations at Fort McKavett. National Park Service, Office of Archeology and Historic Preservation, Archeological Completion Report Series, no. 2. Washington, D.C.

Perry, M. F.
  1986 Historical Analysis of Remains Found in Jesse James Casket. *Kansas City Archaeologist, Special Bulletin* 1:11–18.

Petsche, J. E.
  1974 *The Steamboat "Bertrand": History, Excavation, Architecture.* National Park Service, Publications in Archeology, no. 11. Washington, D.C.

Pfeiffer, M. A.
  1982 Clay Tobacco Pipes and the Fur Trade of the Pacific Northwest and Northern Plains. M.A. thesis, Department of Anthropology, University of Idaho, Moscow.

Pomeroy, E.
  1955 Toward a Reorientation of Western History: Continuity and Environment. *Mississippi Valley Historical Review* 41:581–597.

Price, C. R.
  1979 *19th Century Ceramics in the Eastern Ozark Border Region.* Southwest Missouri State University, Center for Archaeological Research, Monograph Series, no. 1. Springfield.

Priess, P. J.
  1980   *Archaeological Investigations at Upper Fort Garry, 1978.* Parks Canada Research
          Bulletin, no. 125. Ottawa, Ont.
Priess, P. J., P. W. Nieuhof, and S. B. Ebell
  1986   *Archaeological Investigation of the Junction of the Red and Assiniboine Rivers, 1984.*
          Parks Canada Research Bulletin, no. 246. Ottawa, Ont.
Pyszczyk, H. W.
  1989   Consumption and Ethnicity: An Example from the Fur Trade in Western Can-
          ada. *Journal of Anthropological Archaeology* 8:212–249.
Reiss, D.
  1979   Preliminary Excavation at South Pass City, 48ER434, Wyoming. Paper pre-
          sented at the thirty-seventh annual Plains Conference, Kansas City, Mo.
Roenke, K. G.
  1978   *Flat Glass: Its Use as a Dating Tool for Nineteenth Century Archaeological Sites in
          the Pacific Northwest and Elsewhere.* Northwest Anthropological Research
          Notes, Memoir no. 4. Moscow, Idaho.
Rohrbaugh, C. L., R. J. Burton, S. S. Burton, and L. J. Rosevitz
  1971   *Hugo Reservoir I.* University of Oklahoma, Oklahoma River Basin Survey
          Project, Archaeological Site Report no. 22. Norman.
Schoen, C. M.
  1990   Window Glass on the Plains: An Analysis of Flat Glass Samples from Ten
          Nineteenth Century Historic Sites. *Central Plains Archaeology* 2:57–90.
Schoen, C. M., and P. Bleed
  1993   The Archaeology of the Lincoln Pottery Works, 25CL42. *Central Plains Archae-
          ology* 3:1–240.
Schuyler, R. L.
  1979   *Archaeological Perspectives on Ethnicity in America.* Baywood, New York.
  1980   *Archaeology.* Baywood, New York.
Scott, D. D.
  1973   The Archaeology of Fort Larned National Historic Site, Kansas. M.A. thesis,
          Department of Anthropology, University of Colorado, Boulder.
  1975   Archaeological and Historical Investigations at the Fort Towson Powder
          Magazine. *Chronicles of Oklahoma* 53:516–527.
  1976a   Ethnic Identification of an Historic Sac Burial from Northeastern Kansas.
          Plains Anthropologist 21:131–140.
  1976b   Preliminary Report on the Excavation of the Commanding Officers Quarters,
          Fort Towson. *Oklahoma Anthropological Society Newsletter* 24:5–10.
  1977   Historic Fact vs. Archaeological Reality—A Test in Environmental Reconstruc-
          tion. Ph.D diss., Department of Anthropology, University of Colorado, Boulder.
  1978   Fort Towson: A Glimpse into the Past. Paper presented at the first annual
          Fort Towson Anthropological Conference, Fort Towson, Okla.
  1989a   An Officer's Privy at Fort Larned and Some Inferences on Status. *Plains An-
          thropologist* 34: 23–34.
  1989b   Firearms Identification for the Archeologist. In *From Chaco to Chaco,* edited by
          M. S. Duran and D. T. Kirkpatrick, 141–151. Archeological Society of New
          Mexico, no. 15. Albuquerque.
Scott, D. D., R. A. Fox, M. A. Connor, and D. Harmon
  1989   *Archaeological Perspectives on the Battle of the Little Bighorn.* University of
          Oklahoma Press, Norman.

Shannon, F. A.
  1945 *The Farmers Last Frontier: Agriculture, 1860–1897*. Rinehart and Winston, New
        York.
Smith, C. S.
  1954 Cartridges and Bullets from Fort Stevenson, North Dakota. *Plains Anthropolo-
        gist* 1:25–29.
Smith, G. H.
  1960a Fort Pierre II (35ST217), a Historic Trading Post in the Oahe Dam Area, South
        Dakota. *Bureau of American Ethnology Bulletin* 176:83–158.
  1960b Archeological Investigations at the Site of Fort Stevenson (32ML1), Garrison
        Reservoir, North Dakota. *Bureau of American Ethnology Bulletin* 176:159–238.
  1968 *Big Bend Historic Sites*. Smithsonian Institution, River Basin Surveys, Publica-
        tions in Salvage Archeology, no. 9. Lincoln, Neb.
  1972 *Like-a-Fishhook Village and Fort Berthold, Garrison Reservoir, North Dakota*.
        National Park Service, Anthropological Papers, no. 2. Washington, D.C.
South, S.
  1972 Evolution and Horizon as Revealed in Ceramic Analysis in Historic Archaeol-
        ogy. *Conference on Historic Site Archaeology Papers 1971* 6:71–116.
  1977a *Research Strategies in Historical Archeology*. Academic Press, New York.
  1977b *Method and Theory in Historical Archaeology*. Academic Press, New York.
Steffen, J. O.
  1975 Some Observations on the Turner Thesis: A Polemic. *Papers in Anthropology*
        14:16–30.
  1980 *Comparative Frontiers*. University of Oklahoma Press, Norman.
Sudbury, B.
  1976 Ka-3, the Deer Creek Site—An Eighteenth Century French Contact Site in
        Kay County, Oklahoma. *Bulletin of the Oklahoma Anthropological Society* 24:1–
        136.
  1978 Comments on Small Metal Household Shaped Decorations Recovered from
        the Fort Sill Dump Site (34-CM-9). *Oklahoma Anthropological Society Newsletter*
        26:3–7.
Switzer, R. R.
  1970 Lead Bars from the St. Louis Shot Tower. *Museum of the Fur Trade Quarterly*
        6:5–6.
  1971 Charles Parker's Britannia on the Steamboat *Bertrand*. *Museum of the Fur Trade
        Quarterly* 7:6–10.
  1972a Munitions on the *Bertrand*. *Archaeology* 24:250–255.
  1972b Maynard Cartridges and Primers from the Steamboat *Bertrand*. *Military Collec-
        tor and Historian* 24:85–87.
  1972c Butcher Knives as Historical Sources. *Museum of the Fur Trade Quarterly*
        8:5–7.
  1972d Tally Ho's from the Steamboat *Bertrand*. *Just Buttons* 30:416–426.
  1974 *The "Bertrand" Bottles: A Study of 19th Century Glass and Ceramic Containers*.
        National Park Service, Publications in Archeology, no. 12. Washington, D.C.
Tate, J. P.
  1978 *The American Military Frontier*. Proceedings of the seventh annual Military
        History Symposium, United States Air Force Academy, Colorado Springs.
Toom, D. L.
  1979 The Middle Missouri Villages and the Early Fur Trade: Implications for Ar-

chaeological Interpretations. M.A. thesis, Department of Anthropology, University of Nebraska, Lincoln.

Trimble, M. K.

1986　*An Ethnohistorical Interpretation of the Spread of Smallpox in the Northern Plains Utilizing Concepts of Disease Ecology.* J and L Reprint, Lincoln, Neb.

Turner, F. J.

1893　The Significance of the Frontier in American History. *American Historical Association, Annual Report for the Year 1893,*199–227.

Utley, R. M.

1973　*Frontier Regulars: The United States Army and the Indians, 1866–1890.* Macmillan, New York.

Webb, W. P.

1931　*The Great Plains.* Ginn, Boston.

Wedel, W. R.

1959　*An Introduction to Kansas Archeology.* Bureau of American Ethnology Bulletin 174. Washington, D.C.

1963　Visit to Caribou, 1963. *Colorado Magazine* 41:247–252.

Wells, R. F.

1975　Frontier Systems as a Sociocultural Type. *Papers in Anthropology* 14:6–15.

Wheeler, R. C., W. A. Kenyon, A. R. Woolworth, and D. A. Birk

1975　*Voices from the Rapids: An Underwater Search for Fur Trade Artifacts, 1960–73.* Minnesota Historical Society, St. Paul.

White, R.

1991　*"It's Your Misfortune and None of My Own": A New History of the American West.* University of Oklahoma Press, Norman.

Whittenburg, J. P.

1987　On Why Historians Have Failed to Recognize the Potential of Material Culture. *American Archaeology* 6:4–9.

Wiley, G., and J. A. Sabloff

1974　*A History of American Archaeology.* Freeman, San Francisco.

Wilson, R.

1971　*Clay Tobacco Pipes from Fort Laramie National Historic Site and Related Locations.* National Park Service, Office of Archeology and Historic Preservation, Washington, D.C.

1981　*Bottles on the Western Frontier.* University of Arizona Press, Tucson.

Wood, G. C.

1977　Fort Mckenzie (24CH242): A Study in Applied Historical Archaeological Methods. *Archaeology in Montana* 18:43–62.

Wood, W. R.

1990　Ethnohistory and Historical Method. In *Archaeological Method and Theory,* vol. 2, edited by by M. J. Schiffer, 81–110. University of Arizona Press, Tucson.

Wood, W. R., ed.

1986　*Ice Glider, 32OL110: Papers in Northern Plains Prehistory and Ethnohistory.* South Dakota Archaeological Society, Special Publication no. 10. Sioux Falls.

Woodward, A.

1956　Sidelights on Bent's Old Fort. *Colorado Magazine* 33:277–282.

Woolworth, A. R., and W. R. Wood

1960　The Archeology of a Small Trading Post (Kipp's Post, 32MN1) in the Garrison Reservoir, North Dakota. *Bureau of American Ethnology Bulletin* 176:241–305.

Yates, C.
　1975　*Archeological Investigations at Fort Griffin.* National Park Service, Office of Archeology and Historic Preservation, Archeological Completion Report Series, no. 3. Washington, D.C.

Zier, C. J.
　1987　Bent's Stockade Hidden in the Hills: A Myth Laid to Rest. *Southwestern Lore* 53:6–32.

INDEX